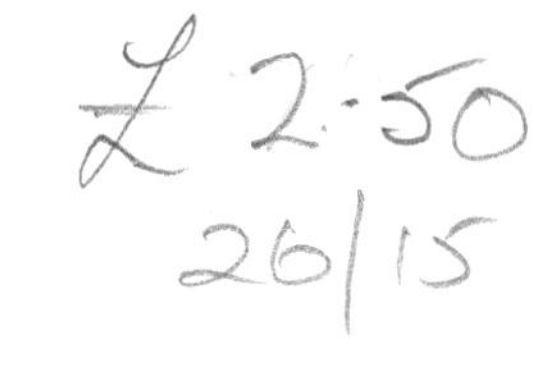

Mountains from Space

Concept:
Professor Stefan Dech, Professor Rüdiger Glaser, Reinhold Messner, Dr. Robert Meisner

Project Direction:
German Remote Sensing Data Center, DLR

Introductions:
Professor Stefan Dech, Reinhold Messner, Christoph Ransmayr

Geoscientific Texts:
Professor Rüdiger Glaser

Climbing and Literary Texts:
Maurice Herzog, Sir Edmund Hillary, Alexander Huber, Dr. Ralf-Peter Märtin, Reinhold Messner, Professor Oswald Oelz, Christoph Ransmayr, Stephen Venables

Picture Captions:
Professor Stefan Dech, Dr. Robert Meisner, Dr. Thorsten Andresen, Nils Sparwasser

Scientific Data Preparation:
Nils Sparwasser, Dr. Thorsten Andresen, Adelheid Craubner

Mountains from Space

Peaks and Ranges of the Seven Continents

Stefan Dech
Reinhold Messner
Rüdiger Glaser
Ralf-Peter Märtin

German Aerospace Center, DLR

HARRY N. ABRAMS, INC., PUBLISHERS

001-013 [INTRODUCTION]

014-061 [EUROPE]

078-121 [ASIA]

062-077 [AFRICA]

Foreword
So Far, So Near

The Alps, the Himalayas, the Andes—for millennia, mountains and mountain ranges such as these were beyond the reach of mankind, and remained a subject of contemplation for philosophers and scientists. Their inaccessible peaks seemed to penetrate into the ether, that radiant heavenly air the Greeks believed filled the upper regions of space. Mountains thus became sacred, the seats of the gods. Even today hikers can hardly resist the pull of majestic, towering mountains. Only in the late nineteenth and especially the twentieth century—a relatively short span of time—has man's thirst for knowledge and experience, along with technical developments, opened up new possibilities in exploration and allowed for a new conception of these ranges. In 1865 the first conquest of the Matterhorn was a sensation. The first 26,000-footer was climbed much later, in 1950. In 1953 Sir Edmund Hillary and the Sherpa Tenzing Norgay stood on the peak of Mount Everest. Reinhold Messner and Peter Habeler entered into what the ancients thought of as the last transition zone, that between air and ether, when in 1978 they were the first to summit Everest without supplemental oxygen. It has also been only a hundred years since mankind learned to fly, and it is not even fifty years now that man has been in space. Only a generation separates us from mankind's first step on the moon. In cosmic terms, these are small strides; we better understand their scale if we translate height into distance. A mountain's 26,000 feet is less than a half-hour's run around a stadium track for an athlete. And how far from Earth does a spaceship fly? Not far, only roughly the distance from London to Paris.

So far if such heights have to be conquered by traditional human means; so close if we negotiate them with the means provided by modern air and space travel.

Man's pursuit of heights has always been a journey into himself as well. Mountains have not been climbed only because they were there, as is often said. Yuri Gagarin's flight into space was considered the triumph of a political system, yet it was more than that; it was an important step toward what modern space travel has become, valuable to science as well as to mankind. The daring of individuals and groups helps all of us advance.

This has to do with the issue of perception, or "aesthetics" as the ancient Greeks called it. The achievement of an individual is perceived by multitudes, and spurs them on. Science and art are closely related, and in this publication they come together in truly artistic form. Viewing these ranges from space brings us close to the peaks we perceive as far away, even though they are right near by compared to the distances of space travel. Geography and geology tell us how they were created, but we crave to explore more fully this *Region between Far and Near*—to borrow the title of a small work by Paul Klee. It is science that helps us do so.

Professor Sigmar Wittig
Chairman of the Board of Directors, German Aerospace Center, DLR

Remote Sensing with Satellites
Technique, Uses, and Fascination

STEFAN DECH

Distance creates clarity—a principle that is especially true of remote sensing. From space, satellites observe Earth, sometimes surveying entire continents and other times focusing on details, and gather valuable data for research and industry. Using radar and infrared radiation, for example, satellites register more than the human eye is able to. Translated into pictures and combined with digital elevation models, their observations provide us not only with impressive perspectives but also surprising information about the earth's landscapes.

The Unusual Perspective

Seeing the planet Earth from space is a fascinating perspective, whether for astronauts in orbit or for the viewers of spectacular satellite photographs. It allows us to see Earth's beauty and vulnerability, and appreciate its wholeness without boundaries. The unfamiliar views of our home planet that space travel offers have given us new understanding, as evidenced by the unprecedented images of mountains and mountain ranges compiled in this book. Satellite photos of mountains such as the Himalayas, the Andes, and the Rockies are more likely the result of research projects than of studies for commercial purposes, and are consequently less well known and less frequently published. From the satellite perspective, mountains and mountain landscapes are full of contrasts. Within the smallest space the landscape changes: lush flatlands with farms and grazing land give way to formidable heights with glistening snowfields, glaciers, and steep cliffs. Light and shadow abruptly change and model the landscape in unique ways. Also, satellite sensors can show us mountains from an artificial radar perspective or in infrared.

What Is Remote Sensing?

Remote sensing is first of all a way of obtaining data about Earth's surface and atmosphere without coming into contact with the targets themselves. An important aim is to collect geophysical data in large-scale images that represent the objects' spectral qualities. These images can also be utilized in cartography and surveying, and the same technique is used in astronomy to study the planets. We speak of terrestrial observation when using Earth-centered remote-sensing techniques from space where Earth's reflected light and electromagnetic radiation are analyzed. The principle: everything on Earth has its own "spectral fingerprint," which can vary strongly depending on its state and the time the image is made. The spectral information gathered by remote sensing devices serves the geophysical and environmental sciences as a database for research and finds numerous other applications. Such data can also be represented in the form of satellite pictures, as in this book.

The Beginnings

Remote sensing was first developed during the space race of the past century, initially for military purposes. It offered an opportunity to observe foreign territories from a distance. But its great potential for scientific study of the earth was also recognized early on. The Earth Resources Technology Satellite (ERTS), launched in 1972 and shortly afterward renamed Landsat-I, marks the beginning of civilian terrestrial sensing from space. Today there are hundreds of highly complex sensors in space, making daily measurements relating to the atmosphere, the oceans, the cryosphere, and the land surface with its unique mountain worlds. The scientific data produced finds any number of practical uses, from forecasting the weather to estimating crop yields in growing regions to monitoring the environment, land-use planning, and supporting humanitarian assistance efforts (after natural catastrophes, for example). Much of the data ends up in international research programs, but it also finds applications in private industry planning, environmental management, and public safety.

Satellites and Instruments

The instruments employed on satellites include the most technologically advanced digital cameras, radiometers, spectrometers, and radar systems. Depending on the objective, they operate in specific wavelengths of the electromagnetic spectrum, and can register both radiation in the optical spectrum as well as radiation invisible to the human eye. Radar sensors also work actively, beaming microwaves at the earth's surface and registering the echoes thrown back from the ground. This method allows images to be generated both by day and by night. Radar waves also penetrate clouds, trace gases, and particulate matter, and optical and radar sensors can detect the tiniest movements in the earth's surface. All of the detailed information the sensors yield can be used to create digital elevation models.

These instruments are operated on satellites and occasionally also on manned carriers (the Russian space station MIR, the International Space Station, or space shuttles), which are placed in different orbits. For high-resolution data, for example in meteorology, geostationary orbits 22,369 miles high are utilized. At this height, the satellite moves with the rotation of the earth, meaning the satellite's view of the earth stands virtually still, and the position on the surface it is focused on can be continually observed from the same angle. For surface sensing, so-called near-polar satellite paths are frequently used with roughly 100- to 110-minute orbits. Their heights vary between 340 and 528 miles. The advantage of these orbits is that virtually every spot on the earth's surface can be seen. The lifespan of a satellite varies, from one year to ten if we are lucky. Up to ten different instruments are operated on the platform of a given satellite, sometimes simultaneously. By far the majority of today's Earth-observation satellites have been put into service by national and international organizations (NASA, ESA, CNES, ISRO, JAXA, DLR) within the framework of scientific or sensing programs.

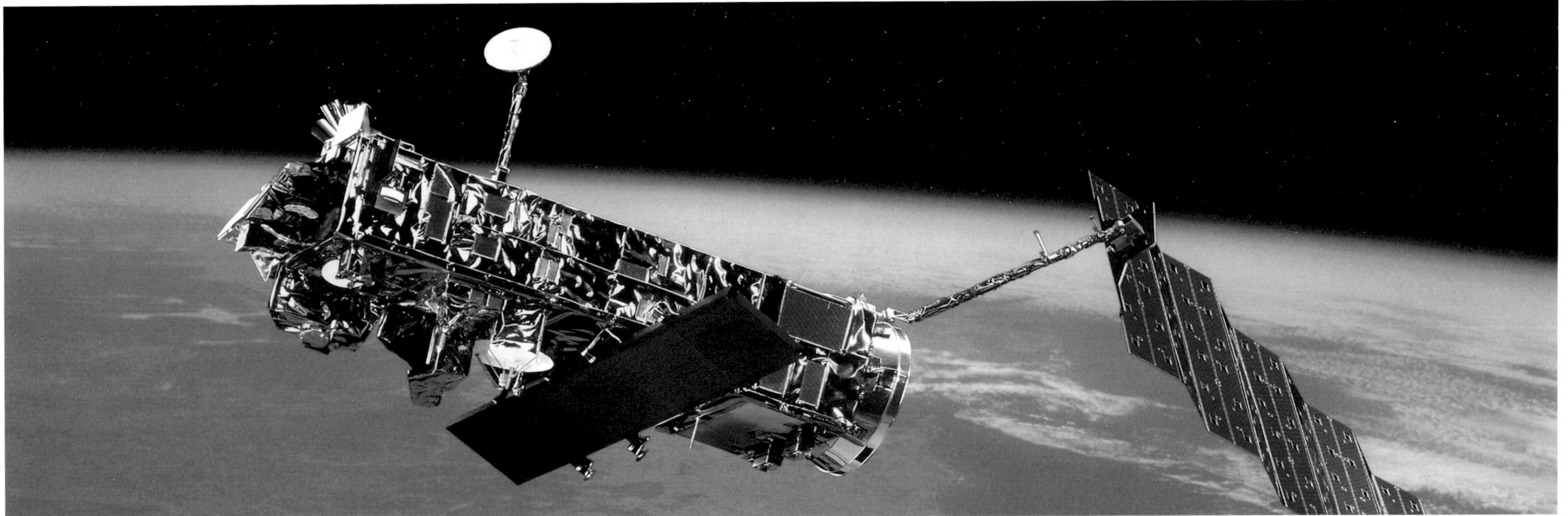

What Kinds of Images Are Provided?

Remote sensors provide comprehensive information. This is their decisive advantage, as it enables us to study larger areas of the earth in context and observe their development. Even the densest network of observation stations on the ground provides only limited data, from which we draw conclusions about larger areas only by way of interpolation and models. Complete images of larger regions, especially those difficult to reach like the polar regions, deserts, or high mountain areas, are only possible through remote sensing. Depending on the sensor, remote-sensing data have different resolutions. Picture sharpness ("spatial resolution") plays a special role. The smaller the pixel resolution, the sharper the image; civilian satellite sensors have pixel resolutions of up to sixty centimeters. Often remote-sensing systems are equipped with pixel resolutions between ten and thirty meters. It is important to be able to classify surfaces as well as secure information about their condition. Here the spectral resolution of a sensor is a key factor; it determines the precision with which significant differences on the ground can be perceived. With high spatial and spectral resolution it is finally possible to determine not only the type and exterior shape of an object but also its physical composition. Such analysis requires elaborate preparatory work. In the end, physics and technical precision come together in products that provide us with complex geophysical information such as the photosynthetic activity of plants, the concentration of pollutants in the seas, or the surface temperatures of glaciers. All this is achieved with computers and by applying mathematical algorithms. Various other steps are required as well: it is necessary to consider atmospheric conditions, the position of the sun, and the observation geometry at the time the image is recorded as well as a number of sensor-specific peculiarities. Finally, it is necessary to calculate the precise geographical correlation between the reading point in space and the entire image.

The Pictures for This Book

For this book we have collected satellite images from various terrestrial observation missions and prepared them digitally, at times through complex conversion steps. The majority are optical satellite data with spatial resolutions ranging from one kilometer to sixty centimeters. Various visualization techniques have been used, among them true color, false color, and pseudocolor images of selected spectral channels or of elevation models. In many cases, data from different sources were digitally combined to achieve a particular expressiveness. This is especially visible in the perspective views, some of which give the impression of being photographs. In these instances, elevation models were specially produced from stereoscopically interpreted data sets (the same area recorded from slightly different angles) or with the aid radar interferometry, an innovative yet highly complex technique. Many elevation models were taken from airplanes or produced by digitizing maps. We maintained the highest standards with regard to expressiveness, brilliance, and accuracy in the selection of the data and its processing. Even so, in some cases recording errors or data gaps had to be mathematically corrected so as to improve the appearance of the image. To enrich the collection, we have also included photographs taken by astronauts with analogue cameras from an altitude of roughly 185 miles. These round out a fascinating and one-of-a-kind collection of space images of the earth's mountains.

The Big Picture
Mountains from Space

REINHOLD MESSNER

The draw of the mountains has to do with overview—the person who stands on top of one comes back down with a new sense of the world, and a new understanding of himself. It is not the mountain but the view from the peak that suggests an increased awareness. Why else do people climb?

The view that extends out from a great height is a gift, even though we are able to retain little of what we saw once we have come back down. But the return is an even greater gift, coming back out of the cold, the danger, and the exposure that intensify any peak tour. Returning from the icy heights to the world of men is like a rebirth. But even so, we were there; we saw the world, or a piece of it, from above. And that stays with you.

The ancient myth of the wise man who comes down out of the mountains has its origin in this view from a mountaintop. Even when myth degenerates into cliché, when teams of hundreds climb Mount Everest in goose step, the seduction of the heights, of standing above everything, remains.

Long before alpinism and tourism began claiming them, mountains were places of refuge for scholars, thinkers, and poets. Even in our age of recreational physical activity, the mountain continues to be a place of exaltation. A peak means expansive views, spectacular light, and fresh air. From its top, the mountain offers a feeling of freedom, transcendence, and joy. It seems only a step from the beyond, as if all our cares, all obstacles—the finite—lie beneath us.

This book *Mountains from Space* takes that next step. In these images, the whole world unfolds, revealing its many geographical, meteorological, geological, volcanic, and tectonic phenomena. These images present a new view of the world's mountains and mountain ranges. For the team of writers, scientists, and mountaineers that developed this project, it was not a matter of parading the highest or loveliest of these peaks; it is their variety that fascinated us. The mountains and mountain ranges created in the long history of our Earth are so endlessly varied that we were able to single out only a few from each continent. The pictures of them give this book the allure of a gem collection. We gaze transfixed at the forces that shape the earth, almost like extraterrestrials.

The concern here is not the who, where, and how of a particular climb, but rather the forces that formed and continue to form our mountains, how they are changed, and how they finally disappear. We can marvel at the movement of the Indian plate, at the eruption of lava, at coral reefs lifted up into massive mountain blocks. We can see sediments piled atop one another and rivers washing away the foundations of mighty peaks. In other places the earth boils over, and cooled magmas form volcanic cones. Wind and weather become visible as well, and with them the erosion that breaks down whole mountain ranges until only sand and shards of rock remain. In the time span of millions of years, even mountains are mortal. They are no more eternal than the ice that covers Earth's extremities—south, north, heavenward.

In our day, glaciation is undergoing a radical change, and the mix of vegetation that clothes our mountains in their lower reaches is being altered. In the Alps, the vegetation has steadily climbed upward over the past few decades; in deserts it is pulling back. Such deserts, decayed mountain ranges such as the Gobi, are gradually being worn away by wind and water, ending up in the sea, where perhaps new mountains are forming.

The eruption of Mount Etna, the rounded shapes of the soft sandstone monolith of Ayers Rock in the heart of Australia, the tilted strata of the south wall of Nanga Parbat, the inland ice that calves into the sea off Patagonia—all of these document forces at work millions of years before human beings began weaving myths about the creation of the world. At Mount Kailash in the Transhimalayas these forces of creation are especially clear, and for that reason the Tibetans consider it a sacred place.

These vast workings—continental shifting, climate change, erosion—have previously been perceptible only to scientists. But with these new, extremely precise satellite images, such fascinating and monumental forces can be observed and studied by interested laymen.

Seen from above, landscapes are made up of mountains and watercourses. Just as a transparent model of the human body consists of a framework of bone and a network of arteries, the earth's crust is structured in mountain ridges, rivers, creeks, and gullies.

Many cultures have envisioned a mountain as the center of the universe, often as a bridge between Earth and heaven. People who live within sight of icy-white peaks that consort with clouds can even be convinced that mountains fly. Mountains are thought of as places for communication between our world and the beyond. Many have become places of pilgrimage, others taboo. Caves within mountains are themselves sacred places, yet we can't witness them from space; the insides of mountains are still mysterious, they keep their secrets. Nor do we see the graves of our ancestors, who have helped to shape the world along with watercourses and mountains.

Mountains are revered for being both protective and perilous. We associate the inside of a mountain with shelter, birth, and the tomb, and envision magic forces and incalculable treasure. Mountain caves and grottoes have served as refuges since mankind's beginnings. Hermits and wise men have retreated to them hoping to discover the meaning of life. But they can also be the haunts of wild beasts, demons and earth-spirits, dragons, and trolls.

In mountains and on top of them, one therefore has to master one's fears. Humans are as helpless at great heights as we are in the dark, and we are always plagued by faint-heartedness, loneliness, and alienation. Seeing mountains from below, it is easy to form a distorted image of their actual shapes. Before setting off on a climb one has to evaluate which is the best route, and during the climb the change in perspective can fuel our fears. Once on top, on the highest peaks in the world, there is too little space for experiments. There is not enough room to stand, the air is too thin to breathe deeply, and there is too little time to linger. There is no revelation, in part because in the dead zone our brains are not getting enough oxygen.

So do mountains only fully reveal themselves from space? Perhaps. From below, the sheer sizes of mountains are impressive, from above and far away it is their colors, shapes, and the play of light on them that enthrall us. From a peak one enjoys an overview of the surrounding landscape, from space one can witness the evidence of millions of years of the earth's history. The processes of glaciation, eruption, sedimentation, and erosion can be seen at work. Looking down from space, we are not only reminded of how small and insignificant we are, we are confronted with our own limited conception of time.

Mountains exist in a wholly different time scale—the history of the earth can be read in their sediments. They contain an archive of knowledge accessible to all. The Himalayas, the Alps, and the Rocky Mountains teach us about the collisions of continental plates. Volcanic eruptions have radically changed the climate, causing the extinction of plant and animal species. And there are surprises: for example, Mount Everest is not the world's tallest mountain after all. That distinction belongs to Hawaii's Mauna Kea, whose peak rises 13,795 feet above sea level but whose base lies a full 18,045 feet down on the ocean floor, giving it a total height of 31,840 feet.

Mankind has settled its gods on mountains, but like mountains they are not eternal. Like them, humans are subject to time and to oblivion.

Here below, in our sprawling urban centers it has become so noisy and hectic that we easily lose sense of ourselves. Seekers of truth head for the mountains as they always have, in search of barren landscapes, the silence, the solitude, and the view from above; as if rocks, water, and wasteland were enough to disclose the way of the world.

The images in this book require us to use our imagination. They provide a new understanding, but only after careful study. Here mountains are much more than aids to orientation, places to experience, playgrounds of the gods and our leisure society; they have metaphysical dimensions. Earth's secrets are exposed here in color spectrums, cloud banks, depressions, and prominences. Only from this great distance does the earth's crust appear viscous and malleable. Down here we are too close to see it as such.

The way mountains rise and fall, the way they are carried back to the sea over millions of years and ultimately folded and raised up again in new combinations is a spectacle that renders our own existence as absurd as it is challenging. Climbing can be instructive; to truly appreciate our world we all need to contemplate mountains from above—especially from space.

The Ballad of the Happy Return

CHRISTOPH RANSMAYR

Enough! Enough. There comes a day when it's enough.
Are we crouched beneath drifting banners of ice?
Lying exhausted beneath the Southern Cross
on a moonless tropical night? It is enough.
How far we've traveled by now
how far we've already climbed, ever higher
till one more step would have led us into the blue
into the clouds, into the void.
Across pack ice, crevasses, boulders
and the scythes of dunes of the Great Sand Sea
on we moved, tumbling, till now
till energies are almost spent.
But there comes a day, and now
it is enough.

How long we did nothing but dream:
of those icy crowns at the poles
of the headwaters of Amazon, Niger, and Nile.
Of shimmering seas of reflected air
in the deserts of the Takla Makan, Gobi, and Tanezrouft.
Dreamt of summits: Nanga Parbat, Shisha Pangma
Dhaulagiri and Chogori and Makalu
and finally that even the highest of them all
lay beneath our feet: Sagarmatha! Chomolungma.
The one that some have baptized with holy names
and that others labeled from afar
with the name of the surveyor George Everest.
The highest of all here beneath our feet!

Enough. There comes a day when our goals
either bear our traces' adornment
wedges of ice-picks on walls of rock
banners and prayer pennants on snowy caps
of the upper troposphere
and the drifting web of our step atop dunes—
or wilderness, snow, sand, and morass
remain unadorned and compel us to return:
Typhoon. Hunger. Wounds. Alpine madness. Fever. Fear.
Exhaustion or homesickness.
One way or another:
there comes a day when we turn our backs on our dreams
and set out down the path to the depths
back to humankind.

How many of those before us
have vanished on this same path, sank there in the ice
in stagnant water, in the abyss, in quicksand?
The way to humankind, back to what we know
devours still greater energies
than the roads to the core of a dream.
But all we really want is to go back
to where we came from
we want, we say, we gasp, we howl
out of here
we want to go home!

Great black heavens! Beneath which we're
now so alone.
What all have we not taken upon us
since that morning when we first left
our bed, our house, what we loved most
and set out, moving up and away.
Up and away!
Nights in snow caverns
northern lights, mirages
were exchanged for iron-hard daily routine
clean sheets for a bivouac in the ice
a coastal promenade edged in roses for quicksand
a candlelight dinner for hunger and cramps
summer evenings for the Arctic darkness.
There the ever-present neighbors,
here abandonment
there almond soap, eye shadow, lavender
here worms and maggots under the skin.
Throat and mouth all in flames
the tongue a charred piece of meat.
And this thirst.
Thirst was the most terrible of scourges.
Or was it fighting for air?
Twenty-nine thousand feet
above the sheen of the sea
we panted and gasped for air.
Like sky-borne sailors to be interred on clouds
laced into sleeping bags
nailed to rocky balconies and battlements
we tried to sleep while still standing
because there was no place to lie down
beneath hanging walls of ice.

The sky high above our goal
was of such a dark and metallic blue
that even at noon constellations
made their appearance:
Swan, Dolphin, Dragon, Andromeda.
Fighting for air, fighting alpine madness
everything that to those where we came from

had seemed unbearable
we had to bear
and then step by step
we reeled toward ridges and pyramids of snow
that retreated before us step by step.
And why all these scourges?

We scaled the highest, the holy mountains
because they were there, simply there.
Ah yes, they stood in the way
between us and the distance
ah yes, and an invisible line
seemed to lead through calvings
and cascades of stone
up into the heights, still further up
a thread visible only to us
through a vertical labyrinth
into the void
our path!
The ocean, the seas, they seduced us
because beneath a horizon plumed
with the crests of waves
there lay what was never seen
unchristened harbors, nameless gardens, our happiness.
What is and what was could not be it all.
And so even in the heart of the desert
we suspected flourishing cities, oases,
white palaces, Zarzura,
paradise itself.

Enough!
Whatever it was, whatever we had
it was never enough.
For there, far beyond and above the clouds
yes even in the gloom of the deepest Pacific trough
somewhere down below, up above
there had to be something to find
that at least bore remotest likeness
to the paintings of our daydreams.

And so we walked and climbed and drifted,
trundled, and kept on swimming
from one pole to the other, across oceans
passing over the white chains
of the Himalayas and Karakorum
along the equator
and wrenched our paths round to a circle.
Then came the day, under fluttering banners of ice
the Southern Cross high above us,
it was enough and we happily or coerced
by some necessity turned our backs
on our dreams and then we said
enough, we want to go home.

Strange, how distant
at the edge of exhaustion, at your goal
the familiar things can appear.
Unattainable the bed, the dwelling, those we love.
The summit of Chomolungma, of Everest
beneath our feet
Zarzura, the white city, palpably near!
But our bed: unattainable.
Our confidence, our energies, water and bread
even the air in our lungs—all exhausted
all running out
just distance, depth, abandonment
of those there's enough both now and always.
A kingdom for a bed!
Let's get out of here, we howl, out of here
the return is all.

Whoever has reached his goal, whoever has arrived
in the distance at the top, at the bottom, meaning us
he must realize
that he does not have even half his journey
behind him yet
that the fight back to the familiar
can be longer and more painful
than the path into uncertainty ever was.
Enough! Return! Go on!
We're prepared to endure anything, anything
just to finally arrive at that spot
from which we first set out an eternity ago.
But how slowly, how reluctantly
all that's familiar comes toward us
unbearable slowly
just like the south peak of Everest that day
or the darkened bays of Novaya Zemlya.
Toward us? It vanishes with our energies
seems already lost.
Now, when we finally want to go home
down into the depths
what is nearest and most loved draws back from us.
Are we dreaming?
Among breakers, ridges, snowcapped pinnacles
of feathery pillows and down? Of our bed?
Maybe, we dream, just maybe, one day
beneath those waving banners of ice?
on a moonless tropical night?
we will arrive.
Doors will open, not abysses
arms, not crevasses in ice.
We shall embrace and be embraced.
Carafes of red wine, gardens, set tables
all shining in the colors of homesickness
everything just as it was.
And in the night after our return
we shall sleep, for the first time in months
in an eternity, a sleep without dreams
overwhelmed by happiness, to once again be
where we were so long ago.
We shall sleep
until some sound awakes us, a word and another
melodious names, Nanga Parbat
Cho Oyu, Gasherbrum
voices out of deeps
that cannot be reached by a plumb line, a rope
Makalu, Amazon, Takla Makan, Annapurna,
the South Pole!
A muddle of voices, a chorus
and its refrain: Up and away! Up and away!

The screws of a ship, the engines
the runners on a dogsled
the crunching of footsteps in snow and in sand
up and away, it whispers, it roars in our ears
up and away, to remain is to be lost
it sings and it gasps in chorus
until our bed, where we lie safe in feathers
spindrift and down, whitecaps, sandspouts
blankets of cashmere and snow, a place
of rest in the web of longitude and latitude
is gently convulsed, and lifted
and slowly inexorably
begins to take flight.

[EUROPE]

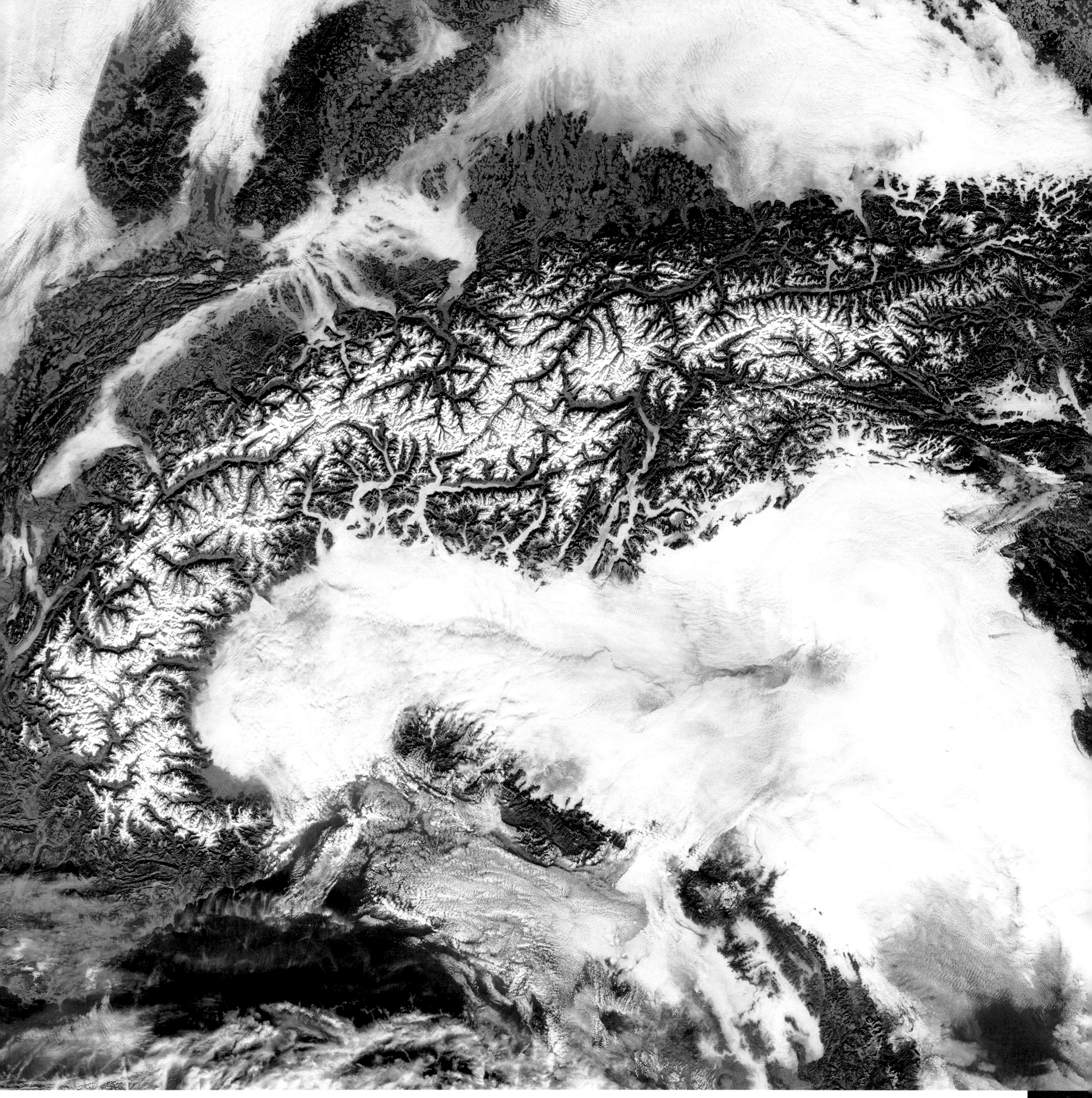

The arc of the Alps framed by cloud

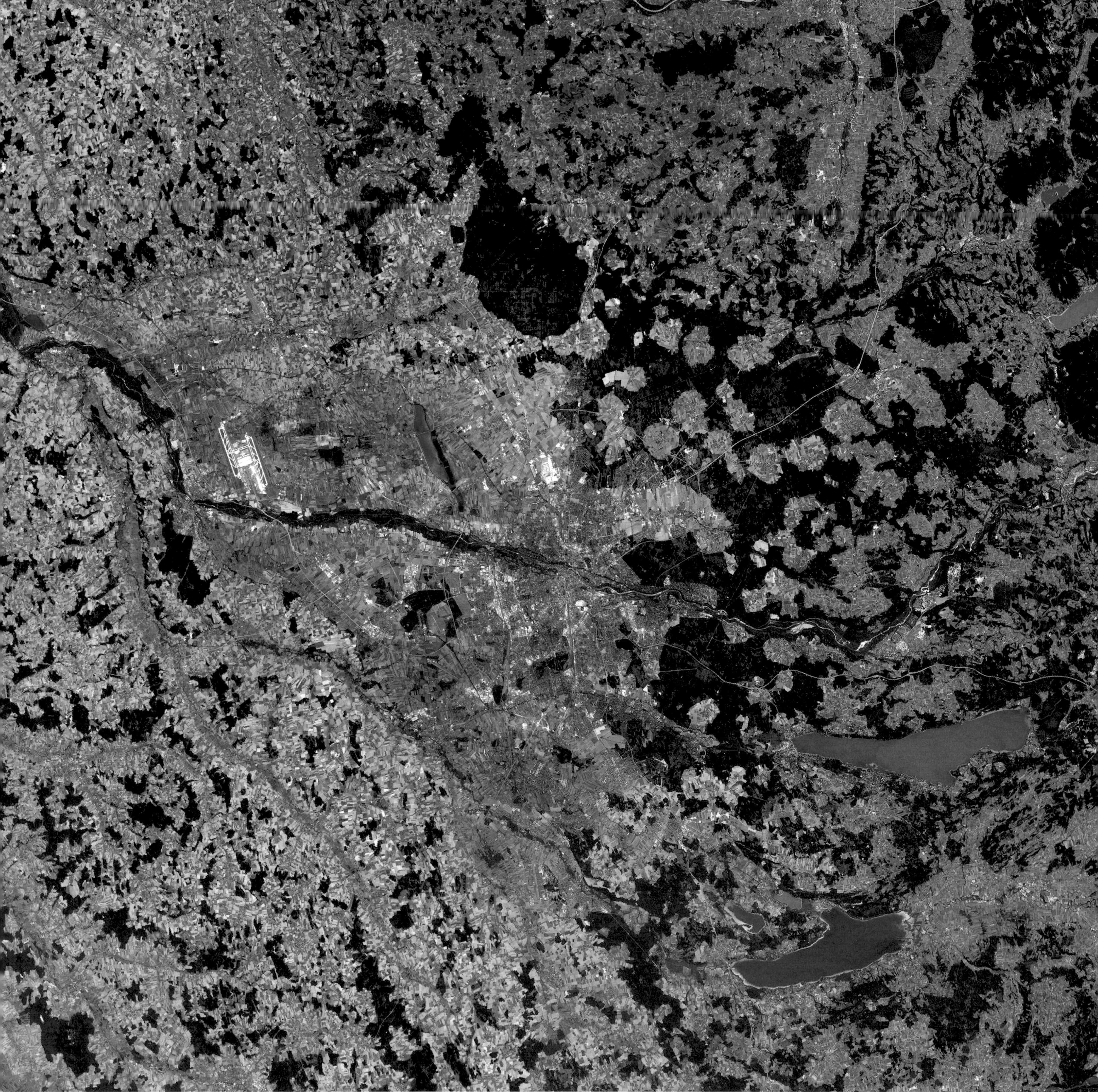

The settled landscape of the northern Alps, from Munich, Germany, to Innsbruck, Austria

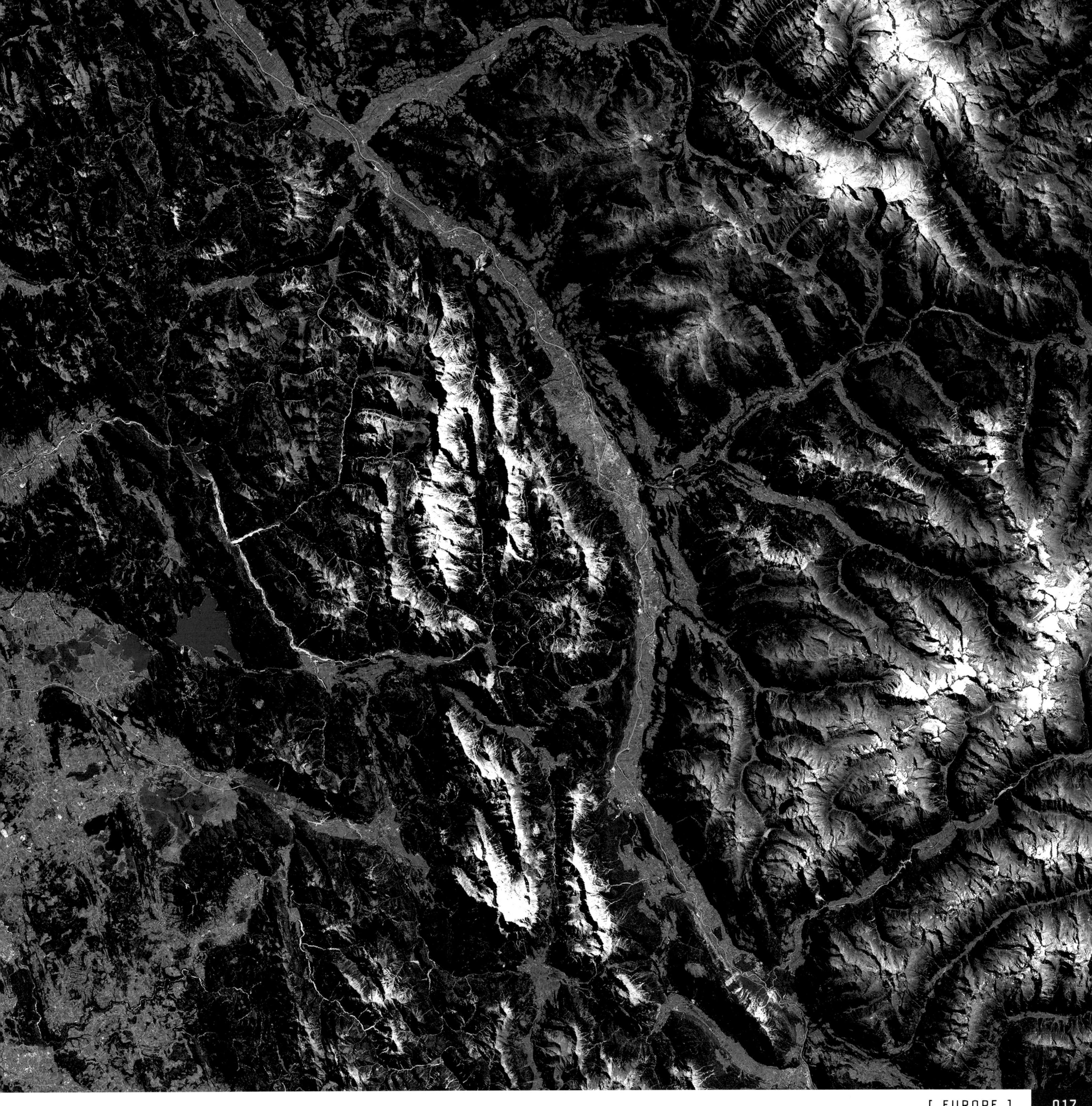

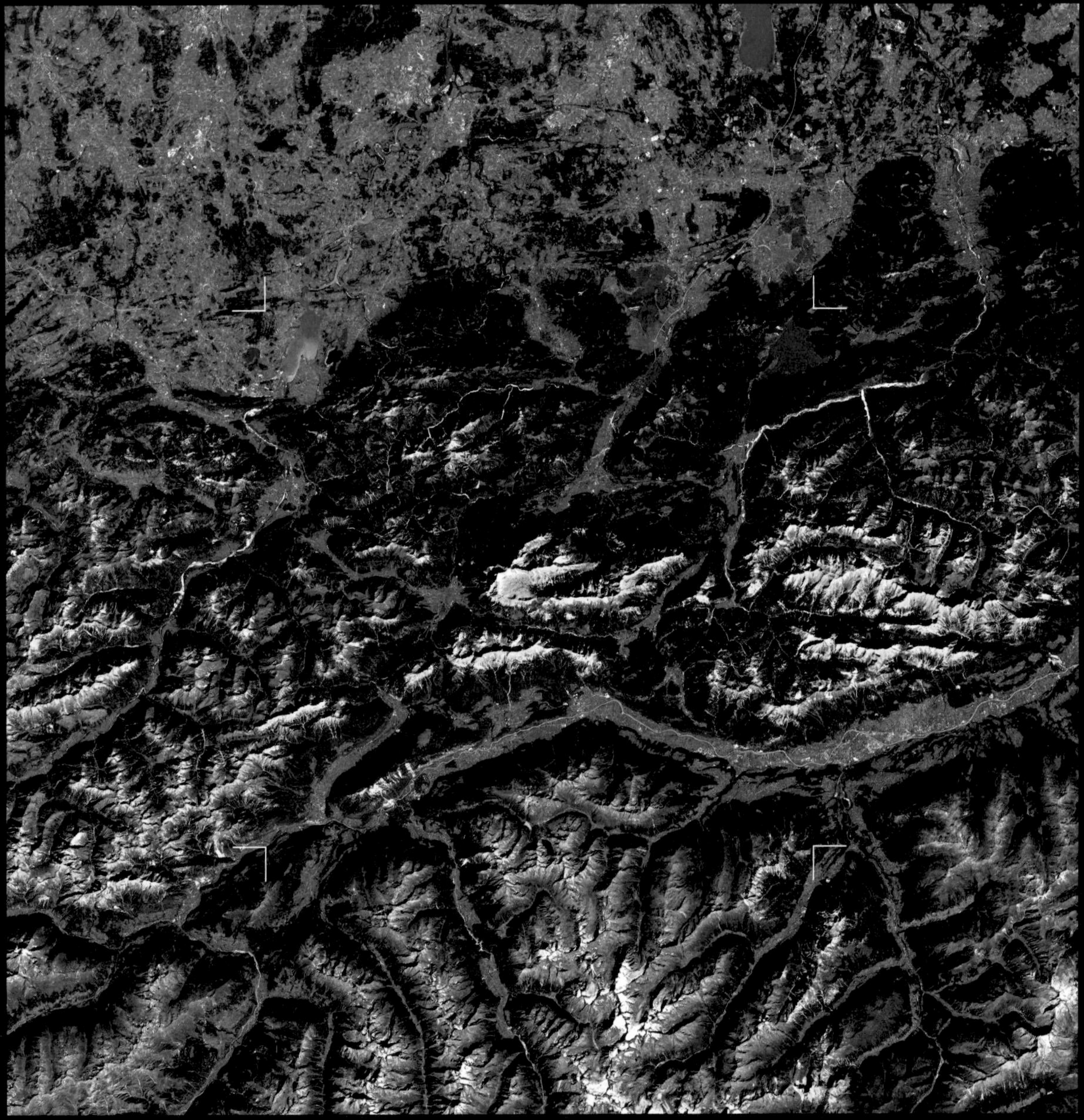

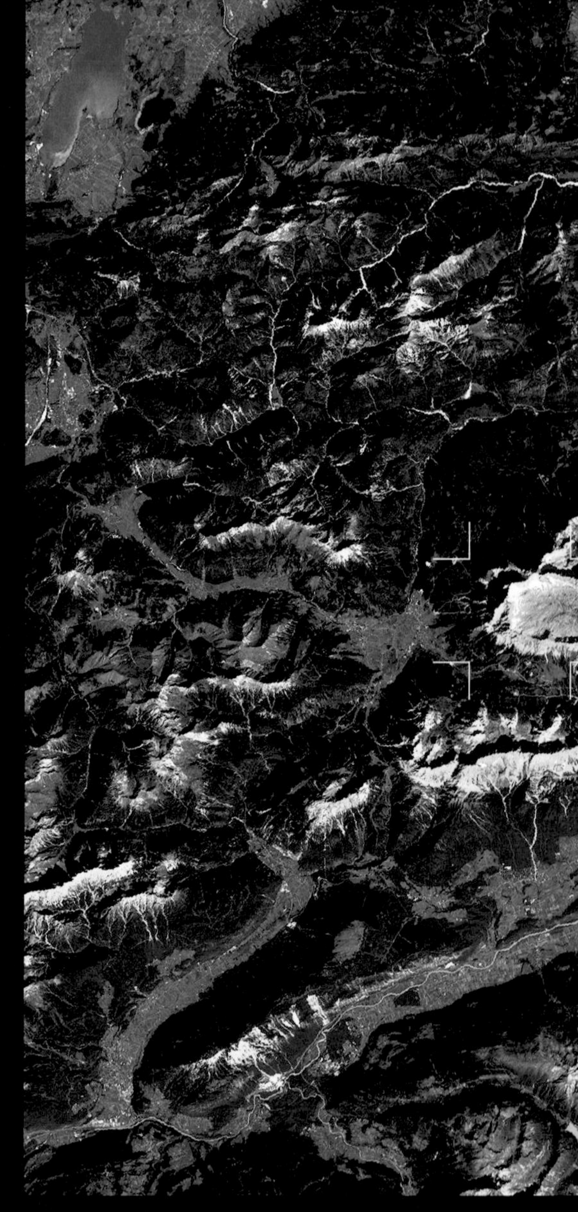

The Zugspitze, Germany's highest mountain, in detail

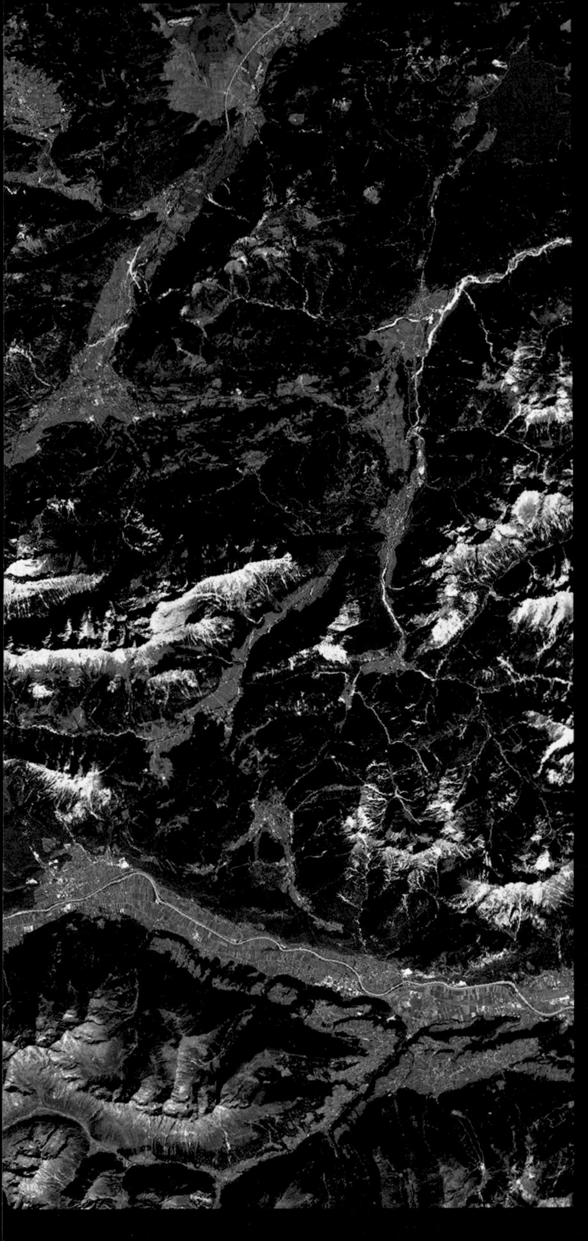

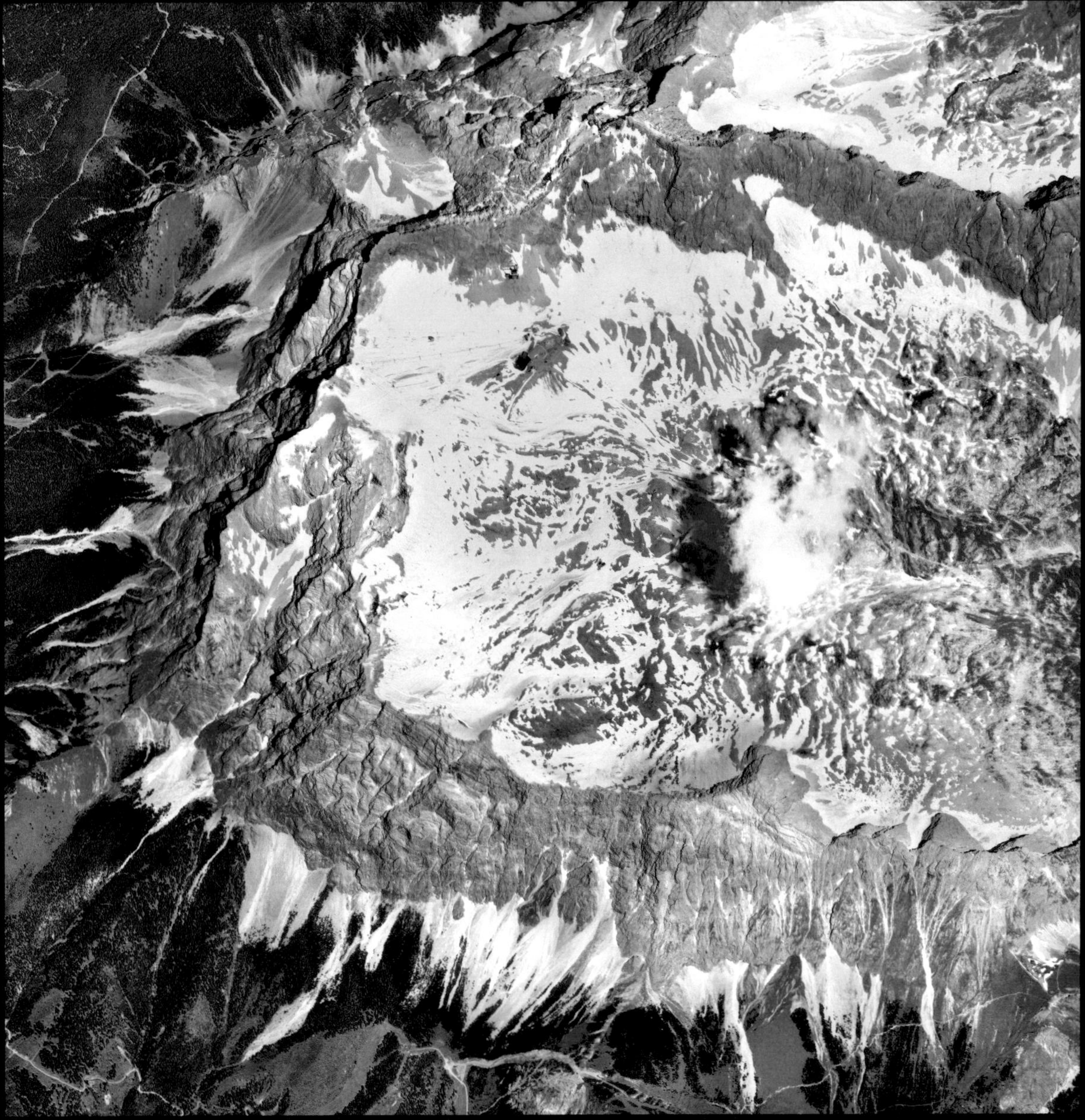

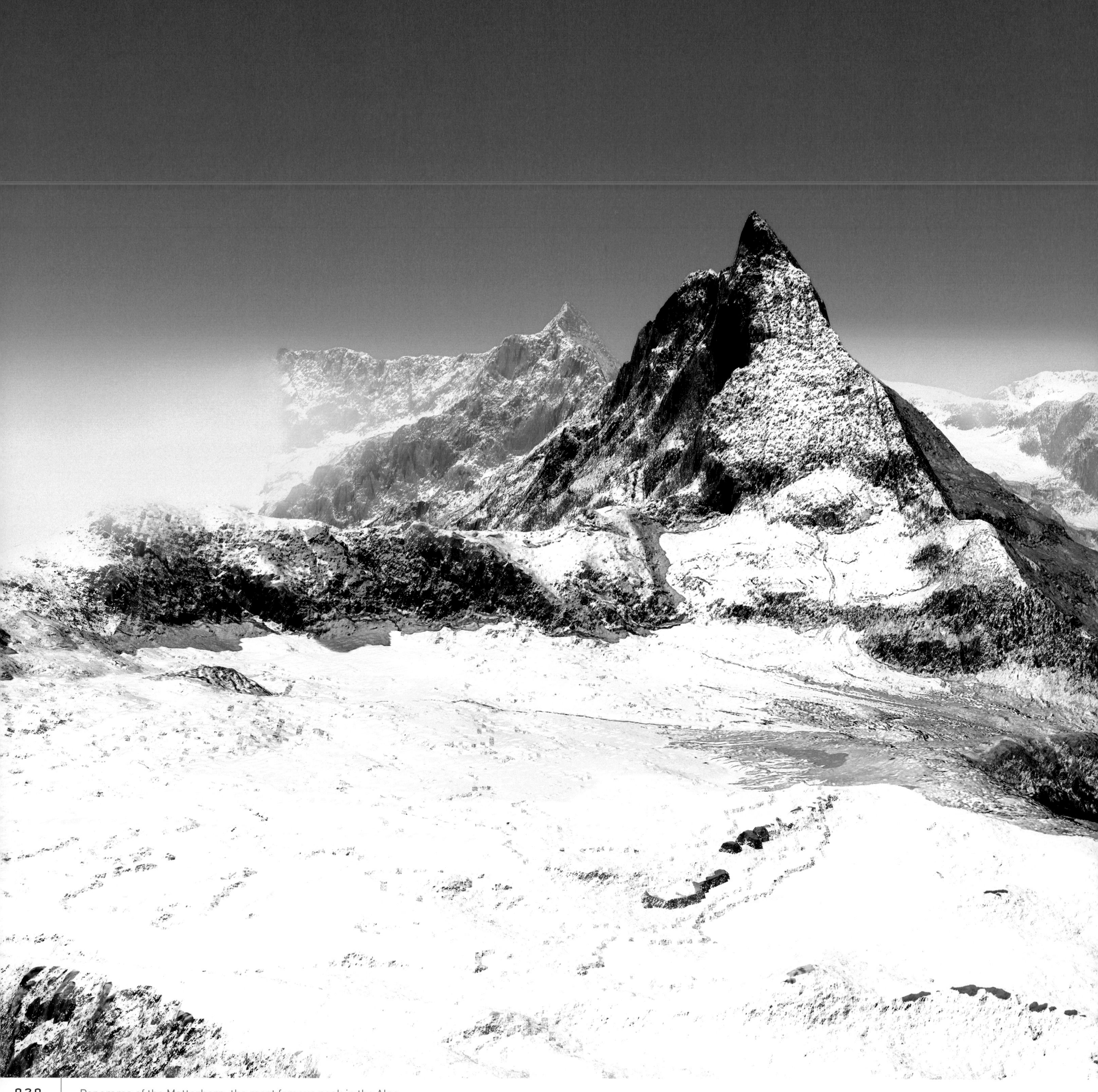

Panorama of the Matterhorn, the most famous peak in the Alps

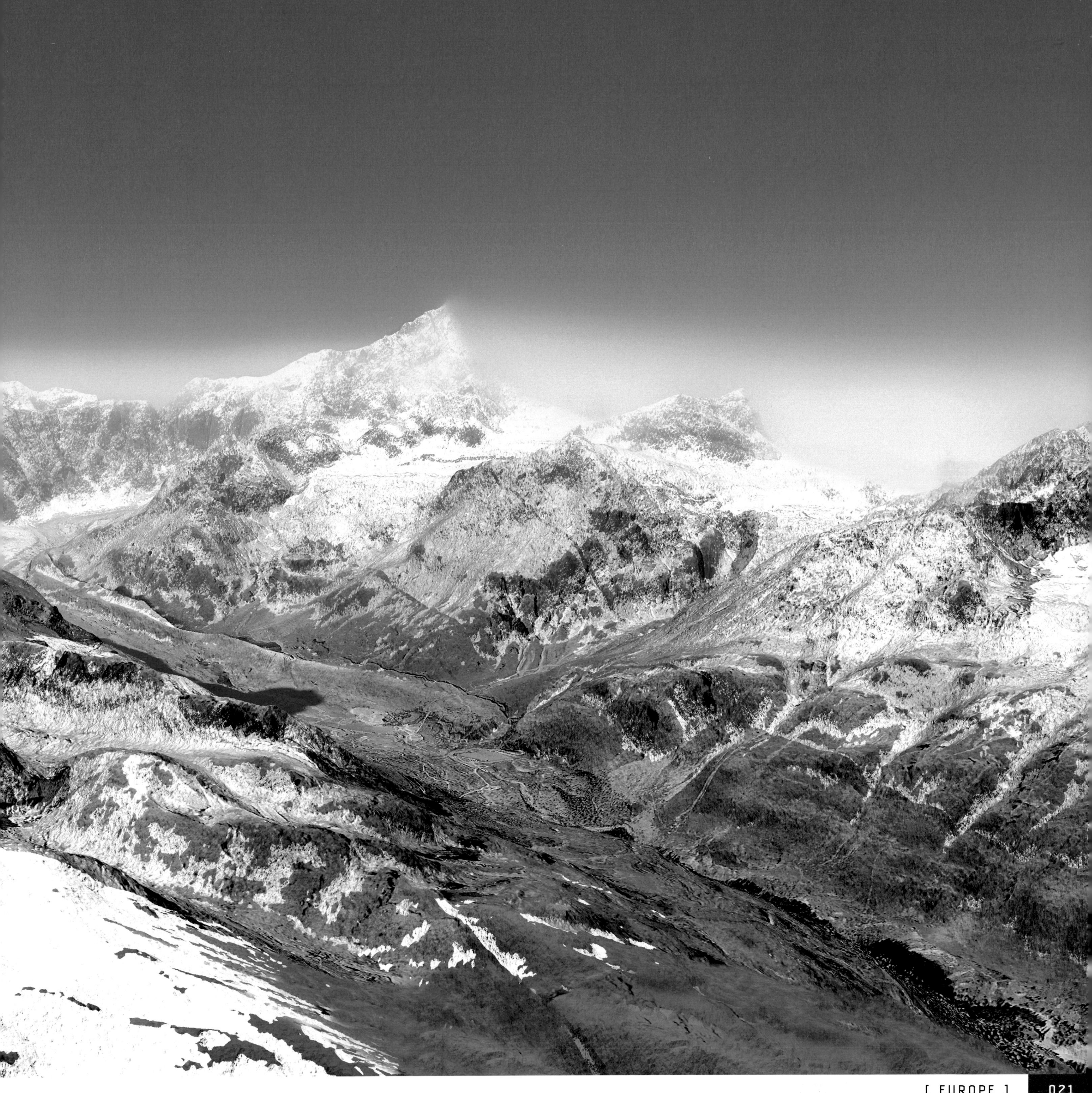

Mountain Building
Zones of Continental Crimping

RÜDIGER GLASER

Mountains are an expression of the earth's constant internal changes. Wherever tectonic plates collide or wherever new crust is created, as it is along the midocean ridges, we discover the answers to questions people have asked since the beginning: How were these huge structures formed? What sort of forces were at work here? Can blocks of stone miles thick really be thrust atop one another? And how is it that we often find petrified shells, corals, and starfish high in the mountains?

Whether as jagged silhouettes, soaring cones, or towering monoliths, mountains are found throughout the world, on every continent and in every climate zone. From an ecological viewpoint, these skyscrapers built of forest, rock, and ice serve as links between different kinds of landscape, connecting the network of life. After the seacoasts, they are the longest feature of the landscape, threading for thousands of miles across entire continents.

The Eurasian mountain belt, extending some 6,000 miles from the Alps through the Caucasus and on to the Himalayas, is a particularly remarkable example of the result of a collision between plates. The Alps owe their existence to a continent-ocean-continent collision, due to their position in the crimping zone between the European and African plates. They were created during the most recent, or eponymous Alpine, phase of mountain building that began some 120 million years ago and continues to this day.

No less impressive is the system of the Cordilleras and Andes, stretching some 10,500 miles long, which border the west side of the American continent. Even though these are big numbers, the surface area of the earth that is occupied by mountains is quite small. Only 3 percent of the earth's surface rises above 6,500 feet. Mount Everest, the highest point on earth, lifts up 29,028 feet above sea level. Yet compared to Earth's diameter, Everest's height seems trivial. From space, mountain ranges appear to be mere wrinkles on the earth's surface, even taking into account the distances between deep-sea trenches and mountain peaks. The maximum rise in height in the shortest distance is that between the Spencer F. Byrd Deep in the Atacama deep-sea trench at 26,456 feet below sea level and the 22,058-foot Andes volcano Llullaillaco.

The most spectacular mountains we all know, the Alps, the Caucasus, the Himalayas, the Cordillera system with the Rocky Mountains in North America and the Andes of South America, and the New Zealand Alps, are all relatively young mountains geologically. They have a number of the features characteristic of high mountains: towering heights, steep slopes, peaks rising above the tree and snow lines. Even height alone is an important criterion. It is overwhelming to see how the Himalayas suddenly lift up to heights of more than 26,000 feet above the low-lying Ganges plain. The way the Andes fall steeply to the lowlands of the Pacific Coast is similarly sublime. Perhaps the most imposing mountain valley is that of the Kali Gandak in Nepal, cut between Dhaulagiri-Himal in the west and Annapurna-Himal in the east. The adjacent flank of Dhaulagiri I (26,795 feet above sea level) rises to a record height of 18,696 feet, while the west flank of Nilgiri on the other side of the valley, part of the Annapurna chain with peaks as high as 23,150 feet, rises more than 13,000 feet. Compared to these, the valley walls in the Alpine region are dwarflike, even though the east wall of the Watzmann rises 6,232 feet above the Königsee, which lies at a mere 1,974 feet above sea level.

Geologists distinguish four phases of mountain building, called orogenies, in Earth's history. The most recent one, the Alpine phase, began in the Cretaceous period 120 million years ago and was largely completed by 65 million years ago, but in part continues to this day. Surviving examples of the next oldest phase, referred to as the Variscan, from up to 350 million years ago are more heavily eroded—the Urals, the Altai, the Tien Shan, the southern Appalachians, and the mountains of northeast Australia. The teeth of erosion have been gnawing for an especially long time on the mountains thrust up in the next oldest period, the Caledonian phase, which began 450 million years ago. Examples are Newfoundland, the Scottish Highlands, and the mountains of Scandinavia. In certain areas, these landscapes have been so thoroughly leveled that now they are scarcely perceived as mountains at all. They are consequently known as rump mountains. The mountains of the oldest, or Assyntian, phase are virtually invisible.

Volcanic mountains like those of the arc of islands in the western Pacific, Southeast Asia, East Africa, Hawaii, and the highlands of Mexico, are very young and for the most part still active. Forms unto themselves are the nunataks that tower above the network of glaciers on Greenland, Spitzbergen, and in Antarctica.

Mountains are formed by dynamic processes resulting from plate tectonics, generally plates colliding or drifting apart. For example, high mountains are produced when an oceanic plate collides with portions of the continental crust, or the heavier oceanic crust slides beneath the lighter continental one, creating what is called a subduction. A deep-sea trench is formed in the area of the subduction, and the edge of the continental plate is compressed and folded. The American Cordillera system was created in just such a subduction zone. Old crust sections, so-called terrains, can be carried along and welded to the continental edges, as on Vancouver Island. Subduction is generally accompanied by volcanic activity. This is predominantly of the explosive type, as in the case of Mount St. Helens in the North American Cordillera, owing to the acidic molten mass and high gas content.

Another type of tectonic movement is the collision of two continental plates. Here, unlike the collision between an oceanic plate and a continental one, neither of the two massive plates can dive below the other. Though this may sound less spec-

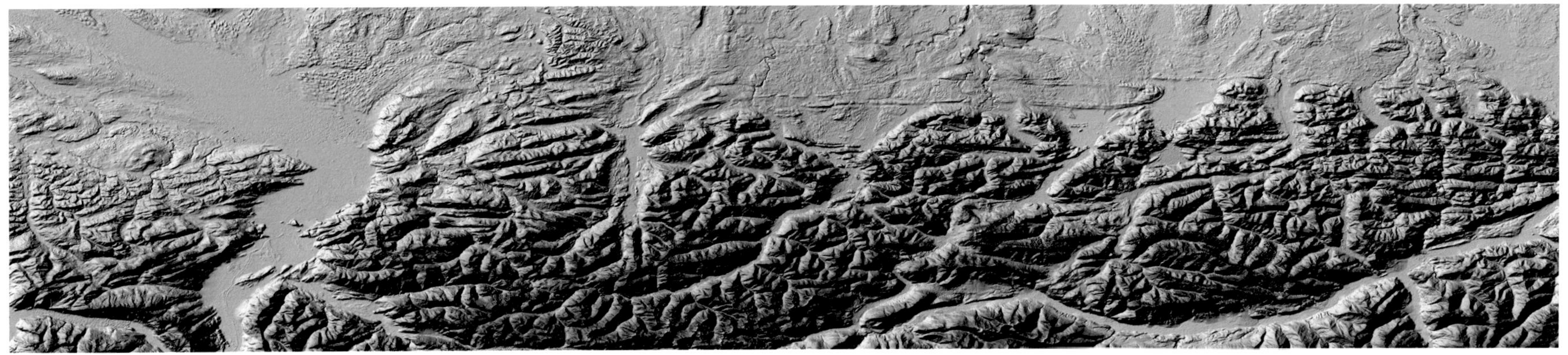

An elevation model of the central northern Alps in February 2002. The folds and structures of the individual mountain masses and the deeply cut valleys, also the Lake Constance basin (upper left), are shown with striking clarity.

tacular, it is exactly this process that has given us some of the mightiest mountain ranges like the Alps, the High Atlas, the Caucasus, and the Himalayas. At the junction, such a collision results in the thickening of the continental edges and the elevation of chains of mountains. This compensatory movement, as the collision forces the lighter crust down into the denser mantle, continues to this day. The Alps are rising from one to two millimeters a year, the Himalayas a whopping two to five centimeters. Seen in this light, our most typical high mountains are zones of crimping between continents, the Alps between the continents of Africa and Eurasia, the Himalayas between India and Eurasia.

The third type involves the collision of two oceanic plates, when one or the other is pressed into the earth's mantle. A common result of such a collision is a basic to intermediate level of volcanic activity where the lava flows out rather smoothly as opposed to erupting explosively. This kind of activity produces strings of volcanic islands like the so-called Ring of Fire circling the western Pacific. Such plate tectonics are often accompanied by major earthquakes and tsunamis, as the world witnessed with the devastating events of December 26, 2004.

Plates not only collide, but they can also drift apart. This occurs on a massive scale along the midocean ridges where sea-floor spreading is a major mechanism of plate tectonics. As the name suggests, most of this process occurs at the bottom of the ocean. On contact with water, the extruded basal magmas are formed into typical pillow lavas. The midocean ridges where this occurs are thus the opposite of subduction zones: in the latter the crust material is being melted, but in midocean ridges new crust is continually being formed. Altogether, midocean ridges form the largest mountain system in the world. In some spots the resulting volcanoes lift above the surface of the sea and form islands; the largest example of this phenomenon is Iceland.

Mountains can also be formed by "hot spots." Hot spots are cylindrical streams of molten magma from sixty to ninety miles in diameter known as "mantle plumes" rising up out of the lower mantle. At the surface, these rising magmas form volcanoes. If a tectonic plate slides across such a stationary hot spot, a chain of volcanoes of decreasing ages results. This is best exemplified by the Hawaiian Islands, with the extinct 13,796-foot Mauna Kea and the active 13,674-foot Mauna Loa. The Hoggar Mountains in North Africa and 12,198-foot Teide Peak on Tenerife in the Canary Islands are also the results of hot-spot activity.

But mountain landscapes are not formed by geotectonic processes alone. The manner in which they are weathered and eroded also determines their appearance. This clearly differs between one climate zone and the next, which helps to explain the variety in our present-day mountains. Moist tropical peaks close to the equator, with their lush hillsides, cloudy forests, and knoll-like glaciers, are very different from high mountains in extremely arid regions, which are too dry for any recent glaciation to have occurred. Except for a few wind-carved nunataks, mountains in polar latitudes are completely encased in ice. Differences in the rock that forms individual mountains also influence their shapes. Impressively steep walls are often carved from limestone, often along with karst features, while granite tends to take on massive, more rounded forms.

Even though the processes of mountain building take place on a time scale remote from our human experience, their attendant earthquakes, volcanic explosions, and tsunamis are the natural occurrences that can have the greatest impact on our lives.

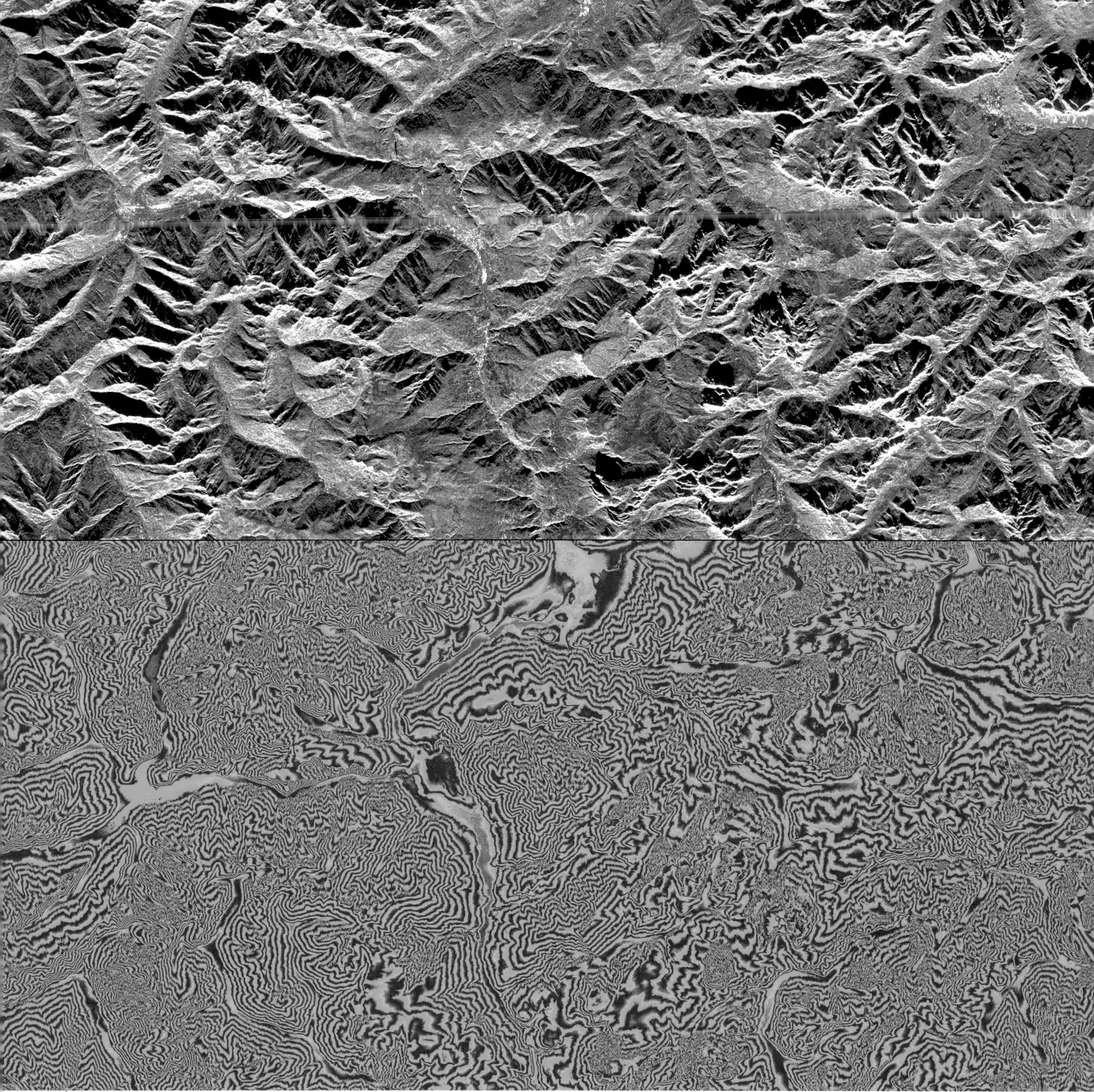

A radar image and interferogram of the Friuli-Trentino region, Italy

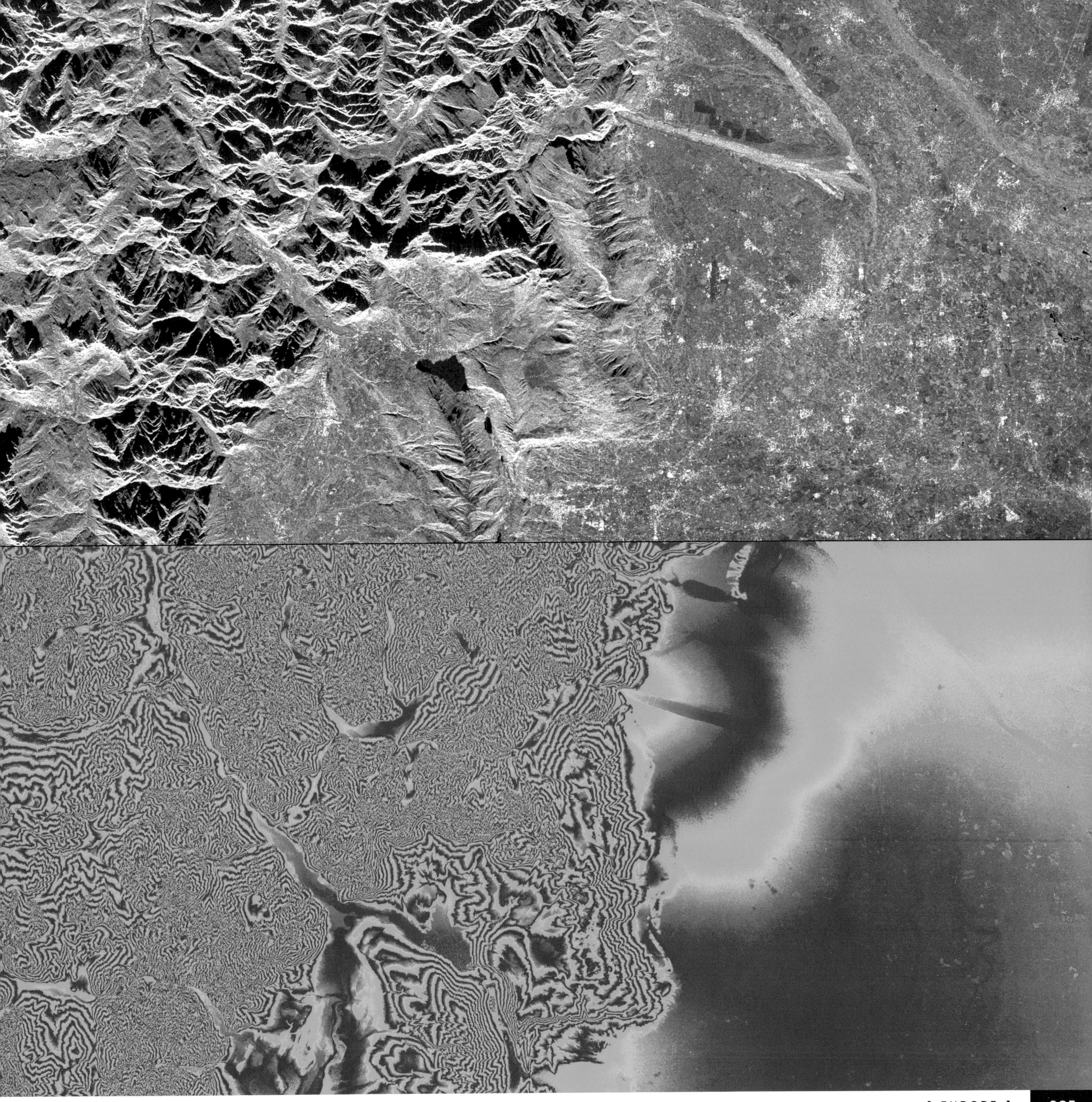

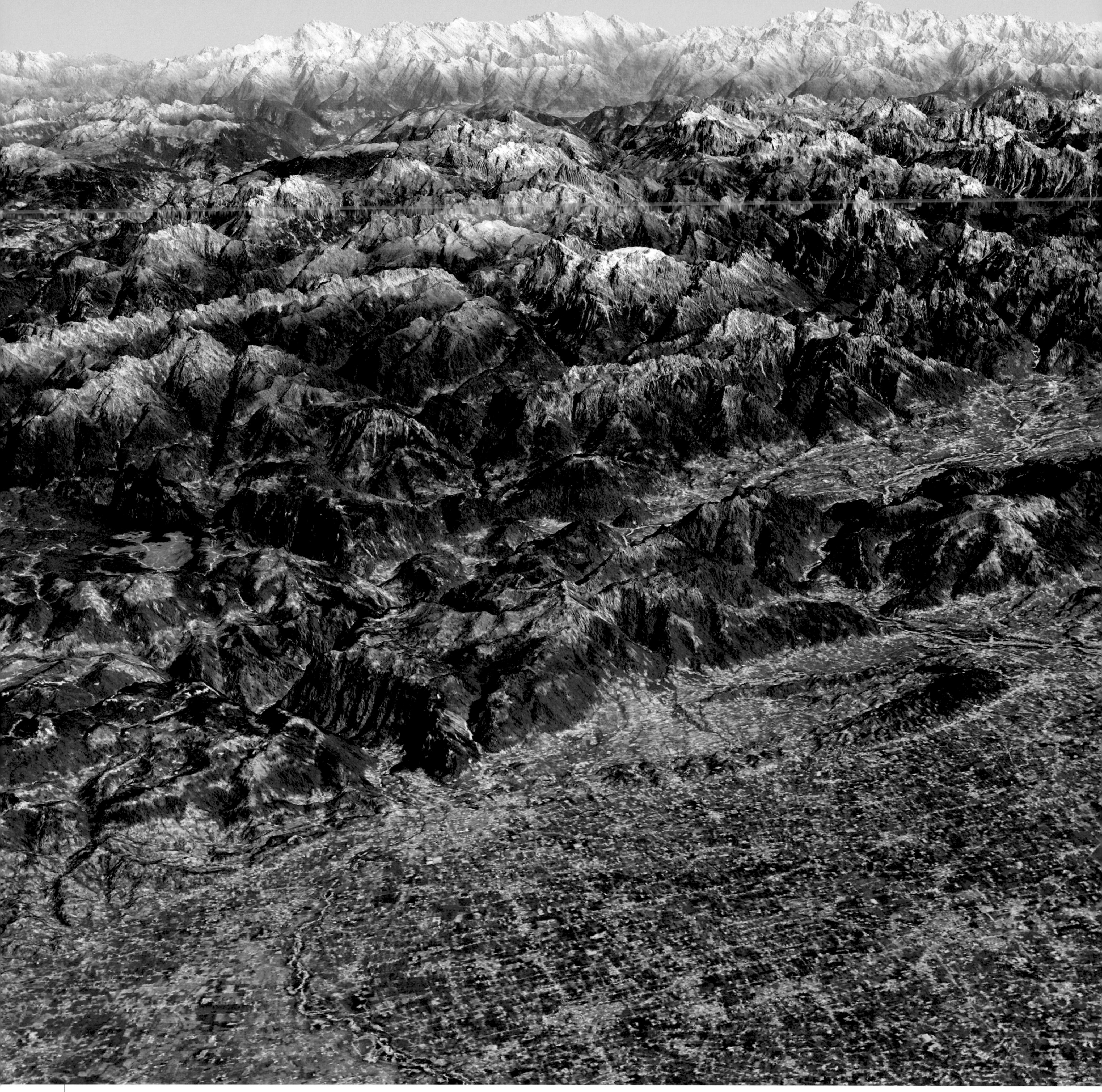

Panorama of the Dolomites from the south, Friuli-Trentino, Italy

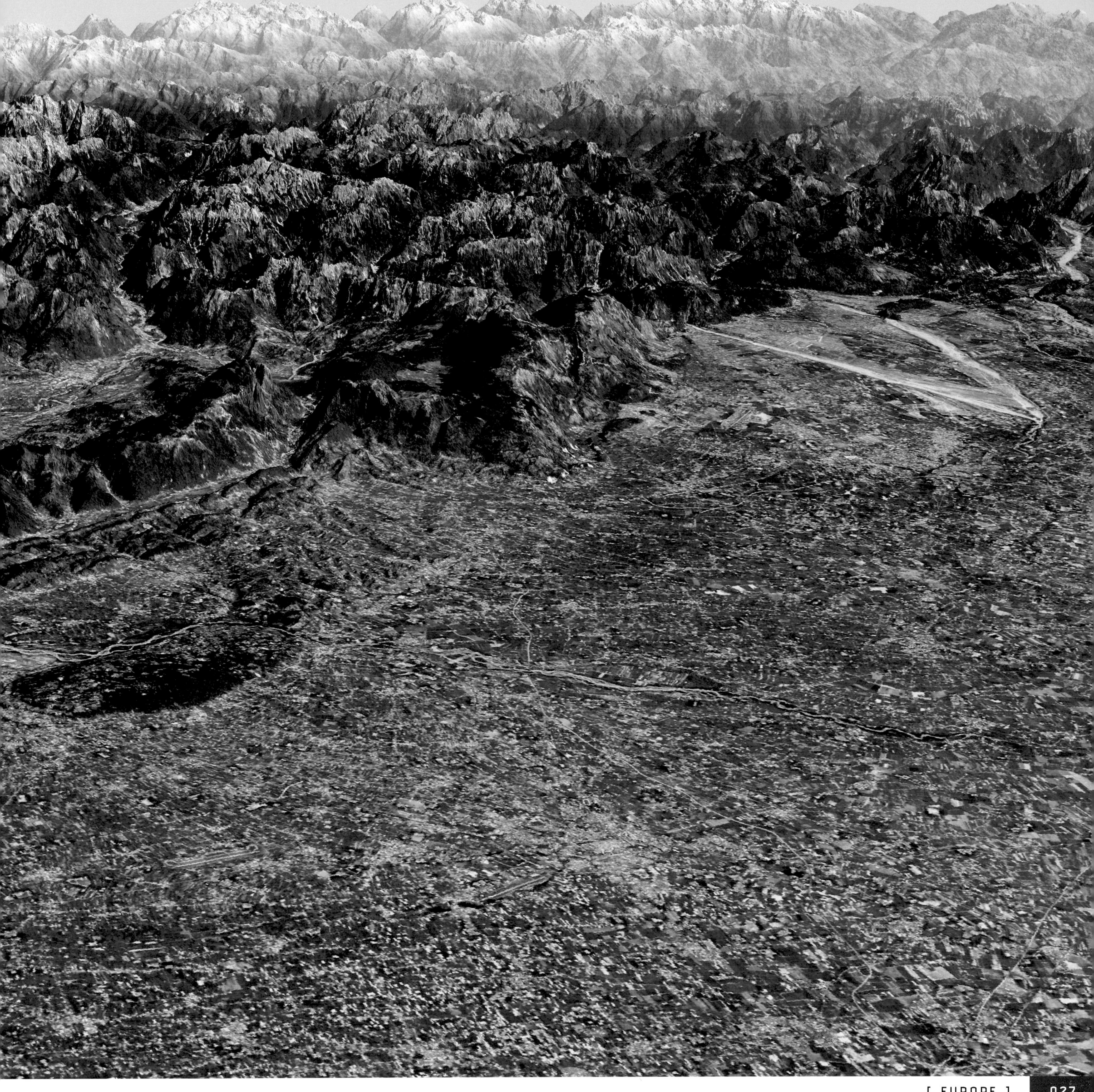

Danger Zones
When Mountains Start to Shake

RÜDIGER GLASER

Mountains call to man, but they also come calling on us. Mountain dwellers have always understood the risks of living in such regions, and have maintained a respectful distance from the dangers mountain life presents. Urban society, however, with its pressing need for living space and continued growth, has seen fit to encroach on mountainous regions more than ever before. Yet all the safety measures and stringent building codes of civilization cannot alter the fact that mountains can be volatile and dangerous places. Only those who are fully aware of this can survive in them for long.

The shape, height, and steepness of mountains present any number of hazards. Avalanches, rockslides, landslides, and mudslides are common occurrences. Peak regions of ice and snow, especially in zones of permafrost, follow a dynamic of their own. When large masses of rock or whole mountainsides give way, they can create bizarrely tumbled landscapes. One such place is Domat, near Chur in Switzerland, with hills up to 230 feet high that are remnants of a prehistoric landslide. Slides can create small lakes on the valley floor, and at times the falling material has enough momentum and mass to surge partway up the opposite slope. This has happened with particular frequency in the Alps since the glaciers of the last ice age melted back out of the lower-lying valleys. Without the ice to support them, the mountainsides, carved to dangerous steepness by the glaciers, are particularly vulnerable to major slides. A textbook case is the prehistoric landslide that occurred at Flims, in the valley of the Vorderrhein, between 10,000 and 17,000 years ago. It littered more than nine miles of the Kästris Valley with some twelve cubic kilometers of rock that the present river has carved into to a depth of nearly 2,000 feet. Other such landscapes are the pass and lake areas on the Fernpass, the Eibsee region at the foot of the Zugspitze, and the mouth of the Ötz Valley.

One of the greatest documented mountain catastrophes occurred in the Blenio Valley, in the Ticino, in the spring of 1515. A landslide off Monte Crenone, presumably in the fall of 1512, backed up the little Brenno River to form a lake two-and-a-half miles long. When the lake broke through the dam, the resulting wave engulfed the town of Biasca and the valley of the Ticino River and swept six hundred people to their deaths.

Landslides are often triggered by earthquakes, as happened in Italy's Friuli region in 1976. Tremors near Gemona and Venzone measuring 9–10 on the Mercalli Scale unleashed a landslide that killed roughly 1,000 people and left between 40,000 and 100,000 homeless. When aftershocks were felt four months later, many people simply left the region for good.

Shears can be thought of as a light variant of landslides. Unlike a rockslide, where the rock is pulverized, or a landslide, where the falling mass is deformed, the stone in a shear holds together. Occasionally, however, such slippage can develop into a rockslide. Layers of sediment with a high clay content are particularly susceptible to shearing. Shears are especially frequent in the Graubünden Slate region of the Alps; one example was the shear at Goldau on September 2, 1806, where nearly 500 people were killed and 200 were left homeless. It was one of the greatest natural catastrophes ever suffered in Switzerland.

Another variant of this natural event is the mudslide. A mix of water and debris, a mudslide only comes to rest when it reaches drier, flatter ground and the water runs off. The edges remain as small ridges a foot to three feet high as the center section flows on a bit farther. Flooding and deposits from mudslides have been observed to effect the surrounding countryside. In the fall of 1868 a mudslide ravaged the village of Zignau in Graubünden, and in late August 1987, a rain storm that lasted for several days caused numerous mudslides and flooding in Austria and Switzerland.

Avalanches are another potential hazard in mountainous regions. In Switzerland, roughly twenty-five people are killed every year by avalanches. In each of the last ten years an average of eighty avalanches has been reported to the Federal Institute for Snow and Avalanche Research in Davos. Avalanches occur as the result of a specific combination of factors: terrain, depth of new snow, wind, structure of the snow cover, and temperature. Unfortunately, they are often caused by people who ignore or misread these conditions; 90 percent of avalanche victims trigger the avalanche themselves. The typical avalanche slope is steep, shaded, close to a ridge, and has a deep accumulation of freshly fallen snow. Most dangerous are so-called snowboard avalanches. In only a few seconds, a whole layer of snow gives way, trapping and often completely burying its victims in an instant. It is possible to check the level of avalanche danger at any time by telephone or on the Internet with local state bureaus that carefully monitor such conditions.

These gravitational events only become disasters when they strike people, herds, or farms; they become catastrophes when whole settlements are destroyed and large numbers of people are injured. Time and time again supposedly safe, recreational vacations are interrupted by such incomprehensible tragedies. The avalanche that struck Galtür on February 23, 1999, is but one example out of many. It raced down the mountain at more than 125 miles per hour, killing thirty-one people. The upper Paznaun Valley was cut off from the outside world and had to be supplied by helicopter.

"Natural catastrophe" is a relatively new concept. Previously such events were spoken of as "frightening omens" or "freak happenings," and considered acts of God. But humans are often not idle victims of such events—they may have made massive intrusions into the regions involved. A classic example is the famous landslide at Elm, in Canton Glarus, in 1881, which was set off by unprofessional slate mining and killed 114 people. The particular tragedy of that landslide was that the deaths could have been avoided. After days of rain, the slide had announced itself with loud

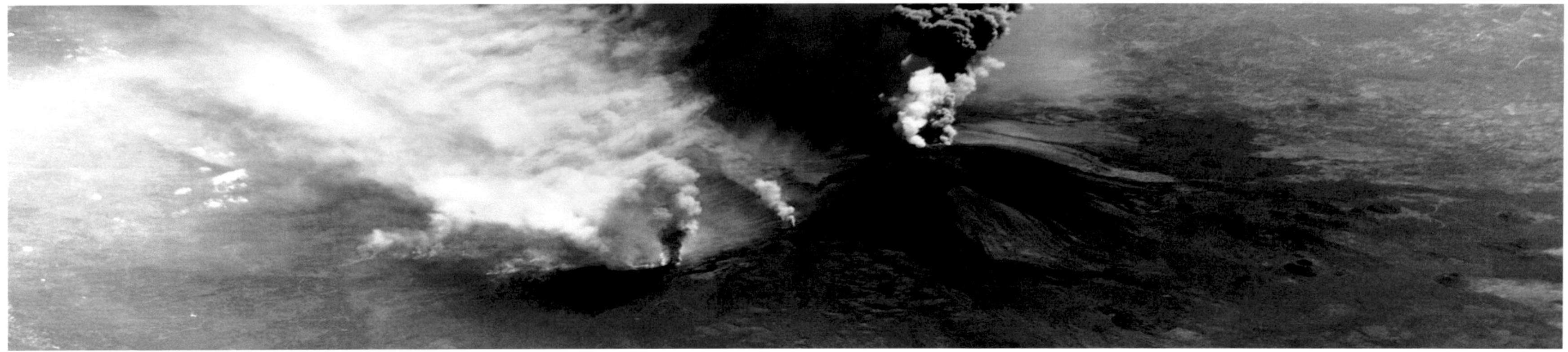

The eruption of Mount Etna, Italy, on October 30, 2001. Volcanic eruptions like this are among the most spectacular natural events, and can cause faulting, landslides, and mudslides.

banging and rumblings. But instead of fleeing for their lives, people were intrigued and stayed to watch. When the slope finally gave way on September 11, hundreds of spectators who had taken up positions on the surrounding slopes were killed as the falling rock surged up the slope on the opposite side of the valley.

In any discussion of such events it is essential to stress the importance of forests. Forests serve as protection against avalanches, mudslides, and shears, but even though they are protected from harvesting they are not protected from other types of damage. They are often harmed by human incursions or by hurricanes, as they were in the 1990s. Even at valley elevations, Hurricane Lothar, on December 26, 1999, reached speeds of up to 75 miles per hour; at altitudes like that of the Jungfraujoch it howled at nearly 155 miles per hour. It felled some 30,000 trees in Switzerland alone, destroying 12.7 million cubic meters of wood, three times the average annual loss. Excessive stocking of wild animals has added to the problem. Yet the protective effect of forests has long been known. All harvesting in the forest above Andermatt, even the gathering of cones, has been forbidden since a ban issued in 1397. And in 1804 Schiller would write in his *Wilhelm Tell*: "So it is, and avalanches would have buried the town of Altdorf long since if the forests up there had not stood guard against them."

The effects of climate change brought about by mankind are also quite obvious in mountainous regions. Glaciers are disappearing and the permafrost is retreating with alarming speed, dramatically affecting the stability of many slopes. How have these things begun to happen in recent years? People continue to ask whether it is simply a matter of overreporting by the media or whether there is a genuine trend behind it. Documenting such serious events is especially difficult. The effects of rockslides, landslides, and shears are dealt with relatively quickly in inhabited areas, and terrain analyses are consequently inconclusive because the results can no longer be observed.

Such latent danger is reflected in the notion of a natural catastrophe. In the insurance business, human responsibility has been more strongly emphasized since the 1970s. Risk management attempts to combine prevention and maintenance; structures such as high-water dams, rockslide barriers, and till collectors or diversion wedges placed in the path of mountain torrents are meant to divert natural dangers. And generally they do. Only in extreme situations do these precautions no longer suffice. There is no question but that we must spend more time in the mountains to come to grips with the natural dangers. Meanwhile the idea of a "culture of risk" has become firmly established, expressing our full-time attention to questions of safety. Ultimately it comes down to how much significance we attach to natural catastrophes—and accordingly the recognition that protecting ourselves from them also has its limits

Mountains do not forgive structural errors and mistaken planning for long. They demonstrate again and again, with floods, mudslides, and avalanches, that we should not try to live too close to them. It is one of their quirks that many of these natural events continue to be unpredictable and uncontrollable. Developing permanent deterrent structures will continue to be our major task, so as to at least reduce the risks.

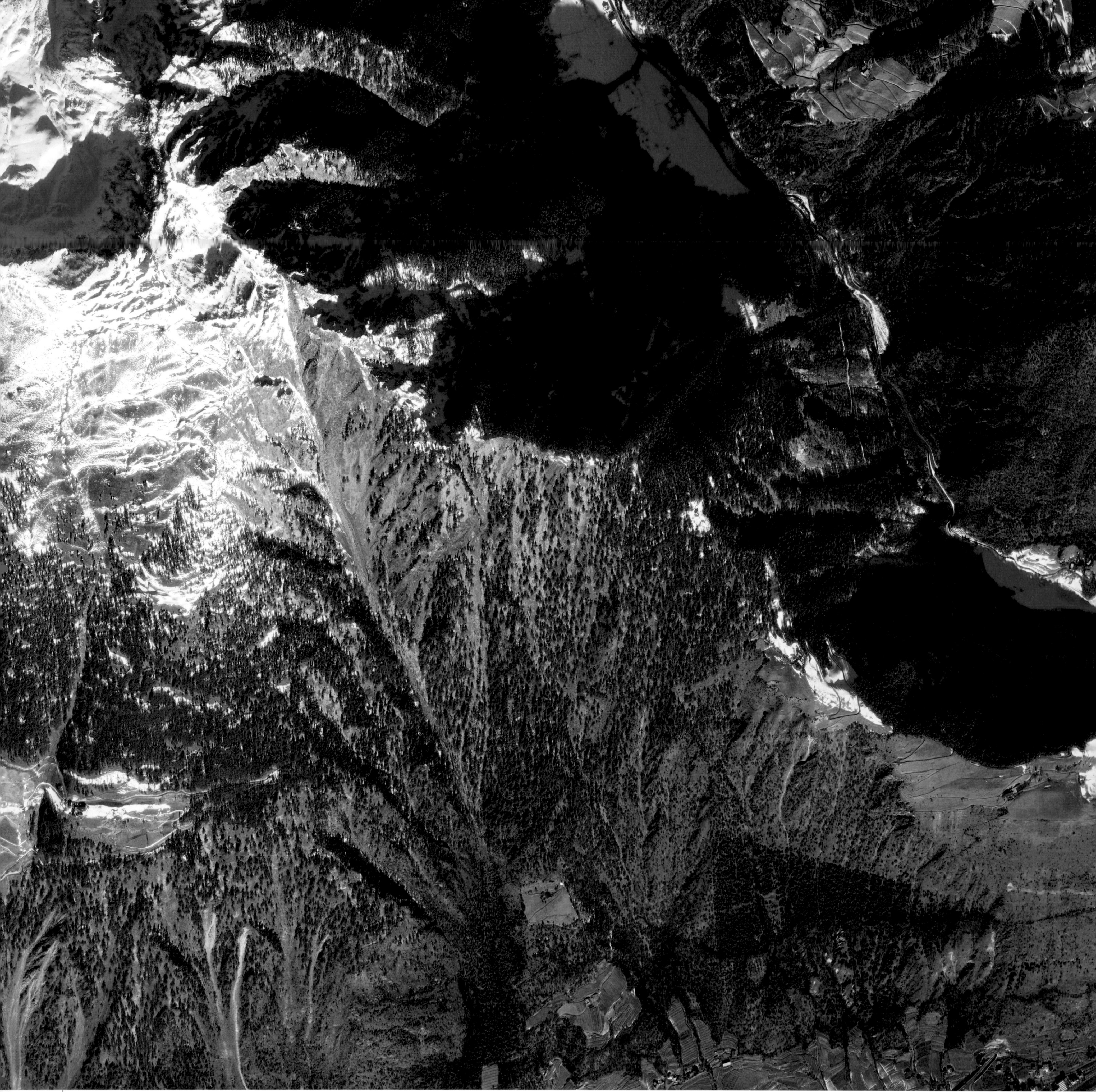

Reinhold Messner's Juval Castle, south Tirol, Italy

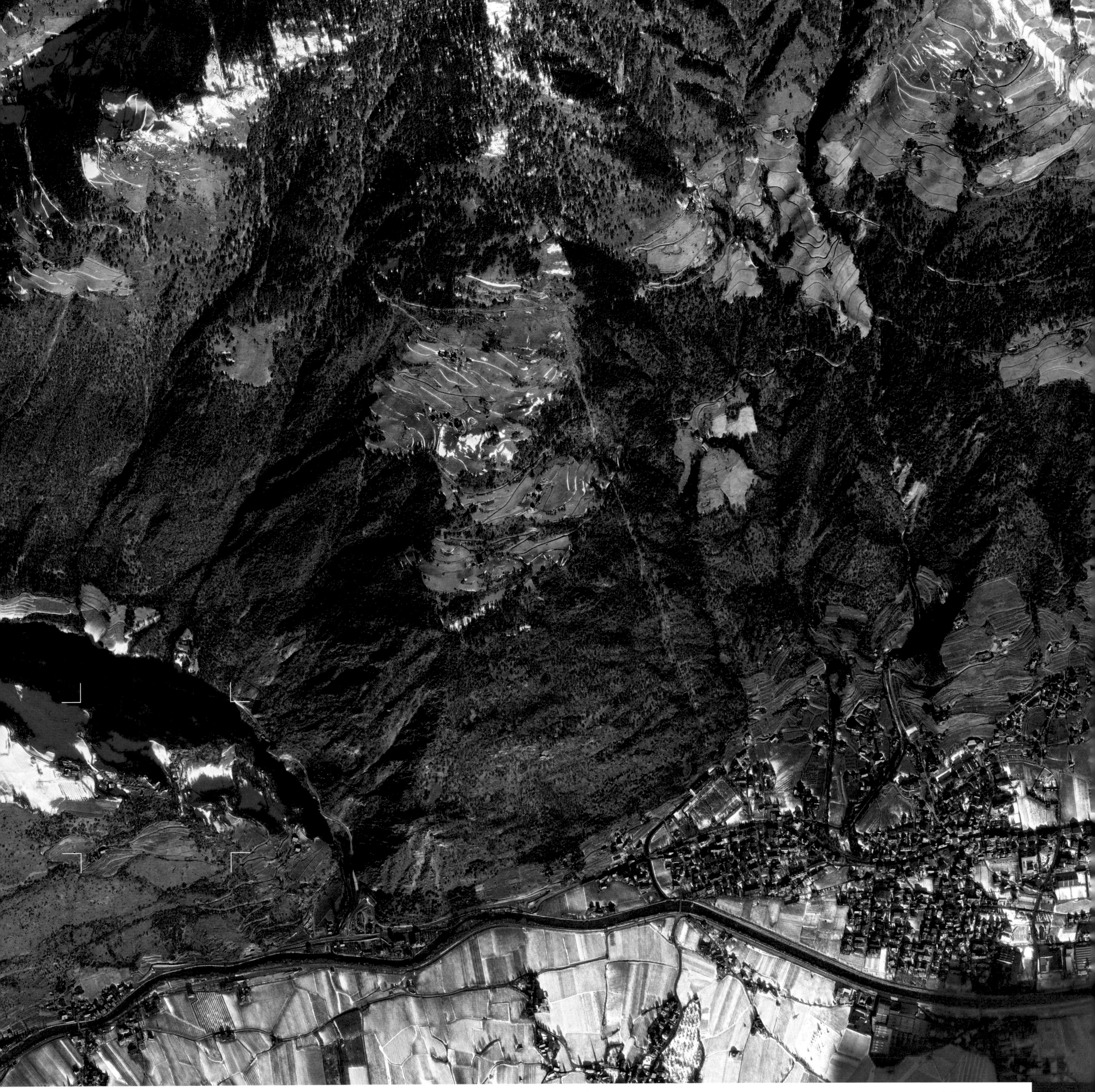

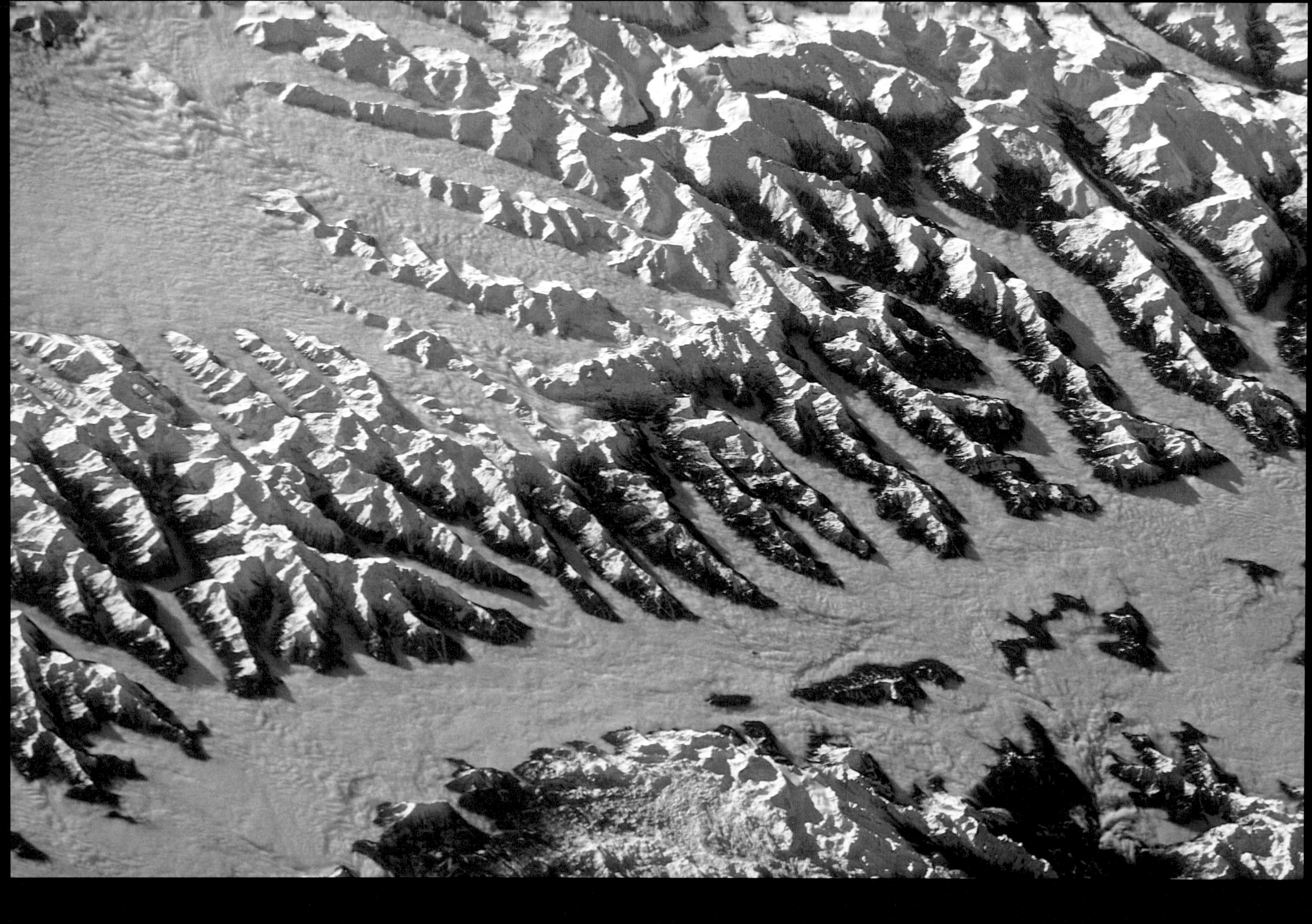

Valleys in a sea of cloud, Hohe Tauern, Austria

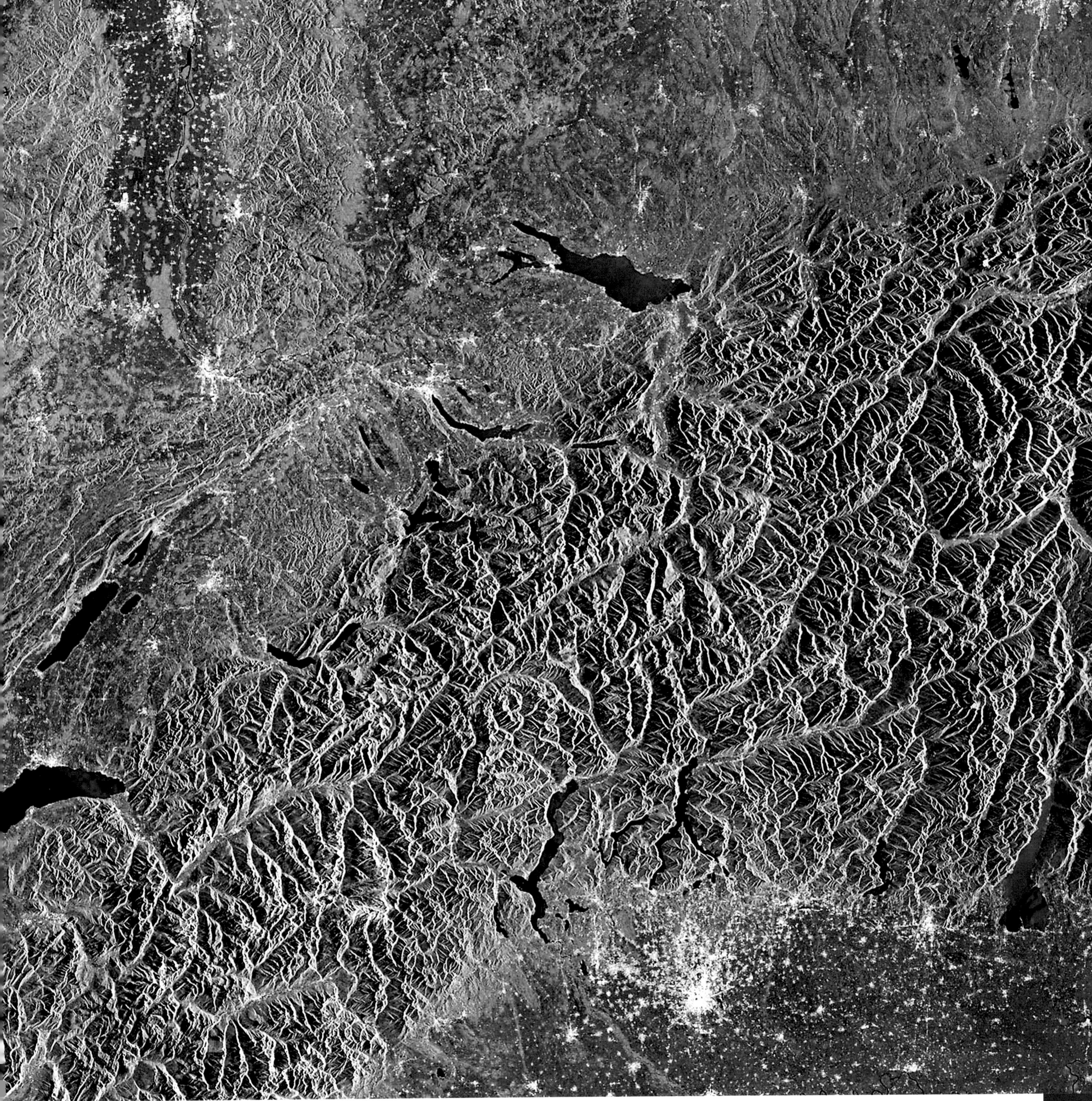

Radar image of the western Alps and large Alpine lakes

Mont Blanc's Peuterey Ridge

MAURICE HERZOG

In August 1944 my brother Gerard and I, along with Lionel Terray and Gaston Rebuffat, decided to attempt the Peuterey Ridge of Mont Blanc. At the time this extremely long climb was considered the most difficult on western Europe's highest mountain, and had never been crossed without a bivouac. Needless to say, this made it especially attractive to us.

It was wartime, and we had to be constantly on the lookout for German mountain scouts and be prepared to hide. We had very little food—foodstuffs were strictly rationed at the time, and because we were such determined opponents of the German occupation neither my brother nor I had ration cards, coupons, or even enough money. Somehow we scared up a few noodles and three pounds of potatoes, and all four of us were in the best of spirits, determined to undertake the adventure.

We had planned to take the cable car from Chamonix to the Col du Midi, which would have saved us six hours of strenuous hiking. But it turned out that the cable car wasn't running that day, so I got to admire Lionel's splendid back muscles as we climbed. At the top we had a quick picnic of cold boiled potatoes, which had sadly become mixed up with the half-raw noodles in the backpack. Fortified nonetheless, we crossed the snowfield of the Vallée Blanche and mastered the extremely steep icy couloir that leads to the Col de la Fourche. The deeply riven Brenva Glacier, which flows down into the Val d'Aosta on the Italian side, separated us from the Peuterey Ridge.

Our climb began on a prominence, the Aiguille Noire de Peuterey. From there the route led from a deep notch to the sharply outlined peaks of the so-called English Ladies. They were our goal for that day, but it was presumptuous of us to think we could reach them by evening. Never before had a roped party managed to conquer the Peuterey Ridge without a bivouac, and we wanted to be the first.

After more than ten hours of climbing, the four of us spent the night in a bivouac box at 12,075 feet. Italian alpinists had used it more than a year before and left behind a few rolls of bread. A greenish mold made them look like Roquefort cheese, but that did nothing to dampen our appetites. We washed them down with ice-cold water then lay down to sleep. After such a strenuous day we scarcely noticed the dampness of the straw bedding, and soon a quartet of snores joined the dull booming of the glaciers and the nighttime roar of the mountain. We planned to set out at two in the morning, so we only had three hours to gather new strength. It was Lionel who wakened us in the darkness: "Three thirty! Get up! We're already late!"

Morning dawned in splendid colors, and we were soon able to see not only one another's faces but also the ice fragments we had climbed down in the dark. At our feet lay the massive Brenva Glacier. With the rising sun all our hesitation disappeared at once, and without wasting words we continued on our way. The Brenva Glacier was flat in its upper part, without cracks and easy to cross. Before us, at the end of a huge amphitheater of snow and ice, rose the Peuterey Ridge. It looked unconquerable. It was time to make some decisions about how we were to proceed.

"We'll have to climb the ridge up the center. If we tackle it from the start, we'll have to bivouac," Gaston declared.

"I'm for that too," I said.

"And where shall we cross?" Lionel asked.

"The route goes across the Dames Anglaises. To get to them we would have to climb down to the glacier and cross all the fractures in it—that will take a long time," Gaston objected. "I propose that we avoid them and climb directly toward the Blanche de Peuterey."

"It's possible that we can do it," Lionel said. "Nobody has tried it before, but who knows?"

"I have another idea," I said.

"The Peuterey Pass?" asked Gerard.

"Precisely. It lies between the Blanche and Mont Blanc. It would shorten our route considerably. It is relatively low and looks easy to reach."

"Not a bad idea," Gaston grumbled, looking across at the pass.

"Count me in." Lionel liked the suggestion. "Nobody has yet gotten through that way. I like that."

After a difficult stretch of climbing ice, we unexpectedly reached a band of rock. To the left of it was a couloir filled with dark bare ice that we had already seen from below. The dark black of the couloir rose up almost vertically, more than 650 feet above us. It was exposed to falling boulders up to the size of a piano. Blocks of granite would crash down the wall, strike together, and break apart with a thundering crack—an apocalyptic scene that was horrifying to look at. But a few feet more, and behind a large block of rock we could see a slight depression covered with snow—a small pass—our "Col de Peuterey."

By now it was afternoon. We had been on the wall for seven hours, and we desperately needed a rest. Lionel was having trouble with his stomach. Apparently the Italian rolls had not agreed with him. The flanks of the ridge fell steeply down to the glaciers on either side, which were so far below us that we could not make out a single detail. The path was narrow and the snow cover was slippery. Every step had to be placed with extreme care. For hours we balanced on the ridge leading up toward the peak. We were concentrating so hard that we didn't even notice that the weather around us had changed. Suddenly we were enveloped in mist. A first jagged streak of lightning shot out of the dark clouds, followed by a powerful clap of thunder. Suddenly we were standing in the middle of a storm. To our horror, little blue flames formed on our fingers and elbows, flickering higher and lower. If we extended our arms the flames from our fingertips grew to be to two-and-a-half to three inches tall, and if we spread our fingers they would turn into five little flames.

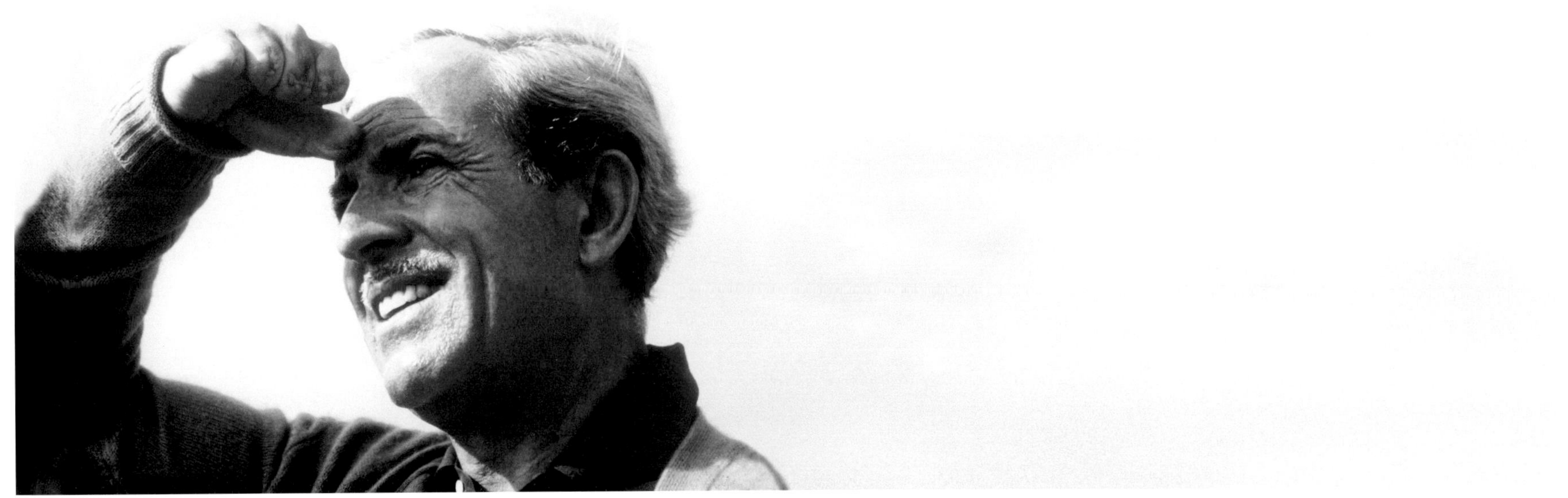

Our hair was standing on end, and sparks were spraying out from the tips. We had become charged with electricity! We were living lightning rods that could burn like straw with the next flash.

The next thunder clap. The wind was growing stronger, nearly knocking us down. Quickly we strode along the now wider ridge that led us to the highest spot. "We did it!" I called back to the others. But I soon recognized that we were standing only on the Italian peak, the Mont Blanc de Courmayeur, which is connected to the main peak by a gentle slope. Despite the poor visibility we could make out the peak by its elongated, tilting form. Driven forward by the storm and whipped by the wind, we didn't waste a second. Without breaking our pace we began the descent. Without saying a word Gaston raised his arm as if in salute. It was his way of celebrating the success we had been laboring for for twenty-five hours and fifteen minutes.

But what is a peak? It is only a spot somewhere and nowhere. At most it is a symbol marking the end. Mixed with the sense of fulfillment at having reached it is the disappointment of knowing the struggle is over. The descent begins, and the peak is already old news, nothing but a quickly fading memory.

From the peak platform we took the normal route back to Chamonix. We knew it by heart, and tore down it at a frenzied speed. At nine o'clock in the evening we were standing next to the Grand Mulets guardhouse and looking bewildered at our naked thighs. The granular snow had torn our pants. "The Herzog Brothers, Rebuffat and Co. in a cancan number!" Lionel laughed. Then with his lovely voice he started singing some nineteenth-century song, but in the hut nothing stirred. Of course it wasn't manned. Who would go mountain climbing in wartime? We all sensed the anticlimax. "Do you really want to spend the night here?" I asked my companions. Instead of answering, Lionel, still singing his song, dragged me in the direction of the glacier.

Night had fallen. Only by straining could we make our way in the darkness along the edge of the glacier toward the middle station of the cable car. We could barely see our hands in front of our faces. Suddenly Gerard, who was racing ahead, let out a scream of pain. He had banged his nose against the cable-car station wall. It offered truly sparse accommodations: four walls and a hard floor. But it allowed us to eat our Spartan supper of potatoes and a few scraps of bread with water protected from the wind. After thirty-six hours of climbing we were grateful for even that. We stretched out on the floor, back-packs flung aside, legs naked, hands still cramped around the shafts of our ice picks. A single breath later and all four of us had fallen asleep. The dark of the night welded our bodies to the mountain, so that we looked almost like rocks. Then there was only silence.

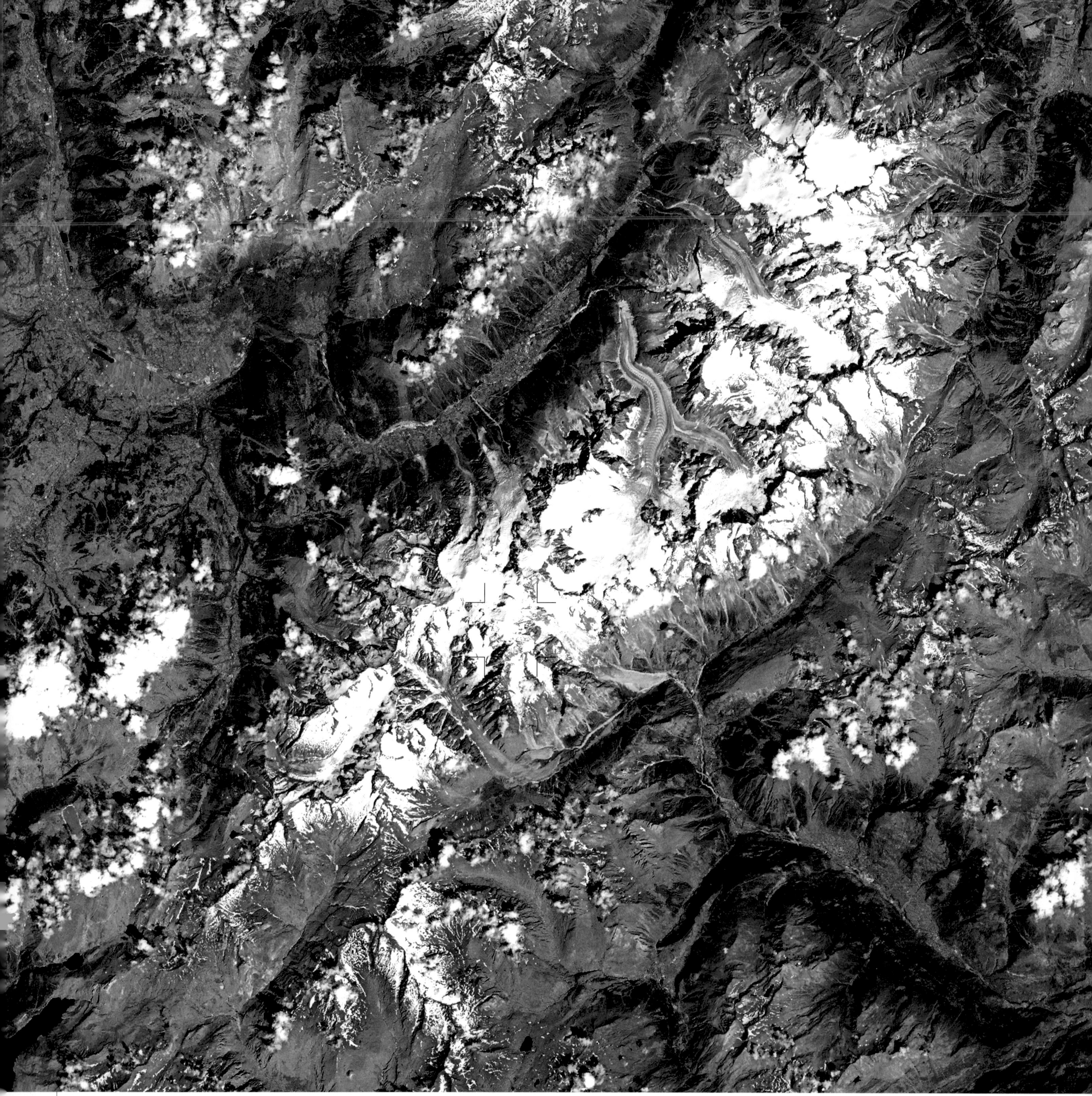

Mont Blanc, the rooftop of the Alps, France, Switzerland, Italy

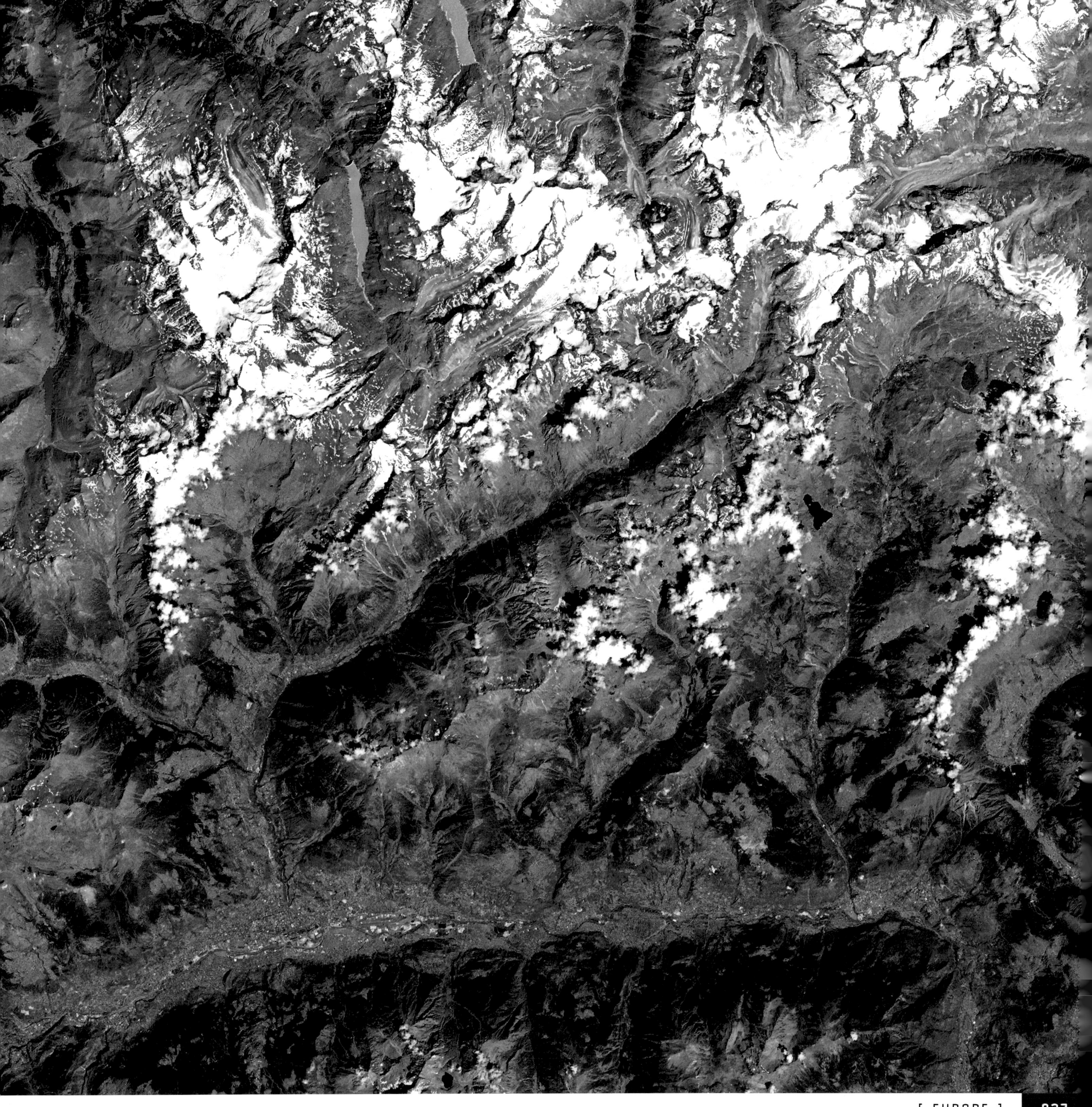

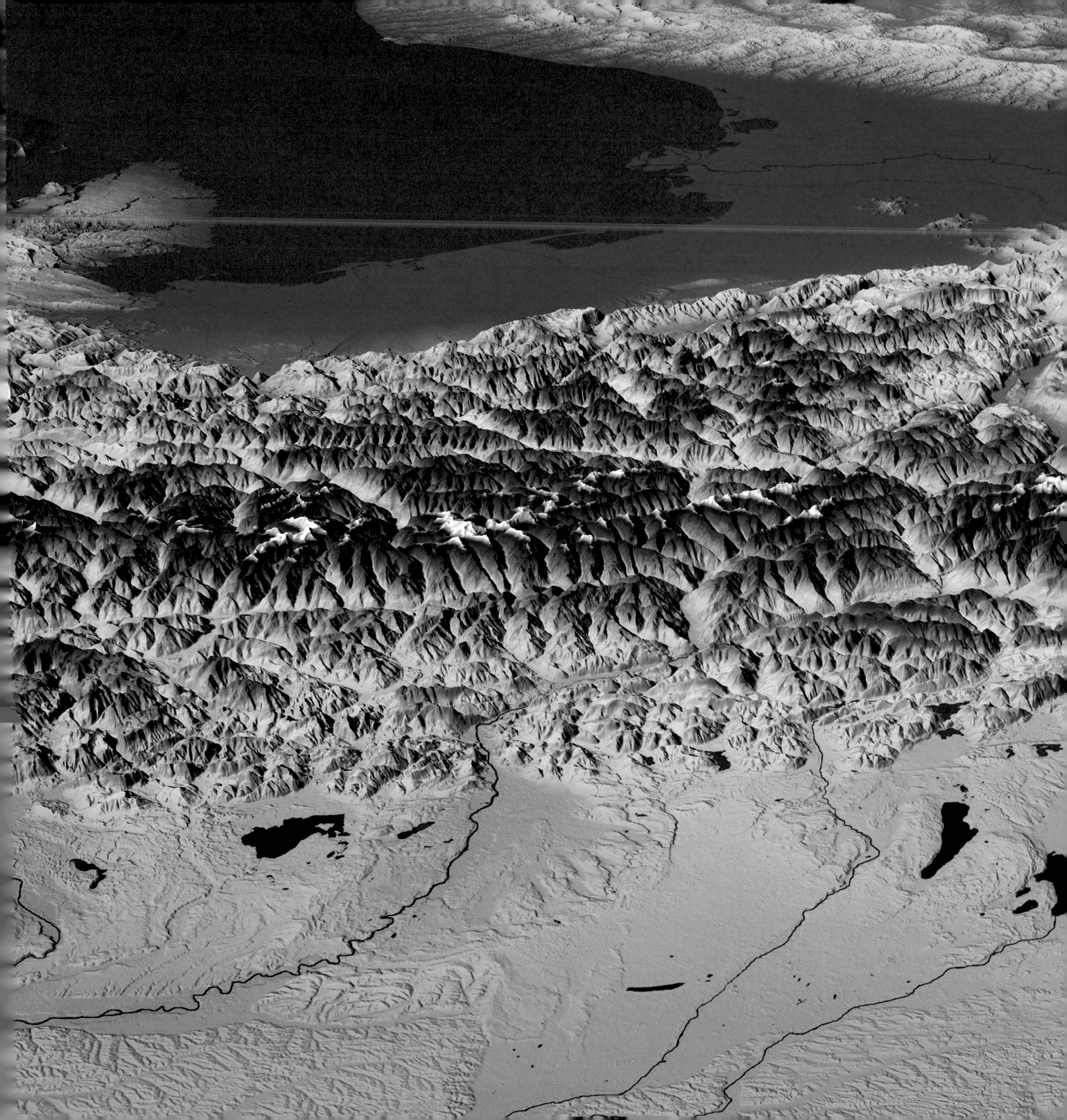

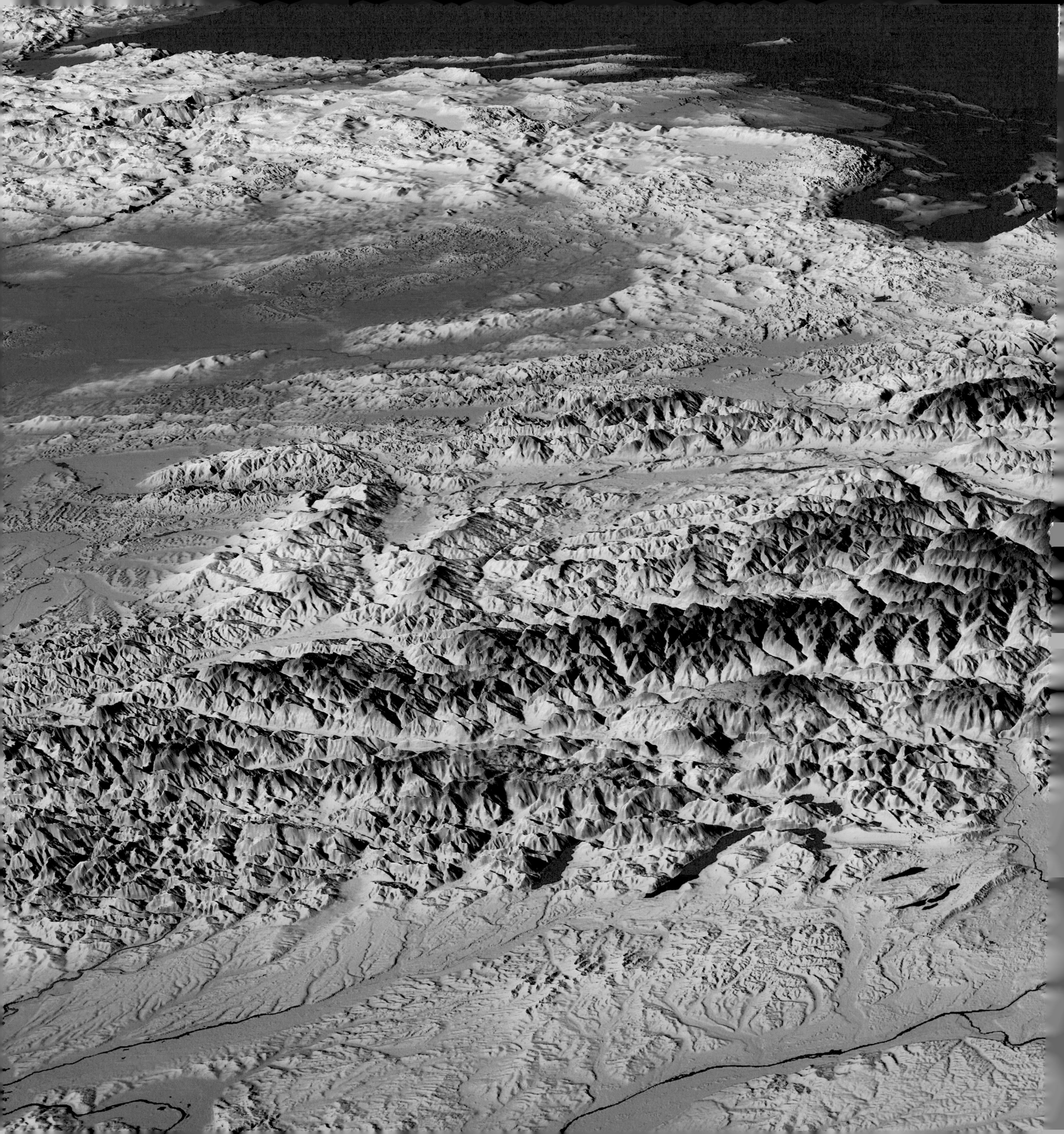

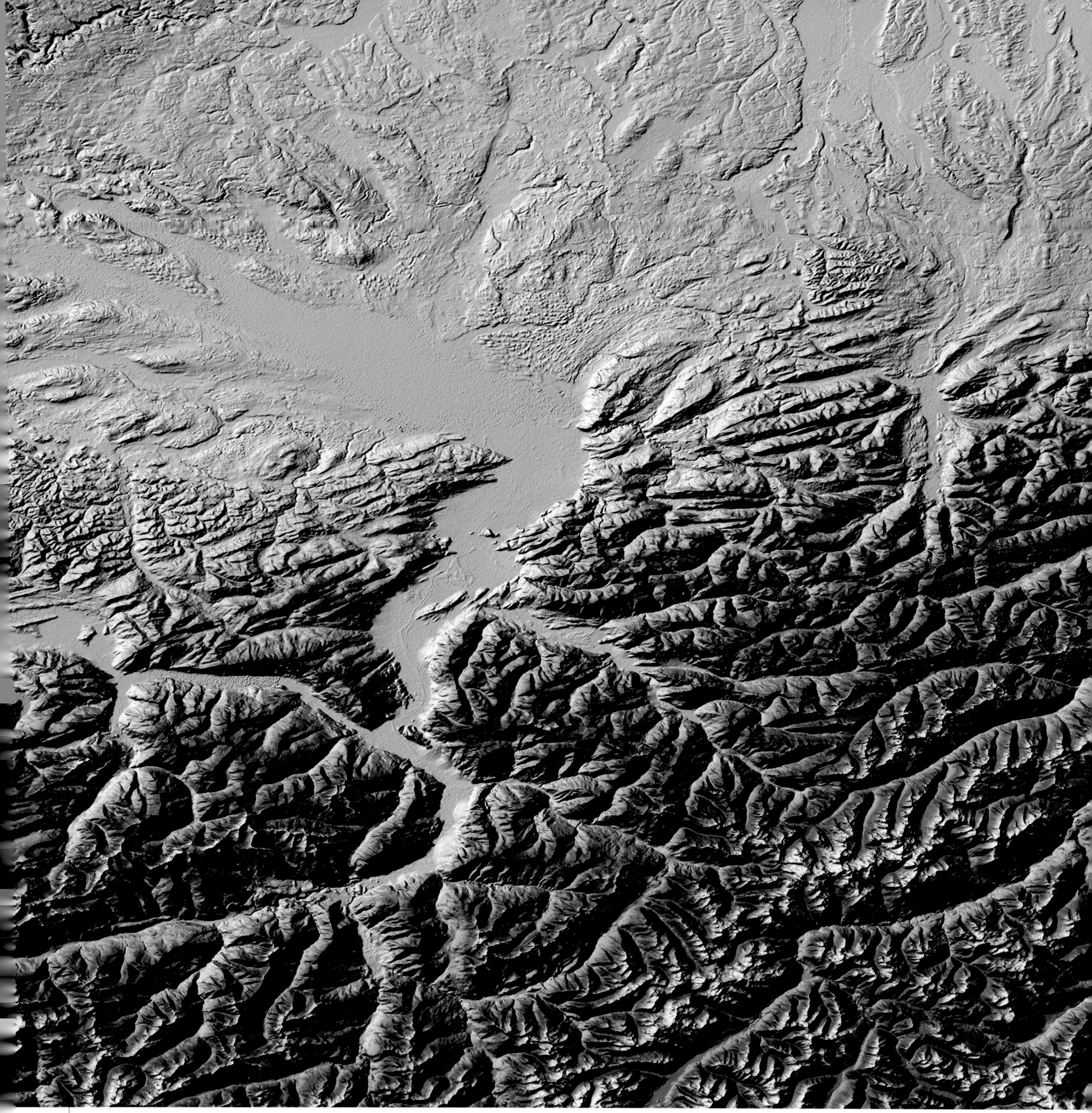

Elevation model of the central northern Alps

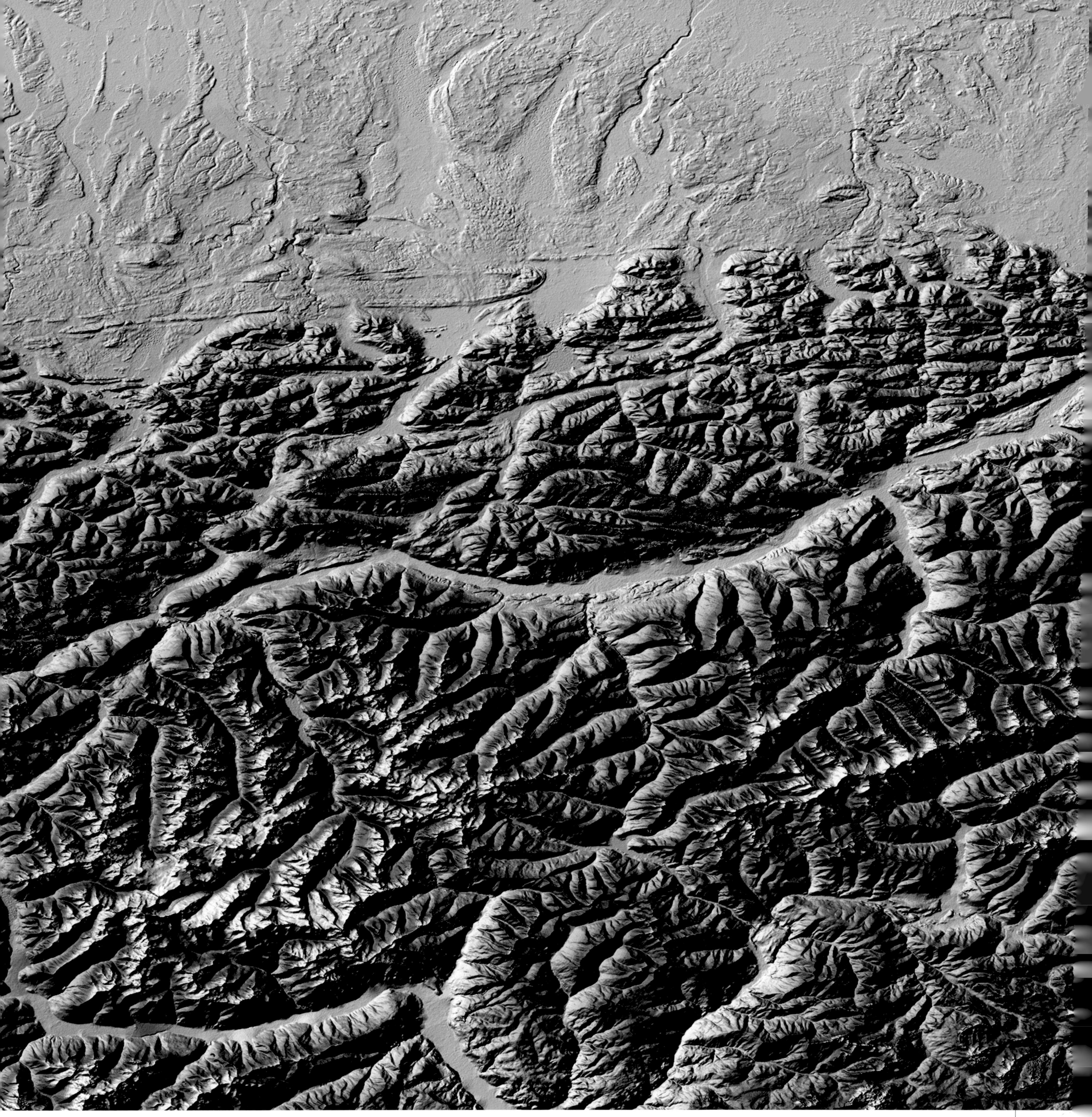

Gatefold: Virtual panorama of the Alps from the north looking south

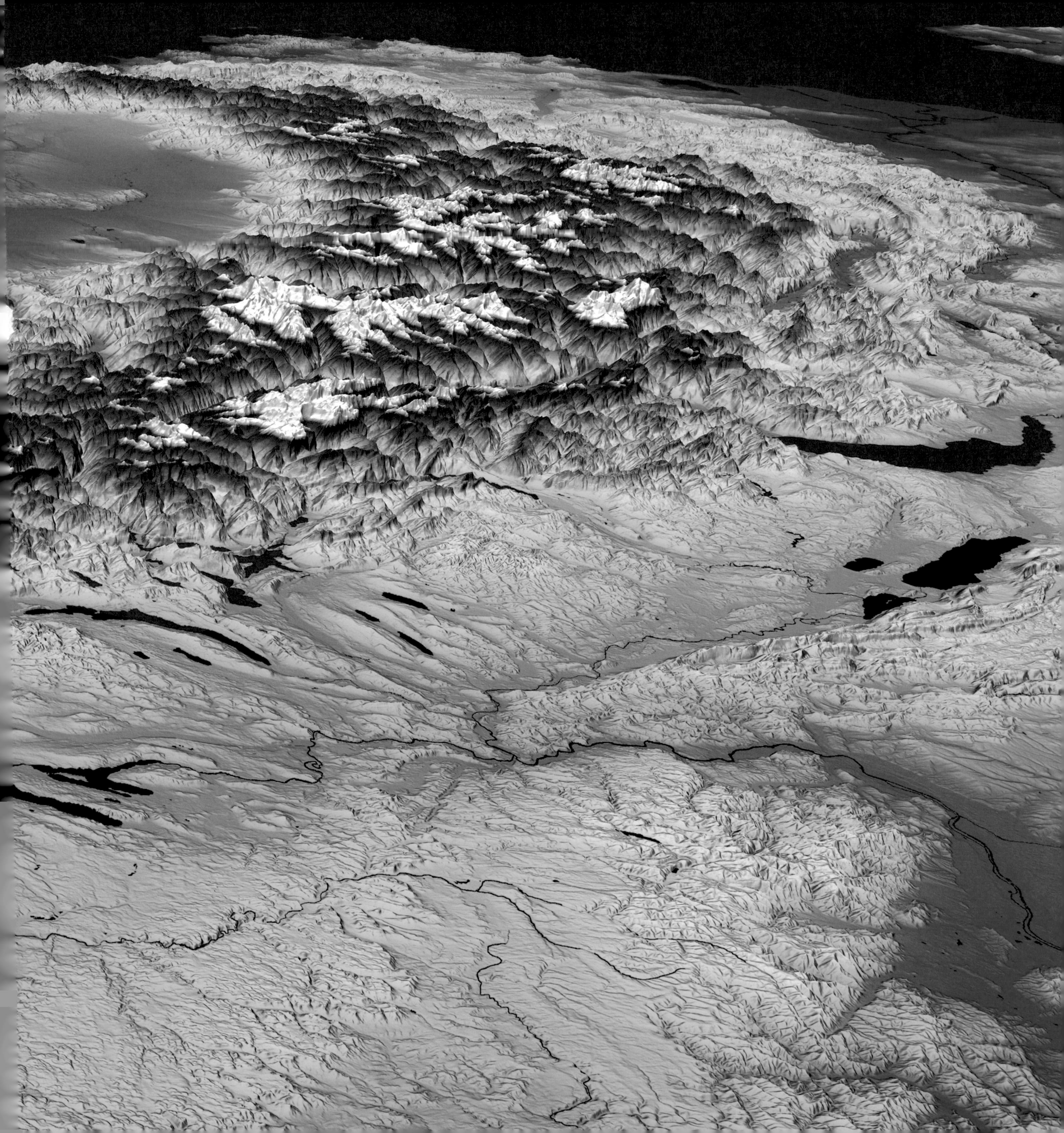

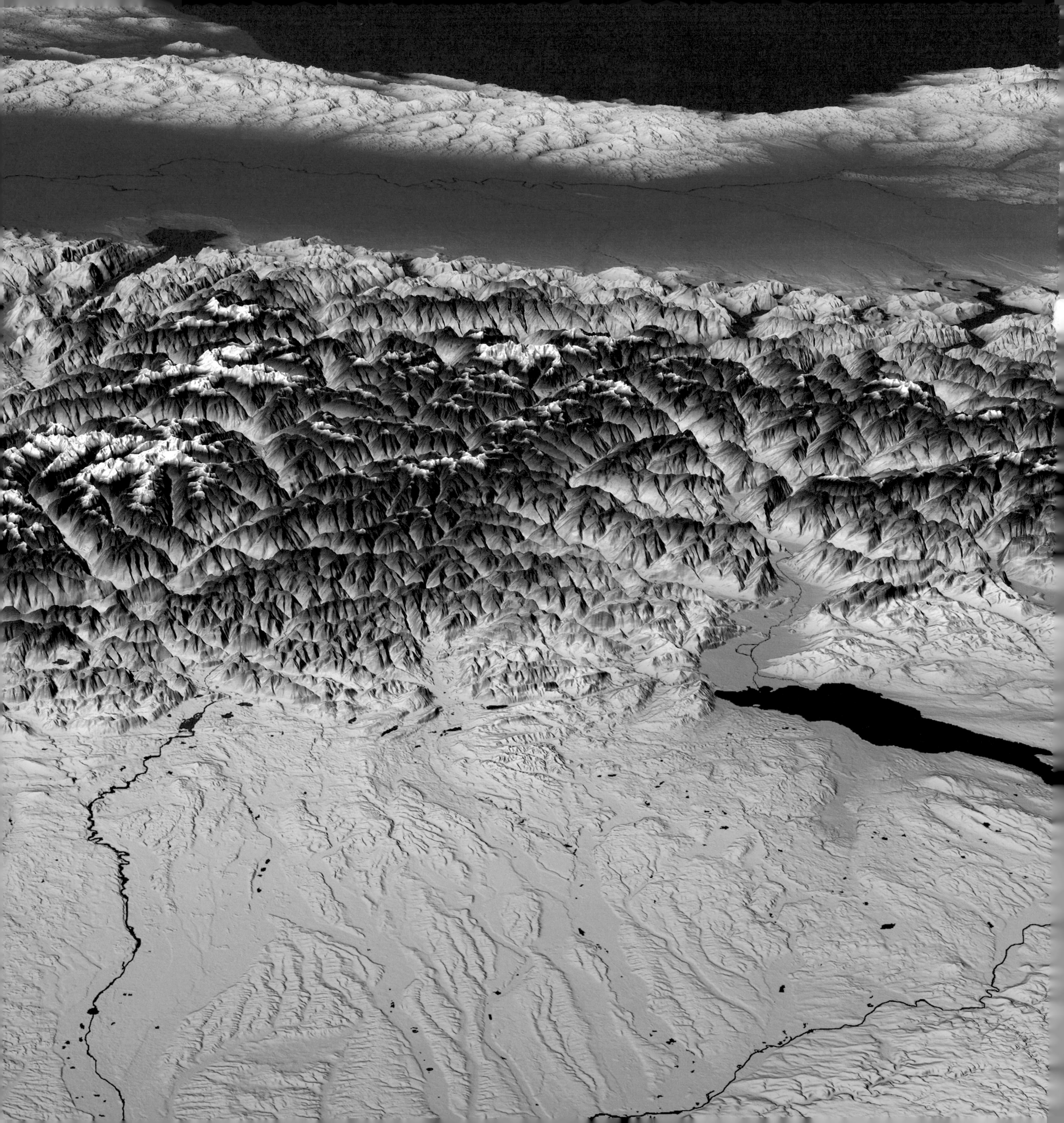

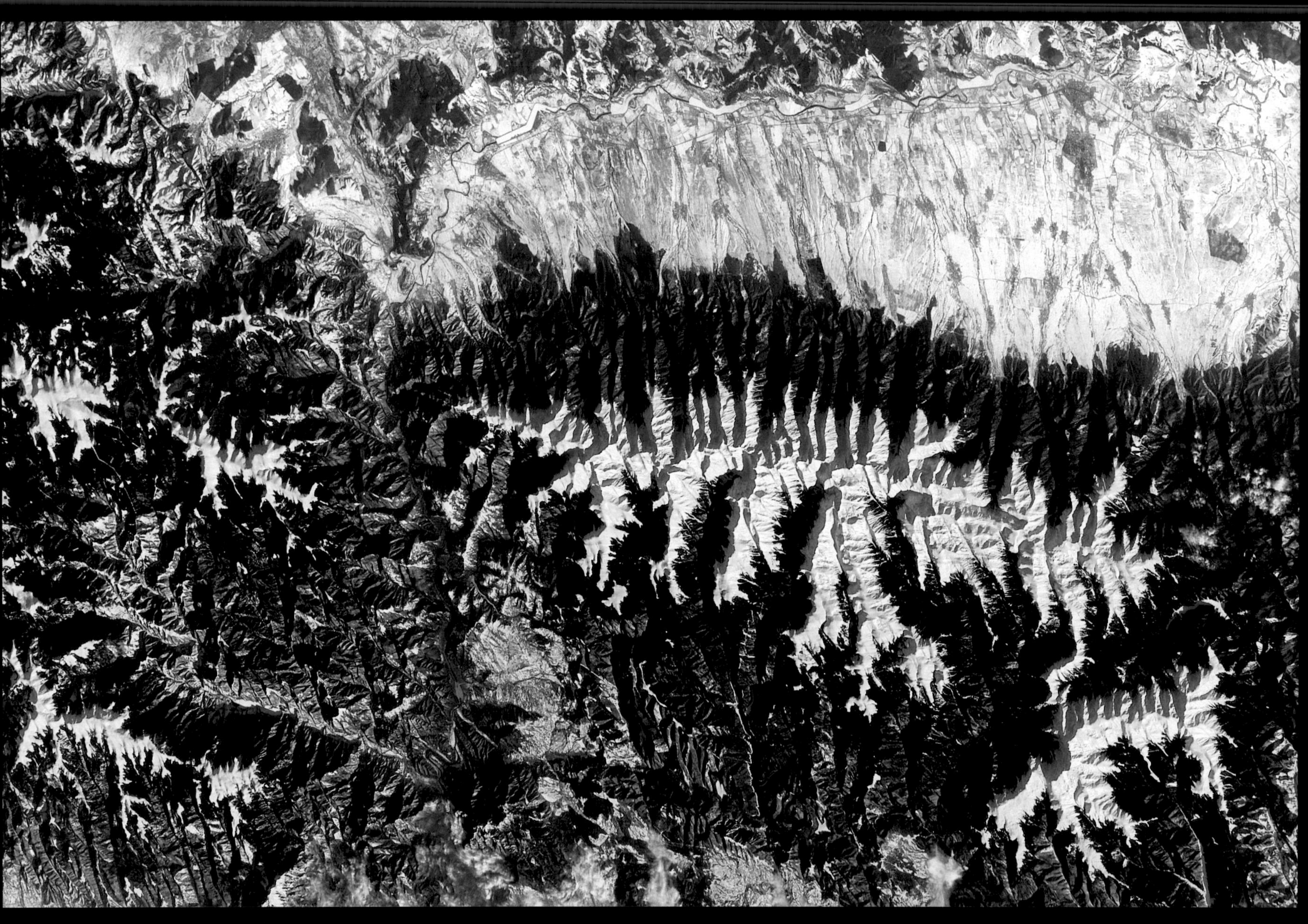

Transylvanian Alps, Romania

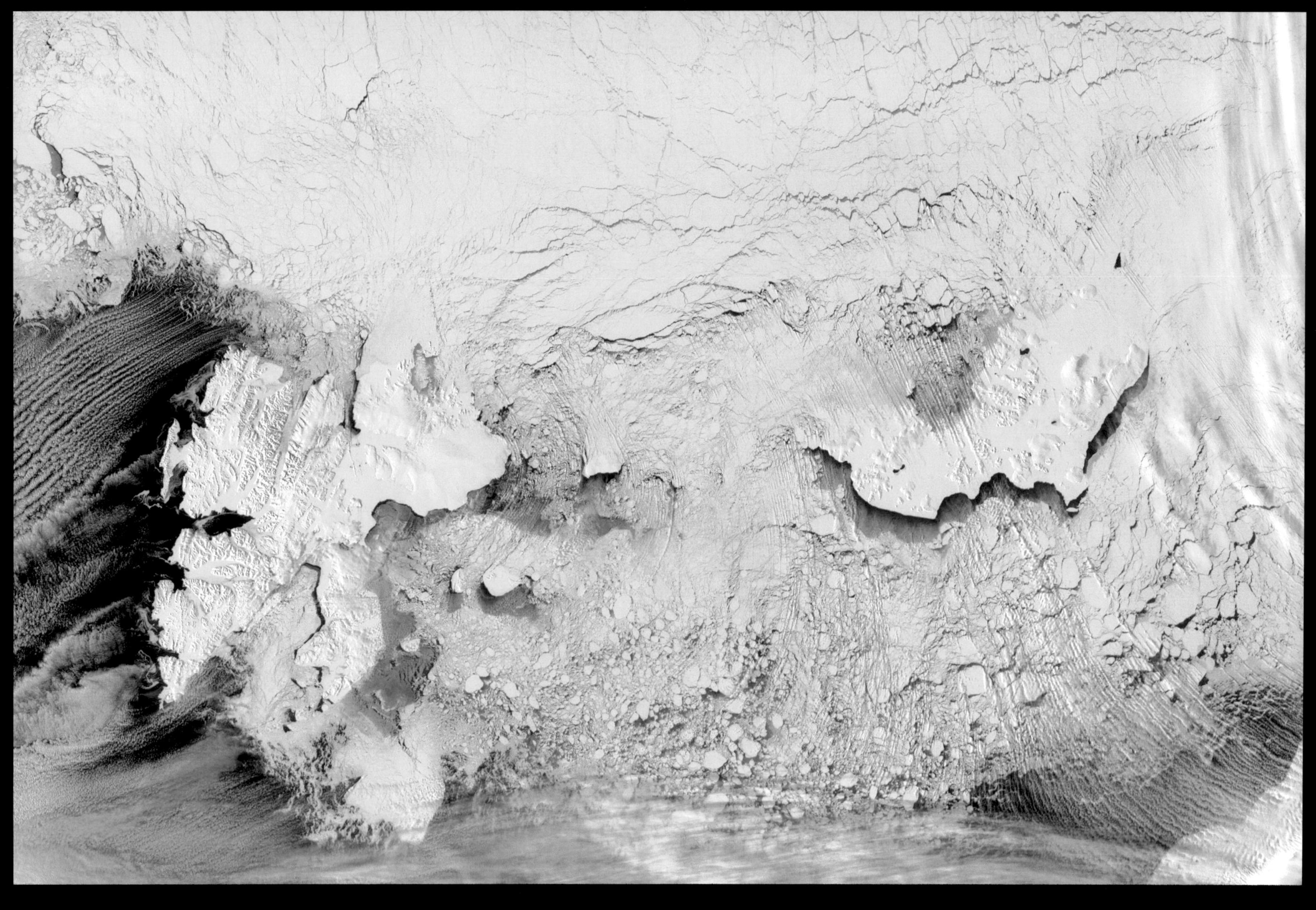

Mountain islands in the Arctic: Spitsbergen, Norway, and Franz Josef Land, Russia

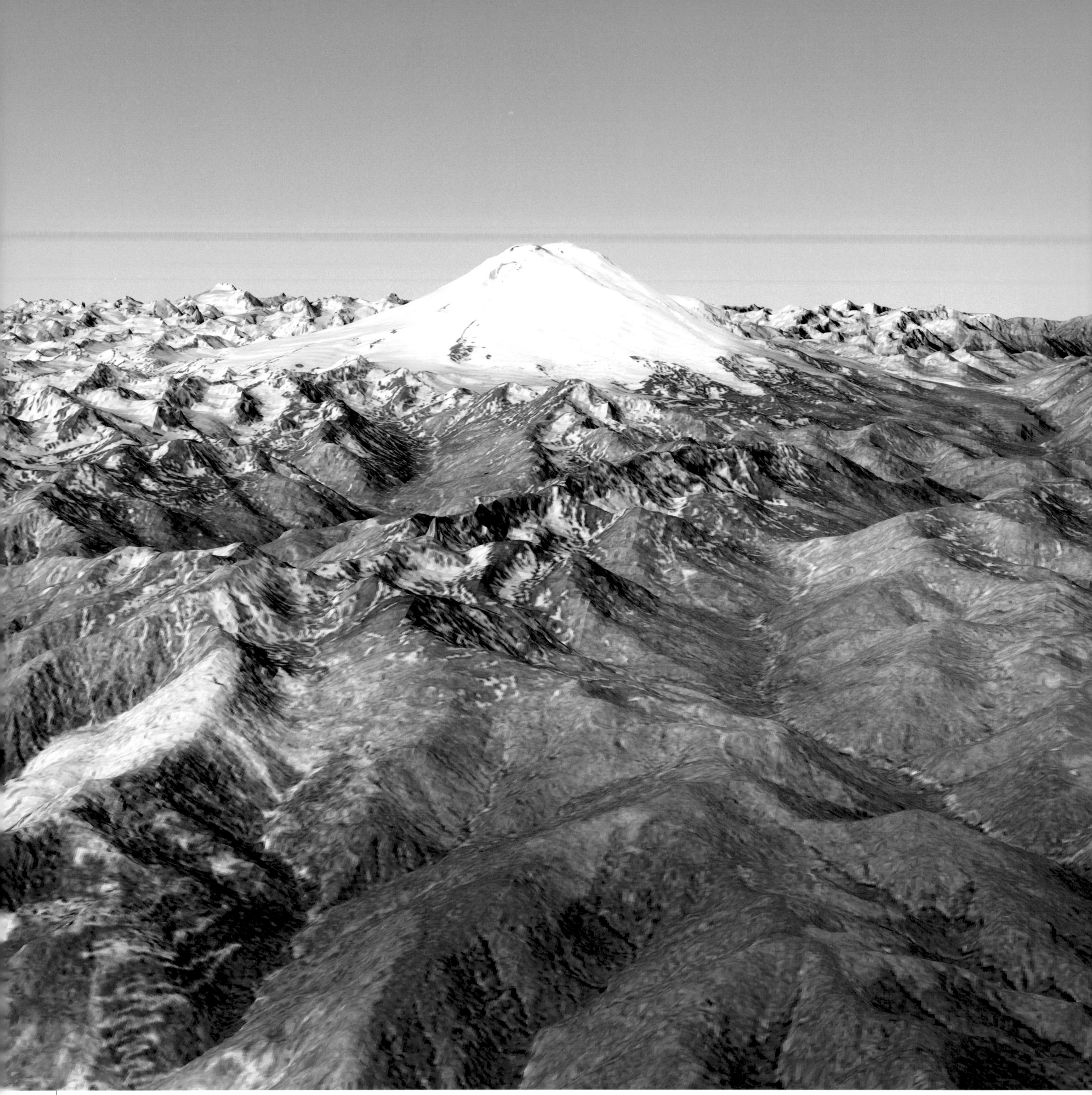

Mount Elbrus, the highest mountain in Europe, Russia

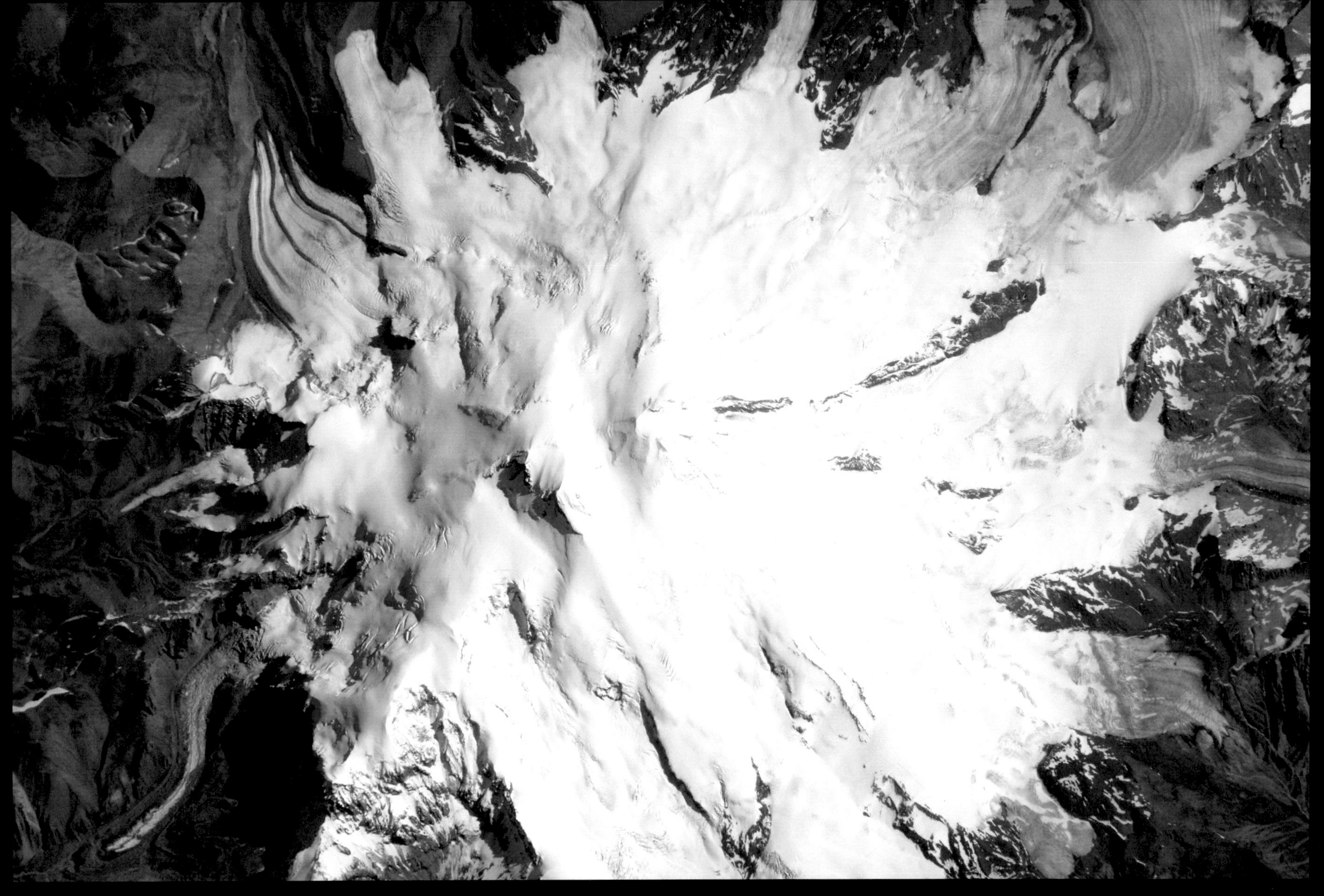

Detailed view of Mount Elbrus, Russia

Glaciers
Memory in Ice

RÜDIGER GLASER

Glaciers are to high mountains as palm trees are to the South Seas; the caps of ice on top of great peaks are synonymous with the mountains themselves, their remoteness, their power. On a geological time scale, though, that seemingly eternal ice has always been subject to change. At present, glaciers all around the world are retreating with increasing speed. With their disappearance, we could lose not only part of the mountains' appeal, but also a valuable resource for solid geographic and climatological information.

June 2050: One of countless foreign tour groups is standing atop the Columbia Ice Field in the Canadian Rockies. From the newly created Icefields Parkway, nature glides by like a Camcorder moment. Around the turn of the millennium it was still possible to drive right up to the tongue of the glacier. Since then it has receded dramatically; signs with dates on them, pointing away from the visitor center across the way, document the glacier's rapid retreat. Meanwhile, a superstructure financed by General Electric spans the last remnants of ice. Critics maintain that the world's largest cantilevered aluminum structure was meant to ease the company's conscience and to polish its battered image after decades in which the global corporation refused to take an active part in emission talks. In addition to the structure, there is an underground refrigeration plant meant to keep the remaining fragments of the once eternal ice alive. Somewhat bored, the visitors listen to stories about the lost ice: of crevasses, for example, that exposed their victims after centuries or millennia.

Can there be such a thing as high mountains without glaciers? The Grossglockner and Mont Blanc, Mount Victoria and Kilimanjaro, clad in only a dirty brownish gray instead of caps of glistening white? That shimmering blue-white splendor, the picturesque symbol of the high mountains and an inseparable element of alpine culture—simply vanished?

The rapid retreat of glaciers worldwide is a fact. Between 1912 and 2000 the ice cap on Kilimanjaro lost more than 80 percent of its area. If this trend continues, the last traces of ice will have disappeared from the peak in fifteen years. In the Alps roughly half of the glaciers' volume has been lost since the middle of the nineteenth century. Their retreat in the past two decades has been particularly dramatic; Alpine glaciers have lost a full fourth of their remaining volume. Wall-like moraines left by the last major glacial advance around 1850 are generally clearly visible. The tongues of the existing glaciers lie far back from the maximums reached during that so-called Little Ice Age. Since that era ended there has been a general retreat, even though there were slight advances around 1890 and again in 1920. But in the 1940s and 1950s especially there was a tremendous loss of mass. A number of Alpine glaciers advanced somewhat once again between 1971 and 1980, but virtually all of them are now in retreat. In the particularly climate-sensitive Kalkalpen region, between the Salzach and the Rhine, there were roughly fifty glaciers in the middle of the nineteenth century. By the 1990s there were only sixteen small remnants, melted far back. When U.S. president William Howard Taft established Glacier National Park in Montana in 1910 there were 150 glaciers within its boundaries. Now there are but thirty, and even they have lost two-thirds of their mass. It is expected that most if not all of them will disappear within the next thirty years.

And it is not only glaciers that have melted back. Permafrost, the ice in the ground, has warmed as much as 3.6°F in the top 150 feet, and this warming is gradually extending to deeper levels. The Alps without glaciers is a frightening scenario, but even more so is the thawing of the permafrost or its retreat to deeper levels underground; it would lead to unstable slopes and the loosening of great quantities of debris, considerably raising the danger of avalanches and slides. Countless mountain shelters, service structures, and lift towers are anchored in permafrost. This alone will give engineers and other responsible experts plenty to work on in the coming decades.

It is generally felt that glacial retreat is a result of global warming. Temperatures in Europe have risen as much as 1.8°F over the past 100 years. The world's climate experts, the Intergovernmental Panel on Climate Change (IPCC) is predicting, based on model calculations, an increase up to 10.5°F by the year 2050. In the Alpine region the rise in temperature already stands at around 3.6°F, of which 2.2°F has come in the past thirty years. The warming of the Alps is comparatively higher than the global trend. This is especially apparent during the winter at higher altitudes. In low-lying areas, nighttime temperatures have clearly risen, whereas maximum daytime temperatures have risen only slightly or not at all. In the twentieth century minimum temperatures in Switzerland rose on average 3.9°F, maximums decreased by 0.40°F. The decrease in maximum temperatures in lower regions has probably been caused the increase in clouds and air particles. In daytime this reduces the sun's heat, whereas at night ultraviolet radiation increases, causing temperatures as a whole to be more balanced.

Snow and ice are essential elements of high-mountain landscapes. They are linked together in a complex reciprocal process, but react on different time scales. Snow is formed by short-term weather cycles. Ice, however, is formed from snow by way of névé, the partially compacted granular snow which has undergone at least one cycle of melting and refreezing and forms at the edge of a glacier. The overall glacial economy, its mass balance, responds in the short term, glacial tongues and permafrost over longer ones, with delays of several decades. These discrepancies make it very difficult to make precise prognoses.

The world's high mountains are ecological fever thermometers, early warning systems for all types of environmental change, especially climate

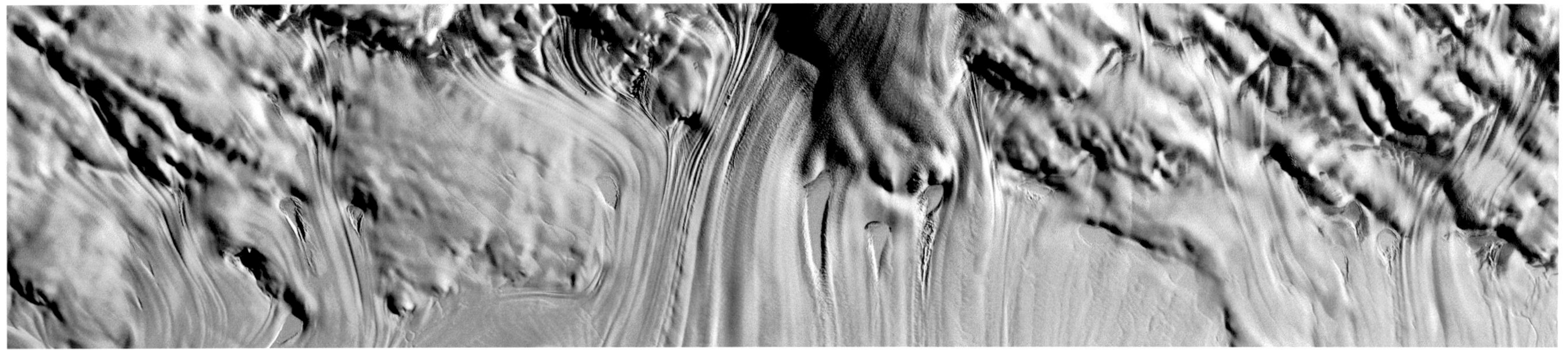

Lambert Glacier, Amery Shelf Ice, Antarctica. Snow and ice are important geophysical archives from which we can deduce temperatures of past centuries and a number of other environmental conditions. The ice has a memory, one which records the environmental changes caused by man as well.

change. They are highly sensitive to any variation, either natural or caused by humans. Because of their structure, especially the way they are layered in different altitude levels, even the smallest encroachment can bring change. The altitude zones can shift, expand, or shrink. For example, the snowline, the treeline, the permafrost line, also the meadow limit can change as a result of climate alteration. Alpine botanists have shown that on a number of peaks certain plants have migrated upward in the past hundred years—that is, they are now colonizing in altitudes that were formerly too cold for them. According to our present state of research, it must be assumed that many such processes do not proceed uniformly, that under certain circumstances the signals can intensify.

Losing mountain ice would mean the loss of important archives relating to environmental changes. Glacial ice cores not only tell us what the temperatures were in any given year, which can be determined from oxygen isotopes, they also record various atmospheric components like sulfate or nitrate and the acid content of the precipitation. From ice cores we can reconstruct long-term temperature changes, volcanic activity, and also other environmental conditions. Among other things, they tell us how drastically concentrations of sulfate and nitrate in the air have risen in the second half of the twentieth century—even far from major industrial areas. Man has left his fingerprints in the ice strata in other ways as well. Atom bomb tests since 1963 are clearly identifiable, and the Chernobyl reactor catastrophe of 1986 is firmly engraved in the ice record.

Ice cores also document dust storms out of the Sahara such as those of 1901, 1902, 1936–37, 1977, and 1990. In the flatland we mostly notice these as a reddish coating of dust on our cars. When this dust falls on white snow it becomes what is known as "blood snow." It is also possible to identify the dust from volcanic explosions like those of Krakatoa in Indonesia in 1883 and Laki on Iceland in 1783.

It has been possible to extract especially long cores from polar ice shields. Studies of high-mountain glaciers are far less common. But geographers and climate researchers at Ohio State University have responded to the current changes: in one impressive research project they extracted cores from the entire depth of the ice on Kilimanjaro and stored them in freezers—in the foreseeable future those cores and the information they provide will be all that we know about Kilimanjaro's ice.

Ötzi, the most famous of the "ice men," could not have told us all he has about his life and his environment if the ice had not preserved him. And he certainly tells us something about climate change as well. According to standard dating procedures he probably died 5,300 years ago, and was gradually buried in snow and névé. By sublimation, the direct transition from solid ice to steam, his corpse was dehydrated and thereby mummified without decaying. He resurfaced only in 1991, which tells us that the temperatures we are experiencing today have not been reached for the past 5,000 years. From the researches of historical climatology we can assume that in the past the Alps were once ice-free. Climate conditions at the time of Ötzi's death were probably not too unlike those of today. In this respect, as well, the glacier man serves as a kind of memento mori.

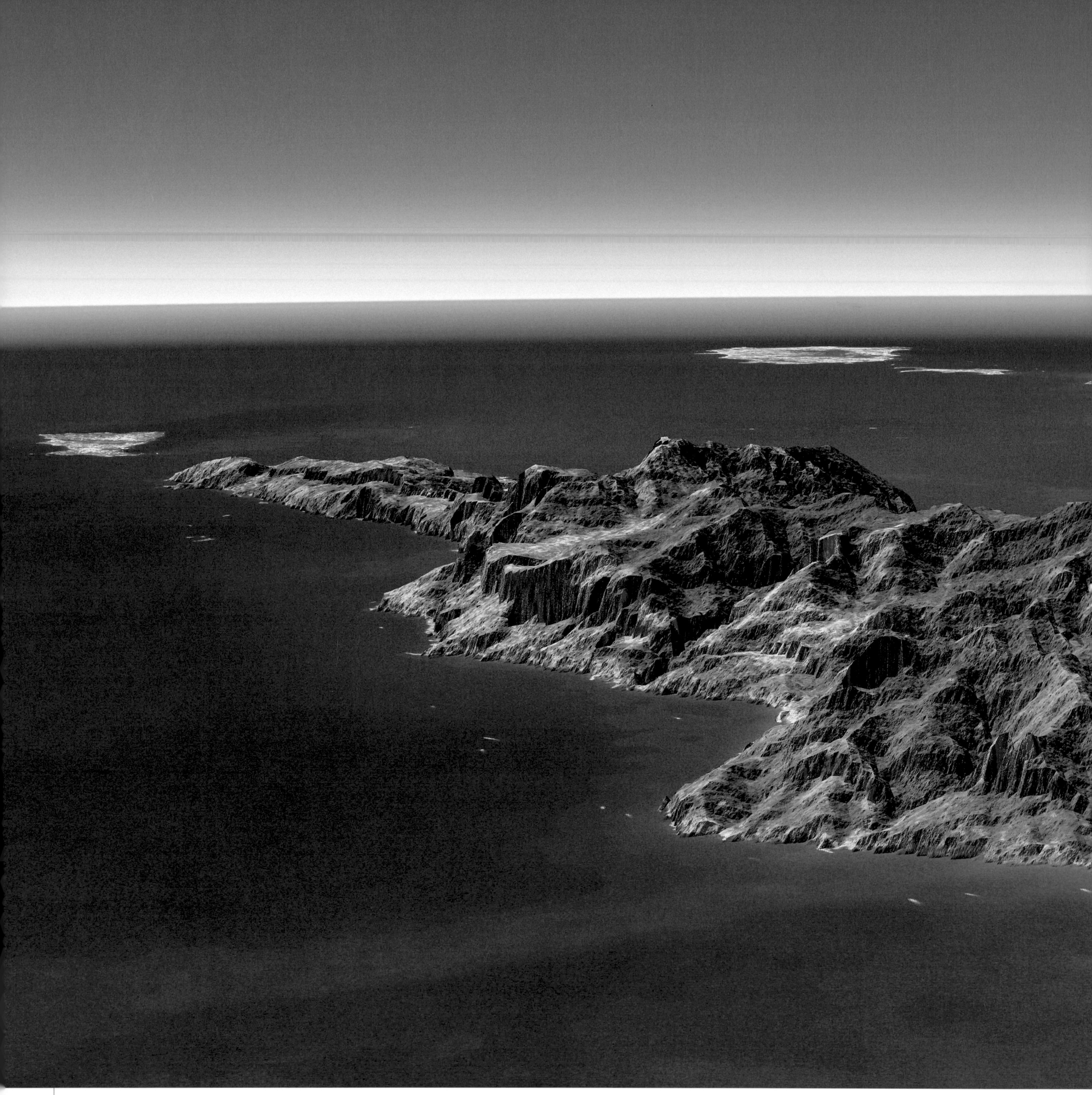

Panorama of Campania and the Bay of Naples with Vesuvius, Italy

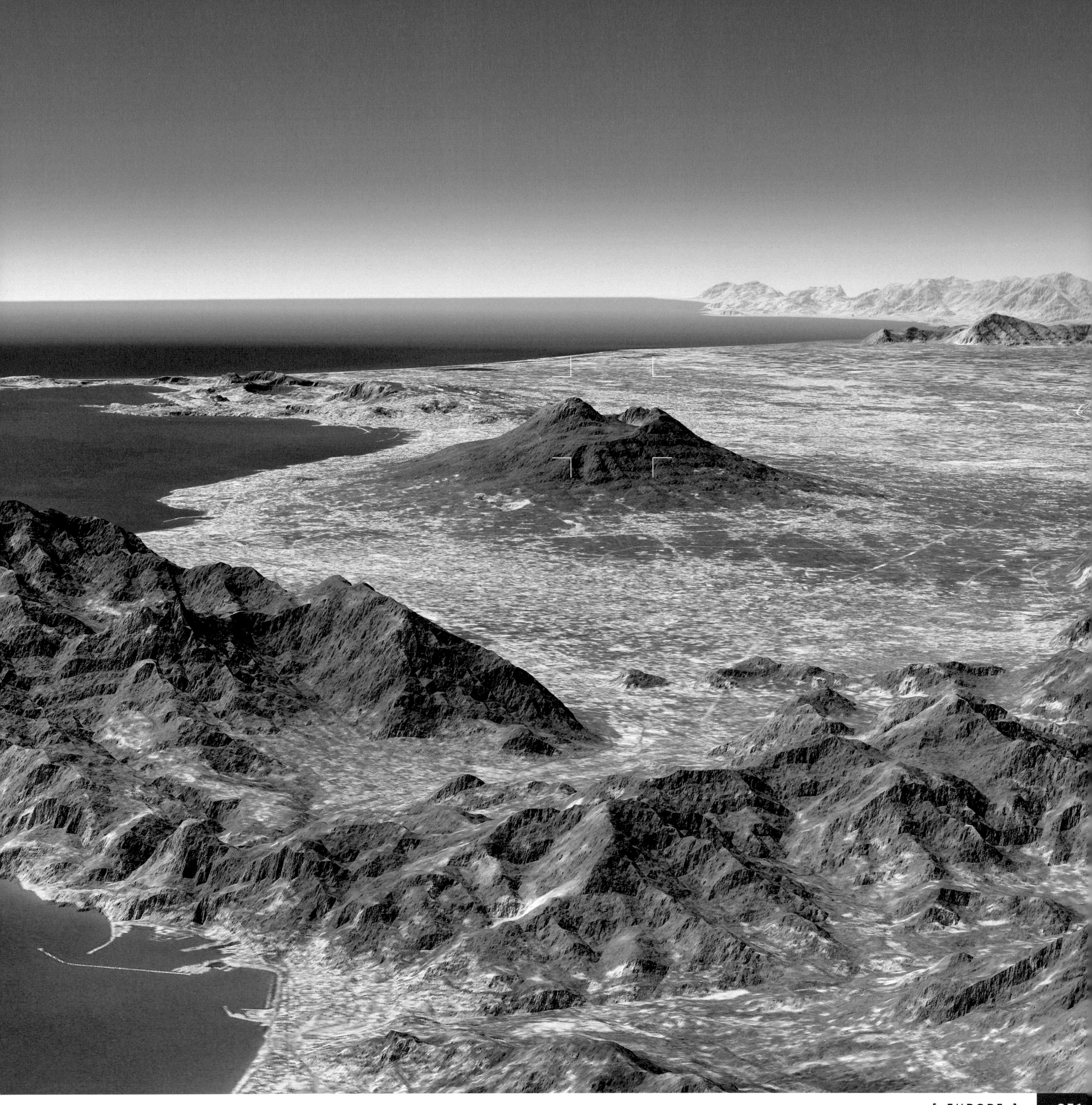

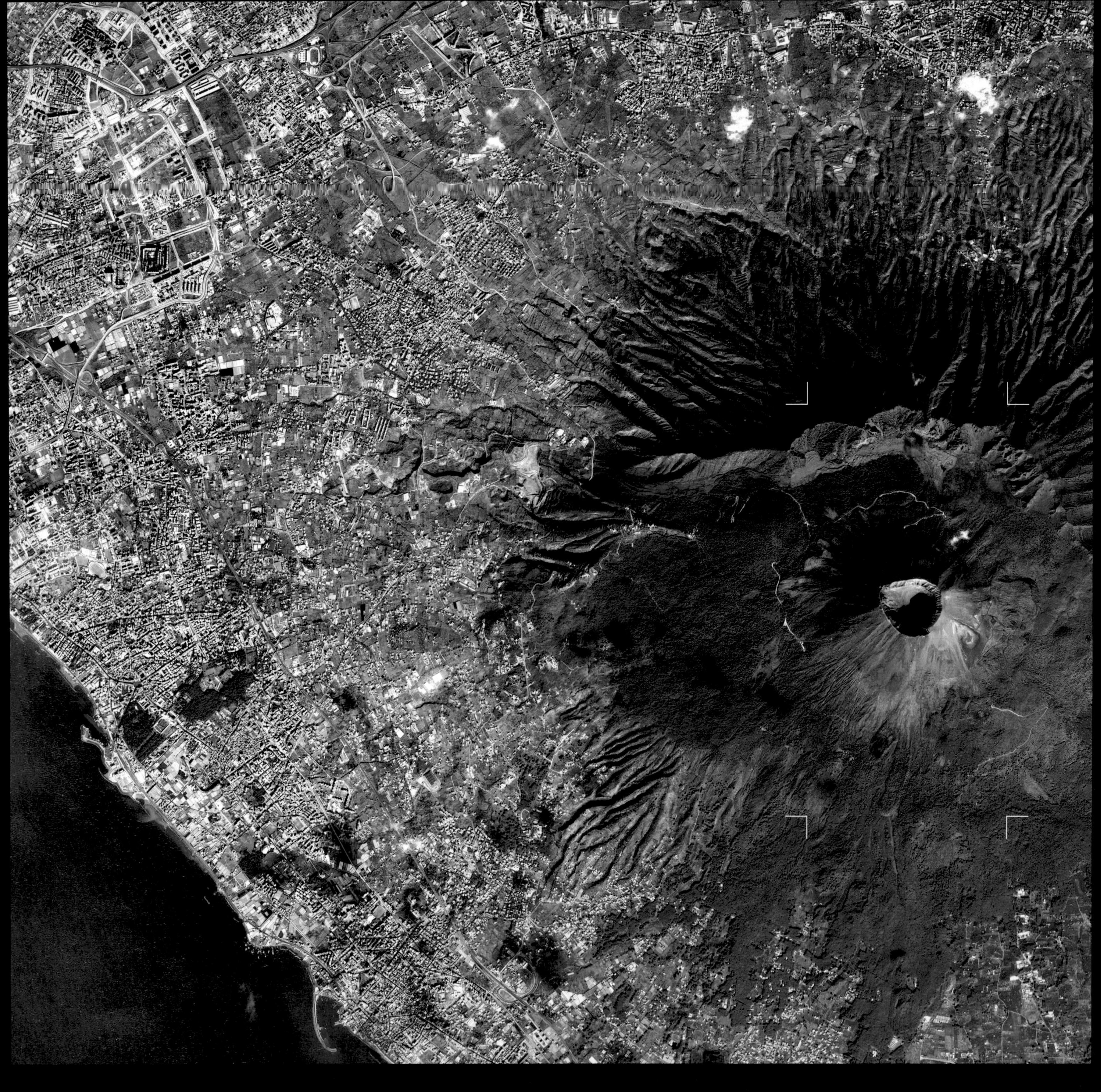

Detailed view of Vesuvius's crater and surroundings, Italy

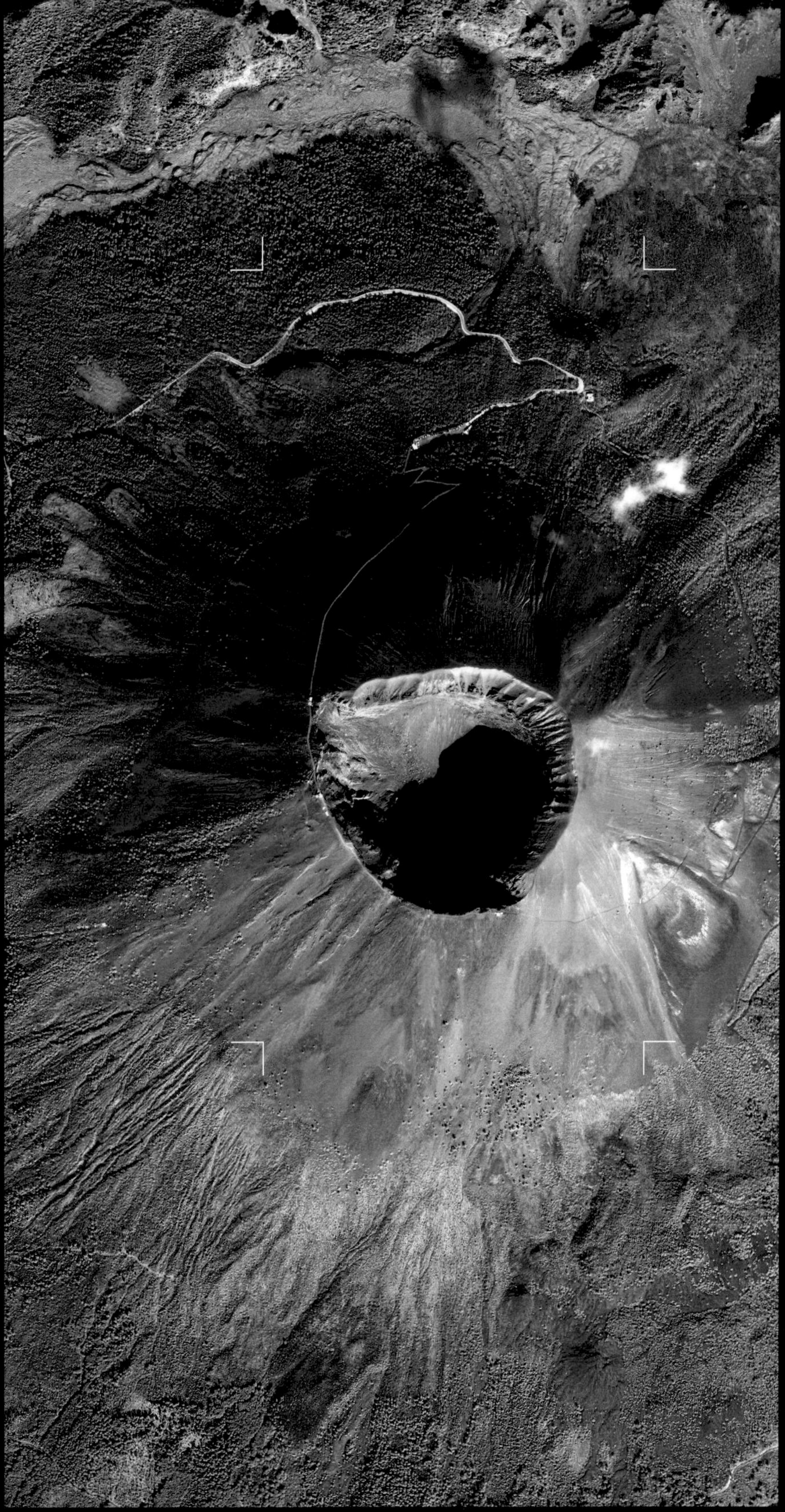

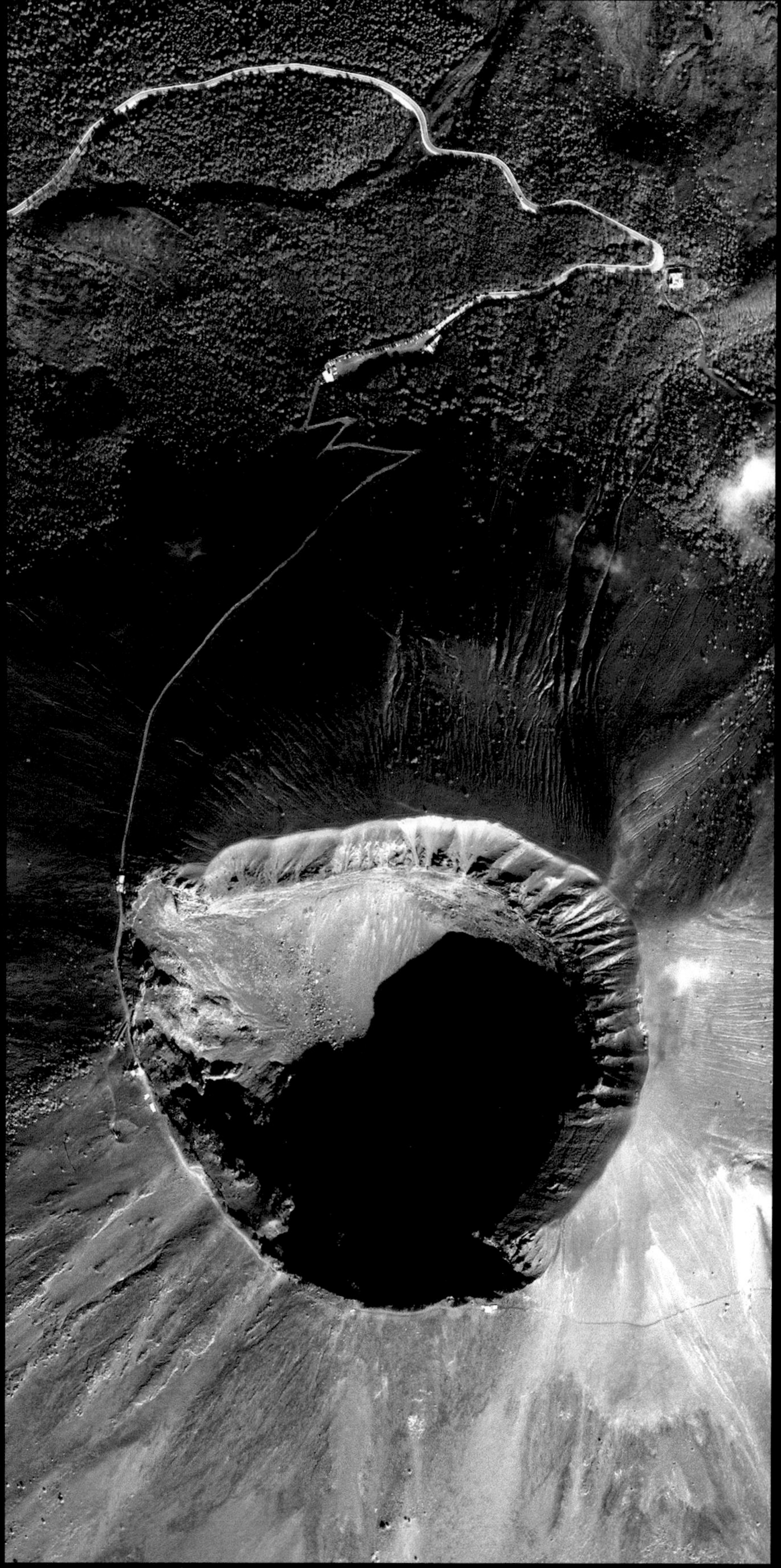

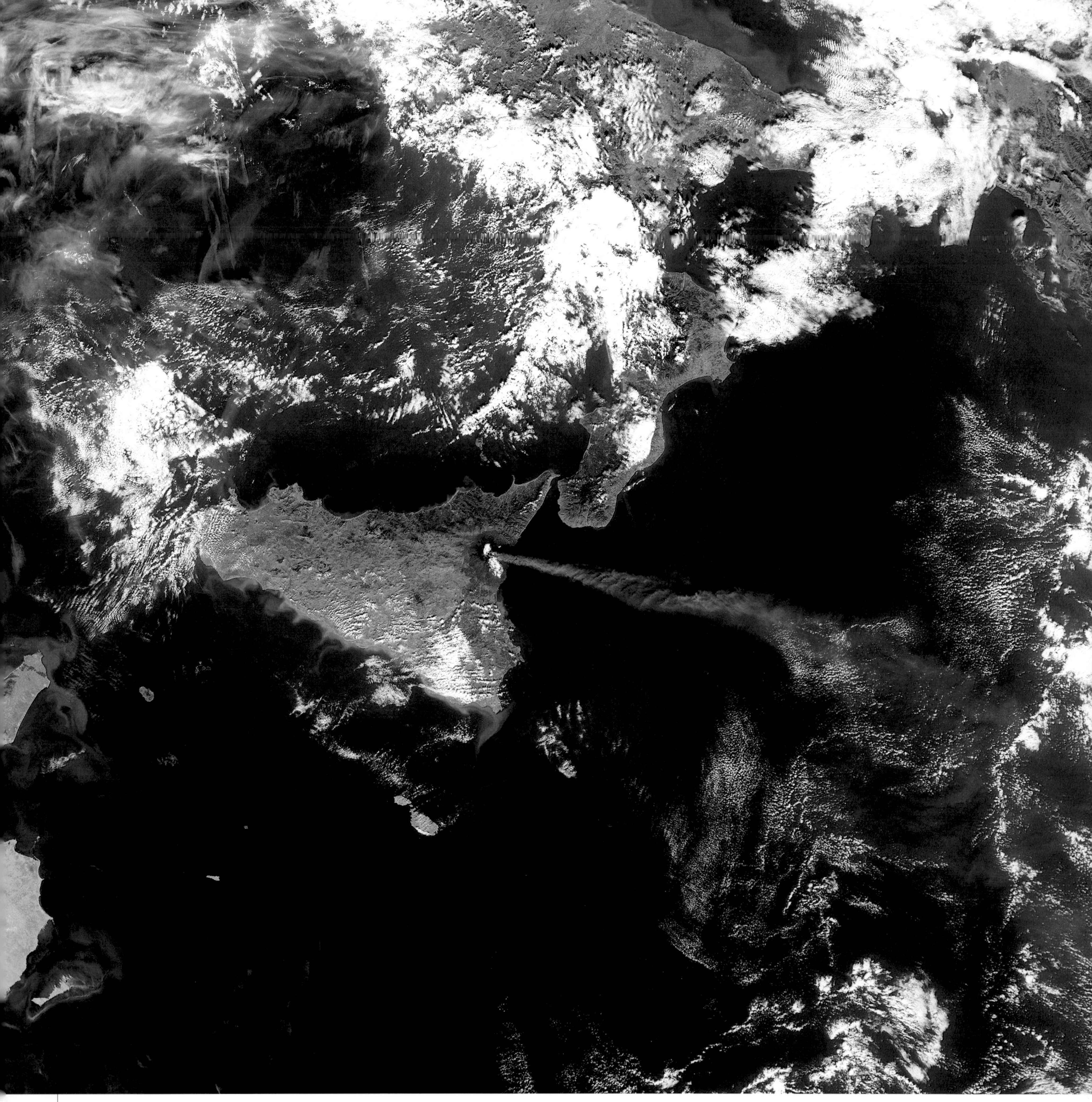

Eruption of Mount Etna in the fall of 2002, Italy

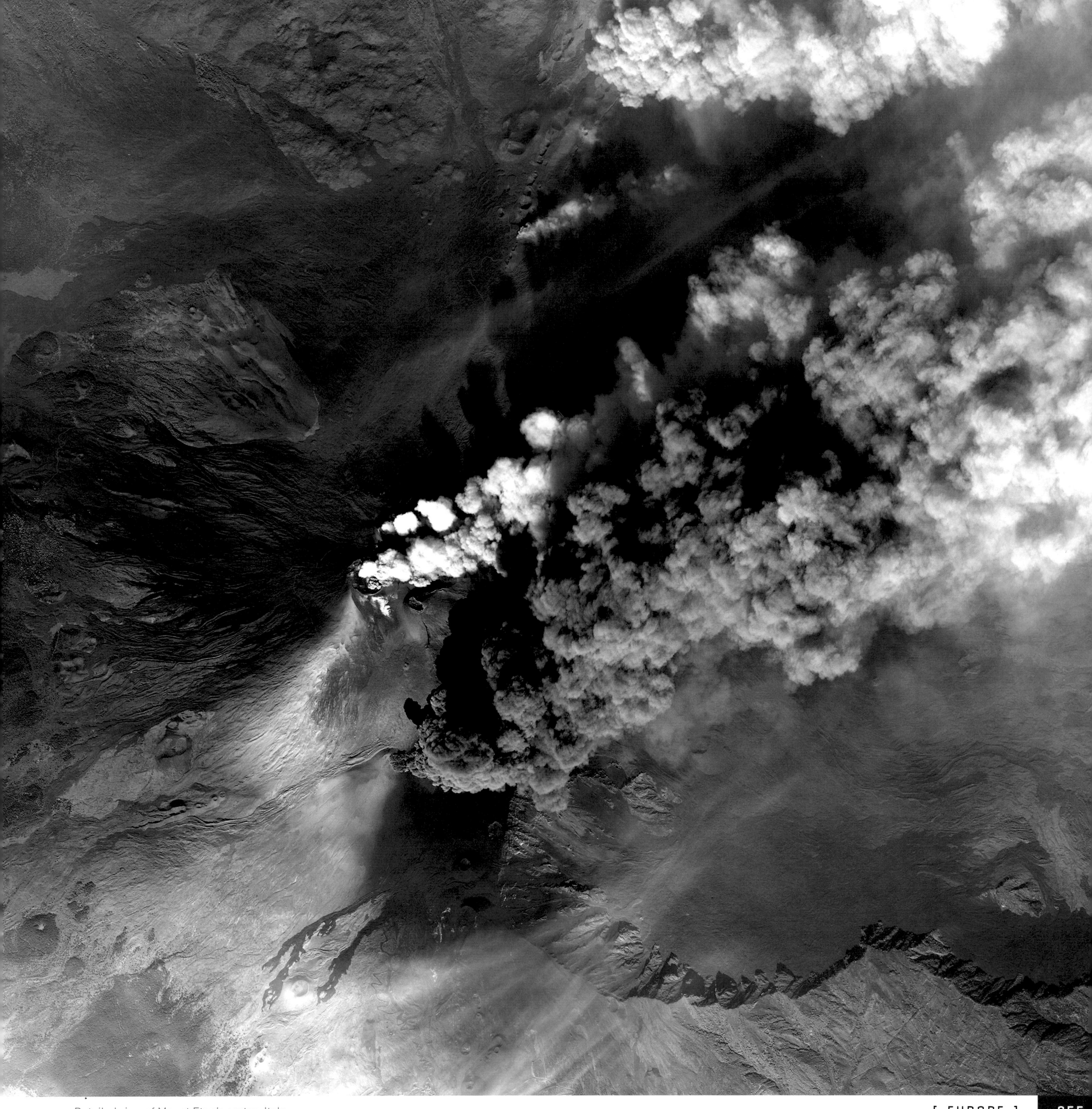

Detailed view of Mount Etna's crater, Italy

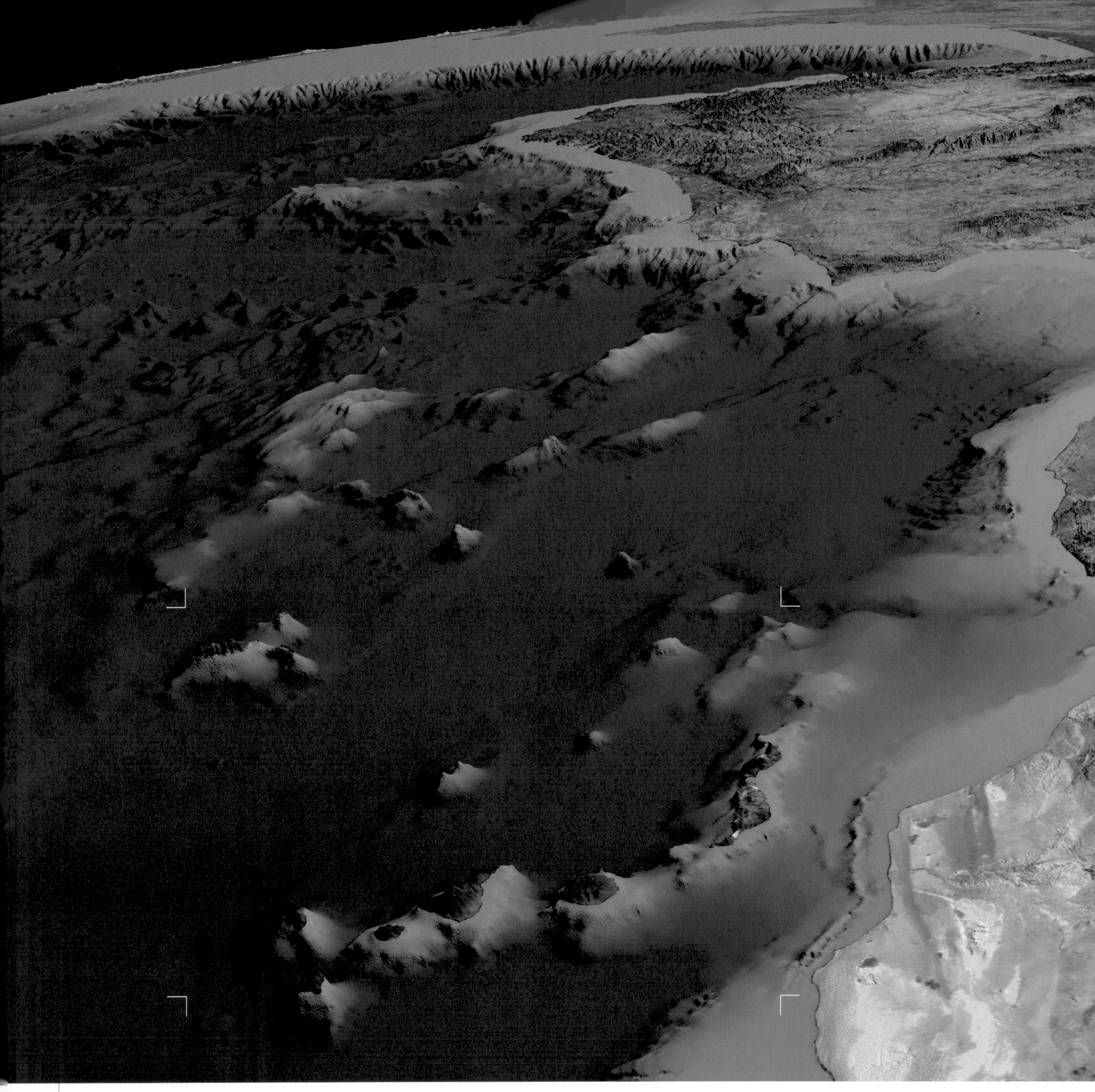

Panorama of North Africa, including the Canary Islands

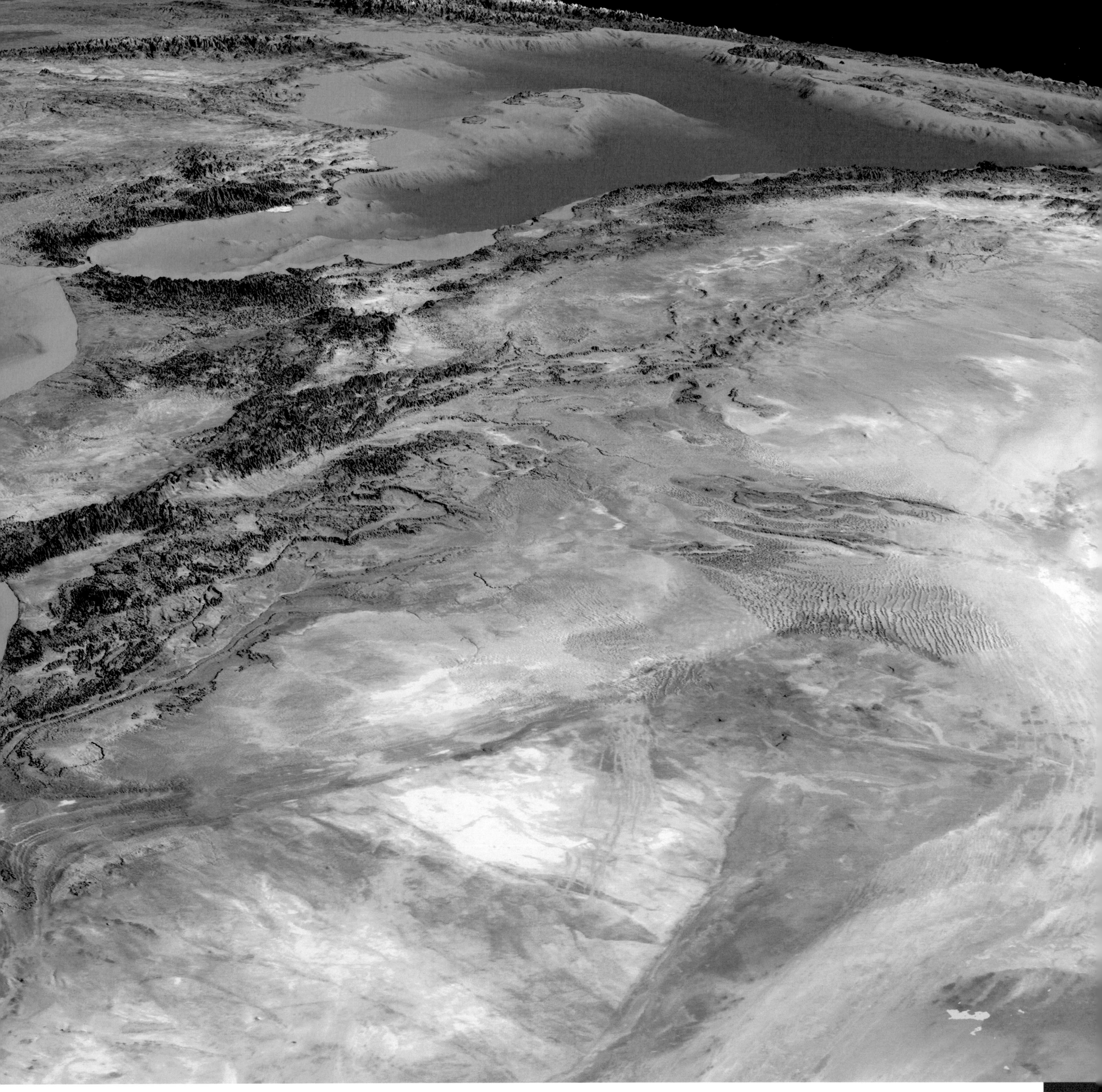

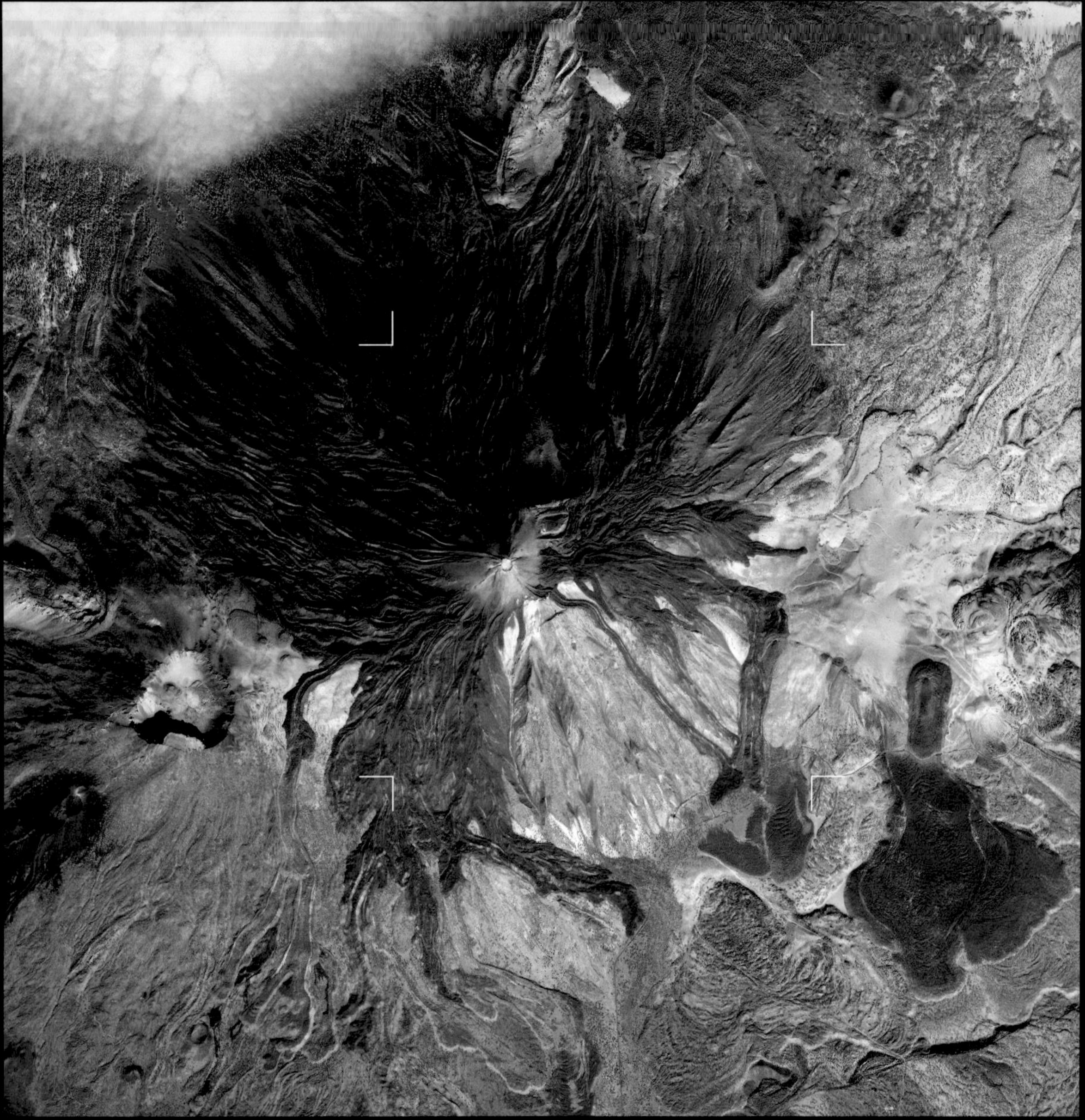

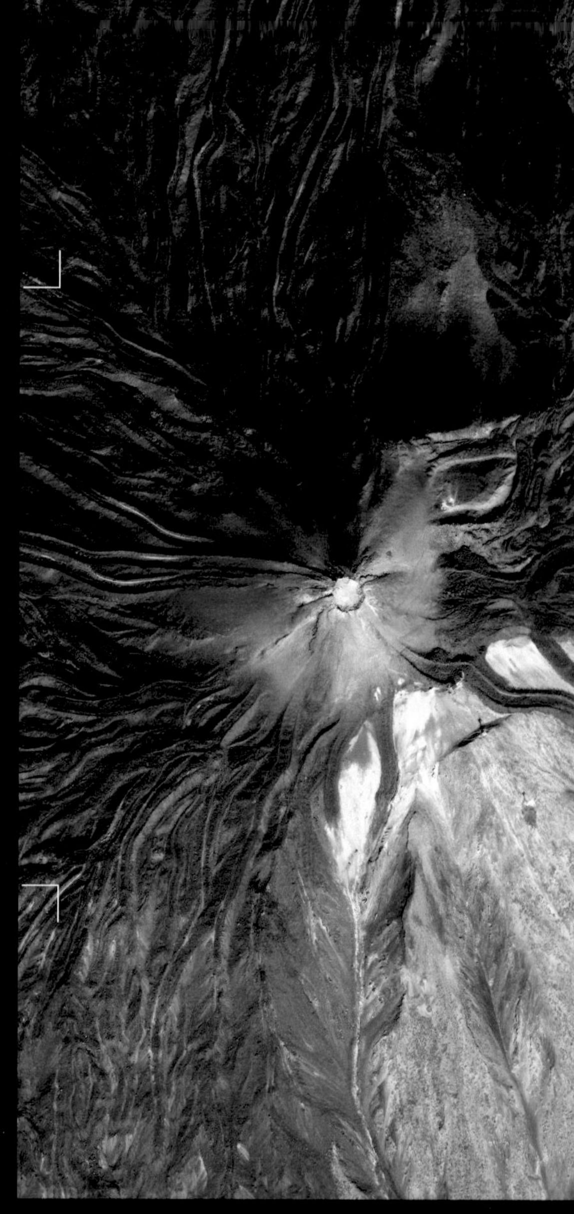

Detailed view of the crater of Teide Peak, Tenerife, Canary Islands, Spain

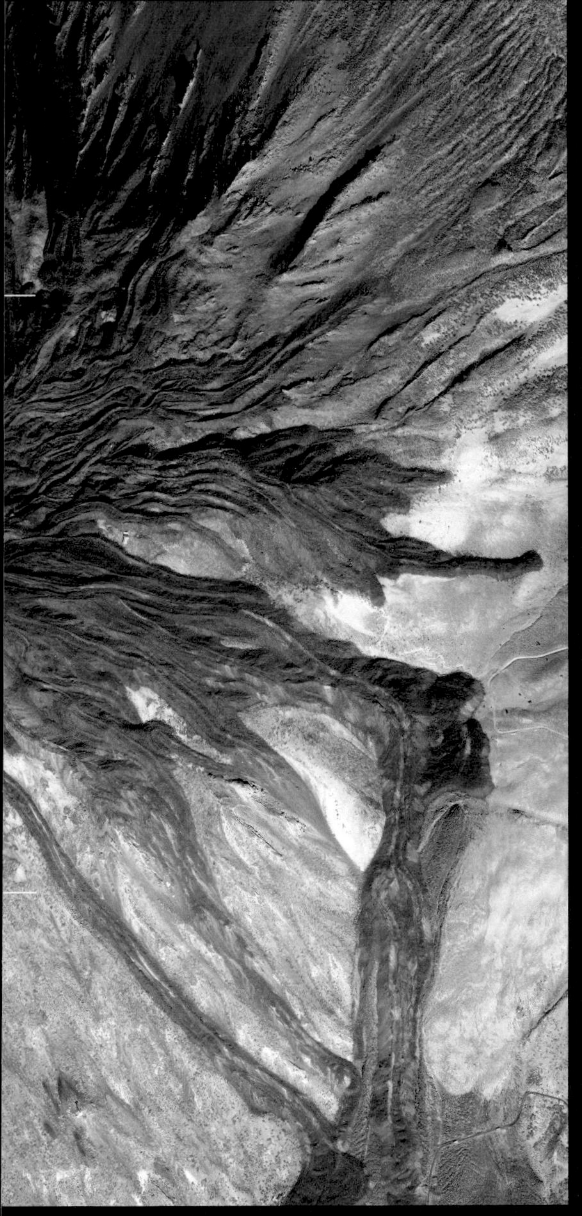

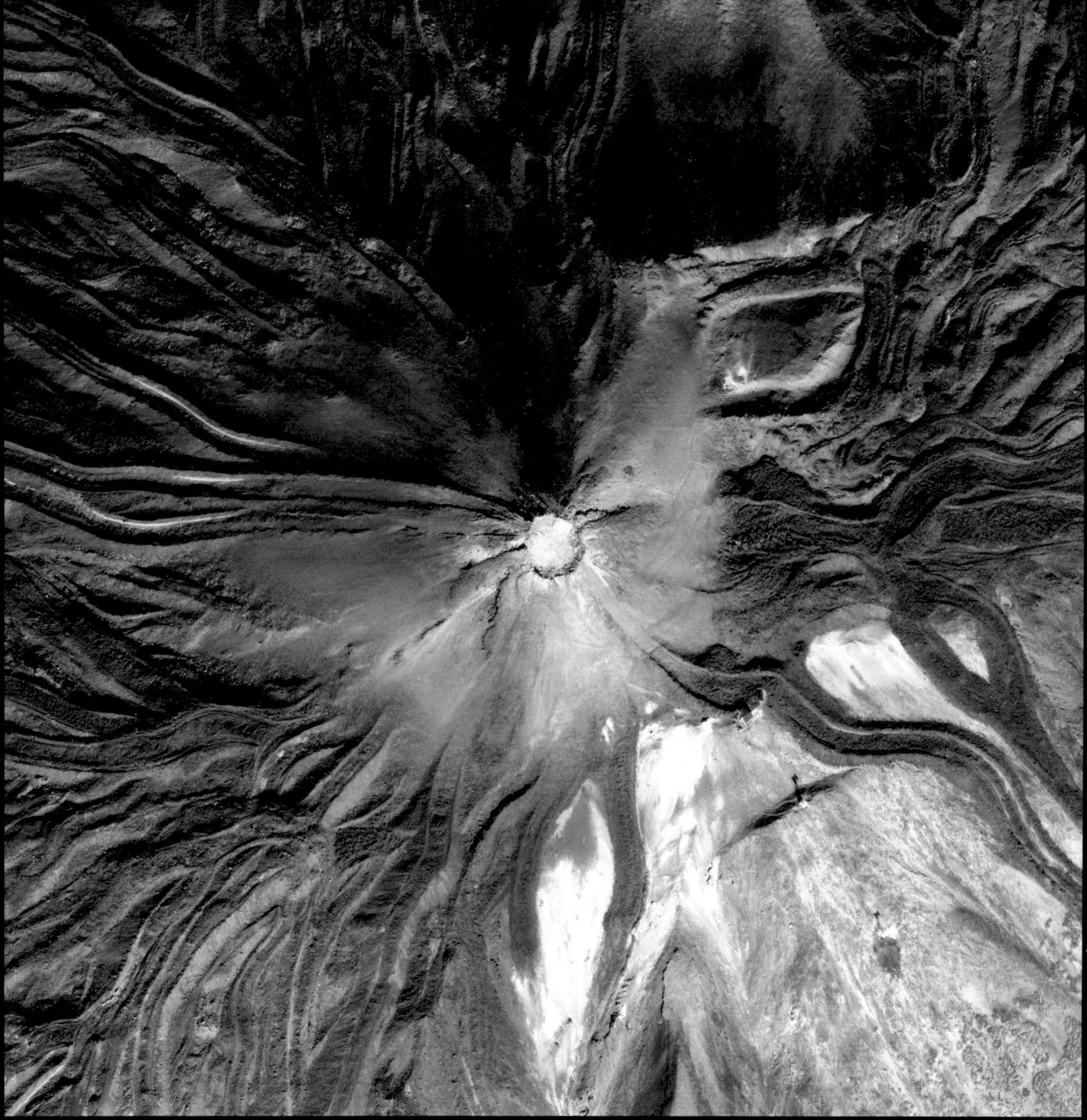

Mountains and Men

RALF-PETER MÄRTIN

In 1780 when the Swiss painter Caspar Wolf exhibited the two hundred alpine landscape paintings he had been working on for seven years in Paris, he was counting on an enthusiastic response. But it turned out to be the greatest disappointment of his life. The French public vehemently rejected his mountains, caves, and chasms as unworthy subjects for fine art.

The visitors to the exhibition who showed such disdain for the artist now celebrated as the founder of alpine painting were an esteemed lot. Wolf's contemporaries, like the archaeologist Johann Joachim Winckelmann, whose writings celebrated the artistic ideals of antiquity, found mountains "horrifying." And the philosopher Immanuel Kant could see nothing grand, let alone beautiful, about "misshapen mountain masses stacked one above the other in wild disarray."

Early historical sources document echoes of the same thinking. For the generals of antiquity, whether Hannibal or Alexander, they represented only troublesome barriers to the mobility of their armies. Mountain peaks were considered the dwellings of the gods, and no one felt the urge to pay a visit to Zeus on Olympus.

Things were no better in the Christian Middle Ages. The pagan gods may have transformed themselves into demons and devils, but they did not change their address. Mountains were teeming with kingdoms of dwarfs, fairy grottoes, and evil spirits banished to the wilderness. One thinks of Pilate, the judge of Jesus, who was said to be up to no good on Switzerland's Mount Pilatus, or of witches dancing on the Brocken in Germany's Harz Mountains. But neither merchants plowing the Brenner and Gotthard passes nor the farmers settled in the valleys ventured to make their acquaintance.

The first mountain climb we read about was undertaken in 1336 out of sheer curiosity. The poet Petrarch climbed the 6,266-foot Mont Ventoux in Provence. Many people pinpoint this climb as the "birth of the alpine idea," but Petrarch's reaction to the experience negates such a claim. Petrarch was not overwhelmed by what he saw; on the contrary, it made him realize that "nothing is so admirable as the soul: nothing compares with its grandeur." Disenchanted, he climbed back down.

The love of mountains and the idea that the world up there with its glaciers, cliffs, and bitter winds, is an appealing destination, is only two hundred years old, an offspring of Enlightenment and Romantic ideals.

The age of discovery and of Encyclopedists with the desire to fill in all the blank spots on the map finally reached mountains at the end of the eighteenth century. There was a whole untrodden world of heights to be conquered in the name of science. Geographers like Horace-Bénédict de Saussure and Alexander von Humboldt took the first steps into the unknown—de Saussure with his climb of Mont Blanc (1786) and Humboldt at Chimborazo in South America (1802), which was believed to be the highest mountain in the world.

At this same time Jean-Jacques Rousseau was preaching his doctrine of "a return to nature," convinced that the untouched world of mountains was the antidote for the corrupted confines of civilization. To Rousseau the ideal scenery was one of "cliffs, dark woods, mountains, rough trails, and frightening abysses." The dramatist and poet Friedrich von Schiller also called such scenery "sublime," Caspar David Friedrich would paint it as "wildly romantic," and Friedrich Hölderlin would invoke such landscape in impassioned verse. In the general consciousness mountains were finally considered beautiful—and so it is to this day.

Taking trips into the mountains became de rigueur. Mountain ranges, both in Europe and elsewhere, needed to be mapped, passes discovered, and peaks climbed for the sake of gathering information. On the level of individual experience, mountains were felt to be instructive. Viewing them was soothing to the soul, which took on something of their ethereal peace. Goethe, on his second trip to Switzerland, took his pupil, the duke of Saxe-Weimar, to Chamonix to show him the glacial world of the Mer de Glace for this reason.

This new positive image of mountains changed the travel habits of Europe's wealthiest populace at the time, the English. Upper-class sons had formerly been sent on a "grand tour" through France, Italy, and perhaps even Greece, so as to further their education and let them get to know something of the world. Now these travelers began making a picturesque side trip into Switzerland, reporting back about its inhabitants and their customs with the same enthusiasm as that heard from modern-day trekkers to Nepal, Bhutan, or Ecuador.

Contrary to their social conventions, the upper echelon accepted flea-infested inns, terrible food, and boorish mountain guides. It became fashionable to be the first to scale still virginal peaks then fill London salons with accounts of perils and close encounters after a safe return. The Alps became an English playground, then Germans, Austrians, Italians, and Frenchmen followed suit. By the end of the nineteenth century, hundreds of thousands of tourists were swarming into the mountains every year. All the Alpine peaks had been climbed, and every country had its own Alpine club committed to opening up the mountains to the general public. But to what end? This was a matter of highly divergent opinion and the subject of passionate debate.

Mountain climbing in the interest of science was generally accepted. Those who went into the mountains with a theodolite and an altimeter, who mapped and collected rock samples, stood in the tradition of the great explorers and discoverers. Even those who haunted mountains for their beauty,

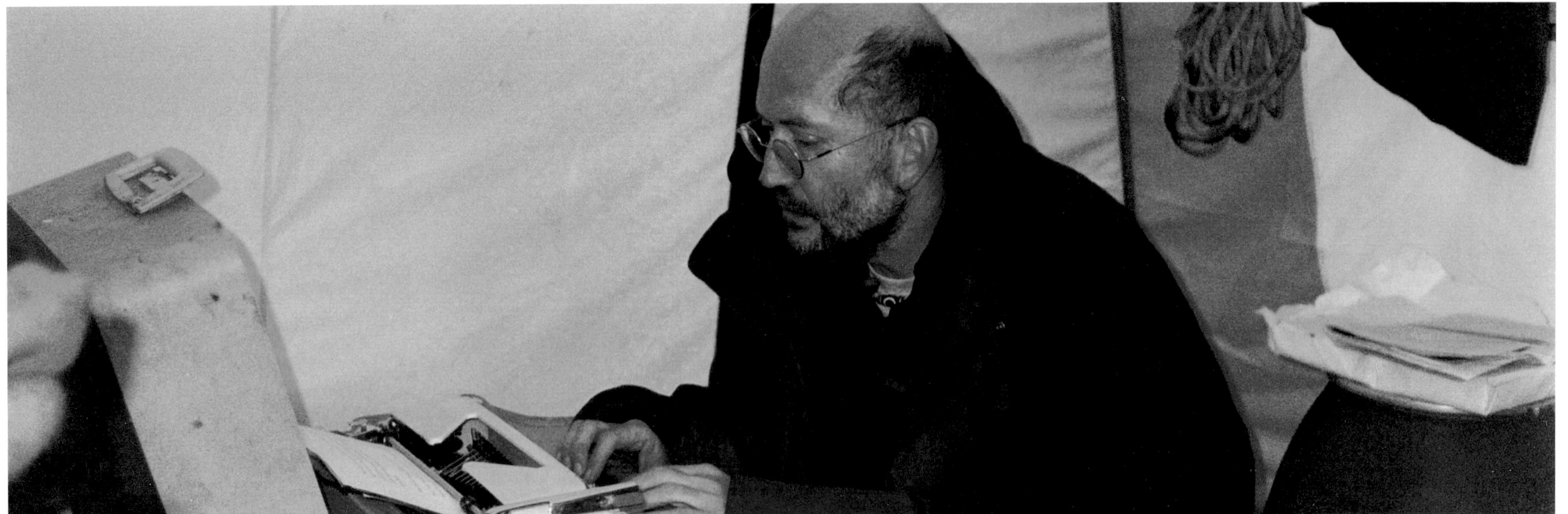

whether as tourists or painters, poets or photographers, were no longer considered unusual. The art critic John Ruskin called mountains "cathedrals of nature," before which one ought to pause in admiration. Scaling peaks is senseless, he insisted, for the "aesthetic beauty disappears, as it lies beneath the climber."

Finally, there were "fugitives from civilization" who found in mountains everything denied them by the industrialized world: silence and solitude instead of hustle and bustle, a peaceful paradise instead of constant competition, and freedom to be oneself instead of succumbing to bourgeois constraints.

But Enlightenment society geared toward practicality mistrusted dedicated climbers, the men driven to the mountains for the sheer joy of testing themselves on rock and ice. All the more so if they "senselessly" risked their lives. Edward Whymper was roundly criticized by the English press in 1865, after the first ascent of the Matterhorn, in which four of his companions lost their lives: the "best blood of the nation" had been sacrificed in a vain search for "glory."

Fifty years and a world war later, pursuit of glory was precisely the driving force behind a new, ideological alpinism. Mountain climbing became the arena for a battle between nations for the highest peaks in the world, the "eight-thousanders" (mountains taller than 8,000 meters, or 26,000 feet). The British on Everest and the Germans on Nanga Parbat no longer attacked these mountains "because they were there," as the Englishman George Mallory once put it, but as nationalistic conquests for their homelands. In the 1930s the National Socialist Party launched a veritable propaganda campaign in its "fight for the Himalayas." Death on a mountain—nearly thirty men died on Nanga Parbat—was glorified as a heroic sacrifice for one's race and the fatherland. The Third Reich's vision of alpinism as a competitive sport had its cost: becoming "a race of mountain climbers," as the Nazi press endlessly admonished, had nothing to do with the joy of climbing or experiencing nature. It was instead about being willing to die, about competing with one's comrades. Mountain climbing was militarized, reduced to mere preparation for the next war.

But parallel to this exploitation of alpinism for nationalist reasons there were always individual mountain climbers to whom self-respect mattered more than the collective will. When the Englishman Albert Frederick Mummery made the first attempt at an eight-thousander in 1895, he paid for his expedition out of his own pocket, and his only allegiance was to family. Mountain fanatics like Eugen Guido Lammer or the Nanga Parbat conqueror Hermann Buhl only felt good about themselves when climbing solo, and in their drive to test themselves against the ultimate, they refused to submit to any sort of regimentation or become members of a "roped party." Extreme climbers like Reinhold Messner or the brothers Alexander and Thomas Huber stand in this tradition; they consciously accept a mountain's dangers, even consider them a requirement if they are to know what they are capable of. For that very reason they scorn mechanical aids and rely solely on their own climbing abilities.

The future of alpinism lies in the view from the top. Beyond the fashionable peaks of the Himalayas and the "seven summits" with their trash heaps of empty oxygen canisters and garbage from countless expeditions, splashes of white and brownish shadows tell of a world of untouched mountain regions and remote valleys where it is possible, even today, to discover the best thing nature has to offer: peace of mind.

[AFRICA]

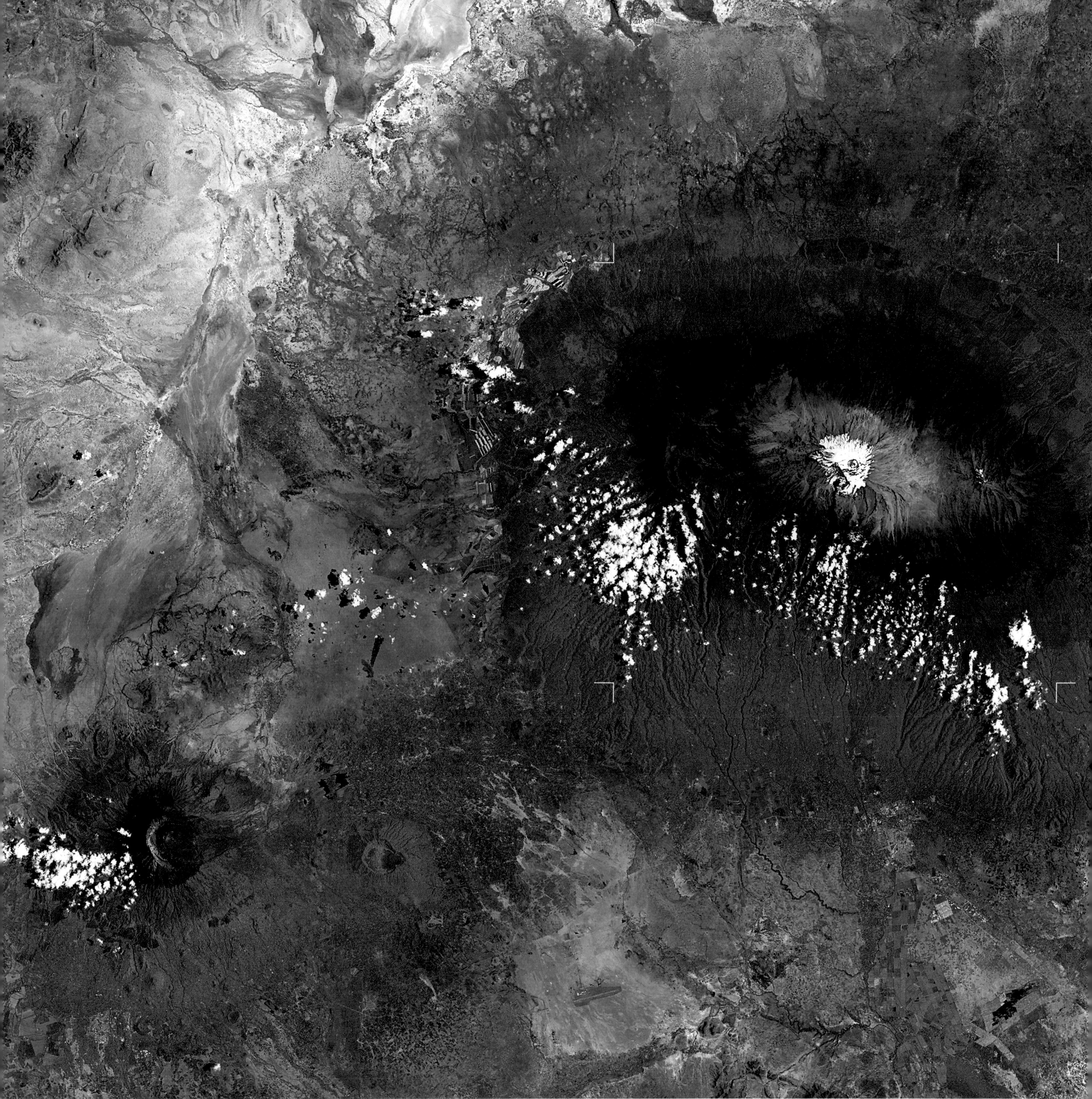

Kilimanjaro, Africa's tallest mountain, Tanzania

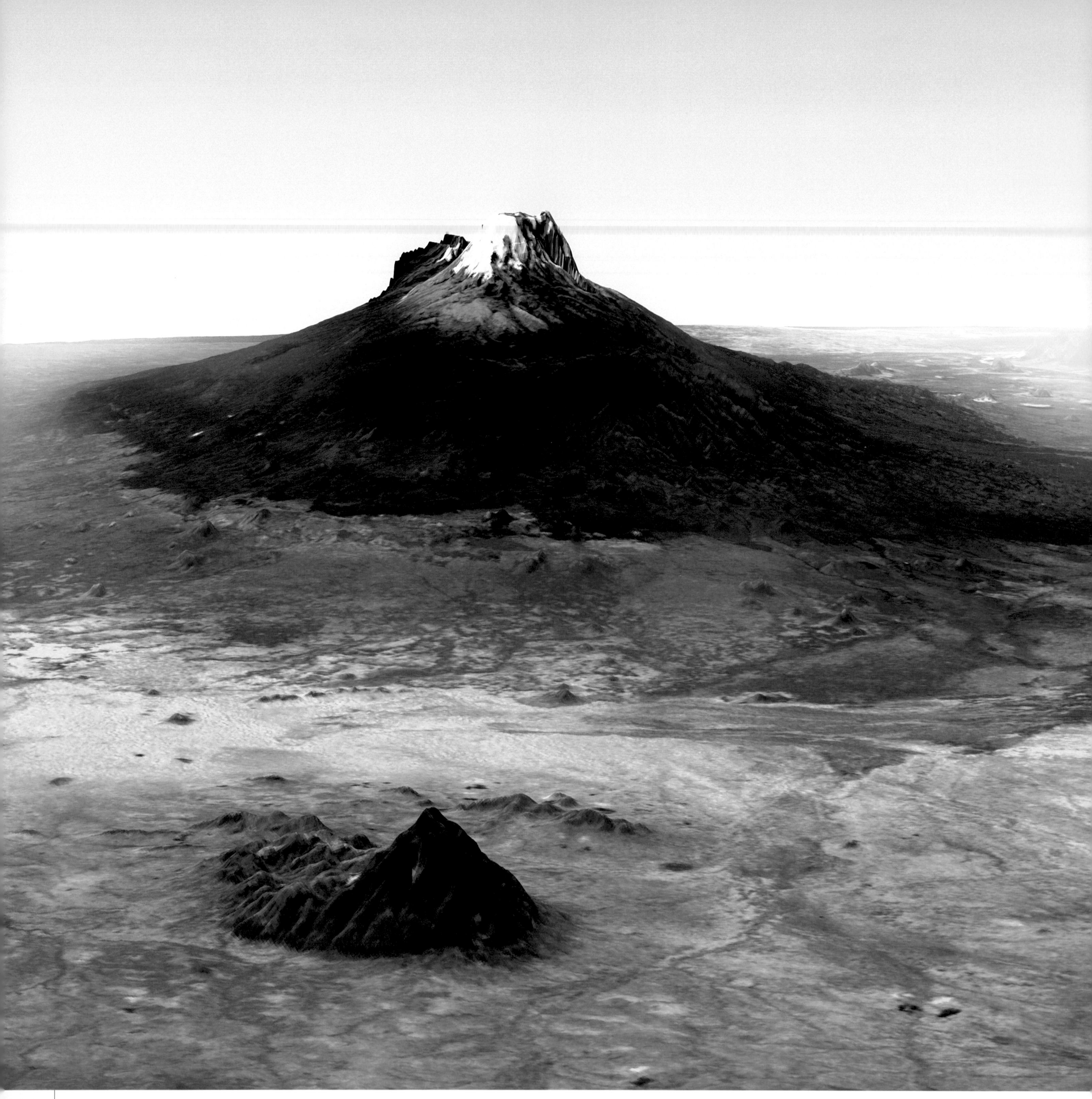

Kilimanjaro in 3D, Tanzania

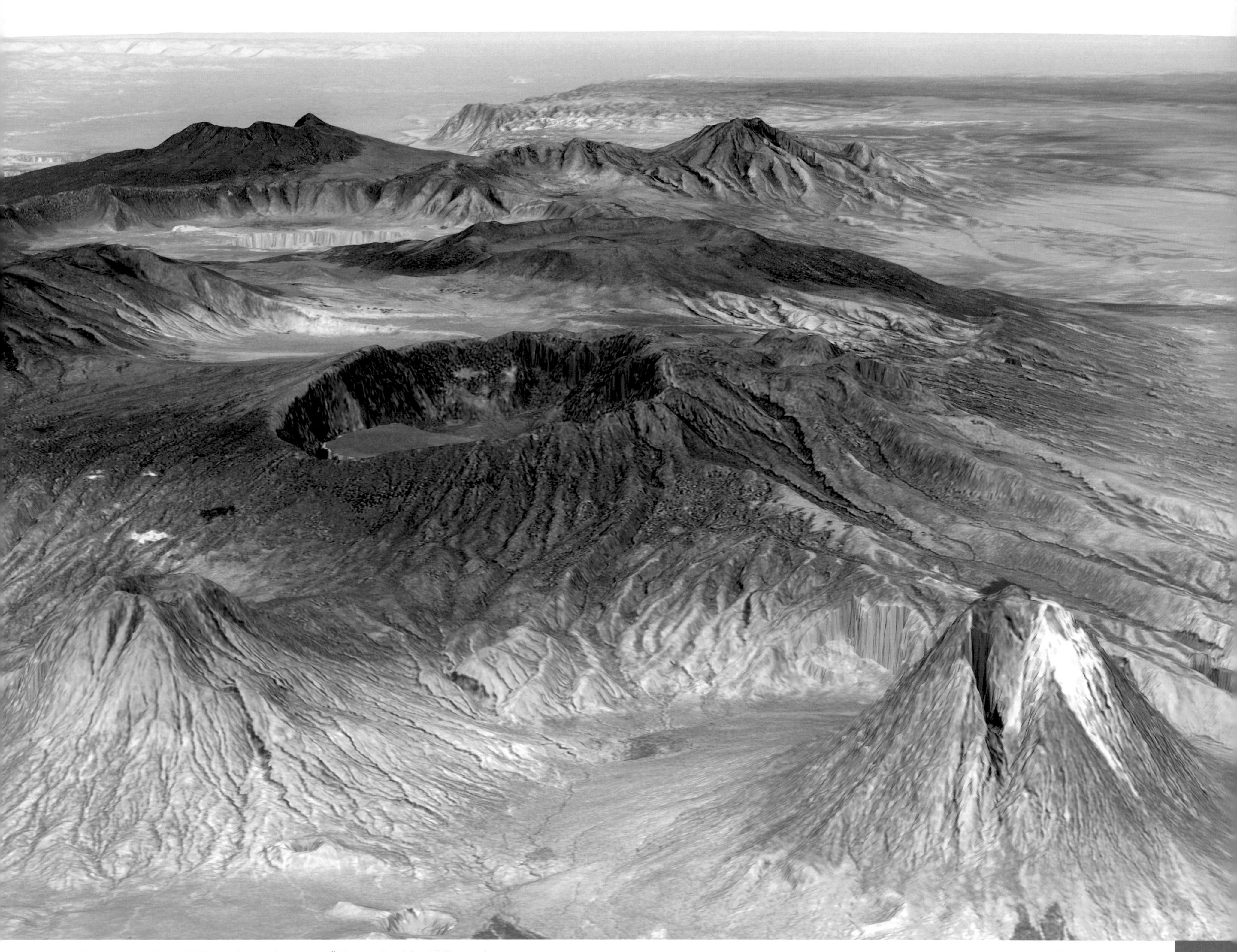

Panorama of the Ol Donyo Lengai volcano, "Mountain of God," Tanzania

Dangerous African Giants
Death in the Snow above the Clouds

OSWALD OELZ

On May 24, 1888, on his longest and most eventful African journey, Henry M. Stanley saw the snow-covered peaks of the Ruwenzori Range for the first time: "When we had gone roughly five miles from the camp at Nsabe, one of the chaps directed my gaze to a strangely shaped cloud with a marvelous silvery color and the shape and appearance of a huge mountain covered with snow. Following its outline I was astonished by the deep blue-black color at its foot, and wondered to myself if the cloud was heralding a new tornado. But I gradually became convinced that I was not looking at simply the likeness of a vast mountain but at a solid, actual peak whose tip was covered with snow."

The cap of Kilimanjaro almost appears detached when the mist rises around the town of Moshi at its base. And Nelion and Batian, the two peaks of Mount Kenya named for local tribal chieftains, sit enthroned in the sky above the greenish-yellow jungle steppe. All three African giants rise up out of seemingly endless plains, making them *über*-mountains that lure dreamers up from below. Many of them perish, like Hemingway's confused leopard at the crater of Kilimanjaro, which really existed. I saw a photograph of his frozen, desiccated cadaver taken in 1924.

What the leopard was looking for up there will always remain a mystery. The prey closer to the ground is fatter, larger, and more plentiful. The first human climbers were motivated by curiosity, ambition, and a desire for fame, of course, but also by politics. Hans Meyer, the first man to climb Kilimanjaro, writes in the introduction to his book *East African Climbing Tours*: "It seemed to me almost a national duty that the peak of Kilimanjaro, probably the highest African mountain and unquestionably the highest mountain discovered by a German (Rebmann), should first feel the print, despite all the efforts of English travelers, of a German foot."

And after he reached the highest point, the middle peak, at 10:30 A.M. on October 6, 1889, he reports, "Then I planted a small German flag I had brought along in my rucksack on the weathered tip of rock with a triple hurrah, strongly seconded by Herr Purtscheller, and cried out: 'By right as its first climber I name this previously unknown and nameless Kibo peak, the highest point on African and German soil, Kaiser Wilhelm Peak.'"

The British did not wish to be left behind. The geographer Mackinder, together with mountain guides César Ollier and Joseph Brocherel, conquered Mount Kenya for England in 1899, a magnificent achievement at the time. From April to September 1906 the Duke d'Abruzzi, after numerous failed attempts by English conquerors, led a highly organized and successful campaign to explore and climb all the main peaks of the Ruwenzori massif. In mountain climbing as in colonization, Africa was divided up among the Europeans. Since then there have been no more claims to be made, and colonial lords returned to tend to the problems in their own countries. The allure of the sublime remains, however, and each year thousands torture themselves in oxygen-poor altitudes we were never meant to survive—on Kilimanjaro alone nearly 20,000—solely to stroke their own egos.

Since man first climbed down out of the trees in East Africa four million years ago, our evolution has continued in jungles and on steppes up to altitudes of 10,000 feet. Above that no bananas grow, only few potatoes, and the few wild animals are shy and meager. But since the end of the eighteenth century at least some of us, no longer forced to wrest a miserable subsistence from a reluctant nature, have sought to test ourselves outside the healthier, denser air of the lowlands, and thus mountain climbing was born. Mount Kilimanjaro is especially seductive, with its technically simple routes permitting a swift ascent. Climbers gain altitude too quickly though, without becoming sufficiently acclimated. People generally attempt to reach the peak on the fifth or sixth day, a murderous pace for the body to try to adapt to. Anyone who has seen the agonized figures on the rim of Kilimanjaro's crater knows what I am talking about.

Climbing too high too quickly leads to the symptoms of acute altitude sickness: headache, abnormal fatigue, nausea, dizziness, insomnia, and a general malaise. The brain, which is extremely sensitive to reduced amounts of oxygen, functions poorly and suffers. If a person continues to climb with such symptoms, high-altitude cerebral edema can develop. The victim suffers severe headache, loss of balance, vomiting, increasing apathy, and finally unconsciousness; breathing ceases and death ensues. A further complication of staying at high altitudes is pulmonary edema, the build up of blood fluids in the vesicles of the lung owing to high pressure in the lungs' circulation. Mountain climbers then suffer excruciating coughing, spit blood, and feel extreme shortness of breath: they then drown in their own fluids. High-altitude cerebral and pulmonary edema often occur in tandem, and good health and fitness are no protection against them. The young and the fit are more often the ones afflicted, as they tend to climb too high too fast, ignoring the warning symptoms. There is as yet no way to test one's predisposition to altitude sickness. Reports of deaths on the great mountains of Africa began appearing some fifty years ago, but still there are no statistics. It is estimated that up to twenty climbers a year suffer the fate of the leopard on Kilimanjaro and die from complications brought on by the altitude. If the administrators of Kilimanjaro National Park keep records on these victims, they certainly do not publish the numbers—the mountain climbing business is too generous a source of income. The frequency of altitude sickness is also unknown, but is surely quite high; it is probable that more than half of the climbers attempting a challenging ascent suffer from it. Moreover, no one knows how many climbers reach the peak and how many are forced to turn around and stagger back down.

The best and most sensible protection against mountain sickness, as altitude sickness is also called, and high-altitude pulmonary edema is climbing slowly, so the body has time to acclimate. As a rule of thumb at altitudes above 8,000 to 10,000 feet it is recommended to sleep each night no more

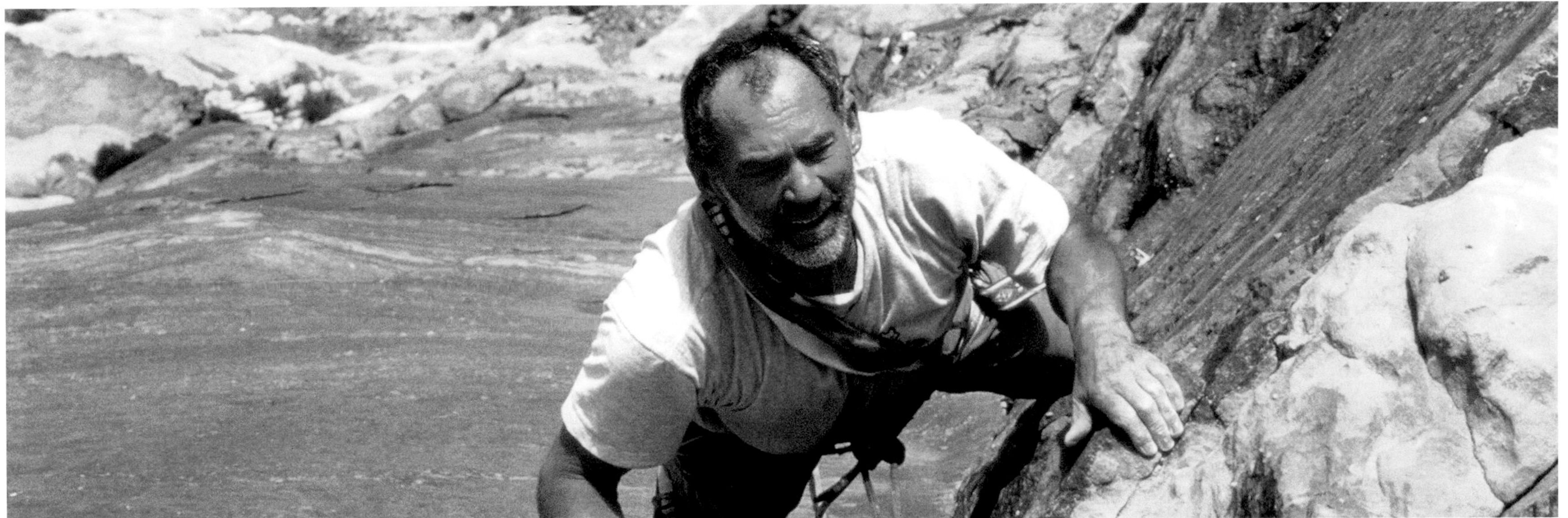

than 1,000 feet higher than the night before. This is an arbitrary figure, but it is a safe one. Every mountain climber needs to gauge his own individual tolerance for altitude and watch himself. This means having the courage to admit, once afflicted, that one is suffering from acute altitude sickness. It can be dangerous to ascribe its symptoms to an upset stomach or the flu. In high altitudes one should always assume that unless there is proof to the contrary, if you are not feeling well you are suffering from acute mountain sickness. When the symptoms are severe, the only remedy is to climb or be transported back down, or be assisted by oxygen. If the symptoms are less severe, one can wait at the same altitude until one has recovered. Under no circumstances should a person with signs of altitude sickness climb to still greater heights. Before tackling Kilimanjaro, one should undergo altitude training on 13,000-foot peaks as a practice tour, and a day of rest at one of the middle camps between 10,000 and 13,000 feet has proven to be helpful. Aspiring climbers have also been helped by medication like Diamox, a drug that in addition to having a slight diuretic effect mainly increases respiration, and has been successfully used in numerous studies to protect against mountain sickness. Whether one wishes to scale Africa's highest mountain by fair means or with drugs is a question of style, time, and medical consultation. I have received a number of enthusiastic reports from climbers who enjoyed a pleasant, successful climb thanks to Diamox.

Anyone who does reach one of the high spots in Africa without major health problems feels detached from the world. High mountains let us see how insignificant we are, none more so than Kilimanjaro, the tallest freestanding peak in the world. Between red banks of clouds, we sense that other world of our evolution below, its gnus racing against death, its lions, its steaming jungle, and its screaming apes. Here we are standing on moon lava, having come up through rain forest, steppe, swamp, sand, and wasteland, at the threshold of the sky. It is understandable why the Masai call the western peak Ngà-ja Ngà, "House of God."

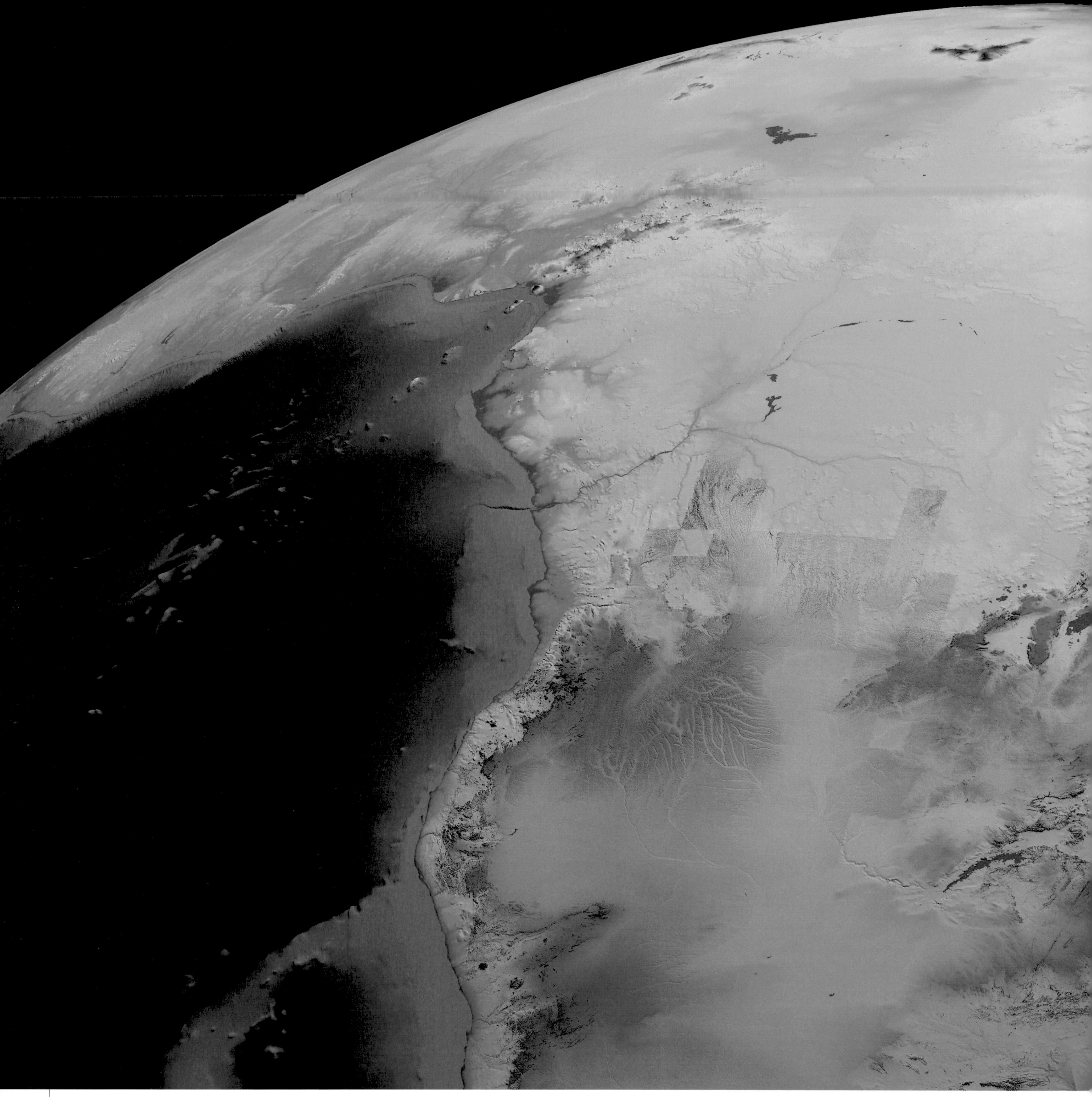

East African Rift, the cradle of mankind

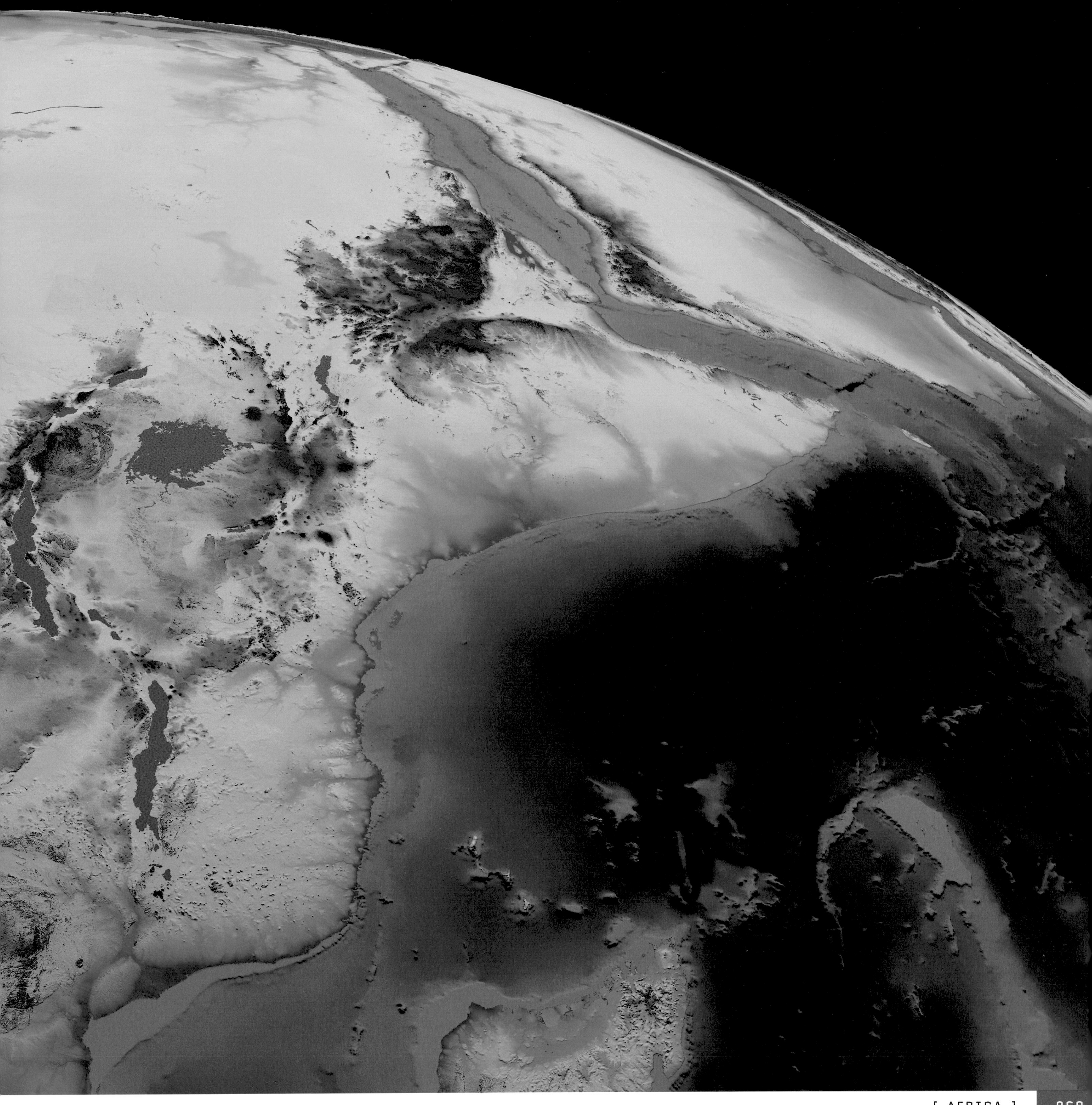

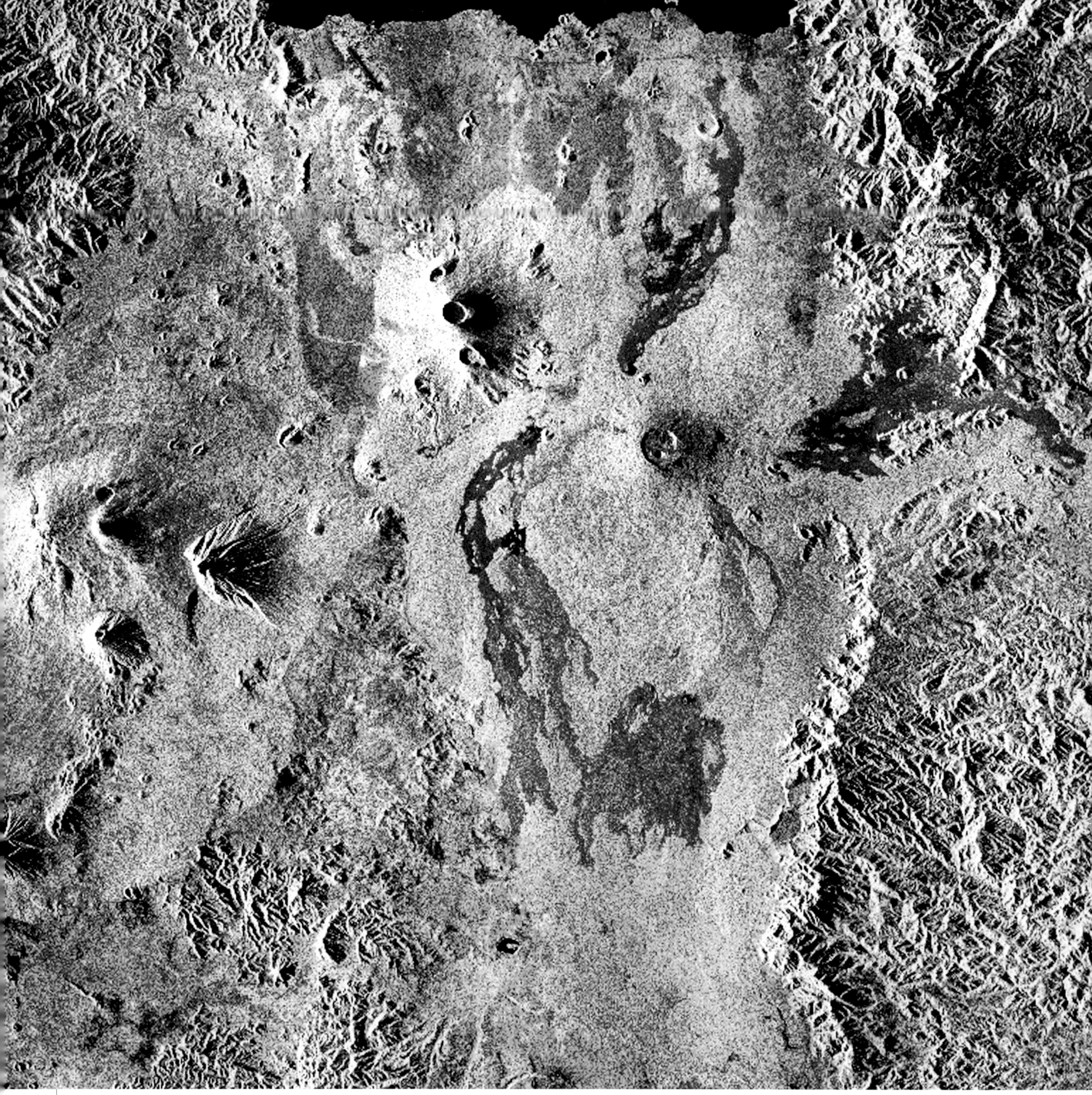

The Virunga Mountains, border of Rwanda, the Democratic Republic of the Congo, and Uganda

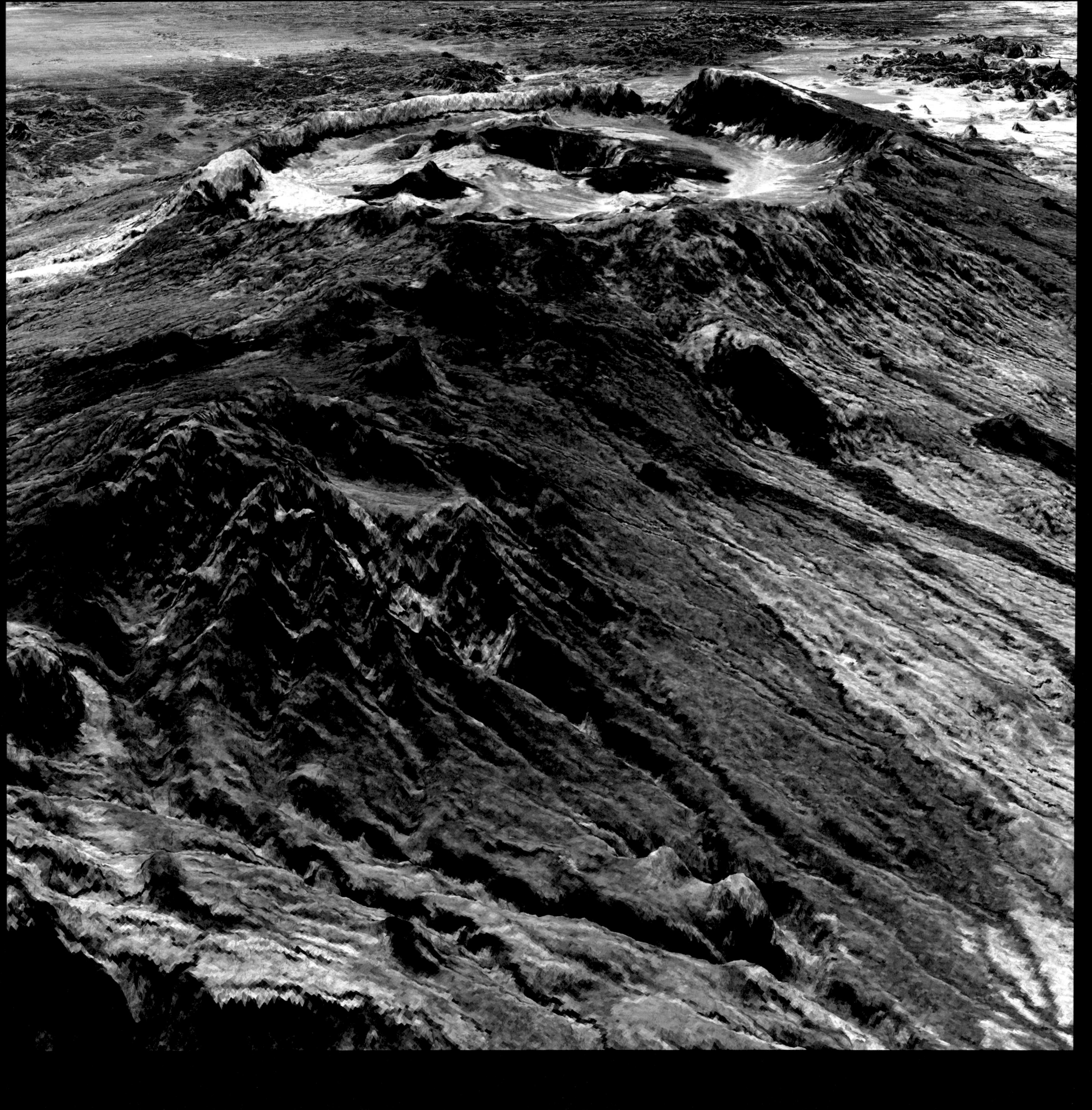

Mount Koussi, Chad

Spirituality
Seats of the Gods, Settings of Myths

RÜDIGER GLASER

In nearly every culture it has been believed that mountains—whether grumbling volcanic cones or menacing ice-clad giants, sharp-edged pyramids or bizarre sandstone monoliths—are the dwelling places of gods. Except for monks in search of enlightenment, no one dreamt of challenging such mountains and attempting to climb them. Only with the advent of alpinism did mountains cease to be unapproachable and become challenges like any other to be conquered—and accordingly robbed of much of their mystique.

Kilimanjaro, Fujiyama, Olympus, Uluru, Kailash. For most of us today, these names read like highlights from the latest promotional travel folder, but the people living near them tend to see them otherwise. These evocative mythological names refer to sacred mountains—dwellings of the gods, symbols of spiritual powers, important pilgrimage sites, home to elves, goblins, or witches, and places where giants and emperors slumber. To many people mountains still have such a spiritual dimension. They keep an appropriate distance from them, and pay homage to their gods.

Spectacular isolated peaks and high mountain chains nearly everywhere on earth have been held to be dangerous and sacred places—Kilimanjaro in East Africa, Kailash in Tibet, Illimani in the Andes, Uluru in Australia (better known to Westerners as Ayers Rock), Devil's Tower in Wyoming, Mount Olympus in Greece, Gunung Agung on Bali, Adam's Peak on Sri Lanka, Mount Sinai in Egypt, Emeishan in Szechuan, and finally the most-climbed and most heavily marketed mountain in the world, Fujiyama in Japan.

For most of our history men stayed away from mountains. It would never have occurred to a member of the Chaga people to climb up to the peak region of Kilimanjaro. No Sherpa or Tibetan would have dared attempt the peaks of the high Himalayas. A number of peaks, Mount Kailash for example, are protected from being climbed as sacred places, and in the Himalayas, the number of religious pilgrims overall exceeds the number of trekkers and mountain climbers. Many an ice-covered mountain figured in the ritual life of the local people, and was revered as a spiritual realm long before climbers discovered the "beauty of the high mountains" or set out to conquer peaks. Even today in many places climbing or otherwise contaminating a mountain is seen as a desecration, and angers the mountain gods who then make the cattle sick, cause drought, or send hail to ravage the fields. In many nature religions it is not only peaks that are sacred; all of nature is animated, every tree, every rock, every body of water, and shamans are able to communicate with their spirits. Every mountain climber who has taken part in a Himalayan expedition can tell of the sacrificial fires and prayer ceremonies of the local guides.

The values of our modern Western leisure-time society are altogether different, with its obsession with conquest and its affinity for adrenaline-charged recreation. Mountain bikes, carving skis, paragliders, high-tech equipment, special clothing, and the appropriate infrastructure have made mountains playgrounds for thrill-seekers. Outdoor experience is hip, and what opinion leaders proclaim as a new cult is swiftly taken up by the masses, or even—here the word "cult" mocks its true meaning—elevated to a kind of religion.

Gradually, however, a reaction to this trend is developing even in the West. There are those who choose not to rob mountain peaks of their dignity, but opt to protect the mountain environment, to enjoy genuine encounters with nature, discovering it to be a source of strength and inner peace, an alternate world for the overstressed. This yearning for transcendental relief, for a retreat from the everyday hustle, amounts to a kind of remystification; the pendulum is swinging back. Today Bhutan is the only country that prohibits all mountain expeditions out of consideration for its populace. In India local protests have led to a ban on climbing sacred Kanchenjunga and seven other peaks.

Sacred peaks of the Western world include Mount Olympus, with its Greco-Roman pantheon, or the Kyffhäuser in Thuringia, where according to legend Emperor Barbarossa lies sleeping. The list of the world's most revered mountains is incomplete without Mount Kailash in Tibet. This 22,028-foot peak is venerated by more than a billion people belonging to four different religions. For more than a thousand years pilgrims have been paying homage to the mountain's mystery by following the thirty-mile path winding around it at elevations of up to 18,000 feet. It is said that a single circuit suffices to erase the sins of a lifetime. Mount Kailash, whose base is rooted in the seventh hell and whose peak reaches up into the highest heaven, stands at the center of Asia's religious cosmography. It is considered the "pillar of the world," and to this day it has never been climbed—all requests for permission to climb to the peak have been strictly declined by the authorities.

A similar aura of myth and legend surrounds Kilimanjaro, which at 19,340 feet towers over the rest of Africa's mountains. Of its three volcanoes, Kibo is the tallest. The main peak Uhuru—or Freedom Peak—is considered a dormant volcano, while the two other cones, Shira and Mawenzi, are ranked as extinct. It was first climbed in 1889 by the Leipzig geography professor Hans Meyer and the Austrian mountain climber Ludwig Purtscheller, which explains why in the German East Africa of the time it came to be known as Kaiser Wilhelm Peak. For nearly two decades it was considered the highest "German" mountain. After Tanzania gained its independence in 1960, it was renamed Uhuru Peak. To the Chaga who live on the east slope of Kilimanjaro, the snow-covered peak symbolizes eternity. They bury their dead with their heads toward the mountain. The Masai named it Nga-ja Nga, which translates as "Castle of Heaven," "Dwelling of God," or "Home of the Engai." The bodiless and sexless Engai manifests itself as either a beneficent black god of rain and fertility or a punitive red god wielding lightning and

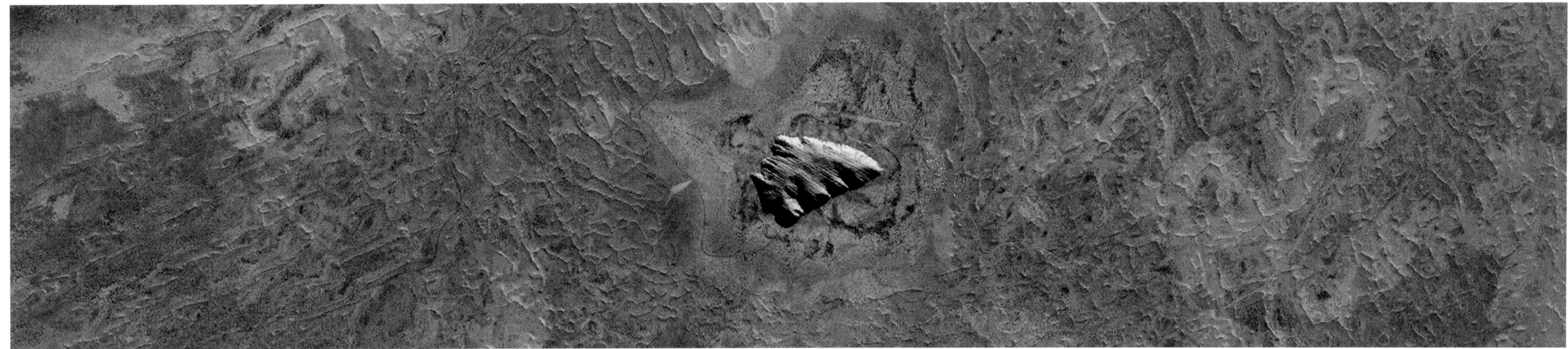

Uluru (Ayers Rock) in Australia on July 12, 1999. To some it is an imposing island mountain; to others, it is the most sacred place on the continent. In any case, it is one of Australia's favorite tourist destinations.

death. But among today's native populace the fervor with which the mountain spirits are venerated is increasingly in decline, as the diversions of modern life continue their triumphal progress even here.

For tourists from Western industrialized countries Uluru, or Ayers Rock, is a magnificent sight: a gigantic block of sandstone in the middle of the Australian desert that presents a grandiose show of color in the sunlight. The huge monolith towers some 1,100 feet above the surrounding desert landscape. It was named in honor of Sir Henry Ayers, Australia's prime minister at the time the European explorer and adventurer William Gosse discovered it in July 1873. To the Aborigines it is the most sacred place in the entire continent. It is where the dream tracks of their legends converge, where the sacred water python landed, and is the place of Kandju, the good lizard, the hare-wallaby people, and the tapestry-serpent people. If to Western explorers this sandstone monolith is an island mountain that owes its surface structure and markings to weathering and erosion, to the Aborigines each fissure, each swelling and indentation has mythological significance. Erosion channels and fluid that seeps from the rock are interpreted as the blood of the evil and despised serpent people conquered in a famous battle in aboriginal dreamtime. Holes in the stone are the eyes of a dead enemy, a protrusion the nose of a sleeping ancestor. The myths of the dream world not only tell how the world was created, where the springs and water holes are that ensure the survival of those to come, they also tell of enemy tribes, battles, annihilations, and deadly clouds. The knowledge of these paths is passed down only in songs and ritual ceremonies. Many visitors claim to have discovered that mythical powers—bringing misfortune—even cling to stones removed as souvenirs. People frequently send their suddenly menacing mementos back to the park rangers.

The Japanese have their sacred mountain too—Fujiyama. It is the country's highest and most famous mountain, and its exquisite profile is nearly synonymous with Japan. A volcano that last erupted in 1708, Fujiyama towers some 12,388 feet above the main island of Honshu. In Japanese Shintoism, Fuji-san as it is called, is venerated as the chief seat of the gods. Ainu, the goddess of fire, dwells on its summit. During the summer months more than 10,000 pilgrims visit its shrines and temples every day. Over the course of a year the mountain has some two million visitors, which has given it the reputation of being the most-climbed mountain in the world. Only in winter months does the bustle subside, for then religious reasons prevent the volcano from being climbed.

Sacred mountains of this sort are unknown in the Alps; in the domain of Christianity, nature itself is considered God's creation. Even so, the Alps once sheltered any number of pre-Christian cult sites—most of which later served as foundations for Christian shrines—and spawned their own ancient traditions, sagas, and myths. King Watzmann, for example, is said to have drunk blood as an infant from his mother's breasts. His whole clan roared across peak and valley and tyrannized the region until a powerful storm washed them down into the valley. All that was left was the Königssee; the evil clan was turned into the striking rock formations that delight visitors today.

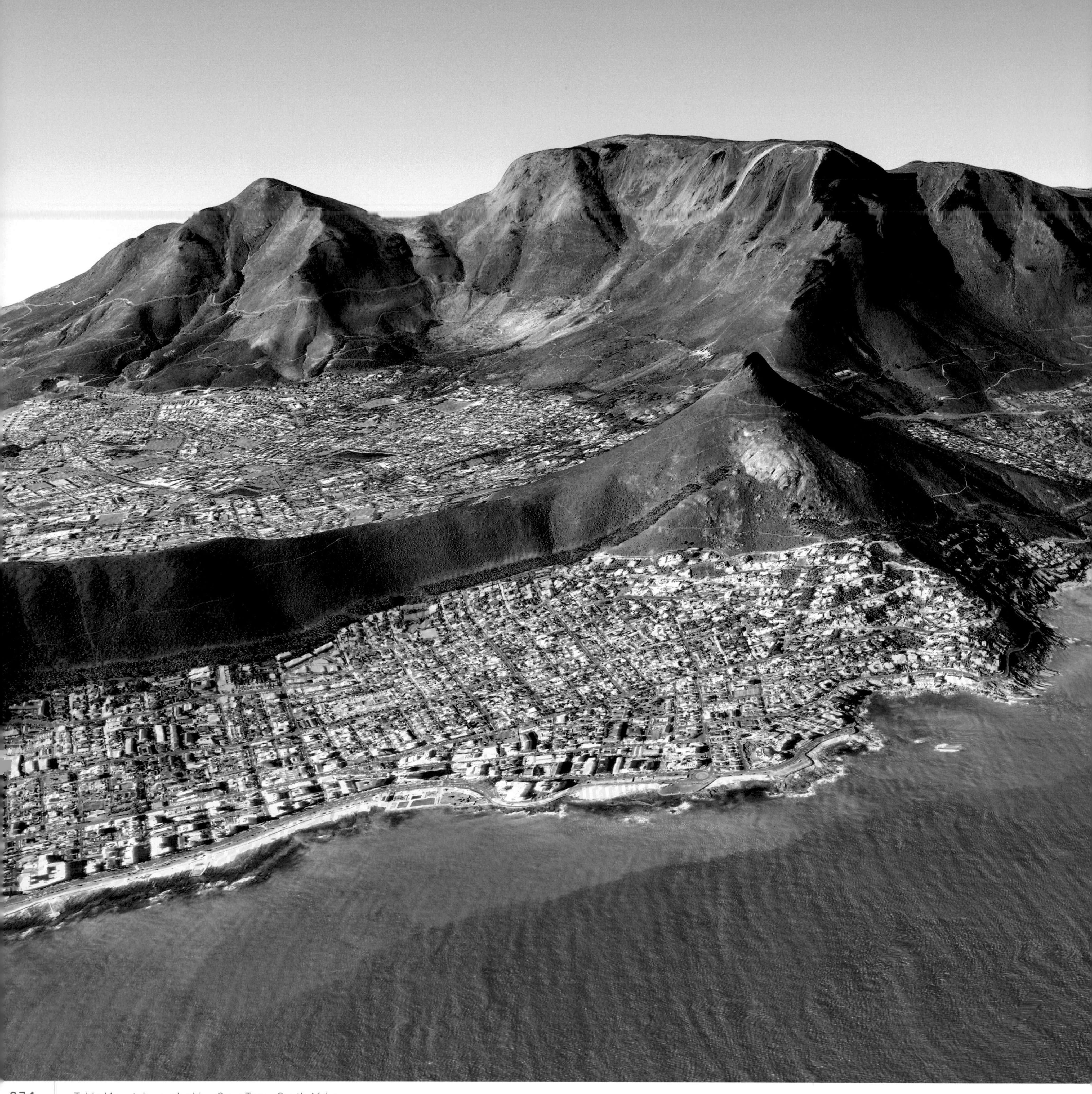

Table Mountain overlooking Cape Town, South Africa

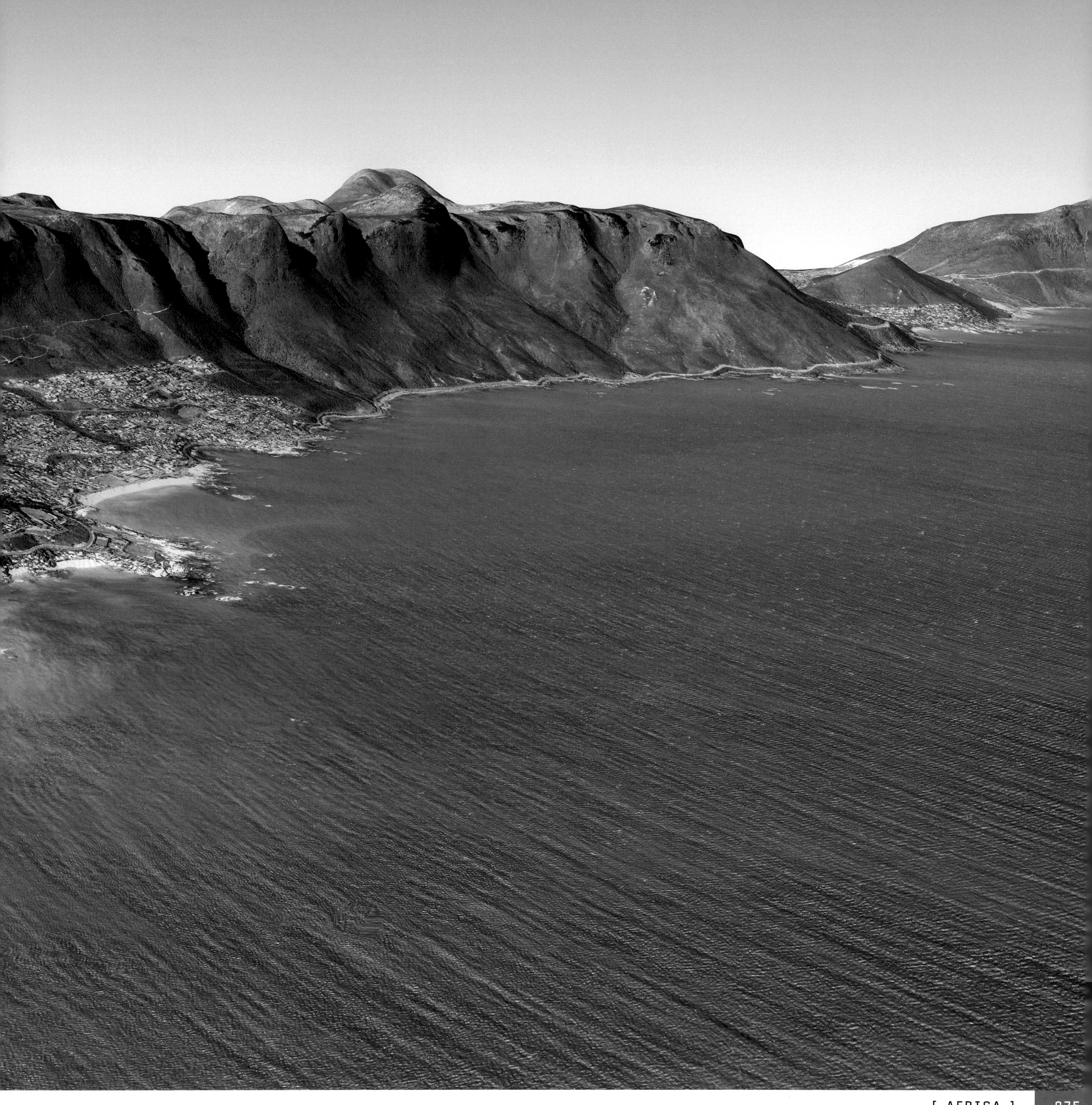

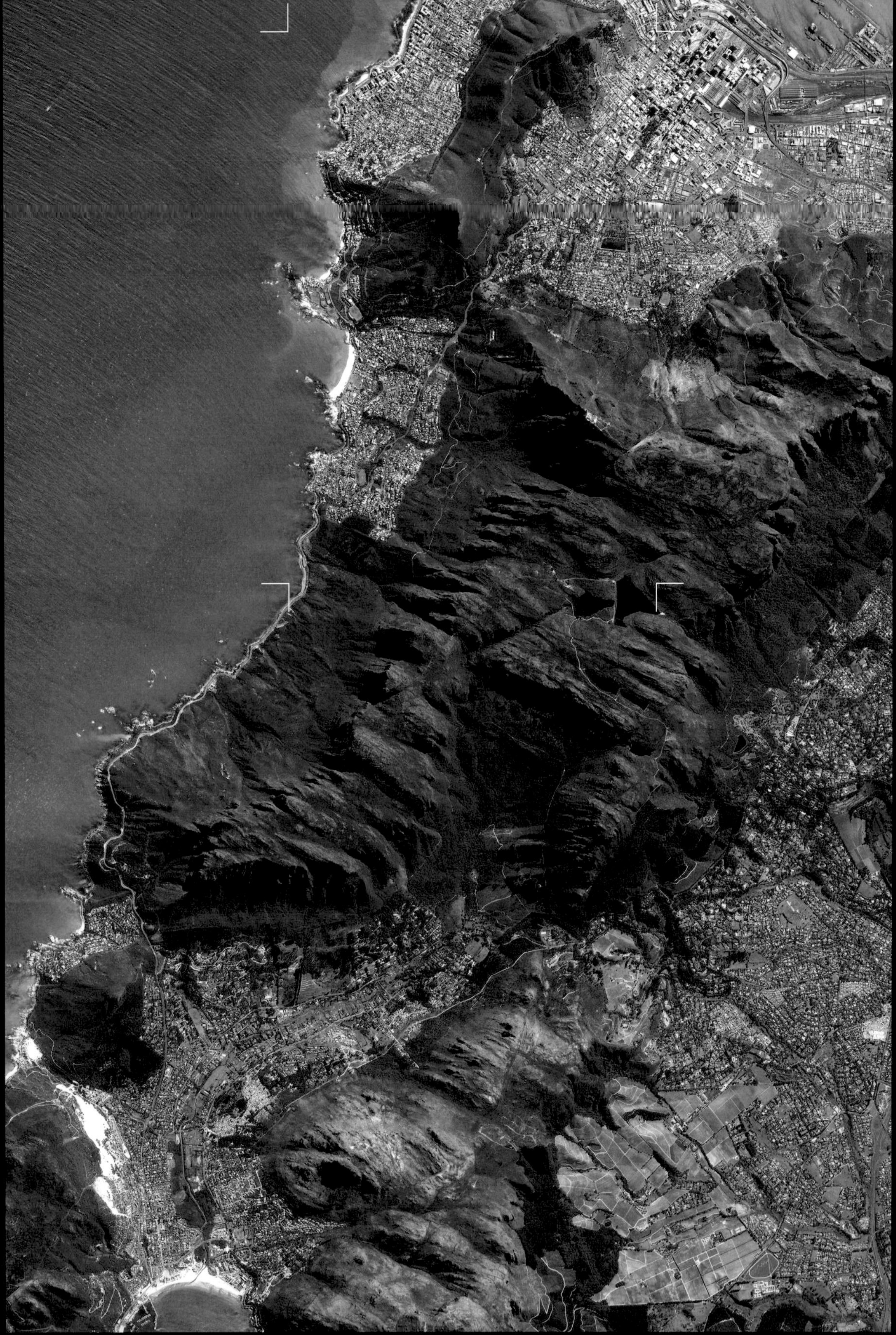

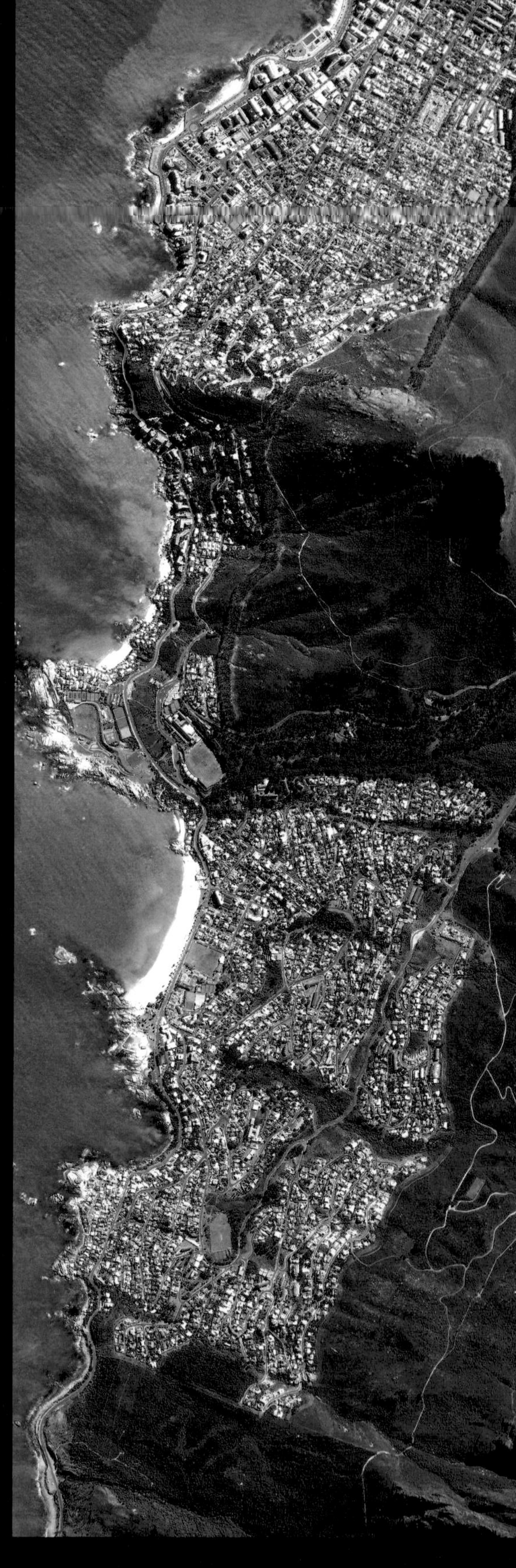

Detailed views of Table Mountain, South Africa

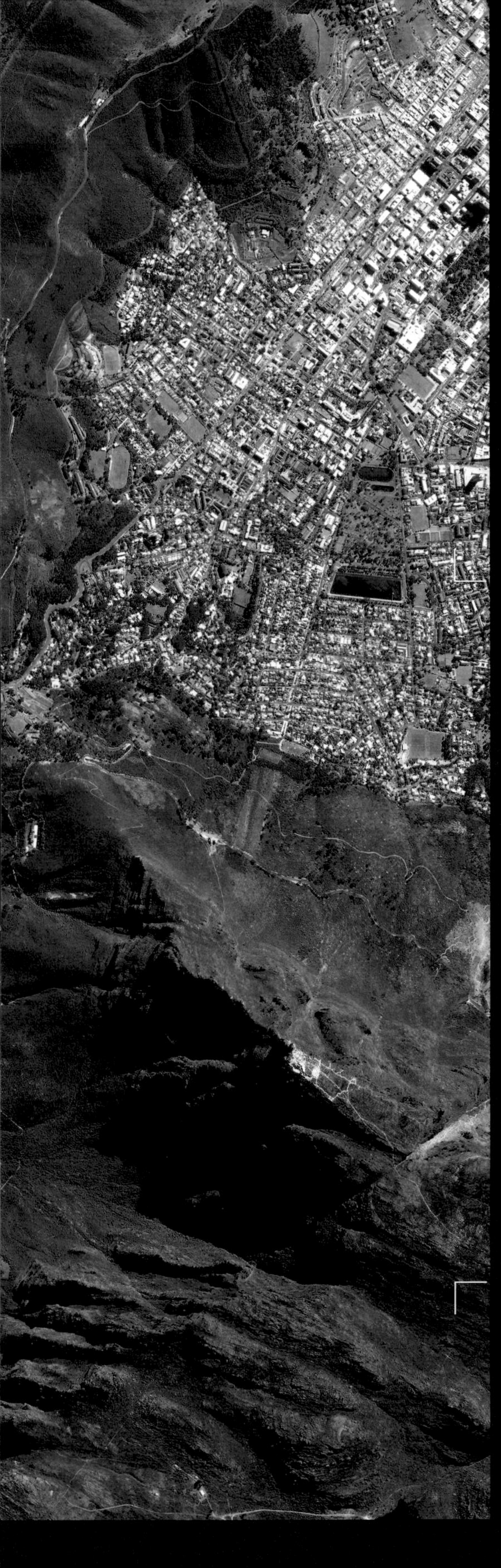

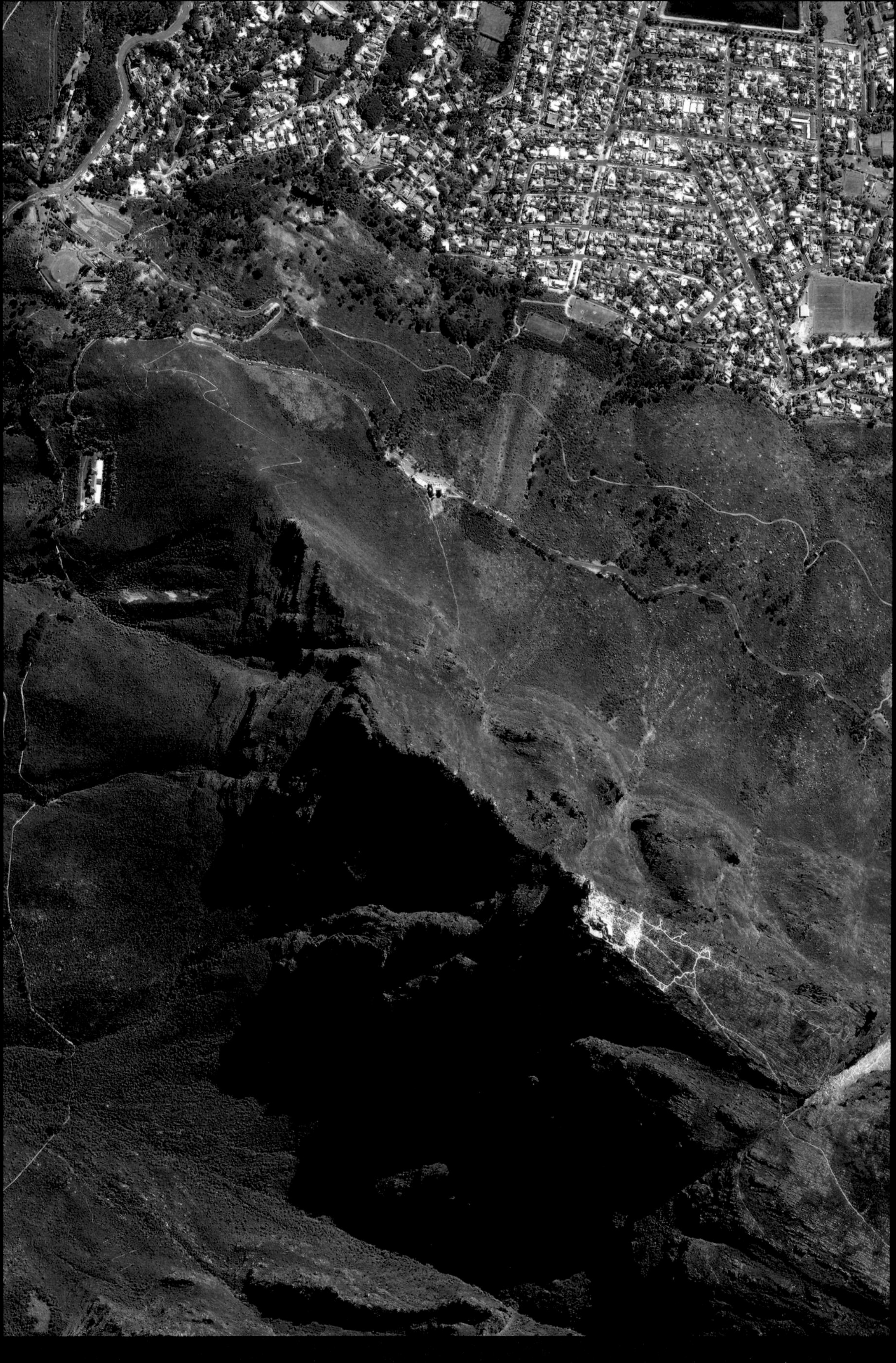

[ASIA]

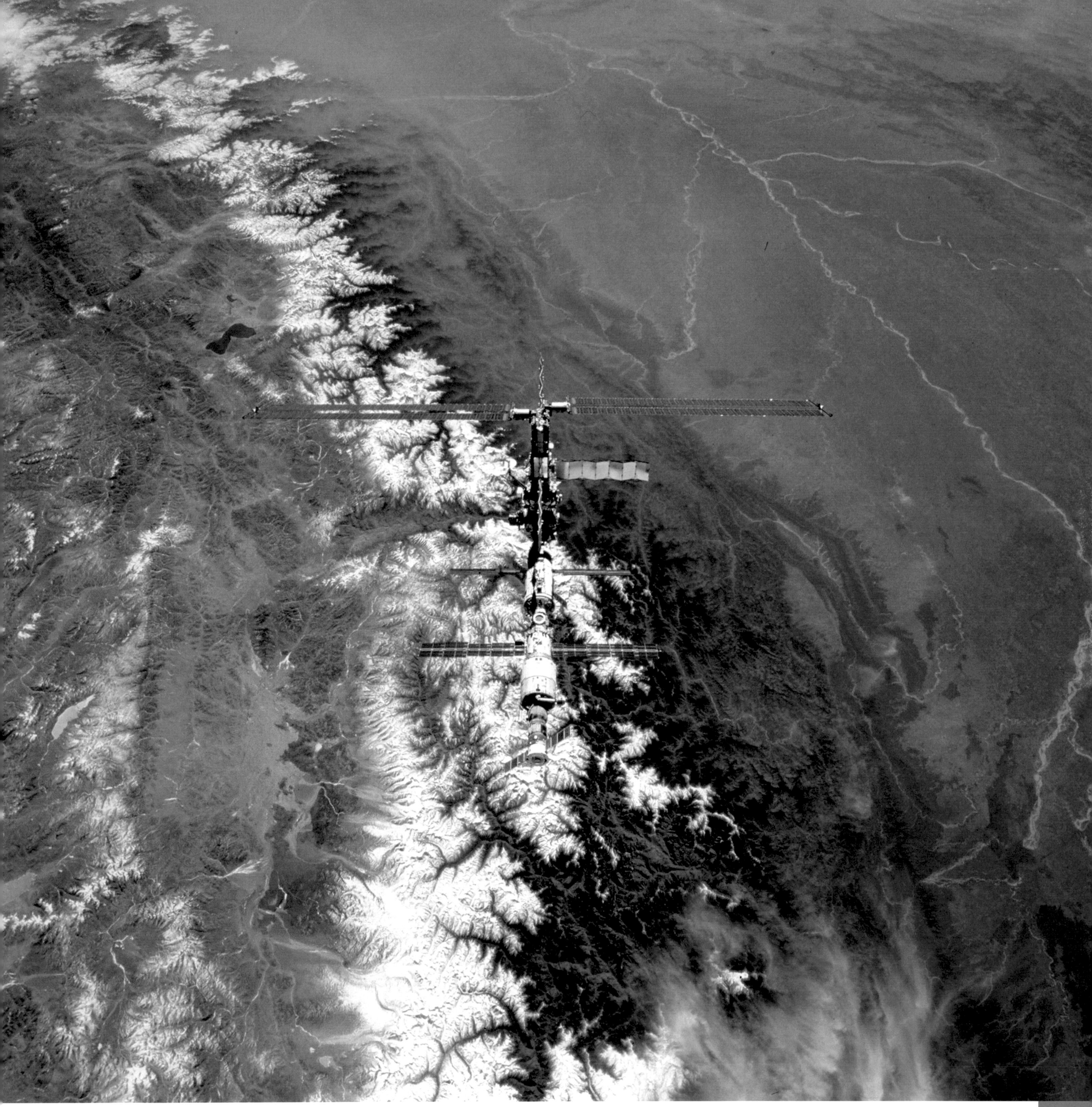

The International Space Station over the Himalayas

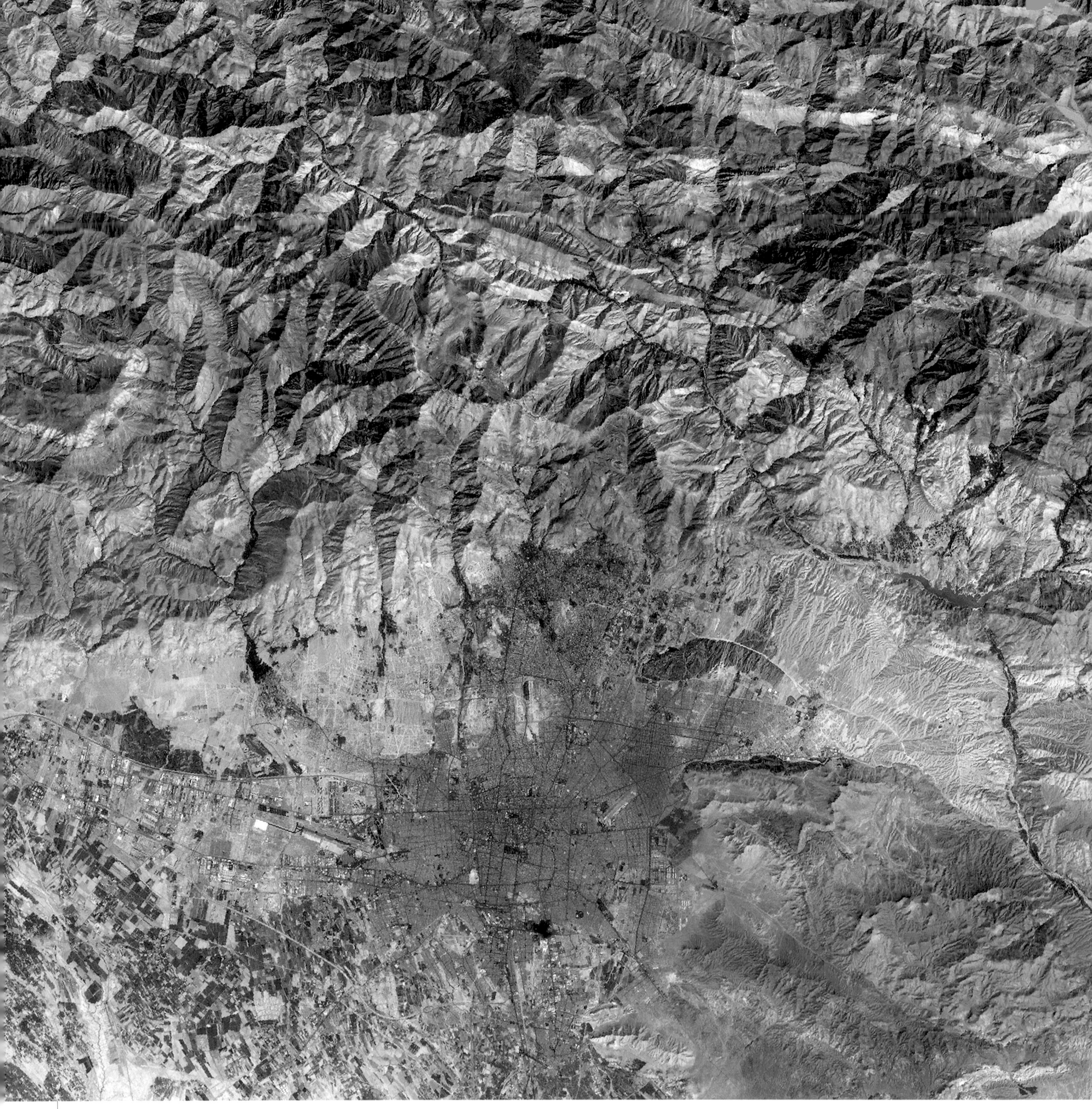

Damavand, the highest mountain in Iran

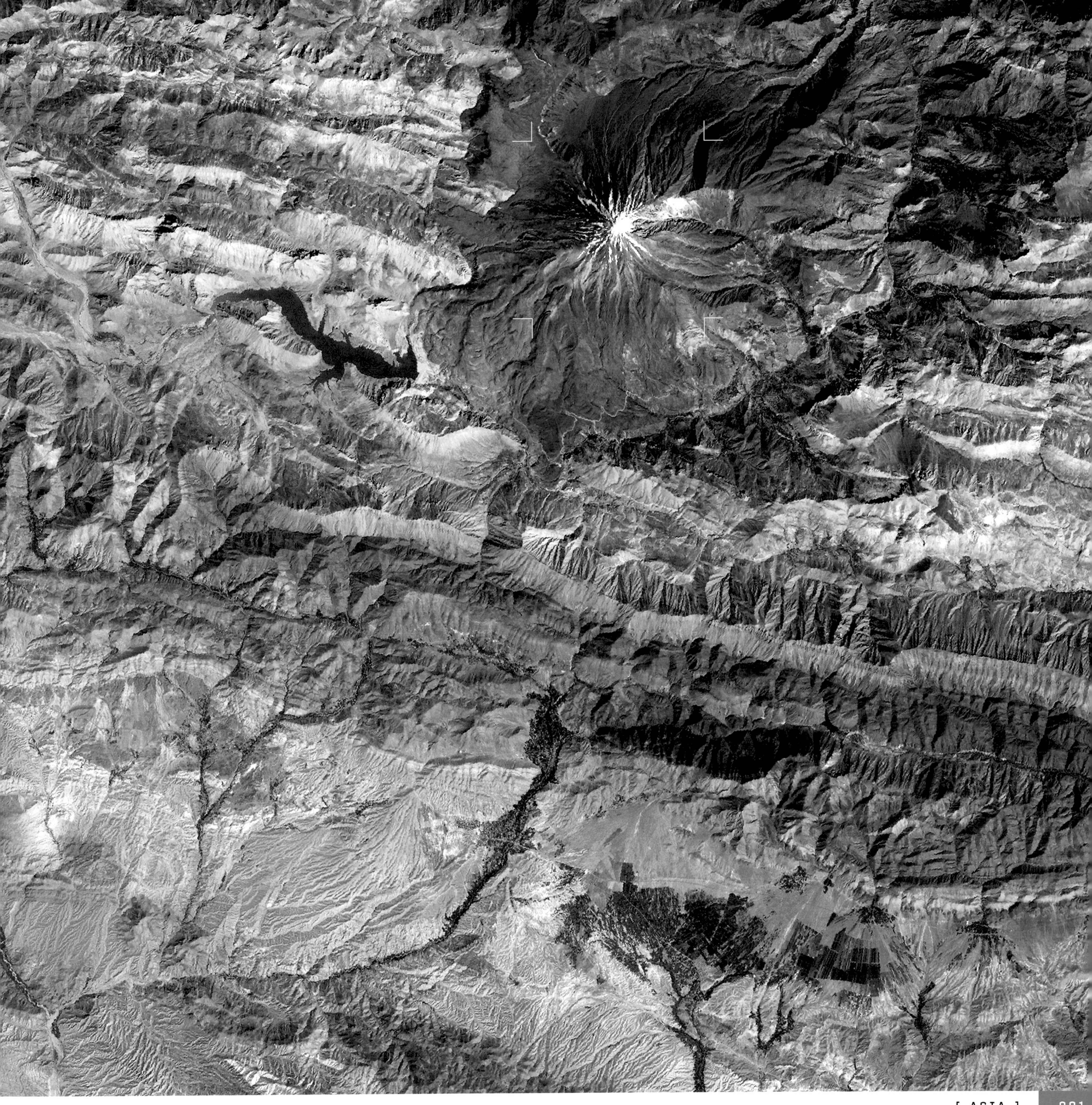

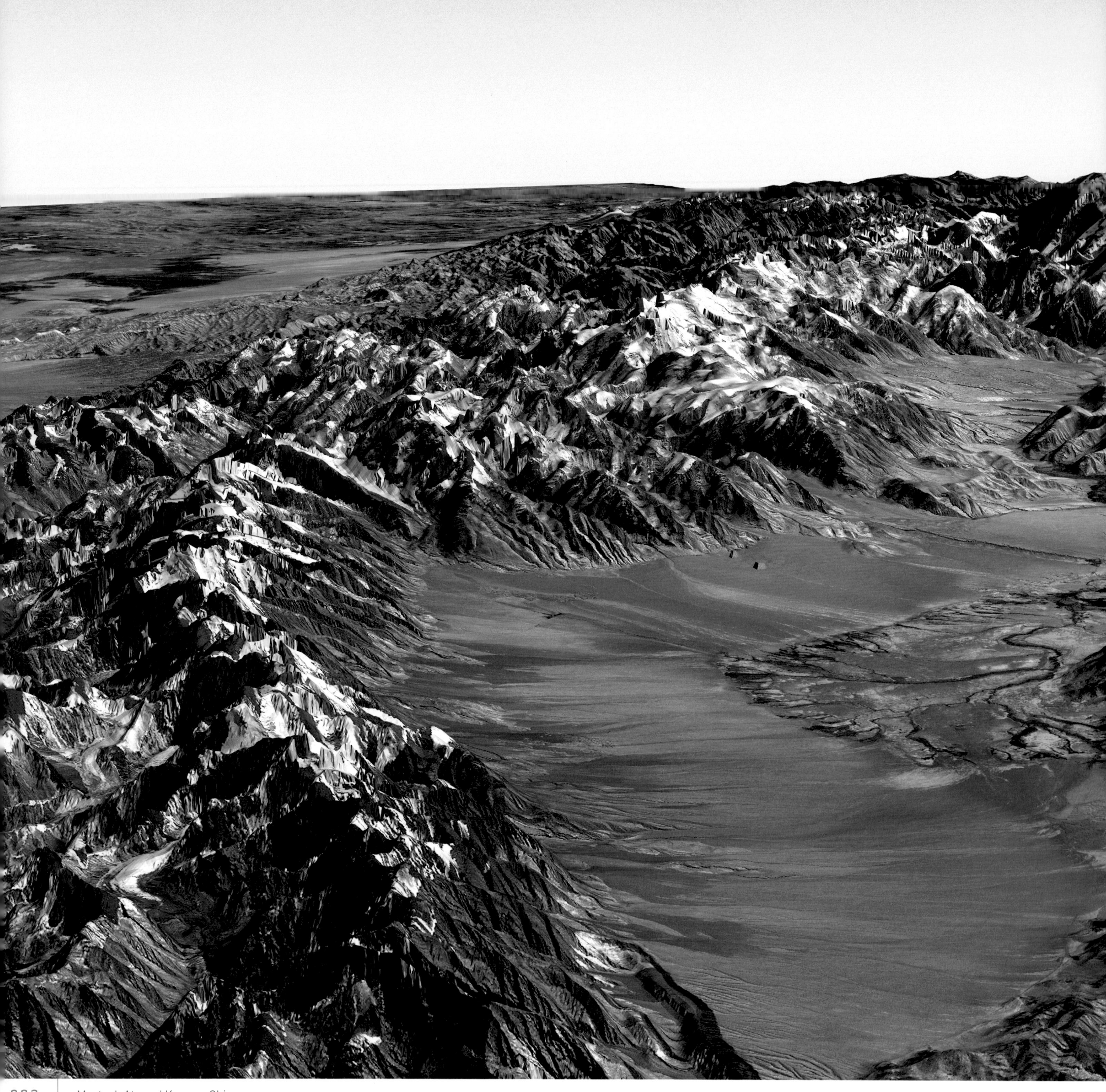

Muztagh Ata and Kongur, China

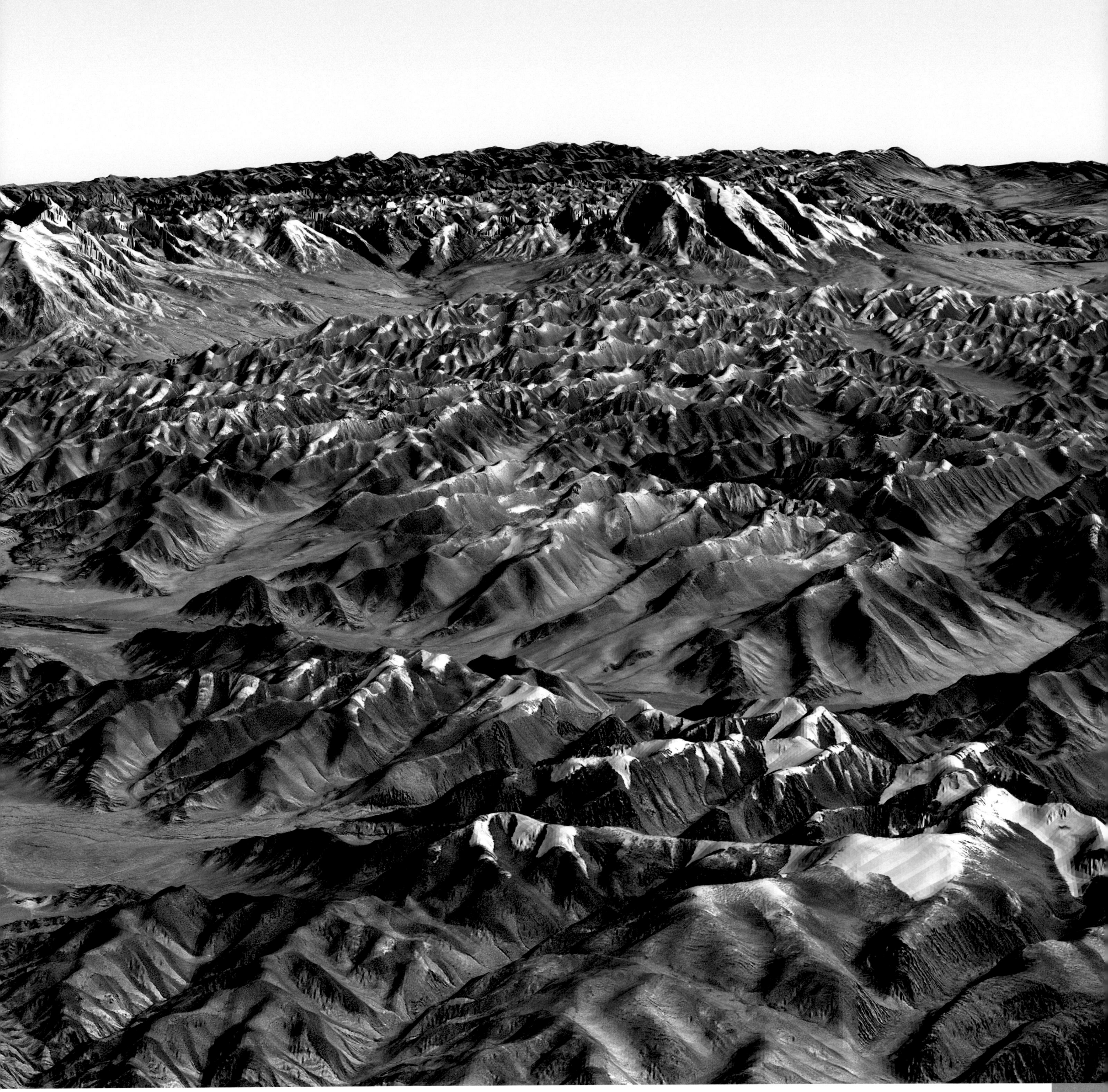

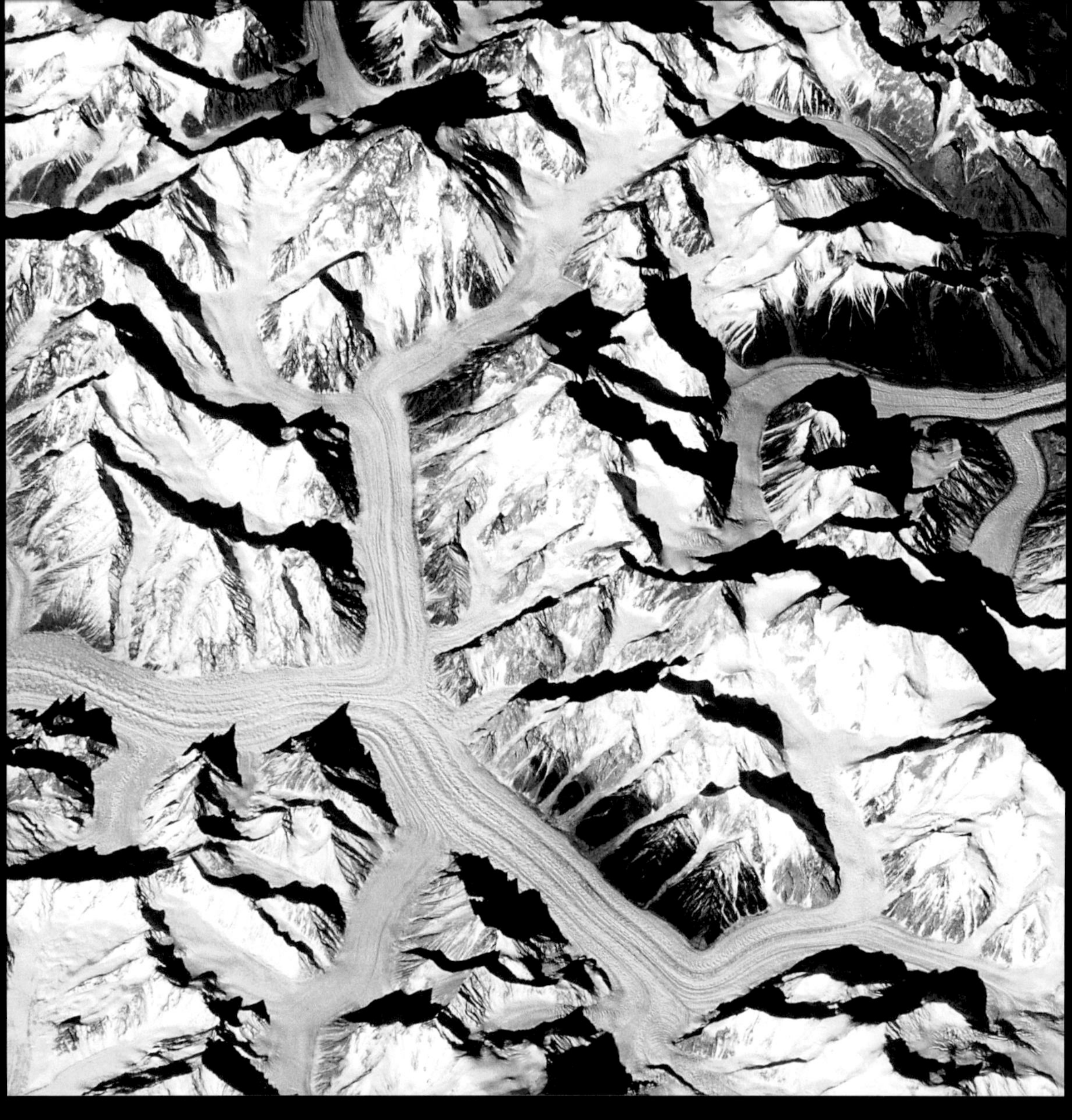

K2, mountain among mountains, Pakistan

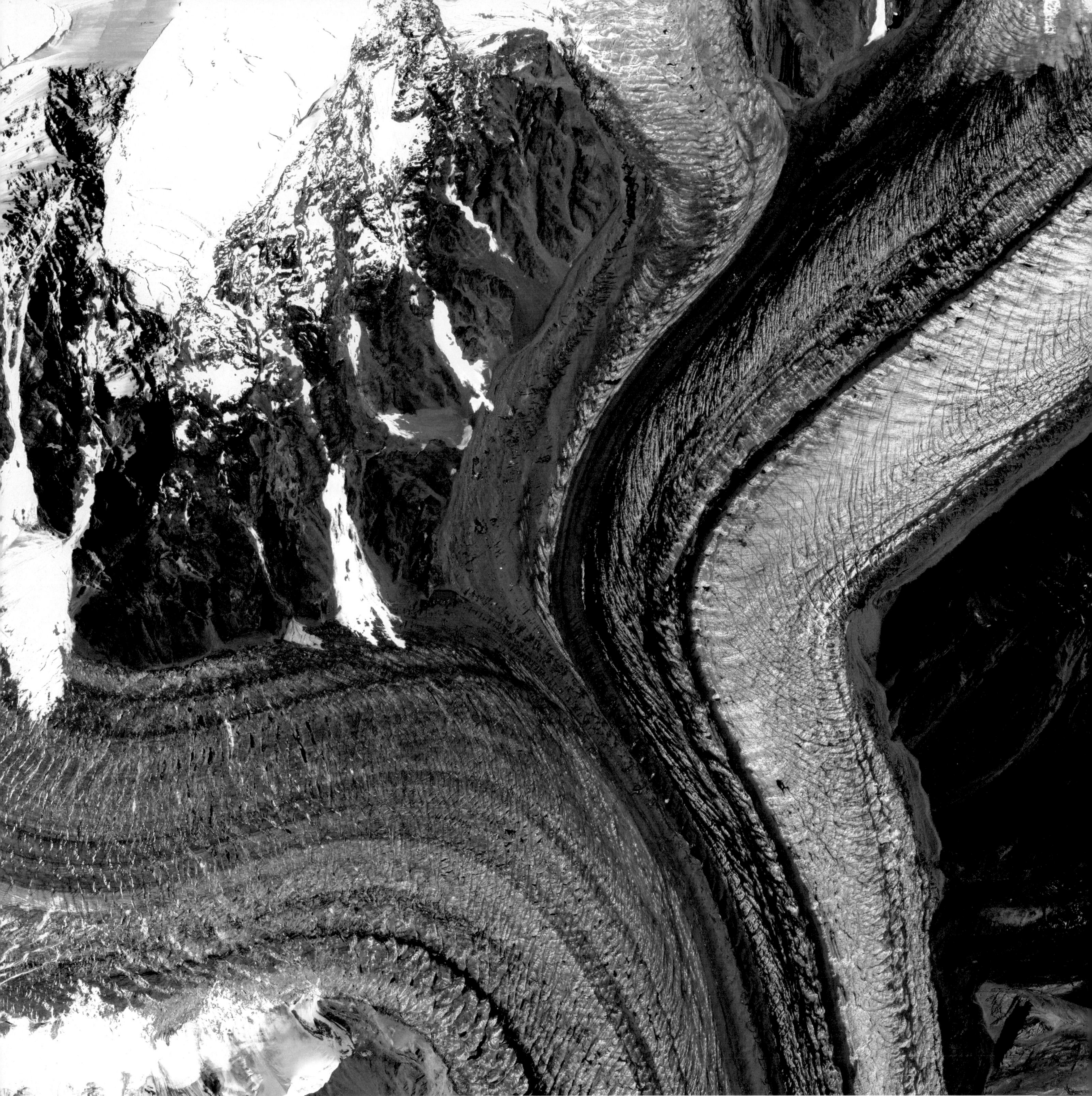

Detailed view of K2 with the base camp in the center, Pakistan

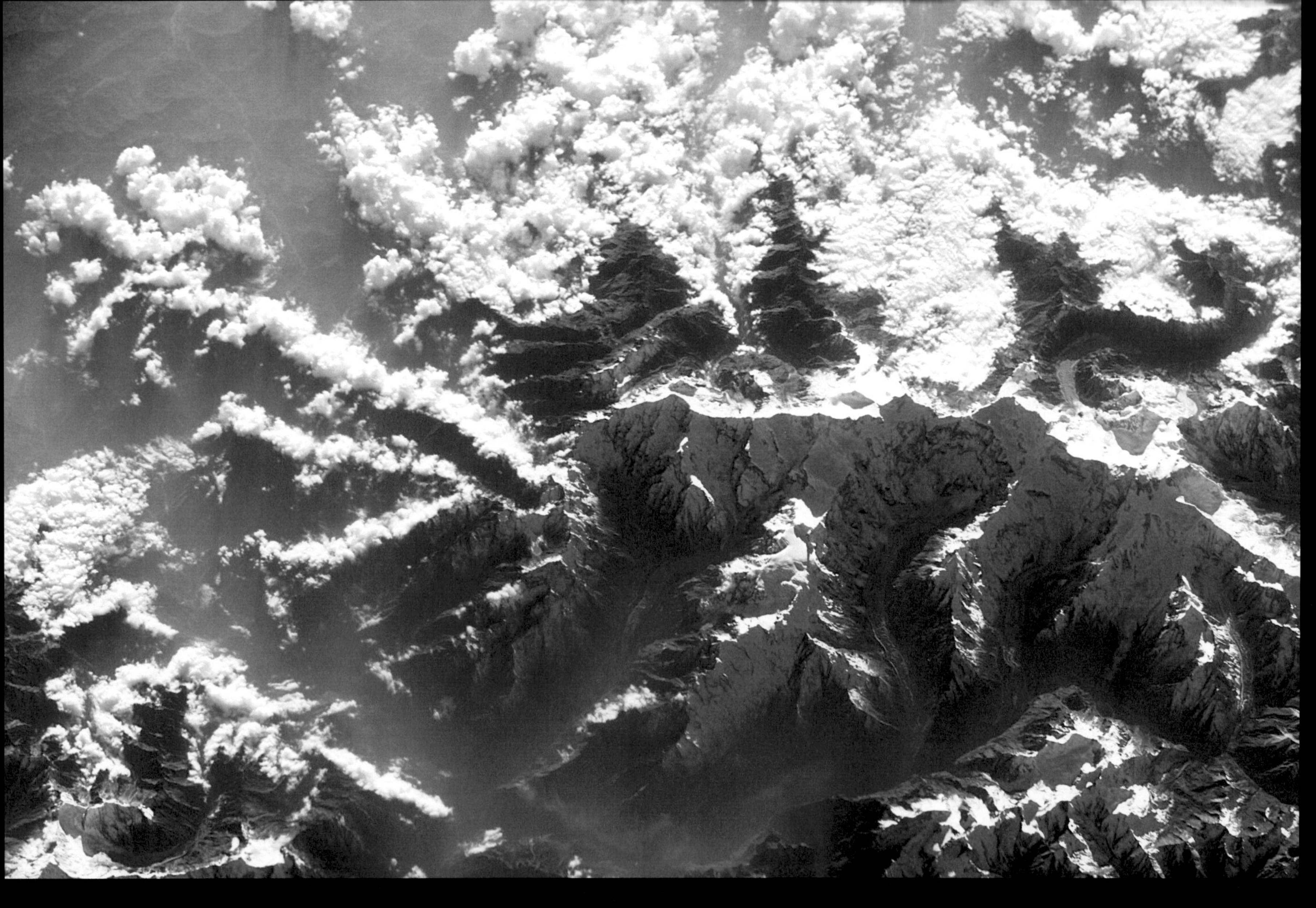

Manaslu, the trekking paradise of Nepal

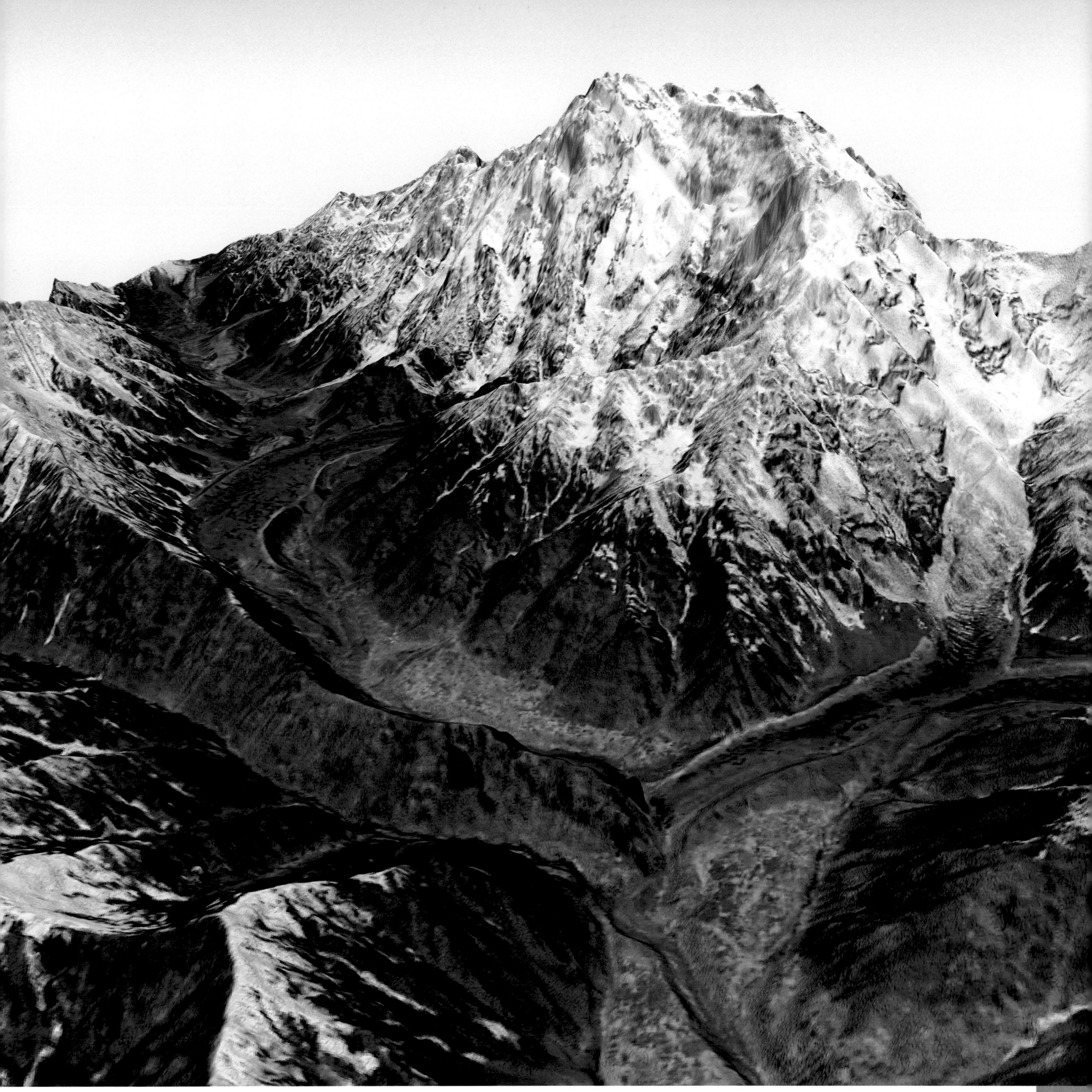

Panorama of Nanga Parbat, Pakistan

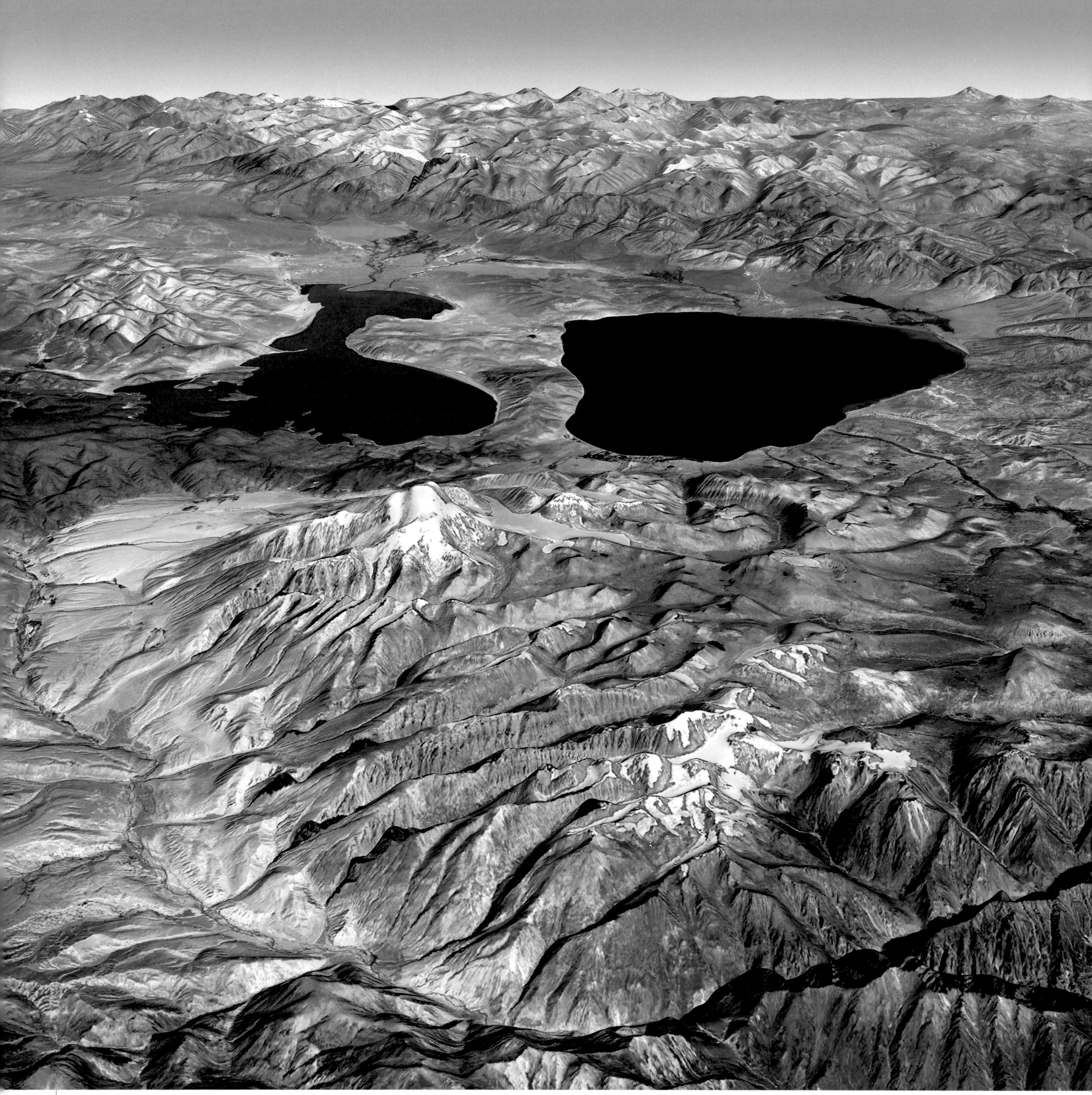

Panorama of Nagari Province, China

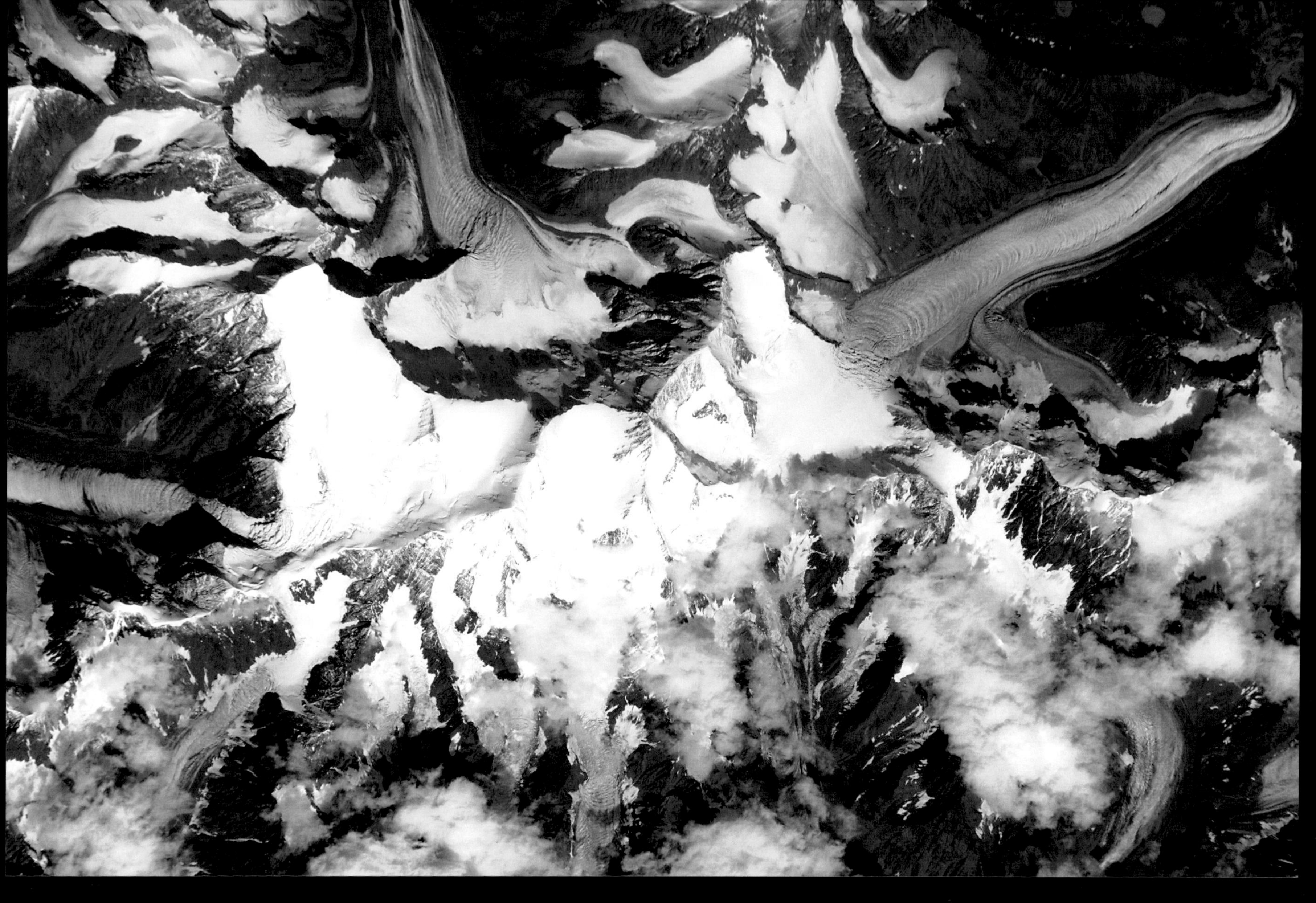

Gora Belukha, Russia

By the Shore of Lake Phoksundo
Portrait of a Happy Man

CHRISTOPH RANSMAYR

On a bitter cold day in February 1993—New Year's Day for the Tibetans—I fell outside of time beside Lake Phoksundo. Days of driving snow had finally ended, the wind had turned, though hardly abated, and now, following the snow-drifted tracks of a friend, I reached the shore of the lake, which lies in the western Himalayas, almost five thousand feet above sea level.

The two of us were trekking across the no man's land between Tibet and Nepal in search of the cloisters and hermitages of the pre-Buddhistic Bon religion and for days now had been taking refuge from the snow in the huts and caves of the tribal kingdom of Dolpo. From the valleys all around us came the steady thunder of avalanches.

We had spent New Year's Eve with seminomads who were wintering in sooty stone huts and waiting for spring to open the passes and allow them to move on with their yaks to the great salt lakes and pastures of Tibet. We didn't want to wait. We had no caravan of heavily laden yaks to lead through the mountains, were not encumbered with household goods and black woolen tents, but had only our backpacks. A day's march, somewhere in the snow clouds ahead of us, was, we were told, Phoksundo Lake and on its shore a village, including a cloister. Inhabited? Or deserted?—as were most such high-lying settlements at this time of year. Our hosts did not know either. When in mid-morning a sunlit glacier emerged like an iceberg floating high above the scudding clouds, we left the camp and set out.

When we pick up and leave, whether on our way to a goal or into uncertainty, we do not simply leave behind people and places, do not merely abandon a refuge, a road, a jetty, a house, landscapes blanketed with snow or shimmering in the heat—no, at the same time we are also following an equally adventuresome route through the more secret world of our own thoughts, where we once again encounter what we have just left behind: memories of people and the places where they live or a longing for what was and what is yet to come. Every road deserving of the name leads both into the distance and into the depths, to the edge of the world and into its heart.

That ridge bristling with pennants of ice that suddenly rises up before us—the minarets of a desert city or the tailings and chimneys of a coalmining district, the ocean!, a beach planted with sunshades, its coastline fortified by cliffs—in our travels do we not at times find even a new somewhere, a place we have never trod before, oddly familiar? We approach the strangeness and begin to recognize things, even faces—the frozen look of palace guards, a stump-limbed beggar outside a silversmith's shop, the muted tumult of a city heard through ragged curtains or the colorful pattern of a nomad's saddlecloth as he crosses our path on a road congested with military traffic, a lakeshore, trees at water's edge, wild roses . . . so many things seem familiar as we pass by. Did we read about this or did someone tell us about it—in a novel? a poem? or was it on the news? And wasn't it in a place exactly like this that we experienced this same light, this same gusty wind, that moment of good luck or bad?

The place that we finally reach, whether exhausted from climbing a steep path or simply stiff and sleepy after a long flight, is so . . . yes, so deserted, as devoid of other people as that book that lives only in fragments in our memory, one single line that keeps running through our mind, while we keep on walking, setting one foot in front of the other and gradually realizing that our path leads not just into the strange somewhere, but into the interior of the world, of a language that knows both what is real and what is possible. Reading, walking, traveling, writing always raises dust, even the proverbial snow of yesteryear, which descends gently again a few heartbeats later, reshaping what is, revealing it more clearly than ever before, or mercifully obscuring it—it all depends on us.

The snow on the path to Lake Phoksundo was so deep that we sank in up to our knees, sometimes to our hips. As long as no obstruction demands joint efforts or no icy rockbound traverses require the security of a shared rope, each person can walk, plod, climb such paths at the rate his energies allow, and so each is often alone. After about an hour, my friend was no longer in view, though occasionally he would reappear as a dwindling figure high up the steep slopes, then vanish in the clouds. When I stopped to catch my breath, I could see our serpentine tracks as they lost themselves in depths or clouds. Now only isolated snow flurries broke away from the bright, increasingly blue sky. The tatters of a dispersing storm front hastened away above my head and at my feet.

It was during one such pause for breath that through a cloud window I spotted the man following us. He was paying no attention to our tracks, but taking the line of greatest slope. I recognized him by his pelt coat and the red scarf he wore like a turban wrapped around his long hair. It was our host from the night before. He waved at me, called out a greeting, came closer, but then stopped at some distance, and only set off again when I walked on. Was he on his way to the top? To the lake? Without a pack? Without a beast of burden? He was following us, but evidently preferred to be alone. To show us the way? To warn us? When I stopped to wait for him, he stopped too and waved at me. Whatever his intentions, I didn't understand them.

Our bartering earlier that morning had been a protracted affair as well. There beside his fire, we had traded a pocket knife and a pair of gloves for yak butter, jerky, parched grain, and tea, and had accepted a little opaque glass bottle of murky rice schnapps as a gift—a drink that, despite his urgent insistence that we enjoy it before departure, we intended to warm ourselves with at our goal. I was carrying the bottle, wrapped in a shirt, in my backpack. My friend's tracks led ever higher and steeper along a face of rock veiled by a

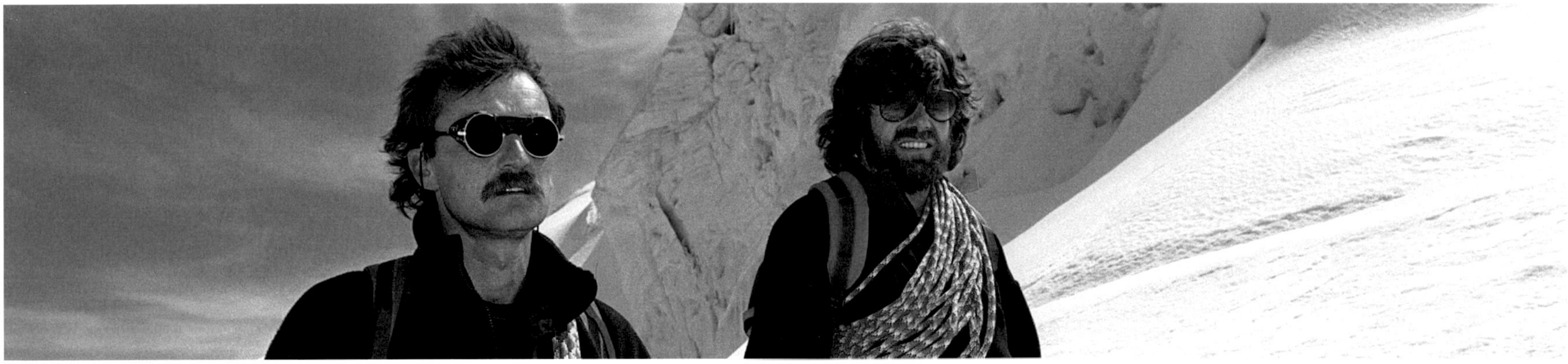

glassy, frozen waterfall and finally to the entrance of a shallow mountain valley filled with Himalayan pines and set between mountain ridges that towered above it like the walls of manmade dams. I stopped to rest under one of the trees with its heavy burden of snow. Only now did my previously unapproachable companion sit down beside me in the snow; he accepted a handful of dried fruit and a piece of jerky, and laughed. Once again he demanded I drink—by sketching the shape of the opaque glass bottle in the air—but then drank only yak-butter tea from my steel flask, and not a drop of rice schnapps. When I moved on, he followed, but soon reestablished his former distance. And so each of us remained all to himself. Finally, after so many hours, how silent and promising Lake Phoksundo appeared at the still distant end of the valley. A blackish green mirror reflected images of clouds and snowcapped mountains back into what was by now an evening sky and was bordered along its rim by just one group of blood-red buildings, the roofs of pagodas adorned with prayer banners, above which drifted a far more delicate, more beautiful banner: smoke! The village and cloister of Phoksundo were occupied!

To be sure its shoreline lay under snow, and layers of ice filled its bays, but anyone who has trudged a long time through high mountains in winter sees more than he sees. He transforms spare, frozen bushes into roses and looks forward to a refuge, even if it is black with soot, looks forward to the company of others, to a fire, to protection from the night. My binoculars told me there were banners of smoke atop every building along the lake.

It would take another hour before I finally reached the hill beside the shore. But the first buildings I came to were houses of the dead—reliquary shrines, chorts, which contained nothing but the ashes of cremated saints and monks, the dust of transmigrated souls. Long garlands of pennants were stretched like tent ropes from the cone-shaped roofs to the ice below—hundreds of pennants inscribed with prayers and the names and ends of all worlds, each frozen stiff and snapping in the wind.

And the banners of smoke above the flat roofs of the village? It was snow—veils of trickling, delicate, crystalline snowflakes, drifting like smoke from the roofs. The houses were cold and locked. No people. No refuge. The village was deserted.

What lake had I arrived at? I glided gently out of time and into the middle of the world from which so many tracks and paths lead to the lakes of cartographers and poets, lead as deep into the past as into the future, so that my companion first had to catch up with me and tug my sleeve—it was Lake Phoksundo. He smiled and pointed to a chort on a barren hilltop ahead of us. There I spotted my friend busy measuring and sketching the house of the dead. He was relieved to see me at last. Another hour and he would have started his search. The night would turn clearer and colder than those that had gone before.

The three of us sat around a fire in a chamber full of echoes, where a prayer mill intended to be turned for all eternity by pilgrims and monks now stood still. A well-worn dictionary and the few scraps of Tibetan that my friend could muster helped us gradually to understand why our host had followed us through deep snow up into the mountains—the glass bottle! He wanted his bottle back. It was the only glass container that he owned. We were supposed to drink the rice schnapps, that was his gift, he didn't want a single sip, but he had to take that little opaque bottle home with him. He had followed us all the way to Lake Phoksundo for an empty bottle.

When at last we understood what the man wanted from us, we emptied the bottle in a few swigs and placed it in his hands. But we wanted to give him a gift, something more than an empty opaque glass vessel—and rummaging our backpacks, we came across an umbrella, one of those Chinese nylon umbrellas that fit into a backpack and that you use to keep relatively dry on treks through the lofty Himalayas during the rain and snow of the monsoon season, instead of having to wrap yourself in a coat that leaves you drenched in sweat. We gave the umbrella to our companion as a gift.

I have seldom seen an expression of such surprise, disbelief, and finally happiness on the face of another human being. Beaming now, he accepted the umbrella and bowed. Although only the sun's red afterglow could be seen along the mountain ridges now, there was no holding him back. He wanted to return to the depths below, to his home, and leaving the echoing chamber behind, ran outside and opened the umbrella, holding it at arm's length triumphantly above his head. The empty bottle in one hand, the umbrella in the other, he bounded away, no, danced away, tracing his own footprints out of abandonment and back to his family. And as if in that moment this umbrella—this filigree refuge, the smallest roof a man on a journey can have over his head—had induced the heavens to reveal their meaning and purpose, there in the clear, now starlit sky to the south, it began to snow again.

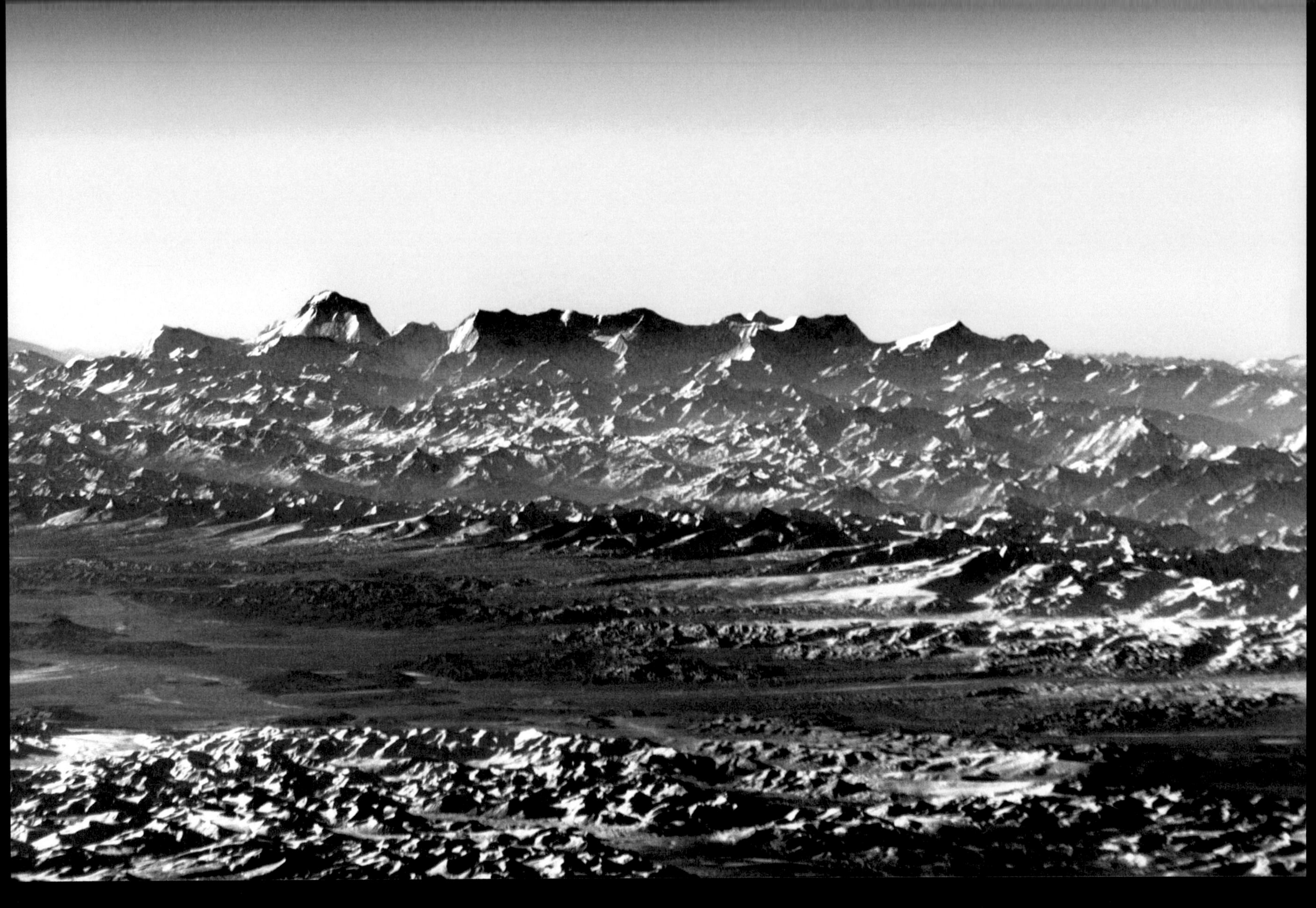

Panorama of the kingdom of Nepal

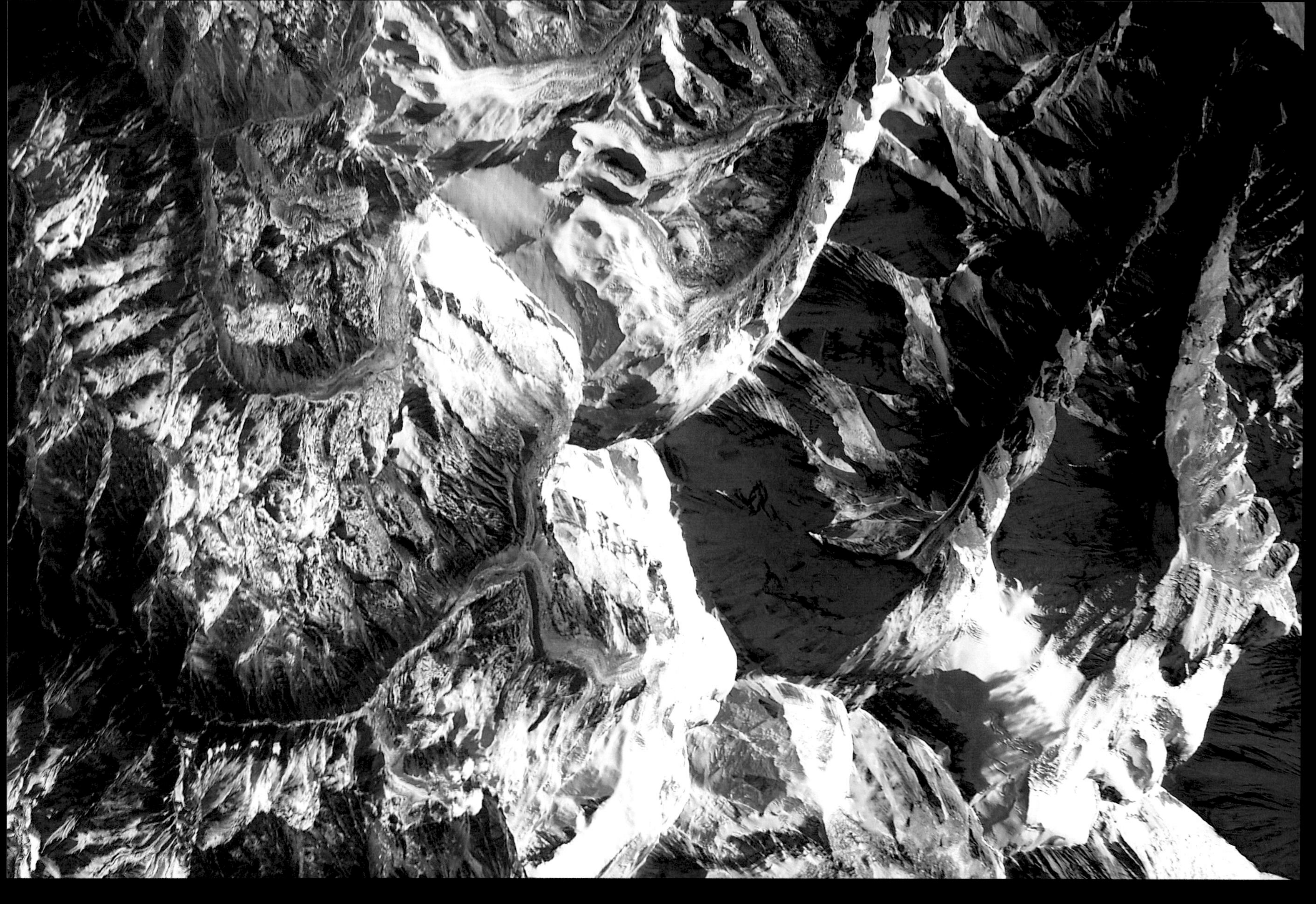

Dhaulagiri, the "White Mountain," Nepal

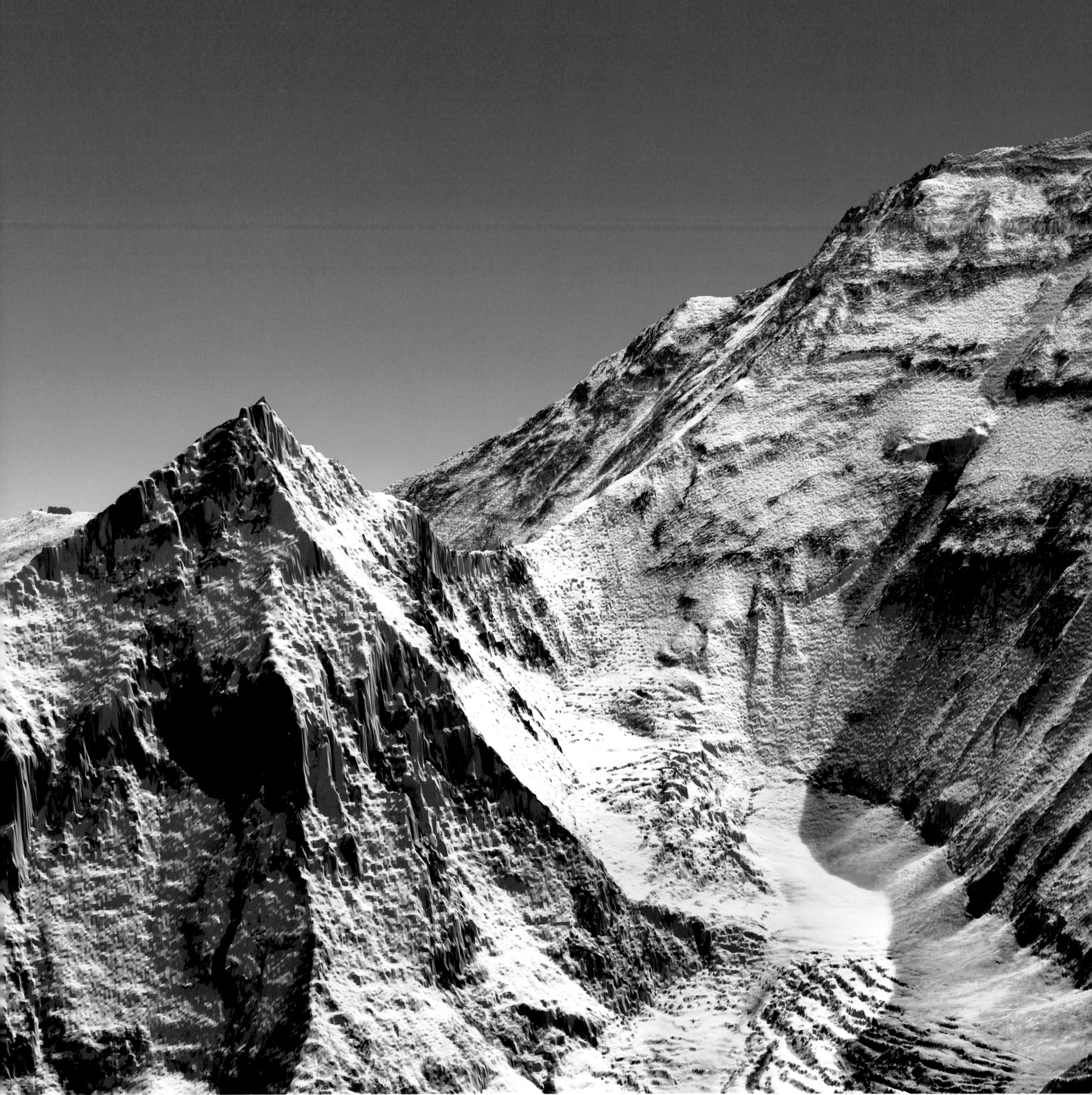

Mount Everest, rooftop of the world, Nepal/China

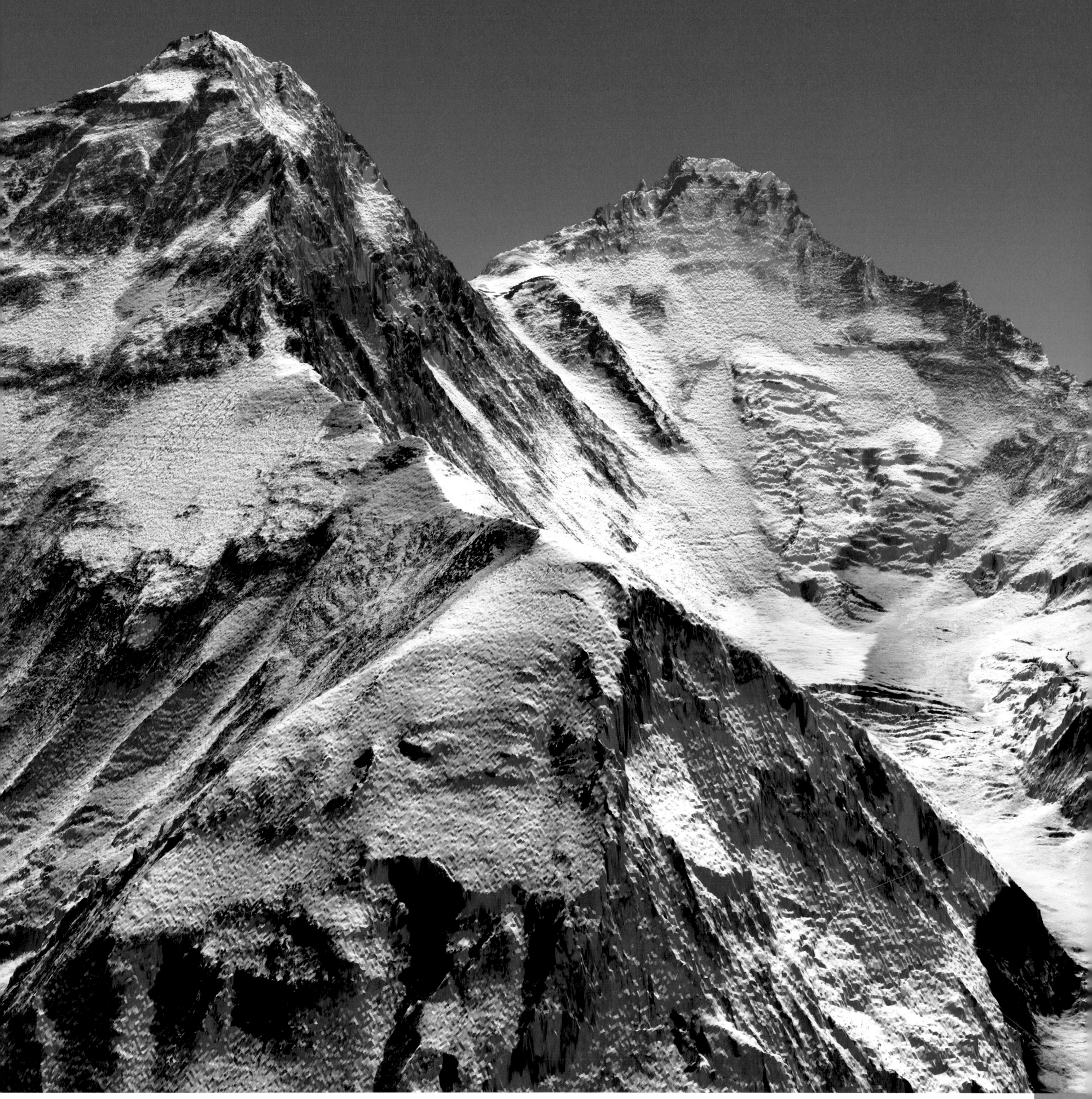

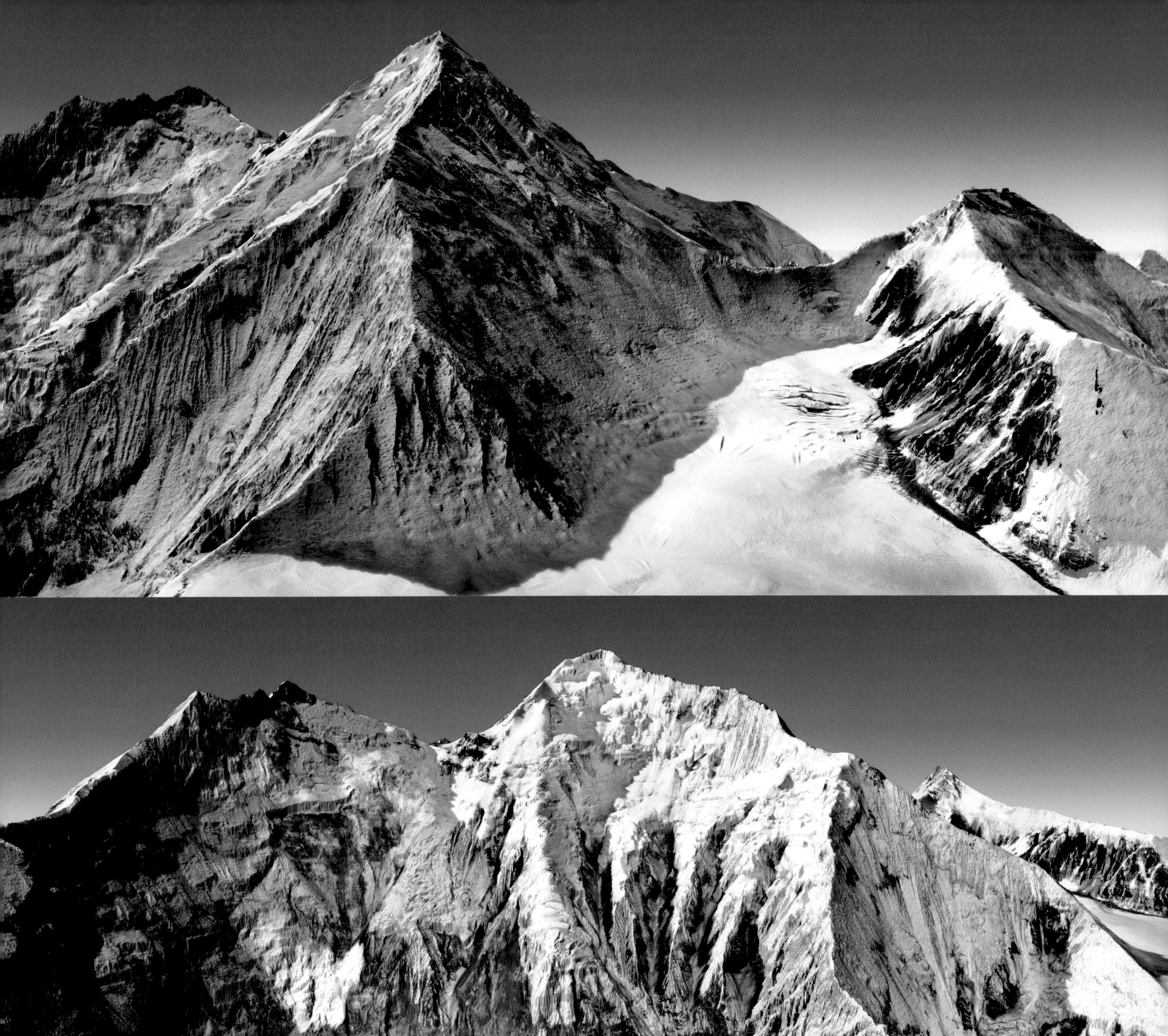

Mount Everest, view from the east

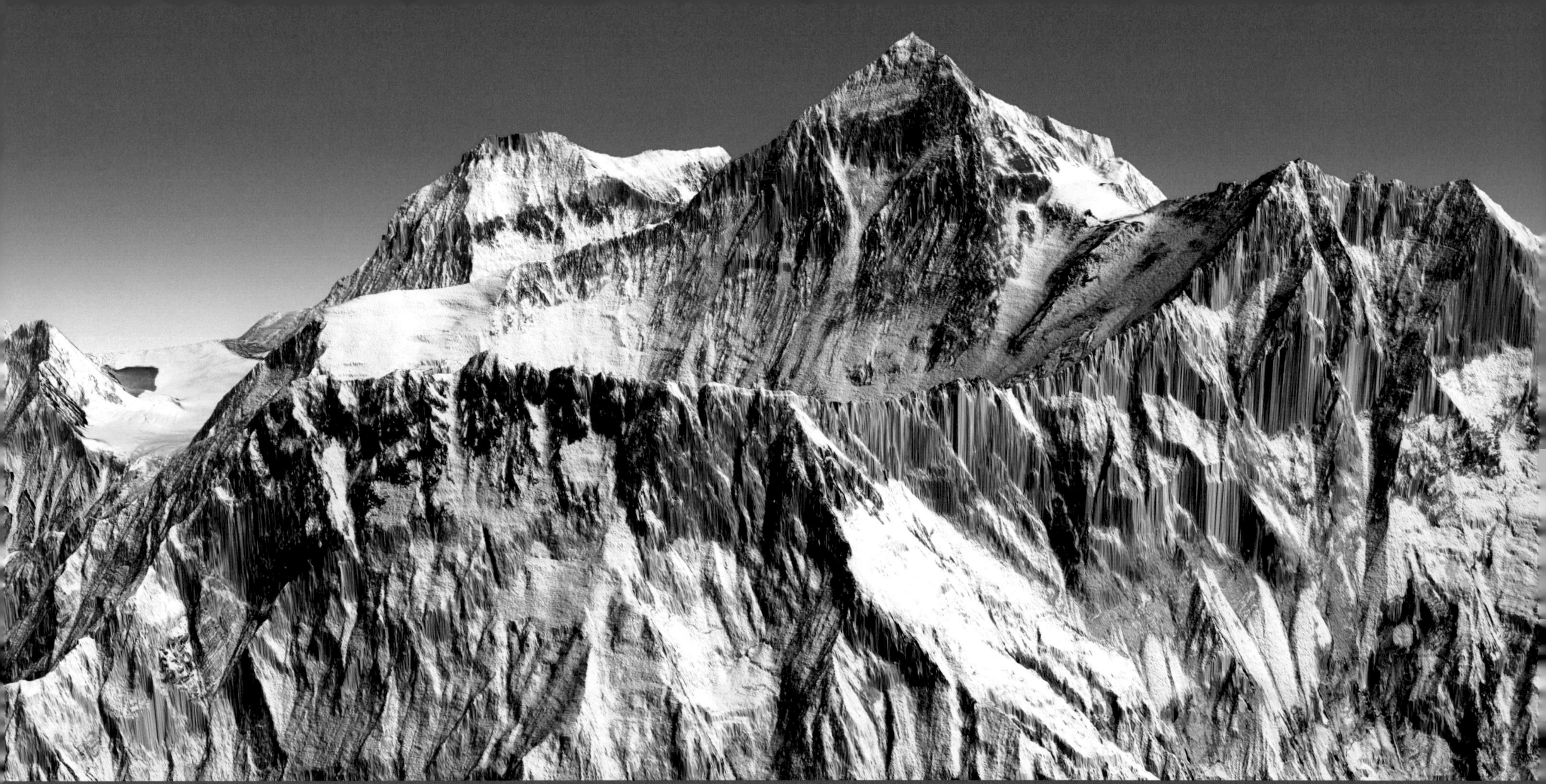

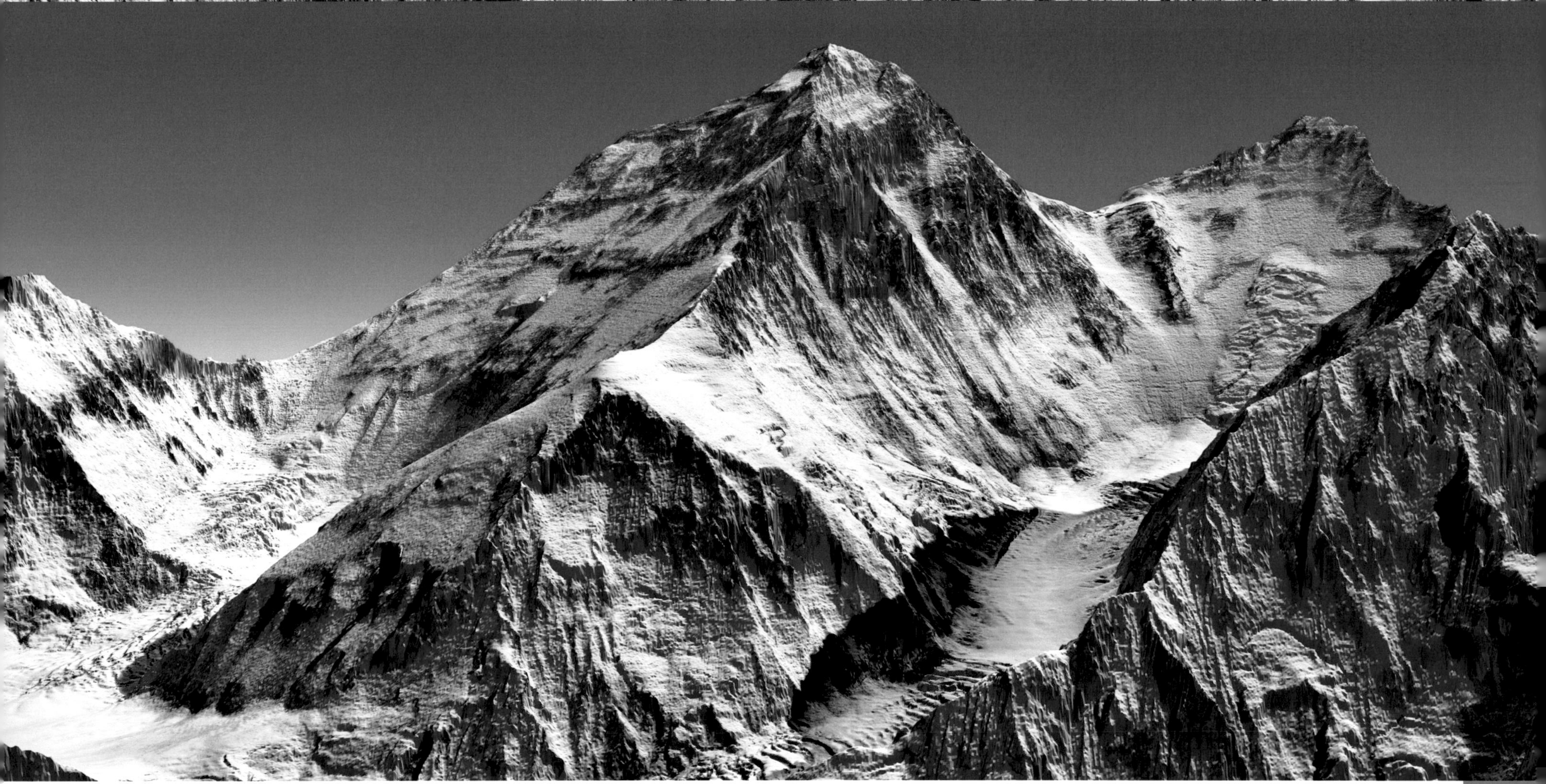

Mount Everest, view from the west

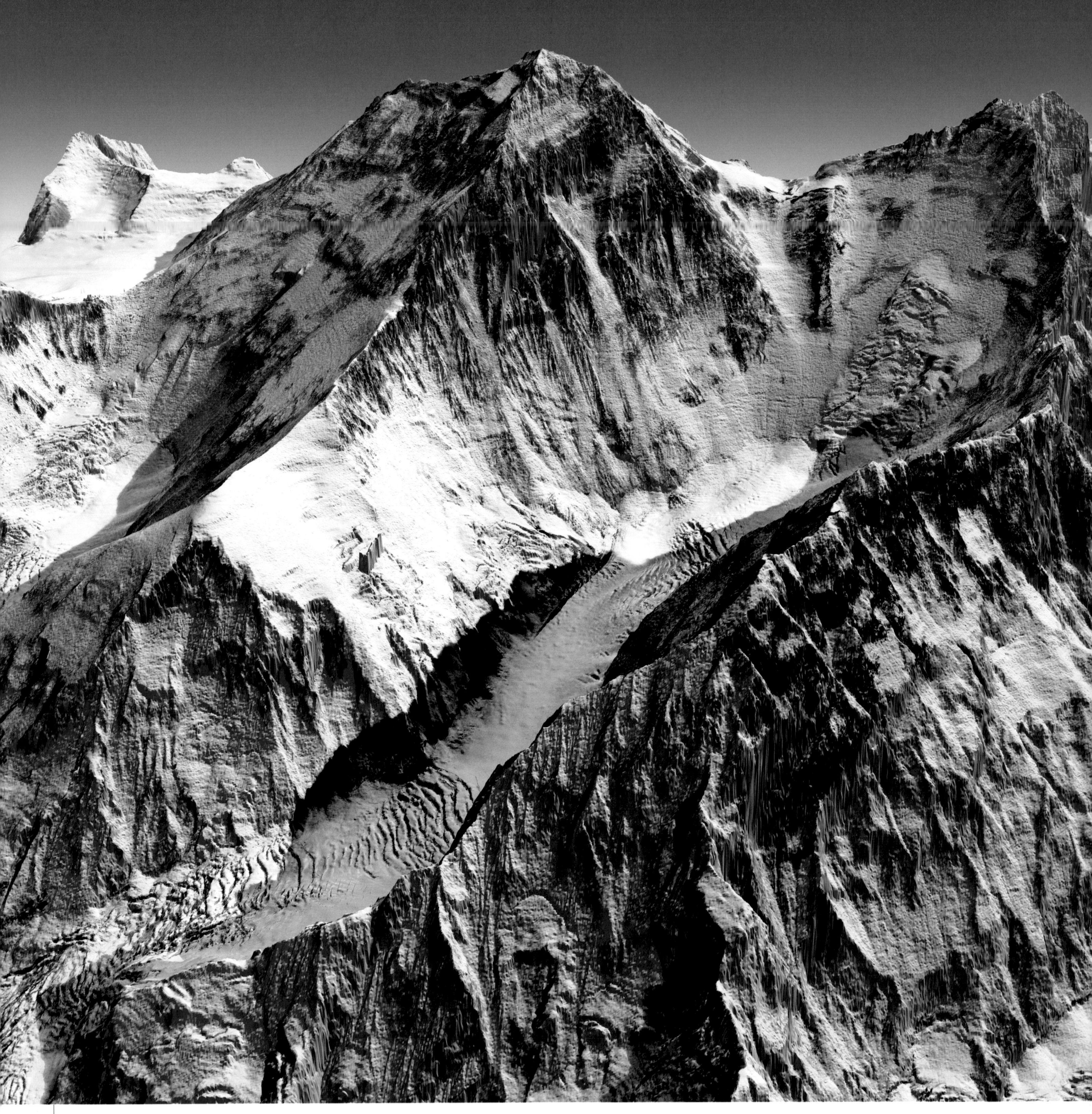

 The route taken on the first climb of Mount Everest

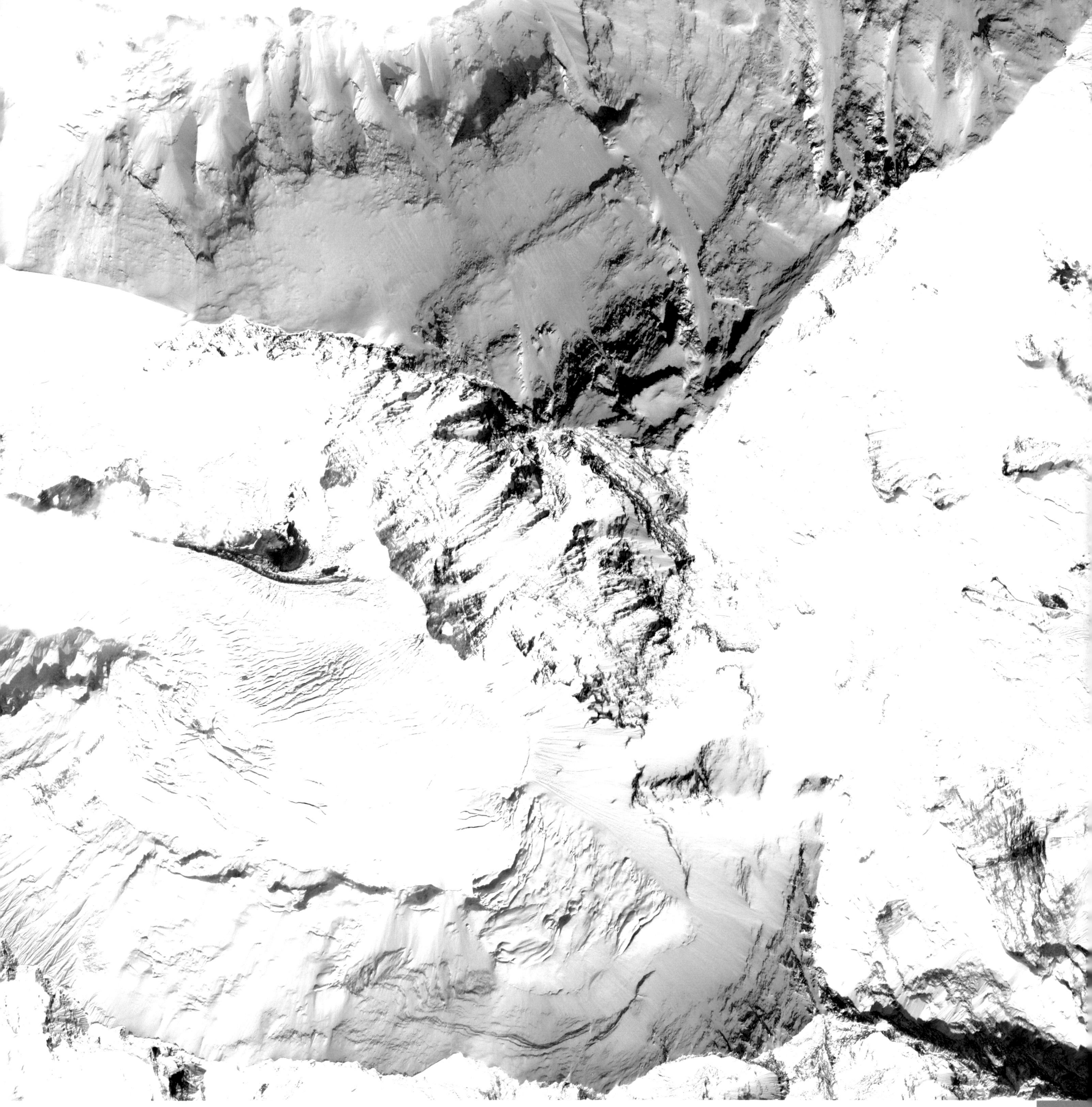

The Mount Everest region after a monsoon

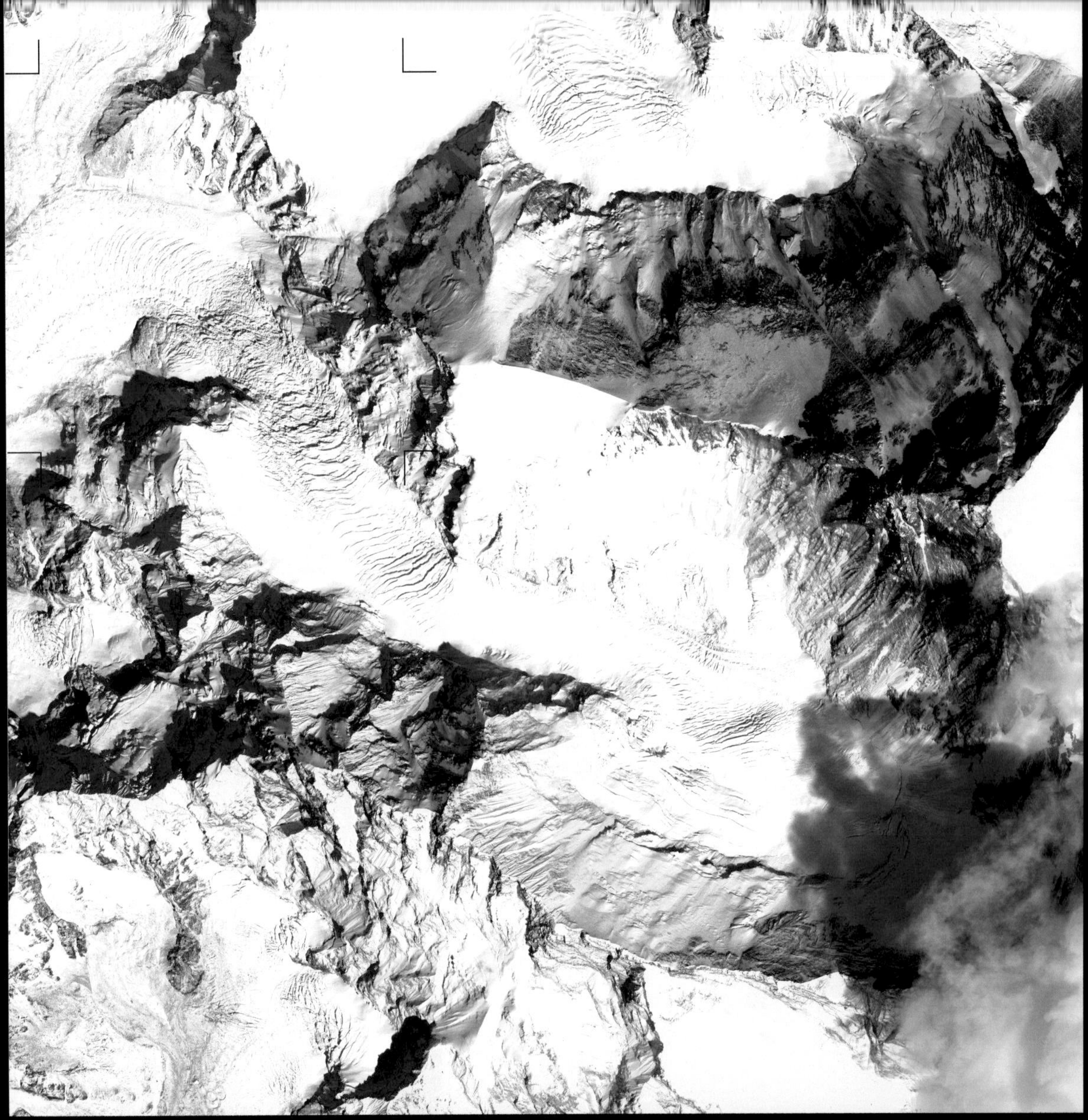

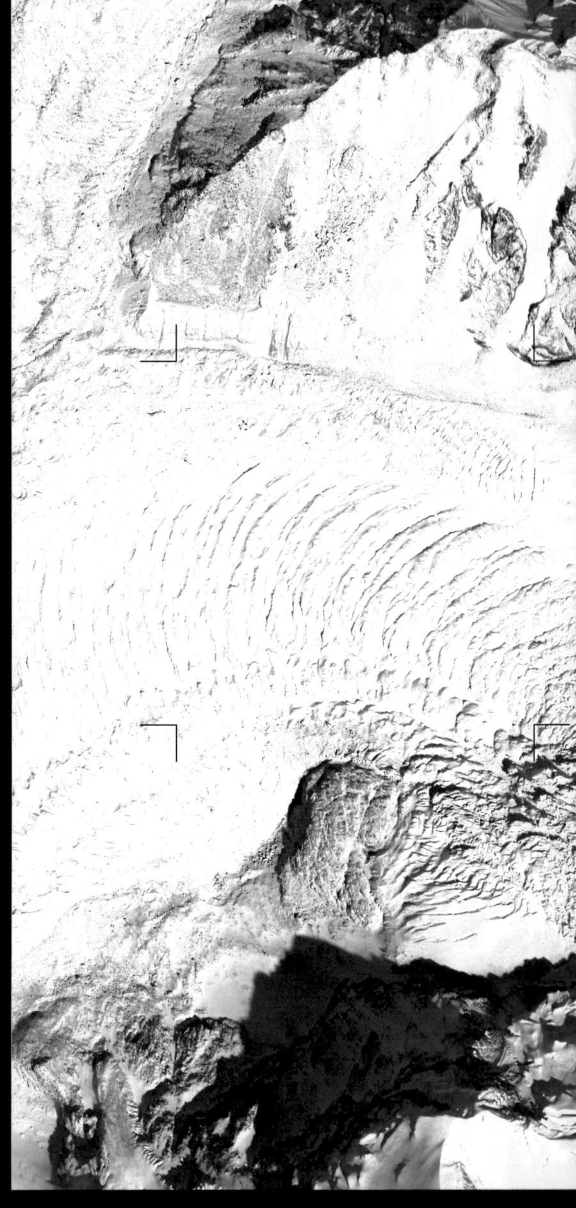

Zoom on Camp I above the Khumbu ice fall, Mount Everest

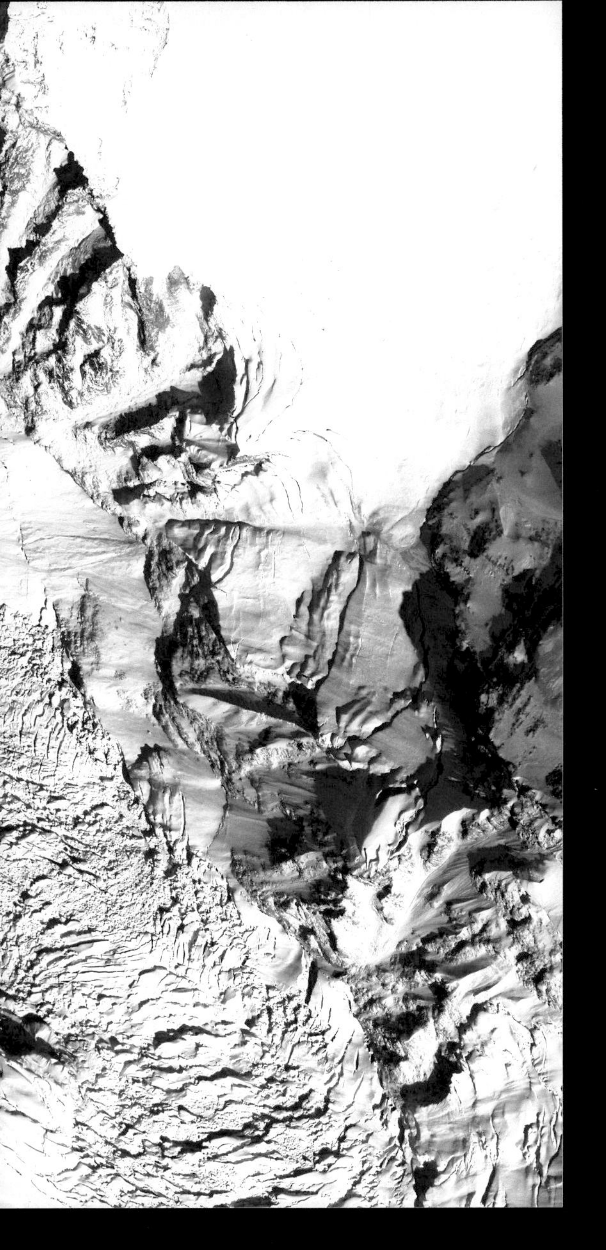

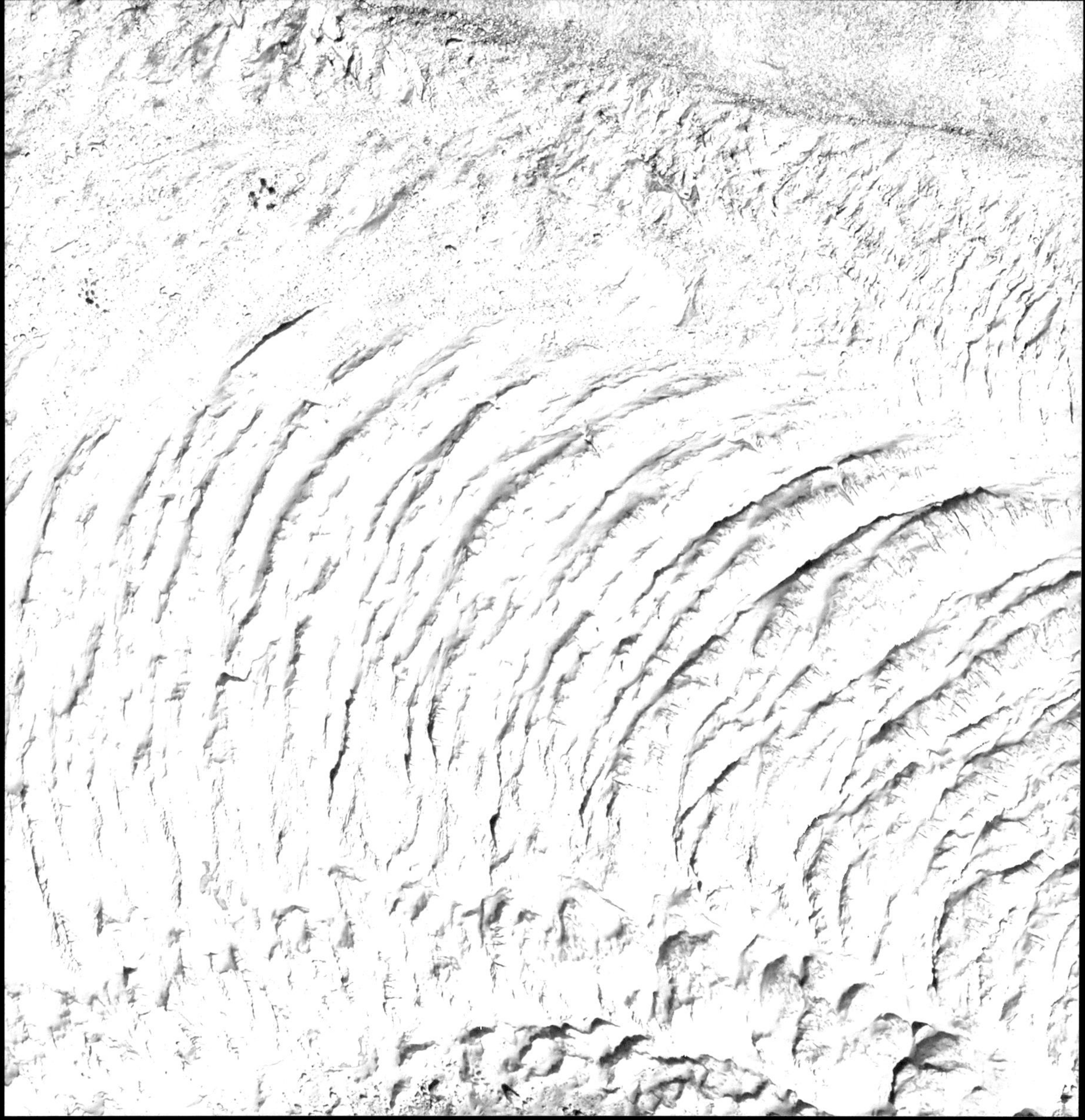

Summit Conference

Reinhold Messner in Conversation with Sir Edmund Hillary

Sir Edmund Hillary was never an excellent rock climber. As a climber of high mountains he managed a single great success, and his famous expedition to the South Pole was assisted by tractor. Nevertheless, Hillary is among the best-known mountain climbers in the world. Ed, as he is called by his friends, became a mountain climber in his New Zealand homeland, where the mountains are neither especially steep nor especially high, but they are remote, unruly, and uncharted.

Anyone who climbs mountains in New Zealand, far from any shelter, to say nothing of cable cars, knows that the chance of being rescued in an emergency is extremely slim. Hillary learned early on that mountain climbing involves great exertion, exposure, and danger. He has always approached mountains with respect, enormous zest, and a trace of self-mockery. This made me take to him from the beginning.

We first met in 1978, shortly after my ascent of Everest, in Solo Khumbu at one of the hospitals Hillary had established for the Sherpas. Sir Ed was curious, but at the same time spoke openly about himself. We have been friends since, and see each other almost every year in either the land of the Sherpas, Kathmandu, or the United States at joint appearances for his foundation.

With the same determination with which Hillary climbed mountains or led the expedition to the South Pole, he has been an advocate for "his" Sherpas. He has helped to finance schools, bridges, hospitals, and two landing strips for small planes in their territory, and in doing so he has created a stable medical and logistical infrastructure. As a result, this mountain people enjoys a unique situation in Nepal. It may be that I admire Sir Edmund Hillary even more for his social engagement than for his daring, without which Everest would never have been bested in 1953. The Englishmen in his team back then were not lacking in mountain-climbing ability, but they lacked the decisive quantum of luck. That Hillary had. We owe the conquest of the mountain with his companion Tenzing Norgay to his enthusiasm and his climbing savvy.

In New Zealand, where Edmund Hillary helped his beekeeper father before he became world famous as the first person to climb Mount Everest, I encounter a cheerful, enthusiastic man with a definite formula for success. Hard work, modesty, and cunning, coupled with his sense of self-confidence, allow him to do what he feels is right, to help where help is needed, and to keep his mouth shut when self-proclaimed experts come on strong.

Hillary still lives in the house he built shortly after his Everest climb. On a slope in a suburb of Auckland, a city of a million inhabitants, the flat structure is nestled in a slight depression, and looks practical and unimposing. One can only approach it from above and on foot. June, Hillary's wife, leads me down a few steps into the living room. Sir Ed has furnished it in country-house style, and decorated it with souvenirs from the Himalayas. Through the picture window one looks out onto a large garden with old trees. The sea glistens far below.

"Sir Ed," I ask him, after exchanging greetings and reviving old memories over tea, "Are you bothered by the trashy articles about you in newspapers all over the world?"

"No," Hillary replies. "I don't have to comment on all the stuff the journalists make up. I know how it was. What outsiders say about it is inconsequential."

"But when it was said that Tenzing was the sole hero of Mount Everest, did you respond?"

"Yes, because the nationalist campaign Tenzing had allowed himself to be exploited by was tasteless. Tenzing was naive, and had no idea what was happening. I was branded as a colonialist who was claiming the 'conquest' alone at the expense of the natives, the Sherpas, when in fact it was the reverse. It really makes no difference who reached the peak first—we had climbed roped together. For that reason, Lord Hunt, Tenzing, and I agreed to say that we had all reached the peak together."

"The southern route on Mount Everest is now called the Hillary Route, and will continue to be. Even if the Sherpas now do all the preliminary work so that hundreds of people can storm the roof of the world."

"My mountain climbing was a matter of responsibility for myself and a love of mountains. Naturally we went ahead and sought the way, built bridges over crevasses, set up the camps. The Sherpas were assistants, bearers. They took care of us after we had blazed the trail."

"Tenzing has not become as famous as you!"

"Tenzing was a lonely man in his old age. I frequently visited him in Darjeeling. We came to be closer friends. Perhaps it bothered him that he did not achieve the living standard that mountain climbers in Great Britain or New Zealand enjoy. Yet after the expedition we shared everything: appearances, lecture honorariums, and the fame. It is possible that the Indian government didn't keep its promises to Tenzing. But he worked as a travel guide, published his autobiography, and traveled a great deal. You have to realize that in 1953 Tenzing could neither read nor write."

"Unlike Tenzing, you have undertaken further adventures."

"Mount Everest was only a single stone in the mosaic of my biography. Perhaps it was the most important adventure of my life. It made me famous. Then came the South Pole. We New Zealanders drove there with tractors, as I had seen them do in Norway. It was a crazy time. The cold, the storms, the breakdowns. I can't tell you how often one of the three Ferguson tractors slipped into a crevasse."

"But you reached the pole before Vivian Fuchs."

"Yes. Fuchs came from the other side, and he wanted us to wait until he got there. We were in radio contact. But we were short of provisions, had too little fuel. We had to go on, and were at the pole before the British. But that's not what mattered. It was all about getting back."

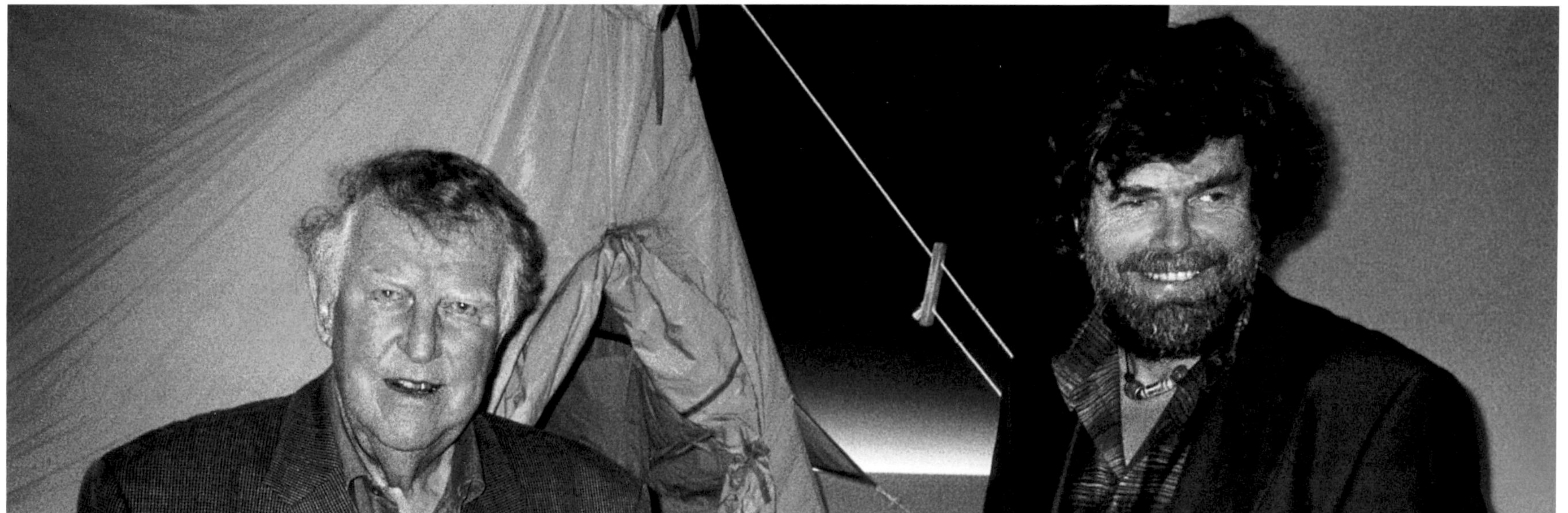

"Then came the 'Silver Hat' expedition of 1959."

"That experiment lasted nearly two years—an altitude medicine laboratory at more than 19,500 feet on the Ama Dablam Glacier. The second focus of the research was the Yeti. My comrades climbed Ama Dablam and there was resentment in Kathmandu."

"But no answer to the puzzling question of the Yeti?"

"No. We found traces, and hides were shown to us. The Sherpas related everything to the Yeti. They were convinced that it exists. But their relics are forgeries. What were we to do?"

"The Sherpas probably brought the legend of the Yeti with them from Tibet at least 400 years ago, when they reached Solo Khumbu after a long migration. The legend goes back to snow bears, and is told everywhere in Tibet."

"Yes. Everywhere the Sherpas presented skins from the "blue bear' as Yeti skins. That seems to be the answer."

"So the 'blue bear' is only a fiction. It was doubtless large male specimens of the snow or Tibet bear. Their fur is dark, glistening with blue, and they behave exactly the way the Yeti legend says they do."

"Ocean to sky," Hillary interrupts. "The journey up the Ganges from its mouth to the source was one of my most beautiful journeys. I was the organizer, we were a cheerful team. People received us very enthusiastically."

"I am most impressed by your social work: The Himalayan Trust, of which you are the initiator and driving force finances hospitals, schools, and bridges."

"Today it is a matter of maintaining all that, training doctors and teachers. Meanwhile the Sherpas have managed to take over the work, to administer the structures that I brought them. It has gotten much better. Communication, transportation, and fund raising are now being organized by professionals. I visit their events and present my projects. June helps me."

"And what about the many tourists who year after year storm Mount Everest?"

"They don't impress me," Hillary says dryly. "But the governments need money, and sell as many permits as possible. And all of them swarm onto the prepared, normal route. No travel company has ever asked me if they might use my name in their advertising. They simply exploit me. For an undertaking that does not please me at all. As if there had never been a different Mount Everest."

We later visited the Auckland Museum, a neoclassical building high above the city that had devoted an exhibit to the fiftieth anniversary of Edmund Hillary's first conquest of Mount Everest. There was the tiny tent in which he spent the last night with Tenzing before the climb to the peak. And the ice pick with which Hillary cut the last steps on the roof ridge of the earth. Like a religious relic, it hangs in a glass case.

I am touched. Perhaps as well because this simple tool represents the life achievement of a man who conquered the world as it was and his own sense of himself with bursting lungs and a pounding heart.

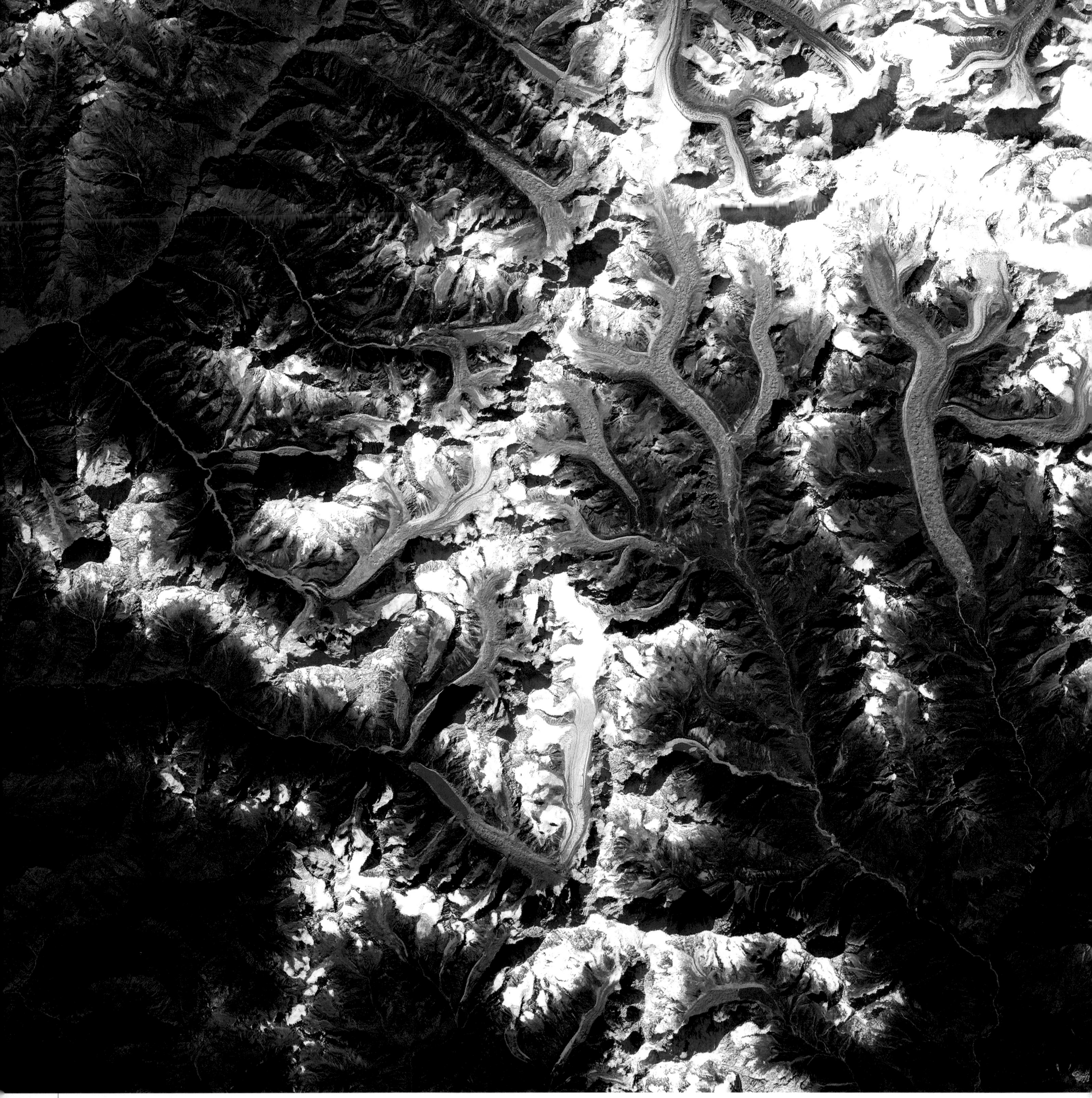

Sagarmatha and Makalu-Barun National Parks, Nepal

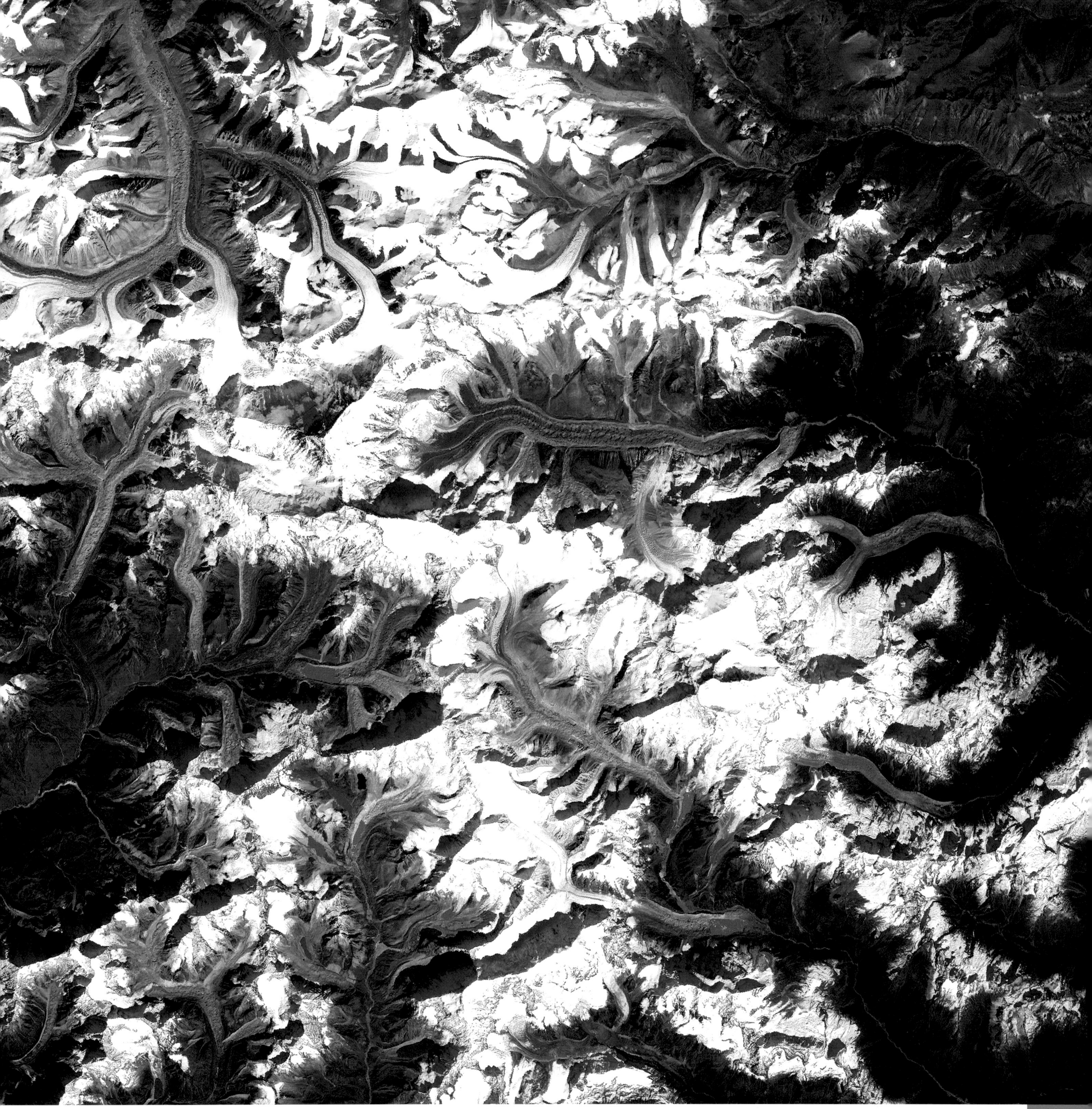

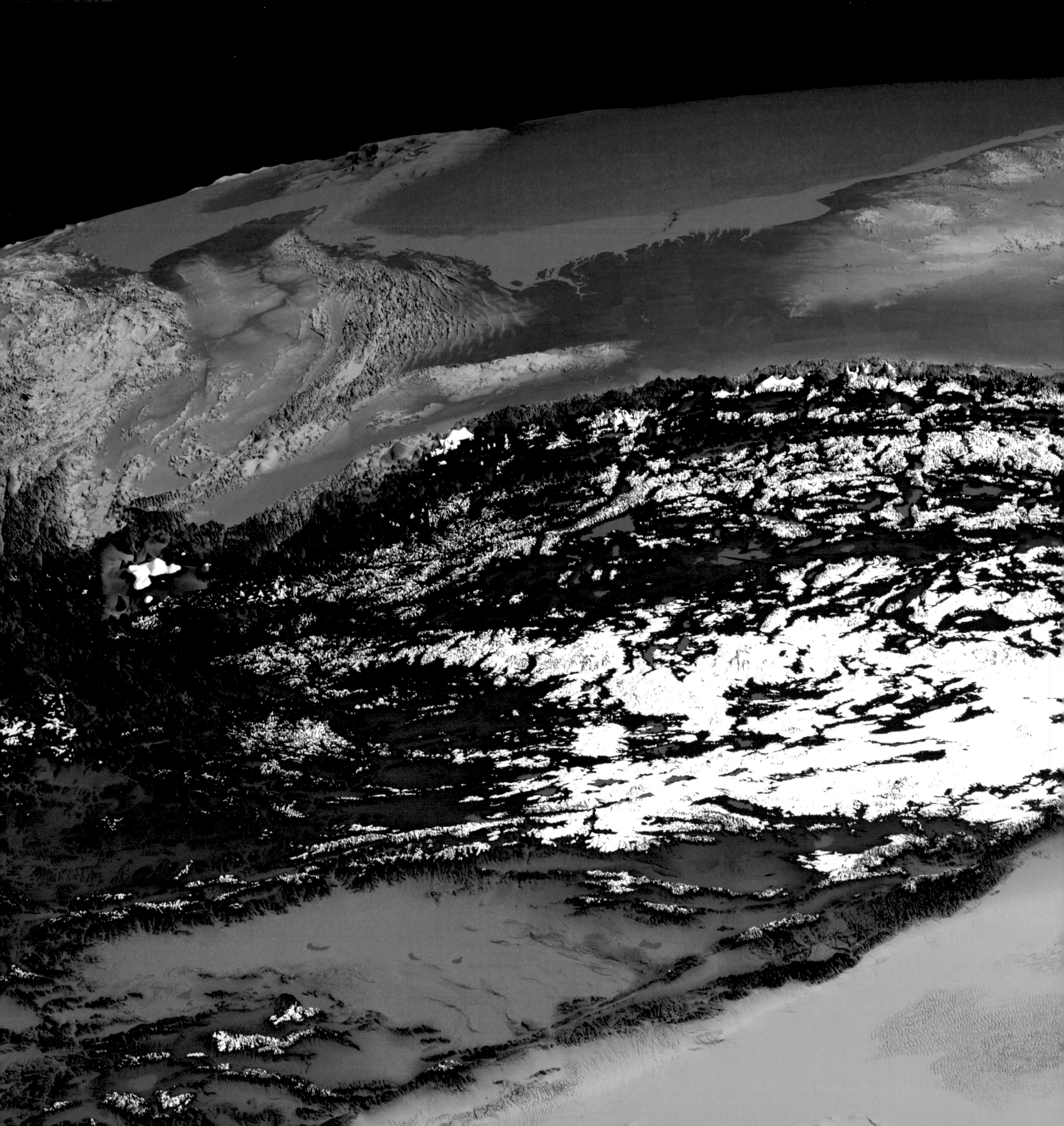

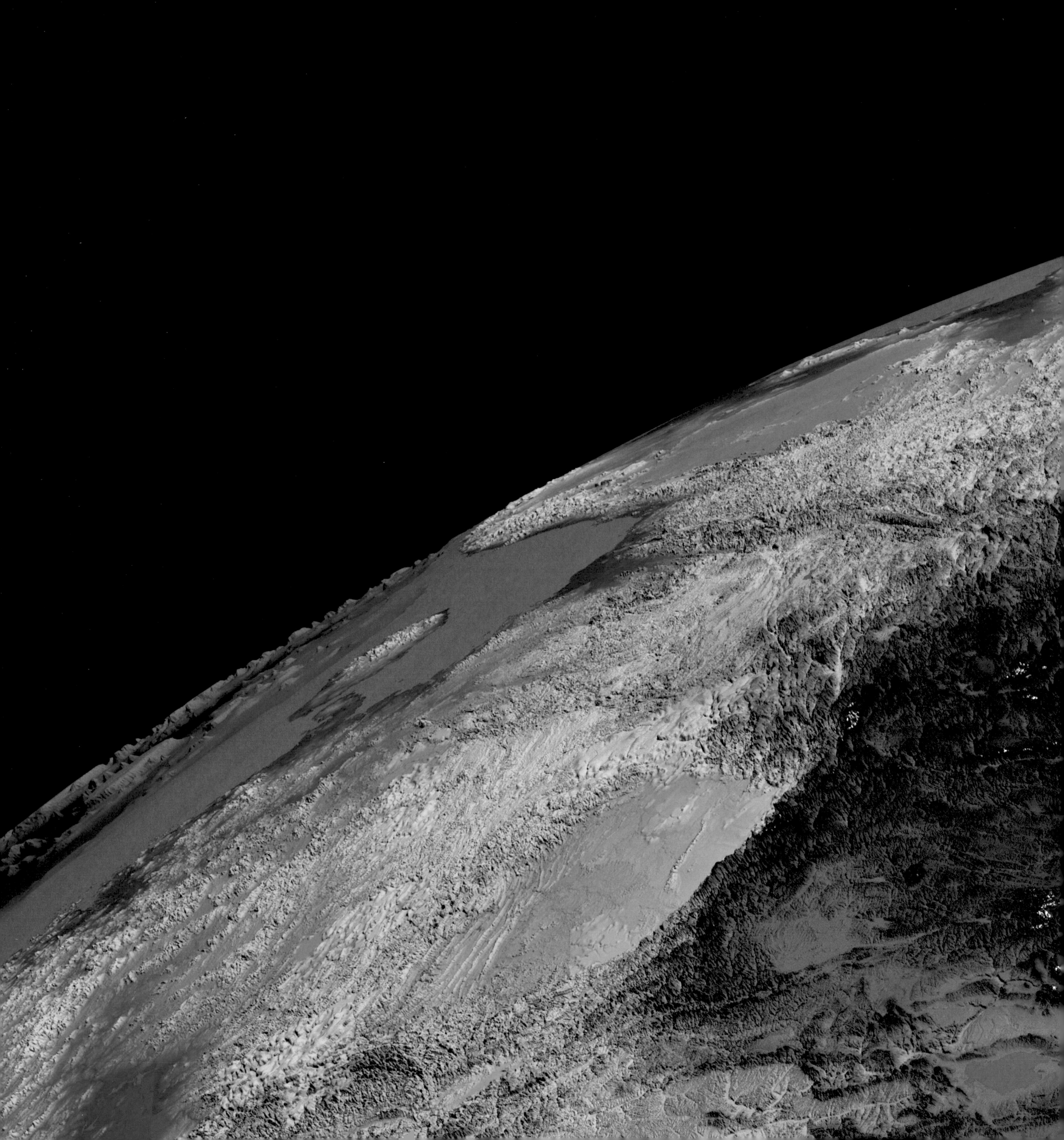

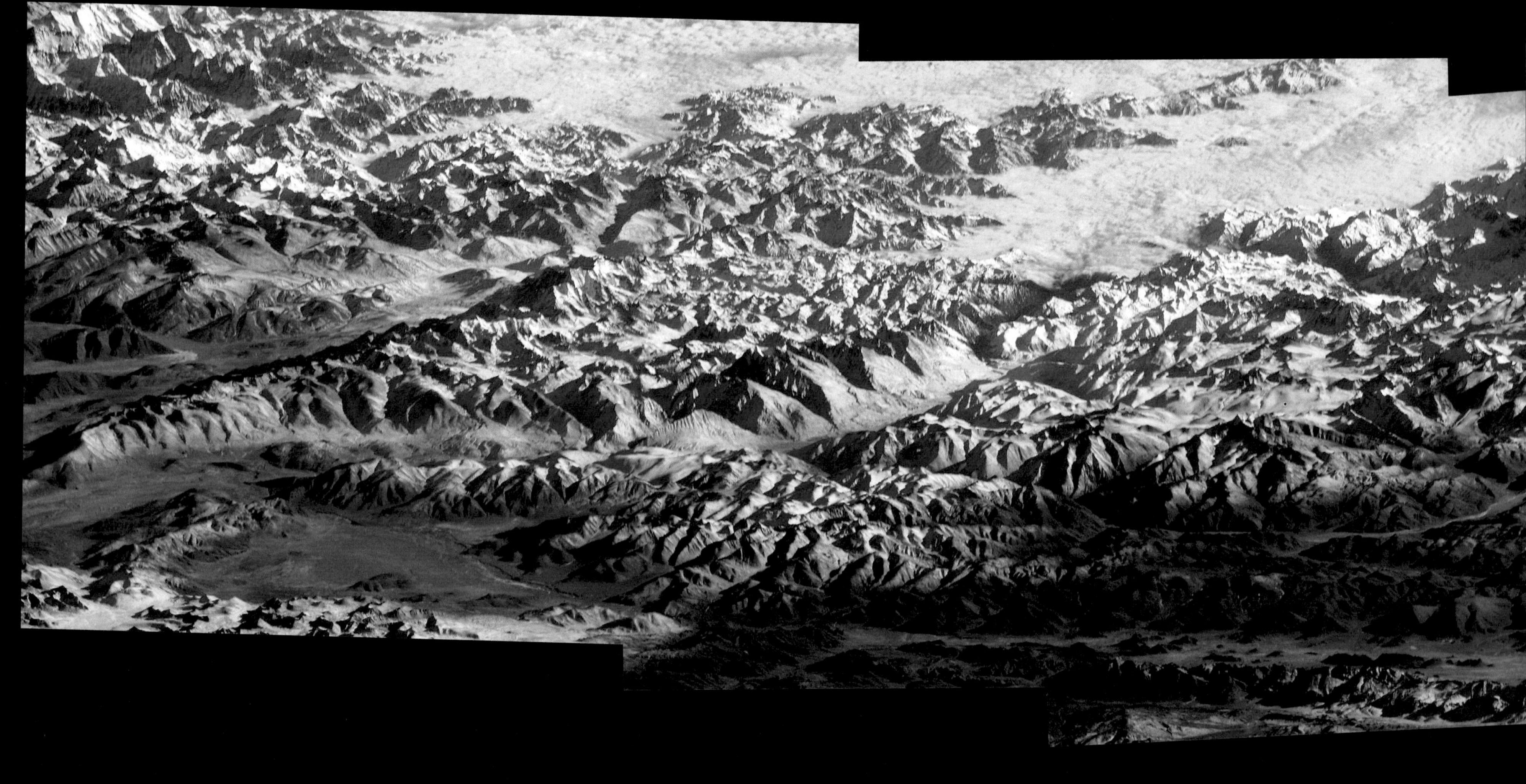

Panorama of the Himalayas as seen from the International Space Station

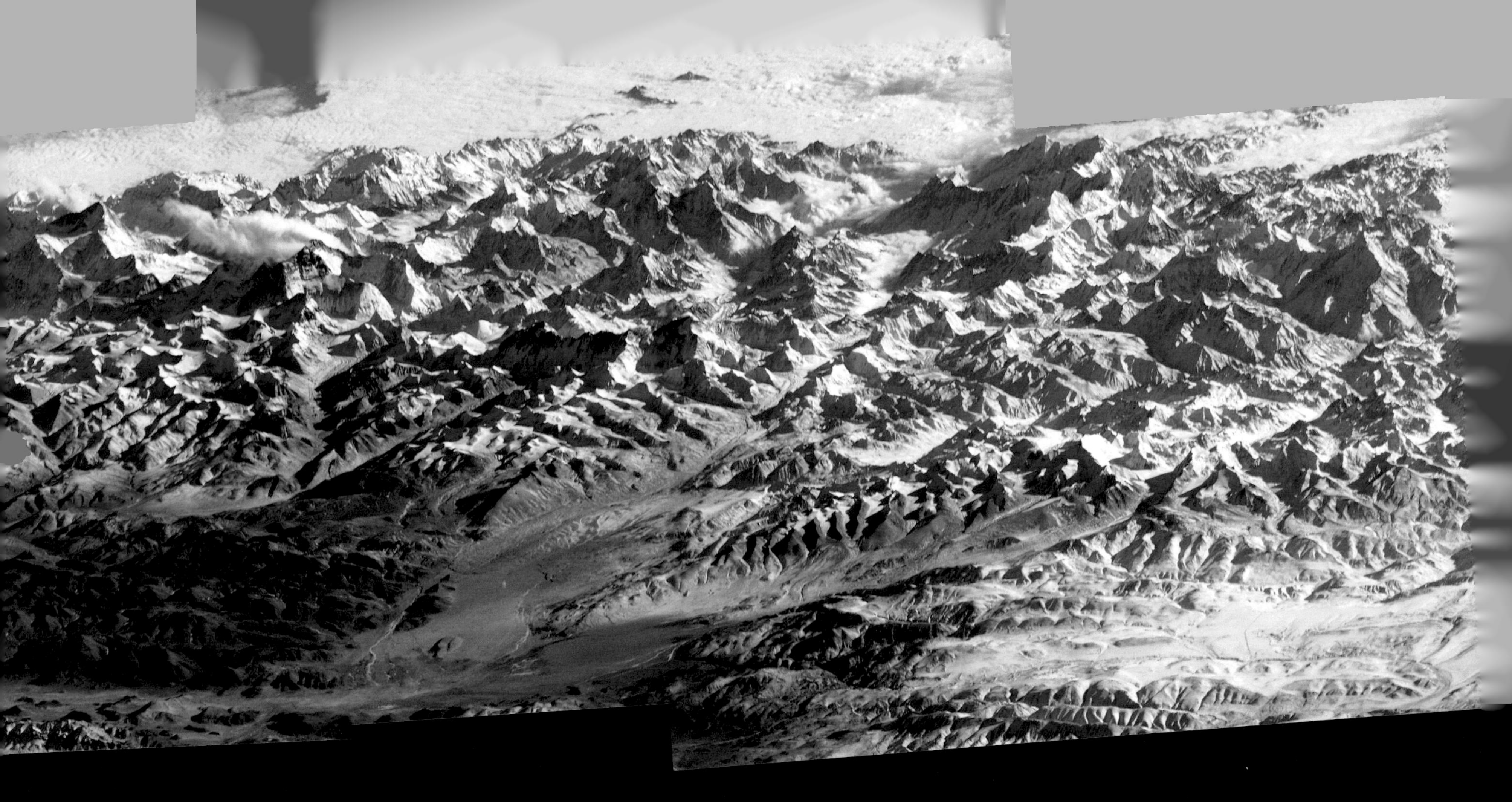

Gatefold: Virtual panorama of the Himalayas

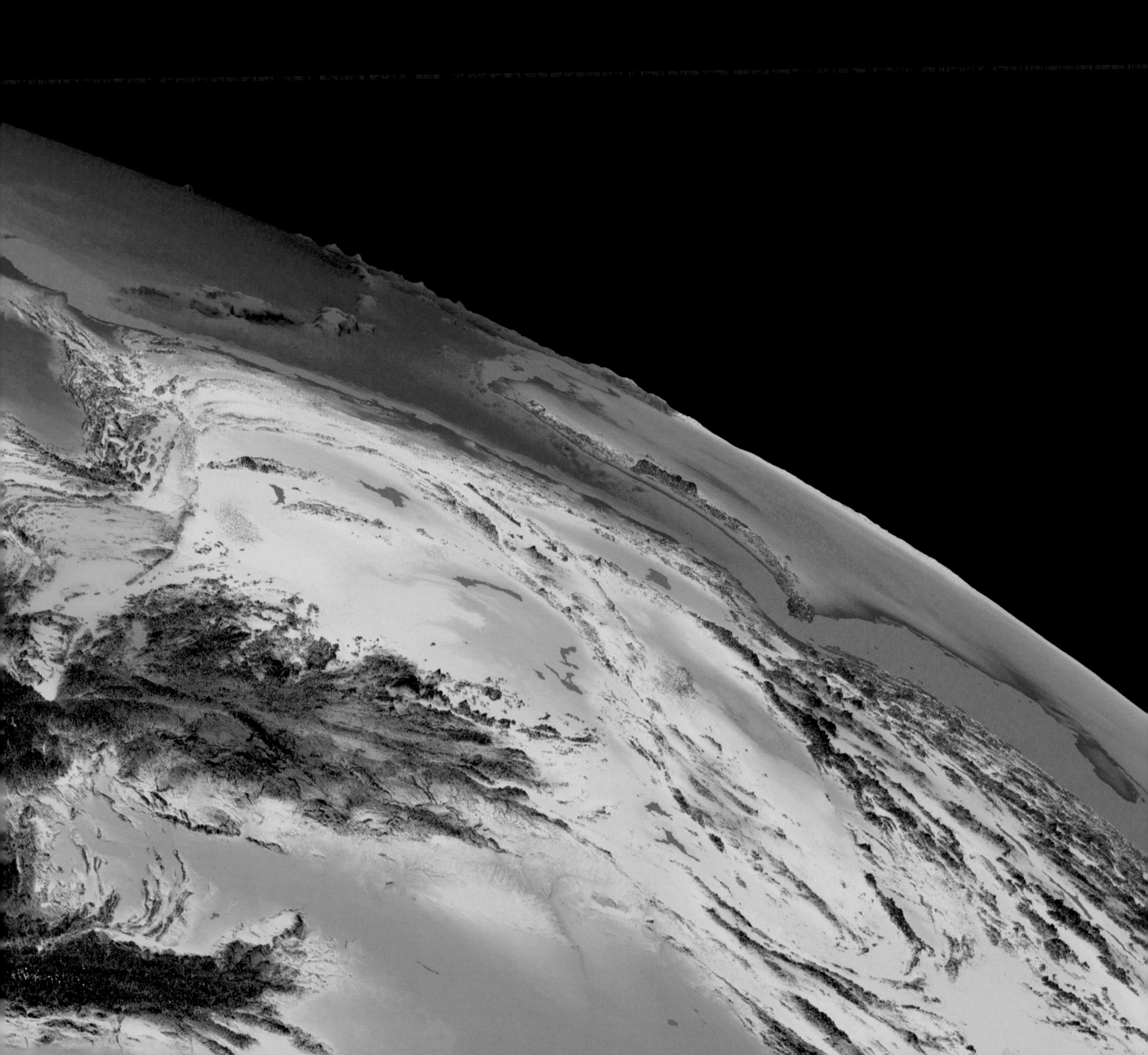

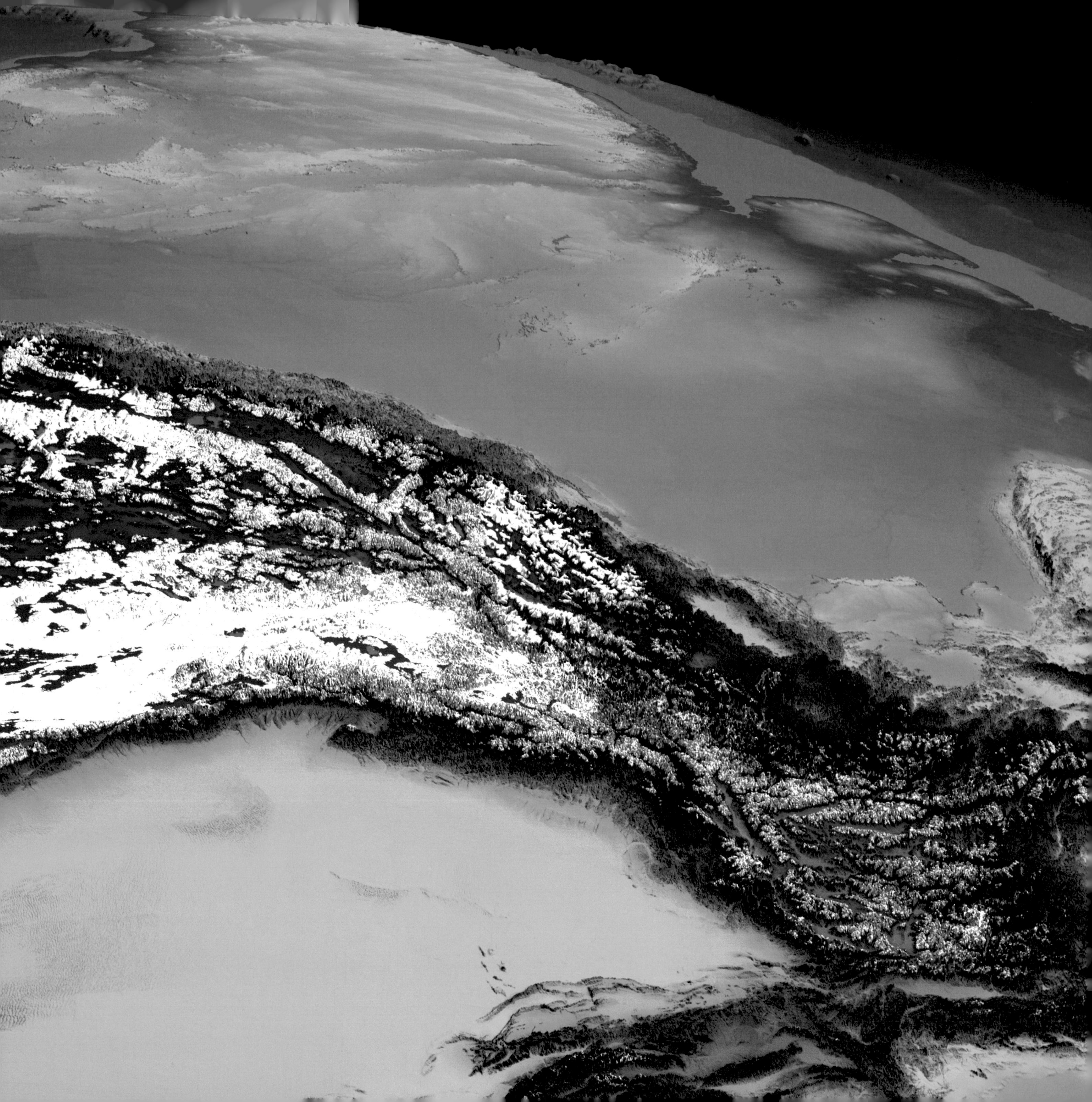

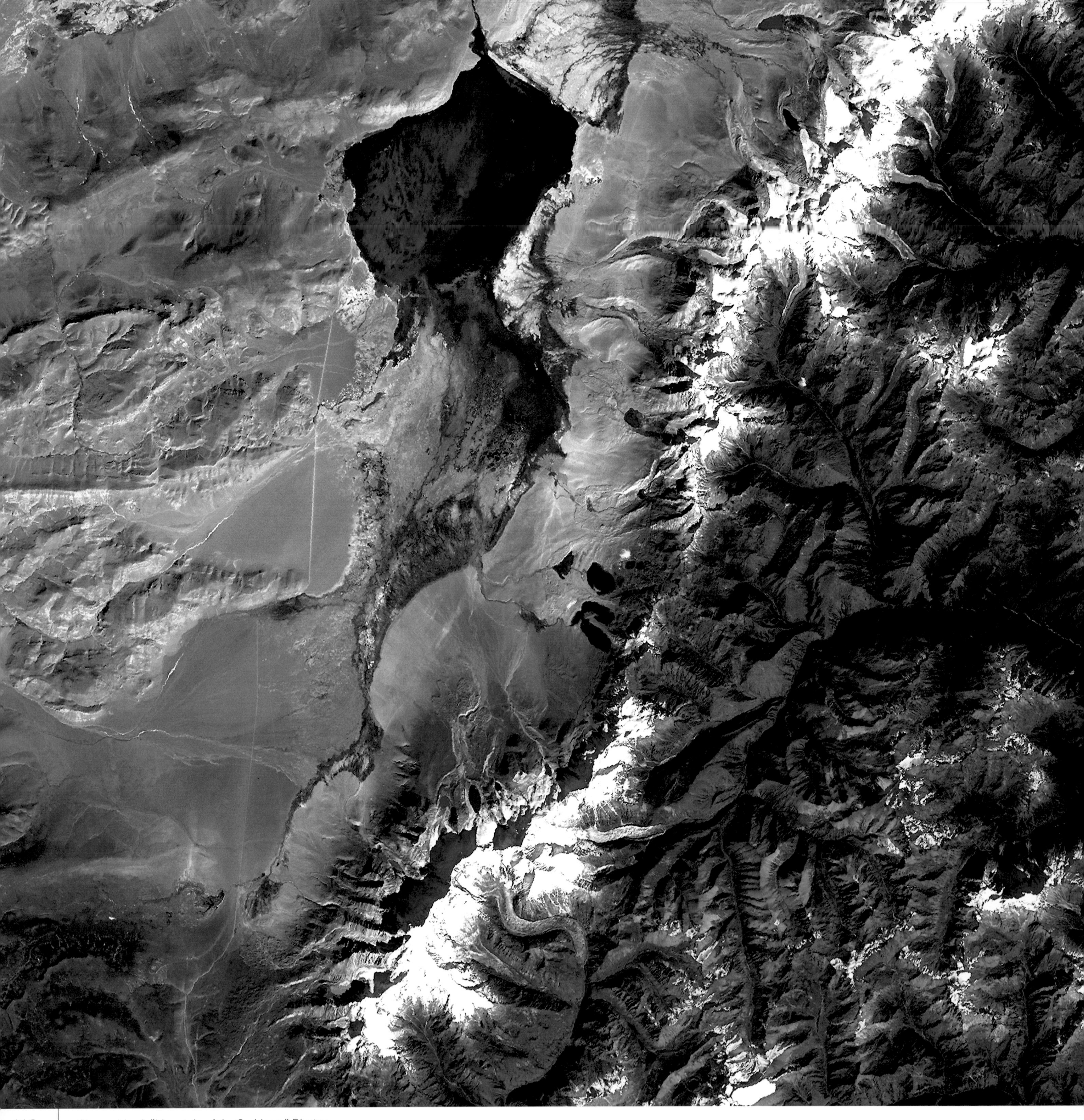

Chomo Lhari, "Mountain of the Goddess," Bhutan

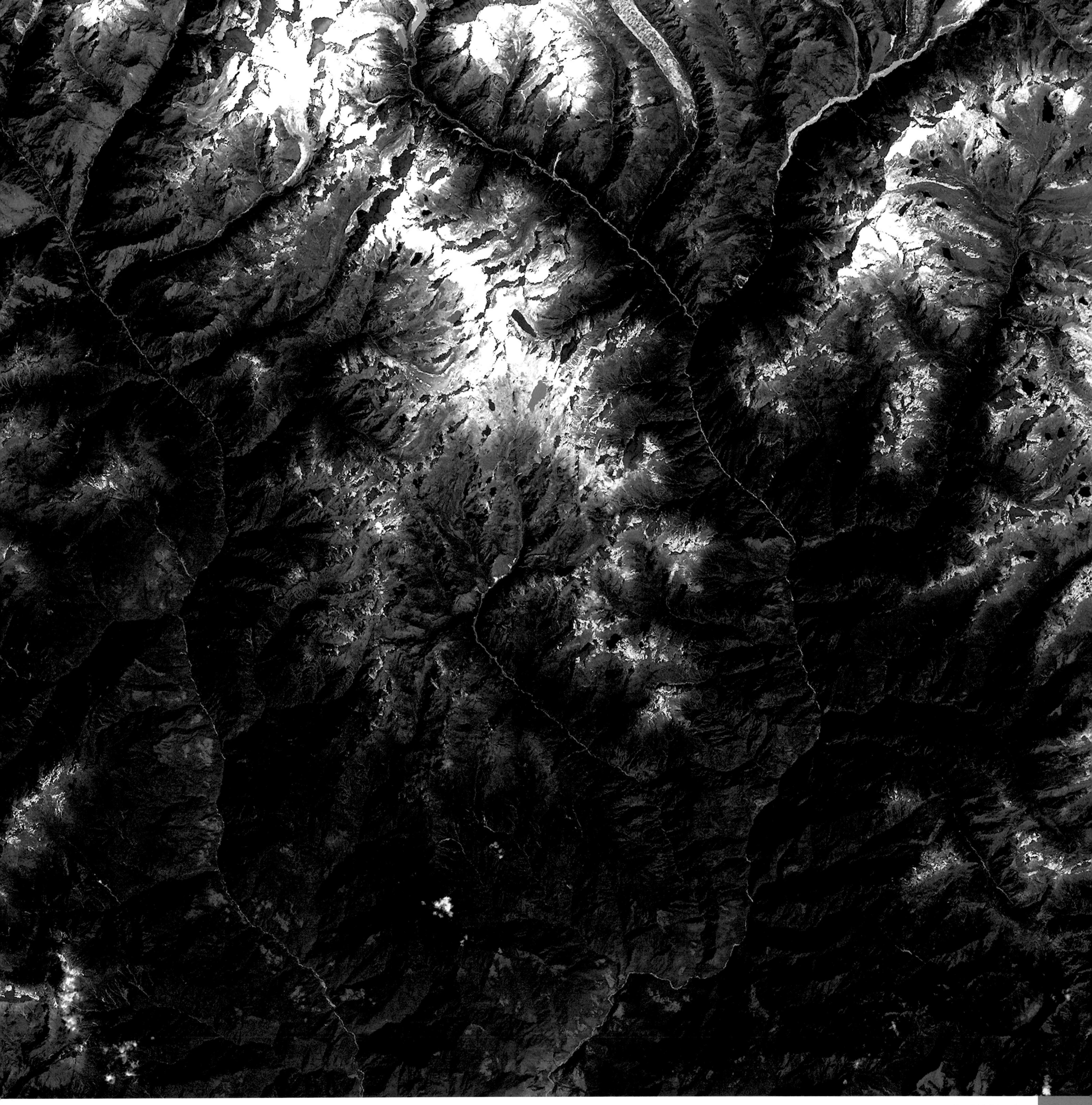

Mountain Climate
Steep Slopes, Wild Weather

RÜDIGER GLASER

Mountains are weather-makers. Their steep terrain and drastic contrasts in elevation insure that they can brew up greater mischief—in less time—than other landscapes. Interplay between mountain and valley air currents, extreme differences in temperature due to peaks blocking incoming wind, and inversion layers in valleys make for an unusually wide variety of weather in a small area. Mountains are not only watersheds but also "weathersheds" that greatly influence the global climate.

The mountain climate is full of surprises. Swift and unpredictable changes in the weather have put many a mountain climber in an embarrassing predicament. Menacing towers of cloud above the high meadows, strong wind howling down off glaciers, frequent inversions above valleys, and the tendency for warm air to linger in the center of a chain of mountains rather than at the edges—all of these are part of the mountain experience. There is also the thinner, high-altitude air, which can either make one sick or have a healing effect, as Thomas Mann explores in *The Magic Mountain*.

The rugged terrain and the complex structure of peaks, slopes, high plateaus, and deeply cut valleys create extreme contrasts: sunlit slopes on one side of a valley, shaded ones on the other; windblown ridges and pockets of no wind at all; rain-soaked flanks and dry ones—all in the closest proximity. Contrasting temperatures and pressures close together can lead to complete changes in the weather in no time at all.

All the elements of climate become more apparent with increasing altitude. The sun's radiation, especially ultraviolet radiation, reaches extremely high levels in higher elevations. Everyone knows that the higher you go the colder it gets; on average, the temperature decreases roughly half a degree Celsius with every 325 feet of elevation, between 0.72°F and 1.26°F depending on the season. The contrast in temperature is greatest in summer, due to lasting snow cover in the higher reaches and more intense heating of air layers on the valley floor. Also a factor in mountain landscapes are the frequent inversions in the valleys, which lead to high atmospheric loading.

Air pressure and oxygen also decrease with altitude, which can afflict the unprepared traveler with the dreaded altitude sickness. At an altitude of 16,000 feet the air pressure is roughly only half that at sea level, and at 24,500 feet the so-called dead zone begins. The air at great heights is cleaner than at lower levels, however, and higher altitudes are a great relief for people allergic to pollens. Together with the stimulation from cold and the radiation effect, higher altitudes can have salutatory effects, hence mountain health resorts like St. Moritz.

In humid climate zones, precipitation also increases with altitude. But this basic pattern is subject to wide variation around the globe, and there are distinct deviations depending on the location of the mountain with respect to planetary air currents, the mountain's orientation, whether it blocks the flow of air or stands in the path of trade winds in the subtropics or in the region of the highest condensation level of the tropics. Then specific altitudinal belts are extraordinarily wet, while those lying above and below them are occasionally much drier. The form of precipitation also plays an important ecological role. If large quantities fall in the form of snow, do these then become transformed into névé and finally ice? Or is there only occasional precipitation as in arid zones? Are fog and dew a factor? Snow fulfills an important ecological function as a storehouse of water, also as insulation for the soil, animals, and vegetation against frost. A blanket of snow a foot and a half thick holds the surface of the ground around the freezing point, even when the outside temperature stands at -54°F.

Other peculiarities of mountains are the periodic up- and downdraft systems during the day, which cause differences in temperature between areas close to the slopes and the open atmosphere. These daily alternating wind systems are very important in that they provide fresh air for the bowl landscapes and valleys frequently suffering from inversions. Glacial winds are another story, as they usually flow downward off the ice-cold surface all day long.

Mountains not only have their own specific climate, they also have a decisive effect on the global climate system. Mountains serve to divert masses of air streaming across the globe far out of their path, thus acting as climate barriers. The Himalayas, the mountains ringing the Tibetan plateau, are a good example. Their effect as rain-catchers is seen especially in the central region. In the summer monsoon season their sides facing the rain receive up to 235 inches of precipitation, whereas protected north slopes only sixty miles away receive a mere six inches. In the southeast, where the peaks are not so high, the winds are no longer blocked, and the moist summer monsoon penetrates deep into the Tibetan plateau. As a result of this buffer from the monsoon, distinct cloud forests have developed in the lower chains of the Himalayas. It is not only there that we see the interplay of precipitation and vegetation; cloud forests have also managed to establish themselves on the shaded sides of valleys, thanks to moisture carried on the prevailing downdrafts. As in all mountains, the blocking effect is associated with cloud formation and precipitation on the south side with foehn winds and descending, warming, cloud-dispersing streams of air on the north side.

In the central High Himalayas the amount of precipitation in winter is significantly higher, and accordingly they accumulate a longer-lasting snow cover. In the northwest, at least, this leads to considerable avalanche activity, as in the European Alps. And as in all mountains like them, alternating daily wind systems are very typical. Here the updraft thermals in the morning occasion clouding on the slopes.This places the higher valley walls in shadow, while valley floors remain unshaded and

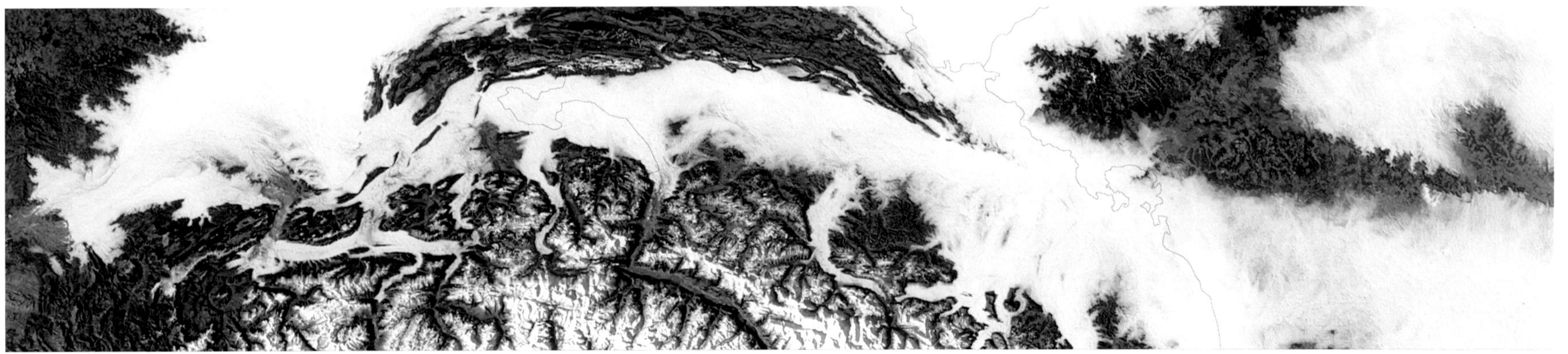

The western Alps on December 11, 2004. While mist billows over large sections of the depressions and larger valleys in the Alpine foothills, the peaks are in radiant sunshine. This is a typical inversion condition.

dry out more. Dry valley winds intensify this desiccation; in the major transverse valleys these regularly attain gale force by afternoon.

The Alps are another significant climate barrier, standing between central Europe and the Mediterranean. When air masses build up in front of the mountains they have to either go around or over, for only a portion of them can pass through the valleys. On the windward side facing the blockage the result can be spells of distinctly bad weather with high precipitation; on the lee side the result is a foehn. And what if the flow of air is from the north? Air masses striking the Alps from a northerly direction drop considerable precipitation on their northern edge. The cold air flows around the Alps to the east and west. The resulting regional winds are known by different names; the people of the valley of the Rhône speak of the mistral, those of the Swiss midlands of the *bisé*, and those of the mountains in Dalmatia of the *bora*. These air masses rejoin on the south side of the mountain range, generally forming a lee-cyclone, another low-pressure area, above the Gulf of Genoa. This is the reverse of the situation resulting from blockage of air flow from the south, when the nothern edge of the Alps experiences foehn. Other well-known foehn systems are the chinook, a snow-melter in the Rocky Mountains, the *zonda* in Argentina, and the *puelche* in Chile.

Mountains are found in all climate zones, and there are consequences to this. While the Alps and the Rockies experience the full range of the seasons, tropical mountains are subject to a so-called time-of-day climate. At the equator there is a uniform alternation of twelve hours of daylight and twelve hours of darkness. The daily variations in temperature can even exceed seasonal ones. Put another way, these mountains experience the alternation between winter and summer on a daily basis. Toward the edge of the tropics summer days are longer and winter days shorter, until finally at the poles the other extreme is reached, the alternation of six months of light and six months of darkness. This rhythm is overlaid by the alternation of dry and rainy seasons. Mountains in different latitudes thus have very different climates.

The Alps are weather-makers. They are centered between the Iceland Low, the Azores High, and the vast continental high-pressure area over Russia and Scandinavia. With both maritime and continental air masses involved, the Alpine climate is highly variable. Even in winter, the Alpine region is very strongly influenced by the Atlantic. The North Atlantic Oscillation Index (NAOI) is a fitting expression of this. Winters are also marked by a large number of Atlantic low-pressure areas. Again and again, however, these are replaced by blocking high-pressure systems with blasts of cold from the northeast. In summer the influence of the Azores High is much more noticeable. It extends into the Alpine region, bringing warm, dry weather. The Alps receive the majority of their precipitation in summer, even though a few high elevations experience an equal amount in winter. The amount of precipitation at high altitudes frequently differs markedly from that in the much lower valleys. In valleys open to the north, some of them funnel-shaped, clearly wetter conditions prevail than in well-protected valleys with an east-west orientation.

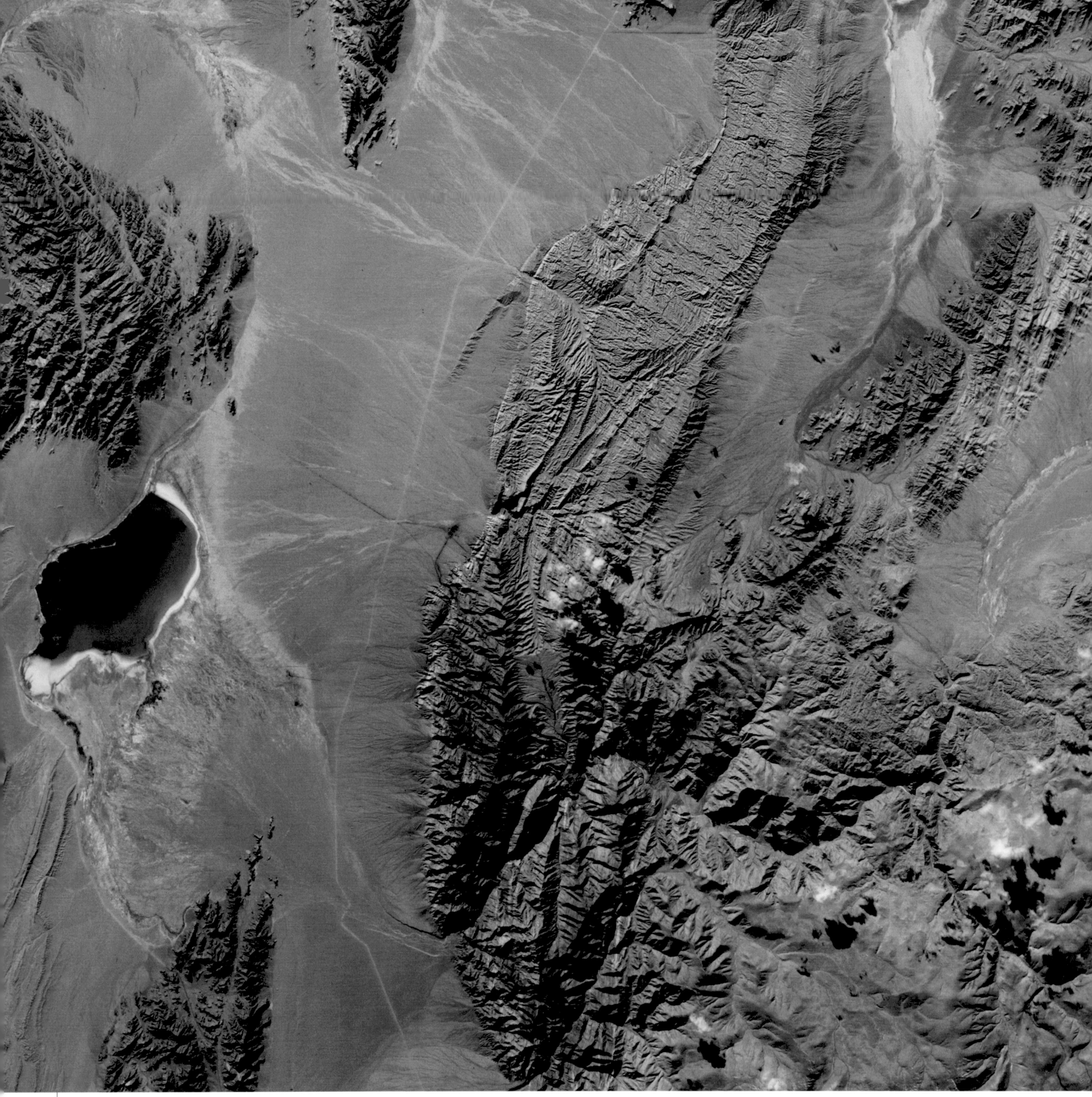

Humboldt Range, China

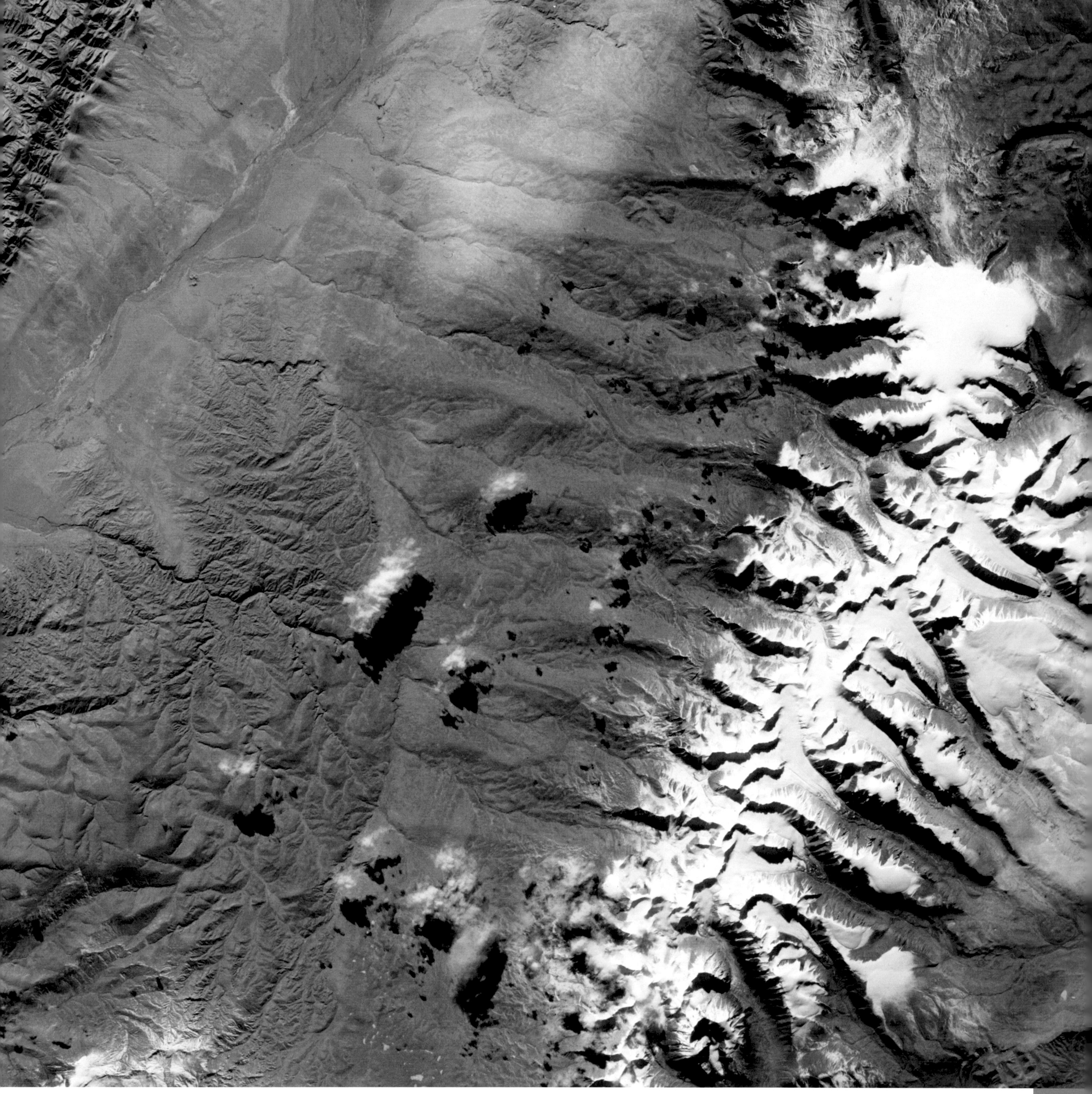

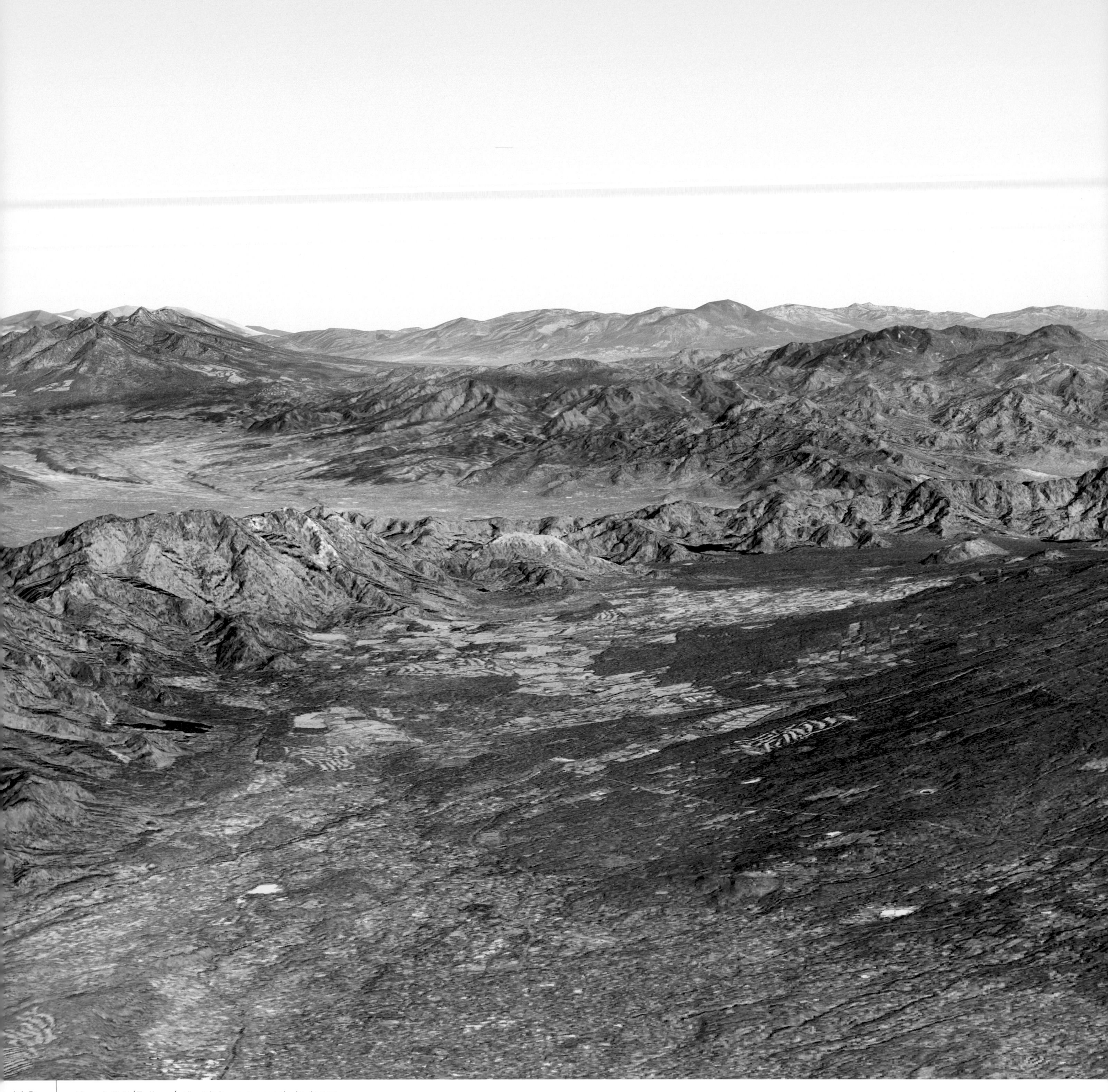

Mount Fuji (Fujisan), the highest mountain in Japan

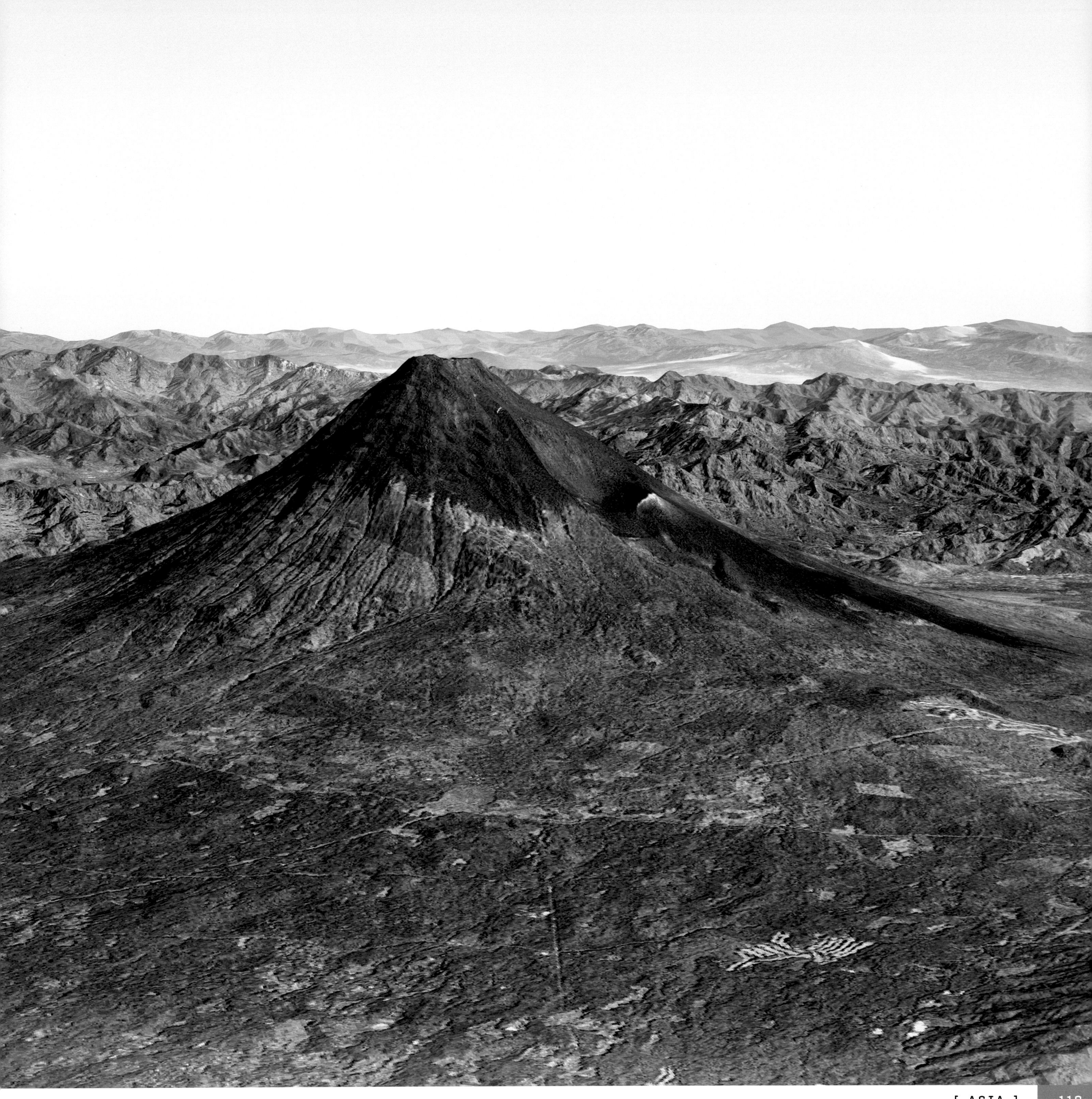

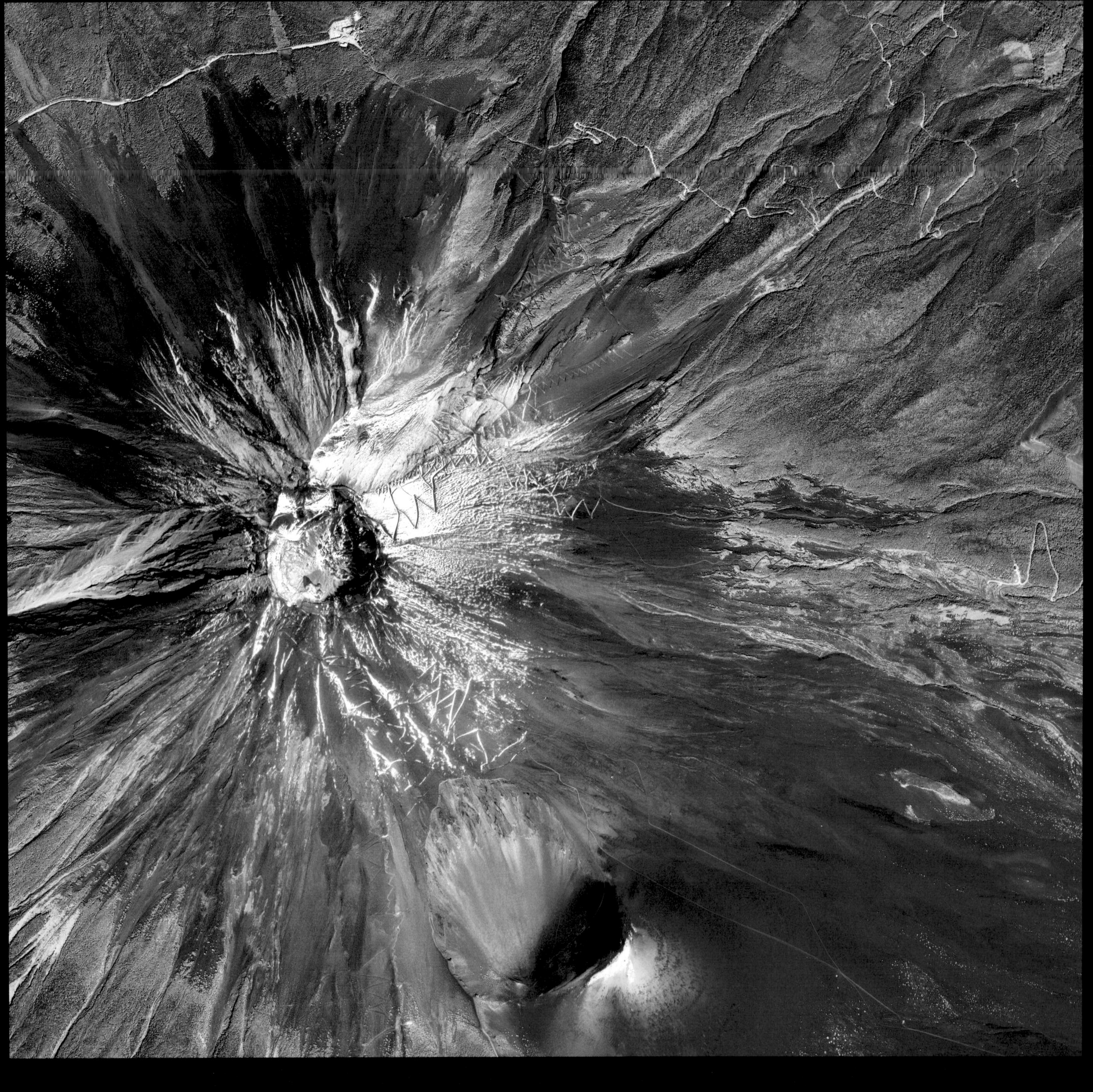

Detailed view of Mount Fuji with and without snow cover, Japan

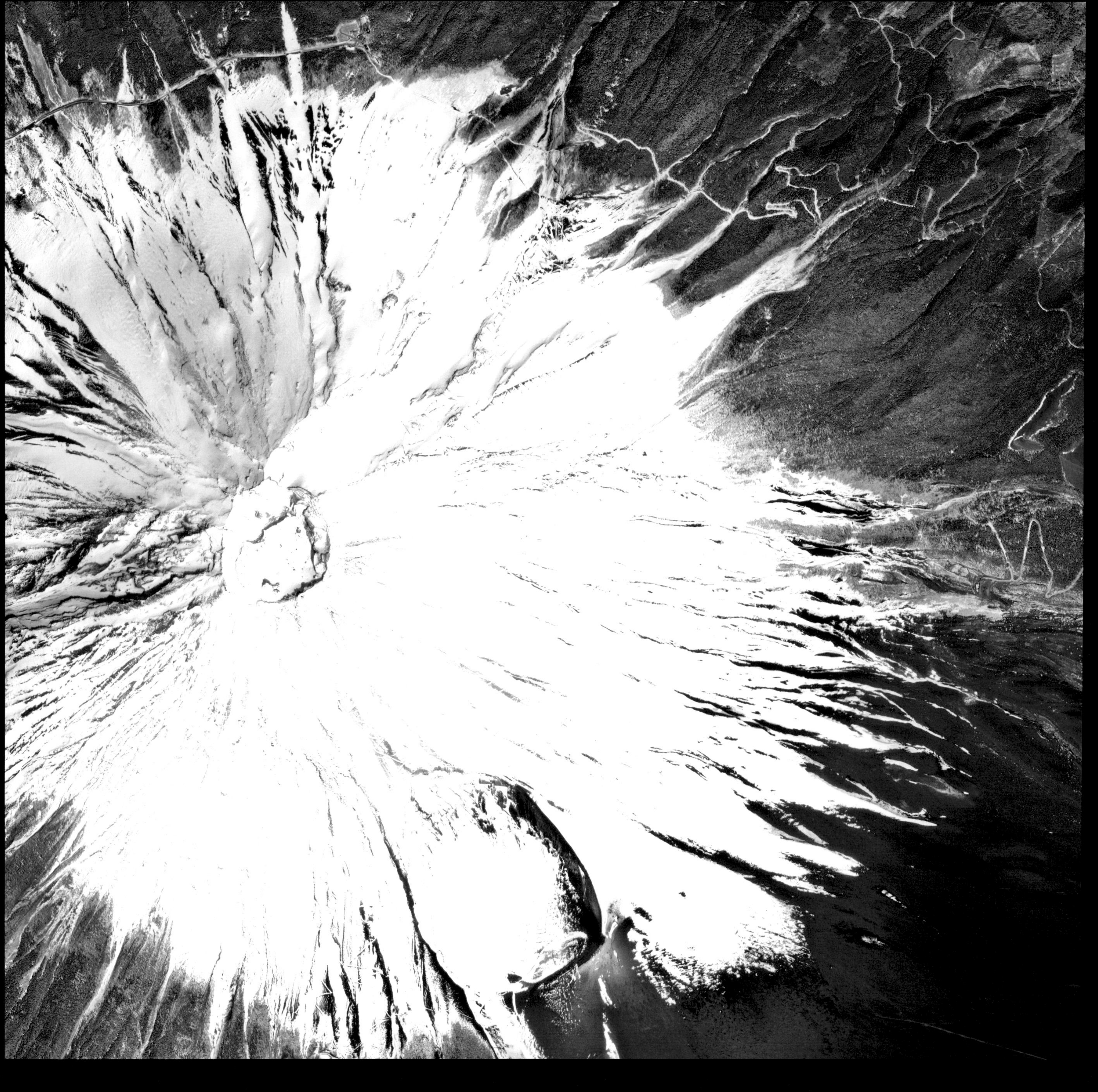

[AUSTRALASIA - ANTARCTICA]

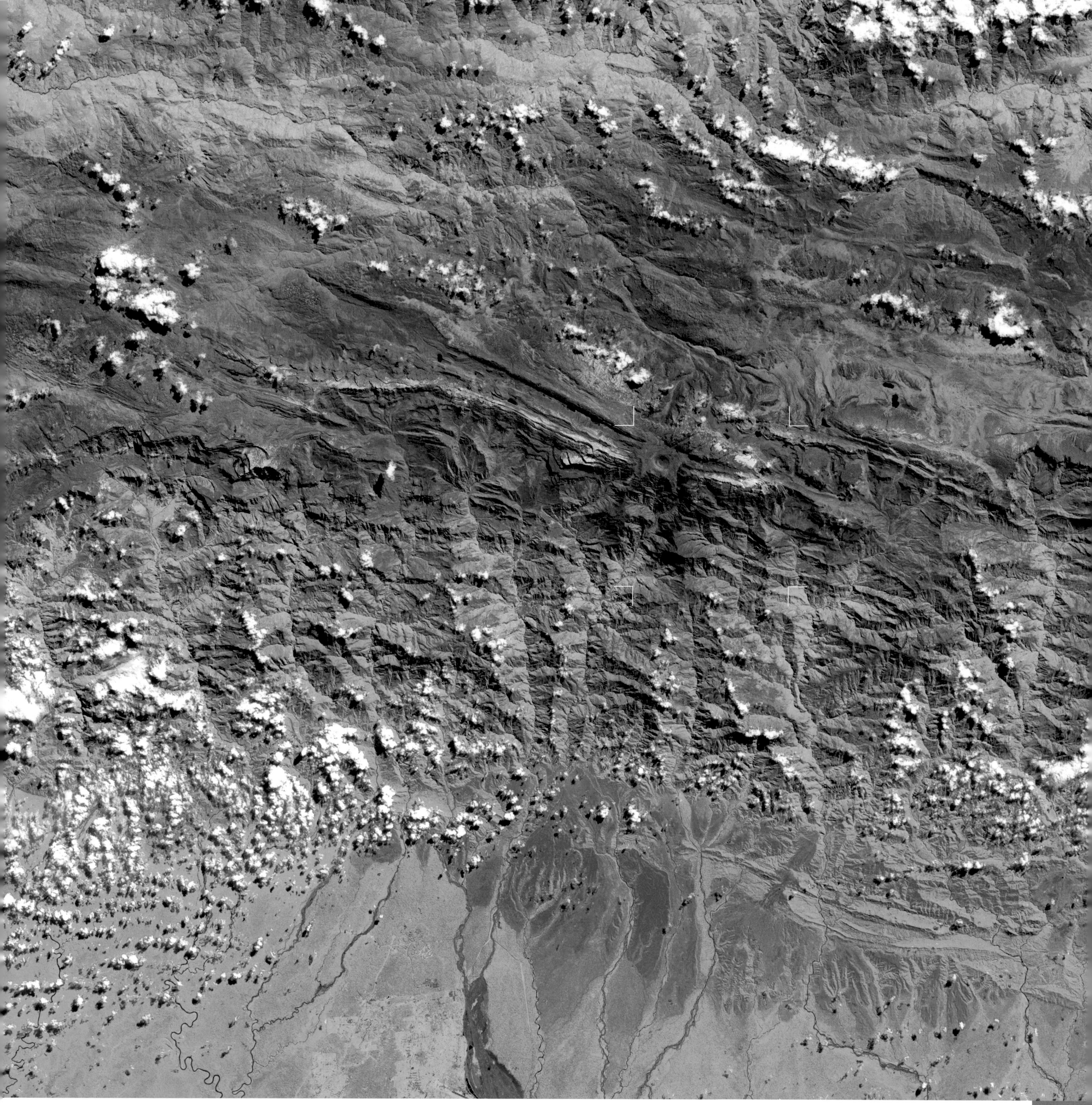

Puncak Jaya, the Carstensz Pyramid, New Guinea, Indonesia

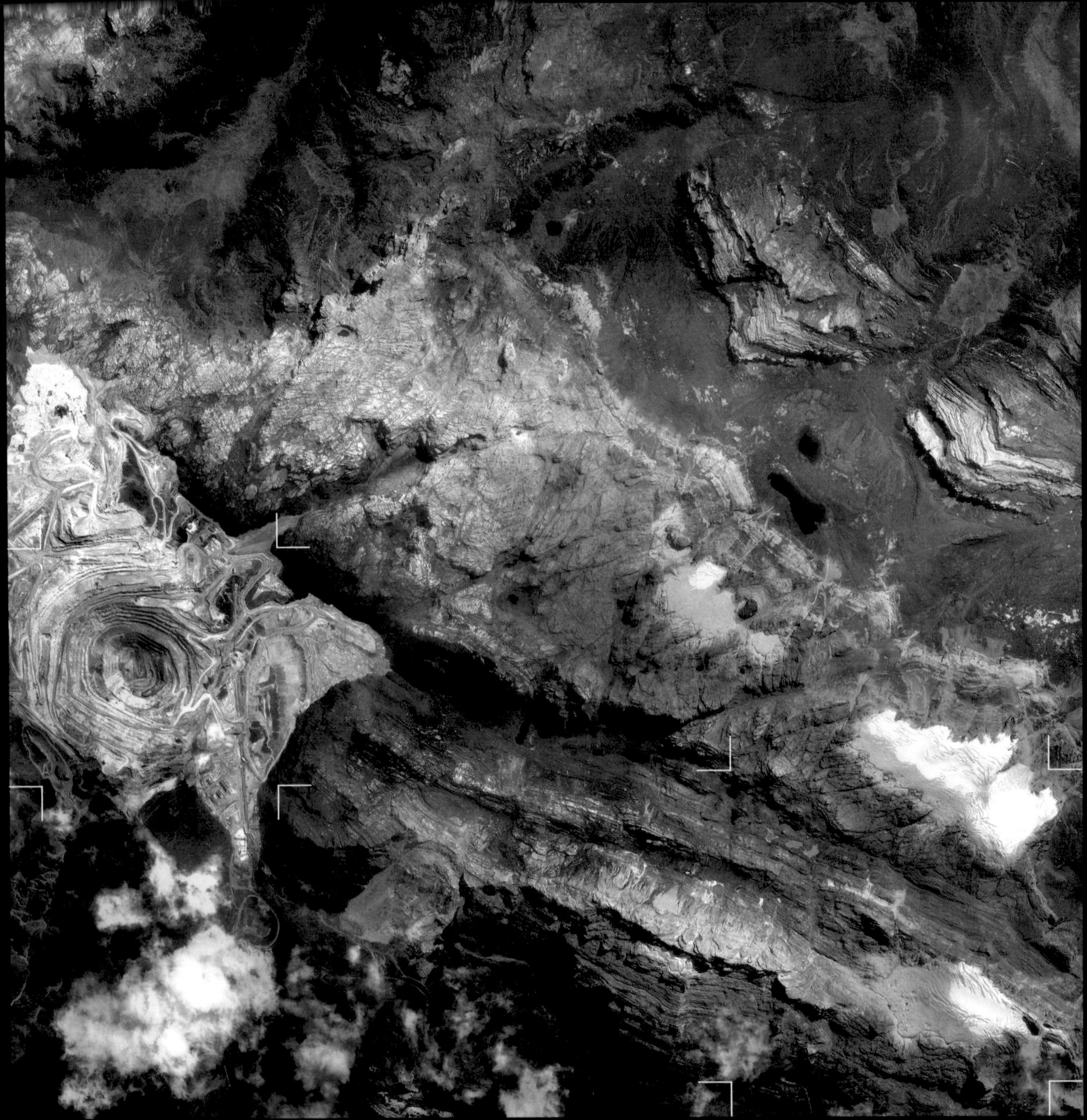

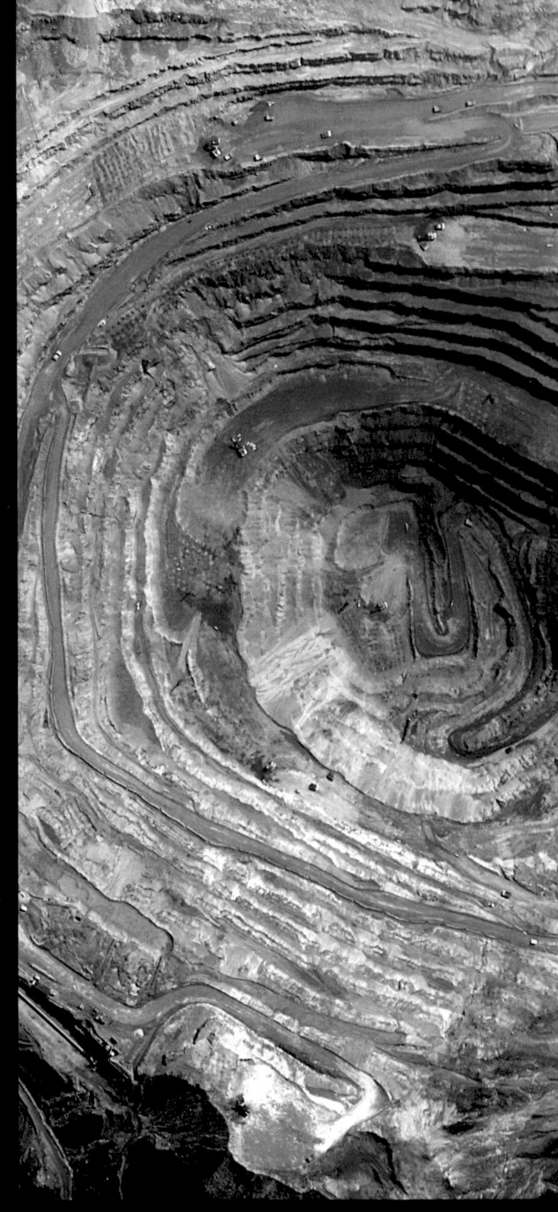

Detailed view of Puncak Jaya, Indonesia

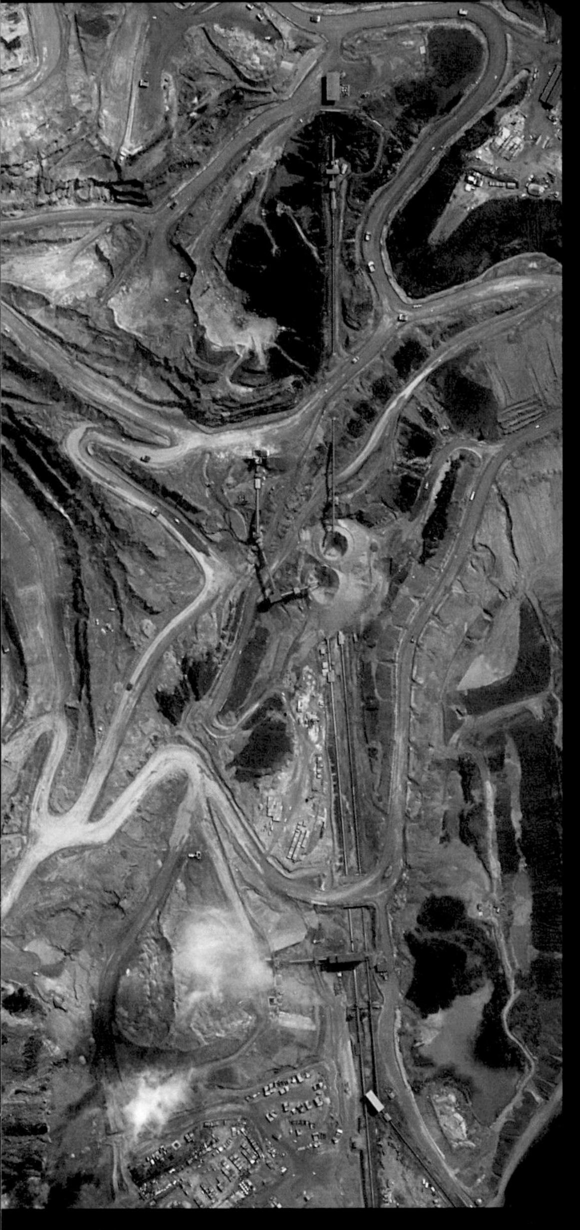

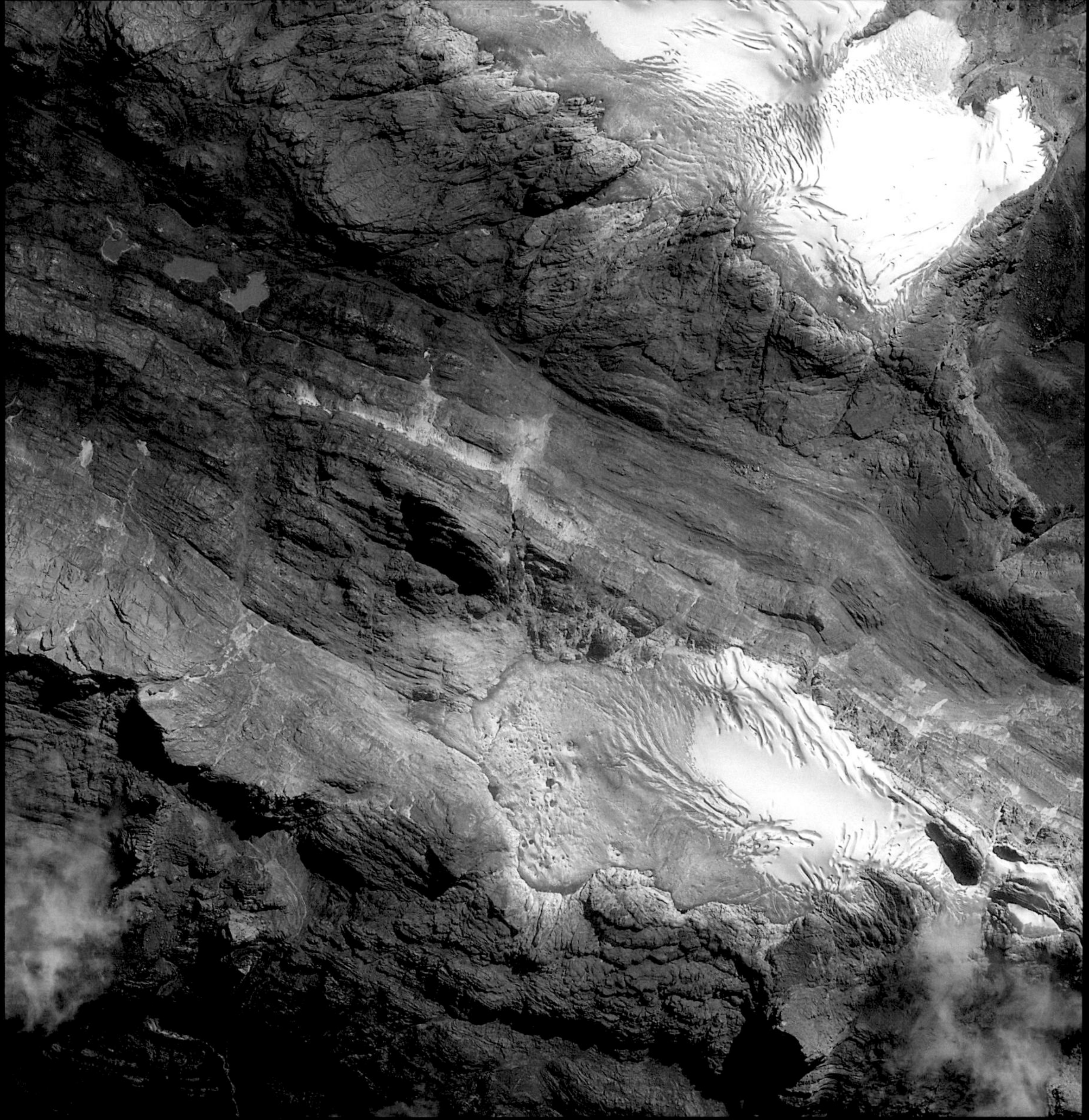

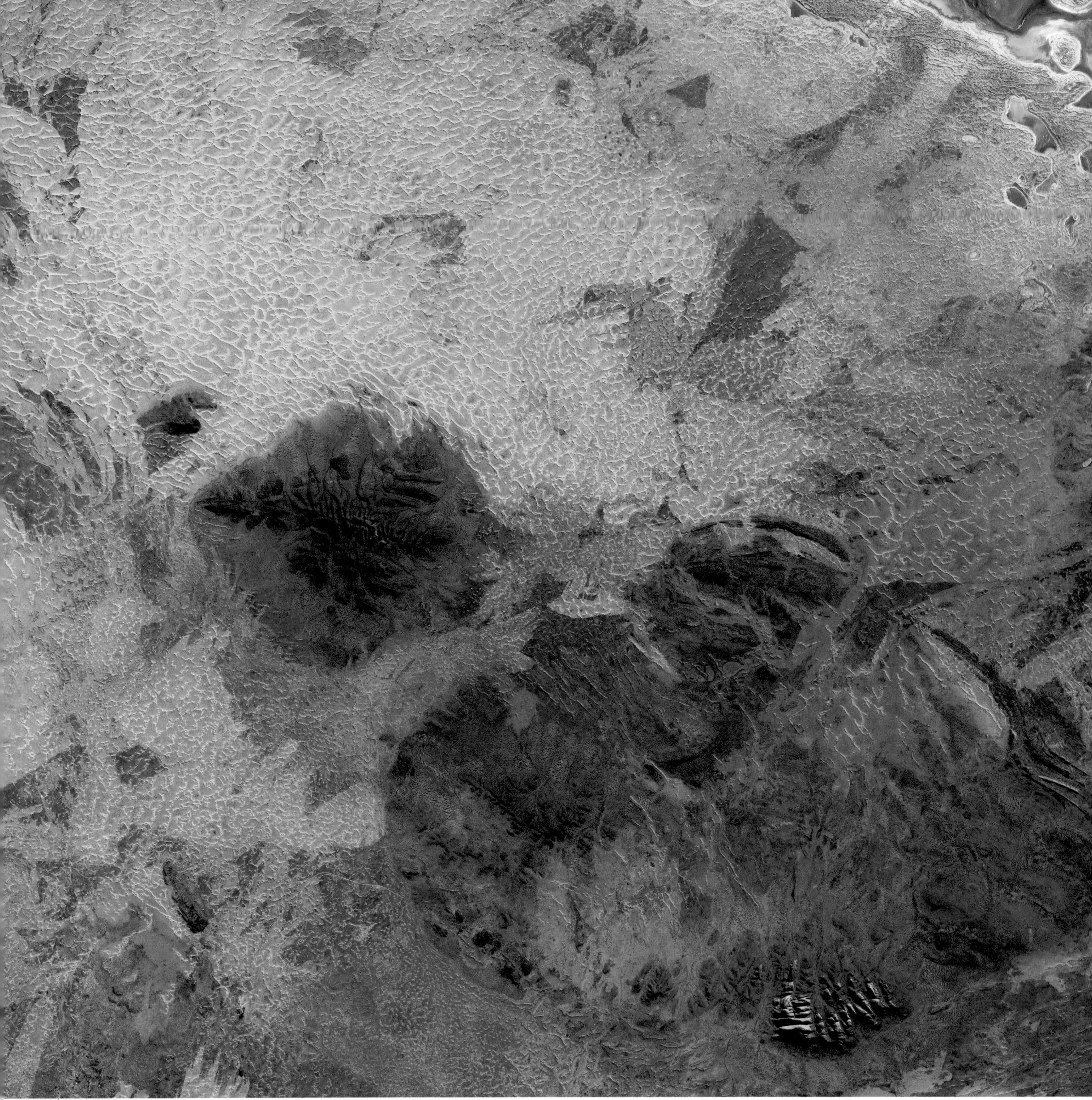

Ayers Rock (Uluru) and Kata Tjuta, Australia

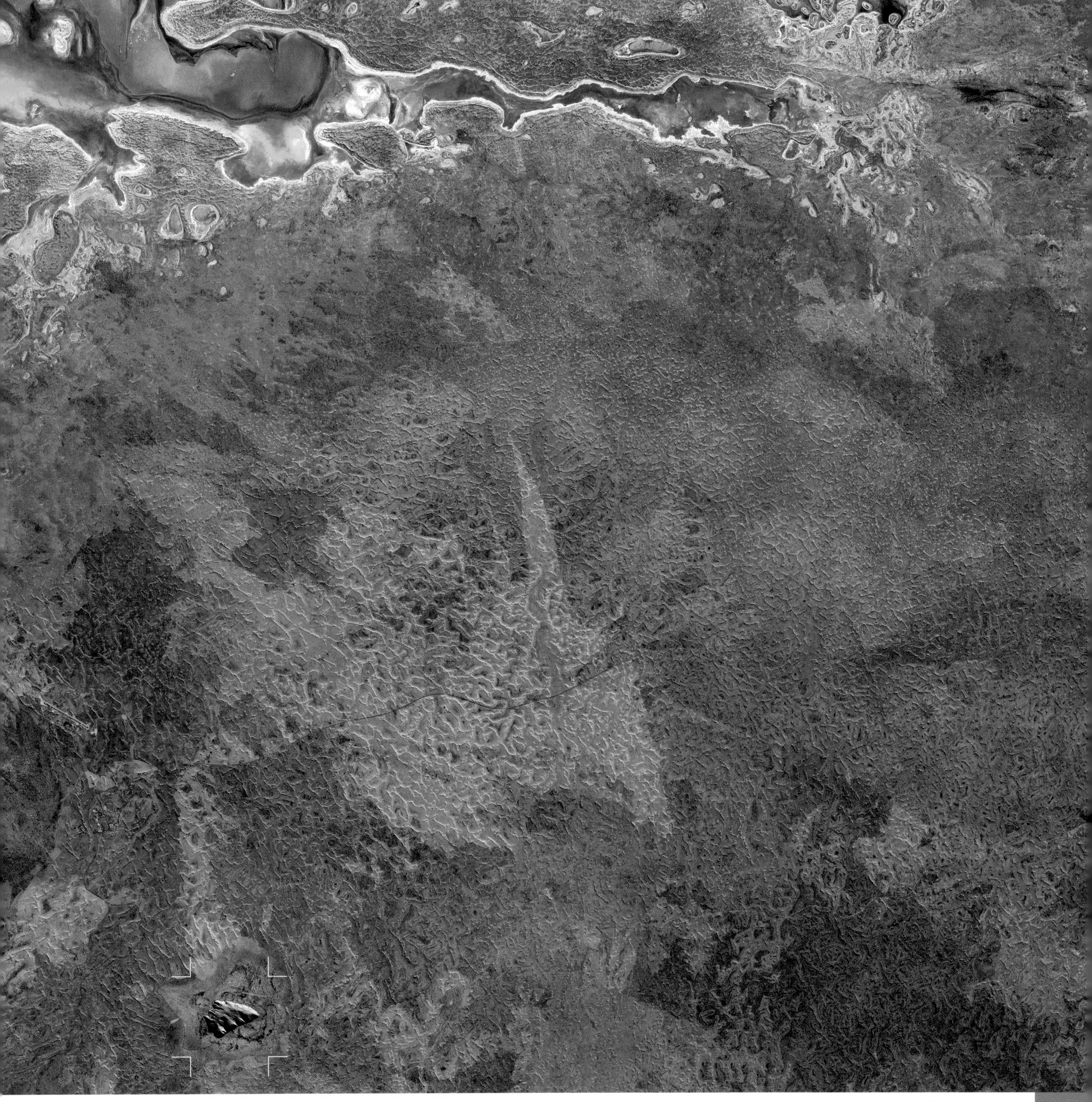

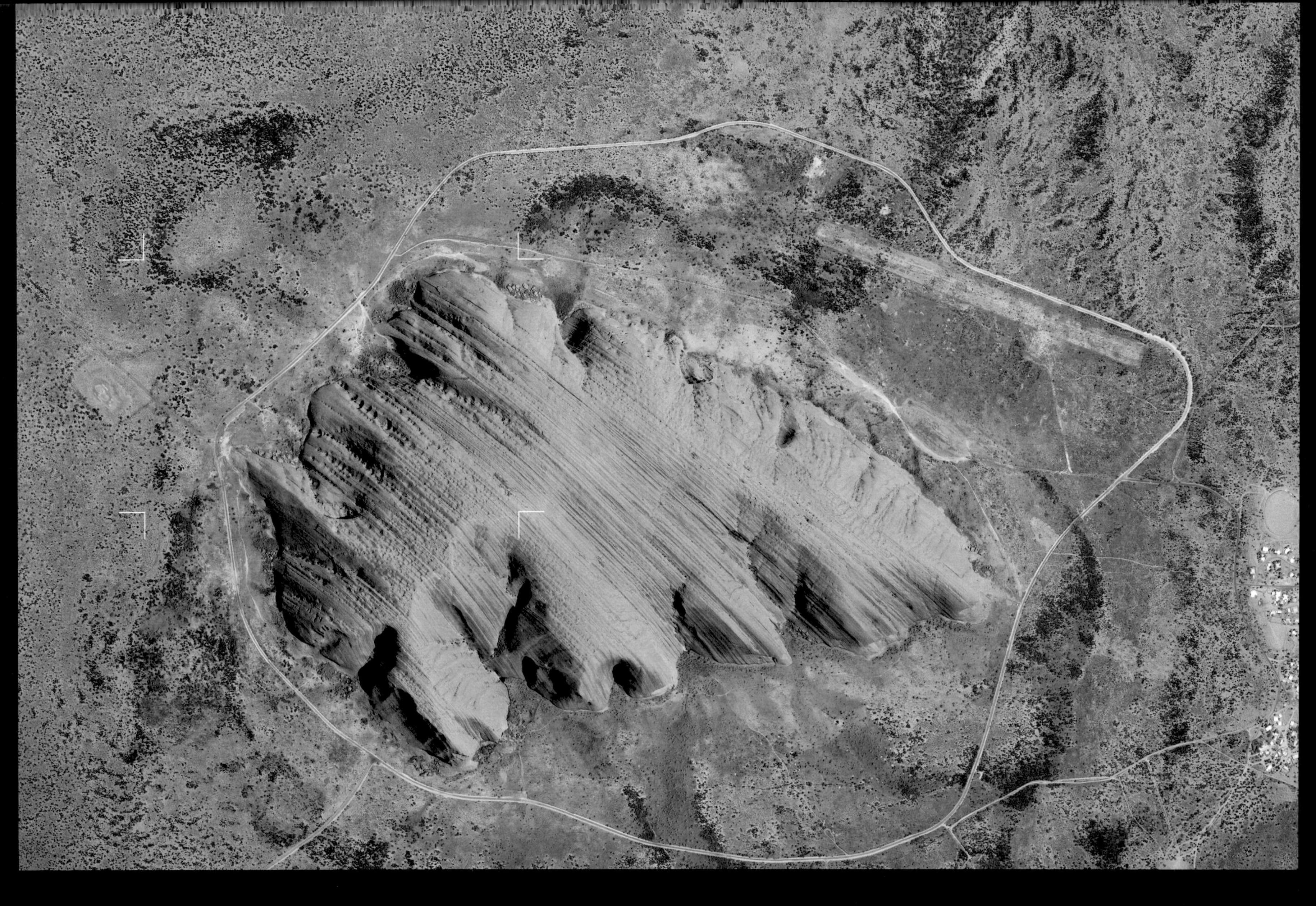

Detailed view of Ayers Rock (Uluru), "Shady Place," Australia

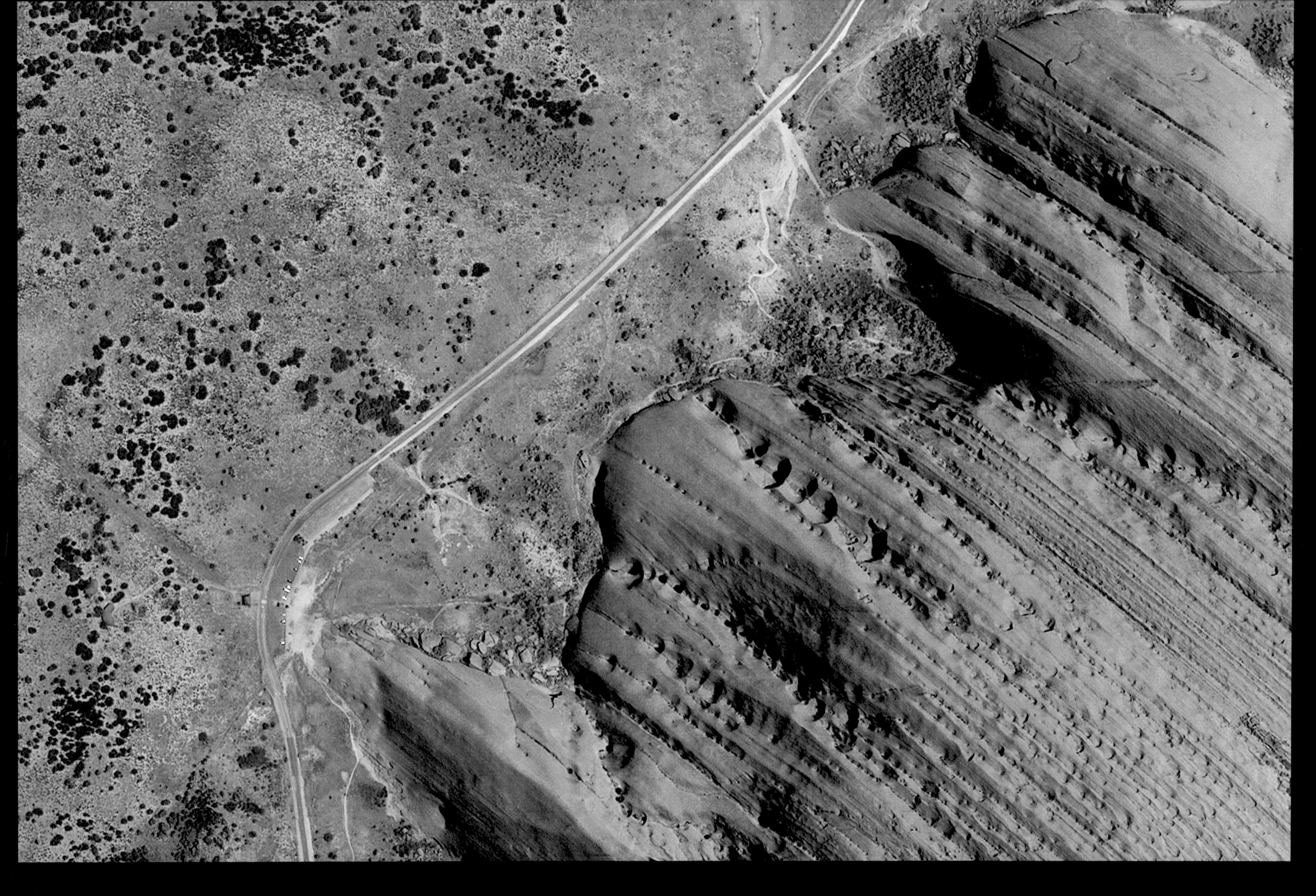

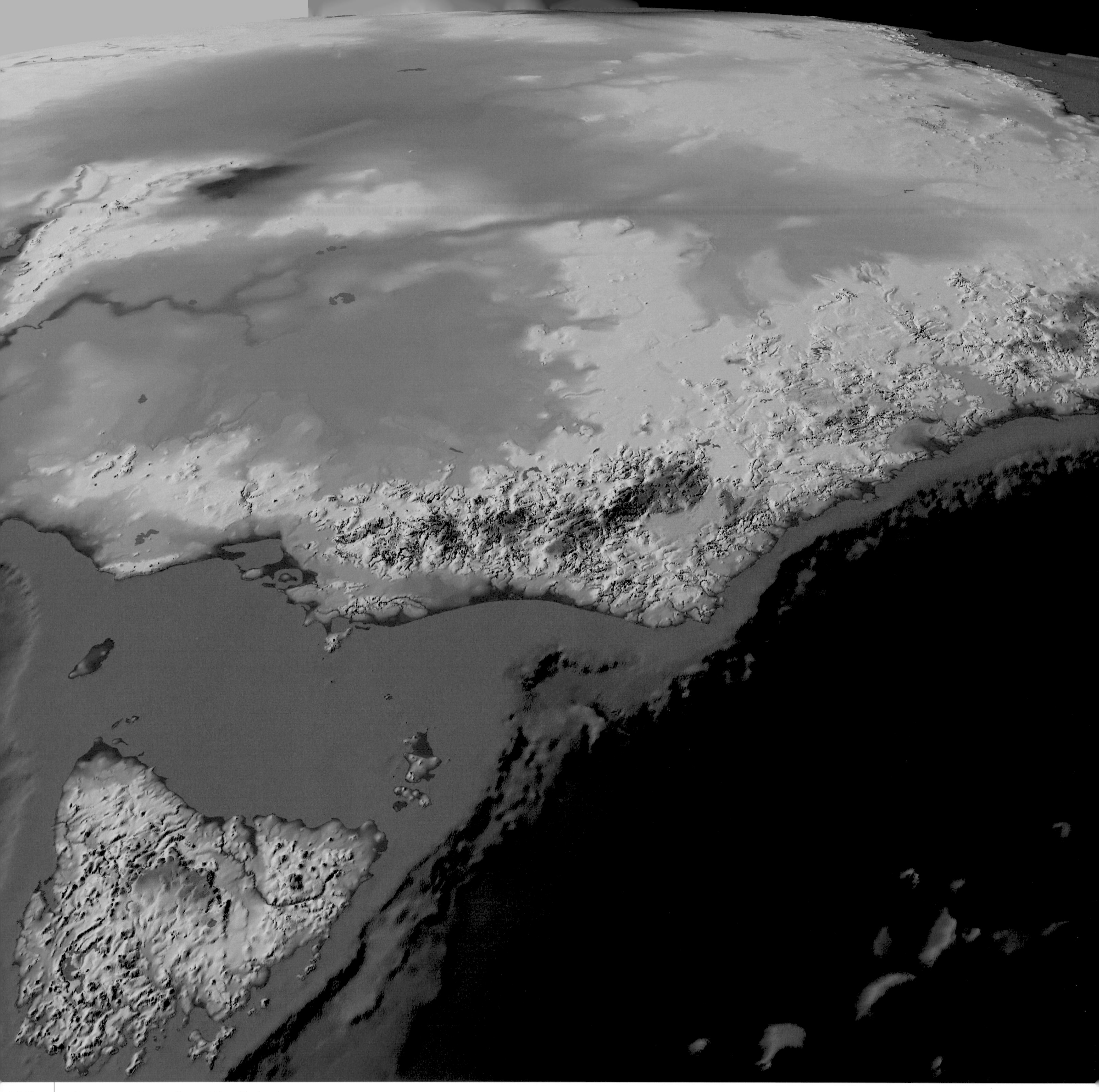

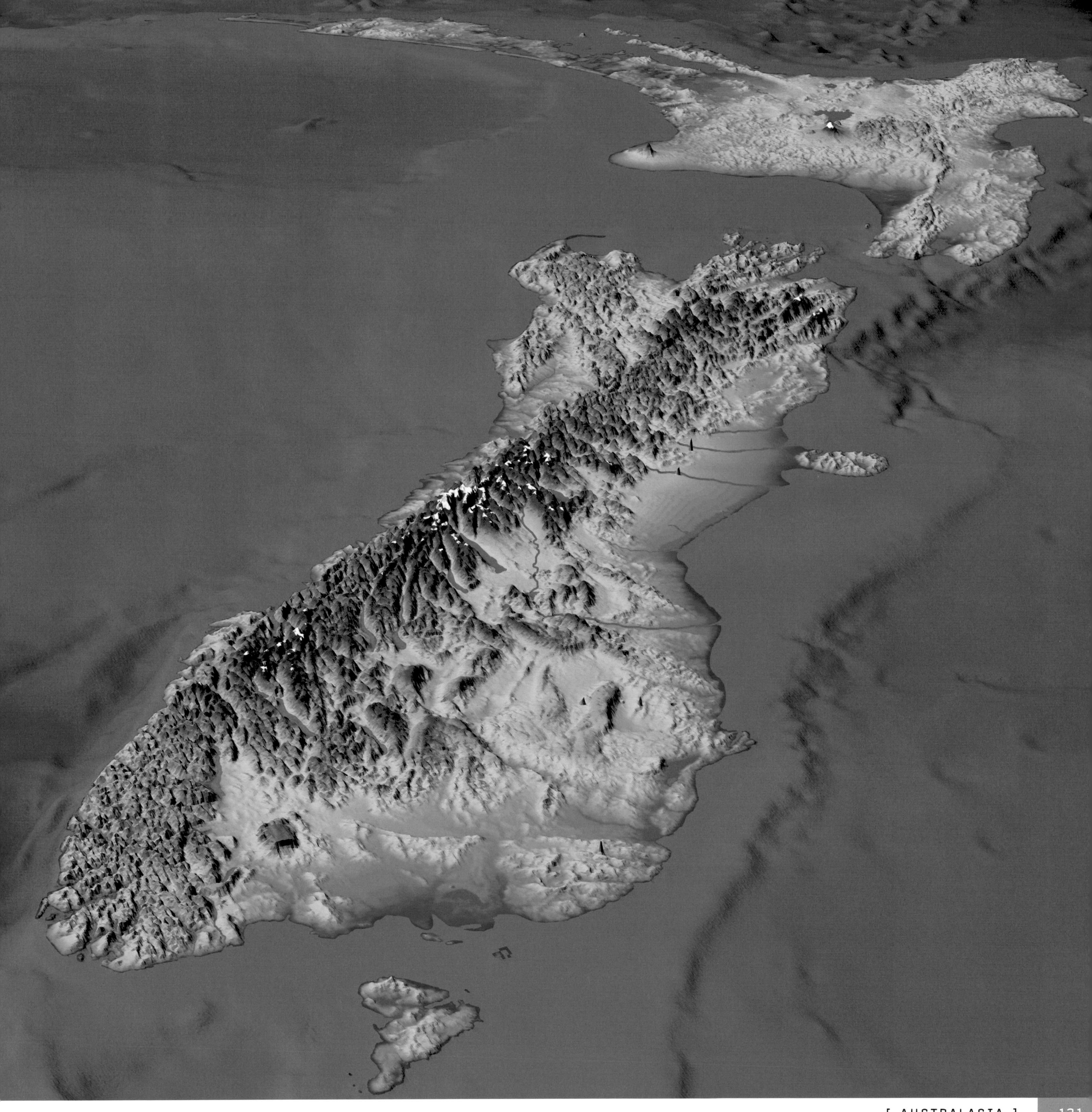

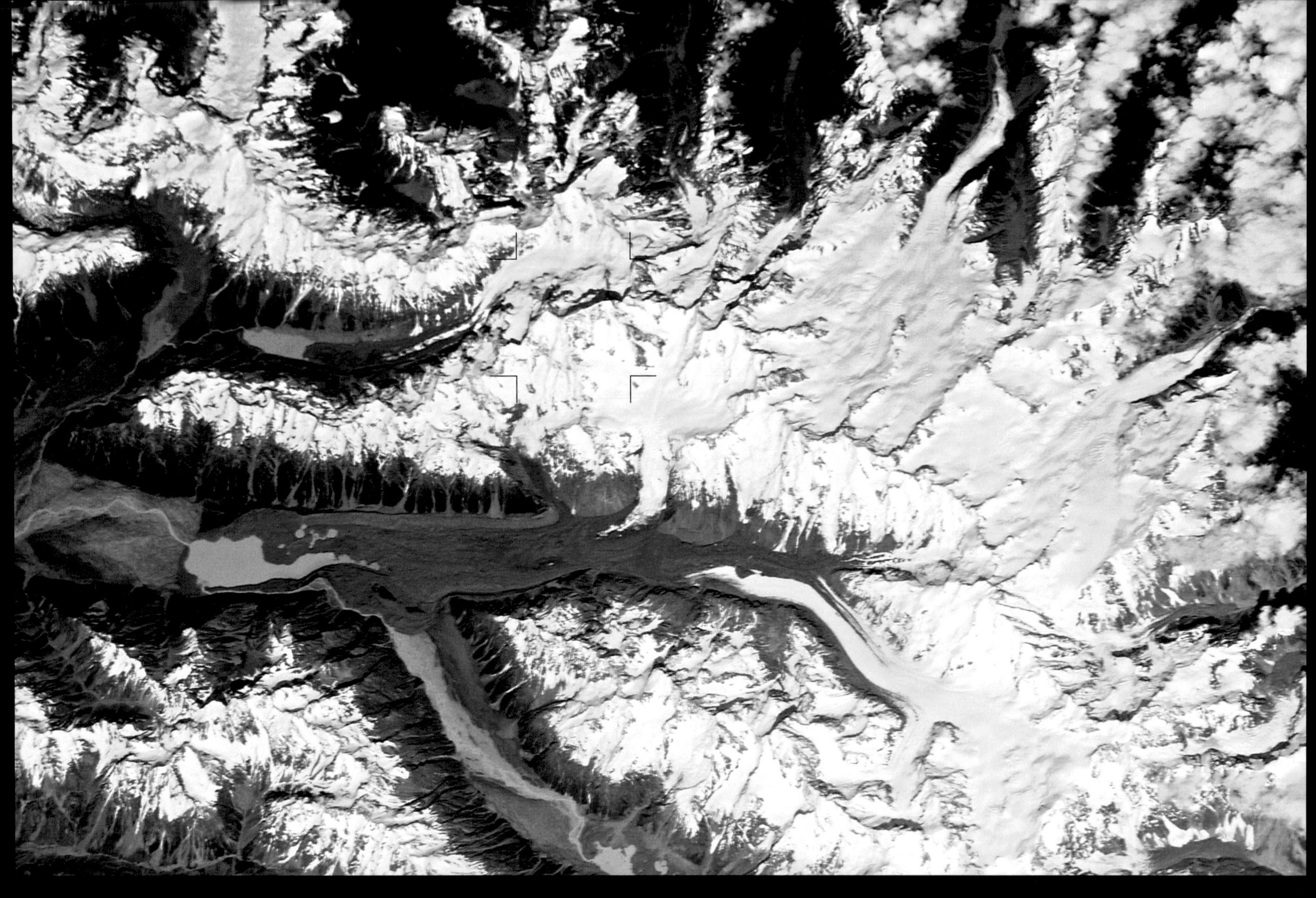

Mount Cook, "the Cloud Piercer," New Zealand

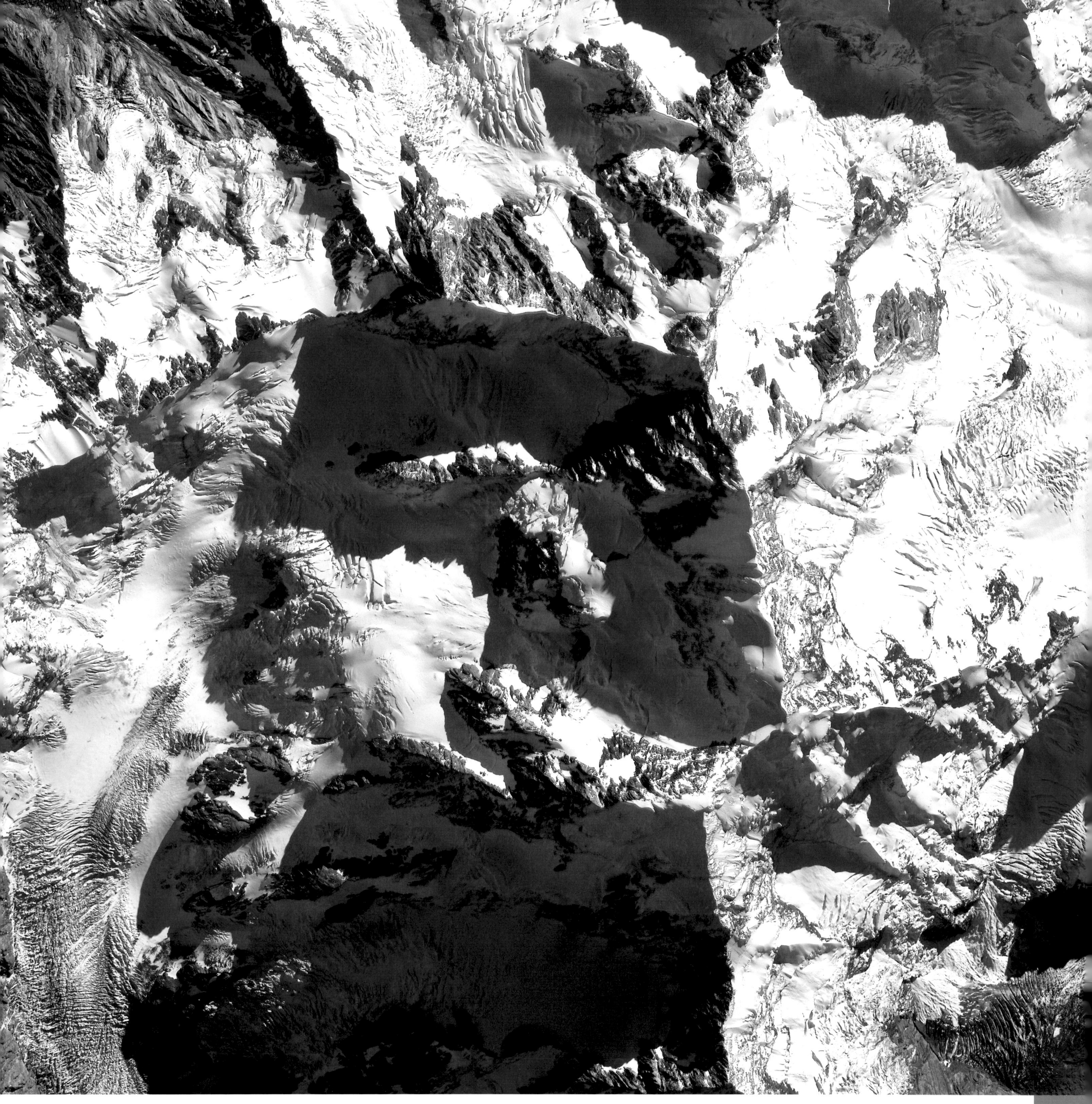

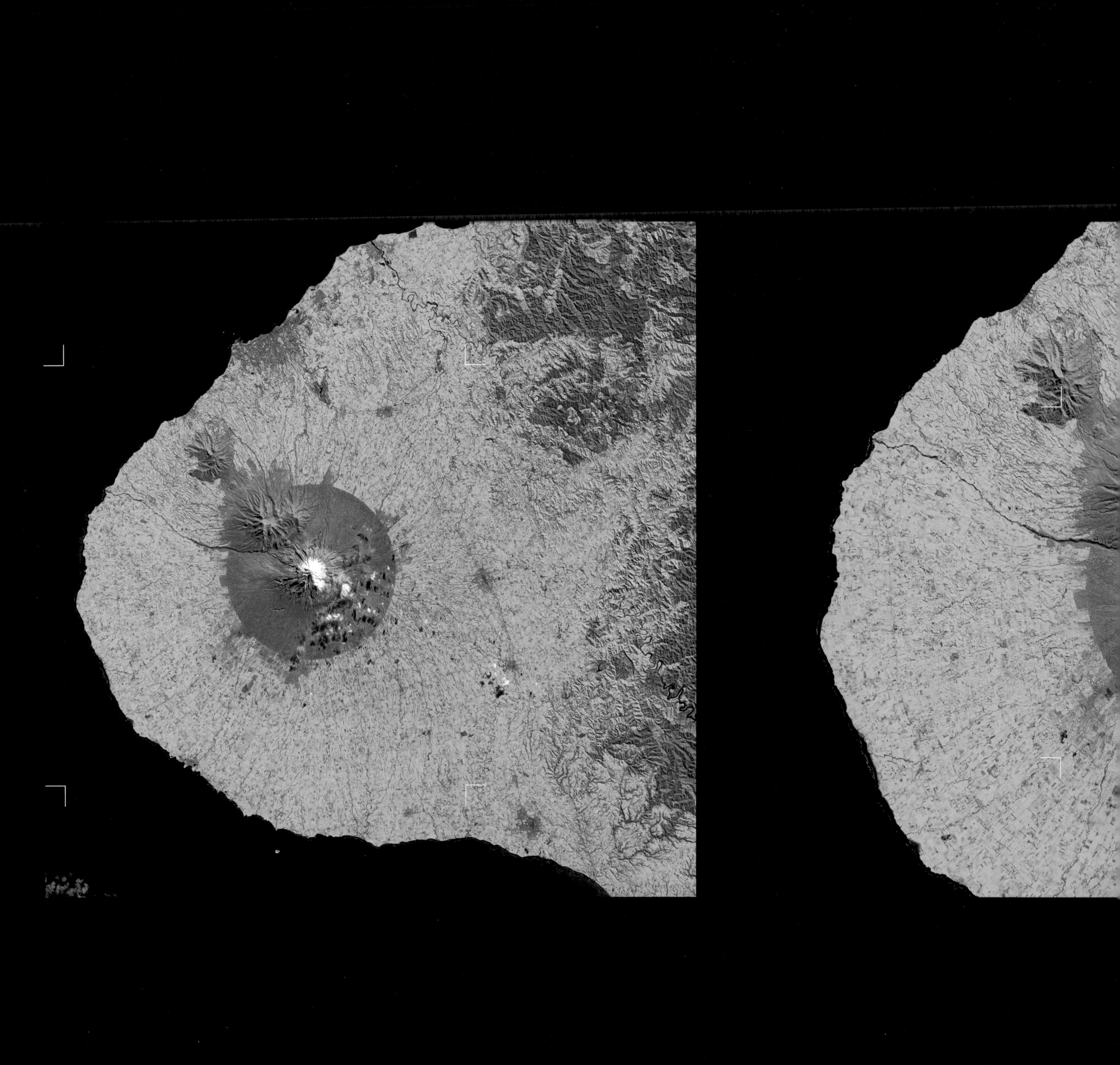

Mount Egmont, a perfect volcano, New Zealand

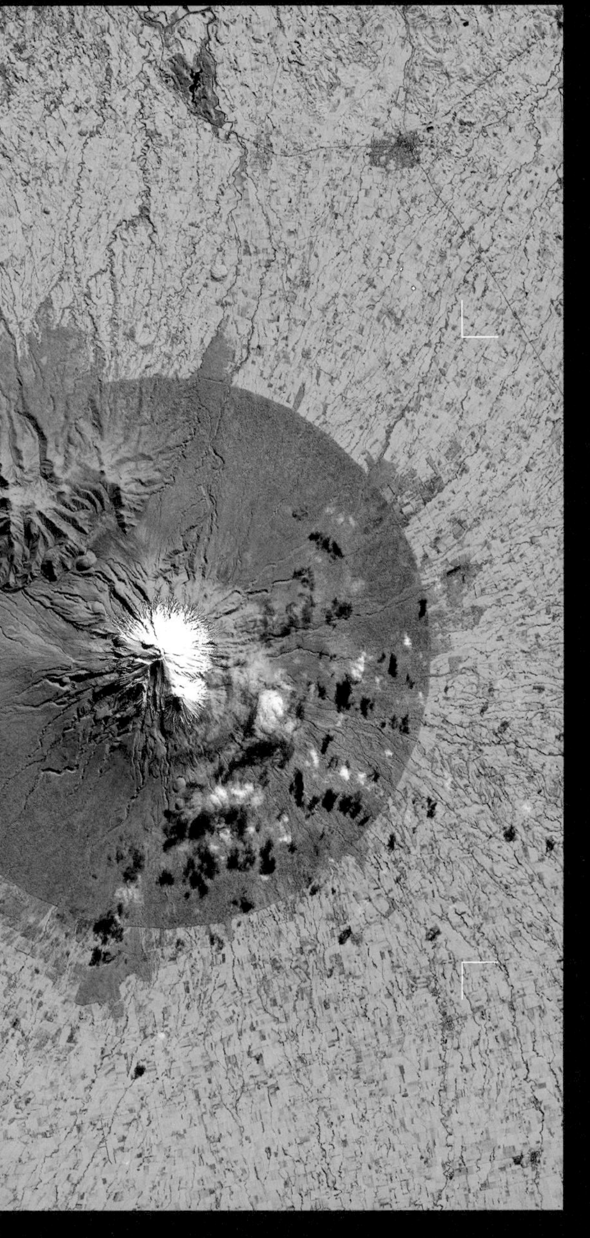

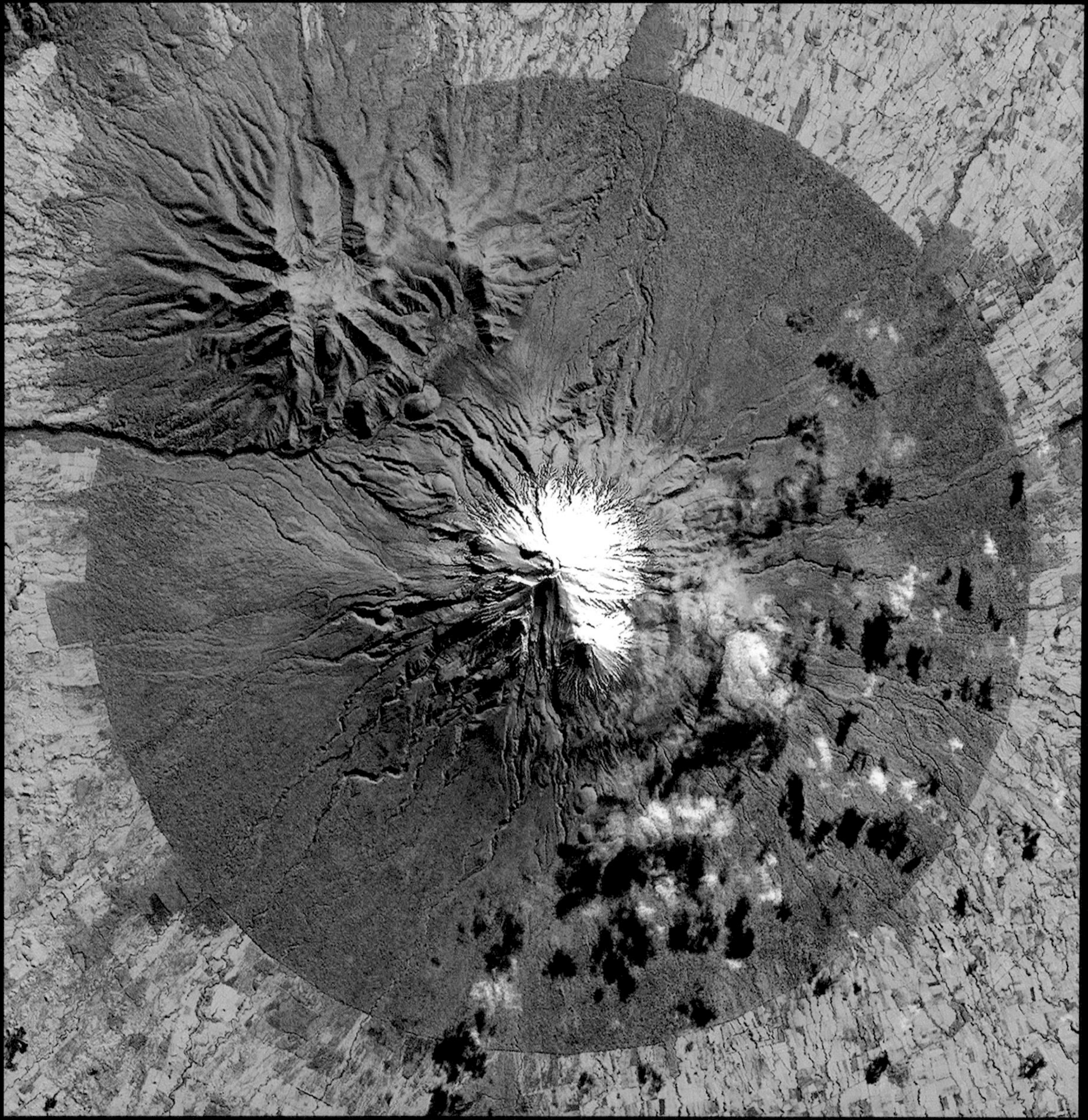

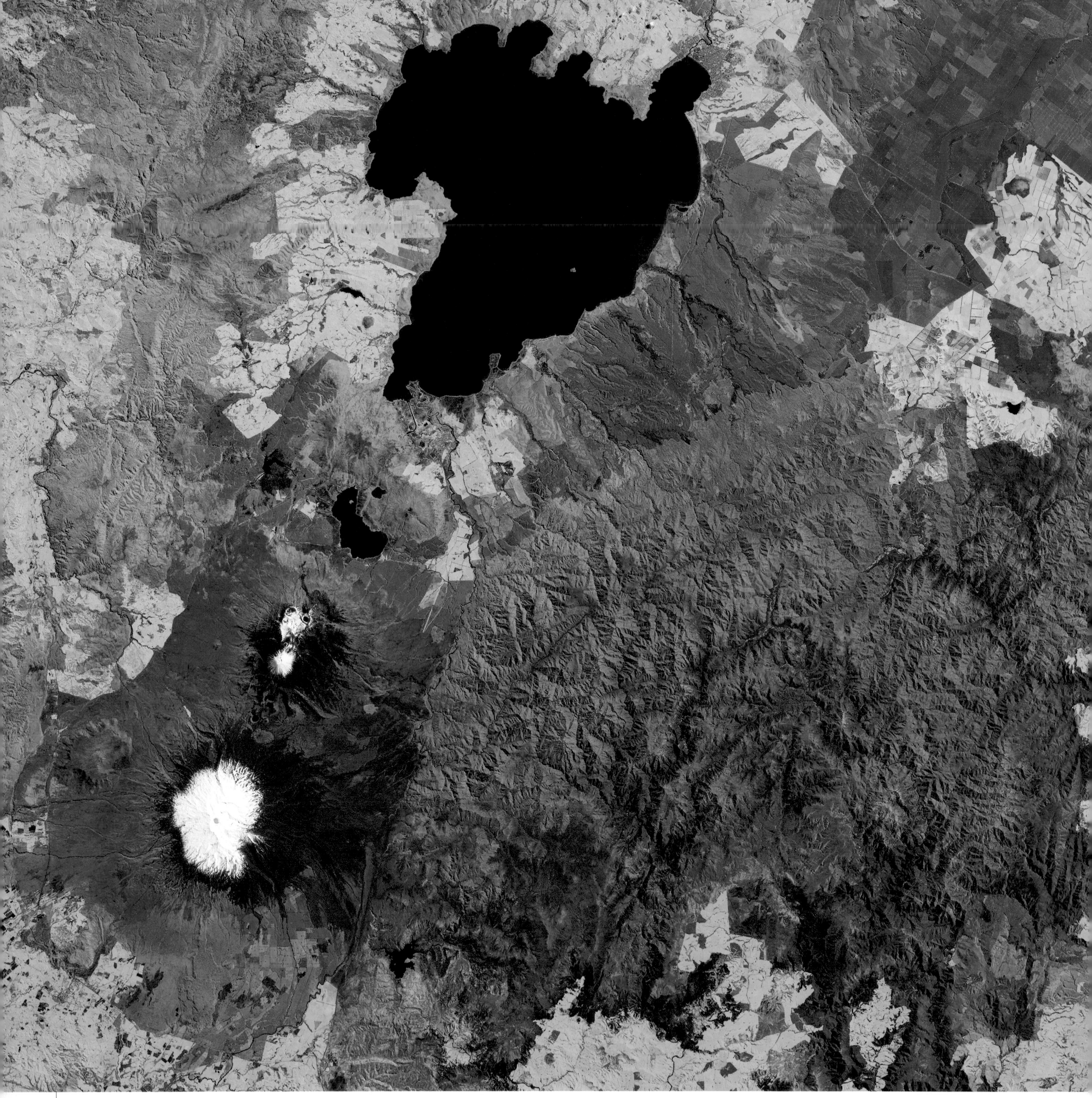

Mount Ruapehu and Lake Taupo, New Zealand

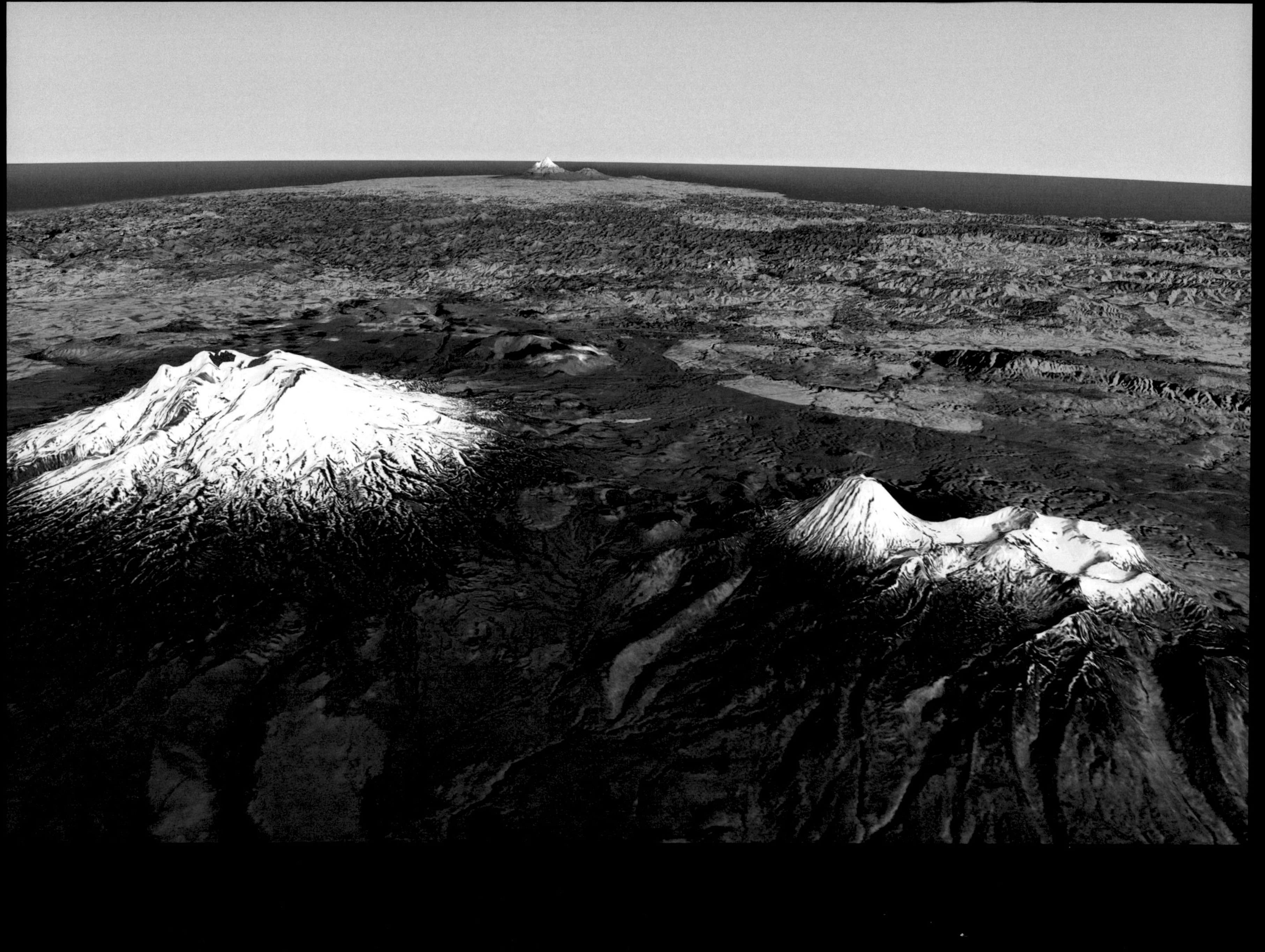

Mount Ruapehu, Ngauruhoe, and Mount Egmont, New Zealand

Antarctica
Earth's Refrigerator

RÜDIGER GLASER

Antarctica boasts one superlative that is generally unrecognized: it has the highest average elevation of any continent. This fact is mostly invisible however, because of its massive ice cap. Only the highest peaks, or nunataks, stand out like the poles of a circus tent. These days Antarctica is the subject of increasing interest because of its role in the global climate economy; three-fourths of the earth's freshwater reserves are locked in its ice shield, which could have a drastic impact on our lives in a changing climate.

Antarctica is a land of many superlatives. The largest icy wilderness in the world is at the same time the driest and windiest of the continents. Its ice masses, covering roughly 98 percent of its surface up to a depth of more than 8,000 feet, are its dominating features, and the continent itself accounts for roughly 10 percent of the earth's surface.

The icy continent is divided into an eastern part, Greater Antarctica, comprising roughly two-thirds of its area, and a western part, Lesser Antarctica, which includes the Antarctic Peninsula, the Usarp Mountains, the Ross Ice Shelf, and the Ross and Weddell seas. These are separated by the Queen Alexandra Range, a mountain system nearly 2,000 miles long, with Mount Kirkpatrick (14,855 feet) its highest peak.

A number of world climate records have been set in Antarctica, among them the record lowest temperature of -160°F at the Vostok Station and the record highest wind speed of more than 185 miles per hour. Antarctica's mean elevation of about 9,200 feet is also a continental record. A few peaks rise to heights of up to 16,400 feet. From the central highlands, a frozen wasteland with year-long temperatures from -90°F to -108°F and only as much as 2.36 inches of annual precipitation, ice-cold winds race down toward the coastal regions. This frigid air meets with milder oceanic air masses, creating a belt of storms, fog, and clouds around the continent. The regions dominated by the circumpolar west winds, the bane of seafarers for centuries, have been given colorful names depending on their latitude: the "Roaring Forties," the "Furious Fifties," and finally, in the region of pack ice, the "Screaming Sixties."

Antarctica's marine boundary is a roughly twenty-five-mile-wide zone, the so-called Antarctic Convergence, in which warmer water from the north encounters the cold Antarctic waters. Antarctica presents not only spectacular scenery of rock and ice, it is also an important player in the regulation of the global climate. And that is not all: its current armor of ice, amounting to roughly 13.5 million square kilometers of inland ice and roughly 1.5 million square kilometers of shelf ice, accounts for roughly 75 percent of the earth's freshwater reserves. The largest ice masses cover the eastern Antarctic plateau area up to 13,000 feet deep.

Antarctica went through a number of drastic geological changes before it assumed its current make up as the "refrigerator" of the earth. Two hundred eighty million years ago, the hypothetical former supercontinent in the Southern Hemisphere, Gondwana, which included South America, Africa, peninsular India, Australia, and Antarctica, was in roughly the same position as the South Pole. It gradually drifted northward into subtropical and tropical regions, and broke apart some 170 million years ago, then with violent and long-lasting volcanic activity the separate plate fragments went their own ways. The first to break free was East Africa, and around 55 million years ago Australia and Antarctica also became separate island continents. After developing the landscape of subtropical conditions, with forests of southern beech and podocarpus dominating the landscape, Antarctica again migrated toward the region of the South Pole—with far-reaching consequences for the world's climate. Today it is assumed that its ice shield has gradually built up since the Miocene, or over the past 15 to 20 million years. During the global alternation of warm and ice ages in the Quaternary period, for roughly 2 to 2.5 million years, Antarctica's glaciers have repeatedly advanced and melted back, until the present conditions, a warm period from a global point of view, set in.

The largest Antarctic glaciers today are the Byrd, Mulock, Nimrod, Beardmore, Shackleton, Scott, and Amundsen glaciers, all of which converge on the Ross Ice Shelf, which is about the size of France and comprises roughly 30 percent of the shelf ice. The Lambert Glacier, roughly 270 miles long, is the largest valley glacier on earth. Only 2 percent of the continent is ice-free—room enough to provide a home for countless lichens and mosses, and two species of flowering plants.

Antarctica plays a unique role in the debate about climate change. If its roughly 30 million cubic kilometers of ice were to melt, the sea level would rise as much as 200 feet. But the somewhat apocalyptic consequences of that scenario are not envisioned even in the most pessimistic climate change models. Realistic estimates assume that the core of the great ice shield will contribute not at all or only very slightly to a rise in sea level, although the edges make up a considerable share. The Antarctic Peninsula is of particular significance here, as it accounts for up to a fourth of Antarctica's ice turnover with some 220 gigatons a year. It is a fact that observations going back many years show a warming trend for the Antarctic Peninsula that considerably exceeds the prognoses from global climate models. In the past fifty years it has seen a rise in the annual mean temperature of roughly 4.5°F. Many areas close to the coast already show large areas of summer wet snow cover or even denuded glaciers. Also, the sea-ice boundary has been steadily retreating, in the Bellinghausen Sea as much as 125 miles in the past thirty years. The accelerated break-up of the ice shelf over the past twenty years has also been fully documented. Another observable phenomenon that has caused the world community to sit up and pay attention is the holes in the protective ozone layer over Antarctica, and it has since

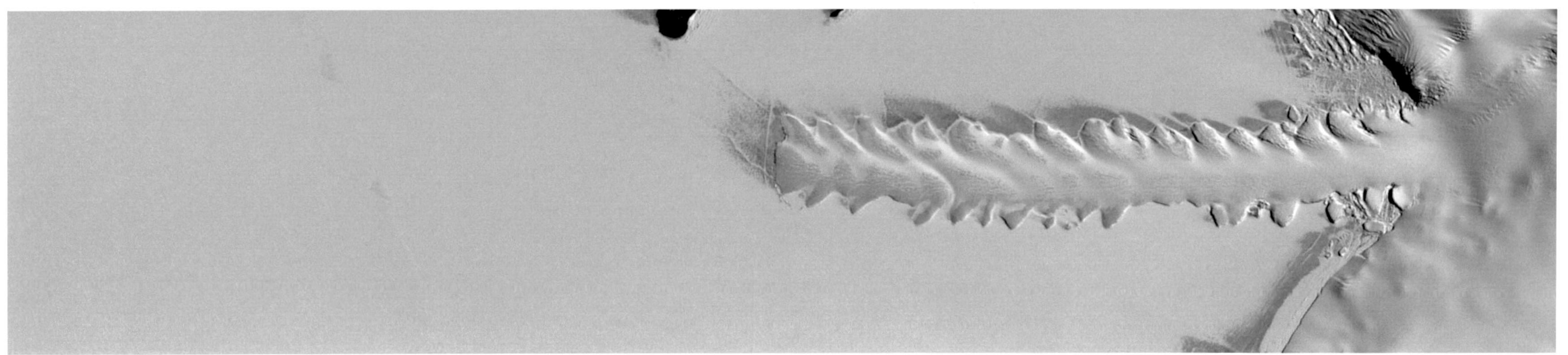

The Erebus Glacier, Ross Island, Antarctica, on November 20, 2001. The earth's refrigerator is not only the highest continent, with numerous climate records and a majority of the world's reserves of fresh water, it also houses a multitude of stunning natural sculptures.

been carefully monitored. All in all, one can say that the earth's refrigerator, which plays a crucial role in maintaining the global climate, is already showing signs of fever.

Since its discovery by Edward Bransfield in 1820 and the spectacular race to the South Pole, reached by Roald Amundsen on December 14, 1911, and by Robert Scott only a short time later on January 18, 1912, the island continent has been the object of a tug-of-war between countries with territorial ambitions and rivalries among scientists. The English, French, Australians, New Zealanders, and Norwegians recognized each other's claims, but not Chile and Argentina. It was only after twelve nations signed the Antarctica Agreement in 1961 that the proprietary confusion was sorted out. Antarctica belongs to everyone and to no one. Seventeen nations are represented at the sixty-eight research stations now in operation there, which have been coordinated since 1958 by the Scientific Committee for Antarctic Research (SCAR). What at first sounds like a pleasant scientific sabbatical can mean joyless surroundings and miserable housing with the same menu for weeks on end in stations built from steel pipes and containers. According to the Antarctica Agreement, all stations are required to be completely dismantled once they are no longer in use.

In 1957 the Russians set up one of the most prominent stations, Vostok, in the center of the eastern Antarctic ice shield near the south magnetic pole. Supplies have to be transported by tractor across the ice from the coast more than 850 miles away, which can easily take a month. At Vostok they immediately began recording record cold temperatures for the planet. One of its main projects, together with France and America, was to drill an ice core through the 12,000-foot-thick shield, which provides useful information to draw conclusions from about climate changes over the past 420,000 years. Since 1994 the first international station has been operating on King George Island, near the Antarctic Peninsula. In the Dallmann lab, Germany, Argentina, and the Netherlands study the ice-free coastal waters and their ecology.

Even though global environmental changes affect this continent especially, the numerous scientific activities and the considerable increase in tourism in the last decades have led to further direct environmental damage. Foreign plants, diseases, and soils have been introduced, noticeably disturbing breeding colonies. Rubbish from the stations stands in piles, and many combustible fuels have been left behind. Stricter policies have been announced in an effort to manage the issues of garbage and pollution. To begin with, a major clean-up campaign is underway to get rid of the worst of the rubbish. Well-meaning as such endeavors are, their effect is minuscule compared to the changes being registered on a global scale.

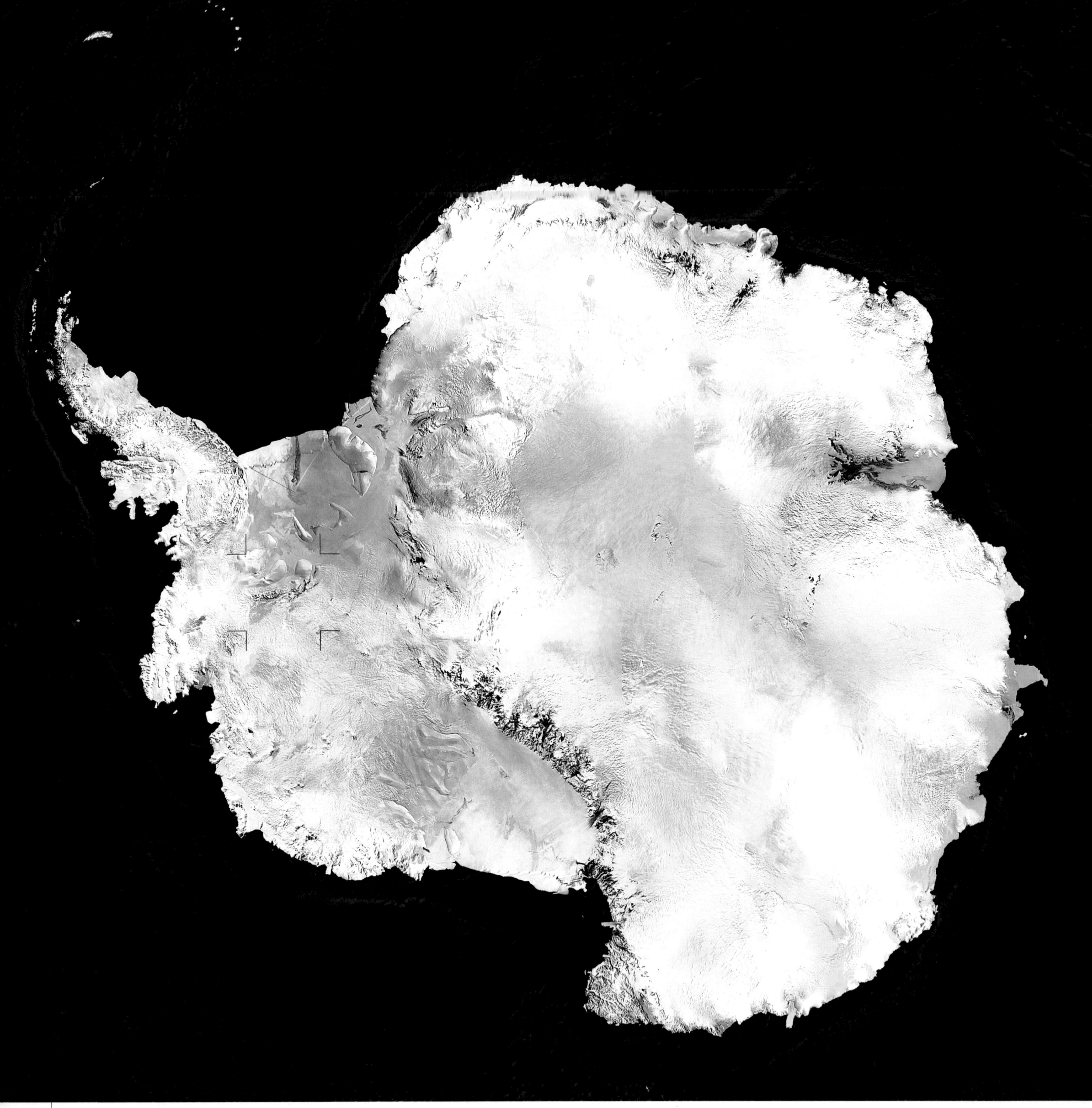

Satellite image mosaic of Antarctica

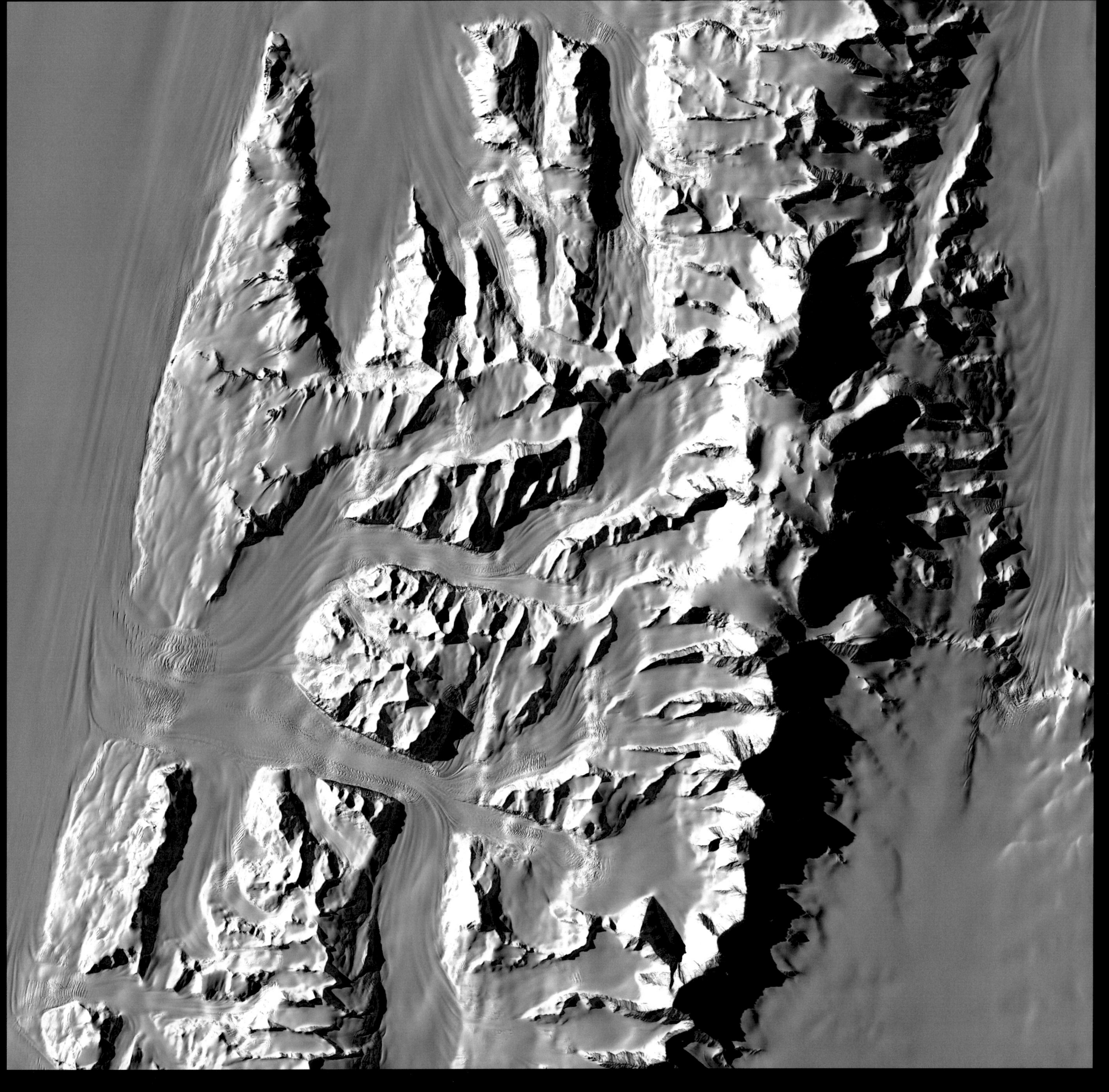

Ellsworth Mountains, mountains beneath and above the ice, Antarctica

Cathedrals of Ice
The Mountains of Antarctica

STEPHEN VENABLES

Antarctica, for me, is a place that exists more in the imagination than in reality—a symbol of everything that is remote, wild, unattainable. When I think of Antarctica, the first images are not of vertical mountains but of tiny figures traveling horizontally across immense white spaces. And of ships—wooden ships, battered by waves, threatened by towering icebergs and, in the most gripping legends, crushed and sunk by the implacable sea ice.

Captain Cook, completing his great southern voyage of circumnavigation in 1775, declaring his belief that somewhere, down there, existed a huge frozen landmass—lands he described as "doomed by Nature to everlasting frigidness and never once to feel the warmth of the Sun's rays, whose horrible and savage aspect I have no words to describe." One hundred and thirty years later, when the Australian scientist Douglas Mawson set sail for Antarctica, most of the southern continent was still unexplored. But the men who came then to unravel its mysteries were driven by a more romantic impulse. Inspired by the magical flickering lights of the Aurora Polaris, Mawson wrote: "Powerless, one was in the spell of an all-enfolding wonder: the vast, solitary snow-land, cold-white under the sparkling star-gems; lustrous in the rays of the southern lights; furrowed beneath the sweep of the wind. We had come to probe its mystery, we had hoped to reduce it to terms of science, but there was always the 'indefinable' which held aloof, yet riveted our souls."

This was Mawson's second Antarctic expedition. His first had been with the British explorer Ernest Shackleton on the *Nimrod* expedition, when Mawson and four others made the first ascent of Mount Erebus, the volcano named after one of the ships of an earlier explorer, James Clark Ross. Mawson and his companions hauled 550-pound sleds up the lower slopes, struggling on hands and knees, before continuing without the sleds, at one stage bivouacking tentless in the open through thirty-six hours of raging blizzard. On the summit plateau at 12,451 feet they discovered a molten-lava lake, with steam billowing through ice-encrusted natural chimneys called fumaroles.

Mount Erebus was one of the first recorded climbs in Antarctica, but it was only a sideline to the expedition's main objective—the South Pole. Although Shackleton's men were forced to turn back about ninety miles short, they did discover a route up the Beardmore Glacier, a laborious gateway through the Transantarctic Mountains and up onto the polar plateau, which Shackleton claimed for his king and emperor Edward VII.

Imperialism aside, Shackleton's 1909 journey was a fantastic piece of exploration, confirming that Antarctica is in fact a huge plateau, the highest continent on earth, which we now know has a mean altitude of 7,500 feet above sea level. The Beardmore Glacier, far grander than any glacier in the northern hemisphere, is just one of numerous outpourings from the plateau—billions of cubic metres of ice bursting seaward through the Transantarctic range. And, in this land of giant extremes, that range is an incredible 1,850 miles long and 37 to 50 miles wide.

In our mad overcrowded modern world, I find it rather comforting to think that virtually none of the Transantarctic Mountains have been climbed; many have never even been *seen*! And the newness of our relationship with Antarctica is emphasized by the fact that the highest Antarctic mountains—in the Sentinel Range—were only discovered in 1935, when Lincoln Ellsworth and Herbert Hollick-Kenyon flew over them on the first aerial crossing of the continent. This range is so remote that it has only ever been approached by plane, first of all in 1966, when the American mountaineer Nicholas Clinch led first ascents of the main summits, including the highest, Vinson Massif, at 16,066 feet. Nowadays Vinson is a popular goal for "Seven Summits" peak-baggers, flying in from Chile to an ice runway at Patriot Hills. Adventure tourism has come to Antarctica, but this is just one mountain on a continent bigger than North America. And, while the tickers follow a now familiar track up Vinson, some of their guides use off-duty days to make some very adventurous vertical journeys on neighboring peaks. Some of the most famous mountaineers of recent years, such as Erhard Loretan, Catherine Destivelle, and Conrad Anker, have pioneered hard new climbs in the range; but the most remarkable was the American Mugs Stump—a safety officer for U.S. government scientists—who sneaked off work to make the first ascent of the west face of Mount Tyree in 1989.

This solo, unroped climb, up a wall of steep rock and ice 8,200 feet high in extreme sub-zero temperatures, was a brilliant feat of daring; but also, I sense, a kind of meditation—one man immersing himself totally in the awesome isolation of the southern continent. South beyond the Sentinel Range the empty white continental dome stretches 870 miles to the Pole; continue another 870 miles on the same line and you reach the subglacial freshwater Lake Vostok—one of Antarctica's still unprobed mysteries. From there you have to travel yet another 870 miles to reach, finally, the Indian Ocean coast. Of all the Antarctic mountains, perhaps the most unearthly are the red granite needles of Dronning Maud Land—fantasy spires piercing the gleaming infinity of the ice cap. For the modern "big wall" rock expert they represent the ultimate climbing dream, but the long flight to the ice runway known as Blue-1 also makes it an expensive dream. For the private mountaineer the most accessible peaks lie closer to the sea, further north, in the area first explored 200 years ago by ambitious seal hunters—the Antarctic Peninsula.

No matter how spectacular the individual peaks on Antarctica, one is always lured back to the great horizontal spaces. Even on the wiggling tail of the peninsula, which looks so slender on the world atlas, there is a huge interior ice cap. And on the peninsula's east coast the ice spills out onto the floating Larsen Ice Shelf, bordering the Weddell Sea. Beyond the ice shelf the sea itself is subject to a gigantic area of temporary winter ice (each winter the

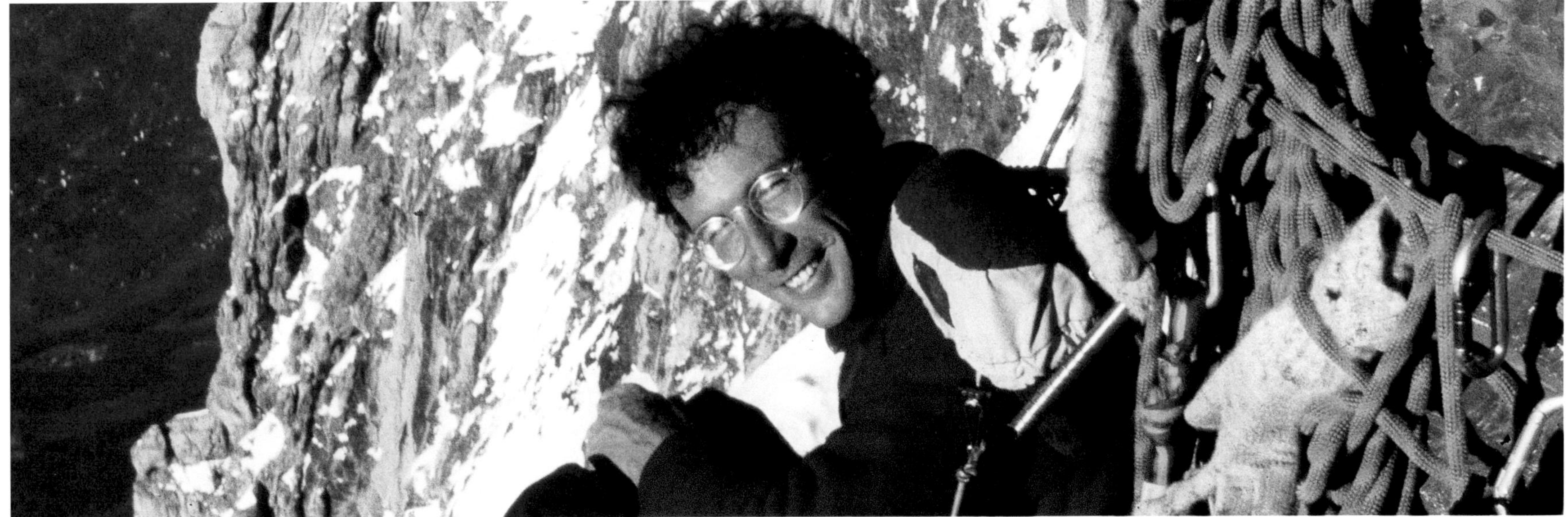

freezing ocean around Antarctica effectively doubles the continent's size) and even in summer, that ice can be virtually impenetrable. It was here that the great Swedish explorer Otto Nordenskjöld lost his expedition ship in 1903, resulting in an epic tale of men struggling across the ice, surviving for months in primitive huts and only just returning to civilization after unimaginable hardship.

It was in the same ice-infested sea, in 1915, that Ernest Shackleton lost his ship *Endurance* and, with his twenty-seven companions, was forced into an even more improbable odyssey of survival. Of all the Antarctic legends, the story of his escape is probably the most remarkable. First there was the eleven-month-long agony of drifting powerless until the ship was crushed and sunk. Then another five months, drifting erratically northward on a floating camp. Then, as the ice broke up, seven days of unimaginable torment as twenty-eight men crammed into three tiny lifeboats and rowed out of the ice's clutches, to make a perilous landfall on the storm-washed shore of Elephant Island. Then the desperate 600-mile, 14-day voyage by six of the men in an open boat only twenty-three feet long across the Southern Ocean to the southwestern shore of South Georgia. And then, as if they had not suffered enough already, the first ever crossing of the mountains of South Georgia by Ernest Shackleton, Tom Crean, and Frank Worsley, to reach the whaling station at Stromness.

In April 2000, I had the privilege of retracing that journey over South Georgia's mountains, with Conrad Anker and Reinhold Messner. With modern equipment, an accurate map, and a well-equipped ship waiting offshore, we were in no great danger. But global warming certainly made our journey awkward. Where Shackleton had walked across smooth snowfields, we found ourselves negotiating a labyrinth of crevasses; where he, Crean, and Worsley had glissaded down a snow chute, we teetered cautiously past crumbling exposed rock. The route had actually become harder. But, as I said, we were not fighting for survival—and the survival of twenty-five other desperate men—having just crossed the Southern Ocean in a boat. We were just tourists, or at best pilgrims, marveling at what those pioneers had achieved in 1916.

That sense of following in footsteps is really at the heart of all mountain exploration. Even though we thrill to the huge white empty spaces, our response to wilderness is not necessarily intuitive: it is an educated, inherited, cultural response built on an accumulated tradition. Visiting South Georgia in 2000—and earlier in 1990—I felt that sense of continuity very acutely. This speck of an island, isolated in the immensity of the Southern Ocean, is the epitome of wilderness. Its beaches teem with seals and penguins. Albatrosses nest on the cliffs and dance their aerial ballet in the crystal sapphire sky. The mountains tower up to nearly 10,000 feet straight out of the ocean. But there are also the rotting remains of whaling stations, rusting hulks of old steamships wallowing offshore, remnants of industrial machinery and cemeteries where whalers and explorers were buried far from home. These industrial relics are a reminder of the ambitious restlessness that first brought men to discover Antarctica. But more than those obvious physical manifestations, it is the accumulated *knowledge* of their exploits that colors our appreciation of Antarctica.

On my first visit to South Georgia, in 1990, Brian Davison and I made the first ascent of a peak called Mount Carse. It had been snowing almost without reprieve, but just as we reached the peak at sunset, the storm briefly cleared. It was a moment of almost transcendental beauty, with the mountains glowing peachy orange, before fading to pink, violet, and blue. Beyond the mountains and glaciers stretched the ocean, with icebergs glinting in the last light of the day. They were tiny icebergs, but when I returned ten years later, an explosion of activity in the Weddell Sea had resulted in a new profusion of icebergs drifting north, cluttering the ocean around South Georgia and nudging into the island's many bays. Dazzling white, blue, green, turquoise, sculpted into a thousand fantastic shapes, they were a part of Antarctica—visible proof of that huge mysterious continent lurking beyond the southern horizon. I hope that one day I will actually go there myself. But even if I, like millions of other people, never actually set foot on the continent, we are all enriched immeasurably just by knowing it is there.

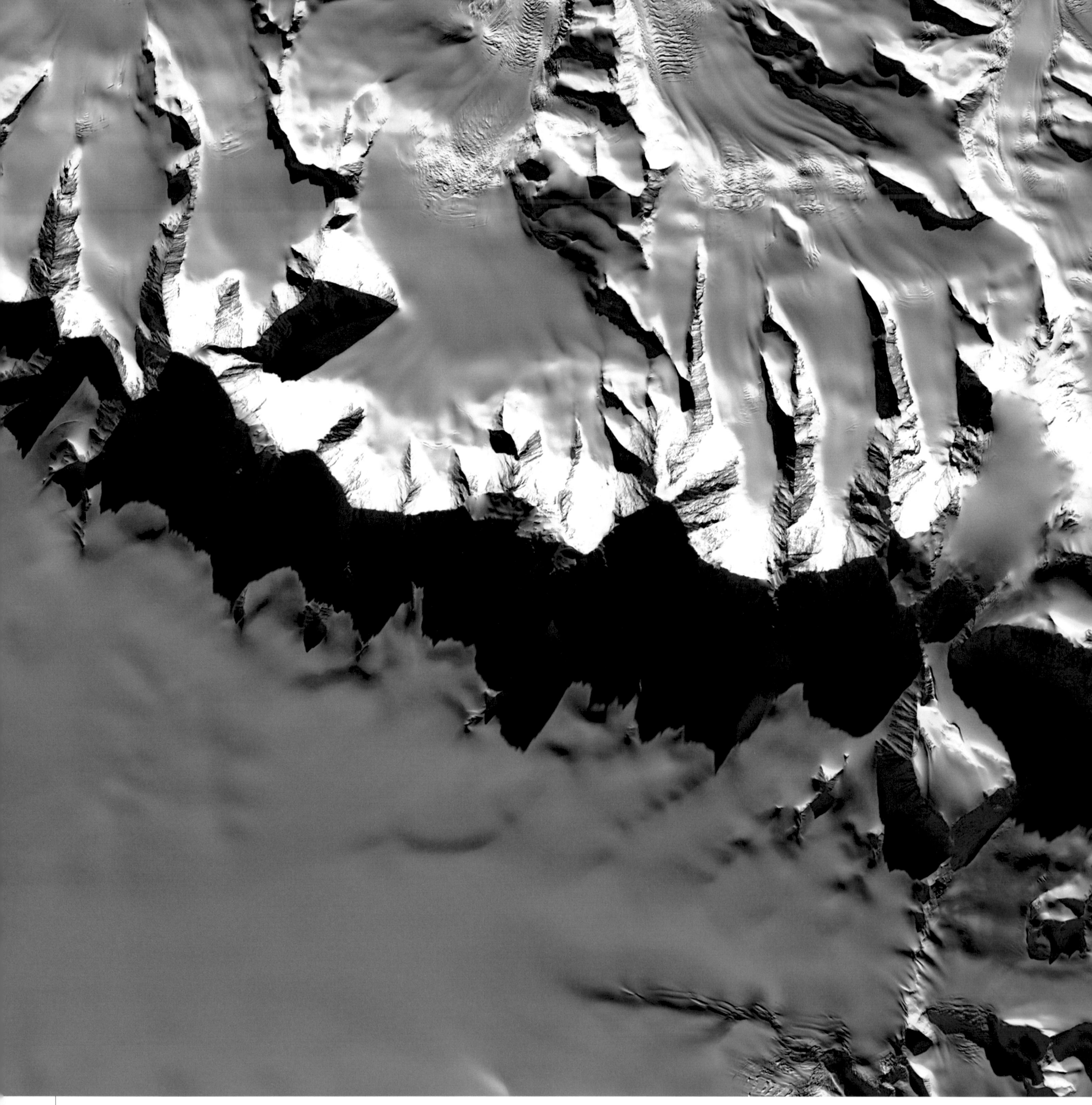

Vinson Massif, the highest mountain massif in Antarctica

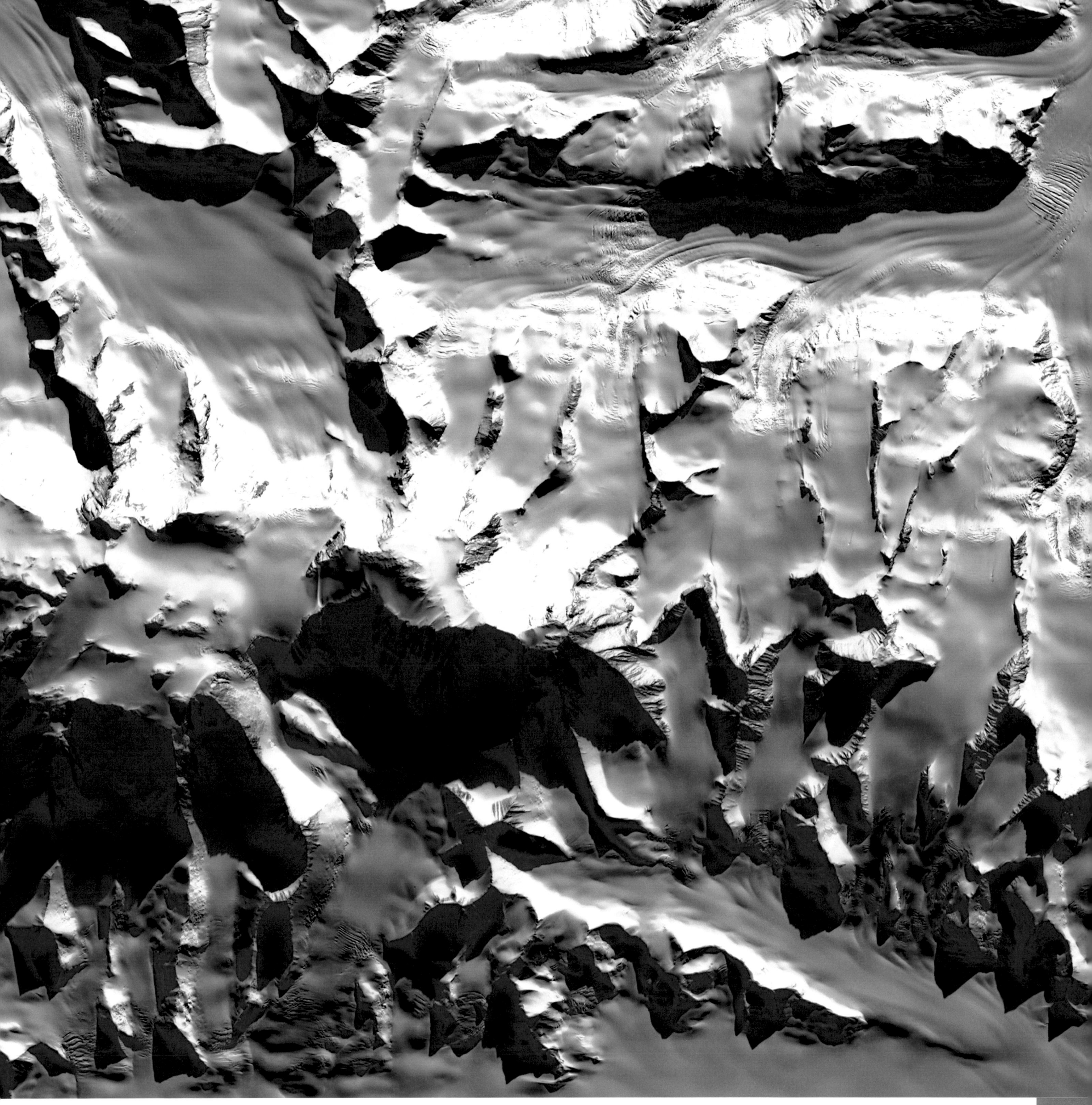

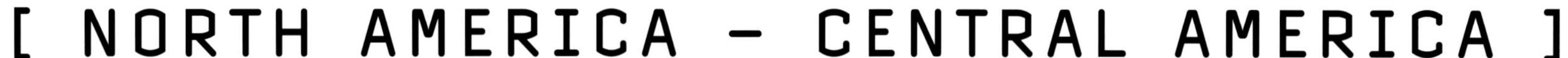
[NORTH AMERICA – CENTRAL AMERICA]

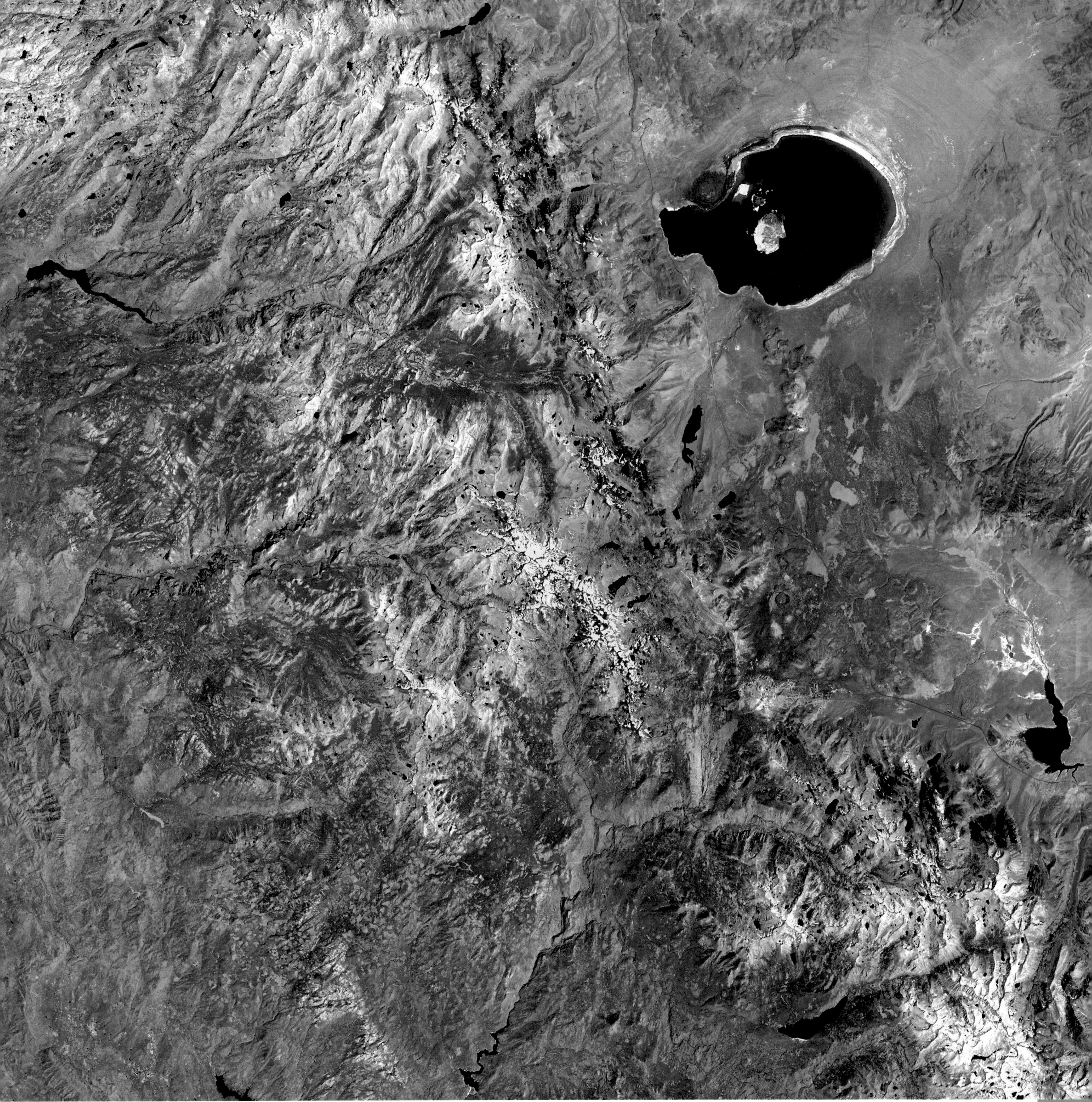

Yosemite National Park and Mono Lake, United States

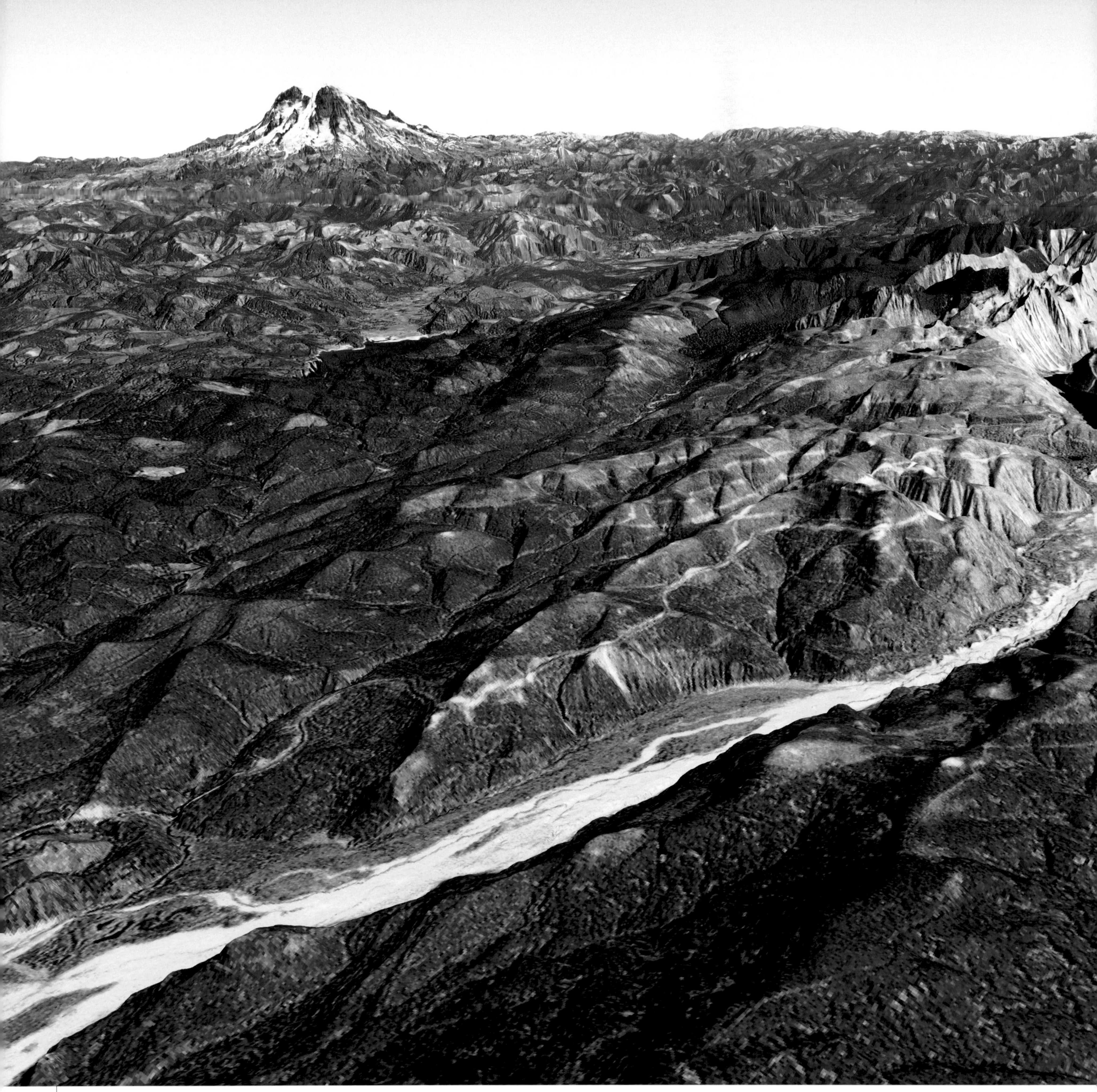

Mount St. Helens, United States

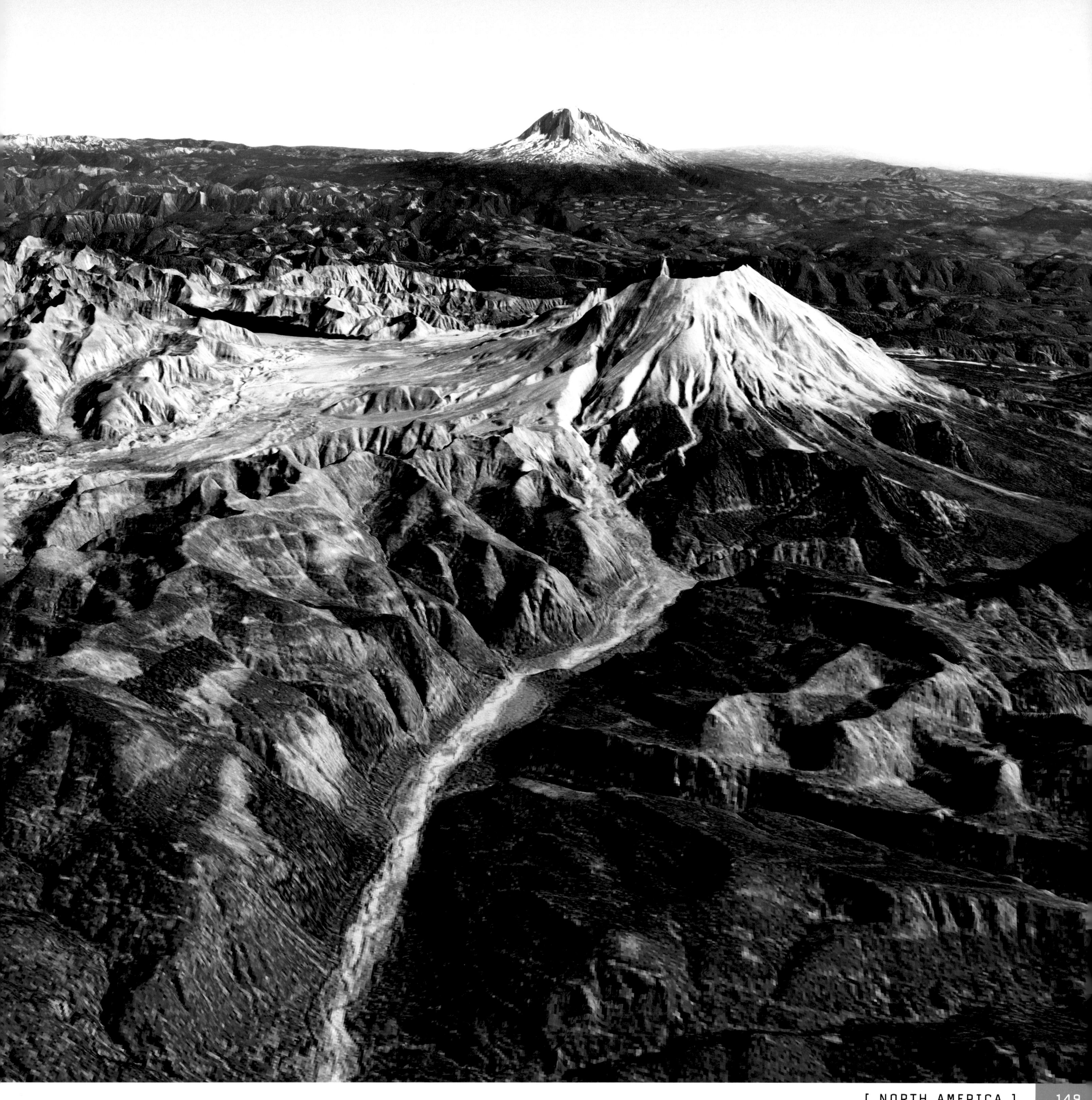

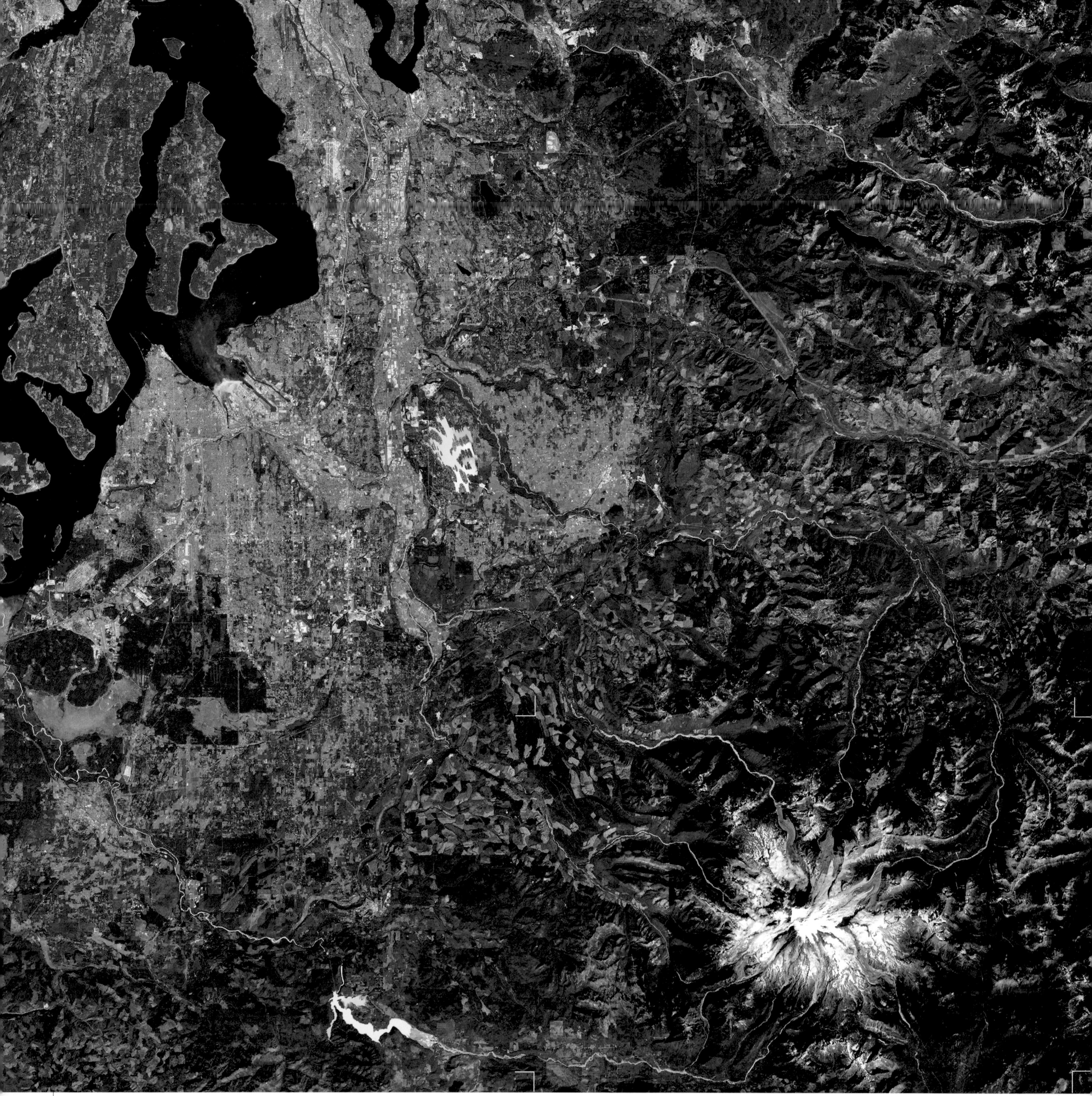

Mount Rainier, United States

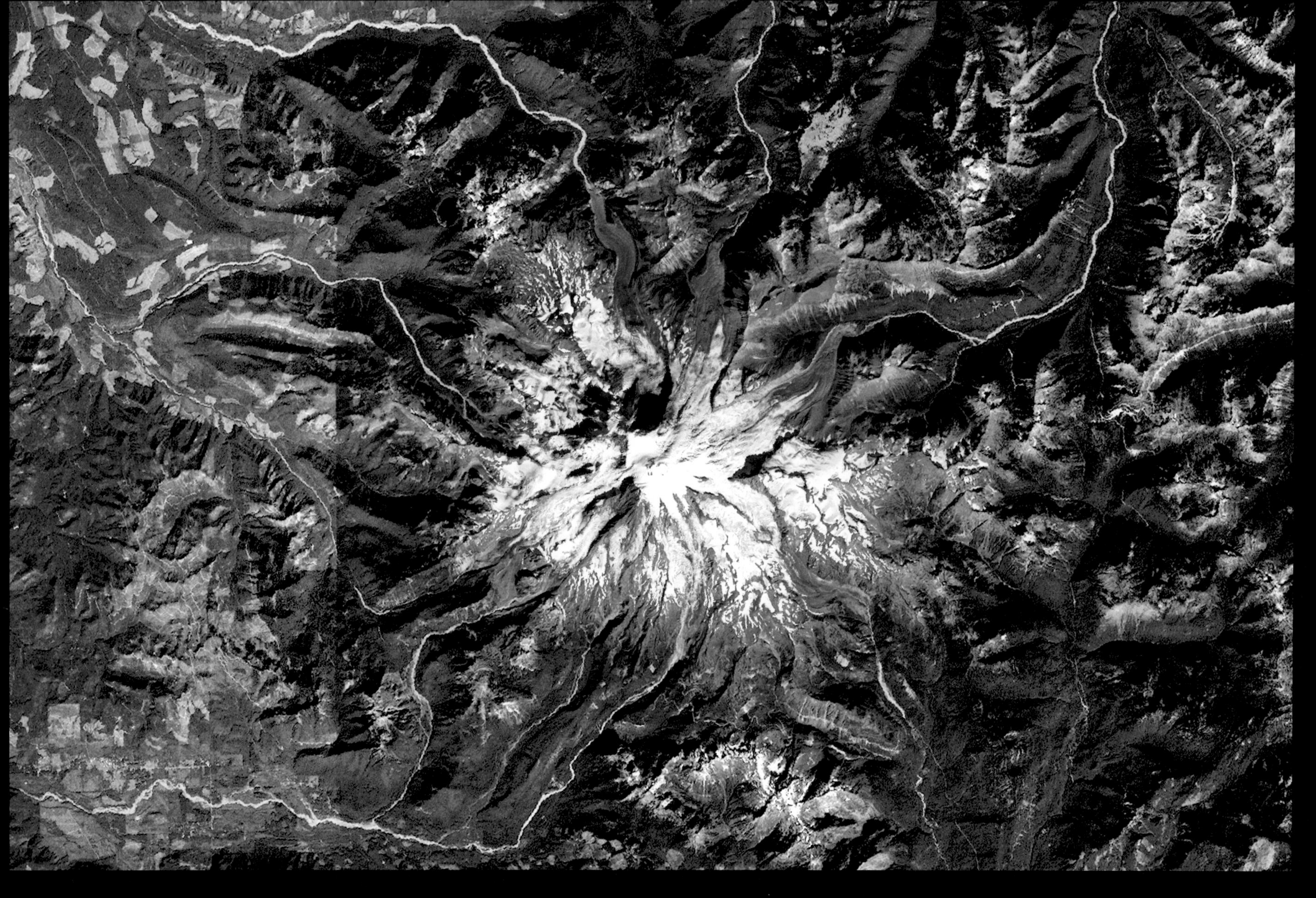

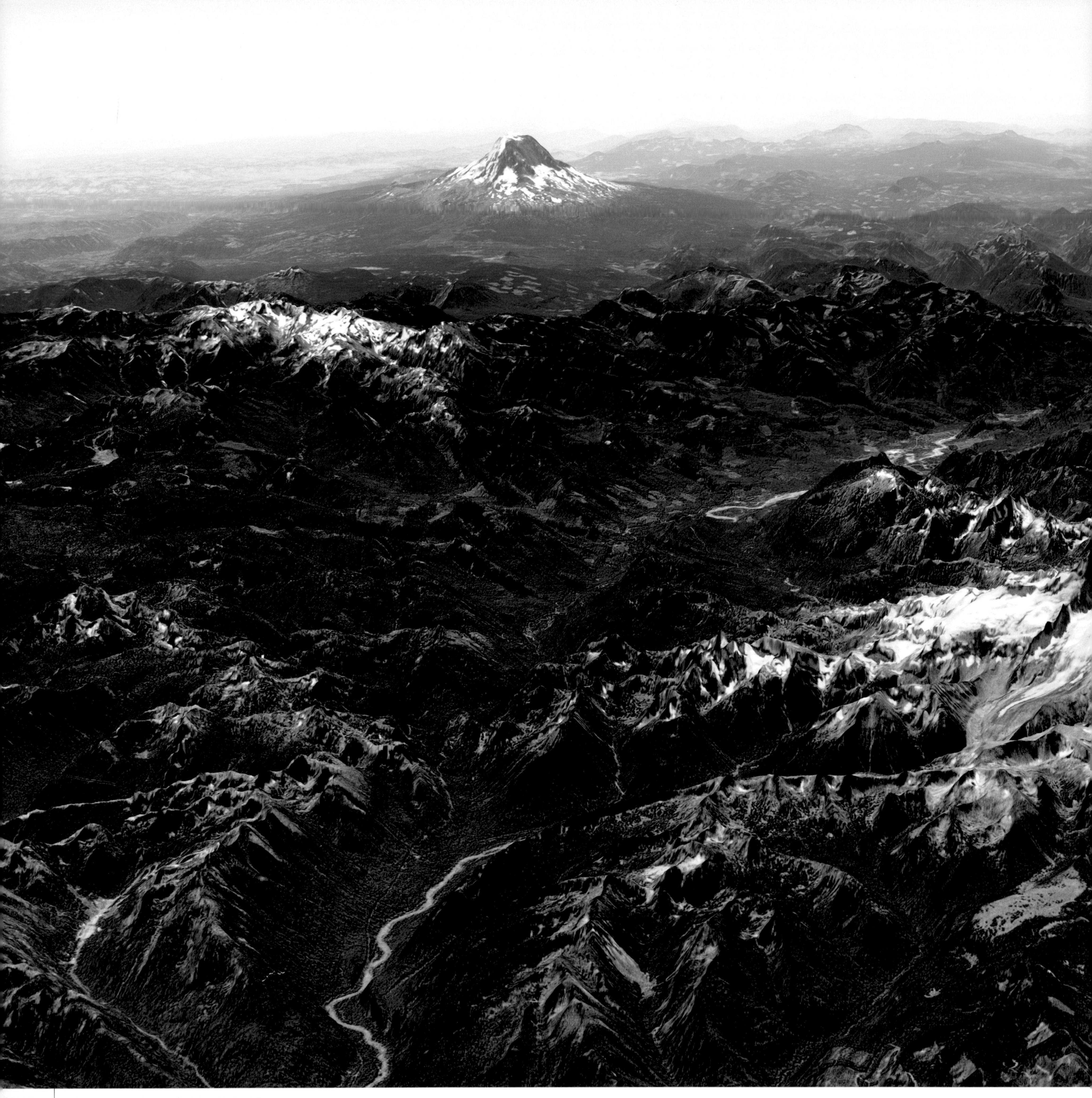

Panorama of Mount Rainier, United States

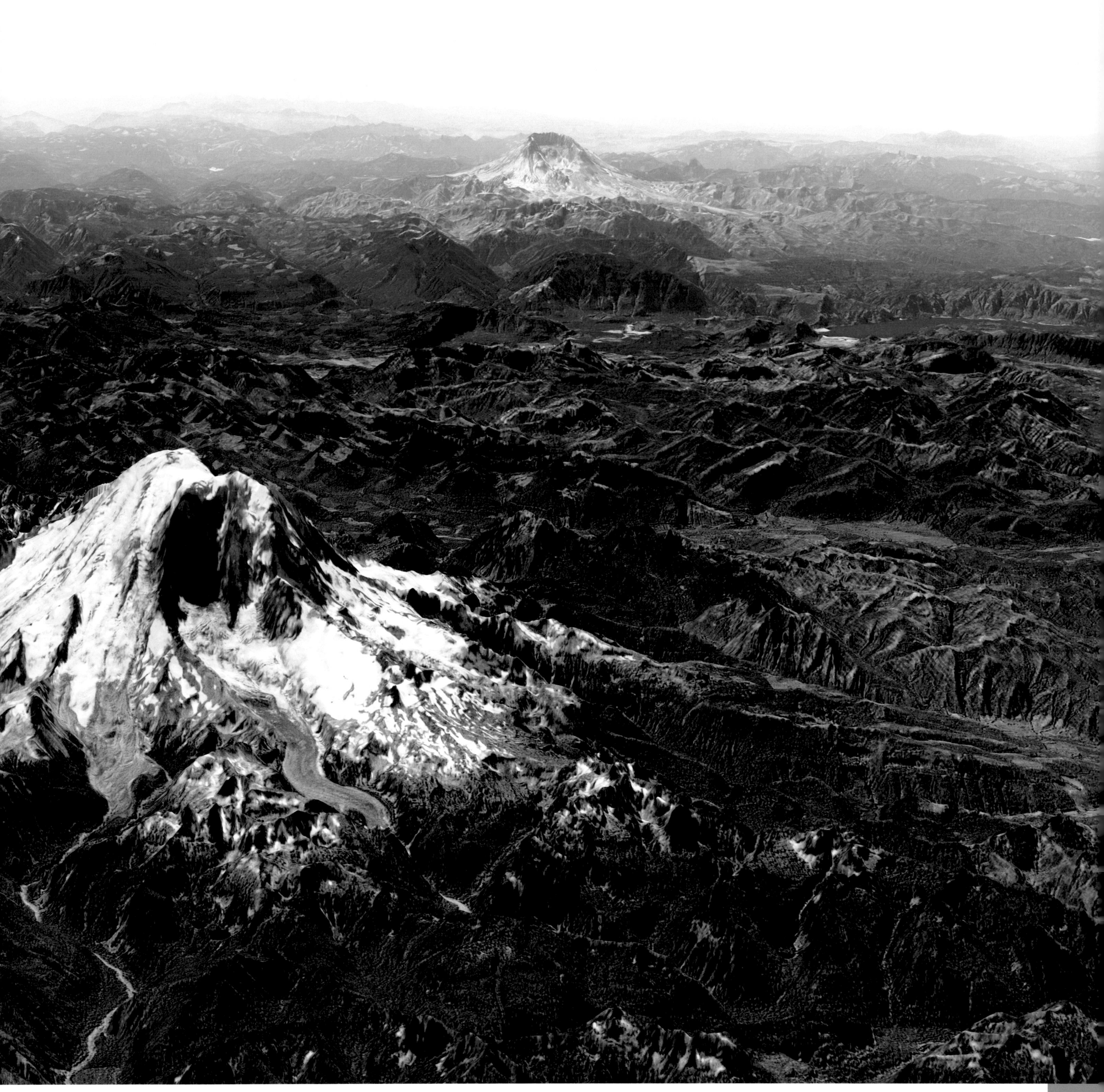

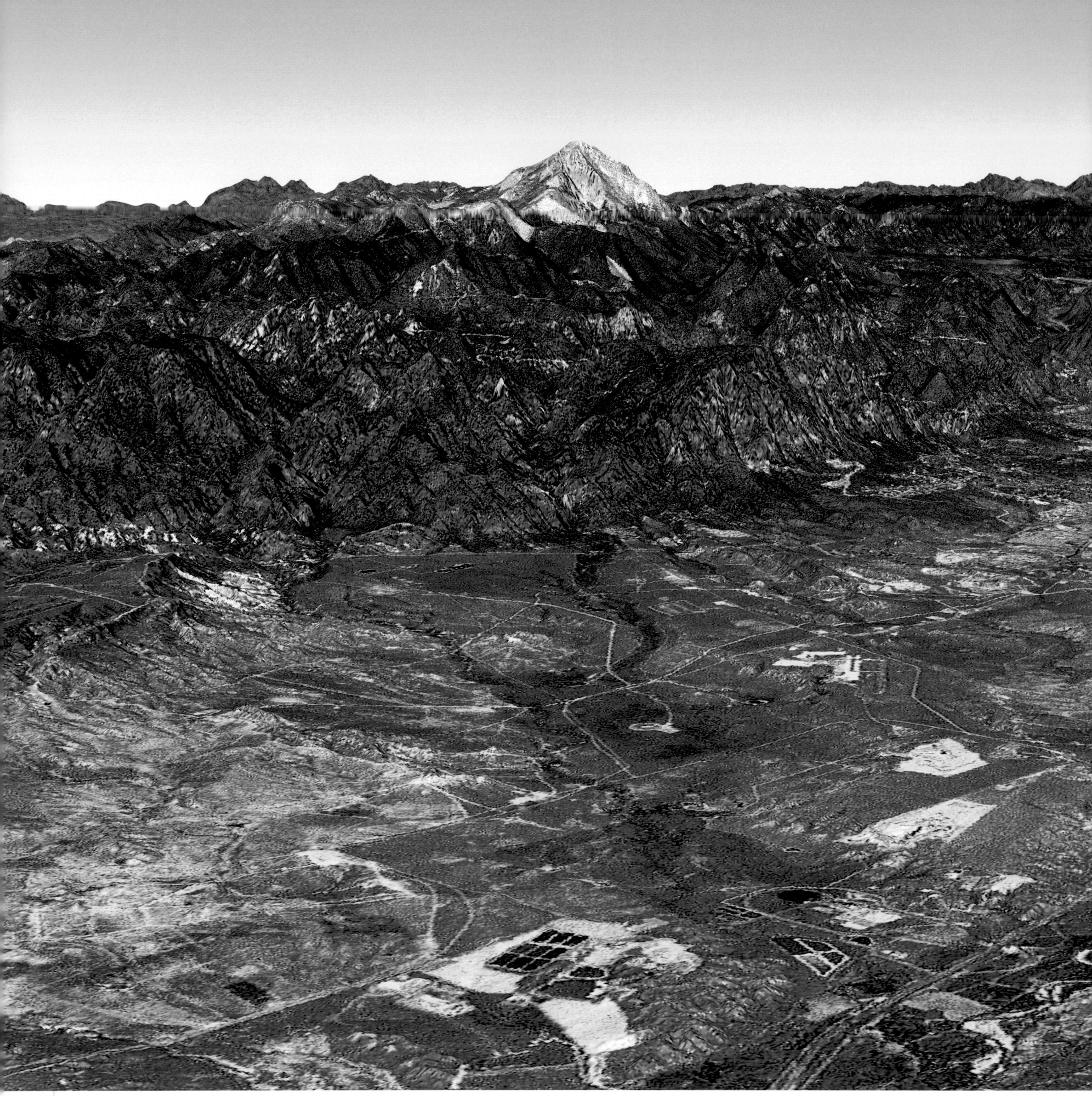

Panorama of the eastern Rocky Mountains with Pikes Peak, United States

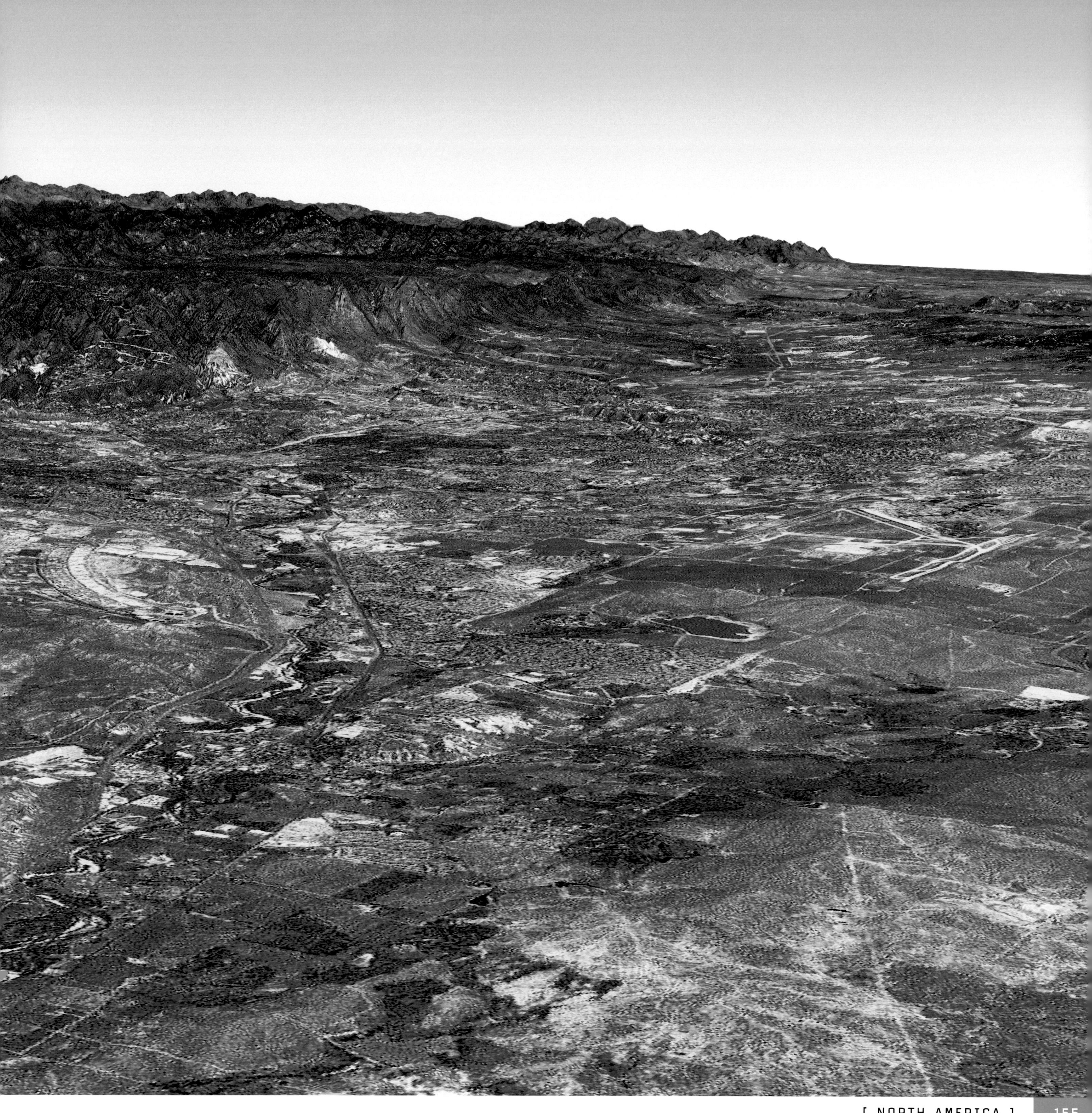

El Corazón

ALEXANDER HUBER

Above me are only a rock wall and the starry sky. I lie awake in my sleeping bag. Here on the southwest wall I am in the shadow of the nose, but Yosemite Valley is bathed in moonlight. My thoughts circle around my free climb. Max lies peacefully beside me, enjoying his first night on a Portaledge. He leans his head over the edge of our sleeping platform suspended above the valley floor and gazes at the lights of the other bivouacking rope teams. There is a lot of traffic on El Capitan.

"So by eleven in the morning you'll be done," Max said with a certain mischievousness. By eleven tomorrow I would have the redpoint, or fall-less, climb of our new route, El Corazón, behind me. Max is an optimist. I had my doubts. I wanted to climb all thirty-five pitches redpoint. Max belays me, watches me, and motivates me: "Eight pitches means four hours; so we start at seven, and by eleven it's over." If only it were so easy . . .

El Corazón—the Heart—is the most prominent rock formation on El Capitan. The heart-shaped, 820-foot-tall outbreak lies precisely in the center of the southwest wall, and through this heart runs the route "Son of Heart"—a classic line dreaded for its deep chimneys. This series of corners and chimneys runs nearly 985 feet through the overhanging wall above the Heart—a natural for free climbing. Only that the giant overhangs above the Heart seemed to present an insuperable barrier in my search for a line that could be free climbed.

Beak Flake: A smooth wall, crossed by the suggestion of a line—for 260 feet this natural wonder draws its trace downward, ending thirty-three feet above a broad band in an overhanging wave of granite—the single most difficult spot in El Corazón. The two-millimeter-thick steel of a Bird Beak, a special rock piton, is the only safeguard, twenty-six feet above the band—this is a no-fall zone. I am tied in, the rope is running easily through the carabiner, a loop connects it with the Bird Beak, and Max is belaying from below—and still I imagine myself moving free solo . . .

Two side pulls, then steps at nearly the same height—leap. Both hands lose their hold, my body flies upward, skimming across the rock in a wave. My eyes are fixed on my goal, my fingers dig deep in the beginning of the Beak Flake. At the deadpoint of my jump my body sags into my extended arm, my drawn-up legs grazing the smooth wall. We are now 325 feet above the overhang of the Heart—goal reached? Not quite, for we are now the same distance to the right of it. The rock structure dictates how to proceed. At the end of the route we reach a zone of black diorite extending upward and to the left as a narrow stripe. Black diorite! Even in areas without cracks there are always little ledges—difficult to secure, but climbable!

Bunny Slope: It is only a few feet more to the huge corner system of Son of Heart. In between: tilted plates. Child's play? Studied by telescope from the valley floor, it hardly seemed a problem— we could simply hike across it. But in fact the Bunny Slope is no piece of cake. What appeared to be a band is too steep for hiking—also too compact for driving bolts. Sixty-five feet, secured by only two Bird Beaks. No straight climbing, just careful creeping with lots of use of edges—a delicate game of nerves. We reach the Heart's main artery. Son of Heart's intersection system with its dreaded chimneys rises vertically some 985 feet above me.

Kierkegaard Chimney: A chimney crack of the "how-am-I-supposed-to-get-through-this" variety. This frightening torture chamber has already cost a number of climbers their lives. At the beginning there is an overhanging gullet impossible to secure that tries to spit you out, then the chimney turns into a claustrophobic nightmare so narrow that you have to exhale if you hope to get through. It is like wrestling when you are in a hopeless position and try once more to break your opponent's hold. Two pitches farther up we now stand under a giant roof, the horizontal cap of the corner system. The crevice, as wide as your fist at the beginning, narrows only slightly above the anchor. That leaves the perfect intersection . . .

Coffee Corner: With each foot of this pitch the crack becomes shallower, and halfway along it is unusable. But the farther up you go, the narrower the intersection angle, and at just the right moment it becomes possible to stem it. Feet on the right side, back and hands on the left, I snake my way upward. Now a roof: change tactics! With a jerk I press my back away from the wall, my left foot swinging across below. Legs spread apart, almost in the splits, leaning far out, and just before tipping over I dig my hand into the crack above the roof. Climbing with all sorts of gymnastics, without the expenditure of energy, becomes an almost playful contest with the rock.

Where now? After 820 feet the corner ends abruptly. A sixteen-foot roof seals off further progress. I first attempt it straight. A narrow trace of a crevice leads upward, but after sixteen feet it ends. Just before the start of a flake the crevice closes completely. Backtrack. To the right leads the line of the first climbers—but here too I soon come to a dead end. Nothing to do but cross 100 feet to the left under the roof.

Roof Traverse: It is like climbing on a ceiling. Feet pressed against the vertical wall, the undercling puts your body under great strain. The roof leaves your body no room, pressing you down hard and trying to throw you off. With your face pressed against the roof, you can't see where you are going. Here climbing is a matter of feeling your way forward on underclings. Only rarely is it possible to turn your body to the side and escape the pressure of the roof—take a deep breath, scan and memorize the next grips. After 100 feet the roof disappears. Following the crevice it becomes possible again—twenty feet upward, twenty-five feet downward, and again twenty feet upward to the Tower to the People, the only horizontal spot on the wall.

Sometime during the night I wake up. It is dark. The southwest wall should be in moonlight. Clouds! The probability of precipitation is slight—in

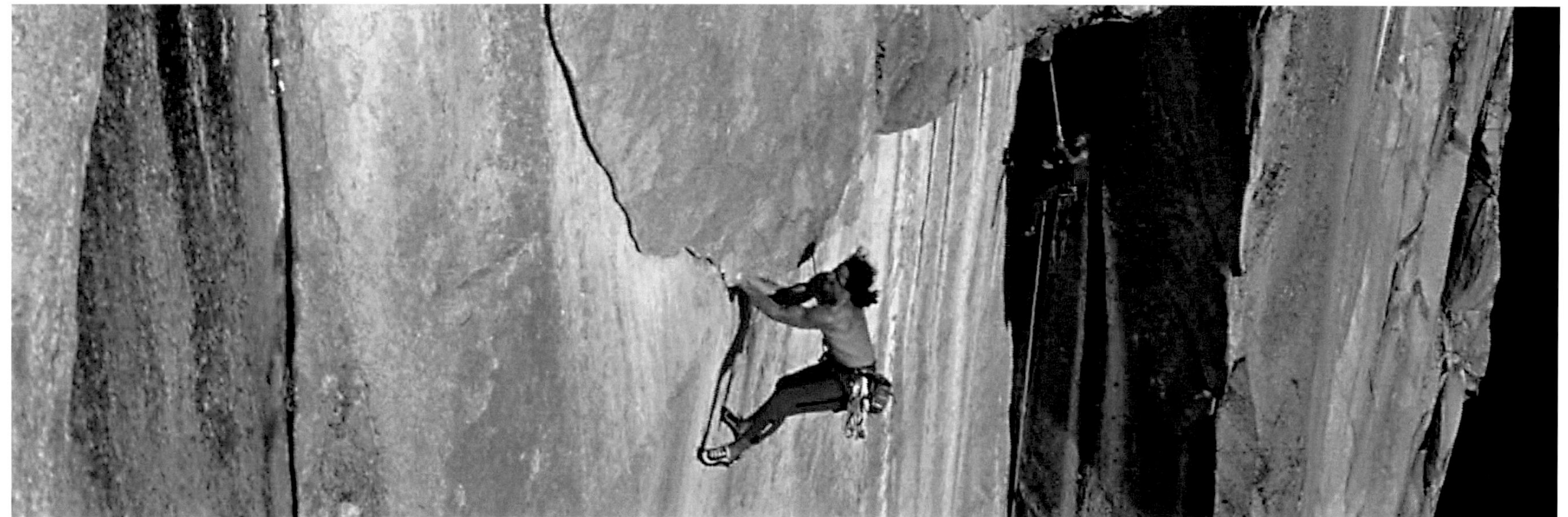

the four weeks I have been in Yosemite it only rained once. Even so, I get nervous, and toss restlessly in my sleeping bag. If it rains it will be impossible to finish—even if the last crux, the A5 Traverse, is already behind me. At the first sign of dawn I wake Max. I simply cannot wait. Half an hour later I am standing in my climbing shoes . . .

Golden Desert: In the midst of this broad expanse of golden granite there is only a single way to get through: a crack that gradually narrows. At first Friends, mechanical climbing devices developed for just such crack-climbing, help my ascent. But for the last few feet even the smallest are too big, and the crevice becomes almost too narrow for free climbing; there is just room for your fingertips. Starting out, my skin is burning—this pitch is not an ideal way to start the day—but my muscles are restored and deliver the necessary strength.

Max follows with the climbing clamps. "By eleven we'll be in the valley." The perennial optimist. But he was right. I see thin stratus clouds, and my panic subsides. And as far as the climbing goes, there is no longer much that could go wrong. Max again secures me. "Let's go!" Just above the anchor the A5 Traverse runs horizontally to the right through overhanging granite. No wall could look smoother. If I hadn't known that precisely at this height a fault runs through the wall, I would have said it was impossible. Three hauls above the shelf I reach the first clinging grips. Now it's out onto the wall, into nothingness. My climbing shoes are pressed against the smooth wall. I can look down at the wall's foot between my legs. My nerves cause my tensed muscles to twitch. Another twelve feet . . . nine . . . six . . . three more. My forearms tense against the edges of the fault one last time. Don't panic. It's all over.

It is a wonderful feeling to get to the top of El Capitan knowing that you were the first to climb a great route across it. I sit down on the edge of the cliff and look down into Yosemite Valley, where I started two days ago. I trace the line I was able to climb free, and again I experience the moment when I reached the top. When I felt so strangely light. All at once all the pressure had subsided and left me flying. Most of us dream of being able to fly, and usually it is really flying. But I would wager that it is also a metaphor for wanting to be better than we actually are. Making such a leap involves risks. For one brief moment in my life I could fly.

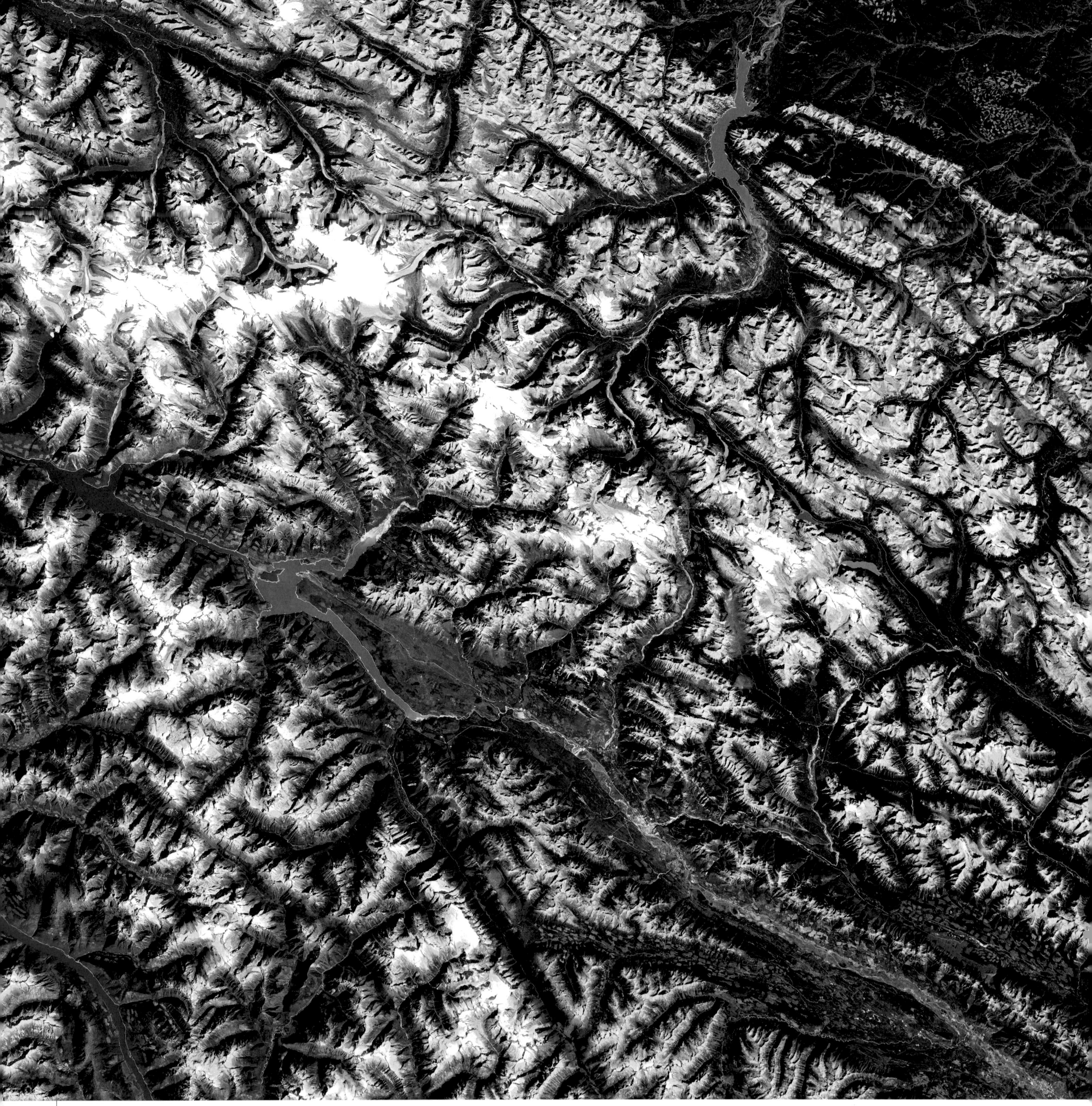

The oldest national park system in the world, Banff, Canada (left), and Yellowstone, United States (right)

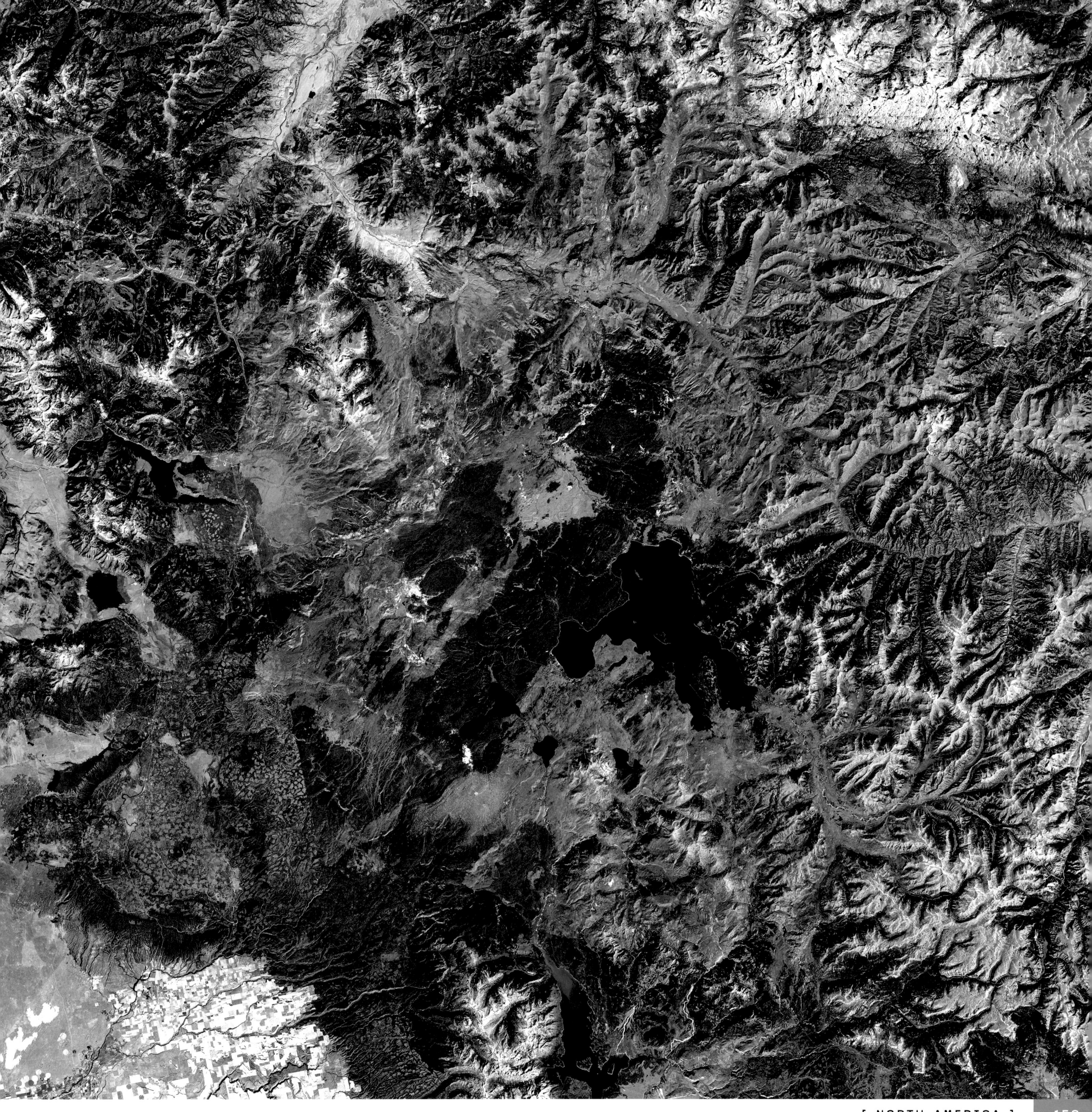

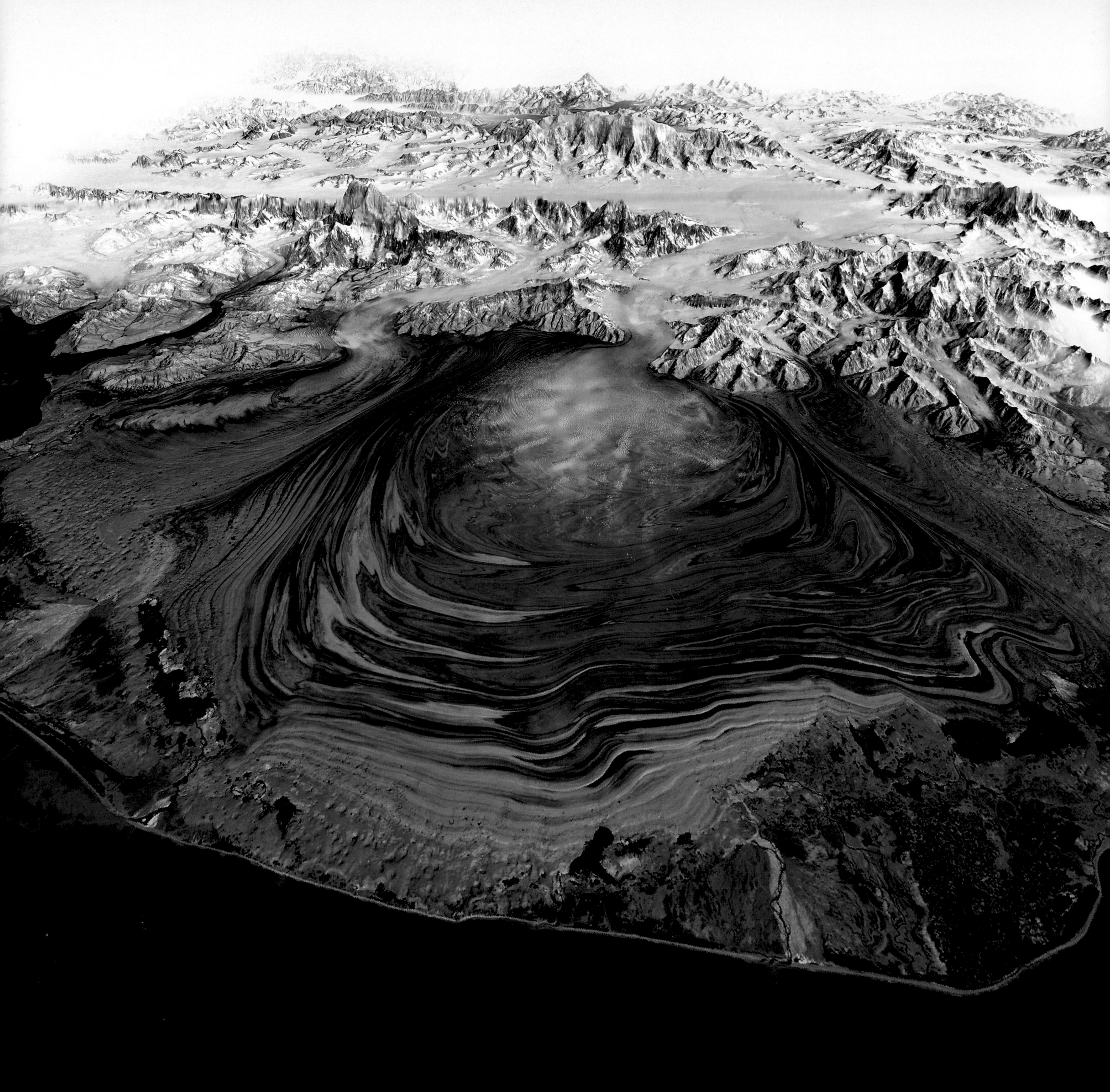

Malaspina Glacier, the largest foreland glacier in the world, United States

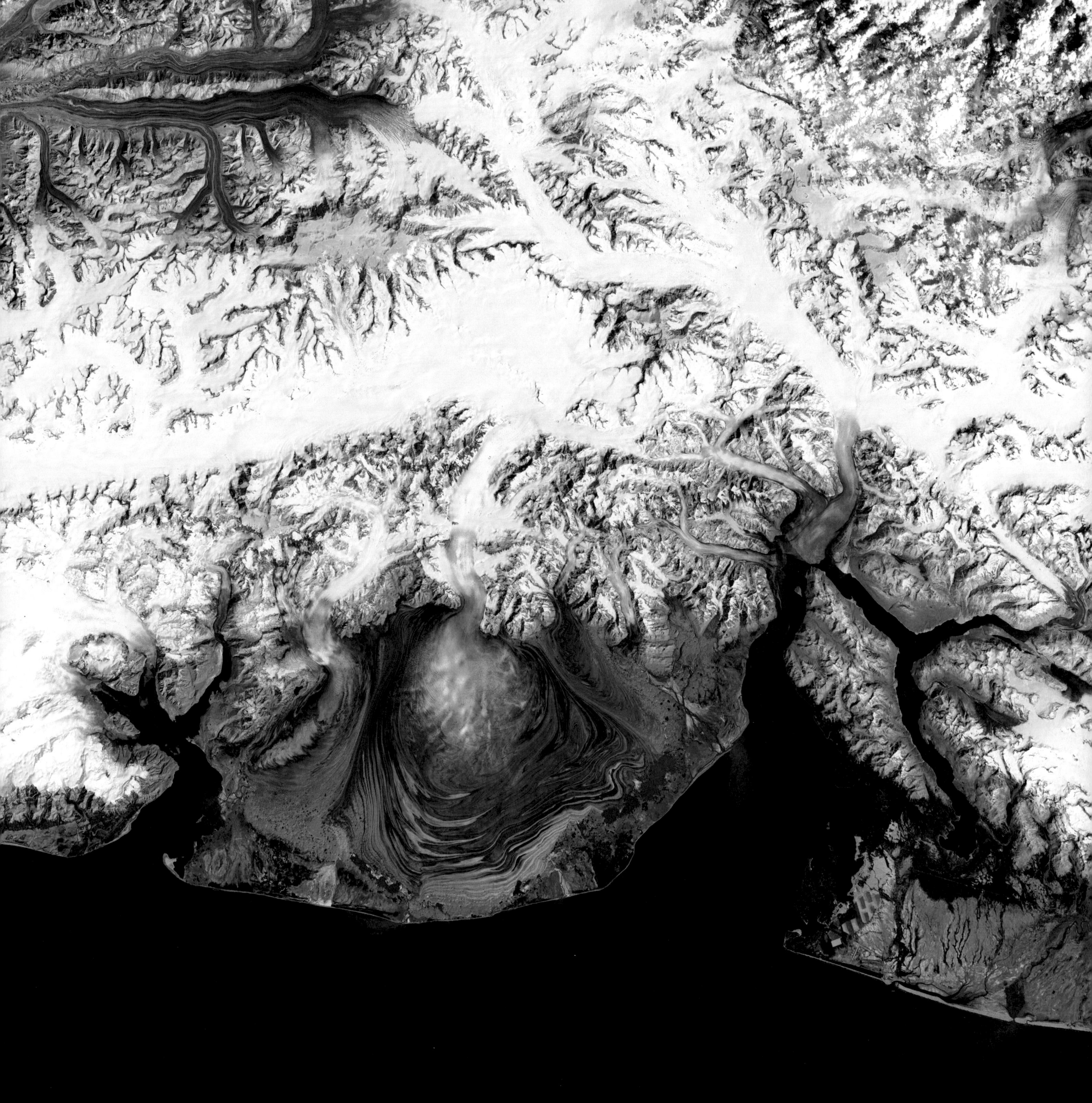

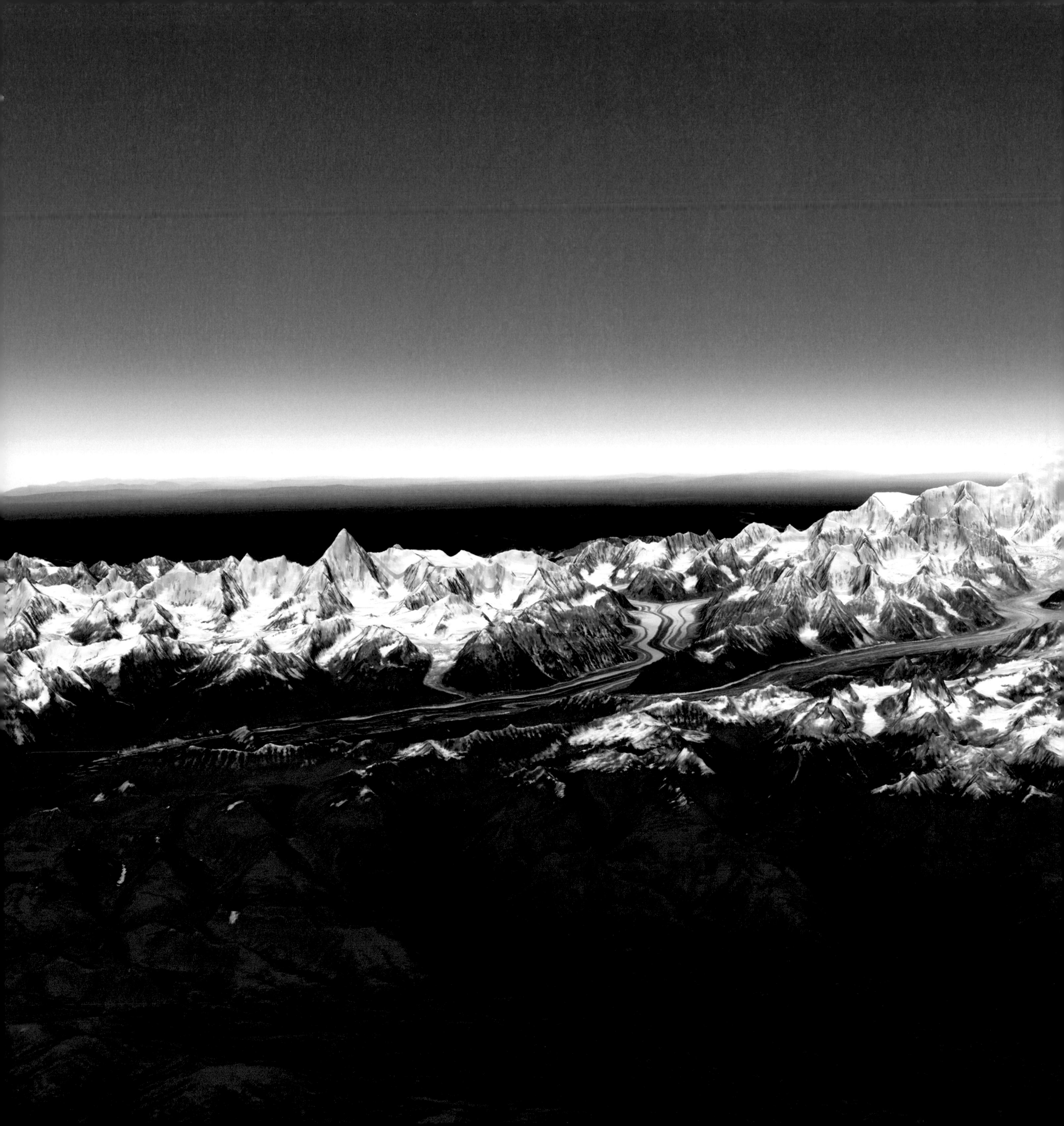

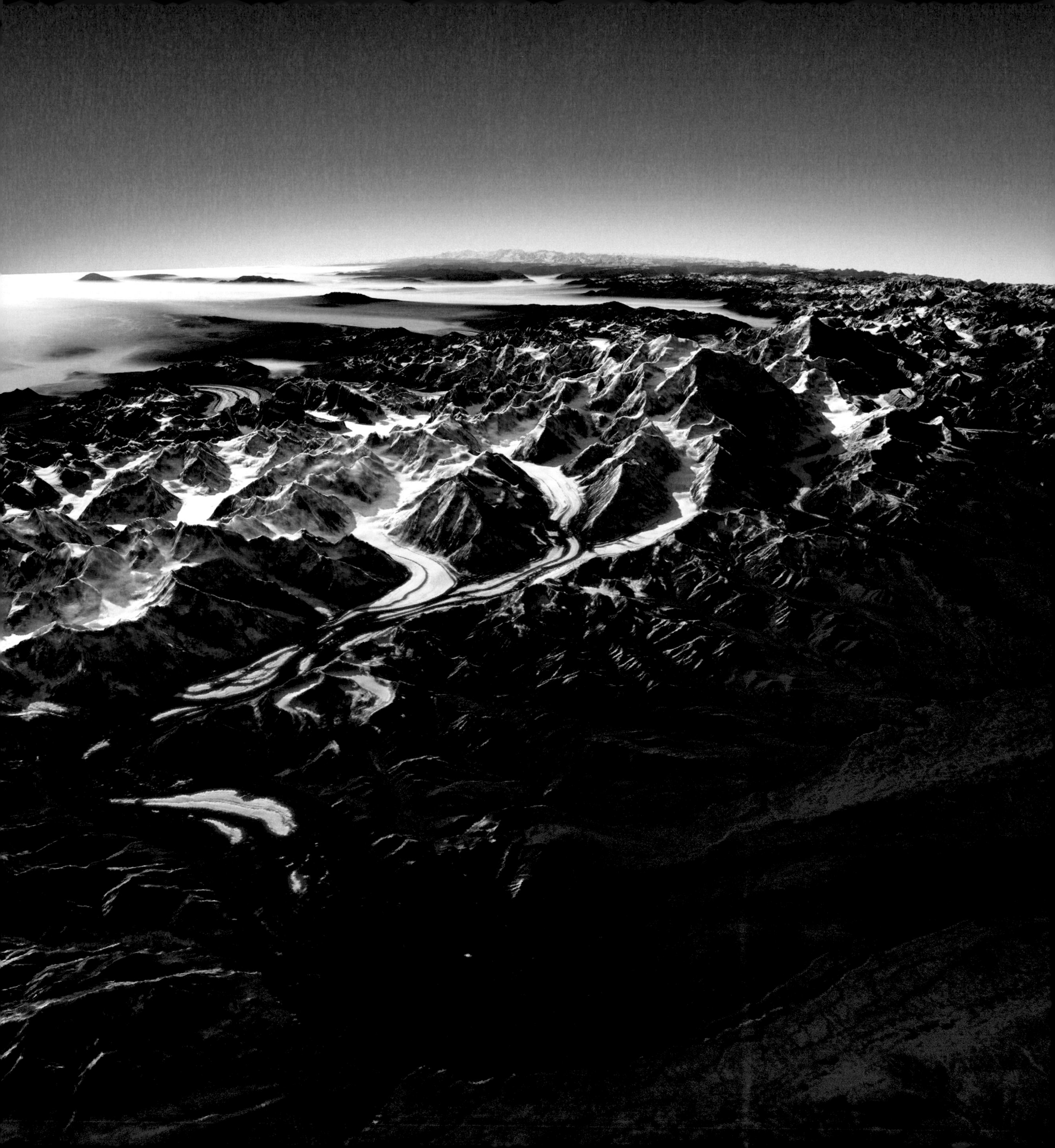

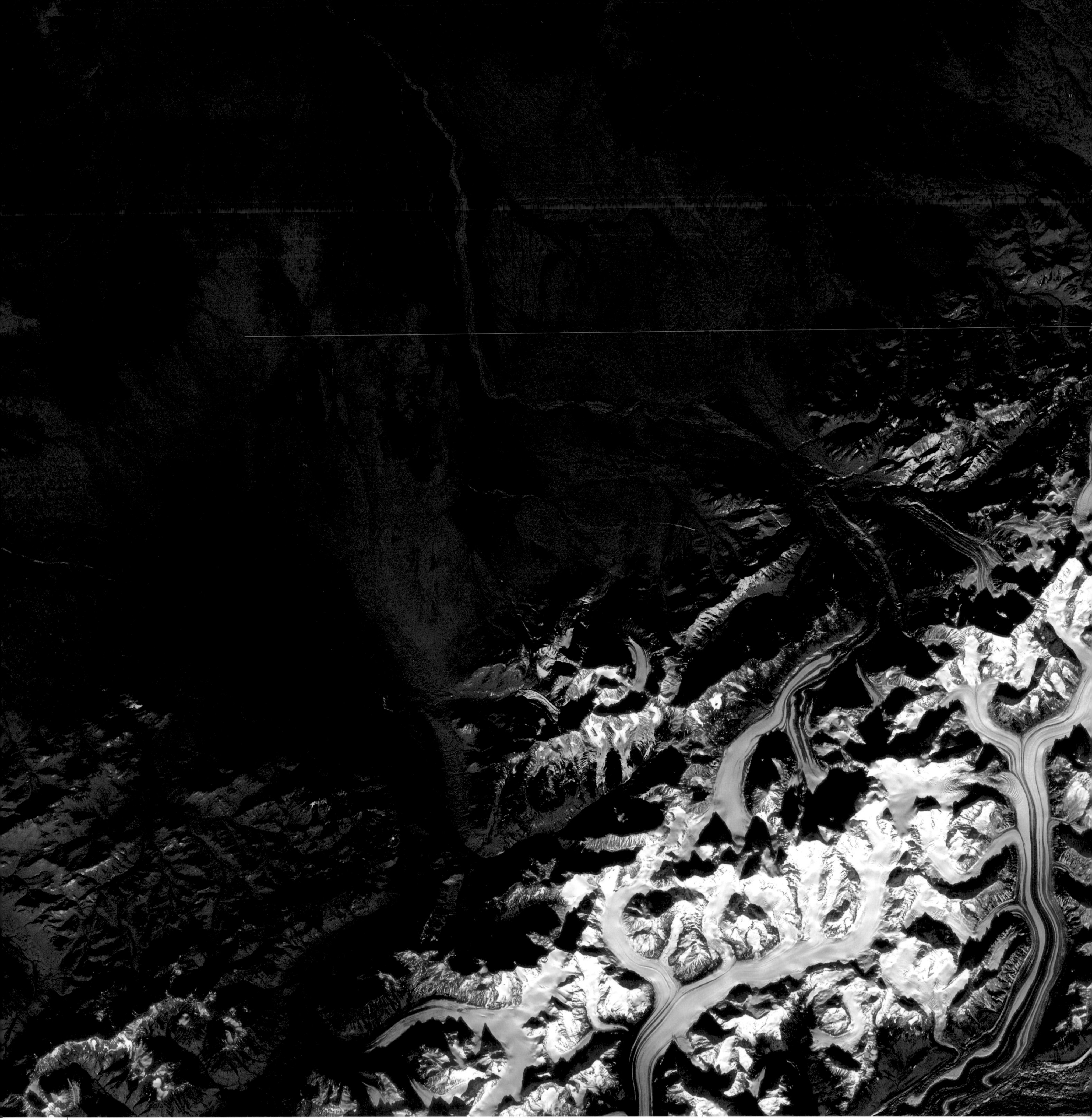

Mount McKinley (Denali), "the High One," United States

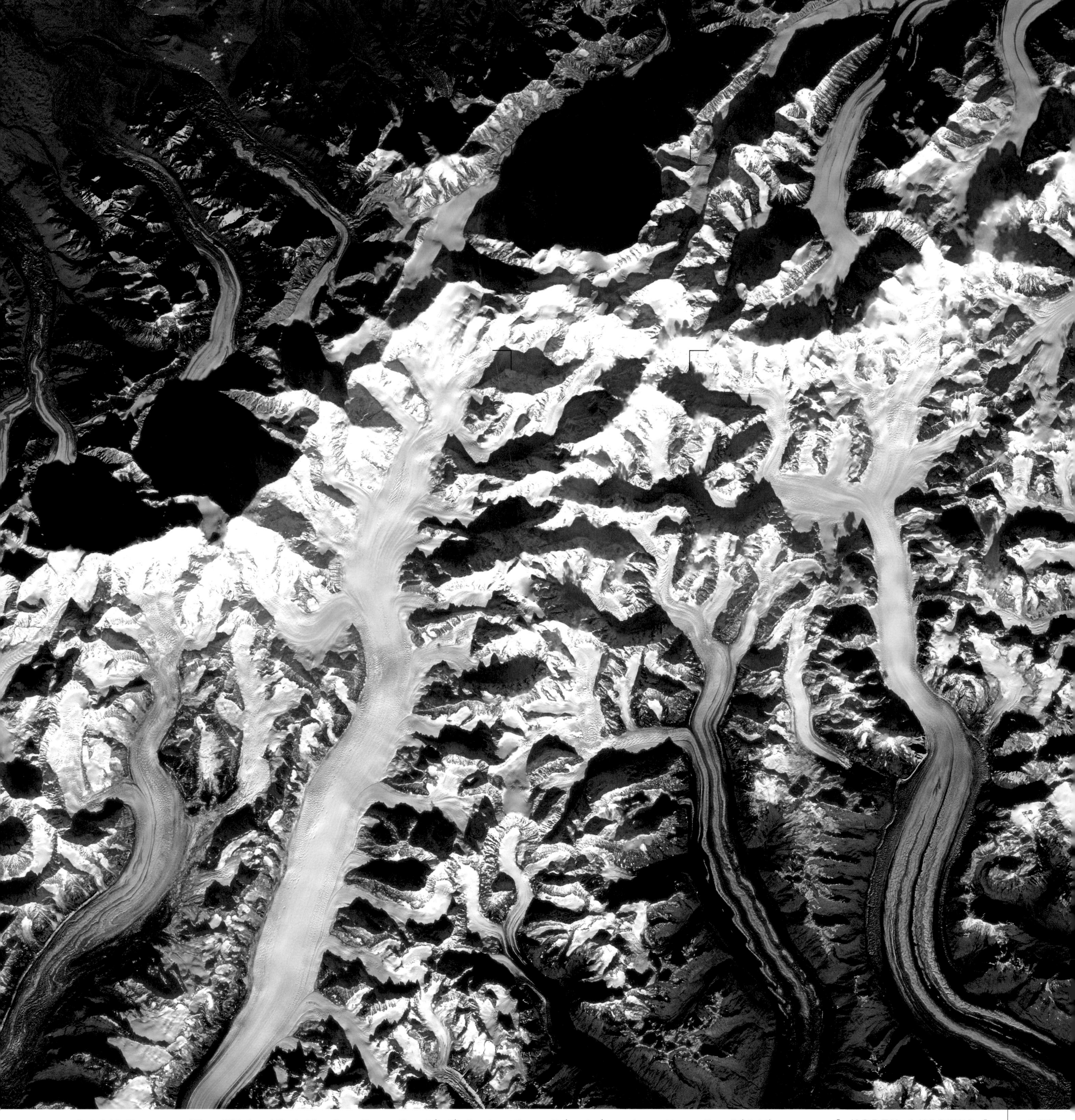

Gatefold: Panorama of Denali National Park. View from the northeast (left), view from the south (center), sunrise on the south wall (right).

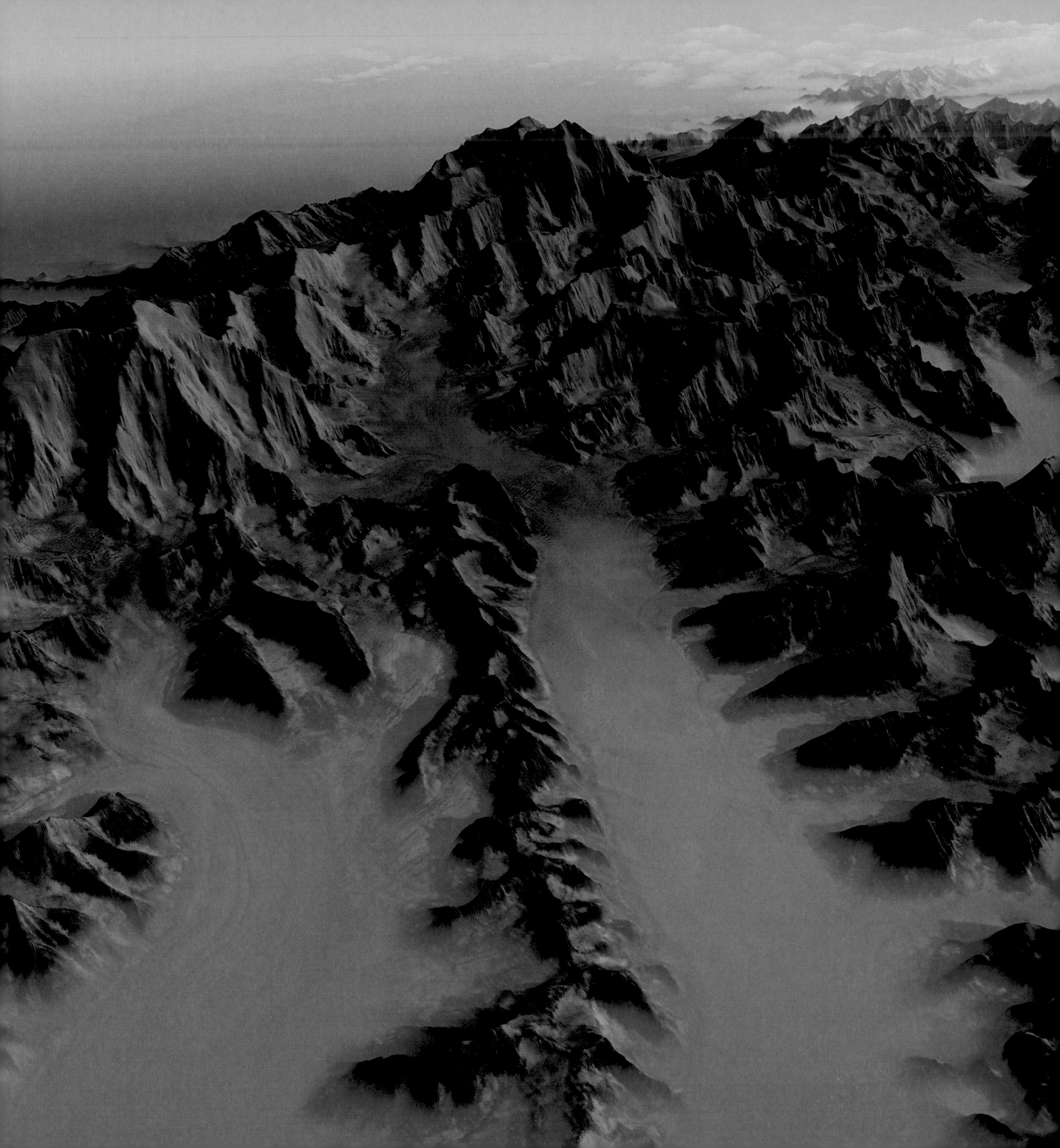

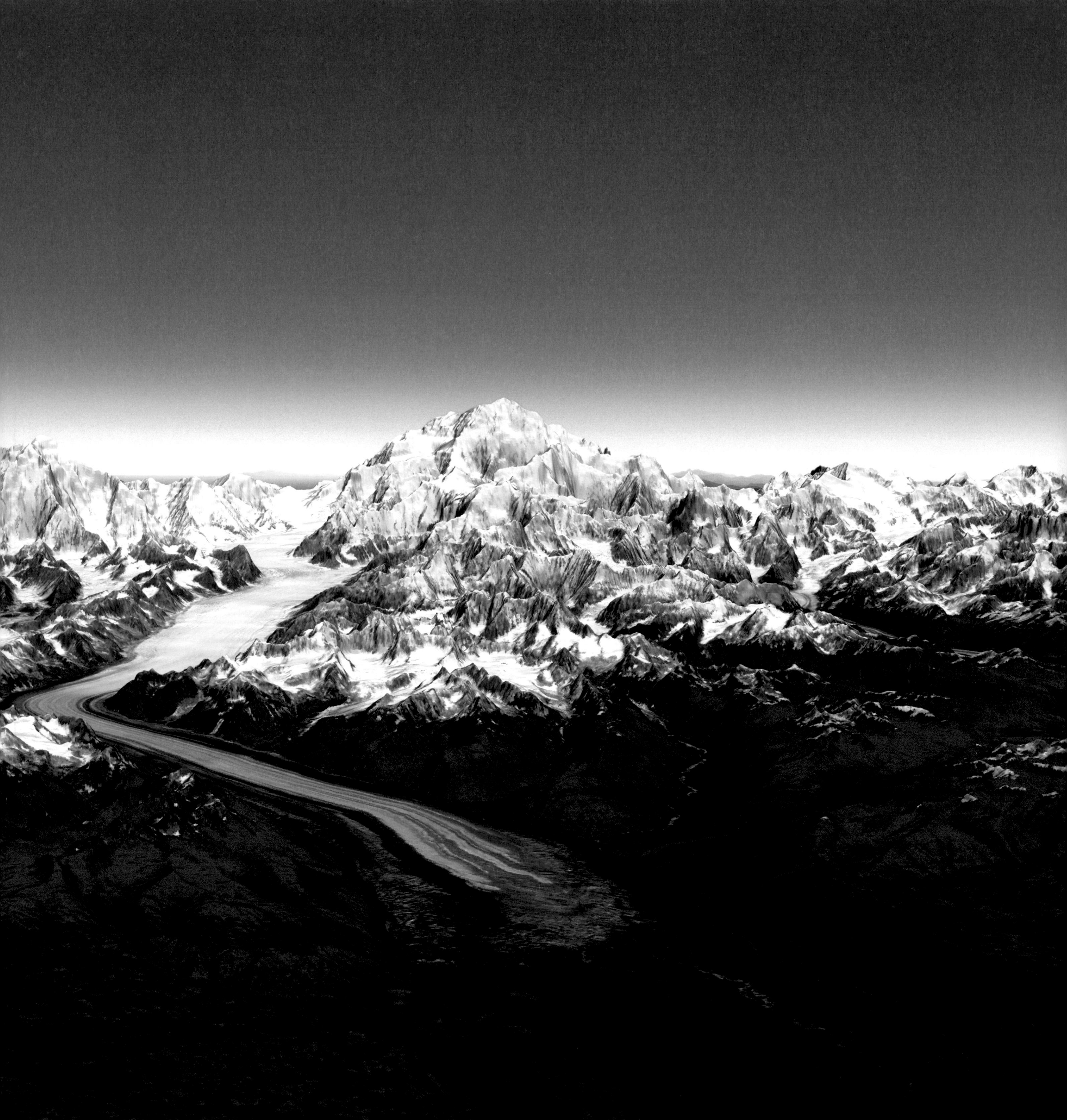

Protected Spaces
Room for Nature, Room for People

RÜDIGER GLASER

Mountain areas were among the first natural environments to be protected by law. Measures taken by the United States to preserve its wilderness areas are achievements that rival the cultural monuments of Europe. But mountains frequently serve as territory boundaries and fall within the borders of different countries, making responsibility for their protection unclear. The Alps are the first mountain region in the world to have been placed under a multinational agreement. This is only a start; the goal is to achieve the same for other ranges.

Traffic jams on the gravel roads of Waterton Lakes National Park. Cars are parked haphazardly, rangers are nervously trying to bring order to the excited crowds; whirring camcorders, digital cameras, and the odd pair of field glasses crane for view of one of the undisputed highlights of a visit to one of the national parks in the Rockies—a sighting of bears, bison, or elk. These stars of North American nature symbolize a pristine nature so very different from that of the Alps, which are almost completely civilized. Primitive campground accommodations, the need to secure toilet doors and garbage cans, and hide edibles from curious bears and brazen squirrels that can even get into sealed yogurt containers are common to the experience.

Untouched forests, high alpine meadows not yet dotted with dairy cows, and the penetrating stillness of nights brightened by the northern lights are less accessible highlights of North America's still uninhabited wilderness. Such places offer space for research removed from humanity in a world where undisturbed fieldwork is becoming increasingly difficult. But global warming, higher nitrogen levels, and other influences are altering ecosystems even far from civilization, and just outside park boundaries the reality is once again clear-cutting, agribusiness, and massive dams.

When man and nature meet, emotions are stirred. In the European Alps, the first victims among grazing animals as the result of the return of wolves, as in Switzerland, have spurred vehement debates. There have been loud demands that these predators be immediately destroyed. People outside national parks are hardly prepared for such encounters. A similar issue has surfaced in one of the best-known national parks in the United States, Yellowstone. Wolves had been exterminated because they preyed even outside the park, allowing the more glamorous bison and bears to survive and flourish—deer were also protected until they became too numerous. Wolves were reintroduced only in the 1990s and nature was again left to itself; not controlling nature's destructive processes like wildfires and not repairing the damage created, like replanting forests thrown down by wind, was a painful path to take, but one that has gradually been accepted.

Yellowstone is the oldest national park in the world, established in 1872. Created expressly for the purpose of giving people pleasure, it was thought of as the American answer to European cultural treasures like Gothic cathedrals. Since then the notion of protecting natural areas has been adopted by a number of nations—with varying commitment. Examples are Banff National Park, the first national park in Canada, established in 1885, as well as Waterton Lakes National Park, established in 1932, which has now been joined to Glacier National Park across the border in Montana to form the first international "Peace Park." The Golden Mountains of the Altai in Russia, which contain three protected areas from the Quiet Zone to the biosphere reserve, have been included on UNESCO's World Heritage list since 1998. The extensive alpine and subalpine meadows below the highest peak in Siberia, grandiose Mount Belukha, 15,157 feet high, are the focus of protection efforts. The sole German example of a national park in an alpine landscape is Berchtesgaden National Park and biosphere reserve, where endangered populations of chamois and golden eagles are now being monitored. Annapurna Conservation Area Project and Langtang National Park in Nepal together protect a total of sixteen national parks, wildlife reserves, and conservation areas that account for 16 percent of the country's area. New Zealand, small as it is, has set aside fourteen national parks.

But not all national parks are alike. What is presented as unspoiled nature is at times a deception, often no more than a label for tourists. Uniform, standardized criteria were only established with the founding of the International Union for the Conservation of Nature and Natural Resources (IUCN) in 1948, which sees to it to this day that its stringent stipulations are adhered to. Hohe Tauern National Park in Austria, already twenty years old, was only granted an international seal in July 2001, and even then only in the Carinthian section, because rampant hunting in other areas disqualified them. It was not until February 2005 that its Tirolean section was recognized. The largest landowner, the Alpine Verein, had authorized the national park to administer hunting rights, given to thirty-two leaseholders, and negotiated hunting-free zones. Routine obstructions in the Alps are such issues as mountain pasturage and, in places, intensive tourism.

An example of how difficult international cooperation can be is the effort to protect the snow leopard in Central Asia. Snow leopards are border-crossers, ecologically and politically. Poaching and the shortage of prey in border regions are threats to such animals. In addition, it has become apparent that border guards and the military go after not only their natural prey but the snow leopards themselves. As a result, the snow leopard, of which according to NABU there are only 7,000 living in the wild, was included in the 1985 Appendix I of the UN Convention for the Protection of Migratory Species. Except for the Tibetan plateau, however, the homeland of the snow leopard happens to be the high-mountain regions that form the natural and state boundaries between the twelve different countries—and in a region where international cooperation is unlikely.

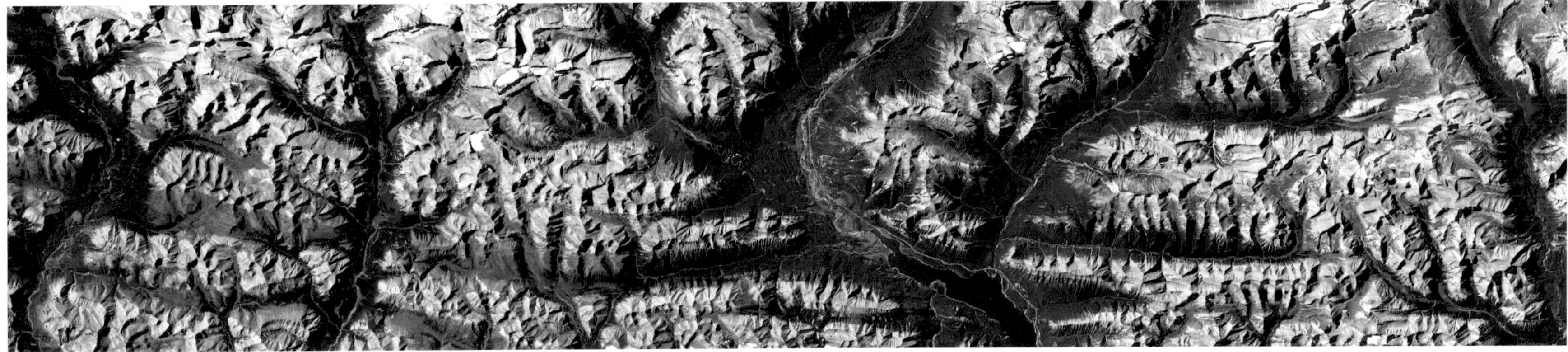

Banff National Park on September 14, 2001. A model of still largely undisturbed forests in the valleys, raging rivers, and deep-blue lakes with mountain meadows towering above suggests an intact environment in Canada's most-visited national park.

Another important and promising protection candidate is the biosphere reserves recognized by UNESCO since 1976. Biosphere reserves combine protection of ecosystems and biological resources, development of sustainable use, environmental research, and environmental education and publicity. These reserves are divided into three zones. The first is a strictly protected core area representative of natural ecosystems where nature is meant to operate undisturbed. These are mostly wilderness areas of a size considered sufficient to sustain their own independent development. Second, a nurturing zone meant to preserve valuable ecosystems of the cultural landscape and at the same time protect the core zone from damage surrounds this core area. Research, environmental education, and recreation are permitted here. Finally, a developed zone accommodates the residential, commercial, and recreational needs of the native populace, surrounding the nurturing zone as a larger area in which cooperation between science, government, and the people can ensure lasting and environmentally friendly regional development.

The goal is to set aside biosphere reserves in all mountain regions and create a long-term research and monitoring program. All elevation levels are to be included, including lower-lying ecosystems used for agriculture and settlement. In 2002 the worldwide network comprised 425 reserves in ninety-five countries, including several prominent representatives in the North American Cordillera like Yellowstone National Park, one of the very first biosphere reserves, also Berchtesgaden National Park in Germany, Mount Kenya in Africa, San Guillermo in Argentina, and Austria's Greater Walsertal.

An example of successful international collaboration is the Alpine Convention concluded in 1991 by Germany, France, Italy, Liechtenstein, Austria, Switzerland, and Slovenia. The convention envisions nothing less than a new negotiating framework for lasting environmentally and socially compatible management. It hopes to see that the Alpine region fulfill the functions brought into the foreground over the past few decades but often seen as conflicting, as an area of commerce and international traffic, a source of drinking water, a recreation area, and an ecologically balanced refuge for animals and plants. Further, it seeks to lessen the economic imbalance between agricultural mountain regions and urban and tourist concentrations and promote the self-sufficiency and self-determination of people living in the Alps. Among the goals included in the protocols of the framework convention are soil conservation, maintaining nature and landscape conservation, land use planning and sustainable development, highland economy, mountain forests, tourism, traffic, and energy—in all some 286 partial aims. Realizing such ambitious goals is not always as easy as one might wish, but there are encouraging exceptions. The Network of Alpine Sanctuaries, initiated by France in 1994, has grown to include more than 300 large protected areas, each more than 250 acres, which together make up more than 15 percent of the Alpine region.

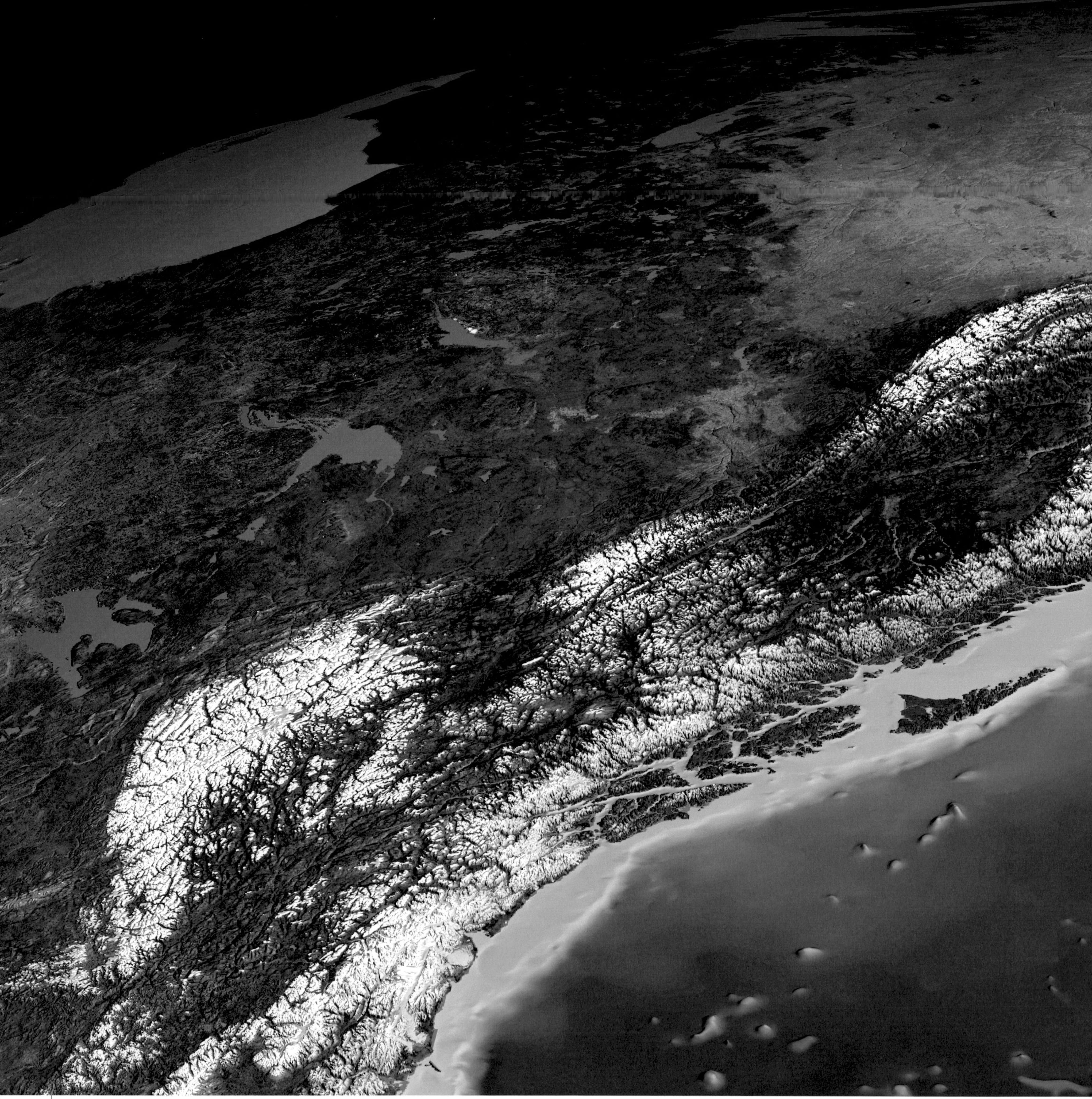

Virtual panorama of North America

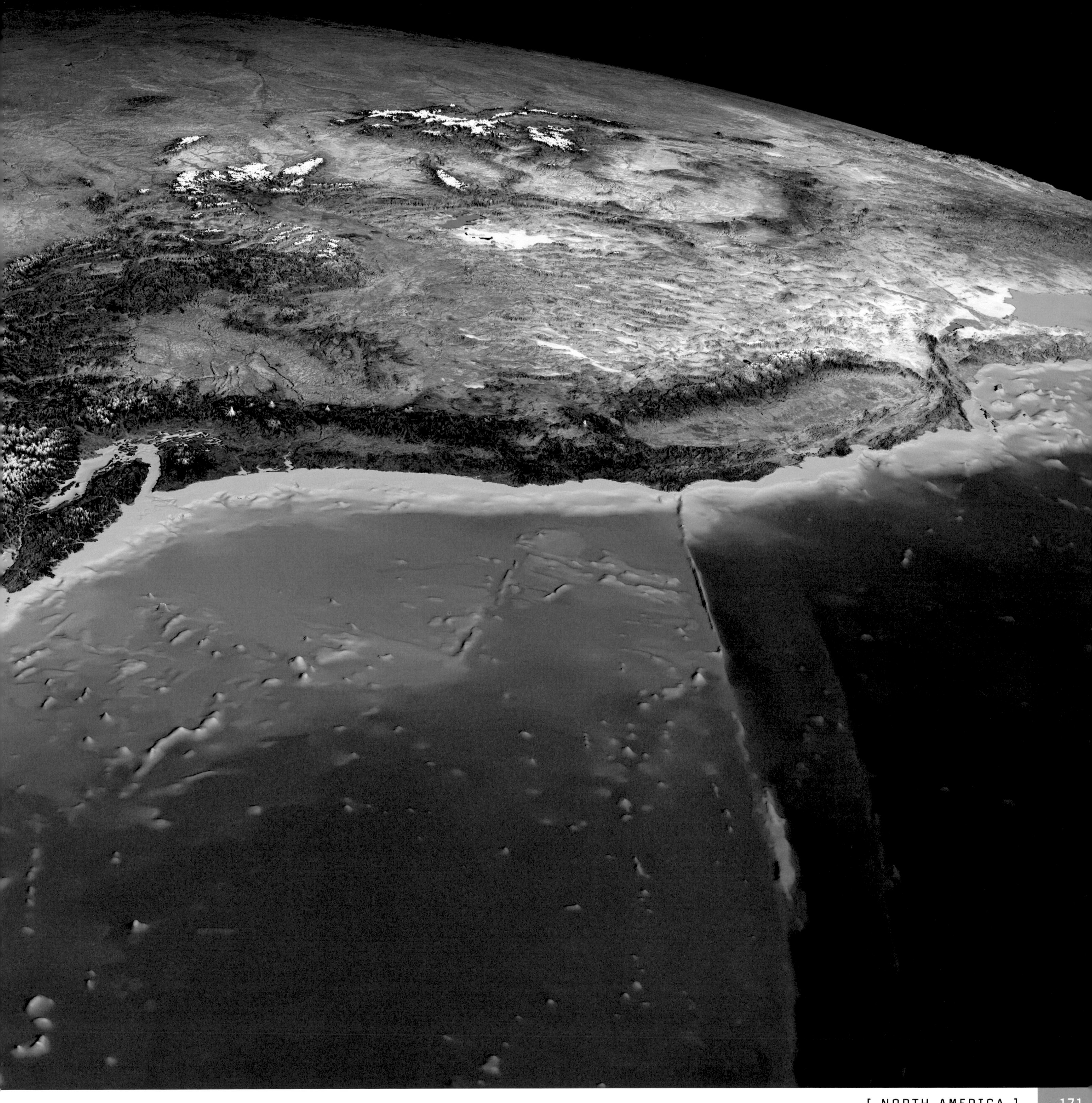

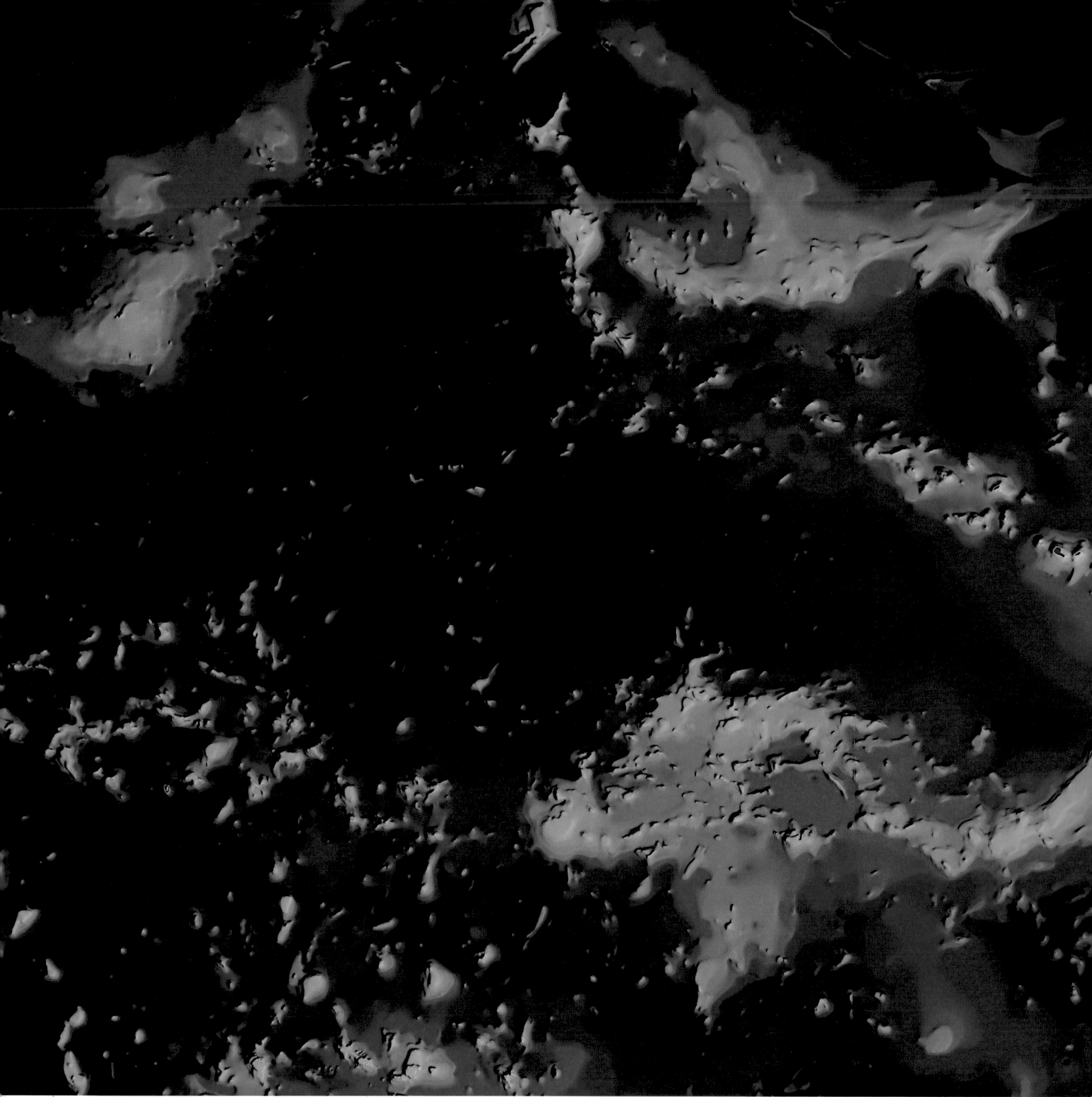

Hawaii, volcanic hot spot in the Pacific Ocean, United States

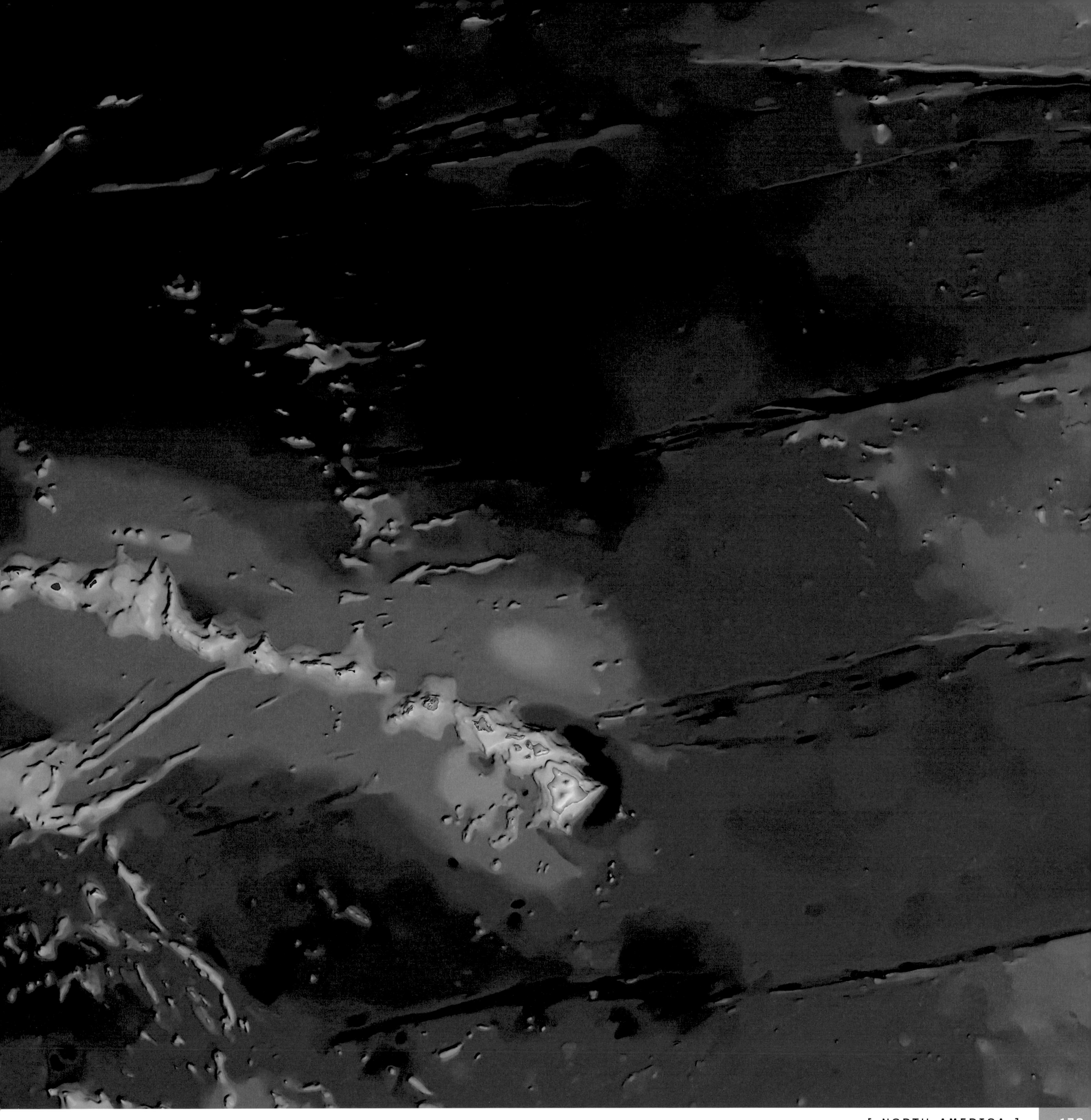

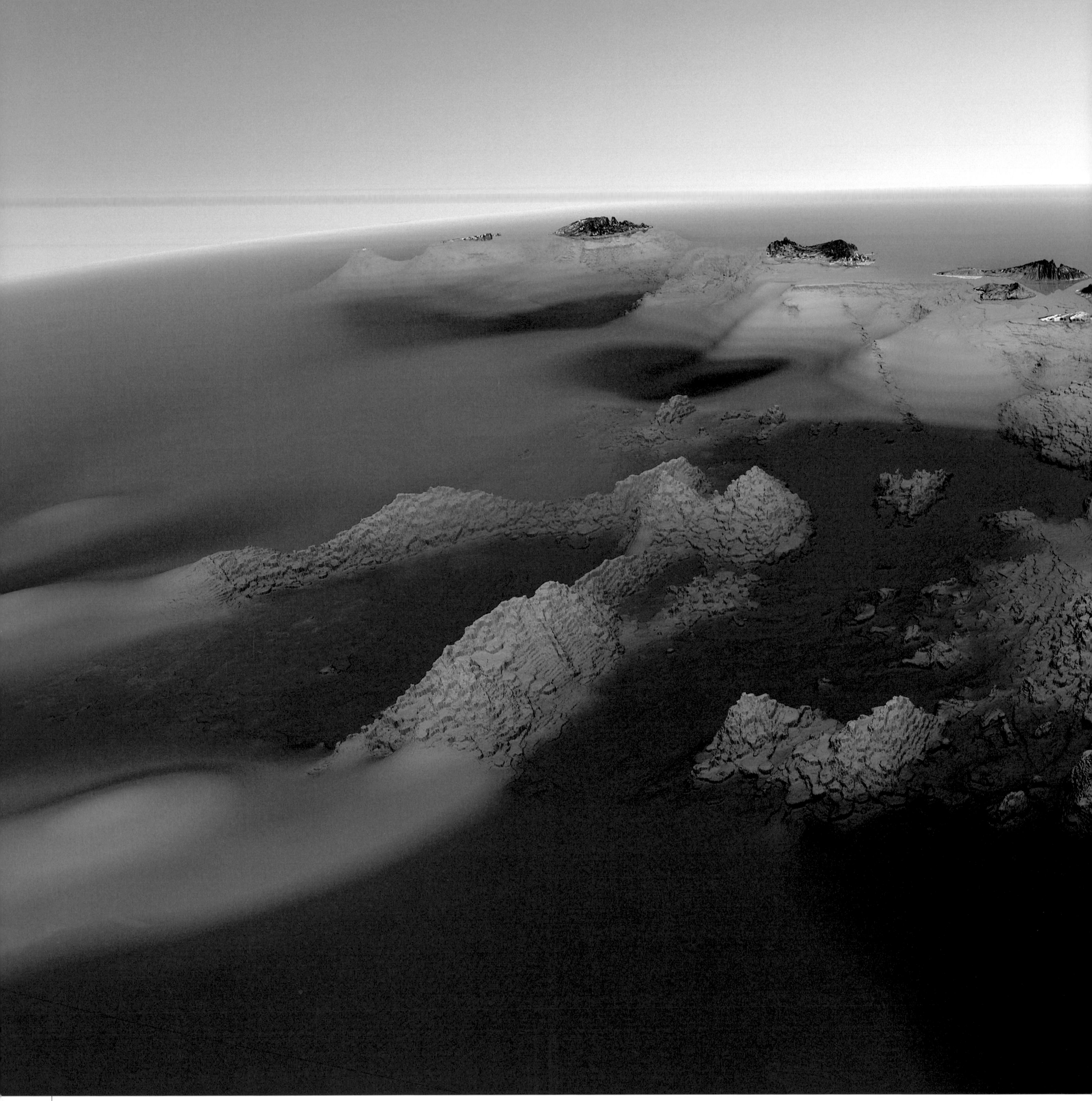

Hawaii, the highest mountain in the world from the sea floor to the peak, Pacific Ocean, United States

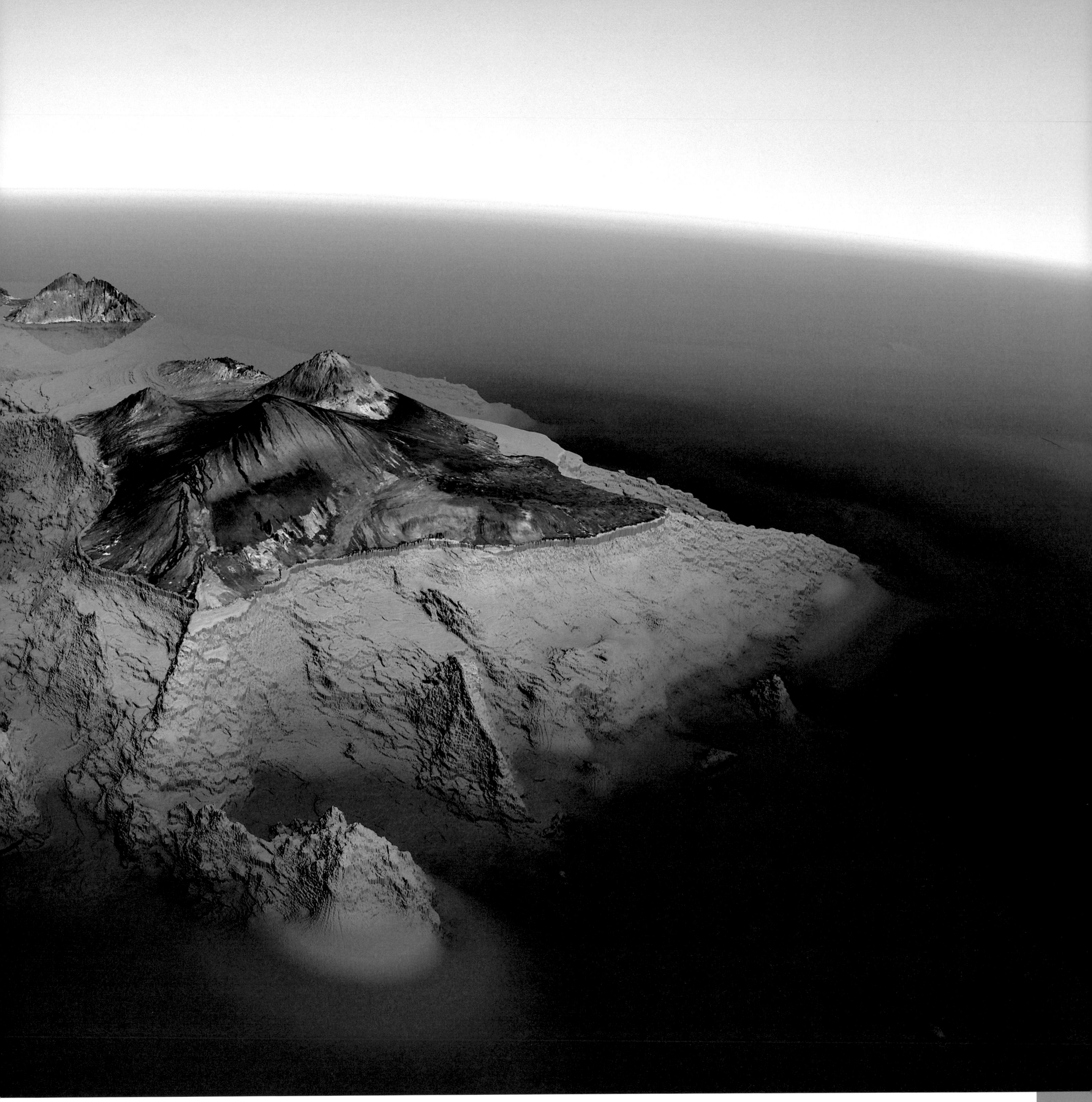

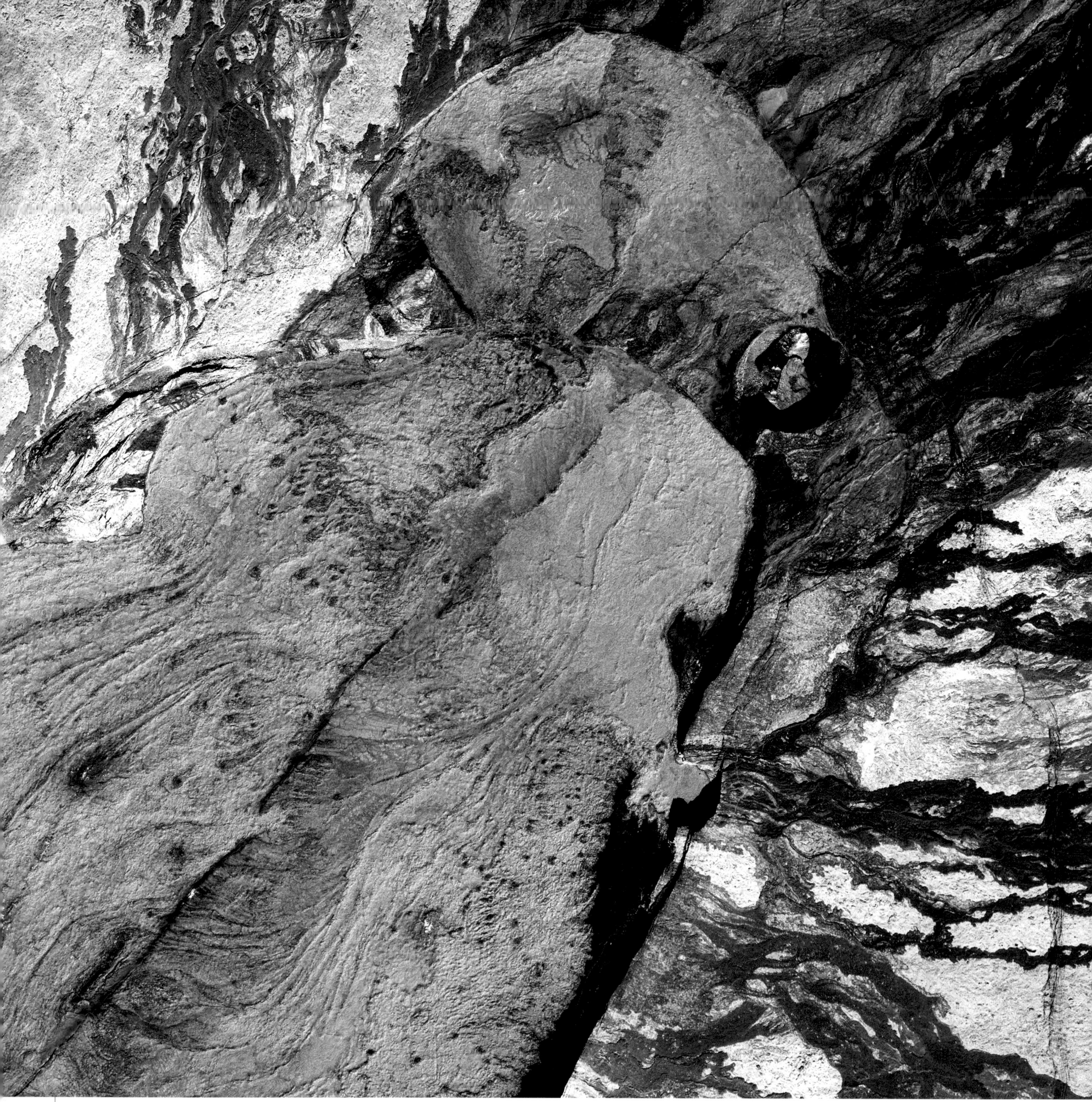

Detailed view of the Mauna Loa crater without and with snow, Hawaii, United States

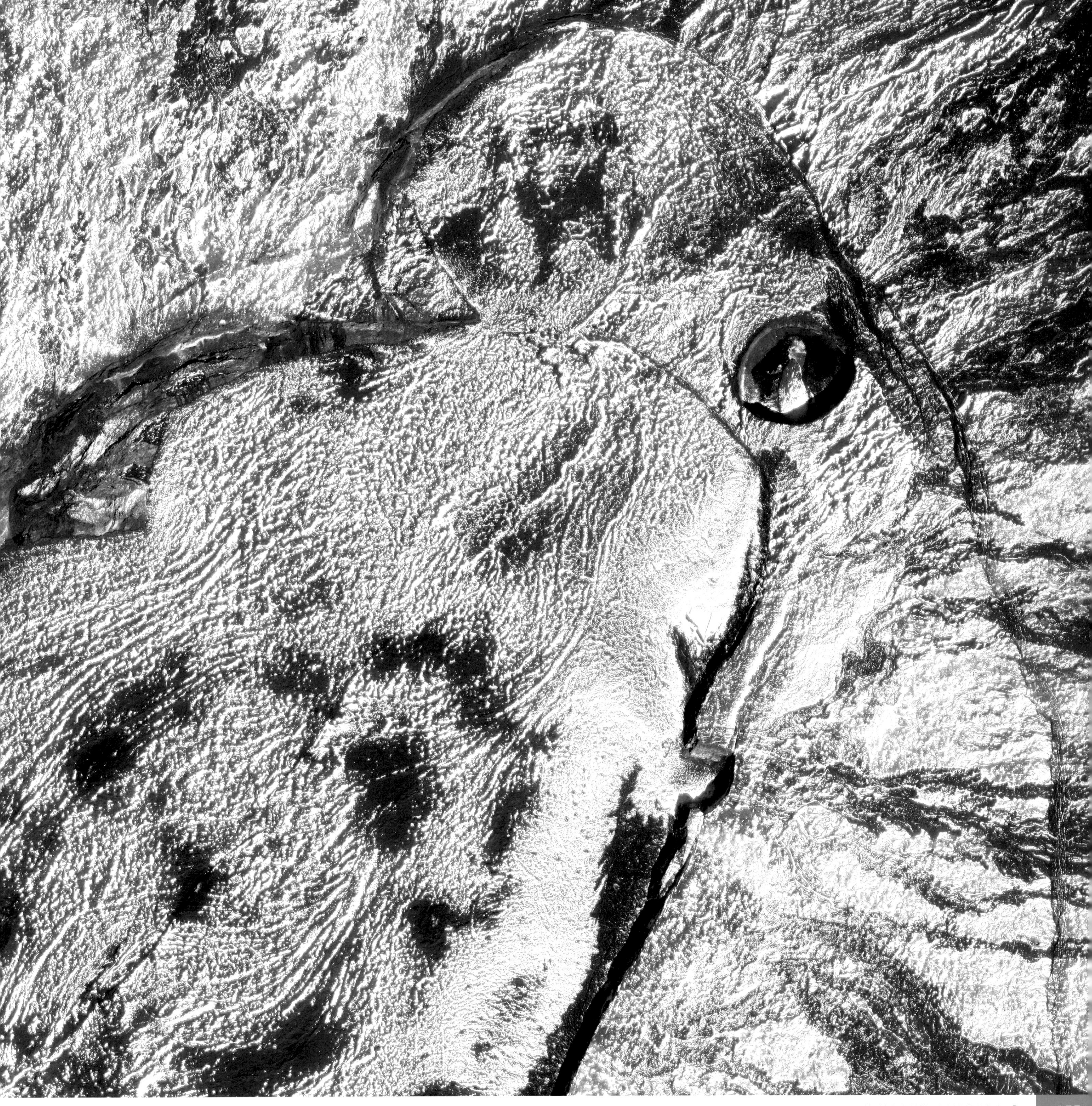

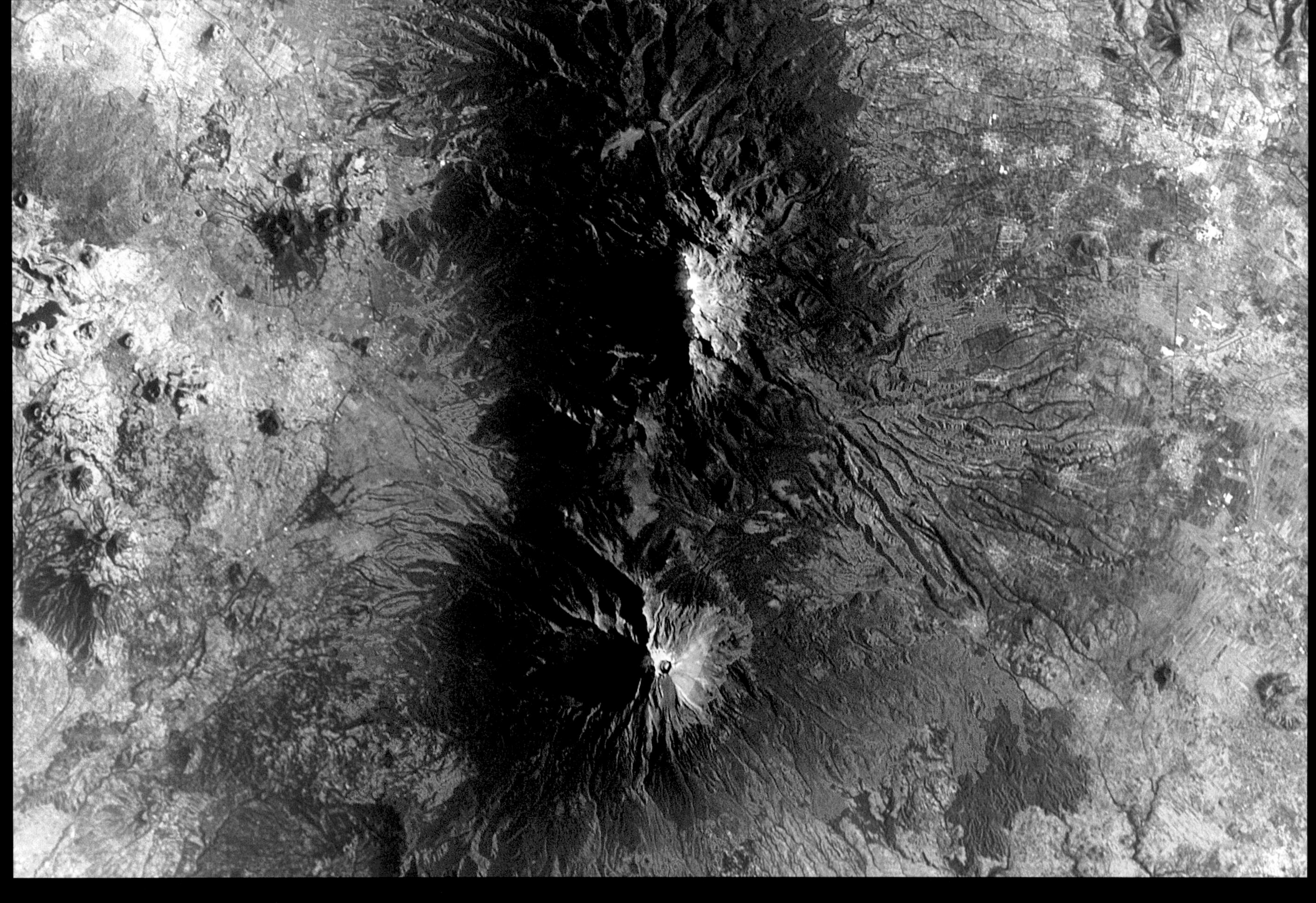

Popocatépetl, "Smoking Mountain," and Iztaccíhuatl, "Sleeping Woman," Mexico

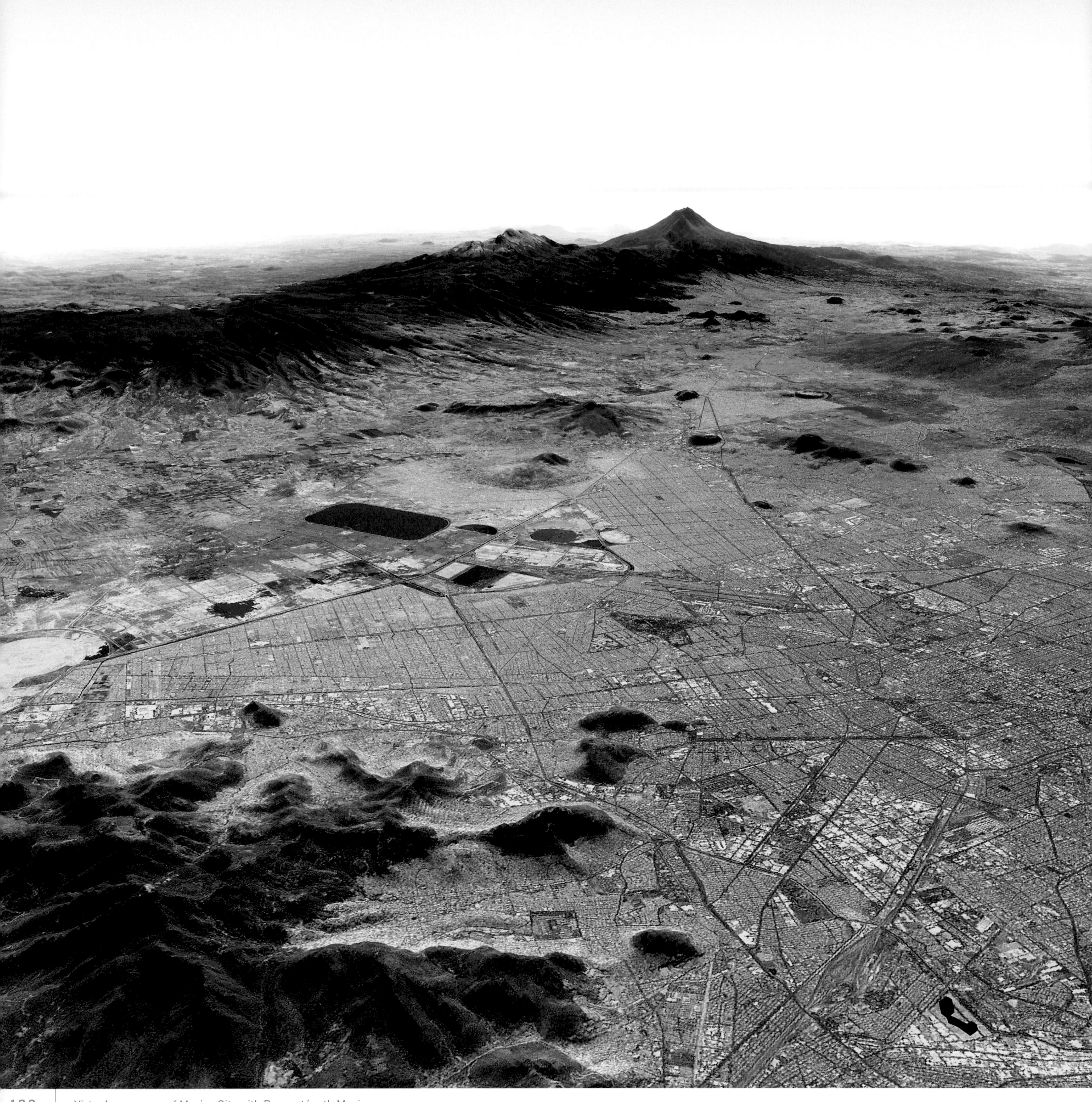

Virtual panorama of Mexico City with Popocatépetl, Mexico

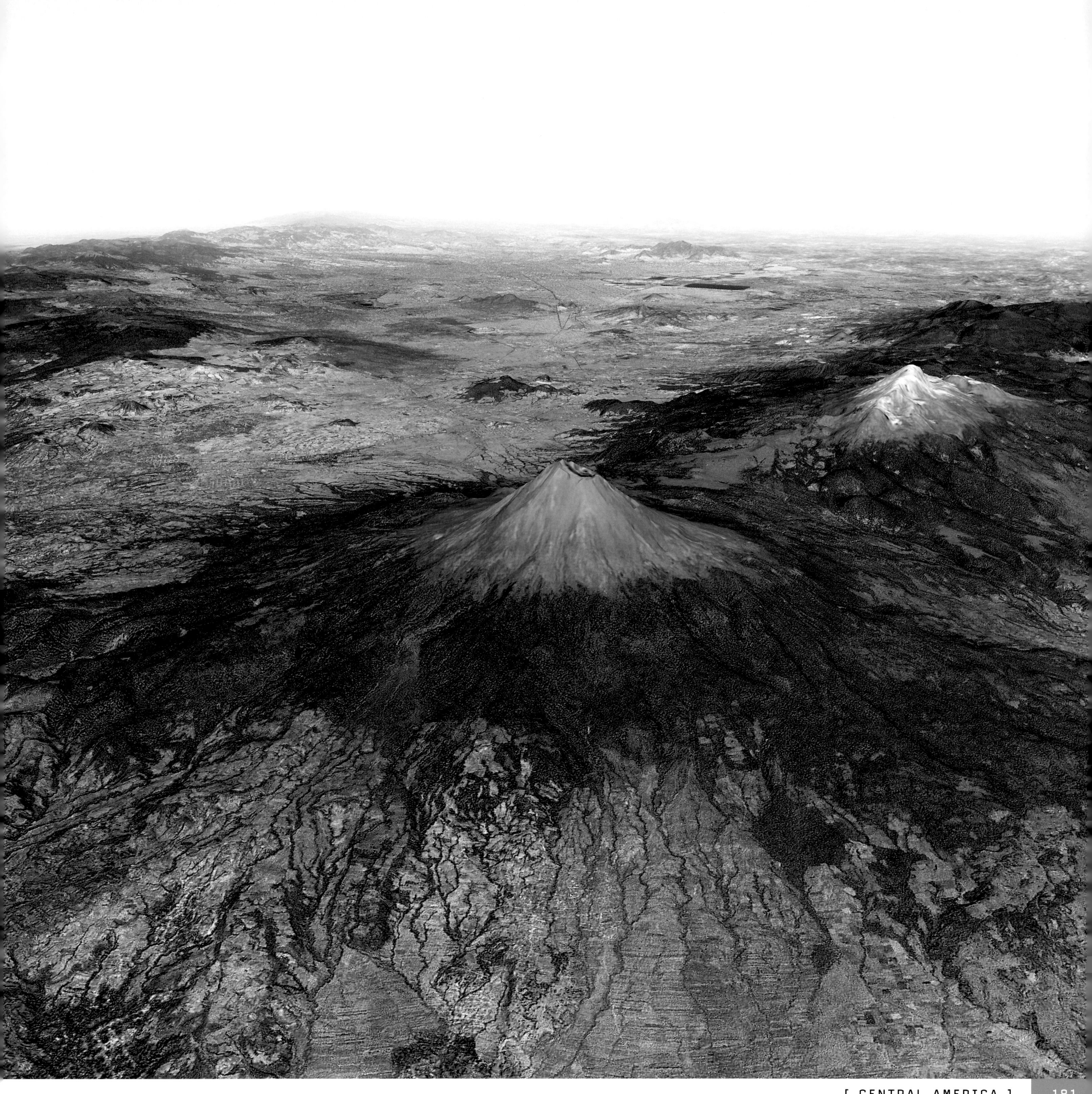

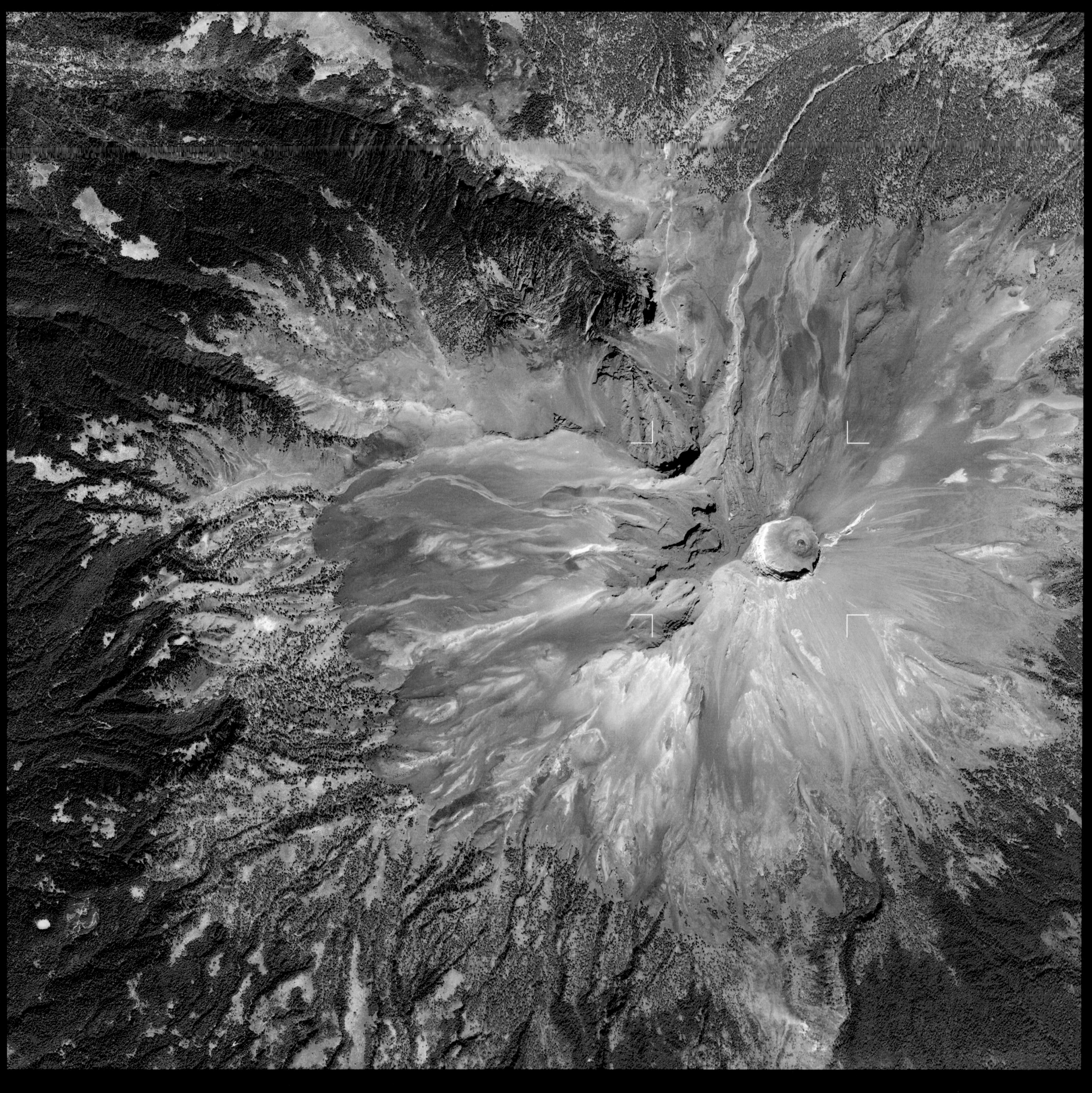

Detailed view of the Popocatépetl crater, Mexico

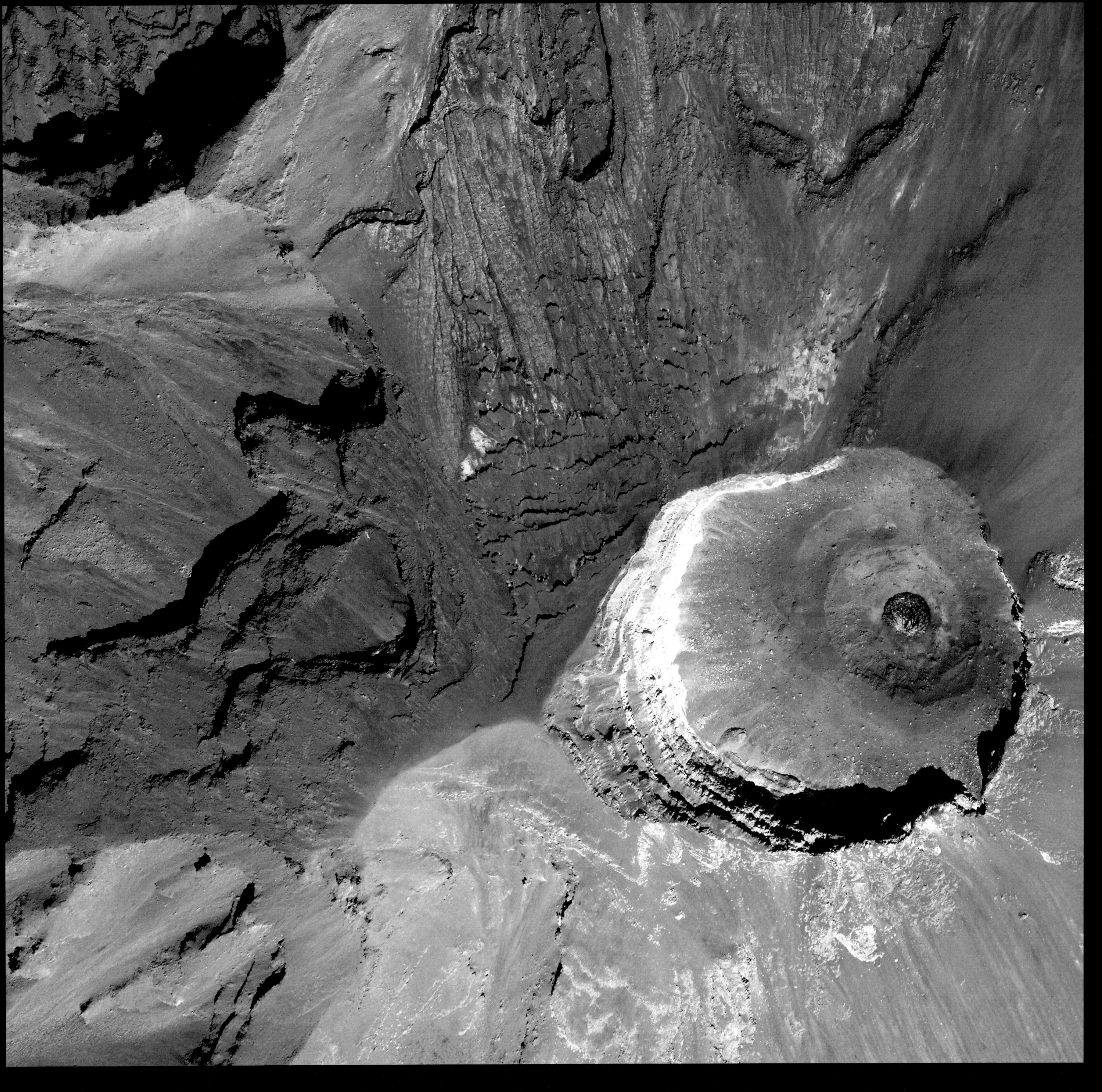

[SOUTH AMERICA]

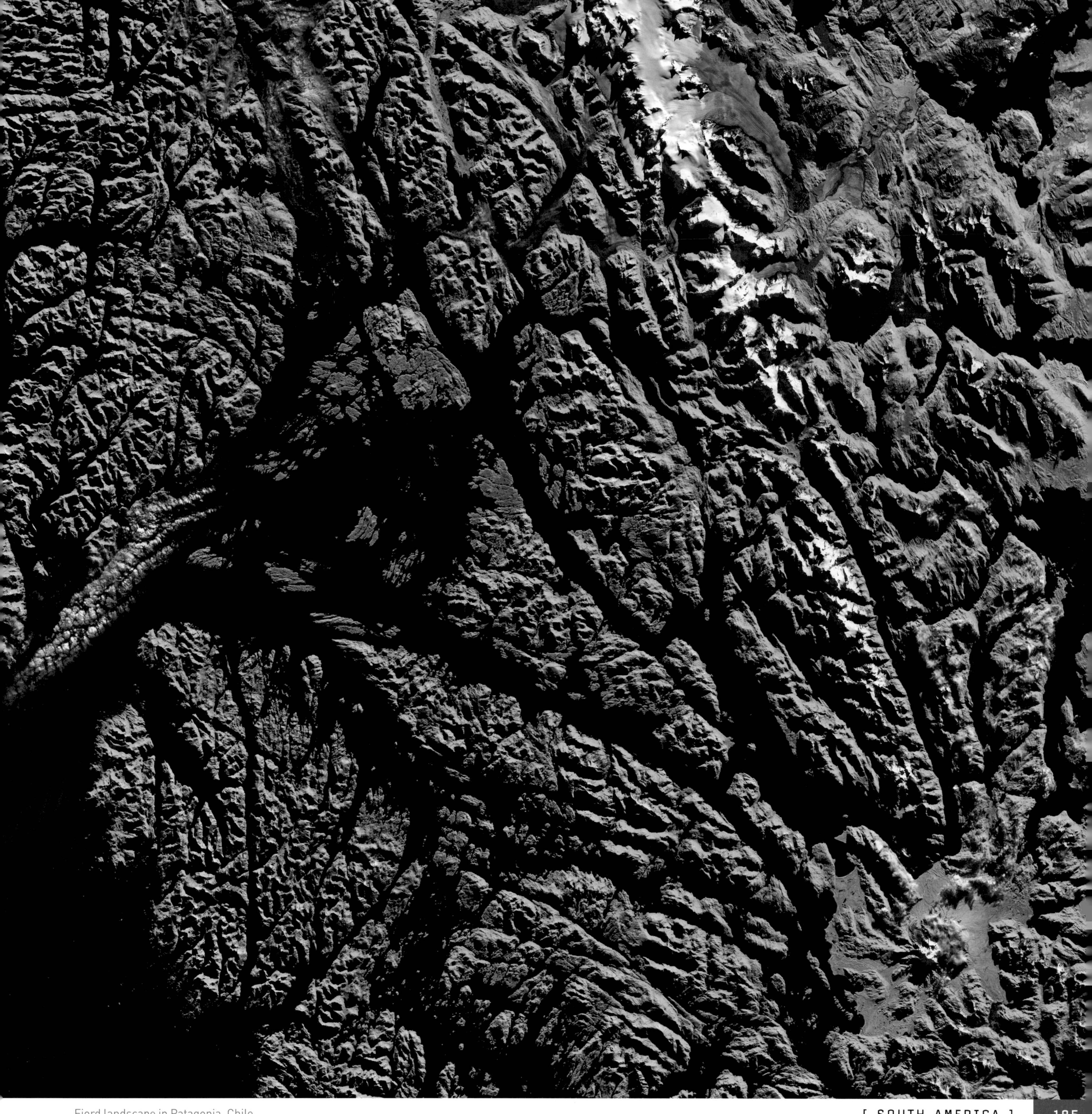

Fjord landscape in Patagonia, Chile

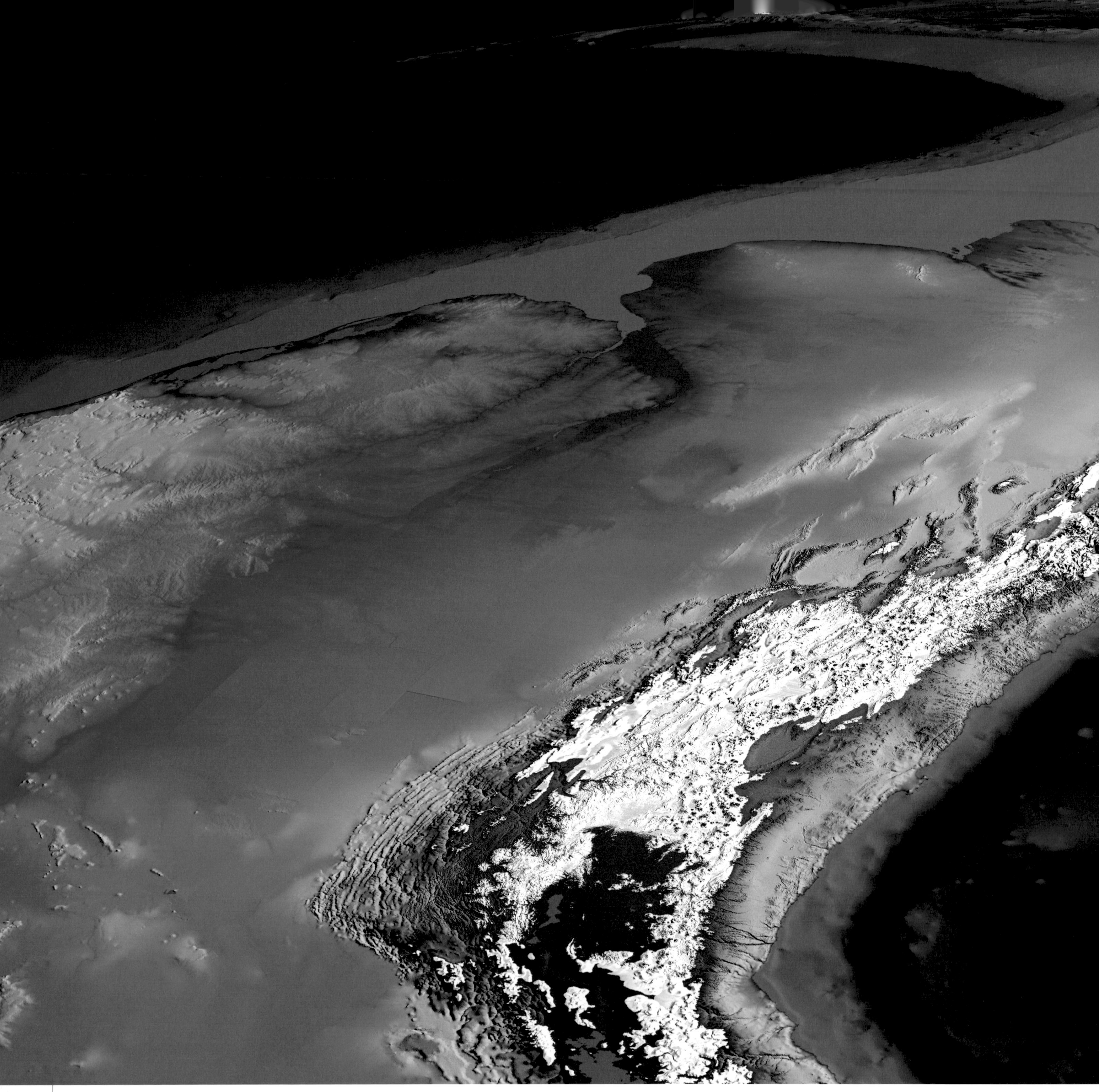

The Andes, the longest mountain range on earth

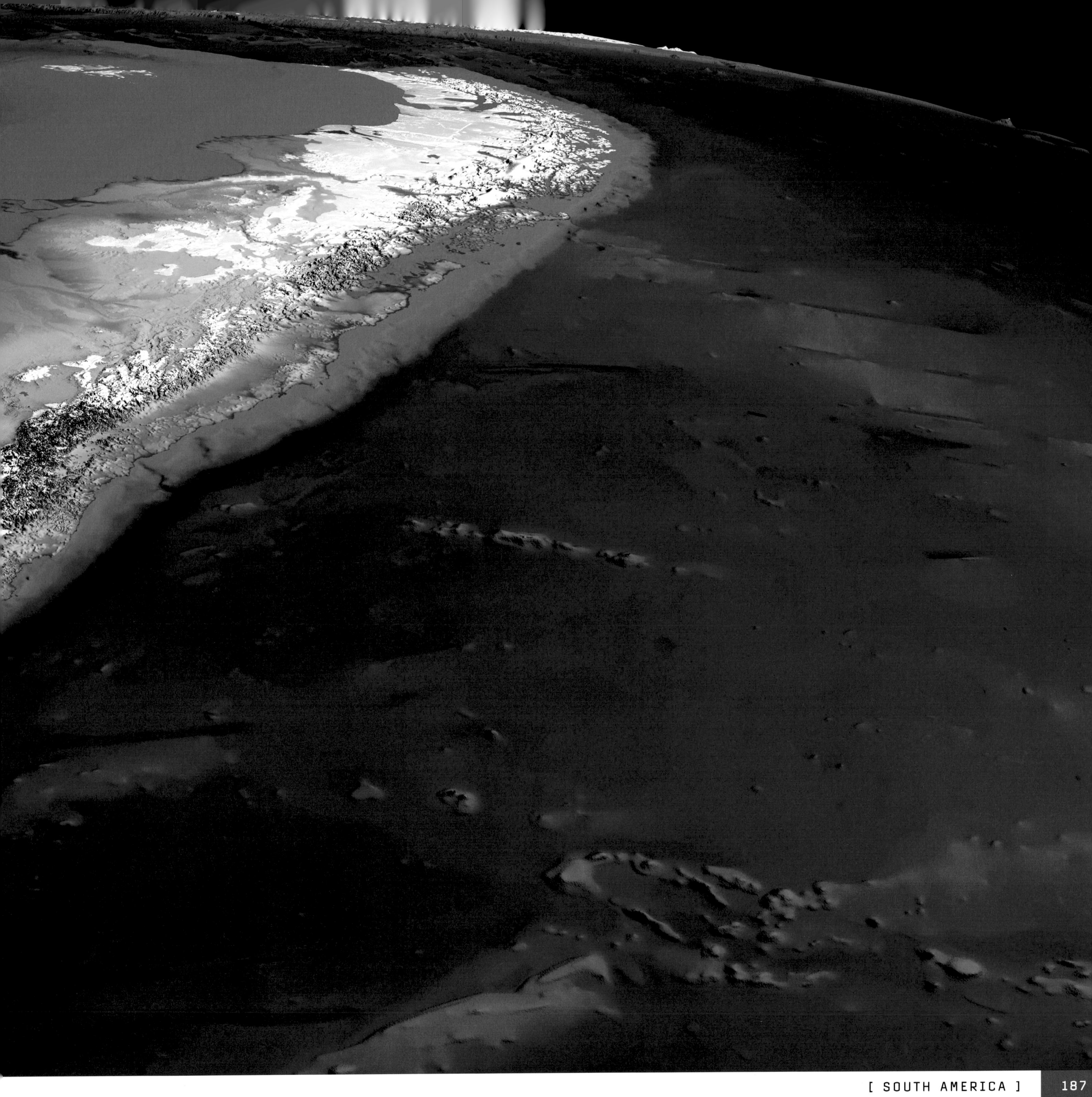

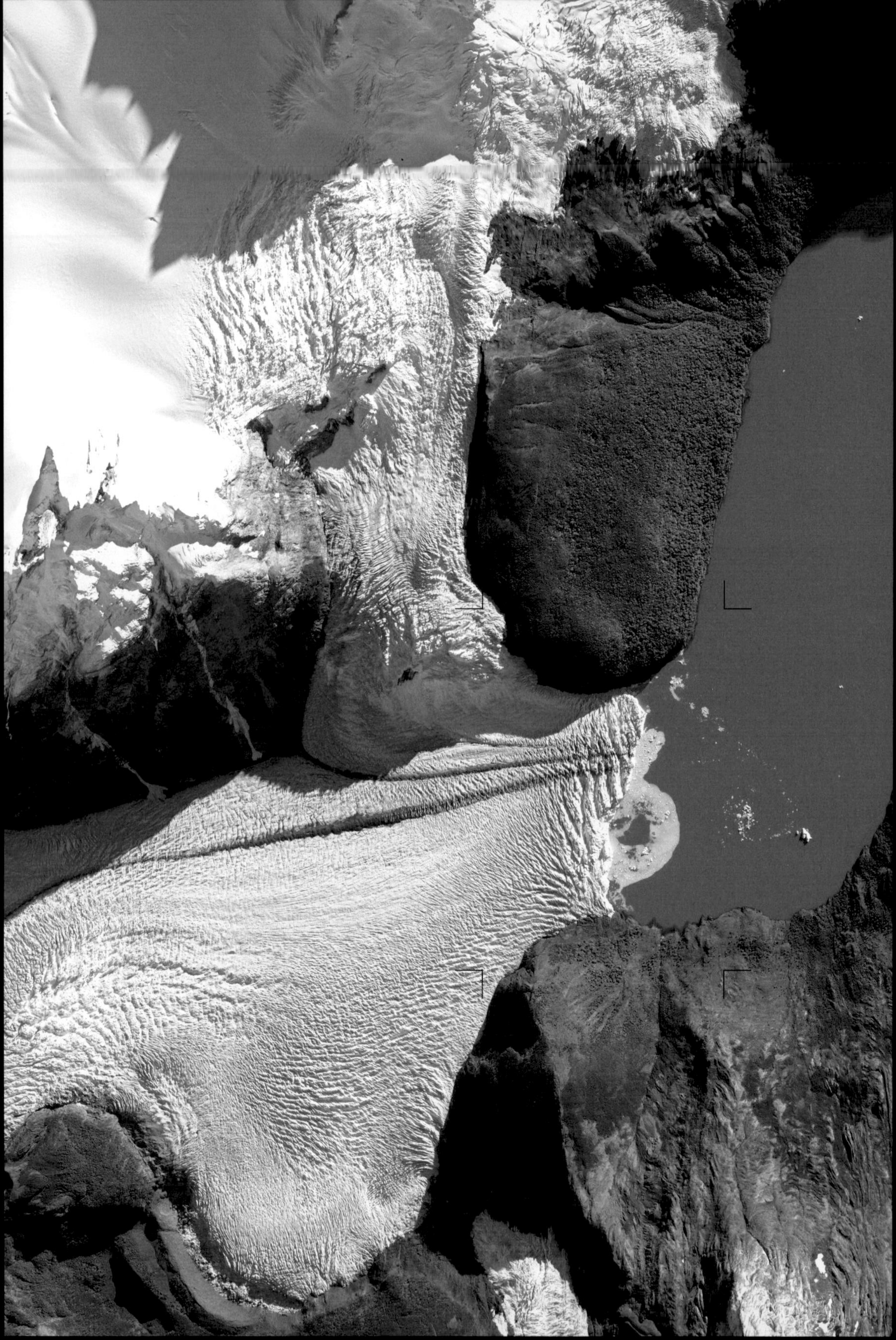

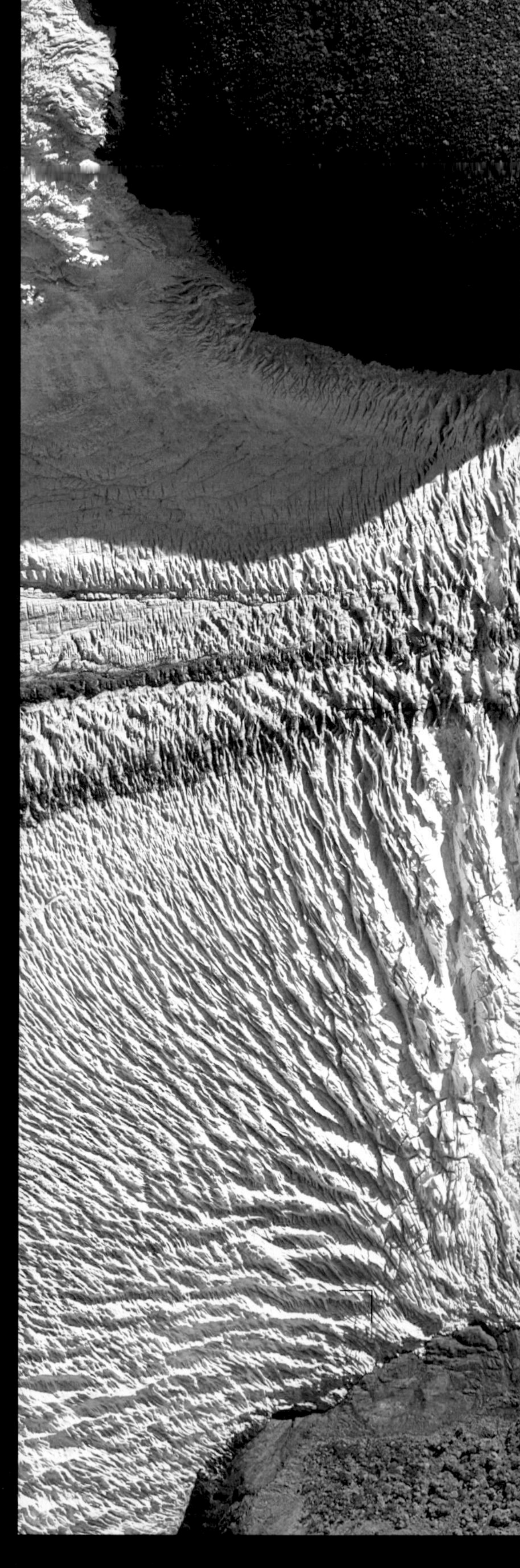

Spegazzini Glacier, Argentina

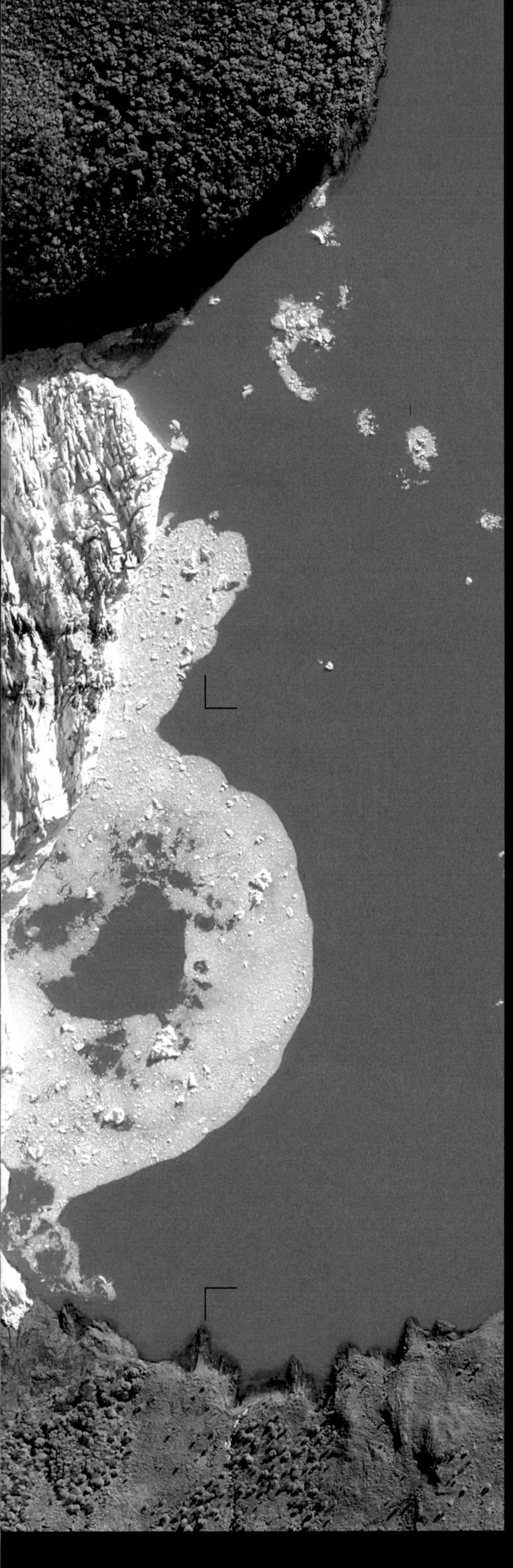

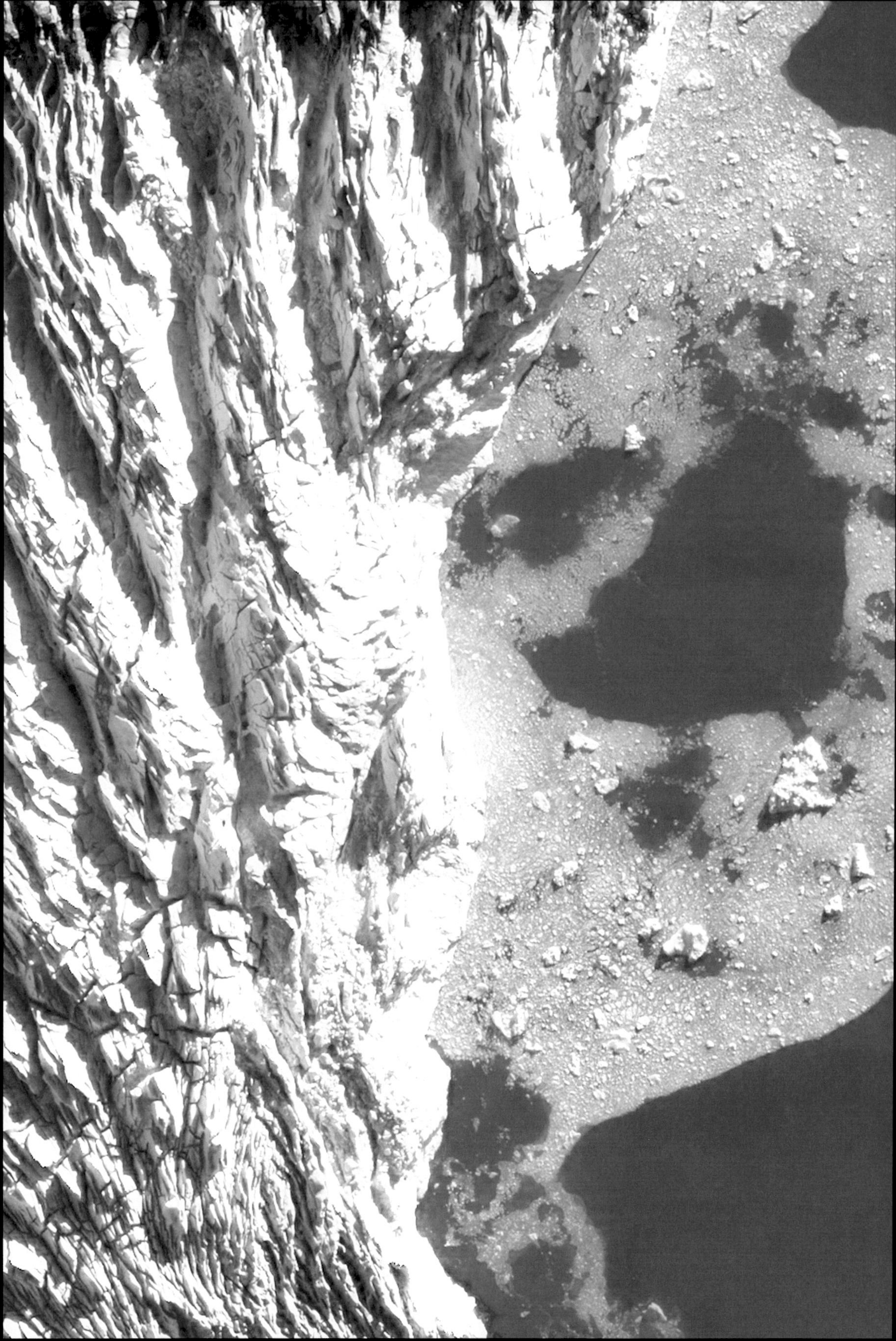

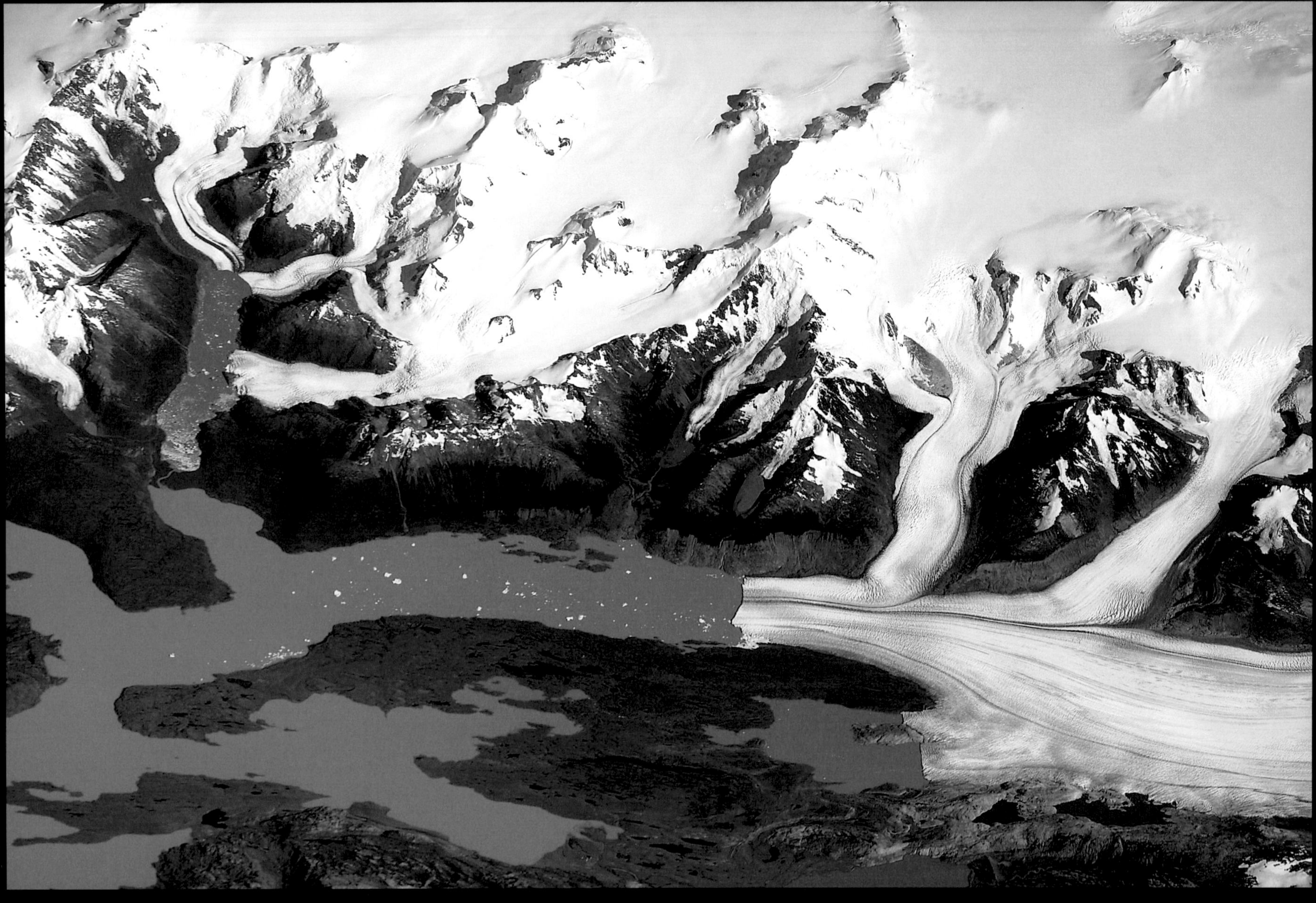

Upsala Glacier, Lake Argentino, Argentina

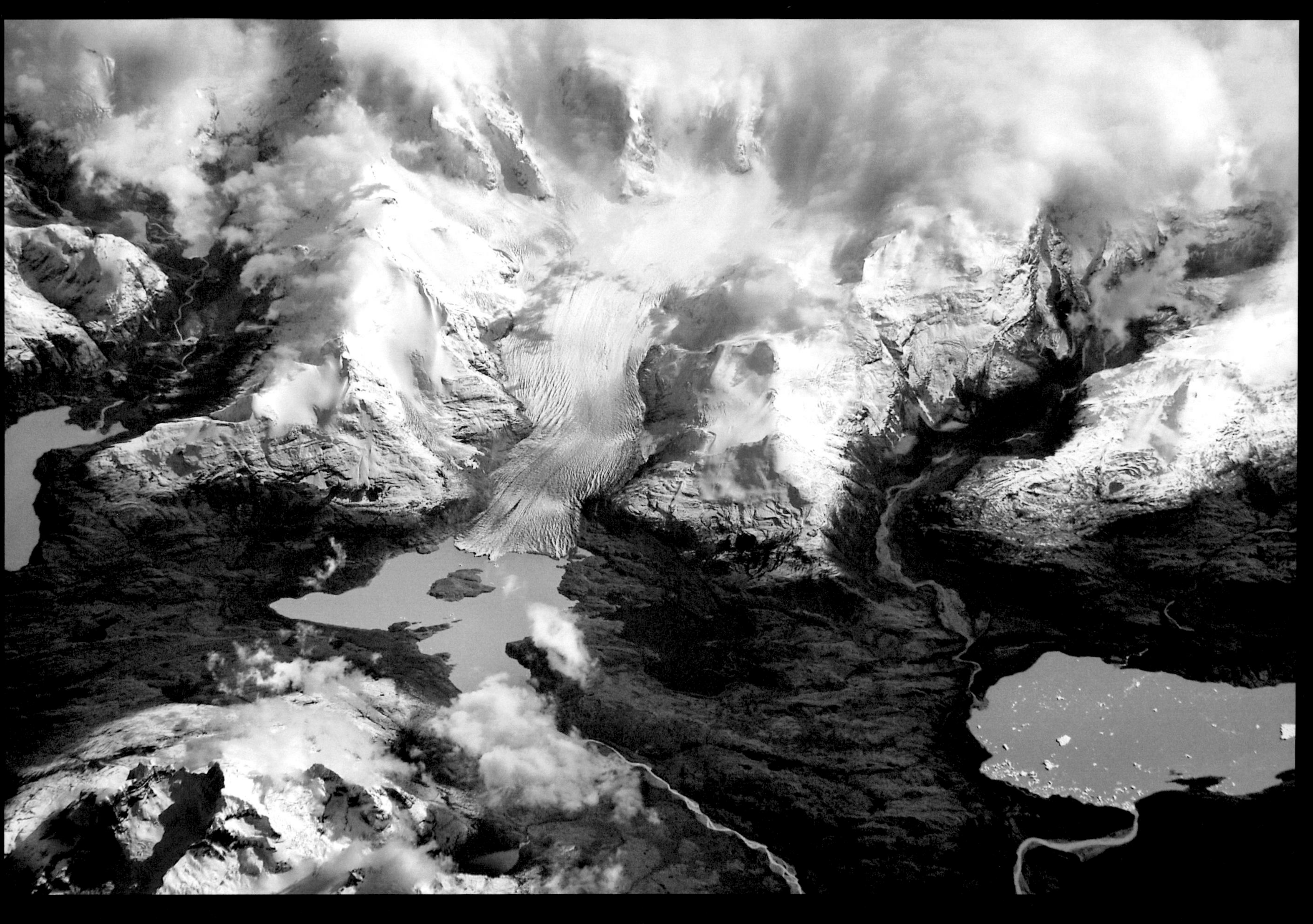

Ultima Esperanza Fjord and Patagonian inland ice, Chile

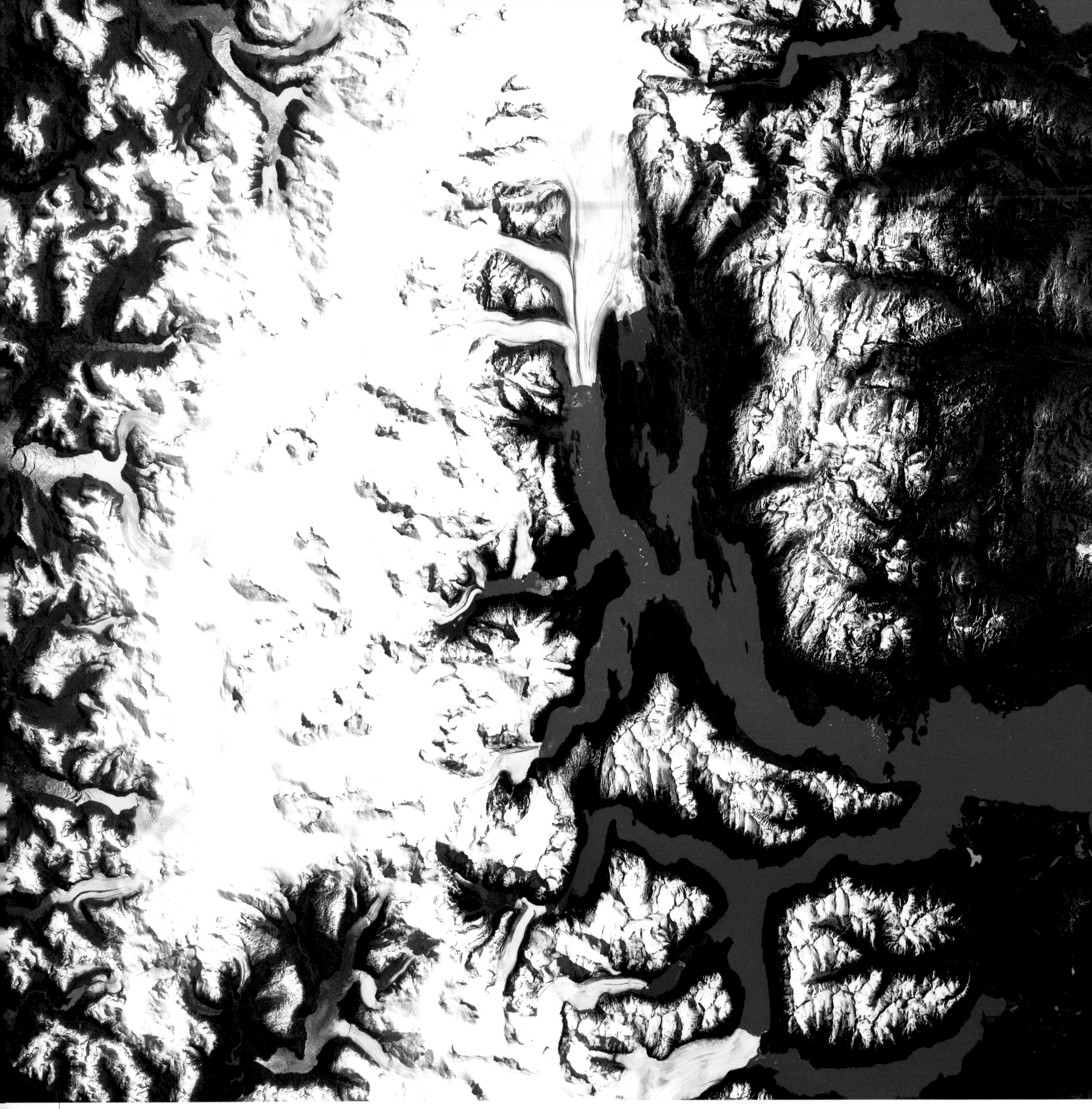

Los Glaciares National Park, Argentina/Chile

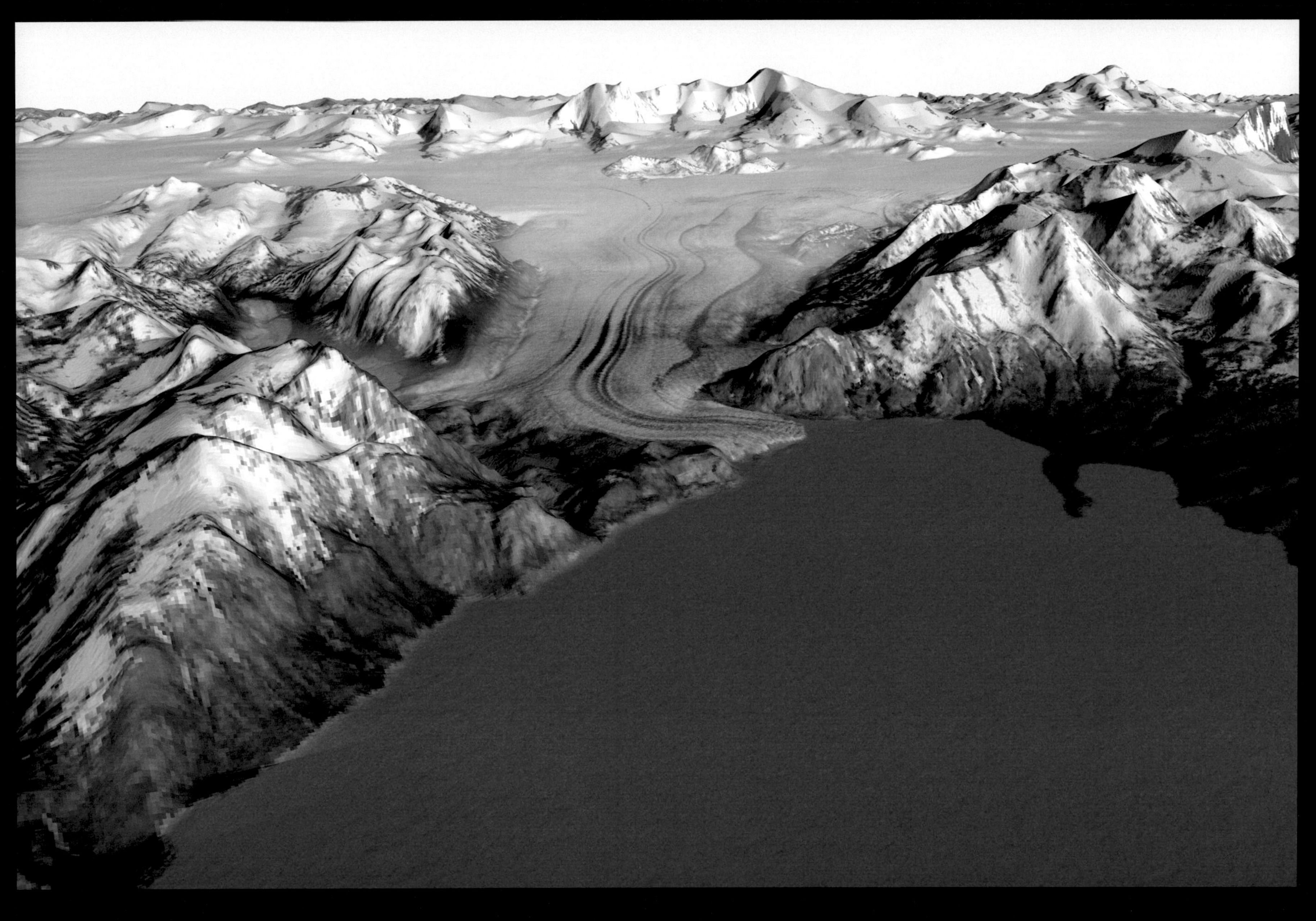

Viedma Lake, Argentina

On the Route of the Volcanoes

REINHOLD MESSNER

I fly on to Quito, Ecuador, home of South America's most beautiful volcanoes. But this time I am not heading for Chimborazo, whose peak Alexander von Humboldt failed to reach by a mere 2,625 vertical feet two hundred years ago. Nor is the planned climb up 19,347-foot Cotopaxi of particular concern. This time I am mainly interested in the highland people of Alao, who get ice from glaciers for the cities.

In Ecuador, the country with the lowest standard of living in Latin America, mountain dwellers are doubly poor. Their currency, the sucre, has been replaced by the U.S. dollar, and this has made life even more expensive for the 13 million Ecuadoreans. Each year half a million people emigrate to Spain and Italy, for today no nation can maintain its economy from agriculture alone. It is understandable that Ecuador's government is counting on the export of oil from wells in the jungle on the other side of the Andes. How else can the country survive? The only question is how to build the pipelines without causing major ecological damage—and where the profits will go.

In spite of everything, there is abundant produce in the markets. After all, the fertile climate of the tropics is ideal for cultivation of potatoes, carrots, peppers, tomatoes, radishes, apples and oranges, corn and rice. There is also meat, especially pork. But only the cheapest cuts find buyers: bellies, intestines, and other innards. Here no one can afford a steak.

In Alao, a village on the edge of Sangay National Park, a few hundred people are attempting to survive as a mountain community. Their fields on the slopes are small and subject to slides. Behind them stretches the nature conservation zone protected by law. And far behind that rises the Altar volcano, the tallest in the region. A few idealists—an architect from Quito, an Italian from Riobamba—got the Alao project running by building a water conduit, then a school. The group also established the first bearers' association in Ecuador, organized like the Sherpas in Nepal. These men carry expedition gear for researchers and tourists to the bases of the peaks of the surrounding volcanoes, making it easier for them to climb Sangay and Altar. Trekking tourism is also a growing source of income for the Alao people. The hope with this project is to improve living conditions and at the same time protect the area's plants and animals. But it is crucial that deforestation be stopped. Seventy percent of Ecuador's forests have been lost in the past thirty years, sacrificed for the export of tropical woods, plowed up for rose plantations and new fields for agriculture. What do the people here have to look forward to, when their slopes are eroding because the rain forest is gone and tourists are staying away because agriculture is in decline?

Working as guides for foreign researchers and climbers, carrying their gear, is not a bad alternative. The small men of Alao organize trekking tours, transport the equipment, do the cooking, and tend to the camp—for eight dollars a day, a decent wage in Ecuador. So this could be the beginning of environmentally compatible tourism. Perhaps a few lodges could be added, offering accommodations for travelers and providing the local women with places to sell their woven rugs and and their llama-wool sweaters. Along with agriculture, handicrafts are basic to existence everywhere in the mountains.

But the people of Alao can only create something lasting if they preserve their culture and do not squander their resources. One must not forget: when help comes from outside, it is at the cost of self-respect. Subsidized development projects have often been doomed to failure because they do not promote the initiative of the people themselves. Mountain people like those of Alao can only survive if they save themselves, if they cultivate their own culture and make the most of the possibilities tourism creates. At the moment the prospects are good. Because classical trekking areas—Nepal, Kashmir, Tibet—are considered politically dangerous regions, Ecuador could fill a market niche in mountain tourism.

Marco Cruz, Ecuador's most important mountain climber, has shown the way with his llama and alpaca hacienda. On a superb site, with a view of Chimborazo, he has created a paradise for his animals and for vacation guests. Buildings of wood and native stone reflect indigenous architecture and provide all the comforts expected by spoiled citydwellers. Cruz, who has made a number of first climbs in Ecuador, Peru, Chile, and Bolivia, is now a tourism pioneer, just as the best mountain guides were in the Alps one hundred years ago. Today he runs his own mountain climbing school, a hotel in Riobamba, and the unique farm on Chimborazo. His sense of style and his enthusiasm for local culture make him an exception. He has created what I envision for many other mountain regions: a sustainable development model.

Ten years ago we climbed Chimborazo together. At 20,561 feet it is not only the highest volcanic peak in the country, it is also important for its role in the development of expedition climbing. When Alexander von Humboldt attempted to climb it in 1802, he approached it with enthusiasm but also naiveté. He was no mountain climber, but he was inquisitive. After he and his companions had made their way to the peak on horseback, they climbed up along a ridge on the Riobamba flank to an altitude of roughly 18,375 feet until a dangerous chasm blocked their way. Humboldt did not set a world altitude record, as he assumed at the time. He only came close to this peak that is, measured from the center of the earth, the highest in the world. On his return he precisely described his physical and mental state at such an elevation: headache, limited perception, incredible exhaustion. His report reads like a treatise on mountain sickness, which was still unresearched at that time.

Three-quarters of a century later the first man to climb the Matterhorn, Edward Whymper, and his defeated rival Jean-Antoine Carrel teamed up to

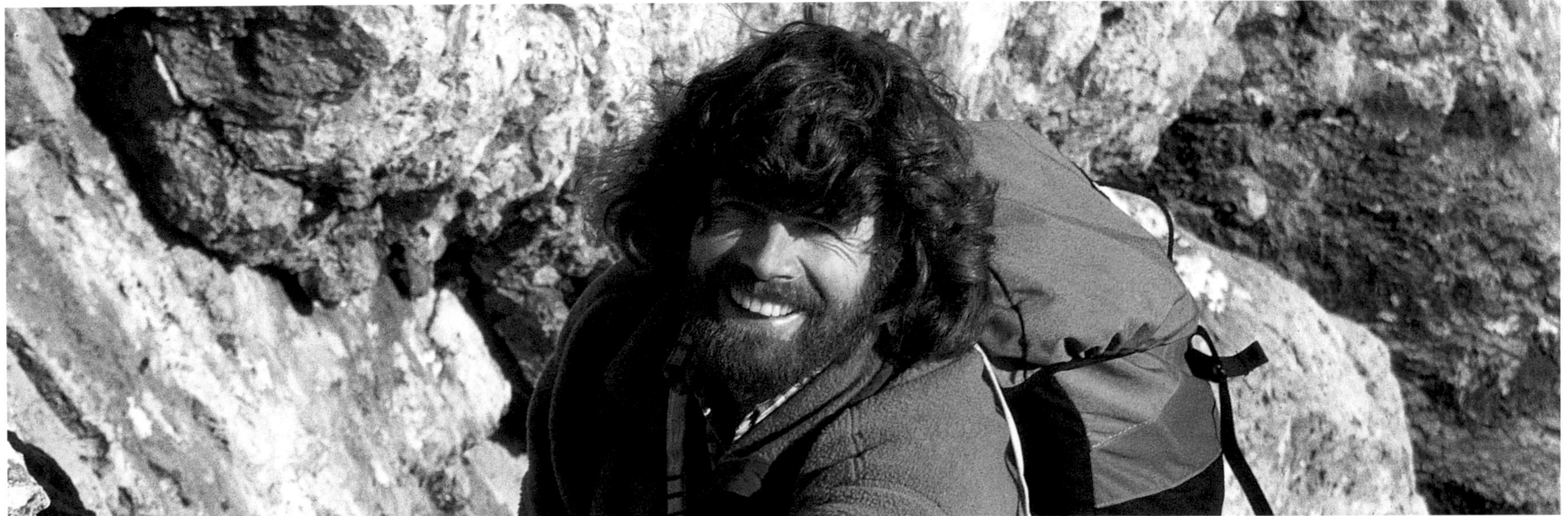

conquer Chimborazo. They managed it with the aid of potassium chloride and red wine, and I consider their climb of this peak in 1880 their greatest achievement.

In 1993 I took both routes, the one followed by the German naturalist until forced to turn back and that of the Whymper-Carrel team up to the icy rim high above the equator. I wanted to experience what these trailblazers had when testing their limits.

After circling Chimborazo—partly in driving snow and partly under burning hot sun—our group moved on to Cotopaxi. During its last eruption a good hundred years ago, a mudslide caused devastating damage. Clear to the coast, where the mud finally stood five meters high, the horror divided the land in two.

Should we have been afraid? Every mountain is dangerous, even more so an active volcano. Nevertheless, we all wanted to scale it and we each set about preparing for the climb in our own way. Some went for a walk, others lay in the tent. I crouched in the sun and read. But I too was nervous, as I always am when setting off into the unknown. I am more alert than usual, full of respect for "my" mountain.

Cotopaxi, the tallest active volcano in the world, is only forty-seven miles from the equator. Its cap of ice can be seen as far as Riobamba. The normal route is not especially difficult, but ice picks and climbing irons, ropes, and climbing belts are indispensable. It is important to set out early, so headlamps are also a must. Whoever stands at the crater at sunrise has won. While I slogged up the icy slopes in the dark, the dots of light from my comrades below me, I thought of the Alpine painter Rudolf Reschreiter, who climbed this mountain in 1903 with the geographer and publisher Hans Meyer, the first man to climb Kilimanjaro. Reschreiter left behind a whole portfolio of watercolors and oil paintings of Cotopaxi, its icy slopes, its glaciers, and the crater. I have collected them in my ice museum in Solda, in the South Tirol, and every time I look at the greens and blues of Cotopaxi's ice in his pictures I feel transported back to the mountain. Not only memories, but physical sensations are revived, as though the mountain were aglow within me.

Above 18,000 feet we continued meditatively, exchanging few words. Fifty steps, a pause for breath, another fifty steps. After a good four hours we were standing on the highest point of the volcano: the stench of sulfur, wind, cold. Then the sunrise provided a glorious spectacle. Incredible colors crept across the sky—first a dark violet, then a bright red. And the silence! Your first sensation is one of being lost, but then the first light strikes you. It warms the soul more than the body, relieves any anxiety, and the sight of the other 20,000-footers on the route of the volcanoes inspires you to hatch new plans.

The descent. The snow becomes soft, and it contracts. But we cannot lose our way, we simply follow our tracks from the climb. If I had the ability, I wish I could capture such scenes as Reschreiter did, who as the expedition's painter played the same role in satisfying public curiosity as does the satellite camera sending imaging data down to earth today.

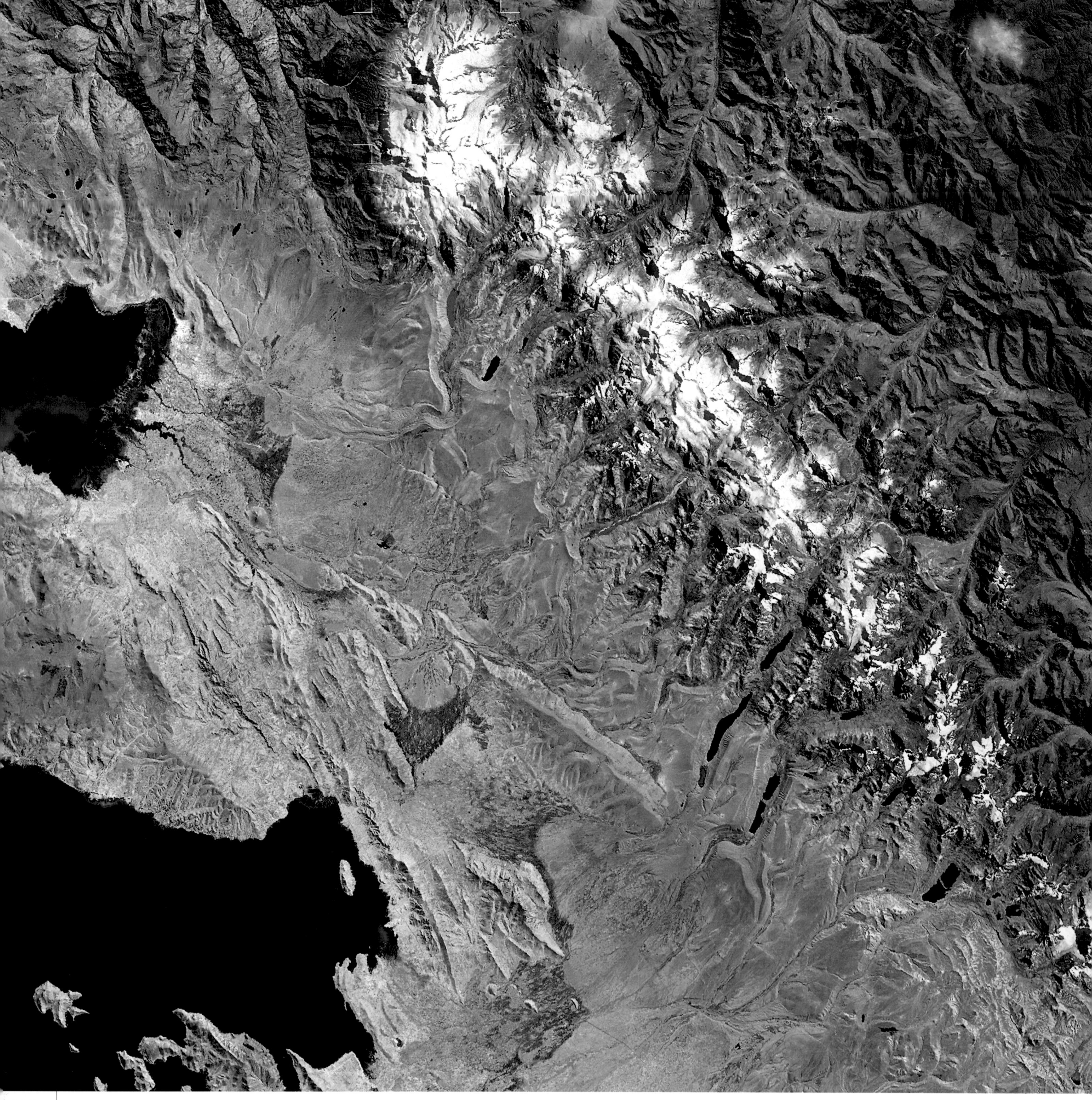

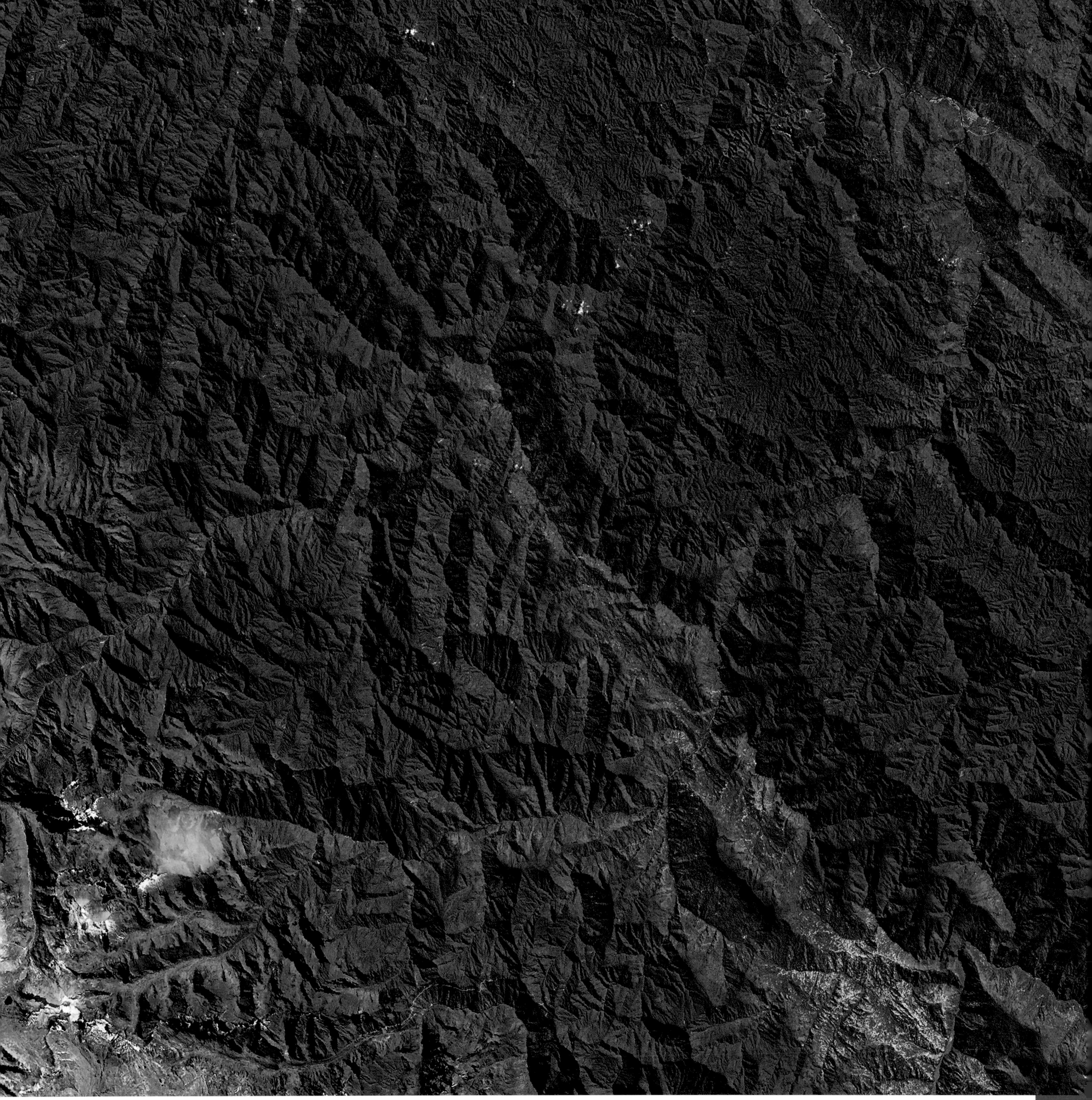

Biodiversity
Endangered Populations

RÜDIGER GLASER

Whether the Caucasus or the tropical Andes, California's Sierra Nevada or the New Zealand Alps, mountains are ecologically rich environments. Their intricate structure, geographic and climatic variety, and differing elevation belts create ecological niches in which a great variety of species can thrive, and even develop offshoots exclusive to the region. Mountains form a network of biodiversity spanning the globe that is urgently in need of protection.

Many high-mountain regions are biodiversity "hot spots"—areas teeming with a much larger range of species than elsewhere. Not only does the unique configuration of mountain environments support the growth of new species, but isolated valleys provide ideal conditions for their evolution, particularly endemic ones. Endemic species are those whose range is highly limited, species found only in a single location, as opposed to cosmopolitans, like human beings and rats, which are found in every part of the globe. Endemic species are especially characteristic of islands that have been isolated for long periods of time, as well as of tropical and Mediterranean climate zones.

The British ecologist Norman Myers developed the "biodiversity hot spot" concept in 1988 in an effort to determine which regions are particularly vulnerable and thus valuable for preservation of species diversity. Hot spots (not to be confused with the geological meaning of the term) are areas in which there are at least 1,500 endemic plant species, or 0.5 percent of the global inventory. They must also be areas that have lost more than 70 percent of their original surface area as the result of human encroachment, and whose continued existence is threatened. As a rule, these regions also contain a large number of terrestrial vertebrate species as well. The concept thus pinpoints areas that are particularly valuable ecologically, and on which protection efforts can be focused and limited financial resources expended most effectively. The twenty-five hot spots identified encompass 44 percent of all plant species and 35 percent of all terrestrial vertebrate species on only 1.4 percent of the earth's surface.

The hot spot with the greatest number of species, the tropical Andes, shelters roughly 15 to 17 percent of known plant species on only 0.8 percent of the earth's surface. Roughly 25 percent of the region's 485,000 square miles is still unspoiled, and not quite 80,000 square kilometers are protected. Roughly 40,000 species of plants have been counted here, half of them endemic. Roughly 3,389 terrestrial vertebrate species pass through the region, among them 1,567 endemic ones. One hundred thirty of these are classified as endangered and twenty are threatened with extinction; two have already become extinct since the hot spot was identified. Its great differences in elevation between ice- and snow-covered peaks and deep canyons, its long north-south extension, its steep slopes and isolated valleys have enabled such a proliferation of species. Among its most remarkable extremes are the world's deepest canyon, the Cañon del Colca (10,574 feet deep), near Cabanaconde in Peru, and the world's highest navigable lake, Titicaca (12,500 feet above sea-level), on the altiplano between Peru and Bolivia.

This wealth of species is a result of specifically adapted vegetation in different elevation belts. Along with the tropical mist and rain forests that have formed at elevations between 1,500 and 5,000 feet, there are various cloud forest formations between 2,500 and 11,500 feet covering more than 193,000 square miles in Peru and Bolivia that are among the most species-rich regions in the world. Above these are grasslands and shrub growth extending upward from 10,000 to 16,000 feet, like the Páramo in the wetter region of the northern Andes and the drier Puna in the colder and drier southern Andes. In addition, there are smaller pockets of dry forest, woodland, cactus groves, and brambles.

It is estimated that there are roughly 10,000 plant species in the mountain rain forests known as the *yungas*, 3,000 of which are endemic. One of the main reasons these valuable forests have been preserved up to now is that there have been so few roads on the eastern slope of the Andes. But since the increase in road building in the 1970s, protection efforts, especially the creation of national parks and the promotion of ecotourism, have had to compete with agricultural interests and economic development. Since the 1980s Bolivia has responded by creating the first protected areas, and to date some 16 percent of that country's total area has been set aside. Despite this favorable development, there are huge expanses of forest with a great wealth of animal and plant species that are threatened by the change.

The Caucasus mountains, which occupy roughly 193,000 square miles between the Black and Caspian seas, is another region of great biodiversity. The region is distinguished by enormous contrasts in climate, with annual precipitation ranging between six inches in the southeast to more than 157 inches along the Black Sea. More than a thousand glaciers dominate the landscape. The region's habitats are correspondingly diverse; a mosaic of desert, savanna, steppe, swamp, deciduous and dry forest, and montane coniferous forests provides homes for more than twice the number of animals found in the adjacent regions of Europe and Asia. Only 10 percent of the area can still be considered unspoiled. Most of it has been turned into desert or semi-desert through overexploitation. Only a little more than 5,400 square miles are protected. Of their 6,300 plant species, 1,600 are endemic. More than 630 terrestrial vertebrate species are at home here, fifty-nine of them endemic. Of these, ten are endangered and three are close to extinction.

Another nodal point in the biodiversity network is the mountainous region of southwest China.

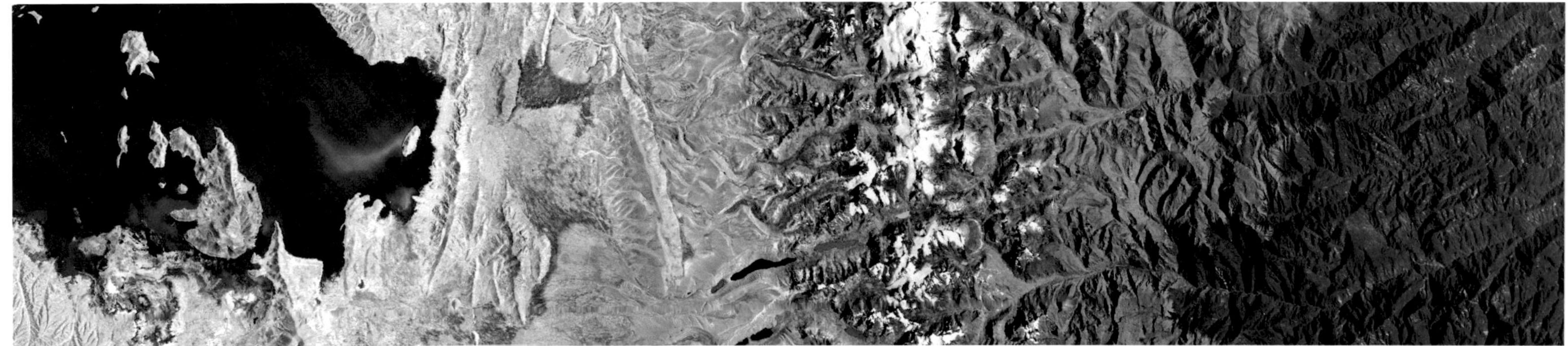

The Cordillera Real and Lake Titicaca in Bolivia on August 2, 1987. The section of the King's Cordillera around Lake Titicaca shows the striking variety of landscape in this region, a biodiversity hot spot with the greatest number of species in the world.

More than 308,880 square miles in area, the region encompasses medium to high mountains with extreme contrasts in altitude, from 3,280 to more than 24,500 feet. In the northwest it is bounded by the Qinghai-Xizang Plateau, in the north by the Tao River, and in the east by the Szechuan Basin and the Yunnan Plateau. In its mountains and valleys a large number of ecosystems have evolved, including deciduous and coniferous forests, bamboo thickets, scrub, savannas, meadows, wetlands, and alpine plant colonies. Only 8 percent of it is considered pristine. Nevertheless, some 12,000 plant species are represented here, 3,500 of them endemic. Of the 1,141 terrestrial vertebrate species, 178 are found here and nowhere else. Thirty-four are ranked as endangered, two close to extinction.

New Zealand, with its three main islands and numerous smaller ones, is a hot spot of a special kind. Its 104,457 square miles represent "ancient life rafts," or evolutionary islands developed long before the spread of mammals. It owes its great biodiversity to the fact that it extends southward from the subtropics all the way to sub-Antarctic conditions. Its highly diverse landscape encompasses soaring mountains, gentle hills, and broad alluvial plains. Tectonically active, it experiences frequent earthquakes and volcanic activity. Its climate is similarly diverse; precipitation on the western slopes of the Southern Alps amounts to as much as 472 inches a year, one of the highest amounts in the world, whereas on the eastern slopes it is less than twelve inches. Temperate rain forest once covered 85 percent of the region, or nearly 89,000 square miles. Dunes, the so-called Tussock Grassland, and wetlands make up the rest. Sadly, only 22 percent of its surface area has been left in its primeval state. The majority of this area is now protected. Because of New Zealand's long isolation, 1,865 of its 2,300 species of plants are endemic. Another indication of its biodiversity is that it is home to 217 terrestrial vertebrate species, of which 136 are considered endemic. A large number, sixty-one species in total, are classified as endangered, five are threatened with extinction, and twenty-five have been exterminated.

The highest peaks of California's Sierra Nevada constitute another biodiversity hot spot, the California Floristic Province, which extends along the west coast of North America for more than 1,100 miles. The greater part of this region of 113,000 square miles lies in California. It is one of the world's five Mediterranean regions, where the distinct alternation of winter rain and summer drought has developed a great diversity of species. Major populations of the kangaroo rat, the California condor, and the worm salamander are found here. The region encompasses a variety of ecosystems: sagebrush steppe, chaparral, juniper forest, subalpine and alpine forest, shoreline and floodplain woodland, stands of Douglas firs, the world-famous sequoias and redwoods, coastal dunes, and salt marshes. Roughly 25 percent of the area is still pristine. An indication of its great biodiversity is its more than 4,400 species of plants.

Mountainous regions in Central America, the Andes in central Chile, peak regions on Madagascar and in the Cape region in southern Africa, in Cuba, in Burma and India, on the Philippines, Borneo and Sumatra, and Sicily are further segments in this worldwide network of biodiversity.

Even though the concept presented here is by no means the only one relating to biodiversity, and its statistics are subject to question, it is still perfectly clear how greatly biodiversity is affected by interaction with human beings. Even slight increases in population and only modest development can occasion a decrease in biodiversity. Transformation of areas of natural vegetation into arable land, the expansion of agricultural boundaries, and especially deforestation all contribute to the decrease in biodiversity. As for the future there are only questions. How will these hot spots evolve in a hothouse climate? Can the extinction of species and loss of biodiversity be stopped? Small wonder that the loss of species stands high on the global change agenda.

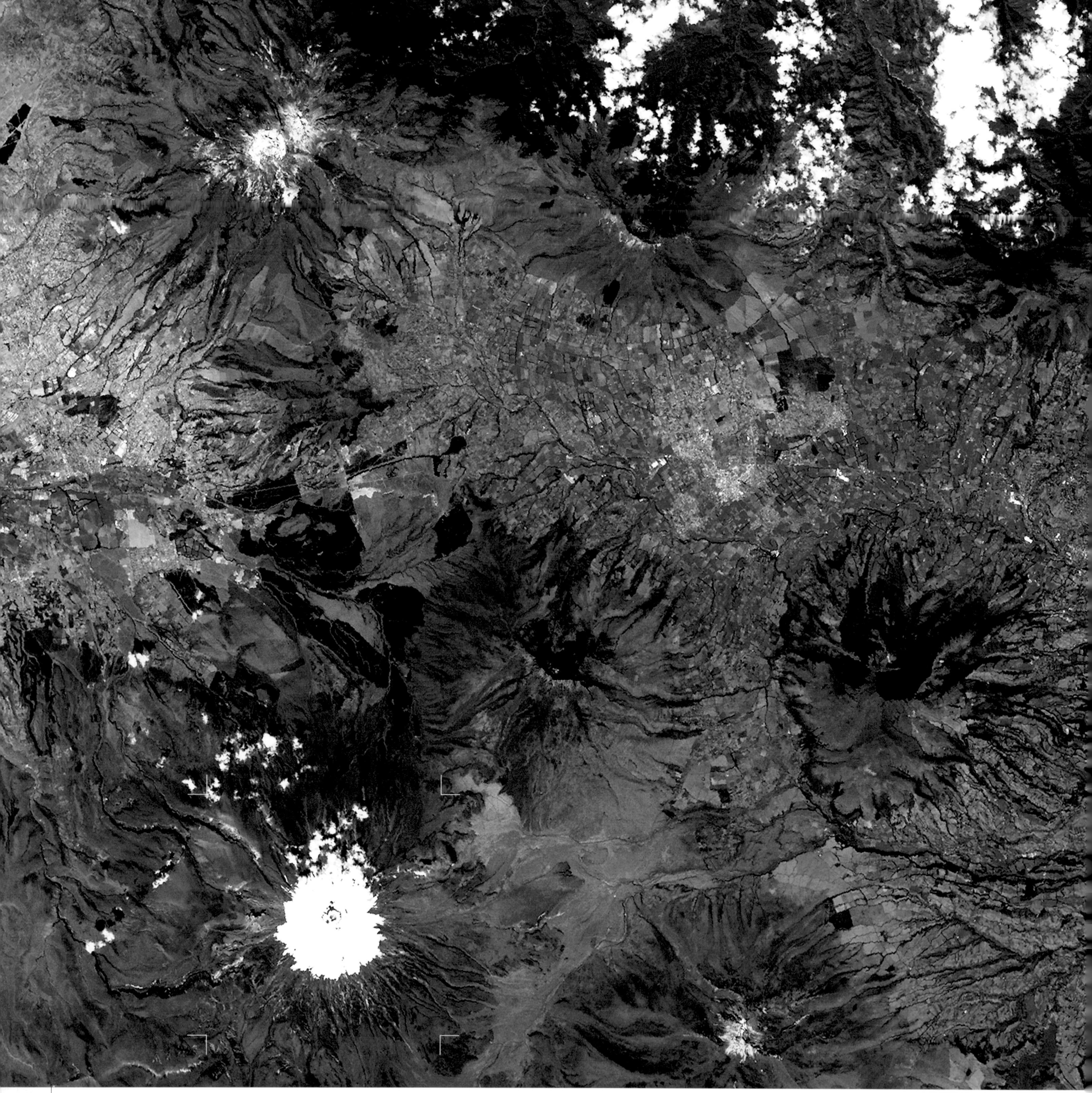

Cotopaxi, Ecuador

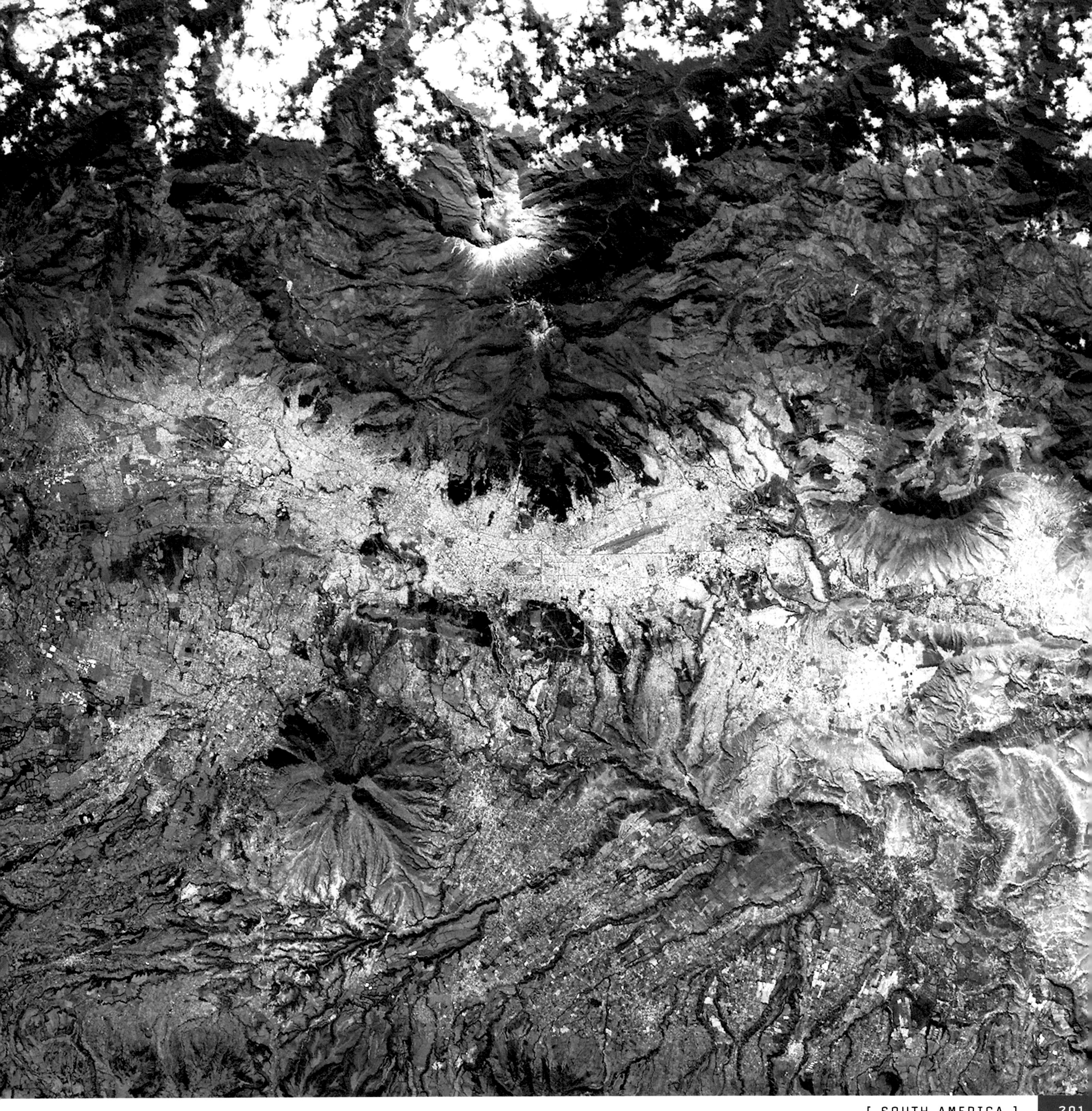

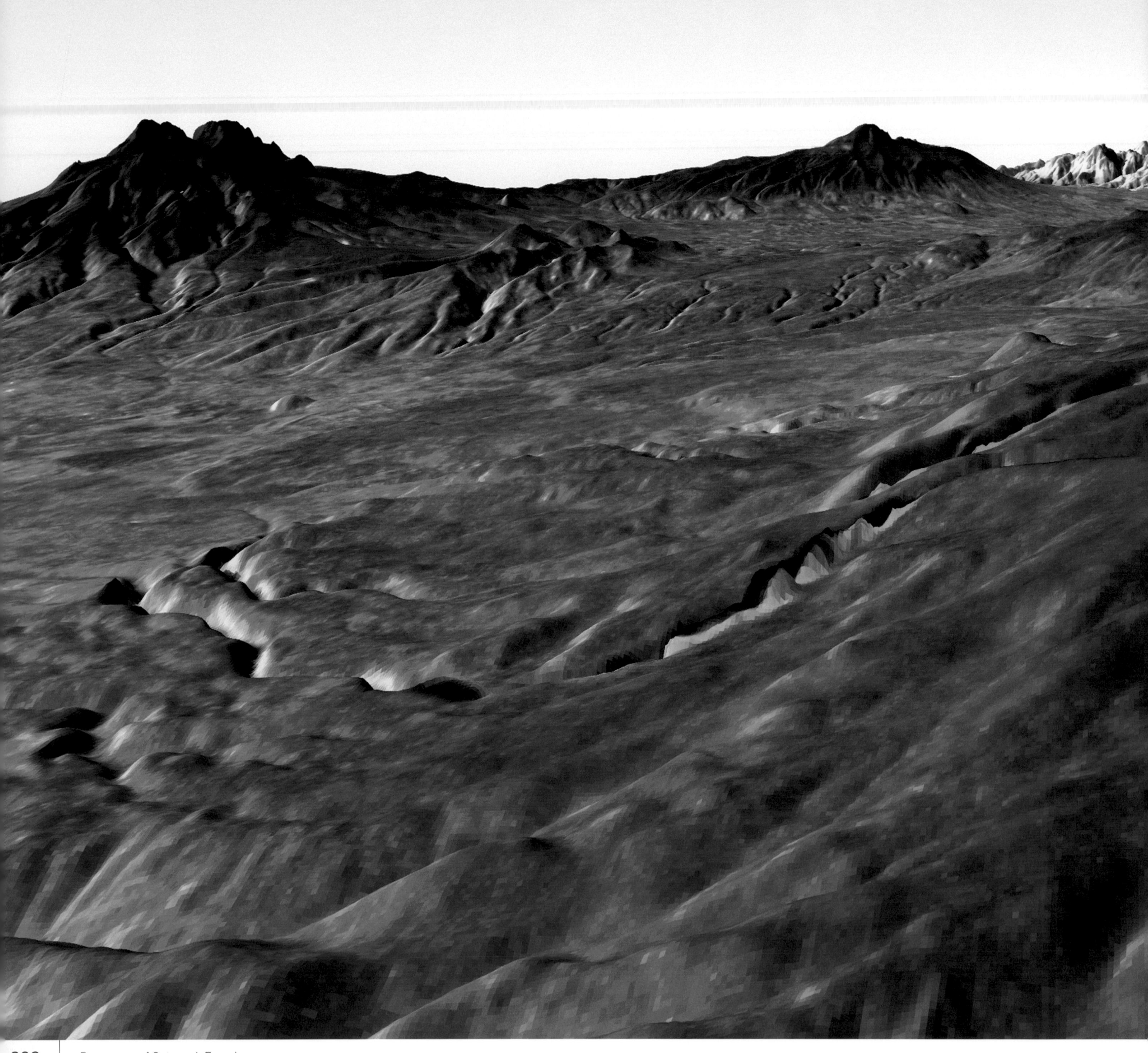

Panorama of Cotopaxi, Ecuador

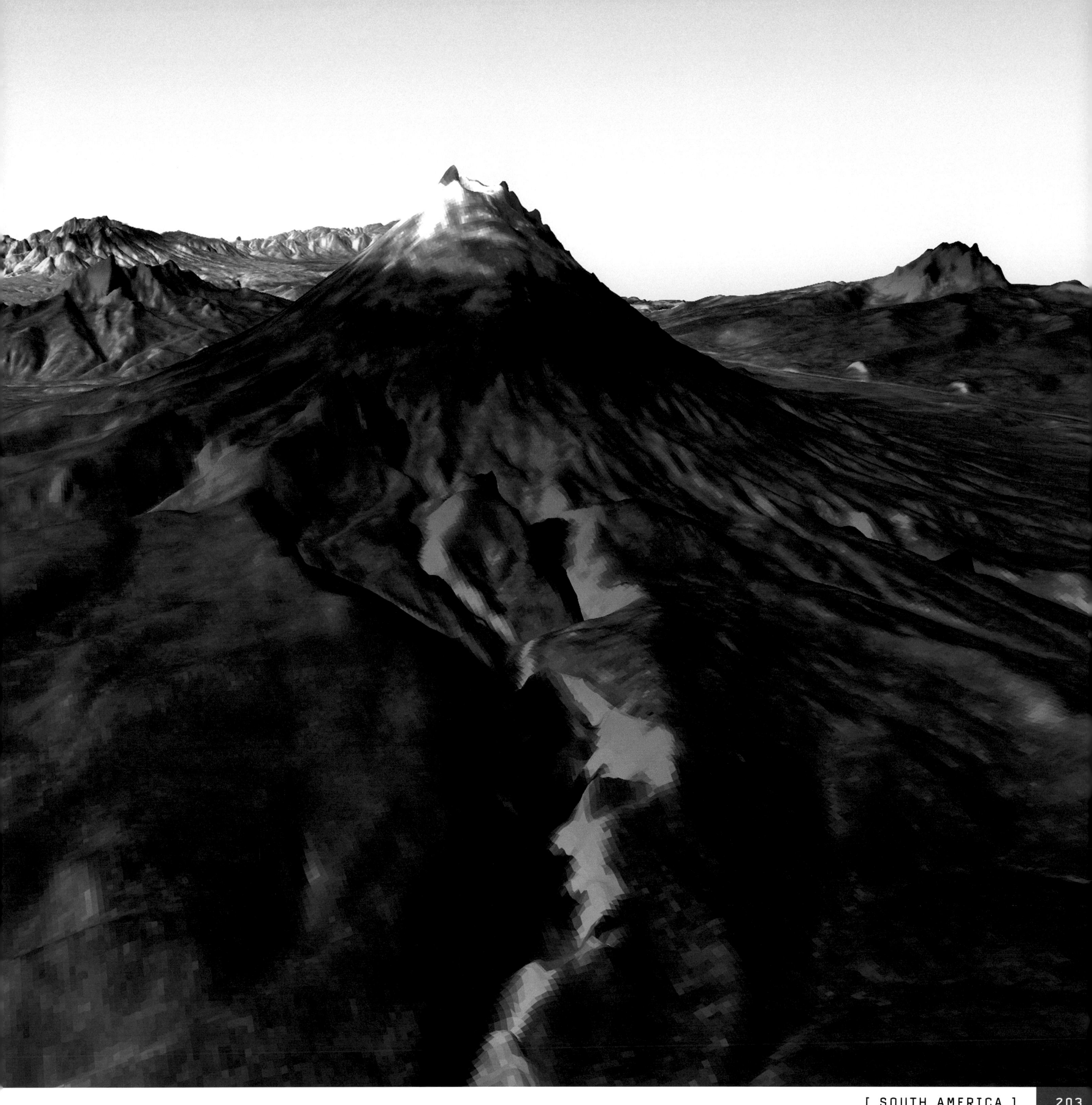

Elevation Belts
Layers of Forest, Rock, and Ice

RÜDIGER GLASER

It is a simple observation: the higher you climb in the mountains, the environment becomes cooler and more inhospitable, the air thinner, and the vegetation simpler. This has been a basic textbook lesson ever since Alexander von Humboldt published the brilliant sketches of his observations during his South American expedition. But it is not that simple; mountain elevation belts and especially vegetation colonies form an intricate and fascinating mosaic.

Seen from a distance, high mountains with their sequence of deciduous, mixed, and coniferous forest, grassland, rock, and ice often resemble the architecture of a layer cake. Elevation belts are among mountains' most obvious characteristics. Humboldt spent a lot of time studying the high mountains of South America, and in his *Cosmos* he reproduced sketches identifying the different elevation belts with the names commonly applied to them today. These are considered the blueprints for a scientific understanding of vegetation habitats. How is Earth's third dimension structured geographically?

A typical example of climatic and vegetation elevation belts of the humid Andes are the *yungas* in Bolivia, the eastern slope leading down to the Amazon lowlands. They follow the classic pattern of South American elevation belts. Up to an altitude of 4,000 feet is the *tierra caliente*, or "hot land." With annual precipitation between 60 and 78 inches, this zone is ideal for the development of lowland rain forest and the so-called *panatal* savanna. Typical crops are rice, corn, manioc, and beans, also bananas, citrus fruits, sugarcane, and pepper. Above this belt, beginning at an elevation of 4,000 feet, lies the *tierra templada*, or "temperate land." Here the mean annual temperature ranges between 40°F and 43°F, the annual precipitation between 70 and 106 inches. The typical vegetation at this altitude is high montane and montane rain forest. Farmers grow coffee, cocoa, oranges, corn, cassava, beans, mangoes, papayas, and sugarcane. Beginning at 8,500 feet the *tierra templada* gives way to *tierra fria*, or "cold land," with average temperatures of 29°F to 32°F and annual precipitation of 60 to 110 inches. Owing to the frequent mist and clouds, this level typically has mountain cloud forest where grains and fruits thrive. Above the *tierra fria* lies the "frozen land," the *tierra helada*, with mean annual temperatures of 18°F to 22°F, more than 100 days below freezing, and 20 to 35 inches of precipitation. At this height there is extensive grazing; typical crops are potatoes, barley, and quinoa.

Worldwide, individual mountain regions exhibit great variation in the development of their respective elevation belts. In the Alps, one distinguishes between the mixed oak forest of the foothills, the layer of montane beech and fir forest just above it, and next a layer of subalpine firs, larch, and stone pine. Above the forest and the adjoining timberline, at which a few dwarf trees and shrubs can still survive, come the alpine and subnival levels, characterized by grassland and dwarf shrubs in the lower one and in the upper one mostly debris and only sparse hardy species and rock plants. Finally comes the nival level, with impressive icy expanses of the glacial level.

Looking more closely at what is perhaps the most imposing level, the nival heights, the sugary icing on the typical alpine panorama is divided into a number of different zones. Temporary, climatic, and current snow boundaries, névé lines, ice-snow lines, névé boundaries, and glacial-snow boundaries are but a few of the distinctions made by geoscientists. The altitudes of these various boundaries differ from region to region. In the Alps, for example, the snow line lies between 8,200 feet on the Säntis to 10,500 feet in the Valais Alps; in Tibet, however, it only begins at 20,300 feet, and in the Andes not until 22,000 feet. The processes at work and the resulting definitions are equally complex at the other levels.

Mountains in arid regions worldwide have a very different sequence from the Alps, with forests, year-round snow cover, and ice caps. In polar regions, by contrast, it is the lower layers that are missing. Mediterranean mountains demand yet another set of distinctions.

Elevation belts are created by distinct climatic gradients, especially perceptible as a decrease in temperature with altitude. Vegetation serves as an expression of this change. But weathering and erosion processes also follow these gradients, which means that two more high-mountain criteria play an important role as well: steepness of terrain and rise in altitude. Mountains with a rise in altitude of at least 3,250 feet generally result in a landscape feature towering over the surrounding lowlands, and echoing a structure met with in similar form in other climate and vegetation zones. Changes with elevation are continuous; seldom are actual boundaries like timberlines developed. At the same time, ecological niches and pocket habitats produce an intricate patchwork. Each level presents its own climatic characteristics and is also distinguished by different mixes of vegetation and morphological processes.

Mountain regions are further differentiated by the way people use them. Grazing on the high meadows in the Alps, for example, has affected the pattern of the highlands. The densely populated and terraced high mountains of Asia are another example. Exploiting natural conditions and perpetuating their own ancient cultural traditions, peoples in a number of mountainous regions have shaped the landscape in their own characteristic ways.

Definitions of the various elevation belts have taken on a new significance in the context of global change. Where are they going to shift on the scale of the global fever thermometer? Simplified models suggest that elevation belts will be shifted upward as temperatures continue to rise. In the

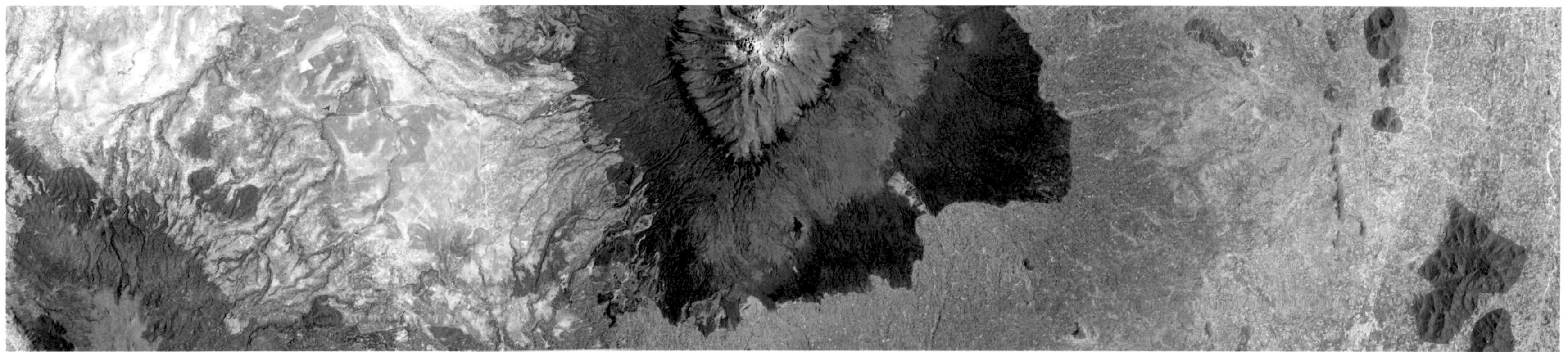

Mount Kenya, Kenya, on February 21, 2000. The individual elevation belts, a characteristic feature of high mountains, are obvious, and underscore Earth's third dimension particularly clearly.

Alpine region this would mean more deciduous forests in the lower altitudes. Timberlines and snowlines would be higher. In the most extreme scenario, plants that now grow in the highest elevations could be crowded out and faced with extinction. It is estimated that roughly one hundred species found only in the Alps would be affected.

More recent models suggest that the vegetation layers exhibit complex reactive mechanisms. This is explained by the mere fact that the various elements of the mountain system—glaciers, alpine meadows, and forests—react with different lag times and not in lockstep. Snowfall, for example, is subject to yearly variations, while the formation of glacial ice follows long-term changes. The vegetation in a given habitat could adapt to changed conditions. Only when this is impossible can it undertake the move to a habitat with a similar environment. Or it could hold out in its present habitat without this possibility of adaptation and become extinct.

Because of the global climate warming of recent decades we have already seen changes in vegetation. But owing to the considerable interference of mankind such observations must be treated with caution. Recent calculations based on a warming of 7°F have foreseen only slight shifts in the type of trees from the montane to the subalpine levels, and thus no essential rise in the timberline. By contrast, however, flowering plants in border habitats are already showing clear reactions. A comparison of fourteen mountain peaks between 1905 and 1985 has shown an increase in the number of species on at least twelve of them. On the one hand this indicates that previously inhospitable peaks have become acceptable to an increasing number of species; on the other hand it means that these plant communities will be trapped if there is further warming, for they cannot migrate any higher. Additional findings from a total of twenty-six peaks in the central Alps also show that various species react swiftly and in different ways to changes in climate. Yet there is clear evidence, for example from the Polar Ural, that in the past 1,100 years timberlines have generally climbed from 200 to 260 feet owing to the changing climate.

There is no question that climate change will alter the water supply. The retreat of the glaciers and change in the amount of precipitation will result in a change in stream runoff. Added to this are the changing demands made by people. Disregard for the natural runoff cycles, winter tourism and the use of snow-making machines are making enormous demands on the available water, especially above the timberline and in months when the water supply is lowest—only one of the many facets of global change.

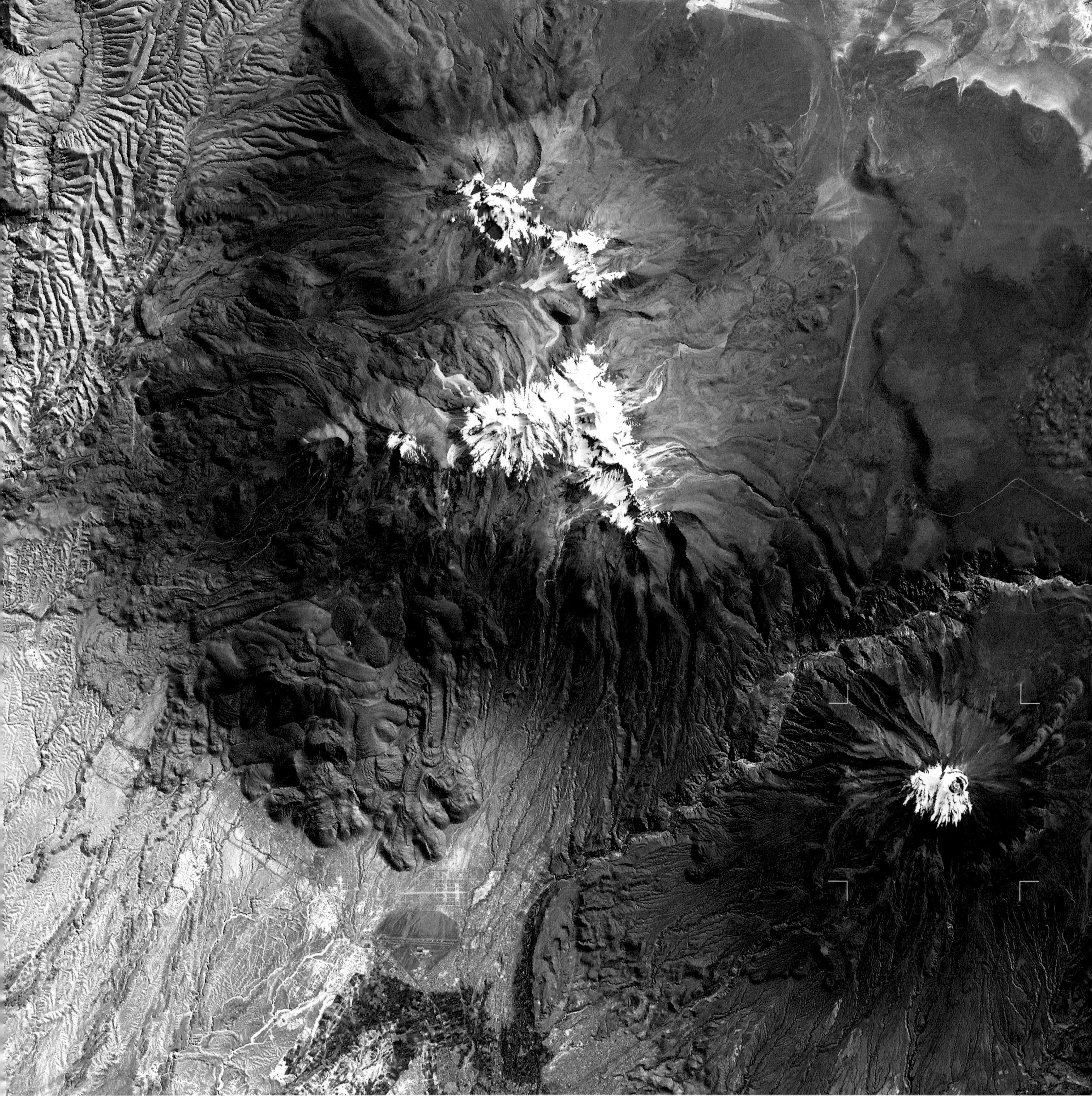

El Misti and Laguna Salinas, Peru

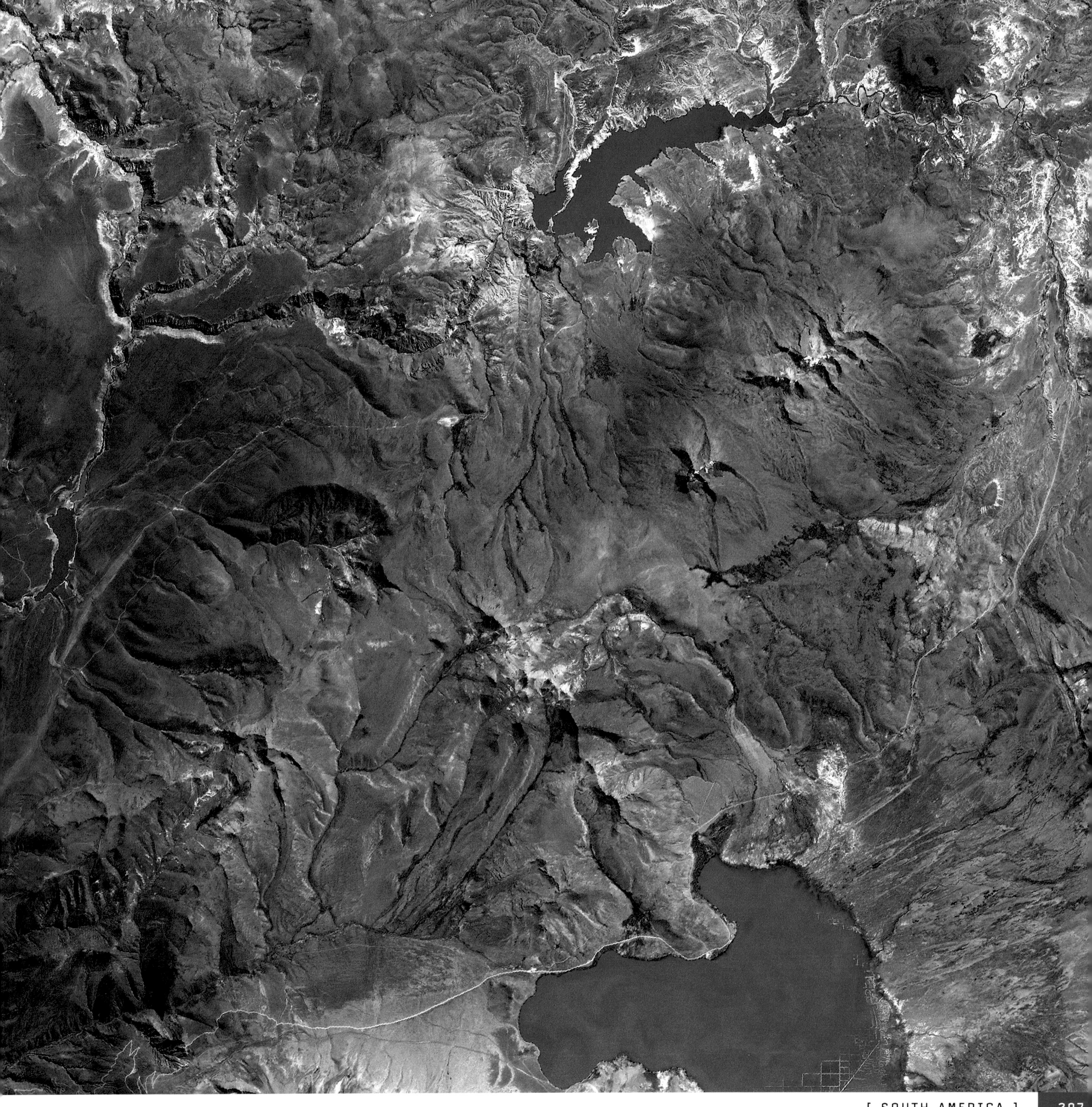

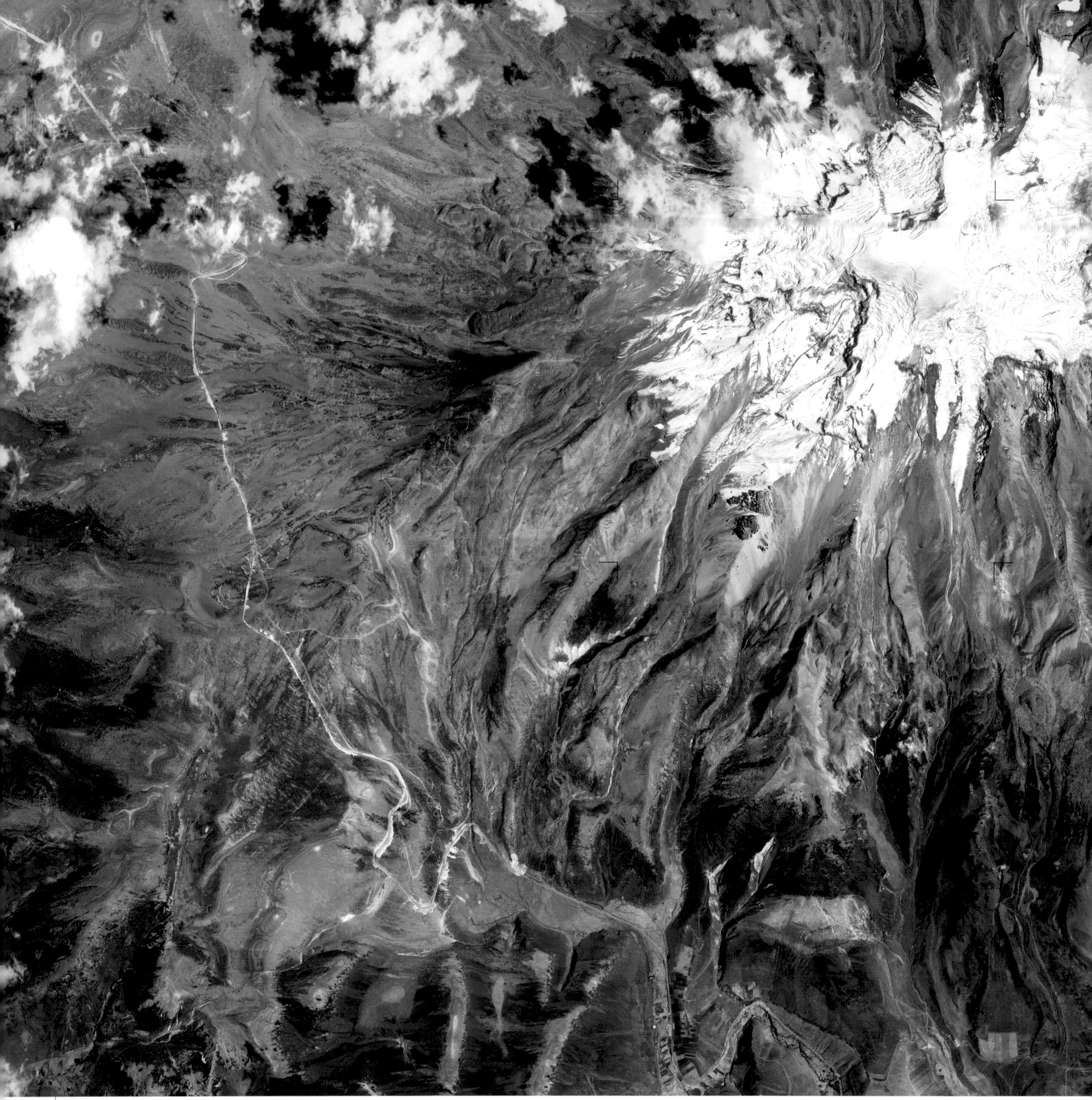

 Chimborazo, Ecuador

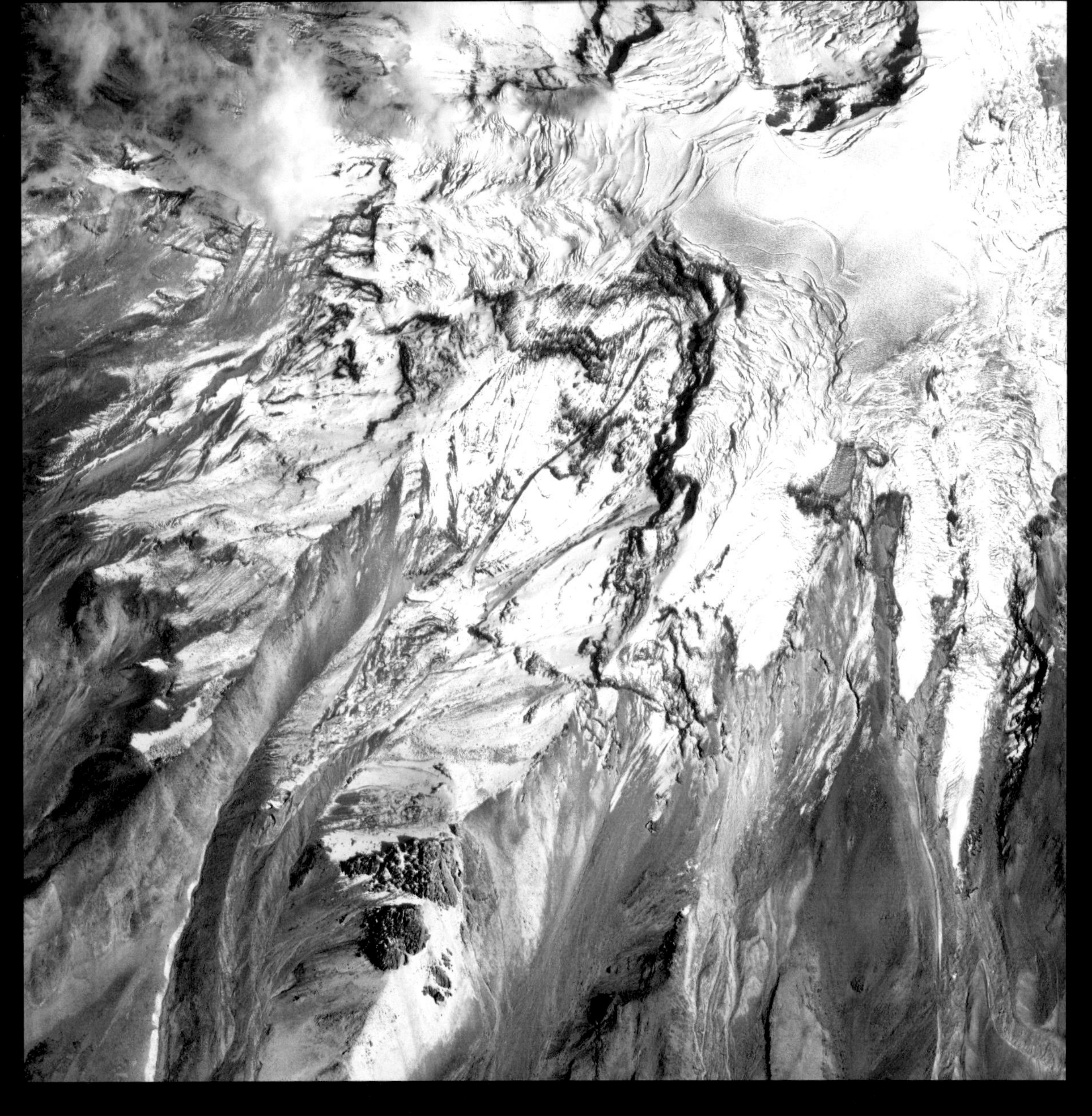

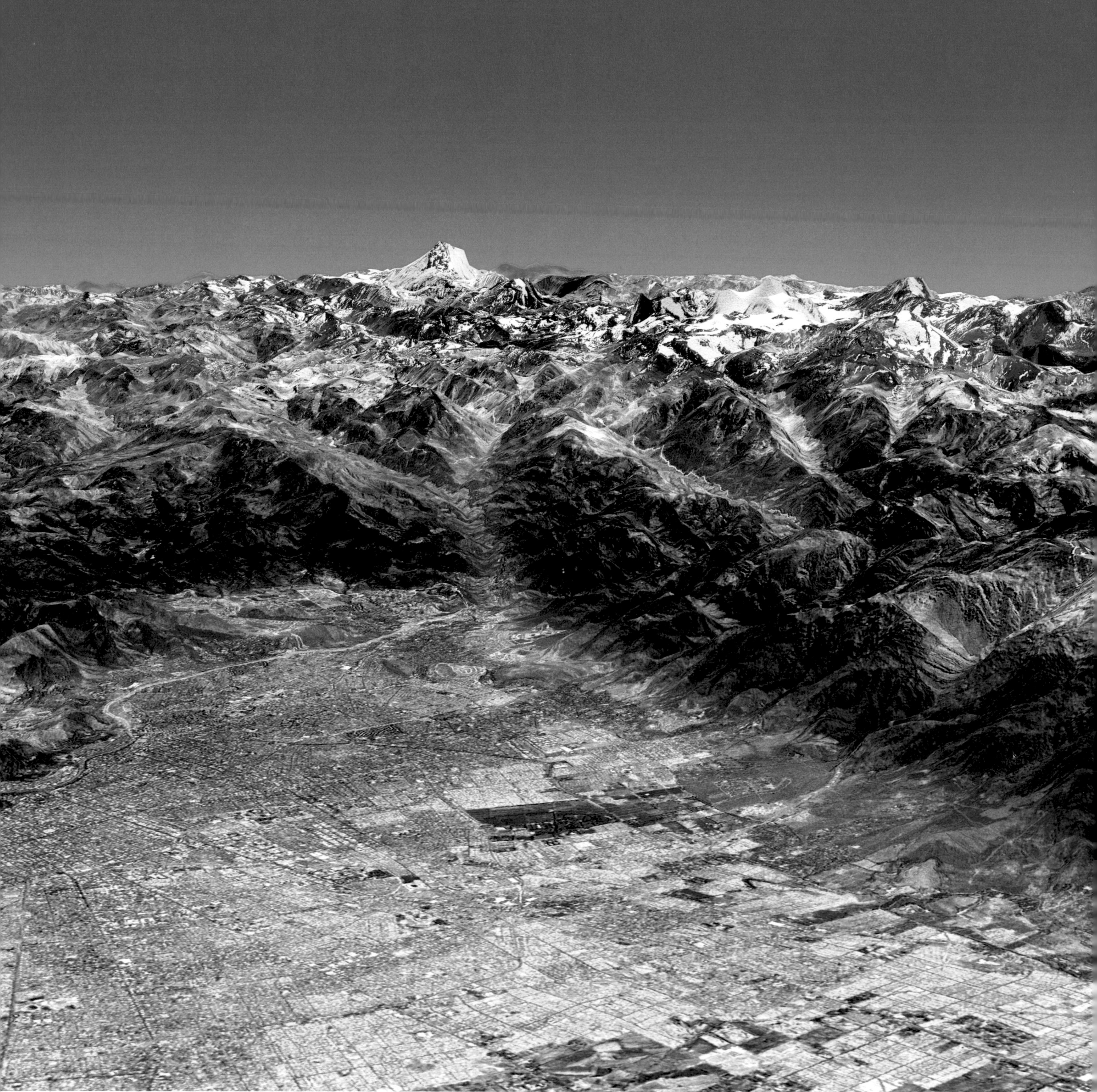

Aconcagua, the highest mountain in South America, Argentina

[APPENDIX]

Page 015

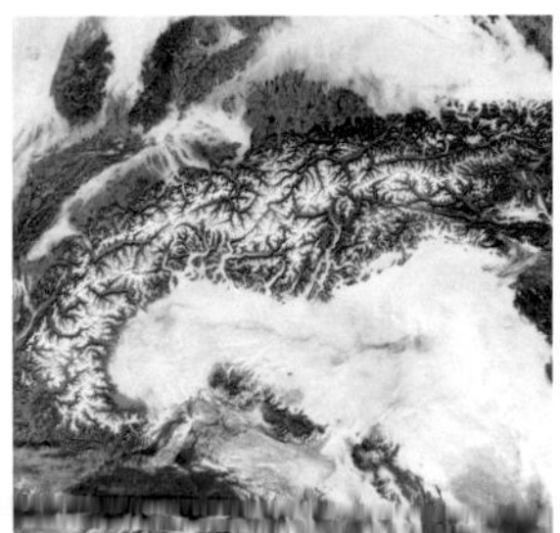

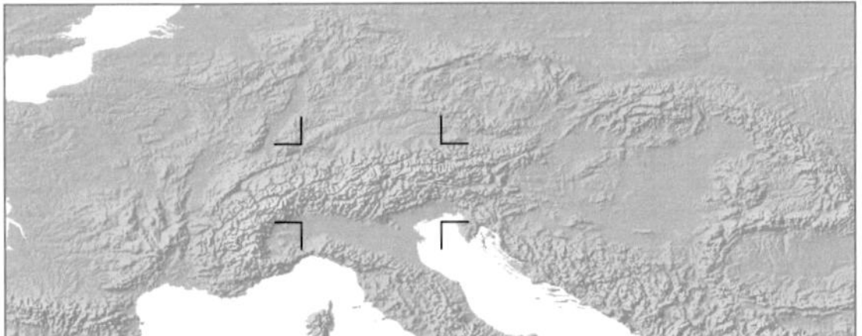

Satellite: Terra / **Sensor:** Moderate Imaging Spectroradiometer (MODIS) / **Resolution:** 250 m / **Recorded:** November 20, 2003, 10:08 UTC / **Visualization:** true colors / **Spectral channels:** 0.62–0.67 µm, 0.55–0.57 µm, 046–0.48 µm / **Image processing:** German Remote Sensing Data Center / **Data source:** German Aerospace Center

The arc of the Alps framed by cloud

In the autumn and winter months, high-pressure conditions settle over Europe, which are often accompanied by continuous, extensive cloud layers. Only the higher elevations remain cloud-free. Thus the entire Alpine chain remains cloud-free for more than 1,200 miles in this unusually clear image. It is easy to make out both the main crest of the Alps and individual mountain groupings.

In this November shot the higher elevations have already been covered with snow, though many of the valleys are still snow-free. Clouds sharply outline the southern edge of the Alps north of the Po plain, some of them extending deep into their valleys well to the north. One finger of cloud extends as far as Bolzano, in the south Tirol. Through larger holes in the clouds north of the Alps, in Upper Bavaria, for example, it is possible to make out the patterns of fields. If one follows the line of the Lake of Starnberg (north of the Alps in the center to the right) to the north, one discovers an almost circular hole in the cloud cover: Munich. The air above the city is a few degrees warmer and functions like a hot plate, effectively dispersing the cloud cover.

Pages 016 / 017

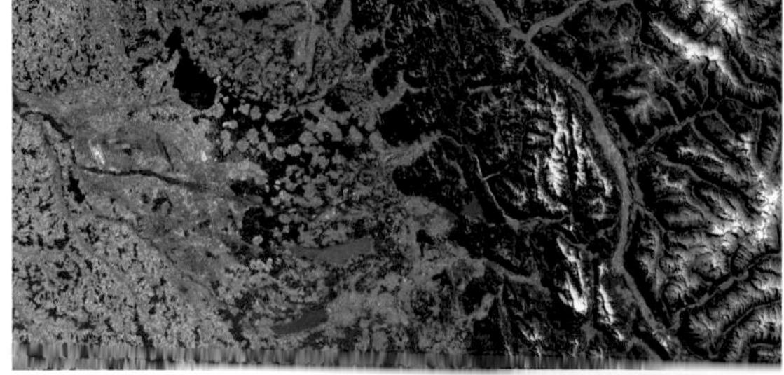

Satellite: Landsat-7 / **Sensor:** Enhanced Thematic Mapper (ETM+) / **Resolution:** 30 m / **Recorded:** September 13, 1999 / **Visualization:** true colors / **Spectral channels:** 0.63–0.69 µm, 053–0.61 µm, 0.45–0.52 µm / **Image processing:** German Remote Sensing Data Center / **Data source:** University of Maryland, Global Land Cover Facility (GLCF)–EarthSat

The settled landscape of the northern Alps

In unusual perspective—left is north, right south—we see one of the most important settled regions of the northern Alps: Upper Bavaria and neighboring Tirol. For this image several satellite pictures were fitted together into a mosaic, providing a view of more than 155 miles north to south. In the center of the left side lies Munich, with the east-west runways of its airport to the north and circular clearings in the forest to the south. These clearings roughly mark the line of end moraines left by the Ice Age, whose glaciers shaped the landscape between Munich and the north edge of the Alps. The glacial basins are clearly recognizable—the present-day Ammer Lake and Lake of Starnberg. South of the line of end moraines the landscape is dominated by the open, green fields of dairy farms; to the north of it, this being September, the fields have already been mowed.

On the right side of the picture the Alps suddenly rise to heights of more than 10,000 feet. In front of Garmisch-Partenkirchen one can see the Wetterstein Mountains, with Germany's highest mountain, the Zugspitze (9,718 feet; lower center). In the center on the right lies the valley of the Inn, with Innsbruck in the center and the snow-covered Karwendel Mountains above. To the right of it are the Stubai Alps, with the 11,499-foot Zuckerhütl, above them in the picture the Zillertal and the Zillertaler Alps with the 11,516-foot Hochfeiler. To the south of the east-west traffic axis of the Inn Valley lies the important route into Italy, the Brenner Pass, at the end of the Wipptal. At the time the image was made the snowline lay at around 8,525 feet.

Pages 018 / 019

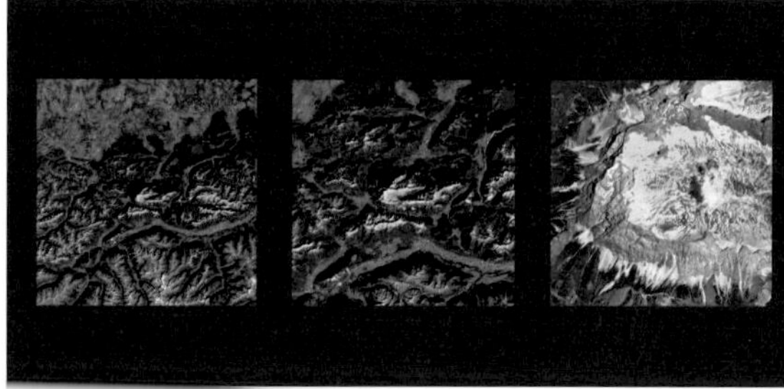

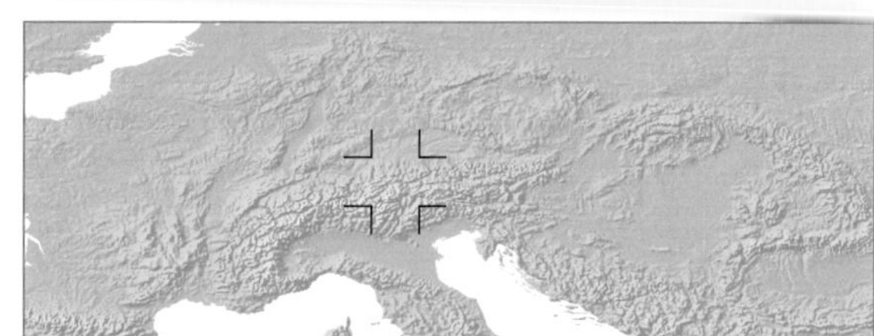

Satellites: left and center, Landsat-7; right Ikonos / **Sensors:** left and center, Enhanced Thematic Mapper (ETM+), right Ikonos / **Resolutions:** left 30 m, center 15 m, right 1 m / **Recorded:** Landsat, September 13, 1999; Ikonos, June 10, 2003, 10:27 UTC / **Visualization:** true colors / **Spectral channels:** Landsat 0.63–0.69 µm, 0.53–0.61 µm, 0.45–0.52 µm; Ikonos 0.63–0.69 µm, 0.52–0.60 µm, 0.45–0.52 µm / **Image processing:** German Remote Sensing Data Center / **Data source:** University of Maryland, Global Land Cover Facility (GLCF)–EarthSat; European Space Imaging

The Zugspitze, Germany's highest mountain, in detail

This picture sequence represents a zoom in on the highest mountain in Germany, the 9,718-foot Zugspitze. The mountain was first climbed in August 1820, when the Bavarian lieutenant Karl Naus set out to survey the peak. The satellite images were produced from spectral channels in visible light (red-green-blue) and thus produce an impression of natural colors. Whereas in the left-hand image the multispectral channels of the Landsat Satellite were used exclusively (30-m resolution), the center and right-hand images were produced after digital "cutting" with higher-resolution panchromatic ("black-and-white") data. Thus both the 30-meter data from Landsat (center) and the 4-meter data from Ikonos (right) were improved to 15 meter and 1 meter.

In the left image one clearly sees the Wetterstein Mountains with the Zugspitze. The roughly 3-square-mile cap of the Zugspitze (in the center picture) is a rocky depression whose upper part is covered by the Schneefern Glacier. Because of its exposed situation, the Zugspitze serves as a very good meteorological-climatological observatory. Weather and environmental survey stations of the German Weather Service and the Federal Environmental Office are located both on the peak and at the Schneefern House, visible just below the peak ridge in the right-hand image. The ascent of the Zugspitze by way of the Rhine Valley opening to the east is still a great experience for ambitious mountain hikers.

Pages 020 / 021

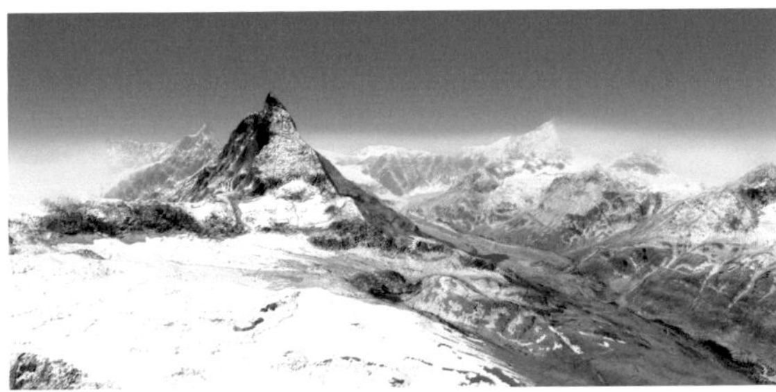

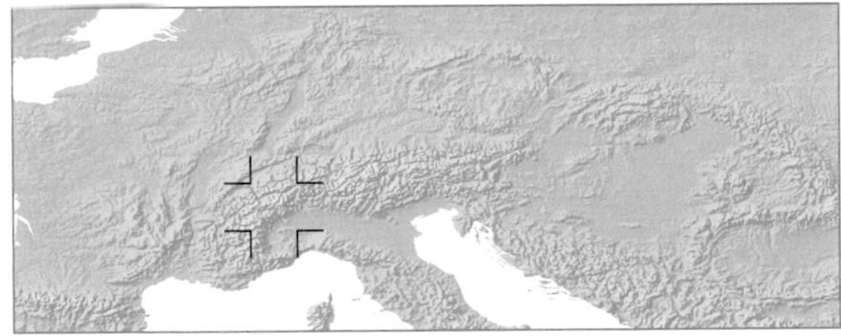

Satellite: aerial view, Landsat-7 / **Sensor:** Wild RC30, Enhanced Thematic Mapper (ETM+) / **Resolutions:** 2 m, 30 m / **Recorded:** Wild RC30, October 1995; Landsat, July 30, 2001 / **Visualization:** perspective view / **Spectral channels:** true colors / **Elevation model:** Wild RC30 / **Resolution:** 10 m / **Height exaggeration:** 1 time / **Image processing:** German Remote Sensing Data Center / **Data source:** ENDOXON AG; Global Land Cover Facility (GLCF)–EarthSat

The Matterhorn, the most famous peak in the Alps

This spectacular view of the snow-covered east wall of the 14,692-foot Matterhorn looks almost like a photograph from a helicopter. In fact, this perspective image was generated by computer, based on satellite-supported remote sensing data recorded from an airplane. From them, with the help of stereophotogrammetric calculations, a precise elevation model of the region around Zermatt, in the Swiss canton of Valais, was produced. The principle: objects on the ground were registered from various angles and imaged out of place independently of elevation. Comparing two photographs from different angles, the altitude above sea level can be determined point by point. Finally, the already adapted pictorial data was overlaid on the elevation model thus produced, then a perspective view created by computer. Gaps in the data and stray clouds were easily retouched. On the left lies the Furgg Ridge, on the right the Hörnli Ridge, across which Edward Whymper made the first ascent in 1865. In that tragic expedition four climbers lost their lives. At the foot of the Matterhorn one can see the Furgg Glacier, while the right half of the picture is dominated by the Zmutt Glacier. In the right center, enveloped in a few veil-like clouds—likewise generated on a computer—one can see the Dent Blanche (14,291 feet).

Pages 024 / 025

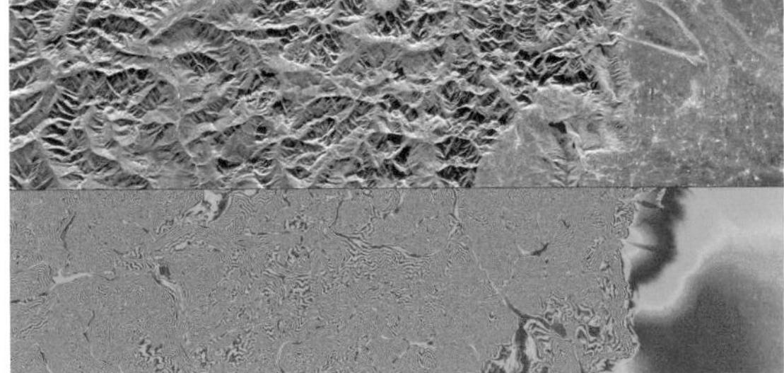

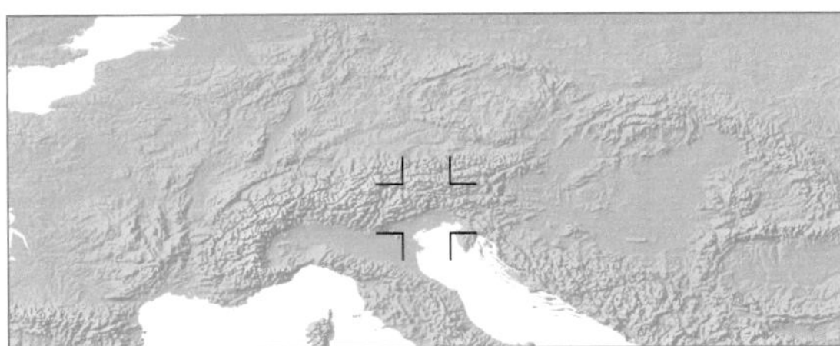

Satellite: Shuttle Radar Topography Mission (SRTM) / **Sensor:** X-SAR / **Resolution:** 30 m / **Recorded:** February 12, 2000, 19:26 UTC / **Visualization:** top, amplitude image; bottom, fringe depiction / **Spectral channels:** X-Band, 3 cm / **Image processing:** German Remote Sensing Data Center / **Data source:** German Aerospace Center

Radar remote sensing: Friuli and the Trentino, cloud-free

This spread presents two very different and unusual images. At the top is pictured a roughly 37-mile-wide and 125-mile-long swath of landscape from southeast to northwest (left to right). It was produced by an imaging radar during an eleven-day mission in the year 2000. To make such images—unhindered by clouds and independent of sunlight—the surface of the earth is radiated with microwaves from an angle. Depending on the direction and the surface structure, the intensity of the reflected signals varies. Slopes turned toward the radar sensor appear brighter, because they reflect directly, those turned away darker. If the signals are received by a second antenna, in this case roughly 200 feet away, a second image is produced from a different angle. The discrepancies between the received radar echos—the so-called phase differences—of the two images can then be evaluated and the ground elevation determined.

The lower image shows such phase differences as a color-coded radar interferogram. Lines of like color correspond to identical phase differences in the recording. These lines are called fringes. Fringes lying close together mark steep terrain. Here this is especially visible on the south edge of the Alps (right side) or in the Alpine valleys. By means of complicated calculations it is possible to derive digital elevation models from interferograms.

Pages 026 / 027

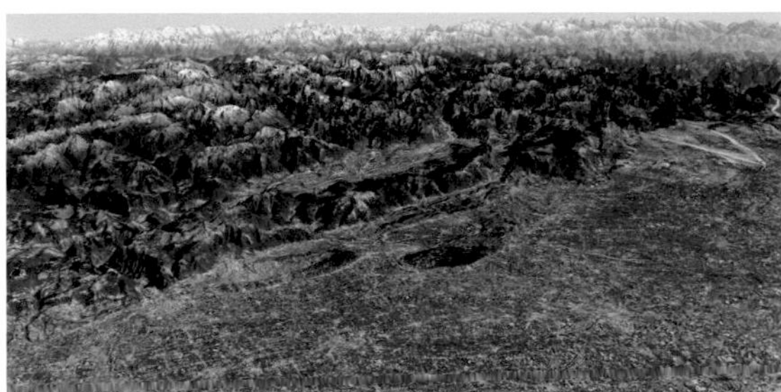

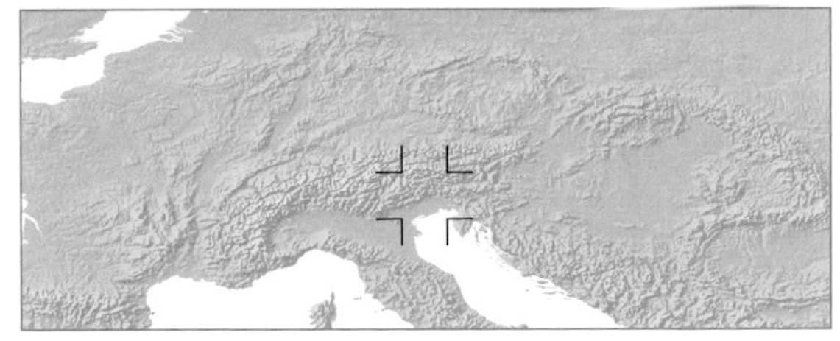

Satellite: Landsat-7 / **Sensor:** Enhanced Thematic Mapper (ETM+) / **Resolution:** 30 m / **Recorded:** August 26, 2001 / **Visualization:** perspective, true colors / **Spectral channels:** 0.63–0.69 µm, 0.53–0.61 µm, 0.45–0.52 µm / **Elevation model:** Shuttle Radar Topography Mission (SRTM), C-Band / **Resolution:** 90 m / **Height exaggeration:** 2 times / **Image processing:** German Remote Sensing Data Center / **Data sources:** University of Maryland, Global Land Cover Facility (GLCF)–EarthSat, NASA

Panorama of the Dolomites from the south

For this image a view looking to the northeast was selected. In the left foreground one can see the town of Bassano del Grappa (pale pink), in the lower right, the city of Treviso. Also clearly visible is the dense network of highways and settlements across the Veneto leading to the Alps.

In the center of the image is the east-west barrier of the Venetian Alps, behind which the Piave River disappears into the Alps. To the east (to the right in the picture) of the Venetian Alps the Friuli begins with its two prominent riverbeds, recognizable from their light-colored gravel, running south toward the Adriatic (see also the previous two-page spread).

In the background on the left tower are the separate peaks of the Dolomites, bordered to the east by the Carnian Alps. The higher elevations are snow-covered even at the end of August. On the horizon is the main crest of the Alps with the Hohe Tauern (right) and the Zillertal Alps (left).

Pages 030 / 031

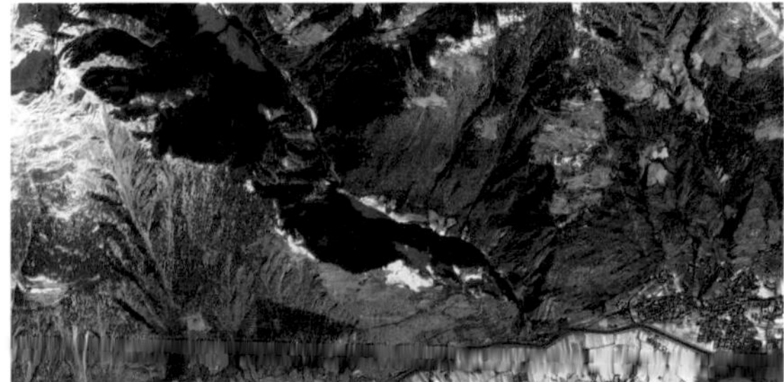

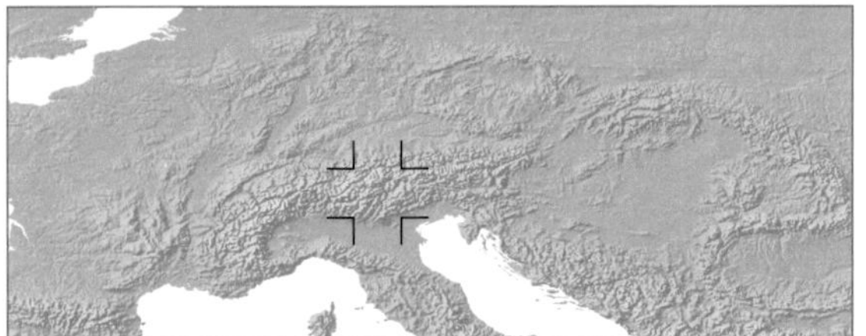

Satellite: Ikonos / **Resolution:** 1 m / **Recorded:** January 15, 2005, 10:35 UTC / **Visualization:** true colors / **Spectral channels:** 0.63–0.69 µm, 0.52–0.60 µm, 0.45–0.52 µm / **Image processing:** German Remote Sensing Data Center / **Data source:** European Space Imaging

Juval Castle

In this winter picture above the Val Venosta with Juval Castle, sited directly above the entrance to the Val di Senales, brown shades predominate. Light and shadow model the mountain ridges in three dimensions. In the lower right are the town of Naturno and the Adige River. The lower elevations in the Val Venosta, mostly planted with orchards, are covered by a moderately thick layer of snow. The field boundaries are clearly visible. The sunlit south slopes of the mountains, rising toward the north into the Texel group, are still snow-free.

For this image, multispectral Ikonos data with a resolution of 4 meters were blended with panchromatic Ikonos 1-meter-resolution data to attain maximum sharpness. As a result, one can make out roads, lanes, houses, even single trees. Only a few minutes above the parking lot at the entrance to the Val di Senales lies Juval Castle, where Reinhold Messner has assembled a collection of art works and mementos of his expeditions around the world. Juval Castle is open to the public.

Pages 032 / 033

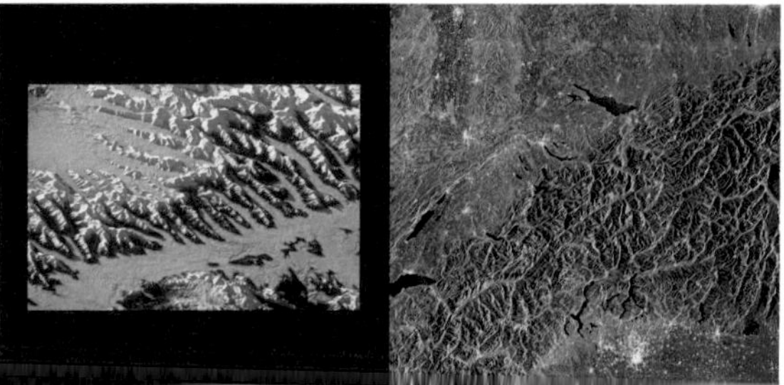

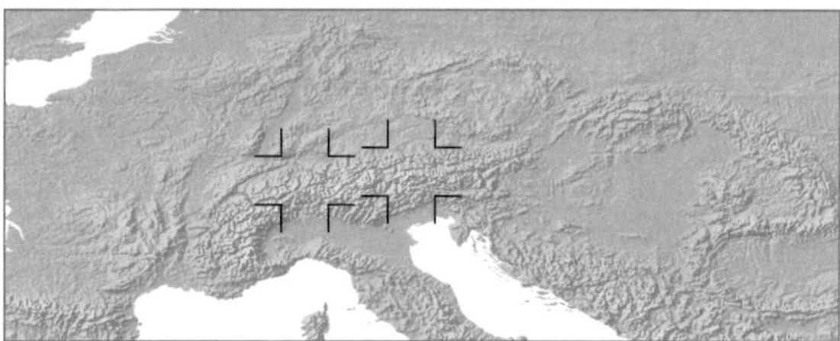

Satellite: International Space Station (ISS 06) / **Sensor:** photograph / **Recorded:** December 26, 2002, 08:39 UTC / **Visualization:** Angled shot / **Spectral channels:** true colors / **Image processing:** German Remote Sensing Data Center / **Data source:** Image Analysis Laboratory, NASA Johnson Space Center, Roll E – Frame 11831

Satellite: ENVISAT / **Sensor:** Advanced Synthetic Aperture Radar (ASAR) / **Resolution:** 150 m / **Recorded:** diverse dates / **Visualization:** Multitemporal radar image / **Spectral channels:** red, October 31, 2002; green, March 20, 2003; blue, January 29, 2004 / **Image processing:** European Space Agency / **Data source:** European Space Agency (ESA)

Left: Hohe Tauern

This image is a digital angled shot made by astronauts from the International Space Station looking from the north. In the foreground lies the fog-shrouded valley of the Salzach, at the bottom of the image is the peak of the Hochkönig (9,669 feet). In a typical high-pressure situation, dense clouds reach like fingers into the Hohe Tauern's smallest mountain valleys. The higher elevations, all snow-covered and some of them glaciated, are free of clouds and present a dreamlike panorama.

Right: Cloud-free radar image of the western Alps

This unique cloud-free view of the western Alpine massif was produced from a number of radar images made at various times. Sections of the earth's surface that have changed over the various imaging times, for example the agricultural areas in the Po plain, the southern Rhine basin, or the area south of the Swiss Jura, can be seen in different colors. Lakes appear as dark spots; the radar reflection is here very slight. Cities and Alpine slopes facing the satellites make very good reflectors and, accordingly, appear quite light. In the bottom right is Lake Como; to the left of it the elongated Lake Maggiore extends deep into the Alps. In the upper right is Lake Constance, below it the cities of Zurich, Basel, and Bern.

Pages 036 / 037

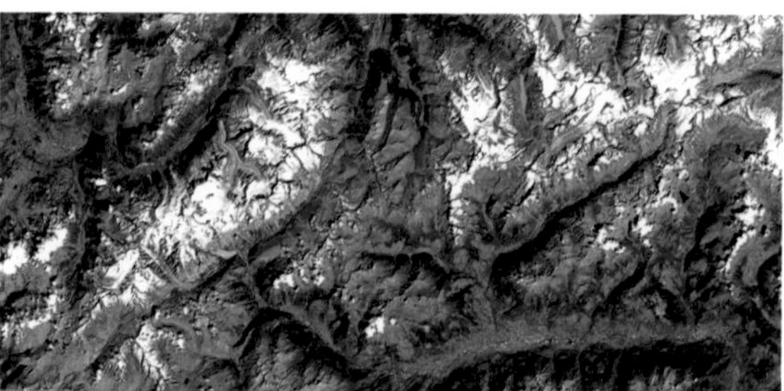

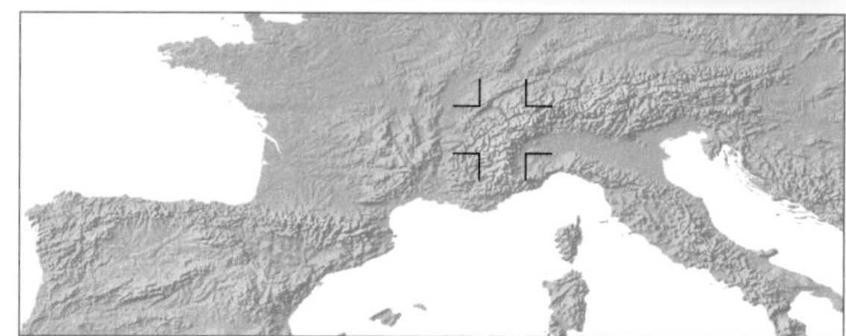

Satellite: Landsat-7 / **Resolution:** 15 m / **Recorded:** July 25, 1999 / **Visualization:** true colors / **Spectral channels:** 0.63–0.69 µm, 0.53–0.61 µm, 0.45–0.52 µm / **Image processing:** German Remote Sensing Data Center / **Data source:** University of Maryland, Global Land Cover Facility (GLCF)–EarthSat

The Rooftop of the Alps—Mont Blanc

Majestic Mont Blanc dominates the Savoy Alps. In the left half of the picture the snow- and ice-covered granite massif can clearly be seen extending from northeast to southwest, extending along the French-Italian border and reaching northeast into Switzerland. Sharp-edged, pyramidlike peaks are typical of the Mont Blanc massif. Mighty glaciers wind downward in the form of elongated gray tongues. The most impressive of these is the Mer de Glace, more than four miles long in the central massif. At the northern foot of the giant mountain, at an elevation of 3,400 feet, the world-famous winter-sports center Chamonix nestles on the slopes in the valley of the Arve. To the north and east, Mont Blanc is framed by the peaks and ridges of the Valais Alps. The southern foothills of the massif are bounded by the Val Veny–Val Ferret. From these the river Dora Báltea flows into the broad Val d'Aosta in the south. From the bottom right edge of the picture the Val d'Aosta runs in a westerly direction and turns into the Valdigne. In its northwesterly extension lies the 7.21-mile Mont Blanc Tunnel, linking the valley systems of Chamonix and Aosta. The highest peak in the Alps, at 15,744 feet, Mont Blanc was first conquered on August 8, 1786, by Jaques Balmat and Michel-Gabriel Paccard. This ascent is considered the birth of alpinism. Mountain climbers dread the peak because of its demanding routes and hostile weather conditions, especially its abrupt weather changes.

Pages 038 / 039

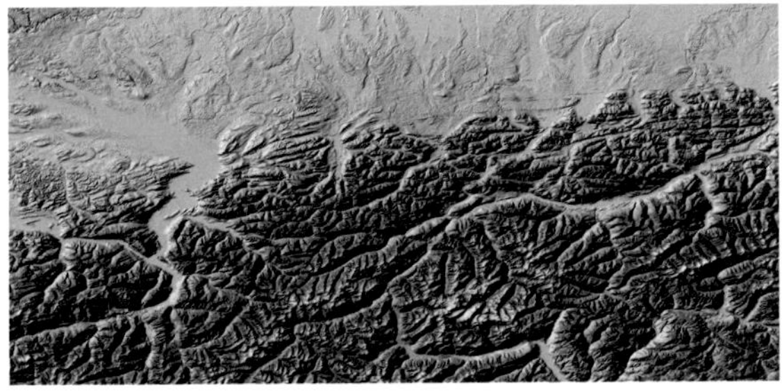

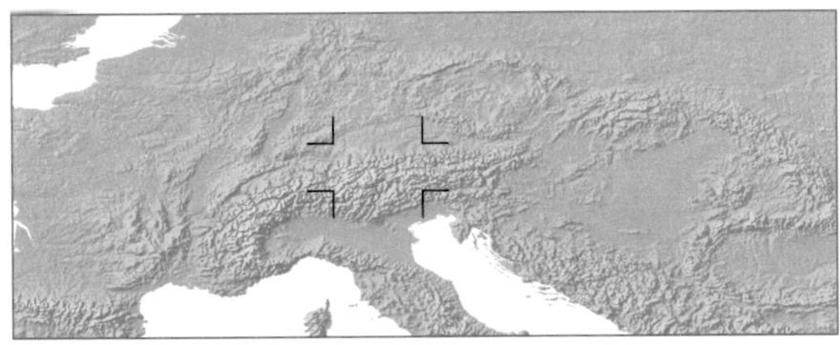

Elevation model: SRTM, ERS-1, ERS-2 / **Resolution:** 30 m / **Recorded:** SRTM, February 2000; ERS, 1995–98 / **Visualization:** shaded elevation model, pseudocolor / **Spectral channels:** X-Band, C-Band / **Image processing:** German Remote Sensing Data Center / **Data source:** German Aerospace Center, European Space Agency (ESA), NASA

Pages 040 – 043

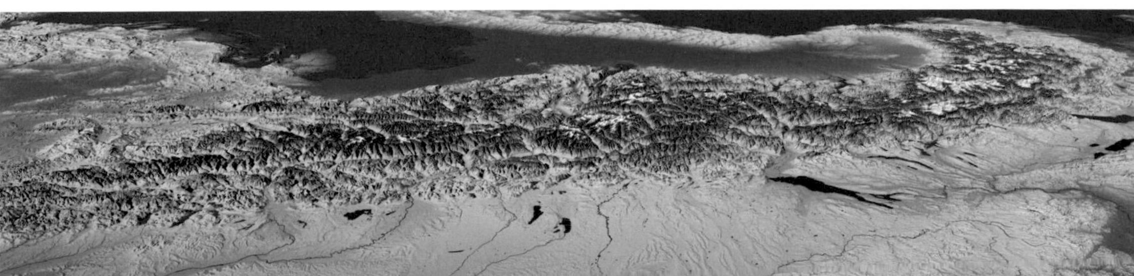

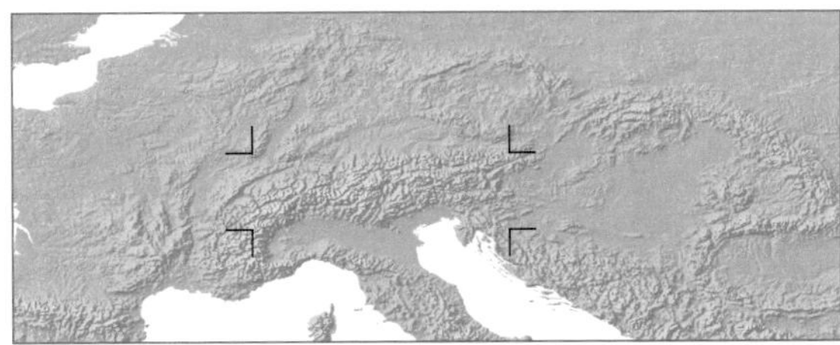

Elevation model: SRTM, ERS-1, ERS-2 / **Resolution:** 100 m / **Height exaggeration:** 3 times / **Recorded:** SRTM, February 2000; ERS, 1995–98 / **Visualization:** perspective, pseudocolor / **Spectral channels:** C-Band, 5.6 cm; X-Band, 3 cm / **Image processing:** German Remote Sensing Data Center / **Data source:** German Aerospace Center, European Space Agency (ESA), NASA

Elevation model of the central northern Alps

This spread presents an impressive view of the central northern Alps. It is a pseudocolor digital elevation model produced with data from two earth-observation satellites (ERS-1 and ERS-2) and a space shuttle mission (SRTM).

It was created on the principle of differential radar interferometry. On the basis of at least two images from slightly different angles, phase differences are evaluated, and from them, with complex calculations, the topography of the earth's surface can be determined. In this instance a number of different pairs of images were combined to achieve maximum precision. Different elevations were assigned standard map colors from dark green (lowland) through light green, yellow, ocher, and brown, up to elevations around 10,000 feet, which are depicted as dark brown. Elevations above 10,000 feet appear in white.

Finally, the elevation model was artificially illuminated from the northwest so as to attain greater three-dimensionality with light and shadow. East-west-running valleys like that of the Inn are clearly visible. The Ötztaler Alps with the 12,382-foot Wildspitze dominate the center of the image. To the west of them lie the Silvretta and Samnaun ranges, to the east, the Zillertal Alps. The northern Alpine foreland reveals a complex mophology created by the various colder and warmer periods during the ice ages. Especially apparent are the tonguelike glacial depressions like the present-day Lake of Starnberg and Ammer Lake.

Virtual Alpine panorama

An unusual perspective looking from north to south shows the entire arc of the Alps from the northern Alpine foreland to the Adriatic. In front of us lie (left to right) Traun Lake, Atter Lake, Chiem Lake, Lake of Starnberg, Ammer Lake, Lake Constance, the Lake of Zurich, the Lake of Lucerne, Lake Geneva, and Lake Neuchâtel, the Alps towering behind them. The great east-west ranges along the main crest of the Alps and individual mountain groups like the Mont Blanc massif stand out clearly.

On the horizon lie the broad plain of the Po River and the Adriatic, with the Apennines stretching off toward the south. This is not a satellite image in the classical sense, but a digital elevation model that was produced from various sources, including satellite-supported measurements. It has a median resolution of roughly 325 feet, but is comprehensive and of consistent quality. Different elevations were assigned the colors familiar from atlases, ranging from dark green (lowland) to light green, yellow, ocher, and brown, up to elevations of roughly 10,000 feet, which appear as dark brown. Elevations above roughly 10,000 feet appear in white. The pseudocolor elevation model was finally presented in perspective and artificially illuminated so as to achieve greater three-dimensionality with light and shadow.

Pages 044 / 045

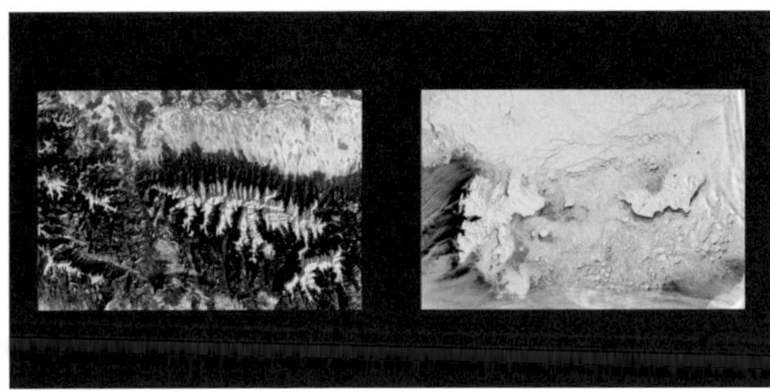

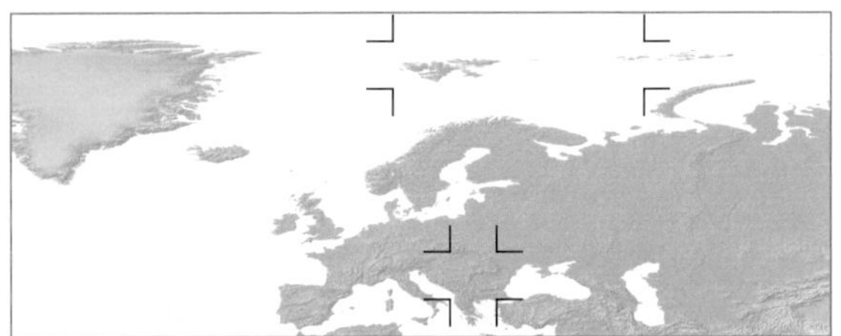

Satellite: International Space Station (ISS 06) / **Sensor:** photograph / **Recorded:** February 24, 2003, 06:53 UTC / **Visualization:** angle shot / **Spectral channels:** true colors / **Image processing:** German Remote Sensing Data Center / **Data source:** Image Analysis Laboratory, NASA Johnson Space Center, Roll E – Frame 31057

Satellite: Terra / **Sensor:** Moderate Imaging Spectroradiometer (MODIS) / **Resolution:** 250 m / **Recorded:** April 23, 2002, 12:25 UTC / **Visualization:** true color / **Spectral channels:** 0.62–0.67 µm, 0.54–0.56 µm, 0.45–0.47 µm / **Image processing:** German Remote Sensing Data Center / **Data source:** MODIS Rapid Response Project NASA/GSFC

Left: The Transylvanian Alps

In February 2003 astronauts photographed the Carpathians in Romania from the International Space Station. Dominating the picture is a small section of the main crest of the southern Carpathians, or Transylvanian Alps, which are still snow-covered at this time of year. The mountain chain, some 43 miles long, is called the Fogarash Range, and is set off from the adjacent southern Carpathians to the west and east by deeply cut north-south valleys. One of these bordering river valleys can be seen in this picture to the left of the Fogarash Range. The region presents Alpine high-mountain character and glacial morphology with trough valleys and glacial lakes created during the ice ages. The 8,343-foot peak of Moldoveanu Mountain in the center of the picture is the highest in Romania.

Right: Spitzbergen and Franz Josef Land

In the middle of the North Polar Sea lie two groups of islands whose mountains can be seen rising above the ocean ice only by looking closely. Spitzbergen, to the left in the picture (4 large and 150 small islands, roughly 60 percent glaciated) and Franz Josef Land, to the right (made up of 191 smaller islands and more than 80 percent glaciated). In this almost cloudless photograph the west coast of Spitzbergen is seen to be largely ice-free up to 80 degrees north latitude. The warm waters of the Gulf Stream make it accessible by ship year-round. From the Arctic (top), covered with ocean ice, cold air masses flow southward. Above the warm, open water surfaces (left and right bottom) convective, parallel strands of clouds quickly form. Around Franz Josef Land and eastern Spitzbergen lie dense belts of permanent ice, or sea ice, that is frozen solid to the shorelines and does not drift with the wind. To the south of this belt of fixed ice the strong northerly wind has already driven the sea ice away from the coast.

Pages 046 / 047

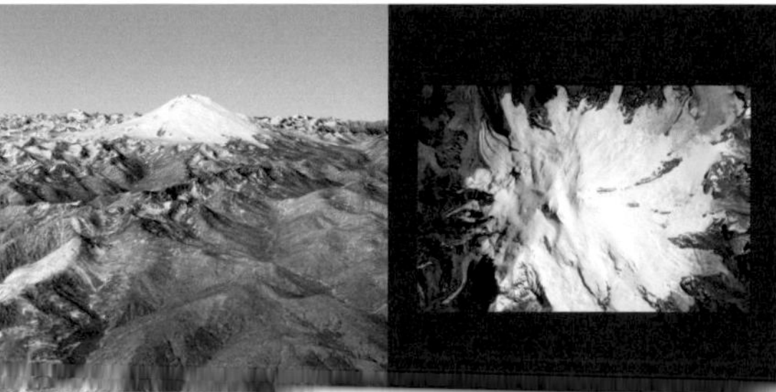

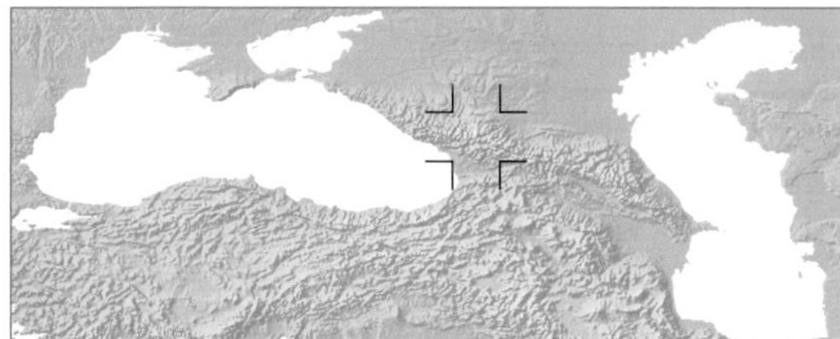

Satellite: Landsat-7 / **Sensor:** ETM+ / **Resolution:** 30 m / **Recorded:** June 17, 2000 / **Visualization:** perspective, true colors / **Elevation model:** SRTM, C-Band / **Resolution:** 90 m / **Height exaggeration:** 1.5 times / **Image processing:** German Remote Sensing Data Center / **Data source:** University of Maryland, GLCF-EarthSat, NASA

Satellite: International Space Station (ISS 05) / **Sensor:** photograph / **Recorded:** August 25, 2002, 06:21 UTC / **Visualization:** angled shot, true colors / **Image processing:** NASA, German Remote Sensing Data Center / **Data source:** Image Analysis Laboratory, NASA Johnson Space Center, Roll E – Frame 11194

Left: Mount Elbrus, the highest mountain in Europe, Caucasus

For this panorama of Mount Elbrus, a satellite picture was laid over a digital elevation model. The image shows the Elbrus area from the northeast in "true colors," or as the landscape would look to a person looking down on it from an airplane. Green areas indicate vegetation; up to an altitude of roughly 7,500 feet this region is one of dark-green mountain forests—an ideal location for conifers, birches, quaking aspen, and ash. In the higher regions up to 9,800 feet, here represented in a light brown, alpine meadows with richly diverse flora predominate.

The double peak of this extinct volcano is seen in the center of the picture, the higher one in the background. Mount Elbrus, at 18,481 feet, is clearly taller than Mont Blanc. Since it lies roughly 12 miles north of the main Caucasus range, which is considered the boundary between Europe and Asia, Mount Elbrus is the highest mountain in Europe.

Right: Detailed view of Mount Elbrus

This detail photograph of the top of Mount Elbrus shows quite clearly the mountain's double peak, connected by a 17,769-foot saddle. The photograph was taken by an astronaut on board the International Space Station (ISS).

The higher peak (18,481 feet) is almost in the center of the picture, to the right of it the smaller one at 18,442 feet. The entire peak area is permanently covered with snow and ice, and down from it flow several glaciers that ultimately feed the Baksan, Kuban, and Malka rivers. The glaciated area on Mount Elbrus covers roughly 56 square miles. In antiquity Mount Elbrus was known as Strobilus, the mountain on which, according to legend, Prometheus was chained.

Pages 050 / 051

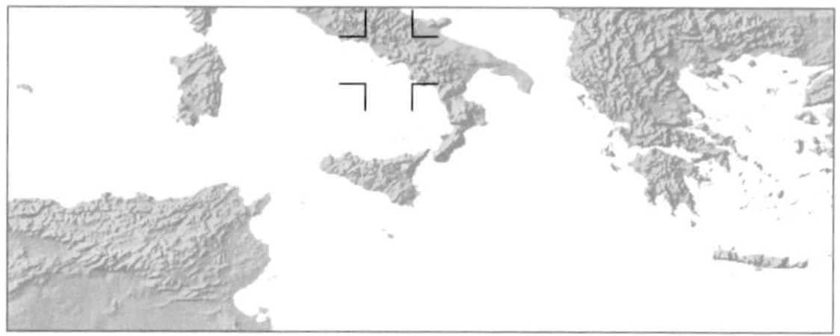

Satellite: Landsat-7 / **Sensor:** Enhanced Thematic Mapper (ETM+) / **Resolution:** 15 m / **Recorded:** August 2, 2002 / **Visualization:** perspective, true colors / **Spectral channels:** 0.63–0.69 µm, 0.53–0.61 µm, 0.45–0.52 µm / **Elevation model:** Shuttle Radar Topography Mission (SRTM), C-Band / **Resolution:** 90 m / **Height exaggeration:** 1.5 times / **Image processing:** German Remote Sensing Data Center / **Data source:** University of Maryland, Global Land Cover Facility (GLCF)–EarthSat; NASA

Panorama of Campania with Mount Vesuvius

Looking from the southeast to the northwest, this perspective view shows the Bay of Naples with Vesuvius rising 4,202 feet above the plain in the center right. In the left foreground the steep Amalfi coast and the Isle of Capri extend far out into the Tyrrhenian Sea. Areas covered with vegetation are seen in shades of green, the densely settled land around Vesuvius and the urban area of Naples in pinks.

In the past, Vesuvius was repeatedly responsible for death and destruction. The mountain last erupted in 1944, destroying two villages at its foot. But most famous is its devastating eruption of 79 A.D., which buried the cities of Pompeii and Herculaneum. Previously, the mountain, then known as Monte Somma, was nearly twice as tall as it is today at an estimated 8,202 feet. A new volcano rose out of the caldera created in that eruption, which now forms the mountain's peak. The edge of the old caldera can be clearly seen in the picture on Vesuvius's right flank. To the left, behind Vesuvius, one can see morphologically well preserved smaller crater remnants. These are part of the volcanically and seismically active Phlegraean Fields (Campi flegrei) west of Naples. The region's volcanic origin is also evident from the many hot springs on the islands of Procida and Ischia off the coast. Today Vesuvius is one of the most closely watched volcanoes on earth—in part with the aid of satellite technology.

Pages 052 / 053

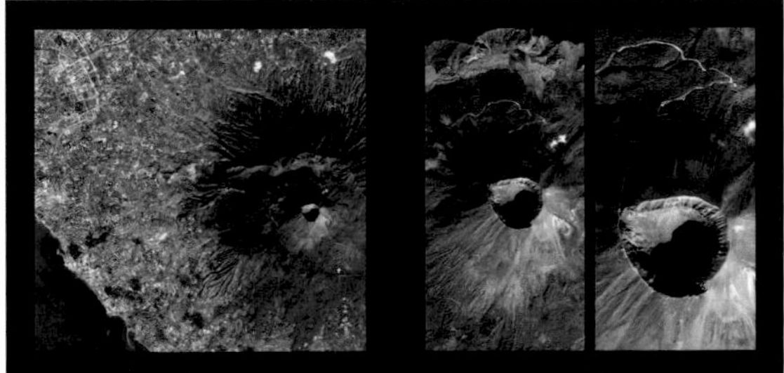

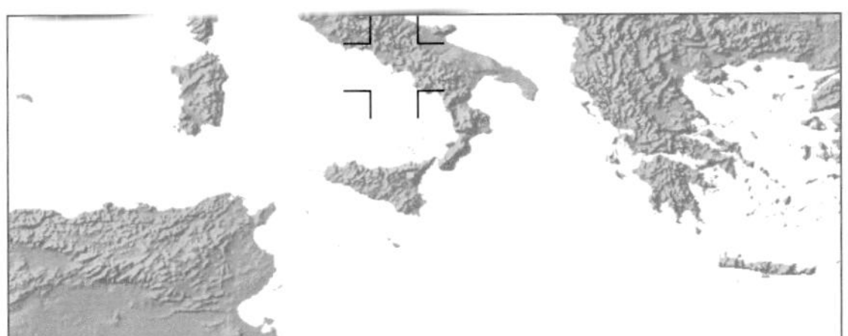

Satellite: Ikonos / **Resolution:** 1 m / **Recorded:** February 17, 2002, 10:10 UTC / **Visualization:** true colors / **Spectral channels:** 0.63–0.69 µm, 0.52–0.60 µm, 0.45–0.60 µm / **Image processing:** German Remote Sensing Data Center / **Data source:** Space Imaging Inc.

Pages 054 / 055

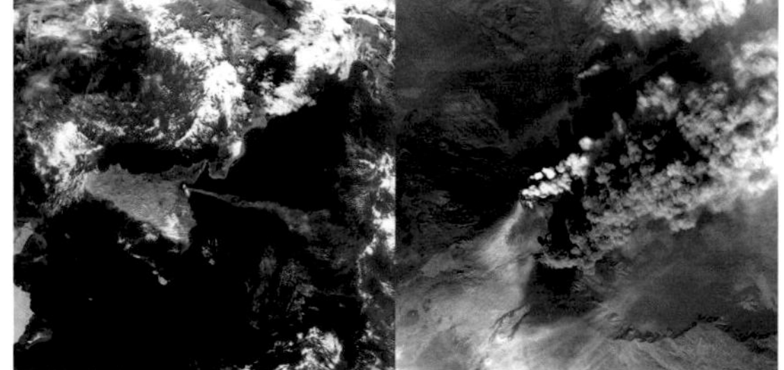

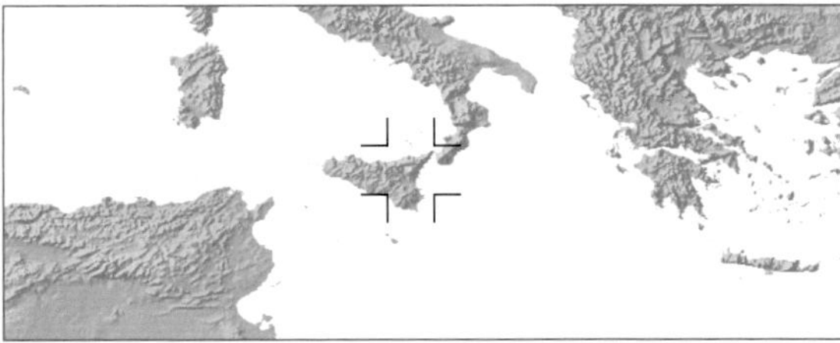

Satellite: Terra / **Sensor:** Moderate Imaging Spectroradiometer (MODIS) / **Resolution:** 250 m / **Recorded:** October 27, 2002 / **Visualization:** true colors / **Spectral channels:** 0.63–0.69 µm, 0.53–0.61 µm, 0.45–0.52 µm / **Image processing:** German Remote Sensing Data Center / **Data source:** German Aerospace Center

Satellite: Quickbird / **Resolution:** 60 cm / **Recorded:** October 31, 2002 / **Visualization:** true colors / **Spectral channels:** 0.63–0.69 µm, 0.52–0.60 µm, 0.45–0.52 µm / **Image processing:** German Remote Sensing Data Center / **Data source:** DigitalGlobe, Inc.

Pages 056 / 057

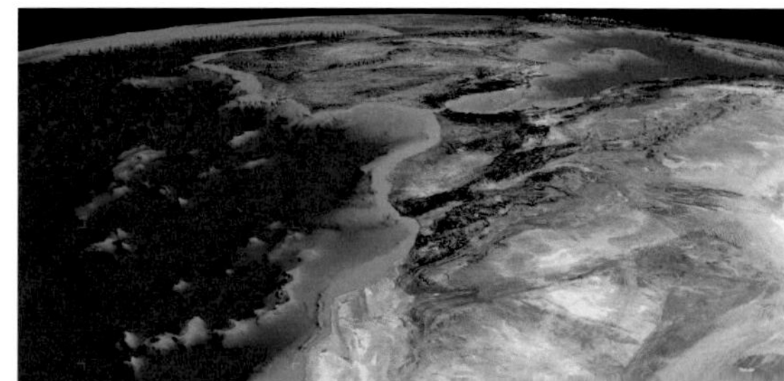

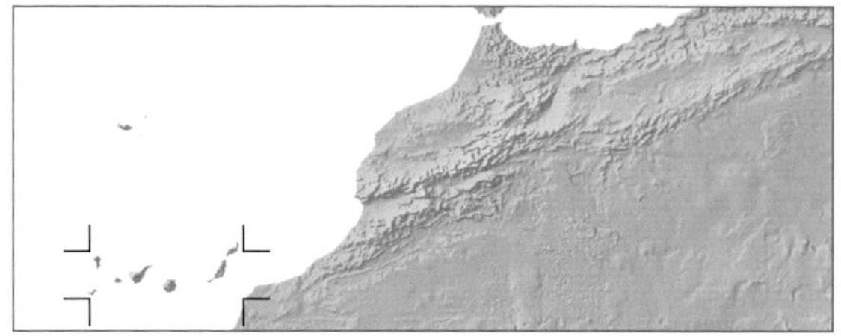

Satellite: Terra / **Sensor:** Moderate Imaging Spectroradiometer (MODIS) / **Resolution:** 1,000 m / **Elevation model:** GTOPO-30, ETOPO-2 / **Resolutions:** 1,000 m, 2,000 m / **Height exaggeration:** 5 times / **Visualization:** perspective, true colors / **Spectral channels:** 0.62–0.67 µm, 0.55–0.57 µm, 0.46–0.48 µm / **Image processing:** German Remote Sensing Data Center / **Data source:** NASA Goddard Space Flight Center, United States Geological Survey (USGS), National Geophysical Data Center (NGDC)

Detailed view of Vesuvius

The right half of the picture is dominated by the crater of Vesuvius, while the left half shows the mountain's thickly settled western flank. At the bottom edge the hook-shaped breakwater in the harbor of Torre del Greco thrusts out into the Bay of Naples. If you look closely, you can make out greenhouses along the coast, recognizable from their shape and silvery color. They are an indication of the importance of fruit and vegetable growing in the region. The entire settled area is laced with a complex network of highways and thruways—as can be seen from the numerous cloverleaf interchanges.

Lava streams from the volcano's various active phases radiate outward like fingers from the crater. One stream broke out northeast of Torre del Greco, and the city extends clear up to it. Even though Torre del Greco was destroyed by this lava stream in 1794, it was rebuilt, and was only barely spared by later eruptions around 1804–5. In the north the present crater is partially framed by the sickle-shaped rim of the Monte Somma caldera from the eruption of 79 A.D. The peak region of the present-day Vesuvius rising out of it is easily accessible by roads and hiking trails, some of which are clearly visible in the picture. A thick network of more than 2,000 modern monitoring instruments covers the region; with them the Osservatorio Vesuviano, an observatory run by vulcanologists in Naples, keeps precise tabs on the volcano. The instruments cannot be seen in the picture, but the dense settlement around the volcano shows the problem: over a million people live in direct proximity to a volcano dreaded for its explosive eruptions.

Left: Eruption of Mount Etna in the fall of 2002

Mount Etna, in the center of the picture, is the most active volcano in Europe, and at 10,991 feet, also the tallest. It lies in the northeast corner of Sicily on the Strait of Messina. This satellite picture shows the mountain during an eruption on October 27, 2002, which was accompanied by more than 200 minor earthquakes and continued until January 2003. The cloud of volcanic ash spewing out from the craters—clearly visible in the satellite photograph—is being blown more than 300 miles to the east by the prevailing west wind. In addition to viewing the ash cloud from a safe distance, satellite observations permit quantitative investigations of volcanic activity. Spectrometers on board make it possible to analyze the chemical makeup of the ash cloud during the eruption. And such analysis allows us to determine the type of eruption and the amount of energy released.

Right: Detailed view of Mount Etna's crater

This detail image was made from an altitude of roughly 280 miles during the volcano's active phase in late 2002. It shows Etna's peak region, with the main crater and a number of active and dormant lateral craters, most of which show lava streams as well. At the beginning of the eruption activity great quantities of ash and gases of varied physical and chemical composition surge out of the craters—this is evidenced by the varied colors. The volcano's dense clouds of ash regularly disrupt air traffic, especially in the capital of Catania. With a resolution of 60 centimeters, the satellite image shows such details as single boulders on the peak. This allows us to make maps of the inaccessible crater region, which is subject to constant change owing to the volcanic activity.

Ocean mountains—the Canary Islands and North Africa

Hovering high above the west coast of Mauretania, the viewer of this computer-generated image is looking to the north. In the left foreground the Canary Islands—peaks of underwater mountains—tower above the surface of the sea. From left to right we see: La Palma, El Hierro, La Gomera, Tenerife, Gran Canaria, Fuerteventura, and Lanzarote. To the right on the African mainland, the Sahara stretches across southern Morocco and Algeria with the High Atlas range in the center. In the background are Spain and the western Mediterranean with the Balearic Islands visible—farther north, near the horizon, rise the Pyrenees and the Alps.

To produce this picture, a digital elevation model was overlaid with a cloud-free satellite picture of the region. Ocean depths were included as well, so that the deep-sea plains, or abyssal plains, with the undersea mountains and projecting islands stand out in three dimensions, just like mountains on the mainland. The Canary Islands are volcanic in origin and belong politically to Spain. At 12,192 feet, the Teide Peak on Tenerife is thus Spain's tallest mountain. Geologically and geographically, however, the Canaries are part of Africa.

Pages 058 / 059

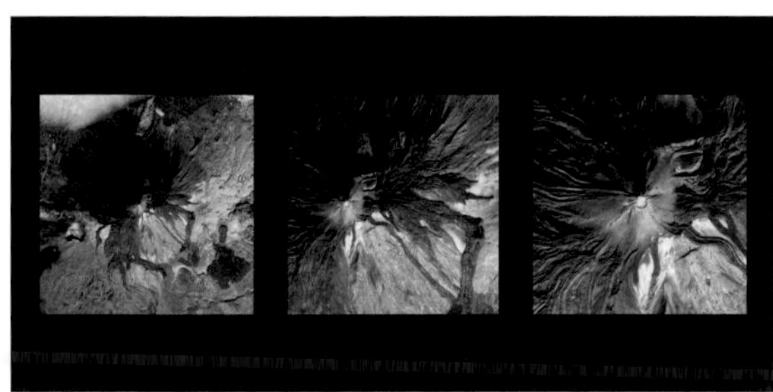

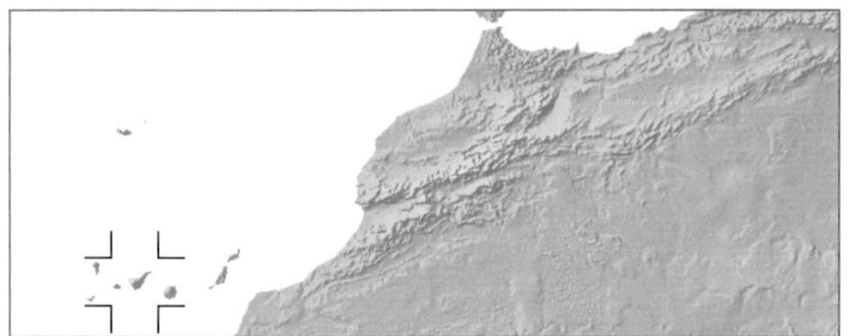

Satellite: Ikonos / **Resolution:** 1 m / **Recorded:** November 27, 2002, 12:06 UTC / **Visualization:** true colors / **Spectral channels:** 0.63–0.69 µm, 0.52–0.60 µm, 0.45–0.52 µm / **Image processing:** German Remote Sensing Date Center / **Data source:** Space Imaging Inc.

Detailed view of Teide Peak

The picture on the left is dominated in the center by the main crater of Teide Peak on the island of Tenerife. The central peak with its relatively small crater and pointed cone lies completely inside a roughly 10-mile-wide caldera—a crater created by a massive explosion some 300,000 years ago. The Canaries presumably owe their existence to a "hot spot," a spot in the earth's crust where magma from the mantle presses close to the surface and produces volcanoes. To the left of Teide Peak, somewhat south of it, lies a larger crater, the "Old Pico" or "Pico Viejo." Teide Peak has partially covered the Pico Viejo in its numerous eruptions. These are documented by the many lava streams radiating outward from the mountain. In the last 500 years, to be sure, there has been an eruption from Teide or one of its surrounding craters only roughly every 100 years. The last eruption on the northwest flank took place in 1909.

In the left-hand picture one can see the base station of the cable car on the right, below the main crater. In the right-hand picture, presenting Teide's peak in detail, its corresponding mountain station clearly stands out. We can even see the shadows of the cable-car supports. Above the top station various trails lead in broad serpentine curves across the lava fields to the rim of the crater. Here the national park administration has also created a volcanic nature trail.

Page 063

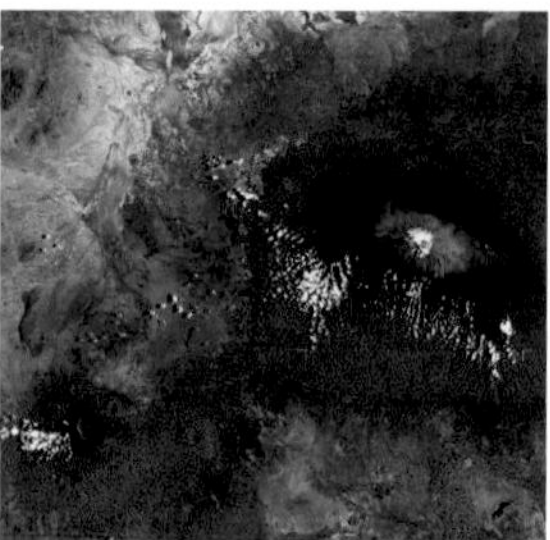

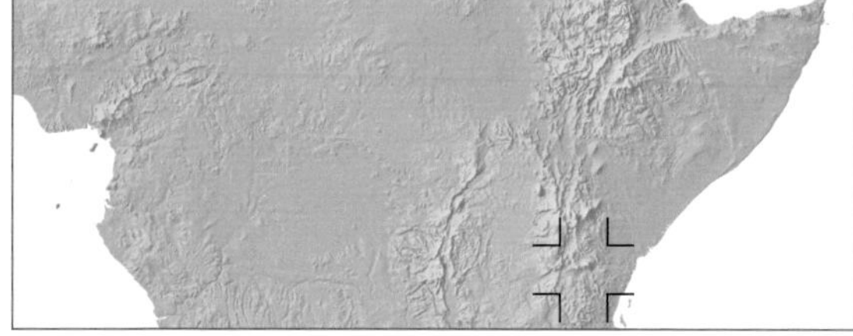

Satellite: Landsat-5 / **Sensor:** Thematic Mapper (TM) / **Resolution:** 30 m / **Recorded:** February 25, 1987 / **Visualization:** pseudocolor / **Spectral channels:** 0.76–0.90 µm, 0.63–0.69 µm, 0.52–0.60 µm / **Image processing:** German Remote Sensing Data Center / **Data source:** University of Maryland, Global Land Cover Facility (GLCF)–EarthSat

Kilimanjaro, Africa's tallest mountain, Tanzania

This satellite picture shows two imposing mountains: in the southwest the 14,977-foot Meru and in the northeast the tallest mountain in Africa, Kilimanjaro (19,340 feet), which lies in the north of Tanzania on the Kenyan border, roughly 210 miles south of the equator.

Kilimanjaro is the result of volcanic activity within the East African Rift system, which began forming in the Pliocene some 20 million years ago. This pseudocolor image—in which areas covered with vegetation appear a bright red—provides detailed information about the elevation bands of vegetation on Kilimanjaro. If one studies it carefully, one notes that the ringlike vegetation belts around the mountain are not symmetrical: on the south side of the mountain the dense vegetation clearly extends farther into the foreland than on the north side. This is a result of the prevailing winds from the southeast—the southeast trade winds, which account for considerable higher rainfall on the south side of the mountain. The higher rainforest zone lies for the most part within the national park established in 1977. Beginning at roughly 10,000 feet the great variation in temperature between day and night and reduced precipitation replace the rainforest with a belt of heath and moorland. This zone is identified in the picture by a considerably less intense shade of red, in places barely visible. Above this follow additional elevation belts in the form of rock, debris, and glacial zones. Kilimanjaro's varied flora is now endangered by settlement, tourism, and commercial tree cutting. Protected since 1968, the area was declared a UNESCO Natural Heritage site in 1987.

Pages 064 / 065

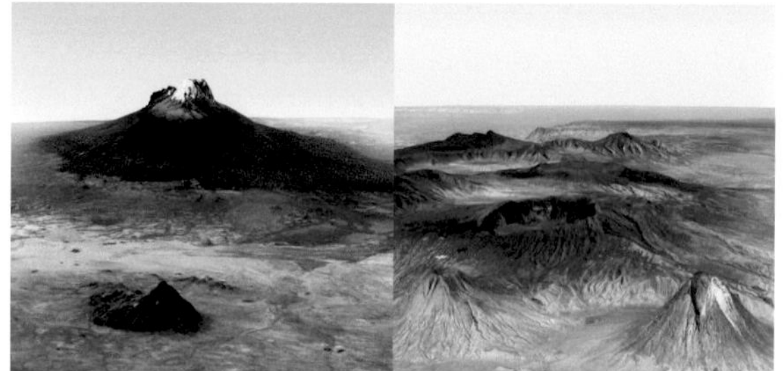

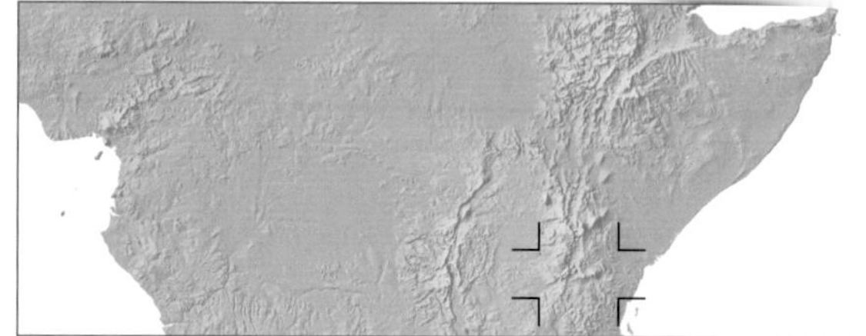

Satellite: Landsat-4 / **Sensor:** MSS / **Resolution:** 80 m / **Recorded:** January 24, 1976 / **Visualization:** pseudocolor / **Elevation model:** SRTM, C-Band / **Resolution:** 90 m / **Height exaggeration:** 1.5 times / **Image processing:** German Remote Sensing Data Center / **Data source:** University of Maryland, GLCF–EarthSat, NASA

Satellite: Landsat-7 / **Sensor:** ETM+ / **Resolution:** 15 m / **Recorded:** February 12, 2000 / **Visualization:** true colors / **Elevation model:** SRTM, C-Band / **Resolution:** 90 m / **Height exaggeration:** 1.8 times / **Image processing:** German Remote Sensing Data Center / **Data source:** University of Maryland, GLCF–EarthSat, NASA

Left: Kilimanjaro in 3D

Only in this slightly exaggerated 3D view can one see how Kilimanjaro rises up out of the surrounding savanna. Because of its exposed situation and altitude of 19,340 feet, the mountain deflects the atmospheric currents and thus creates a local climate different from that of the flatland. The surrounding high plateau is hot and dry, but with increasing elevation the precipitation becomes heavier and the temperature decreases. This has led to the formation of glaciers on the mountain's peak. Since the beginning of the twentieth century, however, Kilimanjaro's glaciers have lost roughly 80 percent of their mass, and pessimistic scientists assume that by 2030, at the latest, the peak will be completely ice-free. What this will mean for the flora and fauna, as well as the population of the region, is difficult to predict. The retreat of the ice masses has already led to a shortage of water in Tanzania.

Right: Panorama of Ol Donyo Lengai

This three-dimensional view shows a part of one of the most unusual volcanoes in the world—the plateau of the 9,501-foot-tall Ol Donyo Lengai. It lies in northern Tanzania and is a part of the chain of active volcanoes on the eastern edge of the East African Rift. Lengai's lava is not glowing red and over 2,000°F, as elsewhere, but relatively cool at only 650°F. It is black and as viscous as mud. But that is not all: as soon as the lava comes in contact with oxygen and humidity, it bleaches out, and after a few months becomes as white as snow due to the lava's high sodium carbonate content. Because of this peculiarity, some sections of the surface of the massif appear uncommonly light in this satellite picture.

Pages 068 / 069

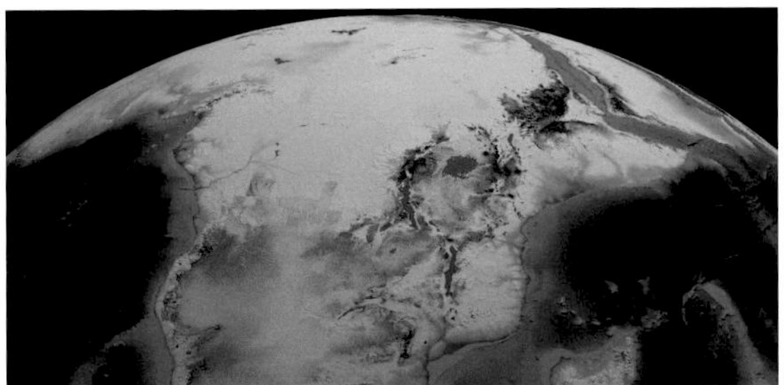

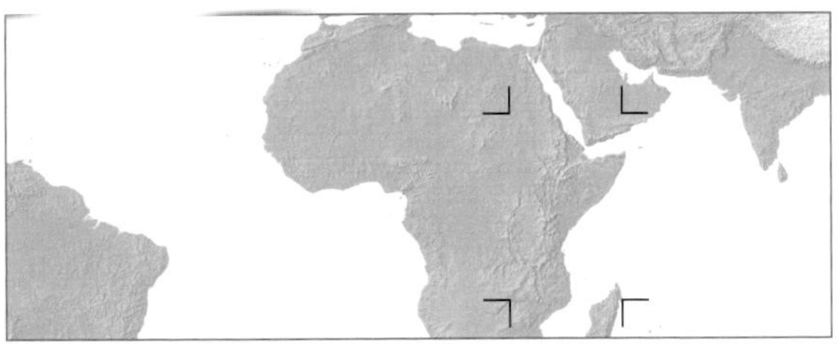

Elevation Model: GTOPO-30, ETOPO-2 / **Resolutions:** 1,000 m, 2,000 m / **Height exaggeration:** 5 times / **Visualization:** perspective, pseudocolor / **Image processing:** German Remote Sensing Data Center / **Data source:** United States Geological Survey (USGS), National Geophysical Data Center (NGDC)

East African Rift, the cradle of mankind

This perspective view of a digital elevation model shows eastern Africa with the ranges of mountains along the East African Rift standing out in brown tones. This structure is part of a geological disruption more than 3,700 miles long, extending from the Red Sea in the north past both sides of Lake Victoria to the Zambesi River south of Mozambique. The rift was created roughly 30 million years ago when huge masses of magma rose up out of the earth's core and caused the surface to bulge upward. The crust broke open, and in the center sank down several thousand feet. Today large areas of this depression are filled with lava, sediments, and water—note the elongated lakes in the center of the picture. Along the vertical flanks of the rift new fissures in the earth's crust are constantly forming. Through them magma repeatedly reaches the surface to form volcanic massifs: Ruwenzori (16,795 feet), the Virunga Range (14,787 feet), Mount Kenya (17,057 feet), and the Kilimanjaro massif (19,340 feet) in Tanzania are among the most prominent of them. The extremely varied landscape of the East African Rift produced a unique variety of animals and plants; the Ngorongoro Crater and the Serengeti are the best-known examples.

The oldest traces of early man also come from this region. The reshaping of the landscape in the creation of the East African Rift possibly helped to spur the evolution of primates into human beings. Climate changes accompanying the rise of the chain of volcanoes led to the creation of expansive savannas. Walking upright, the crucial developmental step in human evolution, is held to be an adaptation by primates formerly at home in the jungle to the new environmental conditions.

Pages 070 / 071

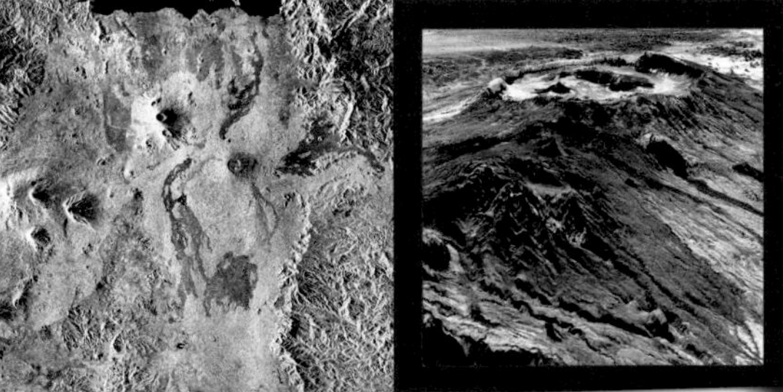

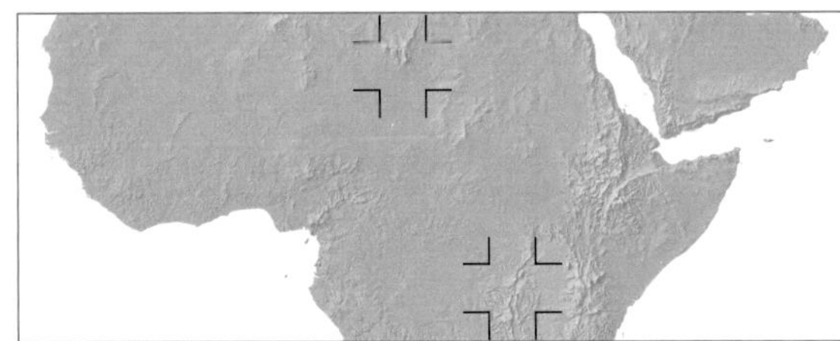

Satellite: Space Shuttle Imaging Radar / **Sensor:** SIR-C/X-SAR / **Resolution:** 25 m / **Recorded:** October 3, 1994 / **Visualization:** pseudocolor / **Spectral channels:** L-Band (HV), C-Band (HH), C-Band (HV) / **Image processing:** NASA, German Remote Sensing Data Center / **Data source:** NASA, Jet Propulsion Laboratory (JPL)

Satellite: Landsat-7 / **Sensor:** ETM+ / **Resolution:** 30 m / **Recorded:** October 27, 2000 / **Visualization:** true colors / **Elevation model:** SRTM, C-Band / **Resolution:** 90 m / **Height exaggeration:** 1.8 times / **Image processing:** German Remote Sensing Data Center / **Data source:** University of Maryland, GLCF-EarthSat, NASA

The Virunga volcanic range, home of the last mountain gorillas

This picture shows the Virunga volcanoes in the border area of Rwanda, the Democratic Republic of the Congo, and Uganda. It is one of a unique series produced from a U.S. space shuttle in 1994 with radar sensors of various frequencies and employing various polarizations. The resulting combination of radar signals has not been repeated from satellites to this day: too much energy is required for the sensors; there is too much weight; as a result it is too costly.

At the upper (south) edge of the picture Lake Kivu appears in black on the border between the Democratic Republic of Congo (right) and Rwanda (left). In the center of the picture the steep Nyiragongo volcano rises up 11,358 feet, with a lava lake in its crater. To the left of it lie the three volcanoes Mount Karisimbi (14,787 feet), Mount Sabinio (11,922 feet), and Mount Muhavura (13,868 feet). The green belt at the foot of Karisimbi (left) is a bamboo forest that forms the core of a protected area that is home to the last mountain gorillas in the world. This was the setting for the famous film about Dian Fossey, *Gorillas in the Mist*.

Right: The volcano Mount Koussi

Mount Koussi, also called Emi Koussi, is an extinct volcano that at 11,204 feet is the highest and the southernmost peak in the Tibesti Range in the central Sahara. The Tibesti Mountains lie in extreme northern Chad, and for political and geographical reasons are very inaccessible. For this image a satellite picture in true colors was combined with a digital elevation model to produced a perspective view of Mount Koussi. Its surface consists of dark lava and is practically devoid of vegetation. Its crater can be seen at the upper edge of the picture.

Pages 074 / 075

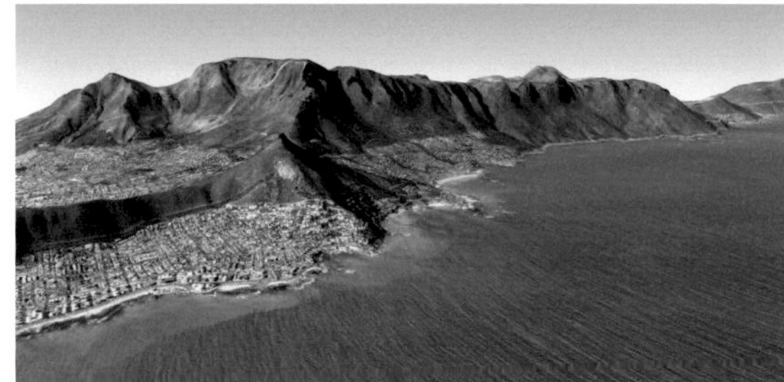

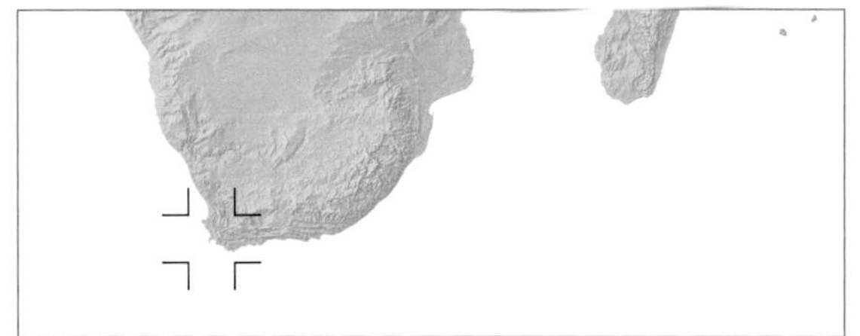

Satellite: Ikonos / **Resolution:** 1 m / **Recorded:** September 14, 2001, 09:06 UTC / **Visualization:** true colors / **Spectral channels:** 0.63–0.69 µm, 0.52–0.60 µm, 0.45–0.52 µm / **Elevation model:** Shuttle Radar Topography Mission (SRTM/X-SAR) / **Resolution:** 10 m / **Height exaggeration:** 1 time / **Image processing:** German Remote Sensing Data Center / **Data sources:** Space Imaging Inc.; NASA; Institute of Remote Sensing Methodology of the German Aerospace Center

Table Mountain, the symbol of Cape Town

We are looking southeast across the rounded top of the Lion's Head at Table Mountain (3,563 feet) near Cape Town in the extreme southwest of Africa. Table Mountain (left half of the picture, in the center) is an extension of the roughly 32-mile-long and 10-mile-wide Cape Peninsula. It is primarily made up of white, hard sandstone resting on a granite schist foundation. Erosional processes have created the mountain's flat tablelike shape, which is particularly clear in this perspective image based on a high-resolution satellite image and a digital elevation model.

Table Mountain, often covered with a dense veil of cloud, its "tablecloth," is the symbol of the city of Cape Town. This cloud veil is noticeable on the north and west slopes of the mountain as downwind, and brings to the mountain an annual precipitation of roughly 79 inches. Thus it rains here considerably more than in Cape Town, which receives only 2.76 inches. The lush and highly varied vegetation benefits from the increased rainfall. Table Mountain was first climbed by the Portuguese navigator Antonio de Saldanha in 1503. Today roughly 500 trails of varying grades of difficulty make the ascent possible. People in a hurry and unwilling to undertake the roughly four-hour hike can take a cable car that was installed in 1928. It carries them up the first 3,280 feet. From the top of it one can look down on bustling Cape Town (left in the picture) and the coastal resorts of Bantry Bay and Clifton on Camps Bay with their long sandy beach (center) at the foot of the mountain—if the view is not obscured by clouds.

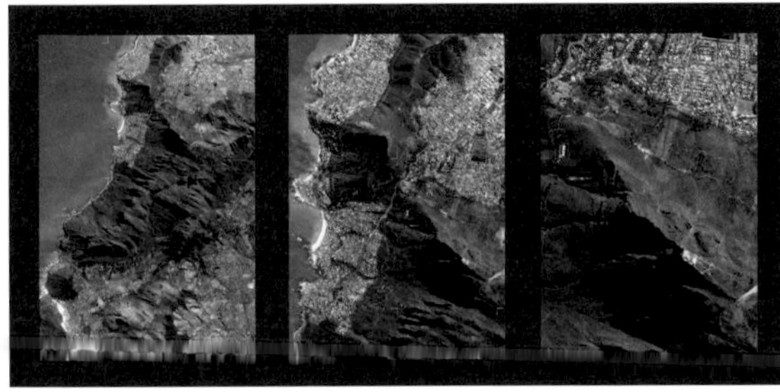

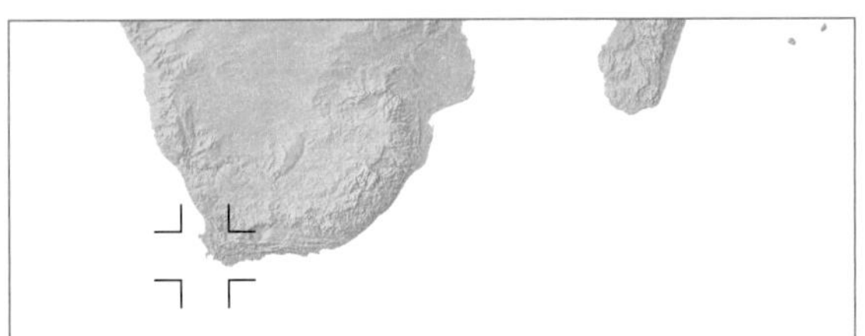

Satellite: Ikonos / **Resolution:** 1 m / **Recorded:** September 14, 2001, 09:06 GMT / **Visualization:** true colors / **Spectral channels:** 0.63–0.69 µm, 0.52–0.60 µm, 0.45–0.52 µm / **Image processing:** German Remote Sensing Data Center / **Data source:** Space Imaging Inc.

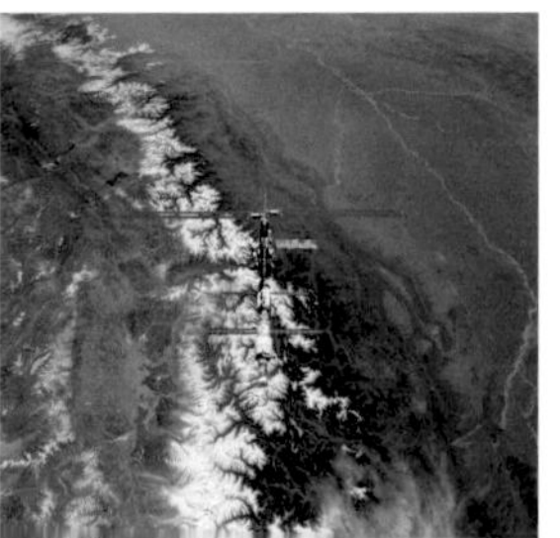

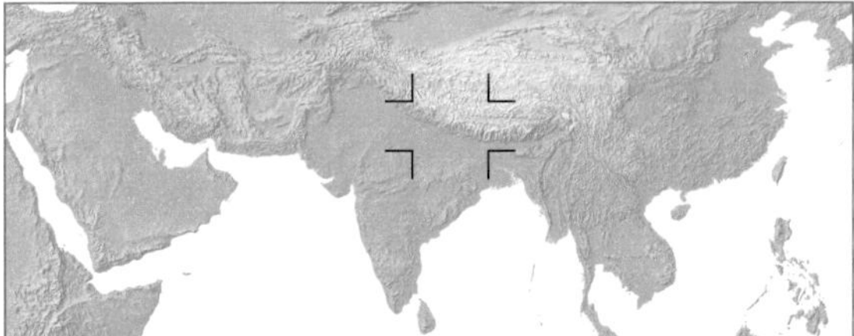

Satellite: Space shuttle (STS 102) / **Sensor:** photograph / **Recorded:** March 19, 2001, 05:06 UTC / **Visualization:** angled shot, true colors / **Image processing:** German Remote Sensing Data Center / **Data source:** Image Analysis Laboratory, NASA Johnson Space Center, Roll 714 - Frame 69

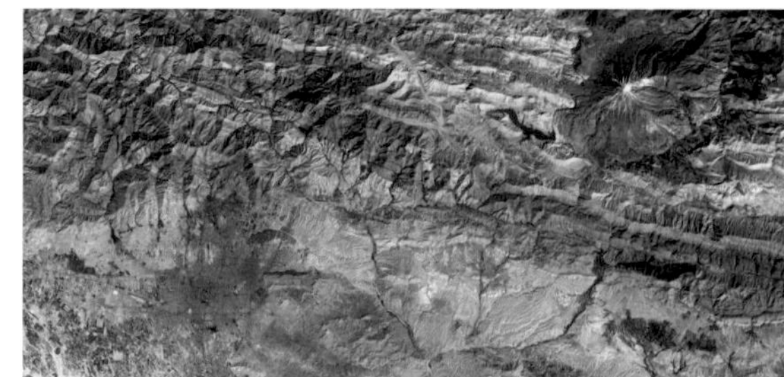

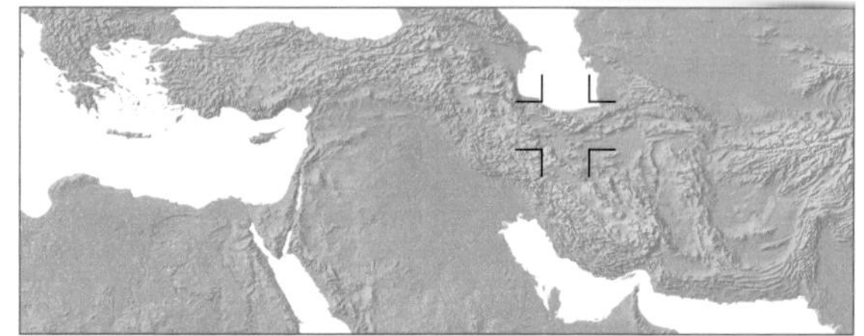

Satellite: Landsat-5 / **Sensor:** Thematic Mapper (TM) / **Resolution:** 30 m / **Recorded:** September 19, 1988 / **Visualization:** true colors / **Spectral channels:** 0.63–0.69 µm, 0.52–0.60 µm, 0.45–0.52 µm / **Image processing:** German Remote Sensing Data Center / **Data source:** University of Maryland, Global Land Cover Facility (GLCF)–EarthSat

Detailed views of Table Mountain

This satellite view looks down vertically at Cape Town and Table Mountain—the pictures from left to right approach the mountain's peak. At the center of the upper edge one can see the elongated ridge of Lion's Head. The flatter extension toward the edge of the picture is the 1,148-foot Lion's Rump, better known as Signal Hill; at one time arriving ships were greeted by a cannon shot from here. In the upper right corner (left-hand image) one can see a section of Cape Town's harbor with the Victoria & Alfred Waterfront—the city's promenade and shopping mile. In the hollow between Signal Hill, the Waterfront, and Table Mountain (marker) lies the city center. In the bottom left corner, south of the mountain massif, lie the rounded mountaintops of the Twelve Apostles and the town Hout Bay (Wood Bay). The fishing village takes its name from the rich forests that once stood here, felled for the building and repair of ships. White spots in the lower left of the picture show the results of that depletion—bald slopes to the west of the town. In the east, the Constantiaberg separates Hout Bay from the town of Constantia. This is South Africa's oldest wine-growing region. One can clearly see the vineyards on the mountain's east flank.

To the west of Lion's Rump and Table Mountain, in the left and center pictures are the sea resorts of Seapoint, Bantry Bay, and Camps Bay, distinguished by their long sandy beaches. In the center picture it is clear how in Bantry Bay the houses were built into the steep slope of Lion's Head. To the east of the mountain two large water reservoirs can be seen in De Waal Park.

The picture at right shows Table Mountain in detail, with the upper and lower terminals of the cable car standing out as white spots in the center and lower right.

The International Space Station (ISS) with the Himalayas

This unusual picture shows the International Space Station above the main crest of the Himalayas, running through the picture from top to bottom. The picture was taken in March 2001 with a Hasselblad camera by astronauts in a space shuttle flying at an altitude of 248 miles diagonally above the space station. Directly beneath the space station lie the mountain massifs of Annapurna, Dhaulagiri, and Manaslu—all famous "eight-thousanders," the term for peaks exceeding 8,000 meters or 26,250 feet.

In the right half of the picture one can see the Indian lowlands. There, near the city of Patna, the Ghaghara, Great Gandak, and Ganges Rivers flow together. The clearly visible haze in the lower atmosphere above the plain is typical, the result of pollutants for which man is to blame.

To the left of the snow-covered mountains stretch the highlands of Tibet, appearing in brown tones. If one follows the line of the space station upward, almost precisely halfway to the edge of the picture lies the city of Kathmandu—the goal of the first climbing stage and hectic entryway for many mountain climbers and trekkers on expeditions to the highest mountains of the Himalayas.

Damavand, the highest mountain in Iran

This satellite picture in true color shows a portion of northern Iran with its varied mountainous landscape. The limestones that form the steep Elburz Mountains were laid down on the ocean floor hundreds of millions of years ago and later folded into these mountain formations. Only much later—roughly 40,000 years ago—the Damavand volcano (marker) pushed its way up through the sedimentary rock. The way its lavas overlay the old rock strata is clearly visible in the picture.

With a height of 18,934 feet, Damavand is the tallest mountain in Iran; it towers above its immediate neighbors by nearly 6,500 feet. There are no records of any eruptions in historical time, however steam and sulfurous fumes repeatedly emerge from its crater.

In the bottom left corner of the picture Iran's capital, Tehran, is clearly visible as a gray spot. Damavand's location only some 37 miles from the center of Tehran makes it a favorite excursion destination for the city's populace. In this arid region water is especially precious. South of the mountain range one can make out irrigated fields in the surrounding semi-desert. Southwest of Damavand is a large reservoir, used both for storing water and for hydroelectric plants. To the west of the lake a broad river valley stands out, running perpendicular to the east-west crest of the mountains. Its course suggests that the river was in existence before the rise of the mountain massif and cut down through the strata as the mountains were uplifted.

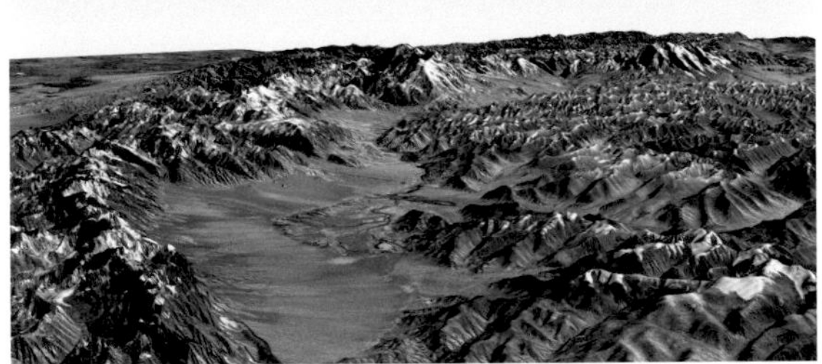

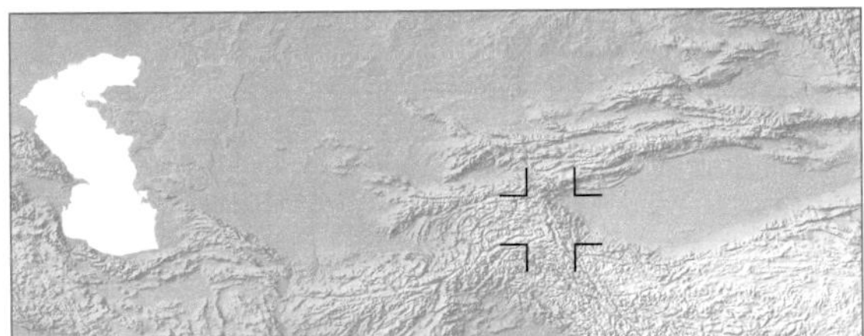

Satellite: Landsat-7 / **Sensor:** Enhanced Thematic Mapper (ETM+) / **Resolution:** 15 m / **Recorded:** October 7, 2001 / **Visualization:** true colors / **Spectral channels:** 0.63–0.69 µm, 0.53–0.61 µm, 0.45–0.52 µm / **Elevation model:** Shuttle Radar Topography Mission (SRTM), C-Band / **Resolution:** 90 m / **Height exaggeration:** 1.5 times / **Image processing:** German Remote Sensing Data Center / **Data source:** University of Maryland, Global Land Cover Facility (GLCF)–EarthSat, NASA

Muztagh Ata and Kongur

This picture shows the view from northwest to southeast from the border region of Kirgiztan and Tadzhikistan in the direction of Pakistan. The mighty range of the Kunlun Shan Mountains runs in a broad curve from the left foreground to the upper right corner. The most prominent peaks of this range are those of Kongur (center, 25,325 feet) and Muztagh Ata (right, 24,75t feet). The brownish tones in this true-color satellite image, which has been laid over a digital elevation model and shown in perspective, clearly indicate that this is an extremely arid region. Although agriculture is practiced on a small scale in the mountain valleys with the help of irrigation, in the upper left corner of the picture we can see the western edge of the Takla Makan desert. This desert is bound on the north by the Tien Shan and on the west by the Pamir and Kunlun Shan Mountains. The Tibetan highlands border it to the south. Its location between these massive groups of mountains explains why it is almost completely shut off from precipitation. The Takla Makan is one of the driest regions on earth, what is called a hyperarid zone. The broad valley in the middle of the picture once lay on the southern branch of the famous Silk Road. Where caravans once transported silks and other precious wares from the Orient to the palaces of southern Asia, tourists now seek adventure on the Karakorum Highway.

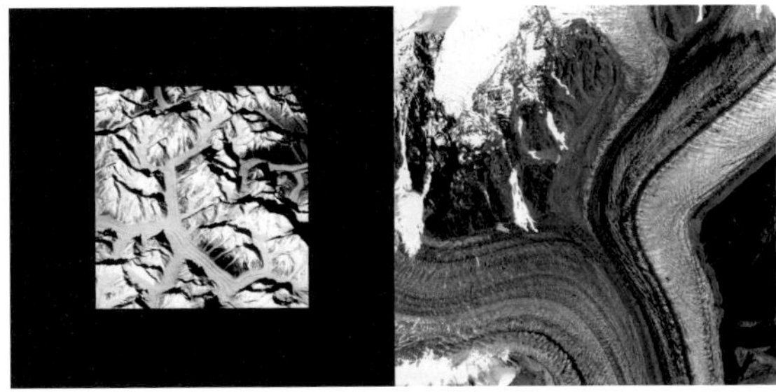

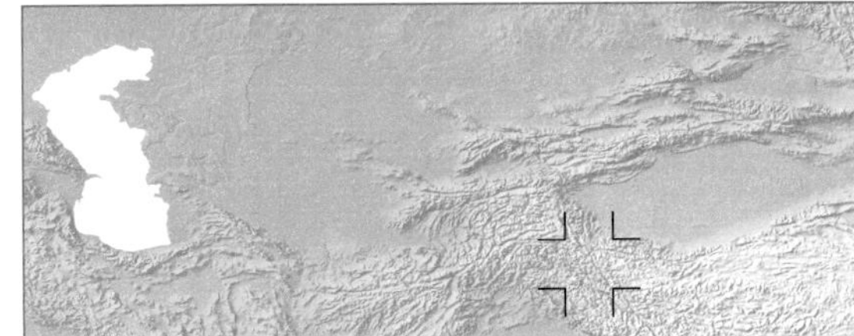

Satellite: International Space Station (ISS 01) / **Sensor:** photograph / **Recorded:** January 11, 2001, 08:13 UTC / **Visualization:** angled shot, true colors / **Image processing:** German Remote Sensing Data Center / **Data source:** Image Analysis Laboratory, NASA Johnson Space Center, Roll 343 - Frame 27

Satellite: Ikonos / **Resolution:** 1 m / **Recorded:** July 8, 2001, 05:50 UTC / **Visualization:** true colors / **Spectral channels:** 0.63–0.69 µm, 0.52–0.60 µm, 0.45–0.52 µm / **Image processing:** German Remote Sensing Data Center / **Data source:** Space Imaging Inc.

Left: K2, mountain among mountains

This photograph from the International Space Station shows the central Karakorum, with no fewer than four eight-thousanders in a very compact area, including the second-highest mountain on earth, K2, which received its name when it was first surveyed and the Karakorum's high peaks were numbered according to height. The natives call it Chogori—"Great Mountain." The center of the picture is dominated by the Baltoro Glacier, which flows to the west. At the famous Concordia ice field it joins with the Godwin Austen Glacier coming from the north. Above stands the massive pyramid of 28,250-foot K2 with its sunlit south wall. Mountain climbers consider K2 the most difficult of all the eight-thousanders; at the same time it is one of the most beautiful, all of which makes it a mountain among mountains. After the first Italian ascent in 1954, Reinhold Messner was the first to climb it without artificial oxygen in 1979. The other three eight-thousanders visible in the picture are Mount Broad (26,400 feet) in the center, followed by Gasherbrum II (26,360 feet) to the southeast, and Gasherbrum I (26,470 feet)—also called Hidden Peak—in the bottom right.

Right: Detailed view of the base camp at K2

In the center of the picture is the confluence of the Savoia Glacier, coming from the northwest, and the Godwin Austen Glacier in the east. The upper part of the picture shows the lower slopes of K2's south wall. The peak itself is not included in the picture. The tremendous erosive force of the glaciers, which constantly carry away material in competition with the mountain's rise, is clear from their large moraines. In the center, on the very dark moraine on the north side of the Godwin Austen Glacier, which is completely free of snow and ice, one can see the K2 base camp used by several mountain-climbing expeditions. Some 45 colorful tents can be seen scattered about in this satellite photograph with a resolution of up to a meter—and this from roughly 425 miles up.

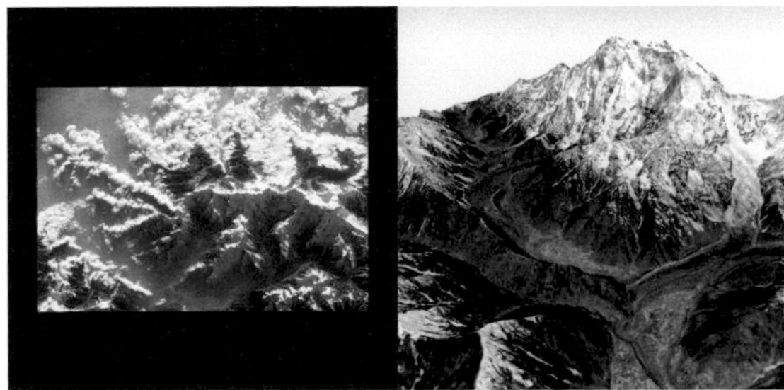

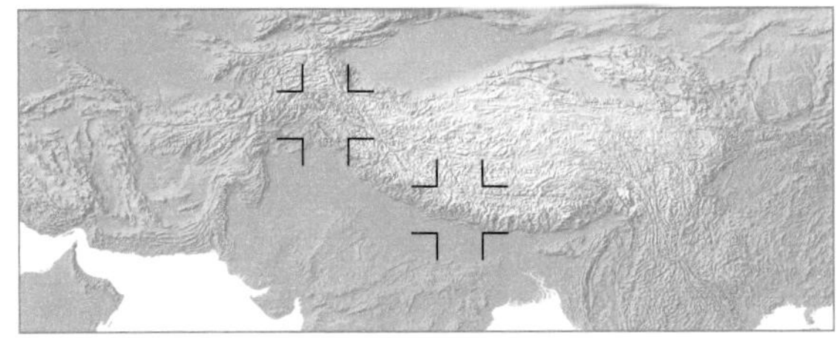

Satellite: International Space Station (ISS 08) / **Sensor:** photograph / **Recorded:** November 28, 2003, 09:40 UTC / **Visualization:** angled shot, true colors / **Image processing:** German Remote Sensing Data Center / **Data source:** Image Analysis Laboratory, NASA Johnson Space Center, Roll E - Frame 6343

Satellite: SPOT-5 / **Sensor:** HRV / **Resolution:** 2.5 m / **Recorded:** June 7, 2003, 05:56 UTC / **Visualization:** pseudocolor / **Elevation model:** SRTM, X-Band / **Resolution:** 10 m / **Height exaggeration:** 1.5 times / **Image processing:** German Remote Sensing Data Center / **Data source:** CNES, Distribution by Spotimage; Institute of Remote Sensing Methodology of the German Aerospace Center

Left: Manaslu, the trekking paradise of Nepal

This photograph from a space shuttle shows the Manaslu region in Nepal from the east. The elongated massif with its ridges and valley glaciers offers manifold but dangerous climbing possibilities. At 26,758 feet, Manaslu is the eighth tallest mountain in the world, and was first conquered by a Japanese expedition in 1956, a year of successes, when three eight-thousanders were finally bested. On this mountain in 1974 a Japanese expedition made the first conquest of an eight-thousander by an all female rope team.

Right: Nanga Parbat

Nanga Parbat (Sanskrit for "Naked Mountain") is the ninth tallest mountain on earth at 26,660 feet, and the westernmost peak over 26,000 feet high in the Himalayas. Hermann Buhl was the first to climb it alone in 1953, in an incredible feat after a number of attempts by German expeditions had failed in the 1930s. For the perspective view of the massif selected here, high-resolution SPOT satellite data were combined with an elevation model from the Shuttle Radar Topography Mission (SRTM). The digital model of the mountain can be turned and any desired view generated on computer. This view from the southwest falls on the powerful Rupal flank of Nanga Parbat, at 14,764 feet, the tallest wall on earth. Günther and Reinhold Messner climbed the mountain from this side in 1970 across the Merkl Gorge in the upper region, but were forced to climb down across the Diamir face, the west side, thus making the—unplanned—first crossing of the entire mountain. Günther Messner was buried by an avalanche at the foot of the wall.

Pages 088 / 089

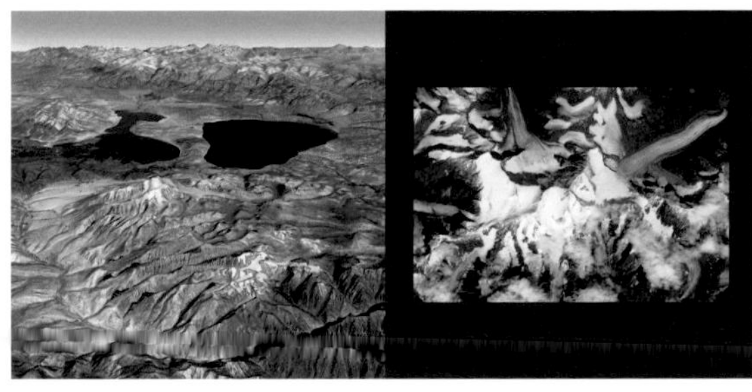

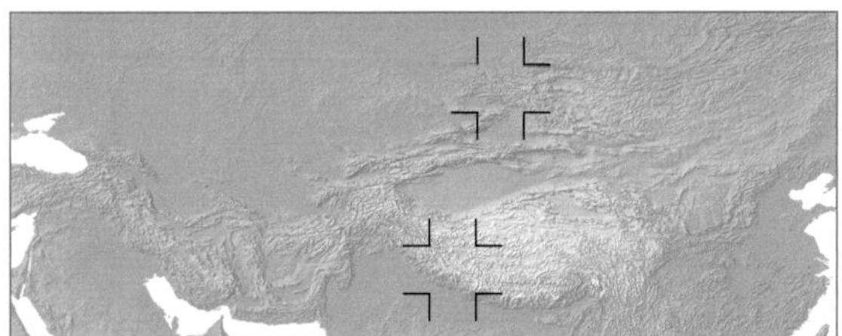

Satellite: Landsat-7 / **Sensor:** ETM+ / **Resolution:** 15 m / **Recorded:** October 13, 2001 / **Visualization:** true colors / **Elevation model:** SRTM, C-Band / **Resolution:** 90 m / **Height exaggeration:** 1.5 times / **Image processing:** German Remote Sensing Data Center / **Data source:** University of Maryland, GLCF–EarthSat, NASA

Satellite: International Space Station (ISS 05) / **Sensor:** photograph / **Recorded:** August 22, 2002, 06:05 UTC / **Visualization:** angle shot, true colors / **Image processing:** German Remote Sensing Data Center / **Data source:** Image Analysis Laboratory, NASA Johnson Space Center, Roll E – Frame 10651

Pages 092 / 093

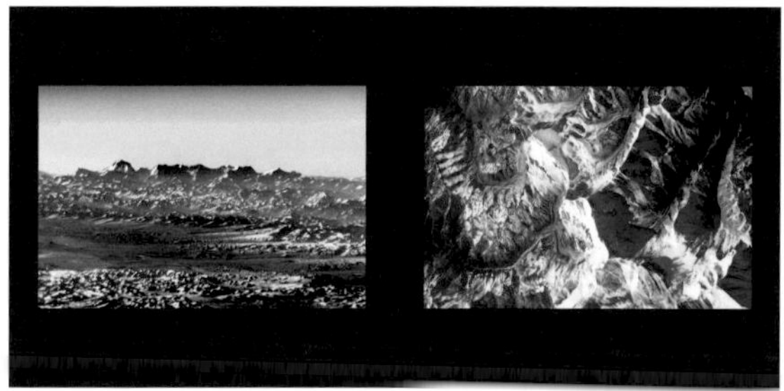

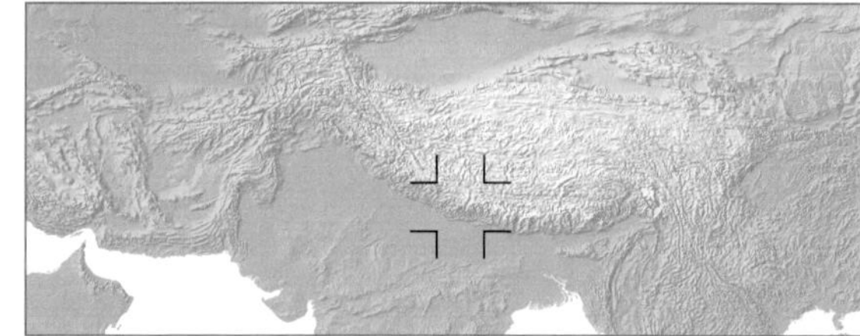

Satellite: International Space Station (ISS 01) / **Sensor:** photograph / **Recorded:** March 11, 2001 / **Visualization:** angled shot, true colors / **Image processing:** German Remote Sensing Data Center / **Data source:** Image Analysis Laboratory, NASA Johnson Space Center, Roll E – Frame 6765

Satellite: Space shuttle (STS 107) / **Sensor:** photograph / **Recorded:** January 21, 2003, 08:31 UTC / **Visualization:** angled shot, true colors / **Image processing:** German Remote Sensing Data Center / **Data source:** Image Analysis Laboratory, NASA Johnson Space Center, Roll E – Frame 5302

Left: Sacred land of Hindus and Buddhists

In the remote western Tibetan province of Nagari, in China, north of the main range of the Himalayas, lie Gurla Mandhata (25,243 feet), Mount Kailash (22,028 feet), and Lake Manasarovar (15,000 feet). The right-hand picture shows a perspective view of the region. It was based on a satellite picture combined with an elevation model. In the upper half of the picture are two lakes, the lighter Lake Rakas (left) and the deep-blue, 15-mile-long Lake Manasarovar (right). Hindus consider the latter to be sacred, and for that reason many of them undertake to run around it, a distance of 53 miles. South of Lake Rakas, Gurla Mandata is clearly visible. The solitary massif has been climbed only four times, first by a pair of Japanese climbers. The light-colored, snow-covered mountains north of Lake Rakas (in the picture at the very top) are the Kailash massif. Climbing Mount Kailash is forbidden for religious reasons. Pilgrims are obligated to walk the circular trail around the mountain, a 34-mile march called the *kora*, or *parikarma*. According to Buddhist belief, those who have circled the mountain 108 times achieve nirvana.

Right: Gora Belukha, Russia

Gora Belukha lies on Russia's border with Kazakhstan, and only 31 miles north of its borders with China and Mongolia. At 14,783 feet, it is the highest peak in the Altai Range. This picture, taken from the International Space Station with a telephoto lens (focal length 800 mm) provides a good overview of the massif. Based on precise analysis of one of the elevation models from the Shuttle Radar Topography Mission (SRTM) so frequently used in this book, Gora Belukha was removed from the list of the 50 highest mountains on earth in 2004. Mount Blackburn in Alaska now stands in 50th place instead.

Left: The Kingdom of Nepal, land of vertical contrasts

More than 26,000 feet of elevation separate the Indian lowlands from Nepal's Himalayan peaks. Thus the highest mountain range in the world presents characteristics and superlatives found in no other range. It was formed by the collision of the Indian and Eurasian plates, which began roughly 70 million years ago and still today accounts for a rise of several millimeters a year. In the course of this uplifting, rivers originating in the Tibetan highlands dug into the young mountain range and created valleys that cut through the Himalayas from north to south. Along with the passes, some more than 16,000 feet high, these form the country's traditional transportation routes.

The most impressive example is the Kali Gandaki Valley, which has cut down more than 16,000 feet between Dhaulagiri and the Annapurna massif (left edge of the picture). Through the valley runs one of the traditional trading routes, along which Tibetan rock salt, Indian grains, and fabrics were transported. Important trading posts were developed along the upper course of the river that are now becoming increasingly touristy. This view looks to the southeast and shows the lightly snow-covered Tibetan highlands near the source of the 930-mile-long Bramaputra River. In the background is the north flank of the main Dhaulagiri crest, abutted to the west (right side of the picture) by the sparsely settled region of Shey Phoksundo National Park. The Transhimalayan mountain range in the center of the picture presents an almost insurmountable barrier against the monsoon rains, which is what makes the high Tibetan plateau so arid.

Right: Dhaulagiri, the "White Mountain"

The photograph shows the highest mountain on Nepalese territory, Dhaulagiri. At 26,794 feet, it is the world's seventh-tallest mountain, taller than neighboring Manaslu and Annapurna to the east. The angled shot was made from a space shuttle and shows most impressively in the lower center the jagged ridge between the main and secondary peaks. The mountain massif is bordered by Myagdi Gorge in the south (lower left edge) and the Kali Gandaki Valley to the east (bottom right corner). To the northwest lies Shey Phoksundo National Park.

In addition to the snow-covered flanks and ridges that shape the roughly 25-mile-wide massif, one can clearly see a few tongues of glaciers and moraine structures. Along the main crest rise several pyramid-shaped peaks, four of which are above 24,500 feet. Dhaulagiri was discovered and first described in 1808, replacing Chimborazo, in Ecuador (20,561 feet), as the world's tallest mountain. For more than thirty years Dhaulagiri maintained that distinction, but was then supplanted by Kangchenjunga (28,169 feet), now recognized as the third highest mountain on earth. Dhaulagiri was first climbed in 1960, the next to last of the eight-thousanders to be conquered, by a Swiss-Austrian expedition. In that effort the expedition used an airplane to transport its equipment and supplies up to an elevation of roughly 18,500 feet, but had to leave it on the mountain at the end of the expedition.

Pages 094 / 095

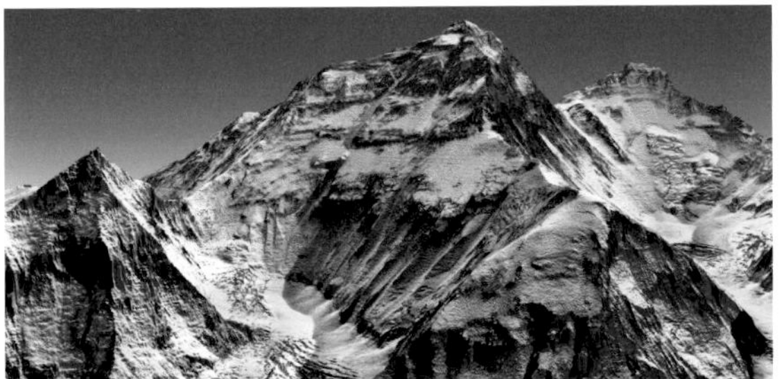

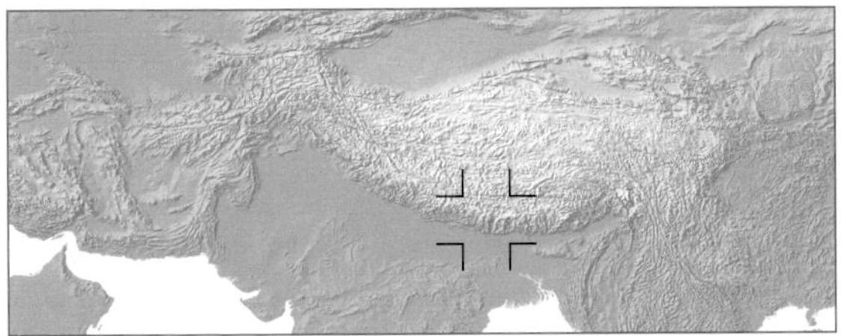

Satellite: aerial photograph / **Sensor:** Wild RC10 / **Resolution:** 1 m / **Recorded:** December 1984 / **Visualization:** perspective, true colors / **Elevation model:** Wild RC10 / **Resolution:** 5 m / **Height exaggeration:** 1.5 times / **Image processing:** German Remote Sensing Data Center / **Data source:** National Geographic Society, Swissphoto AG

Pages 096 / 097

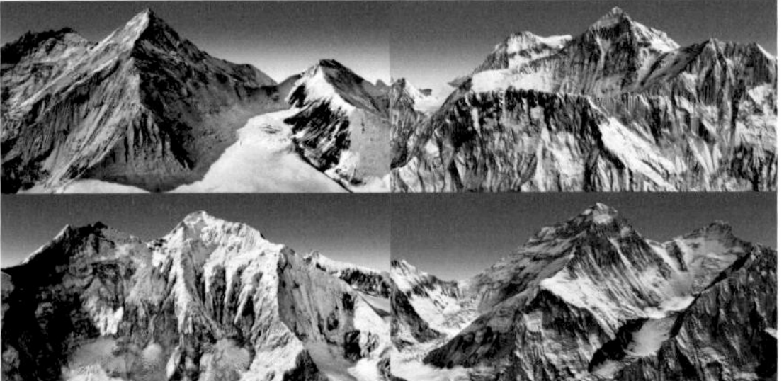

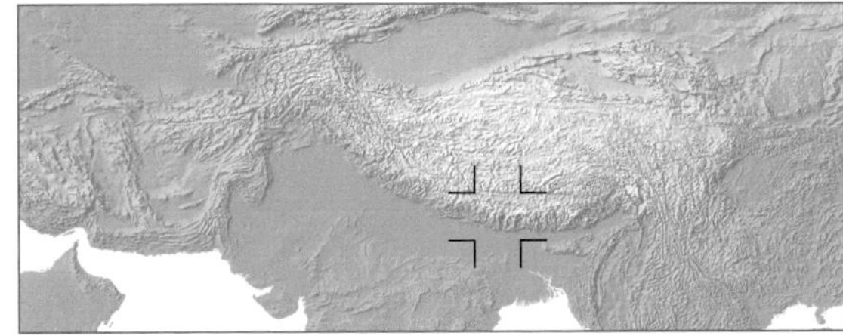

Satellite: Aerial image / **Sensor:** Wild RC10 / **Resolution:** 1 m / **Recorded:** December 1984 / **Visualization:** perspective, true-color elevation model: Wild RC10 / **Resolution:** 5 m / **Height exaggeration:** 1.5 times / **Image processing:** German Remote Sensing Data Center / **Data source:** National Geographic Society, Swissphoto AG

Mount Everest, the rooftop of the world

No mountain on earth can compare with Mount Everest. It is the world's tallest at 29,035 feet, and a magnet for mountain climbers, adventurers, and geophysicists. The spectacular series of perspective, computer-generated images on the following pages is based on data provided by a high-resolution survey camera carried in an airplane. To produce such views a precise digital elevation model was required, and this was created from numerous individual photographs by means of stereophotogrammetry. The principle: from the slightly different angles of overlapping photographs perspective displacements arise. From these, taking into account the photographic geometry and camera position, elevations—here in a 5-meter grid—can be precisely calculated. It is essential to clearly identify corresponding spots in the two images. Given the glaring white glacial and snow surfaces in the Everest region this is especially difficult. Only under optimal lighting conditions and with a powerful camera was it possible to produce the best available elevation model of the Everest region to date (2005).

We are looking at the massif from the northwest. In the center is Everest with its mighty north wall and the Rongbuk Glacier in the foreground. To the right in the background is Lhotse, at 27,939 feet the fourth-highest mountain on earth, and to the left, despite its 24,868-foot height, the almost diminutive-looking Changtse. Between Changtse and Everest one can see the north saddle, from which the "classic" north climbing route passes across the north ridge and on across the northeast ridge. On the right, between Lhotse and Everest, lies the south saddle, from which, by way of the southeast ridge and south peak, the first ascent was made in 1953. Beneath the Lhotse wall lies the upper portion of the Western Cwm.

Left: Mount Everest, view from the east

The boundary between the kingdom of Nepal and the People's Republic of China runs directly across the peak of Mount Everest. The Tibetans call the mountain Chomolungma, or "Mother Goddess of the Universe." We are looking at the mountain from the Tibetan side from a northeasterly (top) and easterly (bottom) direction. In the top image one can see the mighty northeast ridge, from which the north ridge branches off to the right toward the north saddle. This is the climbing route taken by Mallory and Irvine in 1924. Their expedition was fatal: Mallory's corpse was discovered beneath the peak in 1999, while Irvine, his companion and cameraman, is still missing. Whether the two reached the peak or not continues to be the subject of intense debate to this day. In 1980 Reinhold Messner was the first to climb the north flank alone and in Alpine style. Because of the picture perspective the upper part of the northeast ridge appears foreshortened. In fact it is here that climbers face the technical challenges of the rock stages known as the first and second steps. In the opinion of noted mountain climbers, the second would have been impossible in 1924. In the right foreground of the upper picture is the east-flowing Rongbuk Glacier with its great glacial crevasses (at the right edge of the bottom picture). In the lower image the heavily ice-bound and snow-covered east wall, or Kanshung Wall, predominates. This was first climbed in 1983 by an American team with Lou Reichardt following the mighty middle pillar. In the center lie the south saddle, at roughly 25,920 feet, and on the left the peaks of Lhotse (27,940 feet) and Lhotse Shar (27,513 feet). Below the south saddle lies the route used by Stephen Venables to reach the peak in 1988.

Right: Mount Everest, view from the west

These are views of mountain massif from the southerly (top) or southwestern (bottom) Nepalese side. The Nepalese call the mountain Sargamatha, which means "Goddess in the Heavens." The foreground of the top picture is dominated by the powerful rock barrier of the Nuptse-Lhotse massif. The Nepalese name Nuptse refers to the mountain's location to the west of the world's highest peak; it is made up of the elements *nup* (west) and *tse* (mountain). While the main peak at 15,790 feet had already been climbed in 1961, the eastern peak, "Nuptse East" (top, center foreground), stubbornly resisted all climbing attempts until 2003. It was only in the fall of that year that Koshelenko and Babanov successfully made a first ascent. Lhotse rears up farther to the right. Continuing northward, one sees the south saddle of Everest and the normal climbing route across the southeast ridge.

Behind Everest rises the peak of Chuptse. Behind the Nuptse-Lhotse wall nestles the Western Cwm, bathed in sunlight (bottom). The valley is filled by the Khumbu Glacier, which flows steeply downward toward the west before finally issuing from the valley in a great curve toward the southwest. Here, at 17,550 feet beneath the Khumbu Ice Fall, which is famous for its crevasses and breaking ice, lies the base camp for Everest expeditions that approach the summit by the normal route.

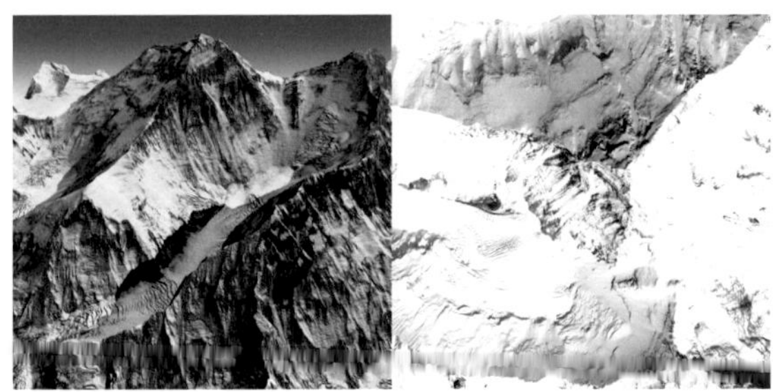

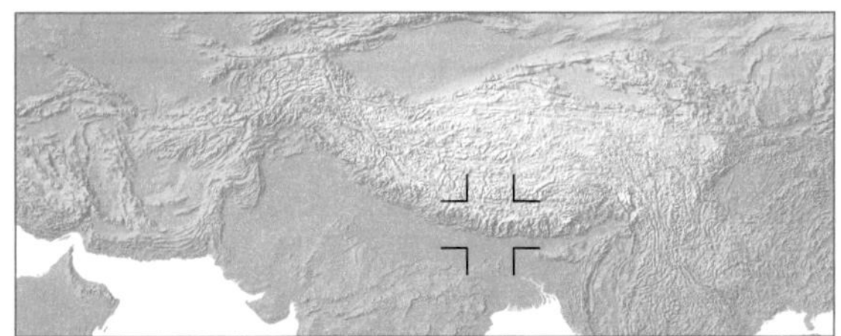

Satellite: aerial photograph / **Sensor:** Wild RC10 / **Resolution:** 1 m / **Taken:** December 1984 / **Visualization:** perspective, true colors / **Elevation model:** Wild RC10 / **Resolution:** 5 m / **Height exaggeration:** 1.5 times / **Image processing:** German Remote Sensing Data Center / **Data source:** National Geographic Society, Swissphoto AG

Satellite: Quickbird / **Resolution:** 60 cm / **Recorded:** September 20, 2002 / **Visualization:** true colors / **Spectral channels:** 0.63–0.69 μm, 0.52–0.60 μm, 0.45–0.52 μm / **Image processing:** German Remote Sensing Data Center / **Data source:** DigitalGlobe Inc.

Left: Route of the First Ascent of Mount Everest

On May 29, 1953, Sir Edmund Hillary and the Sherpa Tenzing Norgay were the first men to stand on the peak of Mount Everest. The view from the west selected here shows major sections of the route they followed—now generally referred to as the normal route. Just above the tricky Khumbu Icefall (bottom left) was Camp I; farther up, in front of the south flank, was Camp II. Their third camp lay in the steep and avalanche-prone Lhotse wall; Camp IV was at 25,919 feet, already in the "dead zone," on the windy and generally ice-covered south saddle. From there they ascended to the peak across the southeast ridge. As the most-climbed of the eight-thousanders, Everest has since that time accumulated any number of records. In 1978 Reinhold Messner and Peter Habeler were the first to climb it without artificial oxygen. Appa Sherpa has by now stood on the peak thirteen times. The youngest person to make the ascent was fifteen, the oldest seventy.

Right: Everest after a monsoon

The satellite picture shows the peak of Mount Everest (center) from an altitude of 280 miles. The mountain's classical pyramidal shape is clearly visible, with its three flanks, the southwest wall, the east or Kangshung wall (right), and the north wall (in shadow). In the lower right one can see the peak of Lhotse. Below the south saddle is a prominent rocky ridge and an orientation point for mountain climbers, the Geneva Spur. On the upper south wall are the prominent sedimentary strata of the Yellow Band. In the summer months, from June to September, Everest is subjected to a long period of high precipitation, the southwest monsoon dreaded by climbers. After it, in the fall, stable weather conditions frequently return, as seen on this cloud-free October day.

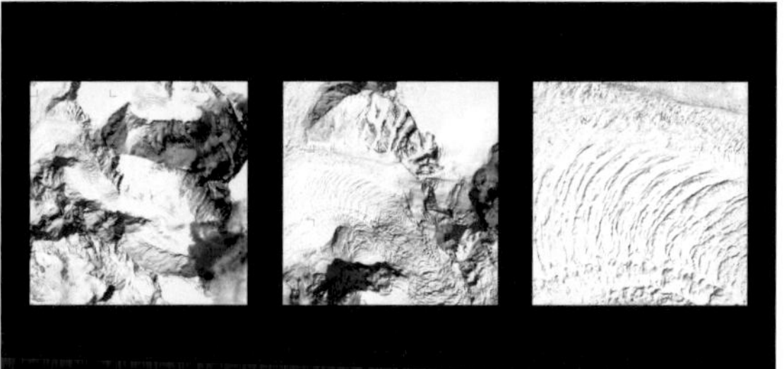

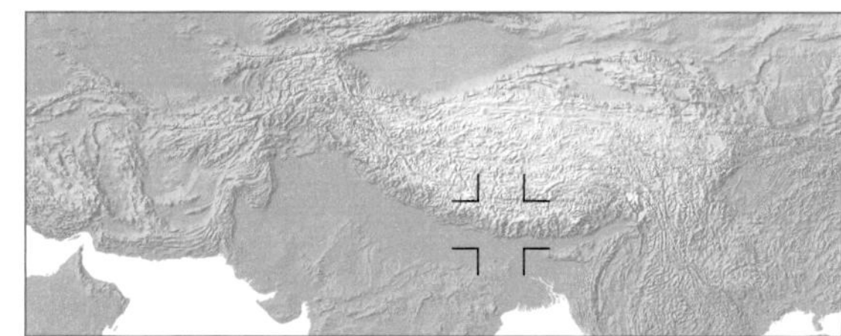

Satellite: Quickbird / **Resolution:** 60 cm / **Recorded:** March 14, 2003 / **Visualization:** true colors / **Spectral channels:** 0.63–0.69 μm, 0.52–0.60 μm, 0.45–0.52 μm / **Image processing:** German Remote Sensing Data Center / **Data source:** DigitalGlobe Inc.

Mount Everest: Zoom on Camp I

From this satellite perspective it is at first difficult to orient oneself. Snow, ice, rock, clouds, and shadows dominate the picture in tones of white, blue, and gray. In the center of the left picture lies one of the highest valleys on earth, the Western Cwm. In the upper left is the Khumbu Icefall, in the center right, Everest's peak structure. In shadow in the upper right lies the mountain's mighty north wall, in the lower right, beneath clouds, Lhotse. If one intends to climb Mount Everest the normal way it is first necessary to master the Khumbu Icefall, which is difficult to cross because of its crevasses and broken ice. Today, at great danger to themselves, Sherpas each spring prepare a route through the Icefall with ladders and technical safeguards. Climbers following these prepared paths then reach the inner high valley, the Western Cwm. Here the sunlight reflected off the glacier and the mountain's flanks produces daytime temperatures that frequently rise above 85°F, making dehydration and sunburn major hazards. Everest stands only at 27° north latitude (that of the Canary Islands), so the sunlight is intense.

In the middle picture we see large crevasses produced when the gradient steepens and at the exit from the valley the glacier picks up speed. In the upper left corner of the right picture, finally a few colorful tents can be seen on the snow-covered lateral moraine. This is one of the first advance camps in this year, one in which more than 500 climbers are waiting at the base camp for good weather. Perhaps the tents belong to the Sherpa Lakpa Gelu, who on his tenth ascent of Everest on May 10, 2003, required a mere eleven hours to reach the peak from the base camp. After eighteen hours and twenty minutes he was back in camp. Another record.

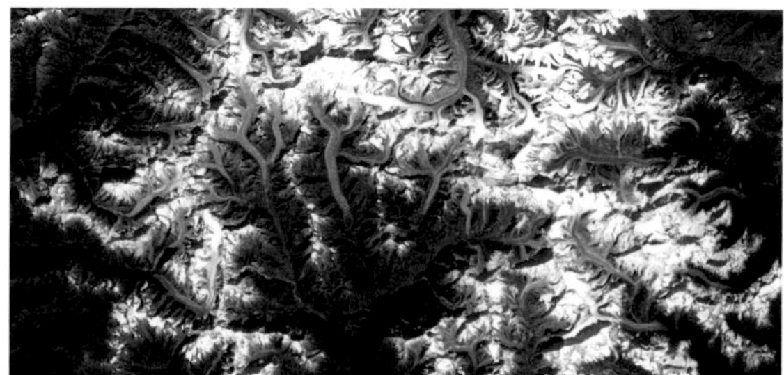

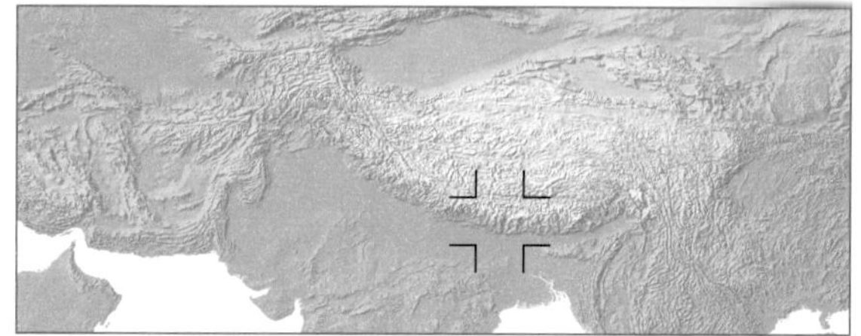

Satellite: Landsat-7 / **Sensor:** Enhanced Thematic Mapper (ETM+) / **Resolution:** 15 m / **Recorded:** October 30, 2000 / **Visualization:** true colors / **Spectral channels:** 0.63–0.69 μm, 0.53–0.61 μm, 0.45–0.52 μm / **Image processing:** German Remote Sensing Data Center / **Data source:** University of Maryland, Global Land Cover Facility (GLCF)–EarthSat

Sagarmatha and Makalu-Barun National Parks

This view from an altitude of roughly 435 miles reveals one of the most fascinating high-mountain landscapes in the world, that of the border country between the kingdom of Nepal and Tibet, in China. In the center of the picture lies Sagarmatha National Park with earth's tallest mountain, Mount Everest (29,035 feet). Everest is clearly identifiable from its distinctive north wall, appearing as a dark, shadowed triangle on the left edge of the right side. In the south (at the bottom of the picture) lies neighboring Lhotse (27,939). Also prominent is the elongated peak ridge of mighty Cho Oyu (26,906 feet; left side, upper right). On the right side, roughly in the center, is another great eight-thousander, the 27,765-foot Makalu (Great Black One) in the heart of Makalu-Barun National Park. In the bottom center lies Solu Khumbu, the land of the Sherpas, with its well-known villages and monasteries. At the confluence of Bhote Kosi and Dudh Kosi lies Namche Bazar (bottom center). Many trekking tours to the Everest base camp lead upriver (to the right) from there by way of Tengboche and Pheriche.

The ridges of the huge mountains are what is left after erosion by frost and ice, which continually wear away at the range in competition with its continuous rise. The powerful effect of erosion can be seen on the mighty glaciers that flow to the north and south from either side of the main crest of the range. This picture was taken during a period of good weather in October, after the heavy monsoon precipitation. The heights are all covered with a fresh layer of snow. Now begins one of the loveliest seasons for trekking tours, with grandiose vistas of the majestic mountains guaranteed.

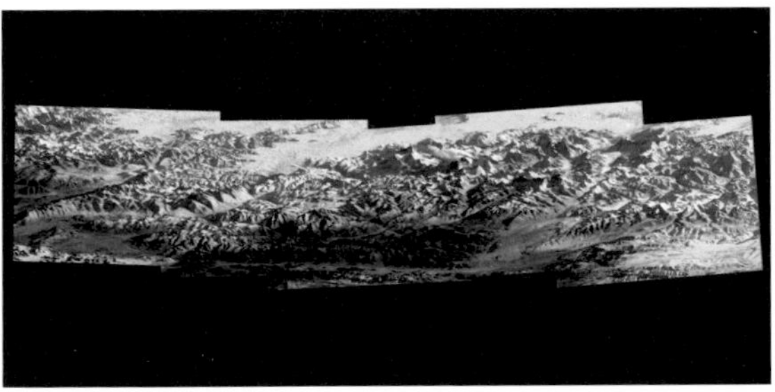

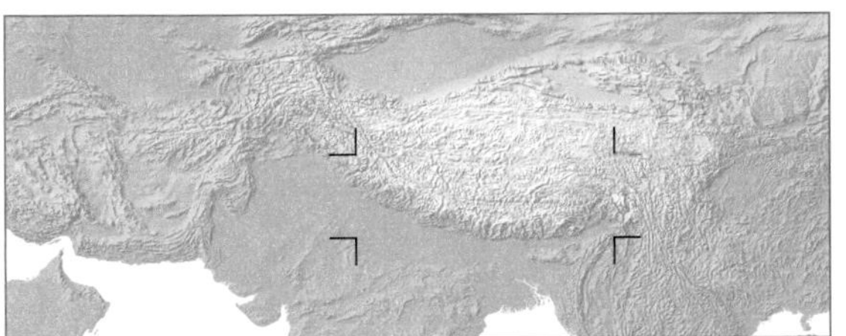

Satellite: International Space Station (ISS 08) / **Sensor:** photograph / **Recorded:** January 28, 2004, 10:01 UTC / **Visualization:** angled shot, true colors / **Image processing:** German Remote Sensing Data Center / **Data source:** Image Analysis Laboratory, NASA Johnson Space Center, Roll E – Frames 13302 to 13310

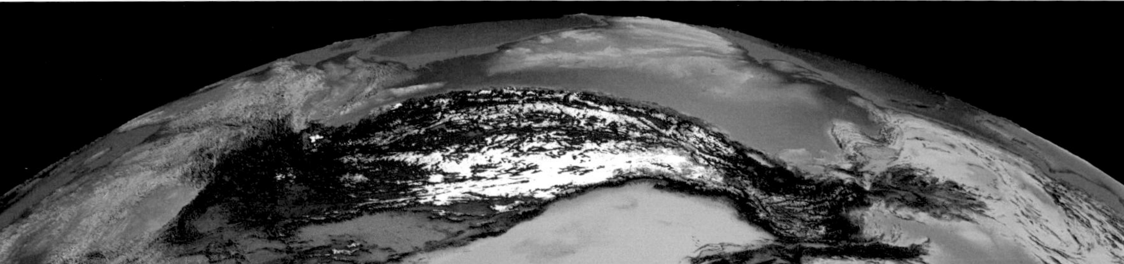

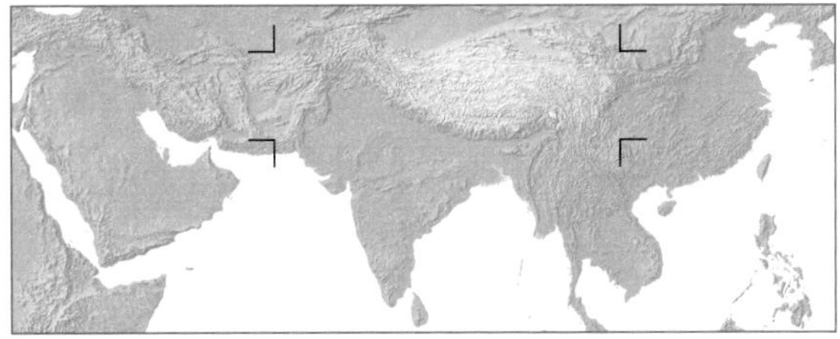

Elevation model: GTOPO-30, ETOPO-2 / **Resolutions:** 1,000 m, 2,000 m / **Height exaggeration:** 6 times / **Visualization:** perspective, pseudo-color / **Image processing:** German Remote Sensing Data Center / **Data source:** United States Geological Survey (USGS), National Geophysical Data Center (NGDC)

Panorama of the Himalayas from an astronaut's viewpoint

This picture montage produced on computer reveals a spectacular panoramic view from the north, over China, looking south onto the roof of the world. The picture mosaic extends some 185 miles east to west. The photographs were made from an altitude of roughly 225 miles by astronauts on the International Space Station.

Clearly visible are the regions Kangchenjunga (left), Khumbu Himal and Rolwaling Himal (roughly the center), and Jugal Himal and Langtang Himal (right). At the left edge one can see on to Sikkim and Bhutan. Sikkim, which belongs to India, is home to Kangchenjunga, the earth's third-highest mountain at 28,169 feet. Roughly in the center of the picture stands the mighty horseshoe of the Nuptse-Lhotse-Everest formation. Everest's dark, almost snow-free north wall and elongated northeast ridge are easy to recognize. From the peak of Lhotse a large cloud floats eastward toward Makalu, the Great Black One (27,765 feet), farther to the left. It has often been mistaken for Everest from the air. To the right of the Everest massif, farther to the west, stand the huge rock wall of the Gyachung Kang (26,089 feet) and the Cho-Oyu massif (26,906 feet). Far to the right at the edge of the picture is the completely snow-covered Shisha Pangma (26,289 feet), one of the easiest eight-thousanders to climb. In the foreground lie the Tibetan highlands, a barren, arid landscape whose brownish tones stand out clearly against the icy, snow-covered heights of the Himalayas. Farther to the south lie India and portions of Nepal hidden under a dense cloud cover.

The Himalayas, abode of snow

This panorama shows a view of the mightiest mountain range on earth, the Himalayas. It is a digital elevation model created from satellite-supported measurements. The coloring from green to yellow to brown corresponds to the altitude layers from the low-lying coastal regions up to the highest peaks. Heights above roughly 18,000 feet are color-coded white, symbolizing snow and glacial areas. The topography of the sea floor was coded in dark shades of blue.

The depiction offers a unique view from an altitude of roughly 4,350 miles. The viewer is looking across central Asia toward the southwest. Below lies the highest mountain range in the world, framed by India to the south and the desert Takla Makan in the north. In the Himalayas (Sanskrit for "abode of snow") and the Karakorum just to the west (to the right in the picture) stand all fourteen of the world's eight-thousanders.

Over millions of years the earth's crust has been folded up here with incredible energy. Mountain building began here some 60 million yeas ago, and continues to this day. Along the collision zone with India the Eurasian continental plate was splintered by the pressure. Huge stone slabs hundreds of miles wide were wedged atop one another as the Indian plate continued to advance. Together with the base rock, the former ocean bed with its sediments was lifted to the earth's surface. Today they form the crest well above 26,000 feet—visible, for example, in the famous Yellow Band on Everest's south flank, where fossils of sealife can be found. As the Indian mainland struck the Eurasian land mass, China was shoved to the east. The primeval sea Tethys, which originally lay off Eurasia, was enclosed and uplifted, and today forms the Tibetan highlands.

There in the north a dry continental climate predominates, but the climate of the regions south of the mountain range is characterized by the monsoon, which reaches its peak in July, transporting moist air from the southwest into the north of India as well. The monsoon is both a curse and a blessing for India. If it is too heavy it leads to flooding and devastation in the Indian provinces and on the southern slopes of the Himalayas; if it is too light the fields wither and the region suffers a shortage of water.

Pages 112 / 113

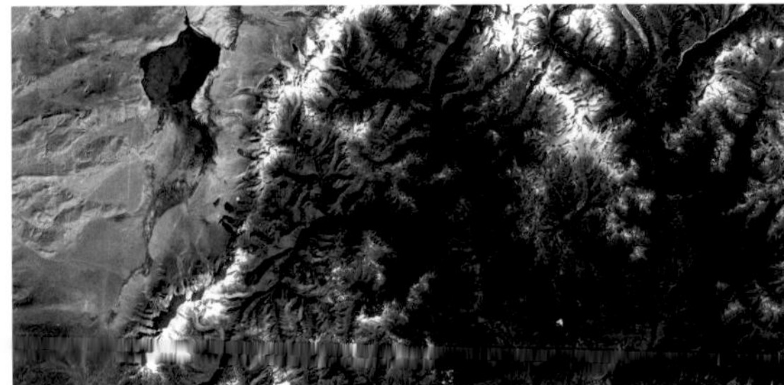

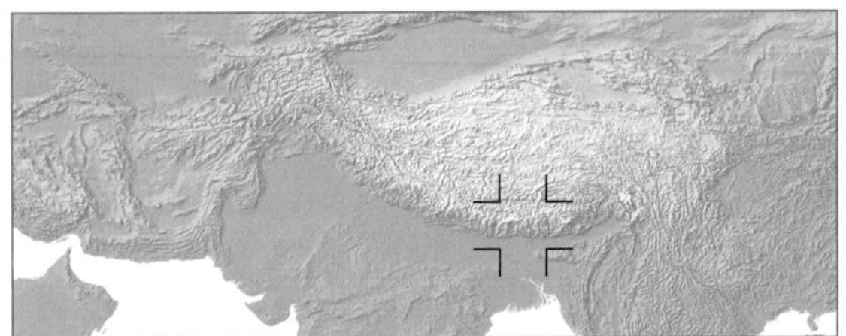

Satellite: Landsat-7 / **Sensor:** Enhanced Thematic Mapper (ETM+) / **Resolution:** 15 m / **Recorded:** November 20, 2001 / **Visualization:** true colors / **Spectral channels:** 0.63–0.69 µm, 0.53–0.61 µm, 0.45–0.52 µm / **Image processing:** German Remote Sensing Data Center / **Data source:** University of Maryland, Global Land Cover Facility (GLCF) – EarthSat

Pages 116 / 117

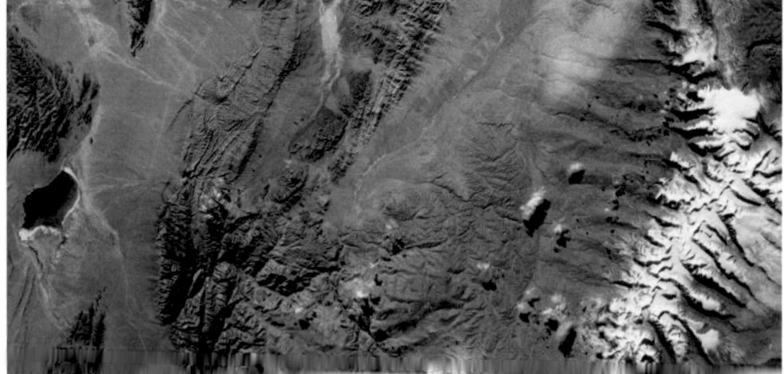

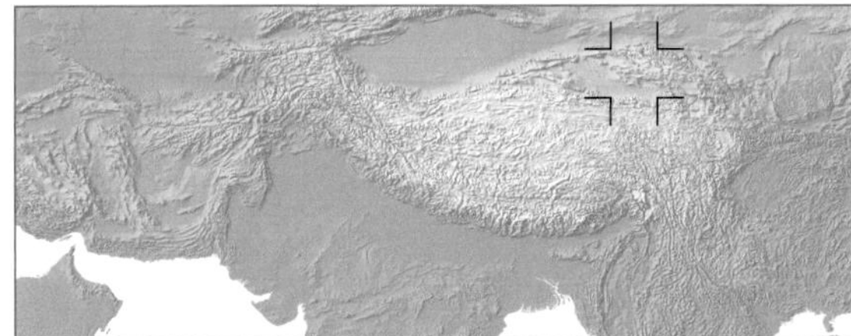

Satellite: Space shuttle (Spacelab Mission STS 9) / **Sensor:** metric camera / **Resolution:** 12 m / **Recorded:** December 2, 1983 / **Visualization:** true colors / **Image processing:** German Remote Sensing Data Center / **Data source:** German Aerospace Center

Pages 118 / 119

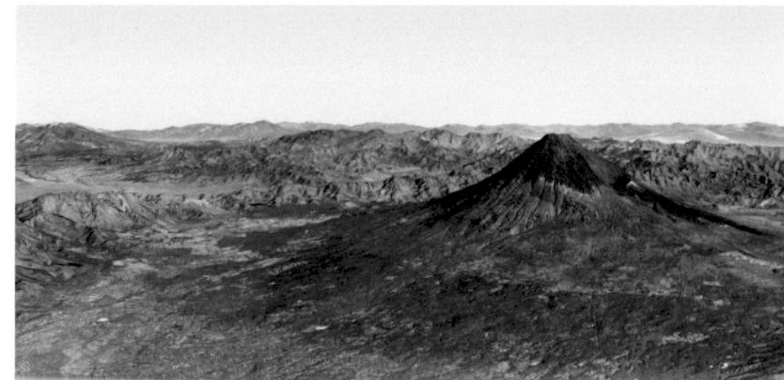

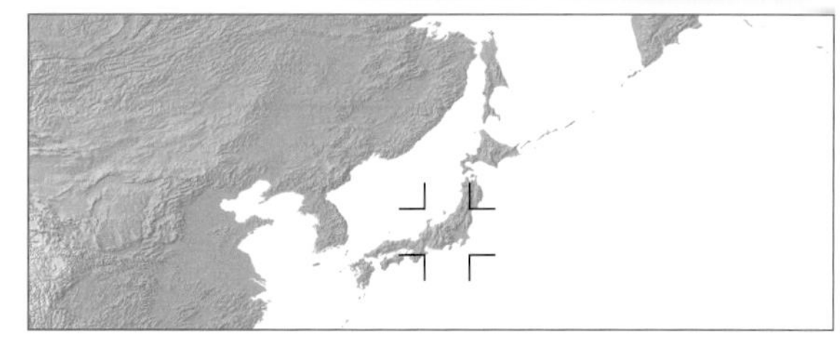

Satellite: Landsat-7 / **Sensor:** Enhanced Thematic Mapper (ETM+) / **Resolution:** 15 m / **Recorded:** October 12, 1999 / **Visualization:** perspective, true colors / **Spectral channels:** 0.63–0.69 µm, 0.53–0.61 µm, 0.45–0.52 µm / **Elevation model:** Shuttle Radar Topography Mission (SRTM), C-Band / **Resolution:** 90 m / **Height exaggeration:** 1.3 times / **Image processing:** German Remote Sensing Data Center / **Data source:** University of Maryland, Global Land Cover Facility (GLCF)–EarthSat, NASA

Chomo Lhari, "Mountain of the Goddess," Bhutan

This satellite image shows a 90- by 45-mile section of the Himalayas, whose main crest runs through the picture from the southwest (lower left) to the northeast. The snow-covered crest sharply separates the barren Tibetan highlands in the west from the southeastern Himalayas, which are cut through with deep valleys. It also marks the political boundary between Tibet and the Kingdom of Bhutan. At the lower left edge of the picture one can see Chomo Lhari (23,997 feet) towering up out of the snow-covered range. From its peak an S-shaped glacier winds toward the bottom of the picture. The peak was first climbed in 1937 by Spencer Chapman and the Sherpa Pasang Dawa Lama. Chapman was deeply impressed: "Chomo Lhari makes a magnificent impression of pure height and inaccessibility, like no other mountain I know. Many people consider it the most beautiful mountain in the entire Himalayan range." To Buddhists it is the "Mountain of the Goddess." Every year pilgrims gather there for a mountain procession. On the Tibetan plateau in the left of the picture (west) lies the lake Dochen Tso, which has formed in a basin with no drainage. A highway cuts through the picture from north to south. This is the traditional trading route from India to Lhasa.

Along the mountain range is a row of basins formed by the tongues of glaciers. These are filled with glacial meltwater, called glacial milk, colored a light blue by its considerable freight of sediment. Bhutanese culture developed in the valleys of the southeastern Himalayas. At the bottom center one can see terraces for rice growing as well as forest clearings.

Historic photograph of the Humboldt Range, China

People in the business of remote sensing view this picture as historic. In 1983 the Zeiss-developed metric camera was sent into space aboard a space shuttle. From there, as part of the European Spacelab Mission, it was to be determined whether high-resolution images of the earth from space would be useful for cartographic purposes. This picture taken by the metric camera shows part of Tibet extending northward from the Qaidam-Pendi highlands. The Qaidam-Pendi is a salt desert at an altitude of roughly 6,500 feet. Also included is the Danghe-Nanshan Range, the southeast extension of the Altun Shan, which marks the northern end of the Tibetan highlands. The Russian geographer Nikolai Przhevalski named this mountain massif the Humboldt Range in honor of the famous German polymath.

North is to the right in the picture, and that is where we see the snow-covered section of the Humboldt Range. To the south of it, on the left side of the picture, is the lustrous blue lake called Hurleg Hu. The prominent white wedge at the upper edge of the right half of the picture represents lower-lying regions with a thin cover of snow.

Fujisan, the highest mountain in Japan

For this perspective, picture data from the Landsat satellite were laid over a digital terrain model. The view is from the coast looking northward at Mount Fuji. The city in the left foreground is Fujinomiya. The familiar designation Fujiyama is based on a mistranslation; the Japanese commonly refer to the mountain as Fujisan. It is a roughly 100,000-year-old stratovolcano whose almost perfect conical shape makes it one of the most-photographed mountains in the world. At 12,388 feet it is the tallest mountain in Japan. The enormous difference in elevation between its base and its peak contributes to its imposing appearance, and makes it visible from Tokyo, some 50 miles away.

Fujisan is classed as an active volcano with only slight risk of eruption. It last erupted in 1707, at which time the secondary Hoei crater visible on the mountain's right side was formed. The mountain's fertile volcanic ash contributed greatly to the development of the capital region Kanto. In Shinto Fujisan is considered sacred. It is possible to climb it only in the snow-free period of July and August. The stations along the hiking trails and the peak station are open only at this time, when some 3,000 people crowd onto the mountain every day. It is thought that the first person to ascend to the peak was a seventh-century monk.

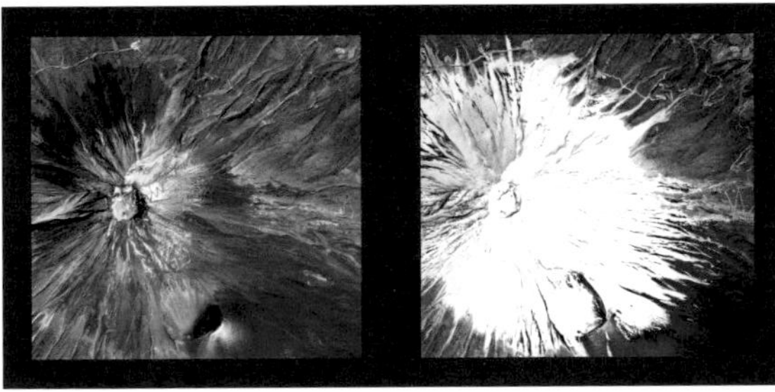

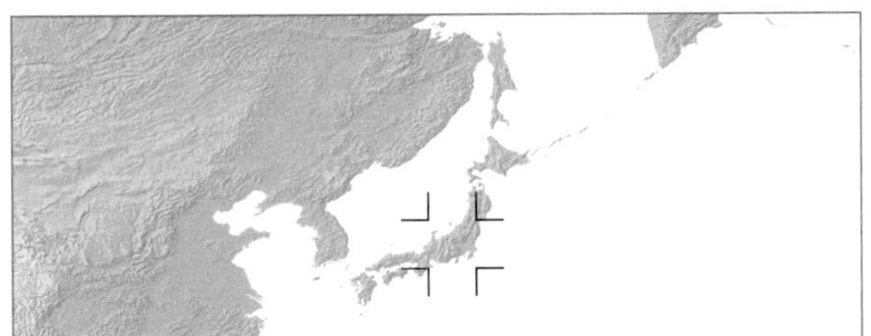

Satellite: Ikonos / **Resolution:** 1 m / **Recorded:** September 24, 2001, 13:38 UTC; April 4, 2002, 13:37 UTC / **Visualization:** true colors / **Spectral channels:** 0.63–0.69 µm, 0.52–0.60 µm, 0.45–0.52 µm / **Image processing:** German Remote Sensing Data Center / **Data source:** Japan Space Imaging Corporation

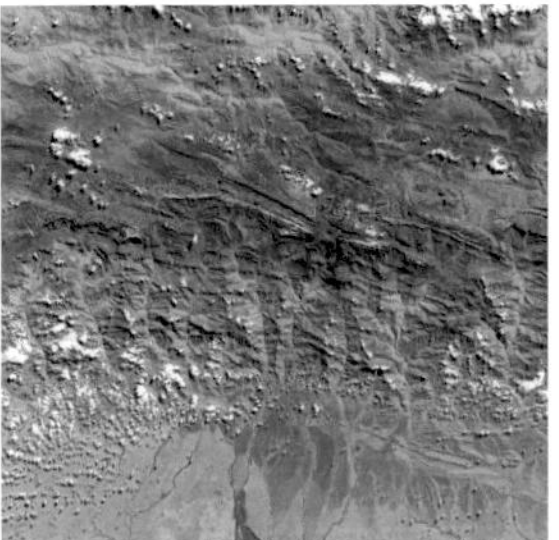

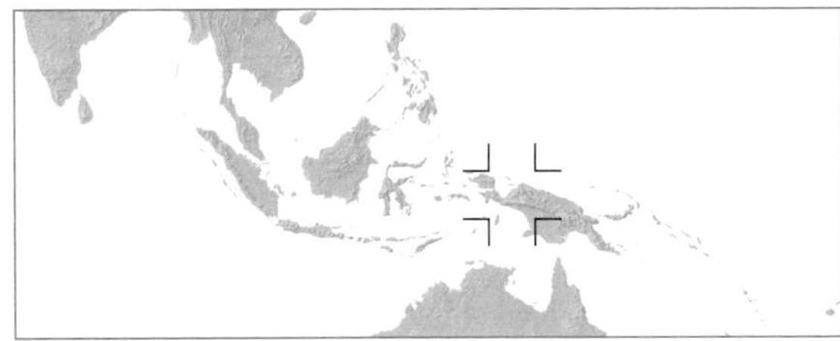

Satellite: Landsat-7 / **Sensor:** Enhanced Thematic Mapper (ETM+) / **Resolution:** 30 m / **Recorded:** May 29, 2003 / **Visualization:** pseudocolor / **Spectral channels:** 2.09–2.35 µm, 0.78–0.90 µm, 0.53–0.61 µm / **Image processing:** German Remote Sensing Data Center / **Data source:** University of Maryland, Global Land Cover Facility (GLCF)–EarthSat

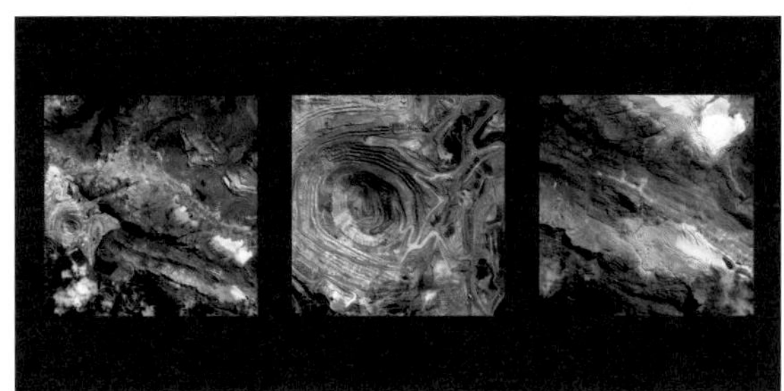

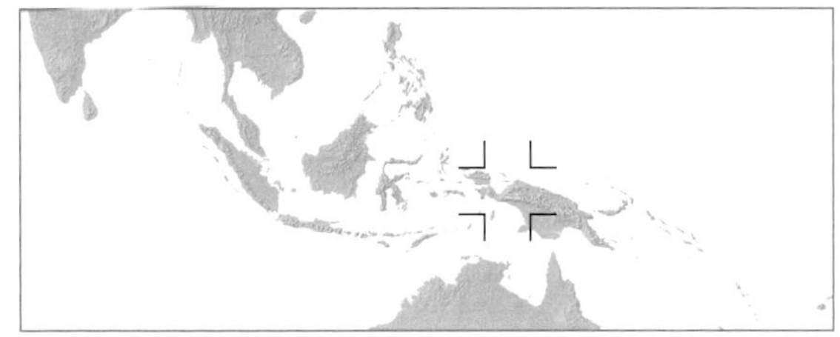

Satellite: Ikonos / **Resolution:** 1 m / **Recorded:** June 8, 2000, 00:59 UTC / **Visualization:** true colors / **Spectral channels:** 0.63–0.69 µm, 0.52–0.60 µm, 0.45–0.52 µm / **Image processing:** German Remote Sensing Data Center / **Data source:** Space Imaging Inc.

Detailed views of Mount Fuji, Japan

The high-resolution picture from the satellite Ikonos on the left shows the peak of Mount Fuji in September, still largely free of snow. Extending from the rim of the crater to the west one can see the collapsed Osawa crater, 1.2 miles long, 1,640 feet wide, and 490 feet deep. Through volcanic activity, alternate layers of hard basalt and soft volcanic ash were created. Rain and frost attack the ash layers first, which are washed away, leaving hollow spaces into which the heavy basalt above them collapses under its own weight. In heavy rains mud and rock slides can also occur here. To the southeast, below the peak, lies the secondary Hoei crater, formed by the eruption of 1707. Also clearly visible are the tree line and portions of the five trails leading up to the peak. These are ancient pilgrimage paths. Many of today's annual 100,000 peak climbers do not follow the whole route, however, but drive or take buses from the north to the top station, climbing the rest of the way on foot.

The right picture shows Mount Fuji in April, still with a heavy blanket of snow. Ambitious Himalayan climbers often train on Fuji in winter, when the trails are covered with snow and the rest stations are closed. The snow-covered upper slopes are also used for skiing in spring.

Puncak Jaya, the Carstensz Pyramid

The Sudirman Range on Irian Jaya, the easternmost province in Indonesia, lies in one of the most inaccessible regions in the world. This mountain chain near the equator is framed by extensive tropical rainforest (green in the picture), in many parts of which the aboriginal inhabitants are still untouched by civilization. Up until the 1970s cannibalism was still commonly practiced. Even today many of the men wear only a penis sheath made of gourd, the women, skimpy loincloths.

The highest elevation in the range is the 16,023-foot Puncak Jaya, or Carstensz Pyramid, named for the first Westerner to discover it. The mountain has become known to mountain climbers mainly because it is the tallest peak in Oceania, and is thus one of the Seven Summits, the highest mountain on each continent.

This pseudocolor picture allows one to distinguish between types of rock, among other things: the pinkish tones indicate sedimentary layers of limestone; violet indicates open-pit mining sites, where copper, gold, and silver ores of volcanic origin are excavated. South of the mine lies a highway built for the transport of raw materials to the coast.

Detailed view of Puncak Jaya

These three detailed pictures are based on satellite data with a very high resolution of 1 meter. The one on the left shows the area around the mountain on the island of New Guinea. In the lower right one can see the Carstensz fern field, and north of it the ice caps of the north wall. To the left are the terraces of the Grasberg open-pit mining complex, in which some 125,000 tons of gold, silver, and copper ore are mined each day. It is difficult to imagine that where a 1,300-foot-deep pit yawns today (center picture) the proud Erzberg and the Grasberg once towered into the sky. Both mountains have been completely removed. At some point the ore forced its way toward the surface in so-called intrusions.

The effects of today's climate change are impressively documented by the retreat of the ice on the Carstensz mountains in the right picture. Sixty years ago the Meren Glacier still thrust its ice masses into the valley, but today only moraines and lakes recall the former glacier. The visible gouges in the rock attest to the grinding effect of the ice and its eroded material. An indication of the speed with which the glaciers have melted is the snow cap of Ngga Pulu in the upper right. Since it was first climbed in 1936, the formerly 16,100-foot peak, once the tallest mountain in Australasia, has lost 164 feet of height, forcing it to surrender that title to the Carstensz Pyramid.

It is expected that because of the warming of the atmosphere the ice will completely disappear from these "Snow Mountains" in the next few years.

Pages 126 / 127

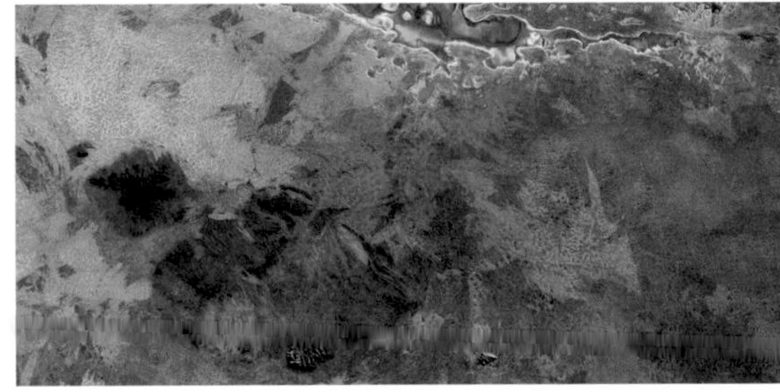

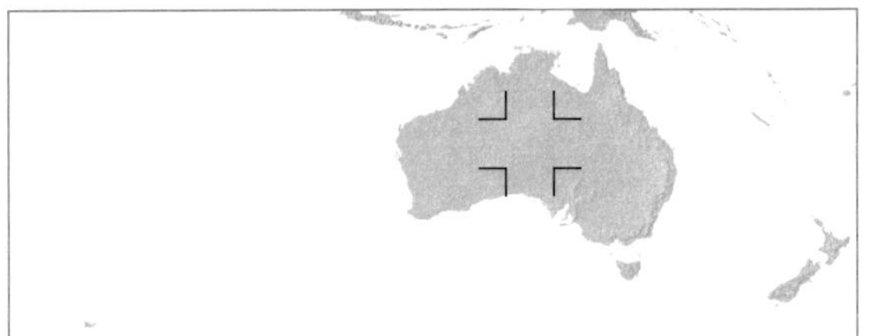

Satellite: Landsat-7 / **Sensor:** Enhanced Thematic Mapper (ETM+) / **Resolution:** 15 m / **Recorded:** July 12, 1999 / **Visualization:** pseudo-color / **Spectral channels:** 2.09–2.35 µm, 0.78–0.90 µm, 0.53–0.61 µm / **Image processing:** German Remote Sensing Data Center / **Data source:** University of Maryland, Global Land Cover Facility (GLCF)–EarthSat

Pages 128 / 129

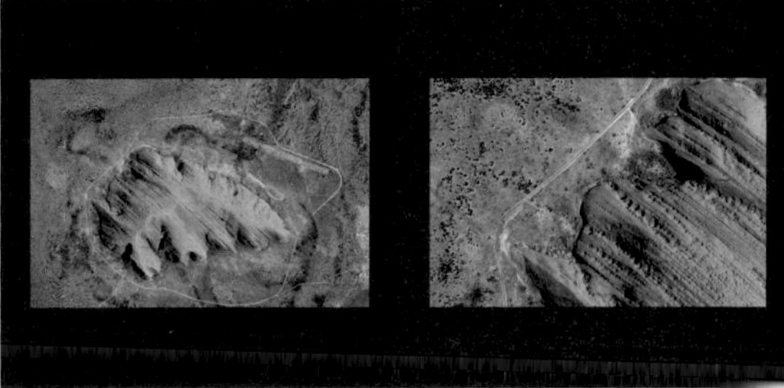

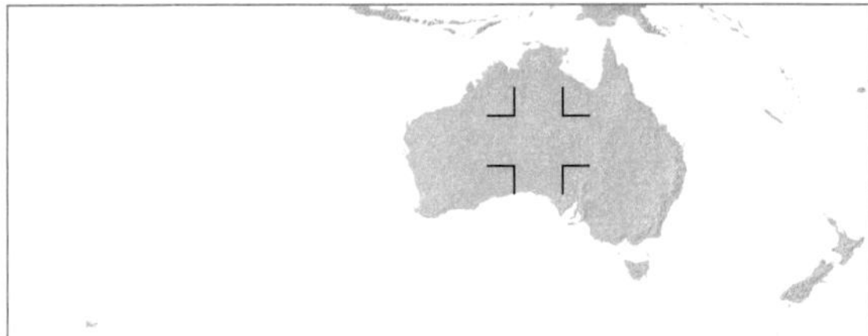

Satellite: Ikonos / **Resolution:** 1 m / **Recorded:** January 17, 2004, 01:45 UTC / **Visualization:** true colors / **Spectral channels:** 0.63–0.69 µm, 0.52–0.60 µm, 0.45–0.52 µm / **Image processing:** German Remote Sensing Data Center / **Data source:** Space Imaging Inc.

Pages 130 / 131

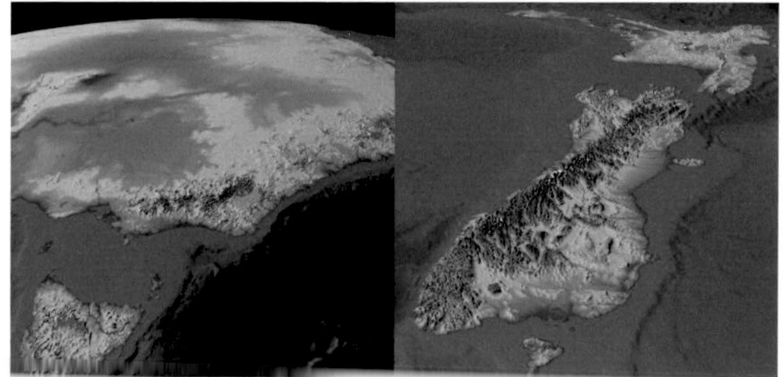

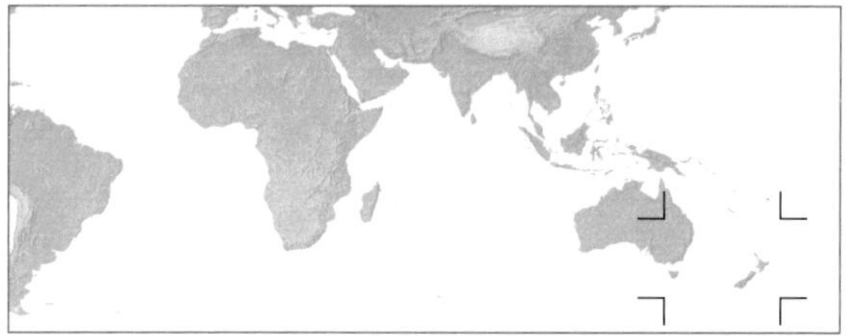

Elevation model: GTOPO-30, ETOPO-2 / **Resolutions:** 1,000 m, 2,000 m / **Height exaggeration:** 5 times / **Visualization:** perspective, pseudo-color / **Image processing:** German Remote Sensing Data Center / **Data source:** United States Geological Survey (USGS), National Geophysical Data Center (NGDC)

Uluru and Kata Tjuta, Australia's Red Heart

This satellite picture shows a fascinating landscape in the heart of Australia. At the bottom edge (marker) one can see Australia's symbol, Ayers Rock—or Uluru, as the Aborigines call it—as a brown spot. This second-largest monolith—the largest is western Australia's Mount Augustus at 3,281 feet tall—lifts up from the background.

Uluru is a remnant of an ancient limestone mountain range uplifted some 340 to 310 million years ago. Over the course of time tectonic forces have raised the sedimentary rock, while water, wind, frost, and sunlight wore it down to its present shape. This form has changed little since the Cretaceous period, roughly 100 million years ago. For that reason the monolith provides geologists with important information about the continent's origin. Eighteen miles west of it lies another of the region's attractions: Kata Tjuta, "Many Heads", or the Olgas. The structure of this mountain range with is 36 rock domes is clearly visible at the bottom left. The Olgas differ geologically from Uluru; they consist of the erosion debris of an adjacent mountain range to the west that appears as a dark-brown surface in the center of the picture. They are made up of fine material and larger stones that have been "baked" into conglomerate under high pressure. Lake Amadeus borders the northern edge of the satellite image; its blue color, the result of using shortwave infrared radiation, falsely suggests a large freshwater lake, whereas this is simply a salt flat on which a few sporadic patches of water form only after heavy rain.

Shady place: detailed view of Uluru

This highly detailed true-color satellite image with a 1-meter resolution shows the monolith Uluru in summer. Thousands of tourist buses circle the ring road around the mountain every year. On the right edge of the left picture one can see a former airfield (light stripes running from east to west), where smaller tourist planes could land up until the 1980s. Although Uluru lies in the middle of desert, its surroundings appear relatively green. But precipitation in December (high summer in Australia) averages only 18 millimeters, in January 38 millimeters. Most of the rainwater runs down the rock, trickles into the ground, and thus adds to the groundwater in the immediate vicinity, so that a considerably larger number of plants can survive here than only a short distance away. Water can be found year-round in some of the shaded depressions and caves on the rock's flanks.

Uluru means "shady place," and to the Aboriginals it is sacred. They only walk on it on specific ceremonial occasions. At those times certain spots are reserved for men, others for women. Tourists need a special permit to climb the 2,848-foot mountain—from its foot to the top is a rise of 1,142 feet—along a fixed trail. In the picture at the right it is easy to see the starting point, a sandy parking lot. In 1985 the Uluru and Kata Tjuta regions were turned over to the Aborigine Pitjantjara tribe, and in 1987 UNESCO included them on its list of World Cultural and Natural Heritage Sites. This is a clear indication of a change in the way the Australian populations relate to each other. More and more one sees visitors wearing T-shirts that read: "I didn't climb Uluru," an expression of respect for the Aborigines.

Dissimilar neighbors—Australia and New Zealand

Only some 20 million people live in Australia, an area comparable in size to the United States without Alaska and Hawaii. The majority of Australians live along the coasts; only a minority live in the Outback, the arid heart of the continent consisting of up to 80 percent desert or semi-desert. This picture shows the topography of the continent and the ocean floor in a perspective view from the southeast. At the bottom left is Tasmania. Different elevations were assigned different colors, from green (lowlands) to brown (mountains). In the center of the picture is Australia's mightiest chain of mountains, the Great Dividing Range, which extends northward for more than 1,800 miles from Queensland in the southeast. To the west of it, water flows into the Murray-Darling Basin, the country's most productive agricultural region.

Topography is also silent testimony to the origin of New Zealand (Aotearoa), only roughly 3.5 percent of the size of Australia (right picture). Its three large islands (North Island, South Island, and Steward Island) lie on a tectonic boundary, where the Indo-Australian Plate is sliding beneath the Pacific Plate. The massive forces of this collision have not only thrown up the still-growing "southern Alps" of the west coast, but the dipping plate also provides the material for the active volcanism of the North Island. At the same time, the mountains of New Zealand make up the only barrier for the water-laden weather systems of the southern Pacific. For that reason the precipitation quantities in the west of the South Island are among the highest in the world. Rain and snow feed the rivers and glaciers that have also carved its mighty fjords.

Pages 132 / 133

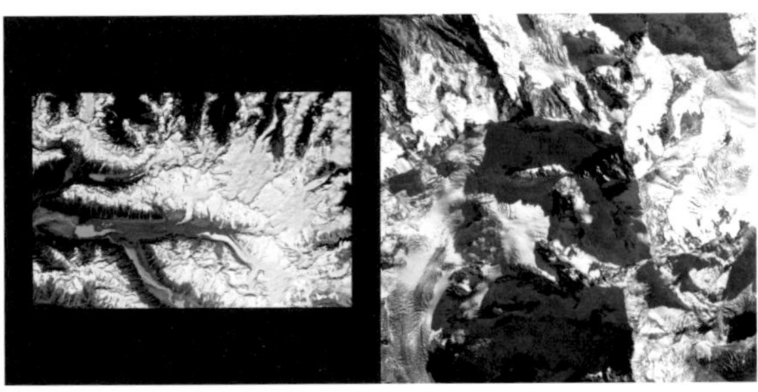

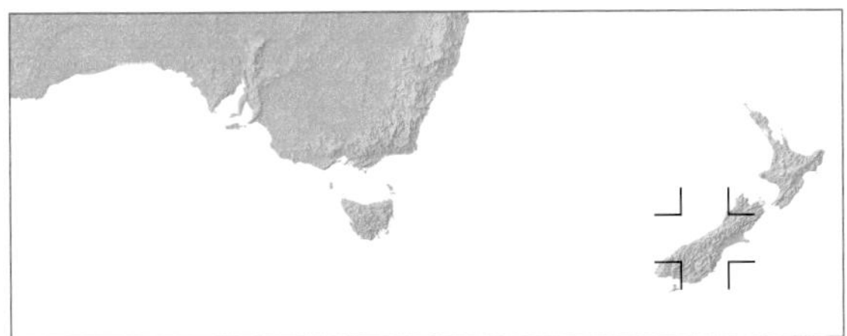

Satellite: International Space Station (ISS 06) / **Sensor:** photograph / **Recorded:** December 8, 2002, 21:14 UTC / **Image processing:** German Remote Sensing Data Center / **Data source:** Image Analysis Laboratory, NASA Johnson Space Center, Roll E – Frame 6599

Satellite: Ikonos / **Resolution:** 1 m / **Recorded:** April 17, 2004, 22:52 UTC / **Visualization:** true colors / **Spectral channels:** 0.63–0.69 µm, 0.52–0.60 µm, 0.45–0.52 µm / **Image processing:** German Remote Sensing Data Center / **Data source:** Space Imaging Inc.

Pages 134 / 135

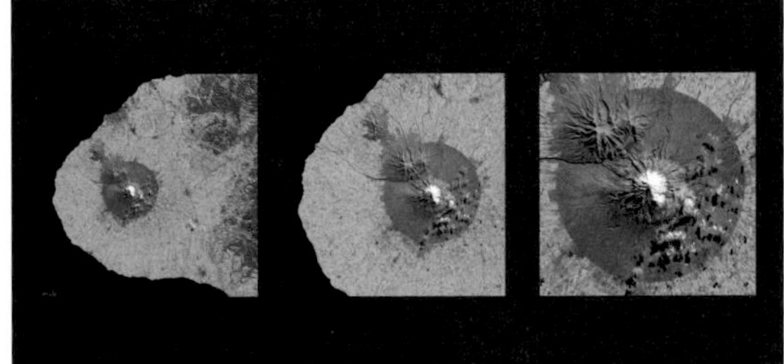

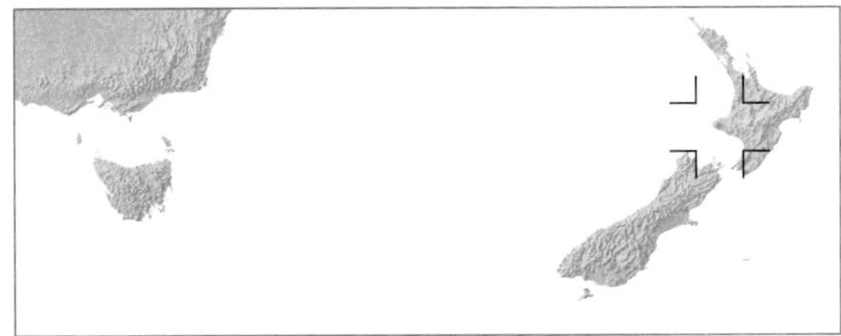

Satellite: Landsat-7 / **Sensor:** Enhanced Thematic Mapper (ETM+) / **Resolution:** 15 m / **Recorded:** October 27, 2000 / **Visualization:** pseudocolor / **Spectral channels:** 2.09–2.35 µm, 0.78–0.90 µm, 0.53–0.61 µm / **Image processing:** German Remote Sensing Data Center / **Data source:** University of Maryland, Global Land Cover Facility (GLCF)–EarthSat

Pages 136 / 137

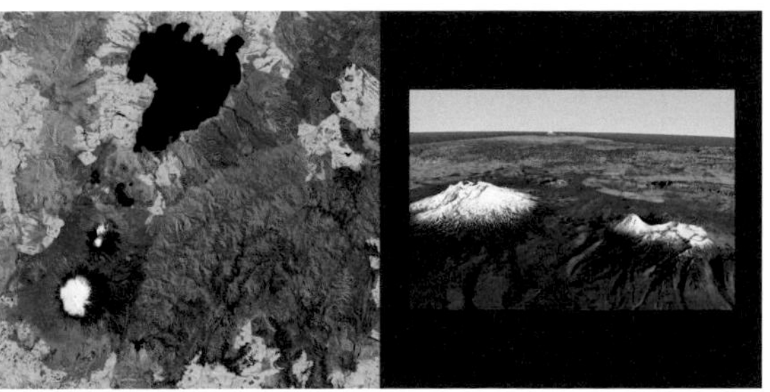

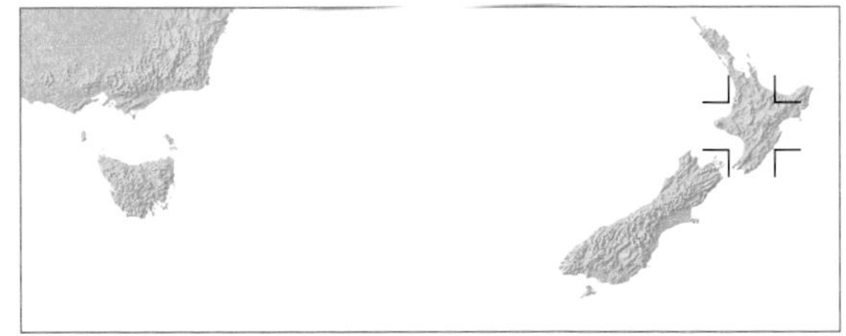

Satellite: Landsat-7 / **Sensor:** Enhanced Thematic Mapper (ETM+) / **Resolution:** 30 m / **Recorded:** October 23, 2002 / **Visualization:** pseudocolor / **Image processing:** German Remote Sensing Data Center / **Data source:** University of Maryland, GLCF–EarthSat

Satellite: Landsat-7 / **Sensor:** Enhanced Thematic Mapper (ETM+) / **Resolution:** 30 m / **Recorded:** October 23, 2002 / **Visualization:** perspective, pseudocolor / **Elevation model:** Shuttle Radar Topography Mission (SRTM), C-Band / **Resolution:** 90 m / **Height exaggeration:** 1.5 times / **Image processing:** German Remote Sensing Data Center / **Data source:** University of Maryland, GLCF–EarthSat, NASA

Mount Cook, "the Cloud Piercer"

Mount Cook—or Aoraki, which translates as "Cloud Piercer"—is the tallest mountain in New Zealand at 12,316 feet. Seen from space, it is barely noticeable against the background of the "southern Alps." This region has a number of steep peaks above 10,000 feet, and is laced with numerous glaciers. Even glacial crevasses are clearly visible in this very high-resolution satellite picture. In the overview photograph taken from the International Space Station (left page) one can see the 17-mile-long Tasman Glacier (bottom of the picture) and the 7-mile-long Hooker Glacier (top). The peak of Mount Cook lies to the right (north) of Lake Hooker. In the satellite picture on the right page the peak is visible in the center. Below it and slightly to the right, linked to the peak by the long south ridge, lies the Middle Peak, only 121 feet lower. Southwest of the Middle Peak one can see the 11,788-foot Lower Peak. To the left at the bottom edge lies Hooker Glacier with its many crevasses. Mount Cook's long south ridge is the symbol of Mount Cook National Park.

Sir Edmund Hillary—who later made history as the first person to climb Mount Everest—and his friend Harry Ayres were the first to ascend the mountain by this route, and thereby reach all three peaks in 1948, more than fifty years after the first ascent in 1894. Mount Cook lies 25 miles in from New Zealand's west coast. There are no comparable elevations for thousands of miles in any direction. Strong winds and heavy precipitation in this exposed location make climbing the higher peaks of the New Zealand Alps highly challenging.

Mount Egmont

The nearly round volcanic cone of Mount Egmont on New Zealand's North Island is especially impressive. The almost perfect shape of this volcano was attained only roughly 10,000 years ago, when it also first reached its height of 8,261 feet. Lava streams from earlier eruptions cover most of the surrounding area. They extend in the direction of the ocean for more than 15 miles and form a circular, clearly visible plateau. The Maori call the mountain Taranaki, which means "without vegetation." Only a few thousand years ago the lower regions were completely covered with dense forests. Today only the jungles of Egmont National Park with their abundant flora and fauna remain. The surrounding area is dominated by pastureland.

On the peak there are a few large snowfields but no glaciers. In summer the peak is often completely ice-free, while in winter the small Manganui ski area is used for winter sports. On the left picture in the zoom sequence, the city of New Plymouth lies directly north of Taranaki on the coast. Towns stand out in light pinkish tones from the rich green surroundings. In truth, this green derives from the strong near-infrared reflection of healthy vegetation. Directly west of the volcano lies the town of Stratford, which documents the European history of the settlement of this area. More details are visible in the pictures at the center and right, especially the intricate network of river courses. These flow outward from Taranaki like rays until they finally flow into the Tasman Sea.

Ruapehu, a picture-perfect volcano

New Zealand's North Island exhibits a variety of volcanic and geothermal activity. The volcanic Taupo region is seen here in a pseudocolor satellite-image overview (left) and in a computer-generated perspective image (right).

In the north of the picture one can see Lake Taupo, New Zealand's largest lake. It lies in a giant caldera created in 186 A.D. in one of the most violent volcanic eruptions in history. In the center of the picture lie the three active volcanoes of Tongariro National Park. In the north (on the right in the perspective view) lies the eponymous Mount Tongariro (6,457 feet). Next to it is the youngest and almost symmetrical Mount Ngauruhoe (7,516 feet), a classic stratovolcano made famous as the Mountain of Fate in the *Lord of the Rings* films.

Ruapehu's three main peaks, Tahurangi (9,175 feet), Te Heuheu (9,038 feet), and Paretetaitonga (9,026 feet) are clearly visible in the perspective view. In the background one can see Mount Taranaki 80 miles to the west on the coast. It is visible from Tongariro only on extremely clear days. Ruapehu last erupted in 1996. Today the main danger is its continually rising crater lake. Tongariro is one of the oldest national parks in the world. In 1887 the visionary Chief Horonuku Te Heuheu Tukino recognized that he could protect the area—sacred to the Maori—from the pressure of settlement by presenting the core of the present-day national park to the queen of England as a gift. The boundaries of the park are clearly visible in the pseudocolor depiction, especially in the west. The intense green outside the park indicates the denser growth of irrigated farmland.

[ANTARCTICA] Pages 140 / 141

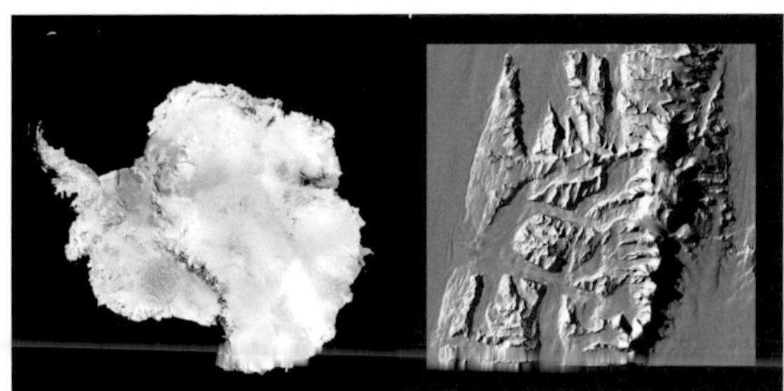

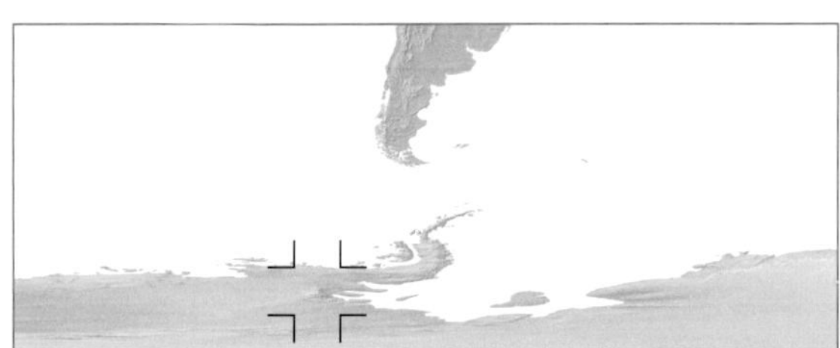

Satellite: NOAA / **Sensor:** AVHRR / **Resolution:** 1,000 m / **Recorded:** 1980 to 1994 / **Visualization:** true colors / **Spectral channels:** 0.58–0.68 µm, 0.725–1.0 µm, 0.58–1.0 µm / **Image processing:** German Remote Sensing Data Center / **Data source:** United States Geological Survey (USGS)

Satellite: Terra / **Sensor:** Advanced Spaceborne Thermal Emission and Reflection Radiometer (ASTER) / **Resolution:** 15 m / **Recorded:** November 15, 2002, 12:43 UTC / **Visualization:** pseudocolor / **Spectral channels:** 0.76–0.86 µm, 0.63–0.69 µm, 0.52–0.60 µm / **Image processing:** German Remote Sensing Data Center / **Data source:** United States Geological Survey (USGS)

Left: Antarctica, the icy continent

In 1820 Russian and English explorers came upon land in the Antarctic region. With this discovery speculations about a southern land mass were confirmed. But it would be another twenty years before it could be proved that the land discovered was in fact a new continent.

This cloud-free mosaic of the entire continent was produced from more than sixty satellite images made by an American weather satellite (NOAA-AVHRR). Data from the years 1980 to 1994 were combined and conformed in color. The Antarctic Peninsula, site of numerous research stations and a receiving station operated by the German Aerospace Center, extends along the left edge of the picture. In the bottom center is the curve of the Queen Maud Mountains which then give way to Victoria Land. To the south of this mountain range lies the gigantic Ross Ice Shelf, which shows up in this picture mainly in shades of blue.

Right: The Ellsworth range

The picture at right shows Antarctica's Ellsworth Mountains. After a successful Arctic expedition, Lincoln Ellsworth turned to Antarctica. In 1935 he made the first flight over the continent, and afterward named the area he had flown over after his father, James W. Ellsworth. The Ellsworth range lies in the south of the Antarctic Peninsula at the end of the Ronne Ice Shelf. The extensive icy wilderness lifts up abruptly out of the surrounding ice fields. These are the continent's highest mountains. The region was pictured by the Advanced Spaceborne Thermal Emission and Reflection Radiometer (ASTER) aboard the satellite Terra. The image has been rotated 90 degrees; south is to the left, north to the right.

Pages 144 / 145

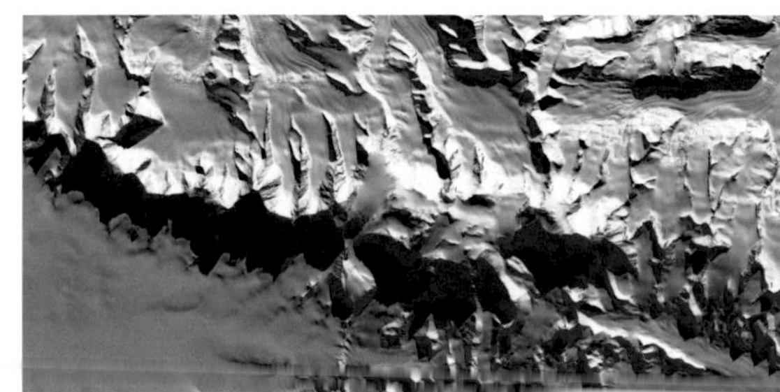

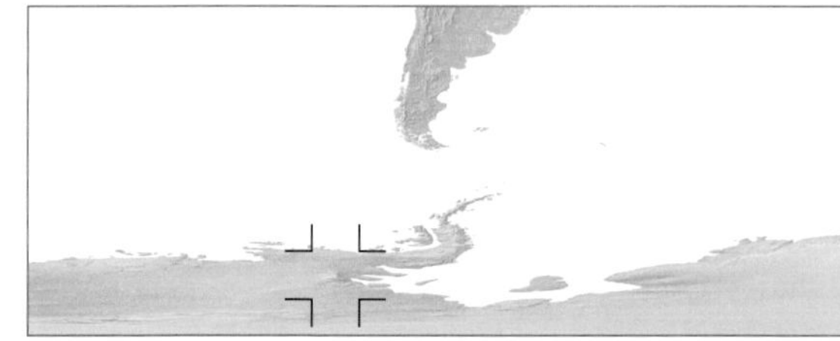

Satellite: Terra / **Sensor:** Advanced Spaceborne Thermal Emission and Reflection Radiometer (ASTER) / **Resolution:** 15 m / **Recorded:** November 15, 2002, 12:43 UTC / **Visualization:** pseudocolor / **Spectral channels:** 0.76–0.86 µm, 0.63–0.69 µm, 0.52–0.60 µm / **Image processing:** German Remote Sensing Data Center / **Data source:** United States Geological Survey (USGS)

Vinson Massif, Antarctica's highest mountain

The Vinson Massif is part of the Sentinel Range of the Ellsworth Mountains, which includes the continent's highest peaks. Very narrow ridges and rock walls rising as much as 6,500 feet, combined with Antarctica's stormy weather conditions, make this region one of the most inhospitable on earth. The peak of the Vinson Massif, at 16,066 feet, is the highest point in Antarctica.

The massif was first climbed in 1966, by an American expedition sponsored by the National Geographic Society, the National Science Foundation, and the American Alpine Club. Today it is one of the favored goals of ambitious mountain climbers. There is little traffic here compared to the rest of the Seven Summits, doubtless because of permanent low temperatures of -18°F and the cost of an expedition, which can reach $50,000. The standard climbing route begins on the Branscomb Glacier, pictured here near the center in the lower half of the picture. The peak of the mountain lies precisely in the center of the picture (marker), somewhat to the left of the large glacier that begins in the center at the top edge.

[NORTH AMERICA] Page 147

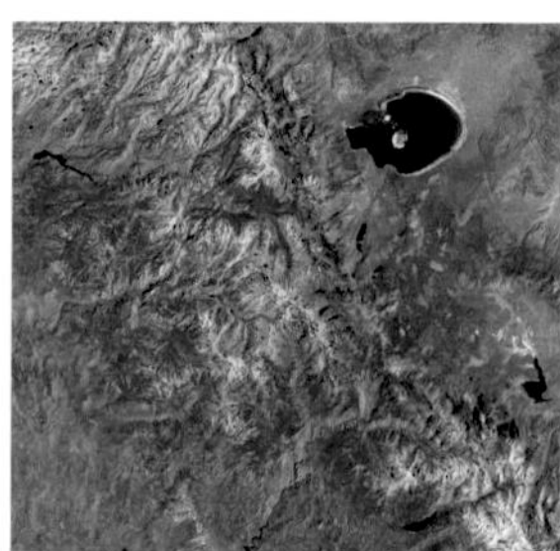

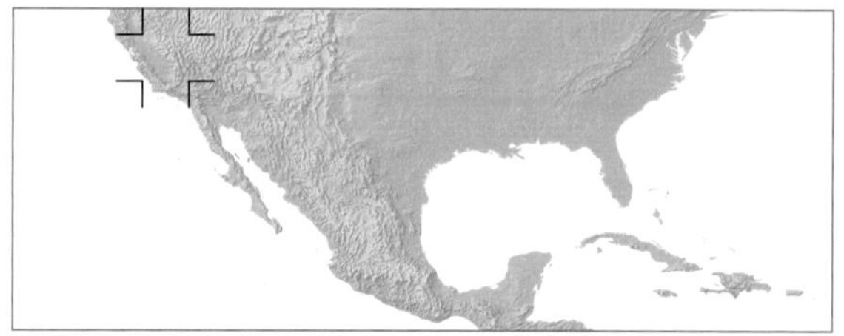

Satellite: Landsat-7 / **Sensor:** Enhanced Thematic Mapper (ETM+) / **Resolution:** 30 m / **Recorded:** July 27, 2000 / **Visualization:** pseudocolor / **Spectral channels:** 2.09–2.35 µm, 0.78–0.90 µm, 0.53–0.61 µm / **Image processing:** German Remote Sensing Data Center / **Data source:** University of Maryland, Global Land Cover Facility (GLCF)–EarthSat

Yosemite National Park and Mono Lake

Yosemite National Park lies roughly 150 miles east of San Francisco, in the middle of California's Sierra Nevada. The area was placed under protection in 1890, and has since drawn climbers and nature lovers from all over the world. This picture clearly shows the effect of the Sierra Nevada as a climate barrier. To the west of it lie lush green valleys filled with fields of vegetables. Moist air masses approaching from the Pacific strike the mountain range and are forced upward. This cools the air, and most of their moisture is precipitated in the form of rain or snow. To the east it is comparatively dry, as is clear from the brownish and pink tones in the picture. The region's landscape was shaped by glaciation during the last ice age. One indication of this is the number of small lakes, which appear as dark spots in the picture. Also visible in the center of the picture is the tallest mountain in the park, Mount Lyell (13,114 feet). On its north flank lies Lyell Glacier, the largest glacier in the Sierra Nevada. Northeast of the mountain range Mono Lake appears like a giant eye in a depression with no drainage. At an age of more than 700,000 years, it is one of the oldest existing lakes in North America. In the last few centuries the lake has clearly shrunk in size, however, reflecting both natural fluctuation and the constantly increasing demand for water over the past several decades. Clearly visible in the picture are the lime-rich deposits and salt crusts in the northeast shore area and dry lake bed in pinkish tones.

Pages 148 / 149

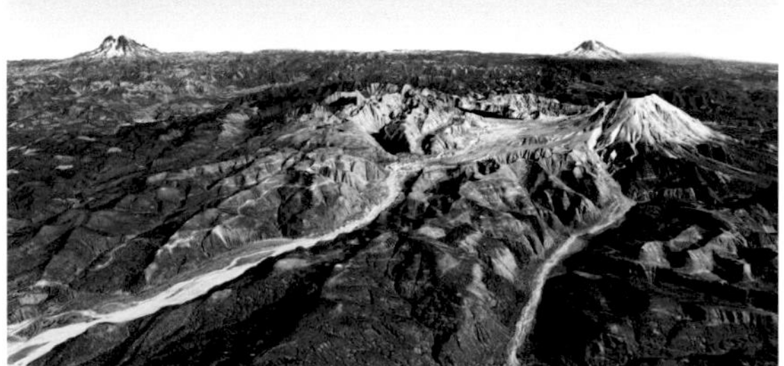

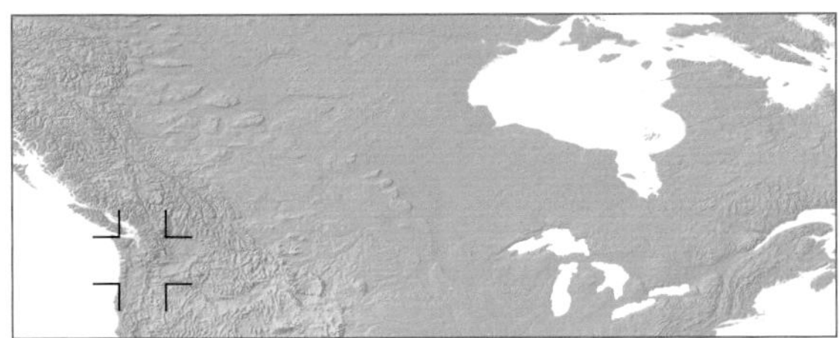

Satellite: Landsat-7 / **Sensor:** Enhanced Thematic Mapper (ETM+) / **Resolution:** 30 m / **Recorded:** September 25, 2000 / **Visualization:** perspective, true colors / **Spectral channels:** 0.63–0.69 µm, 0.53–0.61 µm, 0.45–0.52 µm / **Elevation model:** USGS National Elevation Dataset (NED) / **Resolution:** 10 m / **Height exaggeration:** 1.5 times / **Image processing:** German Remote Sensing Data Center / **Data source:** University of Maryland, Global Land Cover Facility (GLCF)–EarthSat; United States Geological Survey (USGS)

Pages 150 / 151

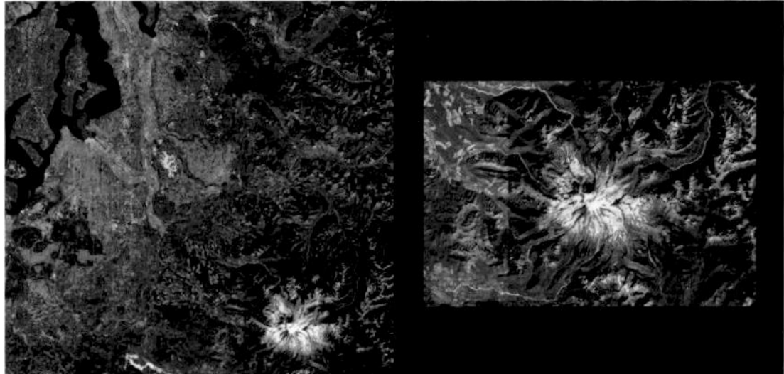

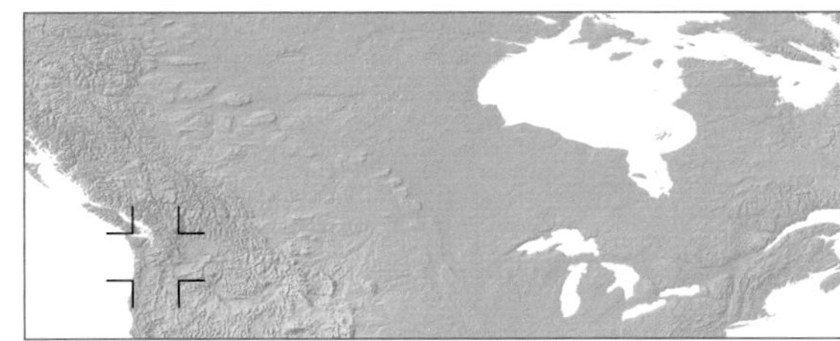

Satellite: Landsat-7 / **Sensor:** Enhanced Thematic Mpper (ETM+) / **Resolution:** 15 m / **Recorded:** September 25, 2000 / **Visualization:** true colors / **Spectral channels:** 0.63–0.69 µm, 0.53–0.61 µm, 0.45–0.52 µm / **Image processing:** German Remote Sensing Data Center / **Data source:** University of Maryland, Global Land Cover Facility (GLCF)–EarthSat

Pages 152 / 153

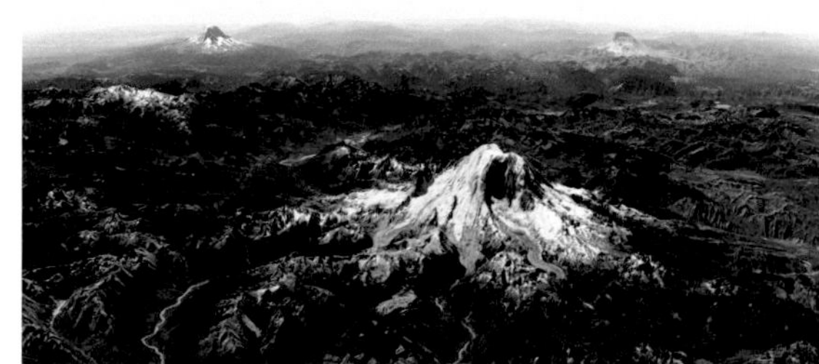

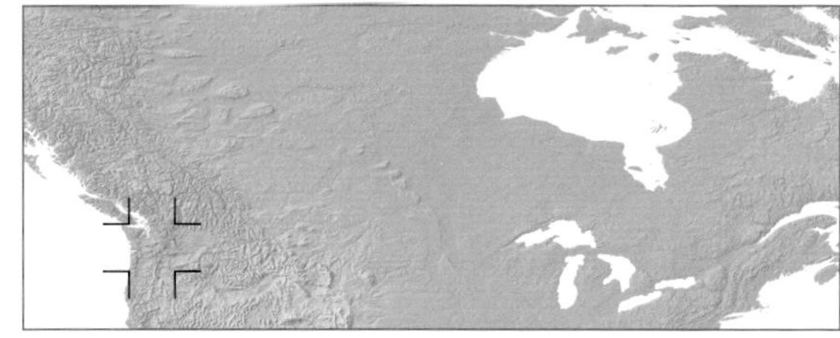

Satellite: Landsat-7 / **Sensor:** Enhanced Thematic Mapper (ETM+) / **Resolution:** 30 m / **Recorded:** September 25, 2000 / **Visualization:** perspective, true colors / **Spectral channels:** 0.63–0.69 µm, 0.53–0.61 µm, 0.45–0.52 µm / **Elevation model:** USGS National Elevation Dataset (NED) / **Resolution:** 10 m / **Height exaggeration:** 1.5 times / **Image processing:** German Remote Sensing Data Center / **Data source:** University of Maryland, Global Land Cover Facility (GLCF)–EarthSat; United States Geological Survey (USGS)

Explosive Mount St. Helens

Mount St. Helens is in the state of Washington in the northwestern United States. It is one of a chain of volcanoes in the Cascade Range, which extends parallel to the Pacific coast from California to northern Washington. The mountain became world famous in 1980, when on May 18, after lying dormant for more than a hundred years, it erupted with a great explosion. In this violent eruption so much rock was blown away from the peak that the mountain lost some 3,280 feet in height; today it rises only 8,363 feet. The explosion was followed by the largest landslide ever documented. The heat and shock waves from the explosion melted a number of glaciers blanketing the volcano, and the surrounding forests were destroyed. A layer of ash up to four inches thick fell on the neighboring cities, and because of the prevailing west wind ash was carried as far east as the Midwest. In that same year the 132-square-mile Mount St. Helens National Volcanic Monument was established—a protected area in which visitors can follow nature's gradual healing process.

The panorama of the area, produced by laying a true-color satellite picture over a digital elevation model, presents a view looking from west to east. The two main valleys of the North Fork Toutle River (left), down which masses of stone and mud rushed after the explosion, stand out in very light colors. The size of the mountain's base and the surviving ridge on the right edge of the picture suggest how high the mountain was before the eruption. In the background are two more of the Cascades' volcanic cones, Mount Adams (right) and Mount Rainier (left).

Mount Rainier National Park

Mount Rainier, at 14,411 feet the highest mountain in the Cascade Range, is in the west center of the state of Washington, roughly a two-hour drive south of Seattle. In the satellite picture at the left, presented in true colors, the mountain appears in the southeast corner (marker). The currently inactive volcano last erupted in 1894. Twenty-four years before, in 1870, it was climbed for the first time by H. Stevens and P. B. van Trump. It is surrounded by extensive forests and is more heavily glaciated than any other mountain in the United States outside of Alaska. The glaciation of the peak can be seen in the detail picture on the right.

The vast Snoqualmie National Forest surrounds the mountain, a protected area with numerous smaller peaks, dense coniferous forest, lakes, and swift mountain streams. This adjacent forest land lies in the east (right) half of the picture, recognizable from its shades of dark green. The central part of the national forest is largely protected from logging and other spoliation as a national park. In the bottom right of the left picture and in the detailed view the boundary between the national park and its surroundings appears as a razor-sharp north-south line on the west side of the mountain.

Northwest of Mount Rainier lies the port of Tacoma, at the south end of Puget Sound. It is identifiable from the man-made canals extending into the city area and the clearly sullied water in the port area. Greenish "veils" attest to high quantities of sediments and effluents in the Sound.

Panorama of Mount Rainier

For this image a digital terrain model was overlaid with a true-color satellite picture to produce a panorama of the region. It shows Mount Rainier, in the northwestern United States, looking from north to south. The light brown spots on the slopes of the mountain are the tongue basins of its large glaciers. From left to right (east to west) these are the terminal points of the Emmons, Winthrop, and Carbon Glaciers. Five of the more than ten glaciers on Mount Rainier originate from the peak, while a number of smaller ones appear as cirque glaciers on the slopes of the volcano. Emmons Glacier, which flows down from the peak for more than 6 miles, is the largest U.S. glacier outside Alaska.

The two ice-filled craters on the peak of Mount Rainier are connected by numerous caves and passages within the mountain. This phenomenon occurs elsewhere only on Mount Baker, another of the Cascade volcanoes, 93 miles to the north, and Mount Wrangell in Alaska. The glaciers feed a number of smaller rivers. The West Fork White River is visible in the center of the picture, the Carbon River to the right (west), and the White River on the left (east).

In spite of the immense masses of ice covering Mount Rainier, the volcano has much to offer not only to mountain climbers but also to hikers. Its slopes below the glaciers are covered with dense coniferous forests and alpine meadows, and every year the splendor of these meadows with their vast array of wildflowers draws tourists and nature lovers to the region.

Pages 154 / 155

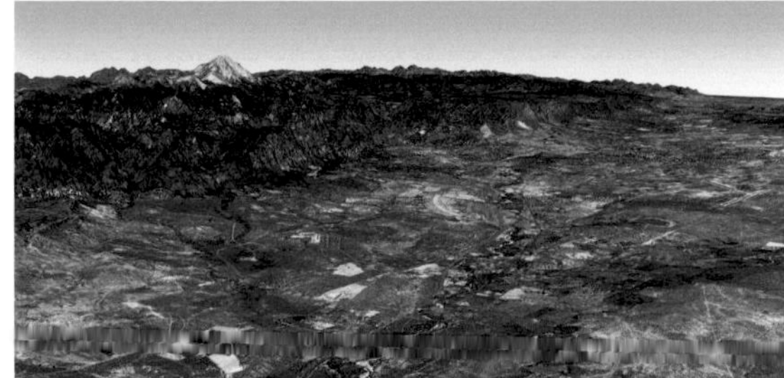

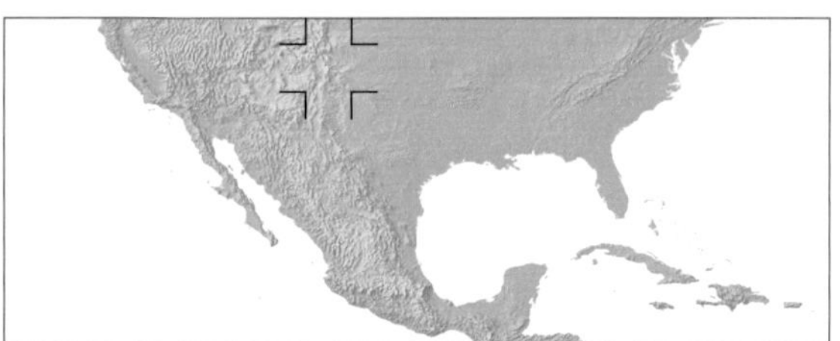

Satellite: Landsat-7 / **Sensor:** Enhanced Thematic Mapper (ETM+) / **Resolution:** 15 m / **Recorded:** September 14, 2000 / **Visualization:** perspective, true colors / **Spectral channels:** 0.63–0.69 µm, 0.53–0.61 µm, 0.45–0.52 µm / **Elevation model:** USGS National Elevation Dataset (NED) / **Resolution:** 10 m / **Height exaggeration:** 1.7 times / **Image processing:** German Remote Sensing Data Center / **Data source:** University of Maryland, Global Land Cover Facility (GLCF)–EarthSat; United States Geological Survey (USGS)

Panorama of the eastern Rocky Mountains with Pikes Peak

Pikes Peak (center left) is one of the 54 fourteen-thousanders—mountains more than 14,000 feet tall—in Colorado's Rocky Mountains. It is the most visited mountain in the United States, and world wide it is second only to Mount Fuji in Japan. In this perspective view it stands out clearly as the tallest peak in this mountain chain. In the foreground lies Colorado Springs, and to the right one can see the start of the Great Plains, America's breadbasket and ranchland extending east to the Mississippi.

One can ascend to the top of Pikes Peak either by hiking trails, car, or by way of the highest cog railway in the world. The first person to climb the mountain was Edwin James, during an expedition with Major Stephen H. Long in 1820. Although Pikes Peak was known to Native Americans and even Spanish explorers, it was first described by Zebulon Pike, for whom it is named. In November 1806 General Pike saw the mountain for the first time, calling it "the great pinnacle." A few days later he tried to reach the peak with a small group of men, but a blizzard forced him to give up at an elevation of 10,000 feet.

Pages 158 / 159

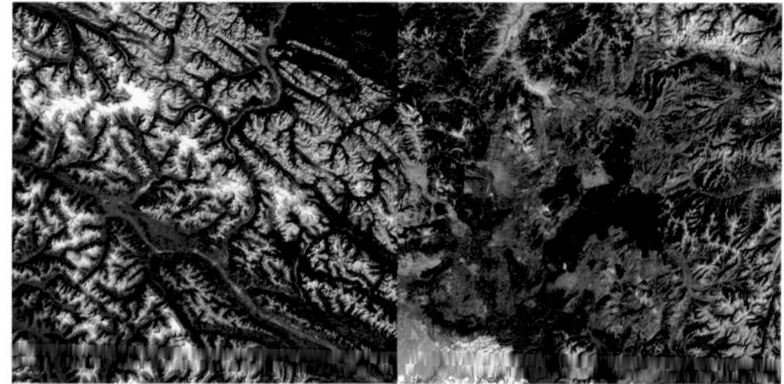

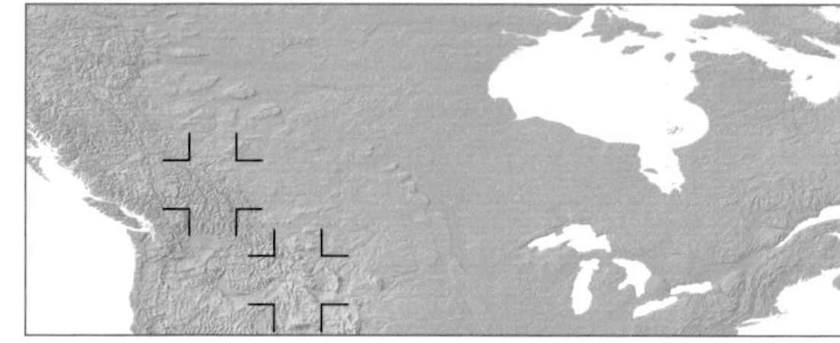

Satellite: Landsat-7 / **Sensor:** ETM+ / **Resolution:** 30 m / **Recorded:** September 14, 2001 / **Visualization:** true colors / **Spectral channels:** 0.63–0.69 µm, 0.53–0.61 µm, 0.45–0.52 µm / **Image processing:** German Remote Sensing Data Center / **Data source:** University of Maryland, Global Land Cover Facility (GLCF)–EarthSat

Satellite: Landsat-7 / **Sensor:** ETM+ / **Resolution:** 30 m / **Recorded:** September 15, 1999 / **Visualization:** true colors / **Spectral channels:** 0.63–0.69 µm, 0.53–0.61 µm, 0.45–0.52 µm / **Image processing:** German Remote Sensing Data Center / **Data source:** University of Maryland, Global Land Cover Facility (GLCF)–EarthSat

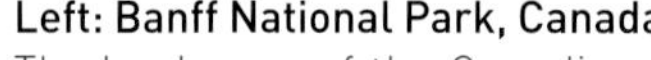

Left: Banff National Park, Canada

The landscape of the Canadian Rockies, on the border between the provinces of British Columbia and Alberta, was shaped by glaciation during the ice ages. Broad valleys and lakes alternate with steep limestone cliffs. From the left center of the picture the valley of the Columbia River extends to the southeast; the elongated Kinbasket Reservoir is clearly visible. Mount Columbia (12,294 feet), in the northwest part of the picture, is the second-highest mountain in the Canadian Rockies and the tallest in the province of Alberta. It was first conquered in July 1902 by James Outram and Christian Kaufmann. Southeast of the peak lies the 100-square-mile Columbia Icefield, a hydrological oddity: its meltwaters flow into the Arctic, Atlantic, and Pacific Oceans.

Right: Yellowstone National Park

A massive volcanic eruption more than 650,000 years ago formed the caldera occupied by the oldest protected natural area in the world, Yellowstone National Park. The park, mostly in Wyoming but extending slightly into Montana and Idaho, lies on a geological hot spot. Several magma chambers lie right below the 6,500-foot-high plateau. They represent a long-term threat to the environment and account for the region's considerable geothermal activity. This manifests itself in the park's numerous geysers, hot springs, and fumaroles. Similar geothermal phenomena can be observed in Yellowstone Lake, which lies just below the center of the right-hand satellite picture. The Greater Yellowstone ecosystem is one of the largest intact ecosystems in the temperate zone, and serves as a refuge for numerous plant and animal species—some endangered—including elk, bison, wolves, and grizzly bears.

Pages 160 / 161

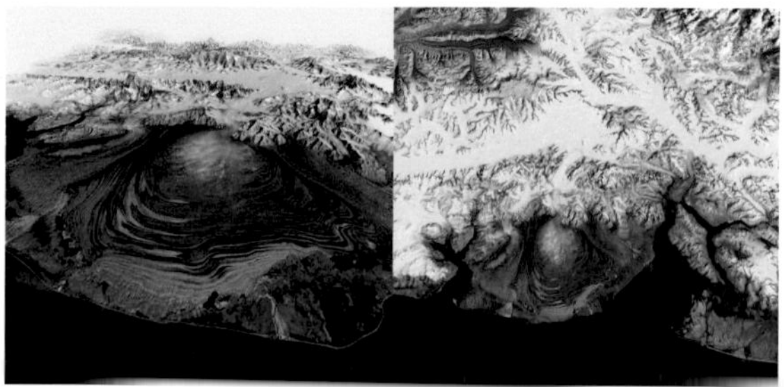

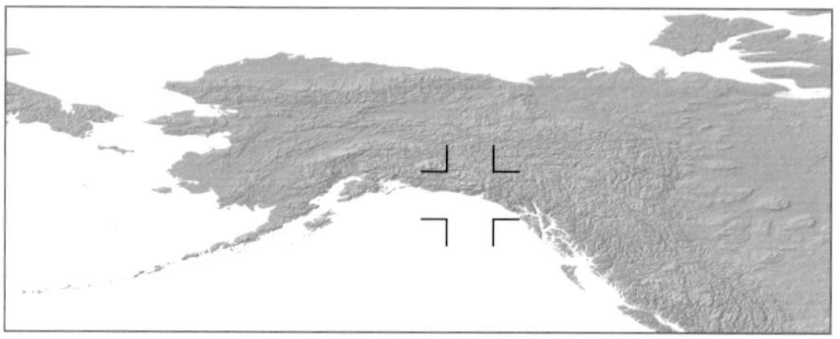

Satellite: Landsat-5 / **Sensor:** Thematic Mapper (TM) / **Resolution:** 30 m / **Recorded:** July 12, 1993 / **Visualization:** perspective, pseudocolor / **Spectral channels:** land, 0.78–0.90 µm, 1.55–1.75 µm, 0.63–0.69 µm; ice, 2.09–2.35 µm, 0.55–1.75 µm, 0.63–0.69 µm / **Elevation model:** USGS National Elevation Dataset (NED) / **Resolution:** 60 m / **Height exaggeration:** 1.3 times / **Image processing:** DFD / **Data source:** University of Maryland, GLCF–EarthSat; United States Geological Survey (USGS)

Satellite: Landsat-5 / **Sensor:** Thematic Mapper / **Resolution:** 30 m / **Recorded:** July 12, 1993 / **Visualization:** pseudocolor / **Spectral channels:** as above / **Image processing:** DFD / **Data source:** University of Maryland, GLCF–EarthSat

Left: Ice Age—Malaspina Glacier, Alaska

This computer-generated view shows a panorama of Alaska's mountainous and icy landscape. The view is from directly above the Gulf of Alaska, looking across the Malaspina foreland glacier to the north. Malaspina Glacier in southern Alaska is one of the largest foreland glaciers on earth, with a length of more than 60 miles and surface area of more than 1,500 square miles. Here it is possible to see first-hand the way glaciers shape the landscape, as they did on a vast scale in North America and Europe during the last Ice Age some 12,000 years ago. The glacier produces all the typical features of glaciated landscape. Even in the picture one can see the brown terminal moraine at the edge of the glacier's ice. The ice is capable of carrying huge quantities of debris, including rubble from the valley walls, and heaps up huge hills at its edges. Somewhat farther from the edge of the ice, its meltwater—decreasing in speed and thus less able to carry large stones—deposits finer debris in so-called sand plains. In the foreground one can see the coastal strip between the eternal ice and the sea, here covered with summer vegetation.

Right: Malaspina Glacier overview

The pseudocolor image on the right shows the same region from above. In the center lies the source of Malaspina Glacier in the Elias Mountains. The foreland glacier, with a thickness of several hundred feet, extends nearly to the coast. There the more recent moraines appear at the edge of the ice in brown. In the satellite picture snow-covered surfaces appear in white, open ice in blue.

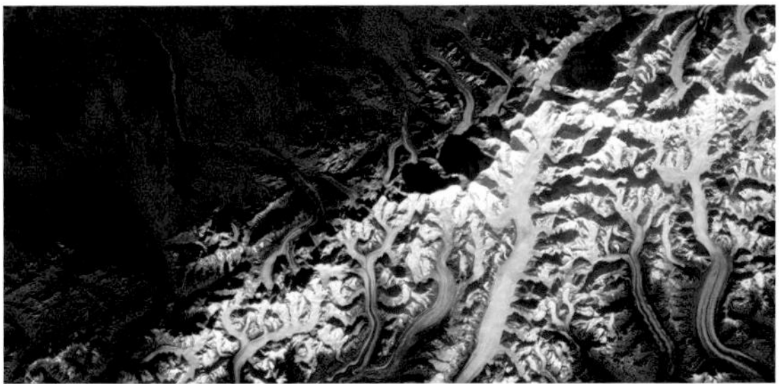

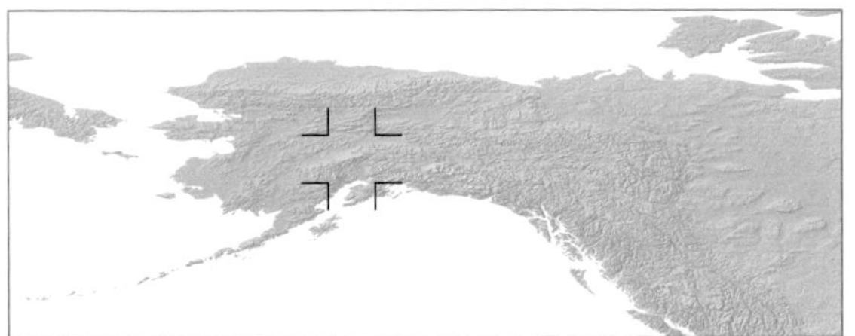

Satellite: Landsat-7 / **Sensor:** Enhanced Thematic Mapper (ETM+) / **Resolution:** 15 m / **Recorded:** September 27, 2001 / **Visualization:** pseudocolor / **Spectral channels:** 0.78–0.90 µm, 0.63–0.69 µm, 0.53–0.61 µm / **Image processing:** German Remote Sensing Data Center / **Data source:** University of Maryland, Global Land Cover Facility (GLCF) – USGS

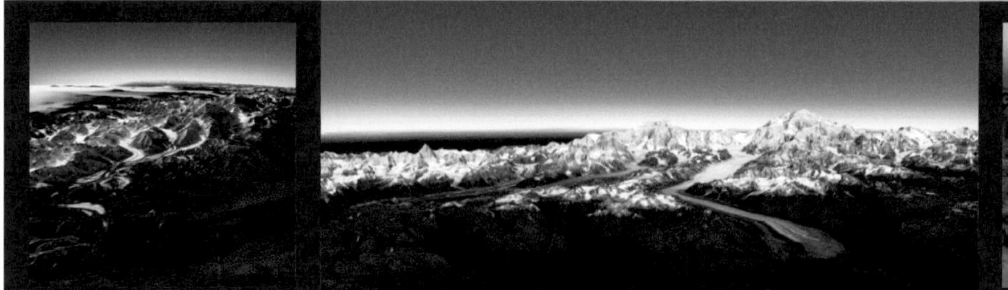

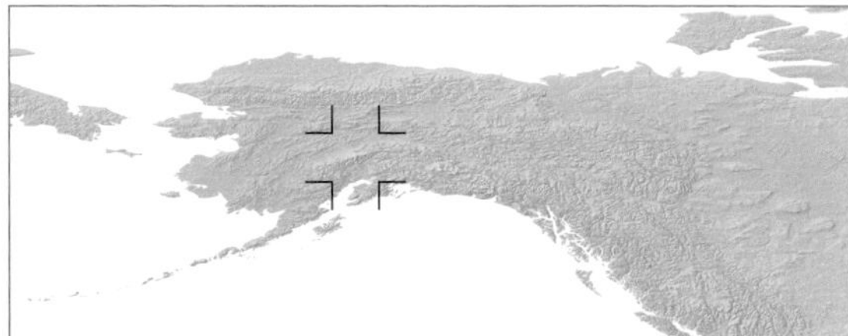

Satellite: Landsat-7 / **Sensor:** Enhanced Thematic Mapper (ETM+) / **Resolution:** 15 m / **Recorded:** September 27, 2001 / **Visualization:** perspective, pseudocolor / **Spectral channels:** 0.78–0.90 µm, 0.63–0.69 µm, 0.53–0.61 µm / **Elevation model:** USGS National Elevation Dataset (NED) / **Resolution:** 60 m / **Height exaggeration:** 1.3 times / **Image processing:** German Remote Sensing Data Center / **Data source:** University of Maryland, Global Land Cover Facility (GLCF) – USGS; United States Geological Survey (USGS)

Denali, "the High One"

At 20,320 feet, Mount McKinley is the tallest peak on the North American continent. The native Athabasca Indians call it Denali ("the High One"), and that is now its official name, though it is still better known as Mount McKinley, named after the twenty-fifth president of the United States. The core of the mountain range that includes Denali, Mount Foraker, and Mount Hunter consists of granite. But these mountains exhibit a broad range of other types of rock as well, mostly metamorphosed sedimentary strata and volcanic rock.

The mountain lies in Denali National Park, established in 1917, in the heart of the Alaska Range—the northernmost section of the American Cordilleras. It is one of the most popular parks in the United States, attracting roughly 700,000 visitors a year. With its almost inaccessible mountains, extensive glacial fields, and subarctic ecosystem, it is home to grizzlies, wolves, Dall sheep, caribou, and elk.

The park has two distinct vegetation zones. Lower-lying areas are covered with boreal forest, a type of vegetation also known by its Russian name, *tiaga*. But the greater part of the park lies above the treeline, which lies at around 2,600 feet, and is covered by tundra. In this pseudocolor satellite image it is possible to distinguish between two types of tundra: dark red indicates wet tundra with its hip-high tangle of birches and willows; bright red alpine tundra in drier areas, with vegetation only a few inches tall.

Left: Panorama of Denali National Park from the south

If you drive north from Anchorage toward Fairbanks in good weather, the Alaska Range towers before you as a seemingly insurmountable barrier. In addition to Denali (20,320 feet), at the right edge of the picture, Mount Foraker (17,400 feet) looms above the numerous 10,000- to 13,000-foot peaks in the Alaska Range. From the lowlands around Wonder Lake, at just under 2,000 feet, Denali rises to its full height of 20,320 feet in a horizontal distance of only 6 miles. The difference in altitude between its base and its peak is more than 18,000 feet, greater than that of Mount Everest. Its far northern location, height, and exposure make for extreme climatic conditions. In winter, temperatures at 15,000 feet often descend to -90°F, and even in summer one can expect hurricane-force winds of more than 120 miles per hour. Denali is therefore considered the coldest mountain on earth, and climbing it is more than a challenge. The first to do so were the Americans Hudson Stuck, Harry Karstens, Walter Harper, and R. G. Tatum in 1913. Today the Kahiltna Glacier on Denali is transformed each summer into an airport: mountain climbers from all over the world fly have themselves set down on the glacier, where they set up their base camps. More than 600 people make the ascent every year.

Center: View from the northeast

This view of the Denali massif from the northeast shows in the foreground the huge Muldrow Glacier, which is fed by the smaller Brooks and Traleika glaciers. The snout of Muldrow Glacier is almost completely buried under the moraine debris that shows up dark in the satellite image. This is what is called a surge glacier; it does not flow at a uniform speed like the typical Alpine glacier but moves in sudden, rapid spurts after long periods of rest. Muldrow Glacier's last surge began in 1956 and continued for about two years. During this time the glacier advanced several miles into the foreland, where some of its ice masses are still thawing to this day. The mechanics of such glacial advances have not yet been thoroughly explained, however it appears that a sudden advance is preceded by a rise in water pressure in the meltwater tunnels of the glacial ice. The glacier floats, and friction becomes almost completely nonexistent. A glacial surge ends when the trapped water is released and the pressure drops.

In this view across the Denali massif it is clear how the Alaska Range curves to the southwest and later links up with the Aleutian Island chain.

Right: Sunrise on the south wall

All the pictures on these pages are perspective views that make it easy for viewers to orient themselves. They are based on digital terrain models depicting the area's surface structure. A satellite image is laid on top of the terrain model to produce a realistic impression of the landscape. On a computer it is possible to view the resulting image from various angles. In addition to varying the viewpoint, it is possible to simulate different lighting conditions. We can, for example, create an impression of sunrise on Denali, when for a brief time the entire massif glows in the light of dawn. To see this in reality one would have to get up very early—the mountain is so close to the Arctic Circle the sun rises by three in summer.

Pages 170 / 171

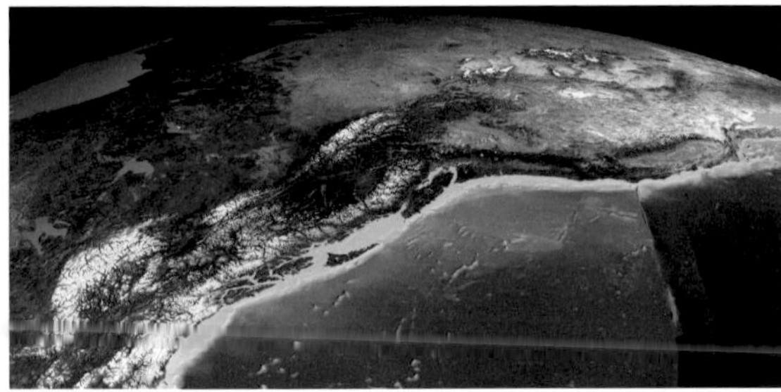

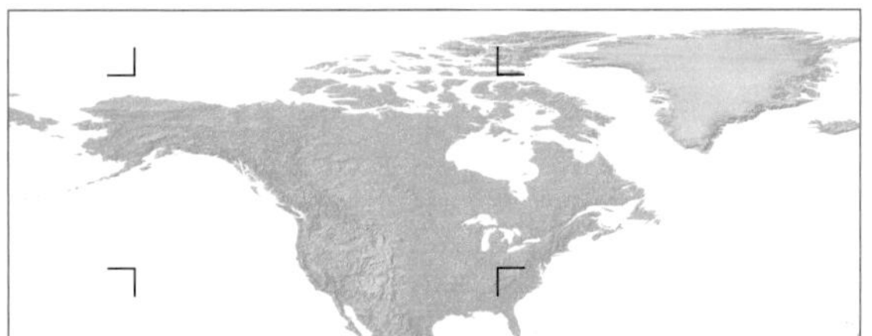

Satellite: Terra / **Sensor:** Moderate Imaging Spectroradiometer (MODIS) / **Resolution:** 1,000 m / **Elevation model:** GTOPO-30, ETOPO-2 / **Resolution:** 1,000 m / **Height exaggeration:** 5 times / **Visualization:** perspective, true colors / **Spectral channels:** 0.62–0.67 µm, 0.54–0.56 µm, 0.46–0.48 µm / **Image processing:** German Remote Sensing Data Center / **Data source:** NASA Goddard Space Flight Center; United States Geological Survey (USGS); National Geophysical Data Center (NGDC)

Pages 172 / 173

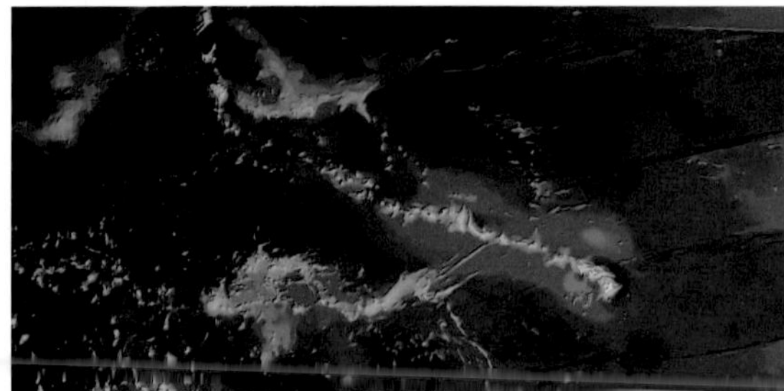

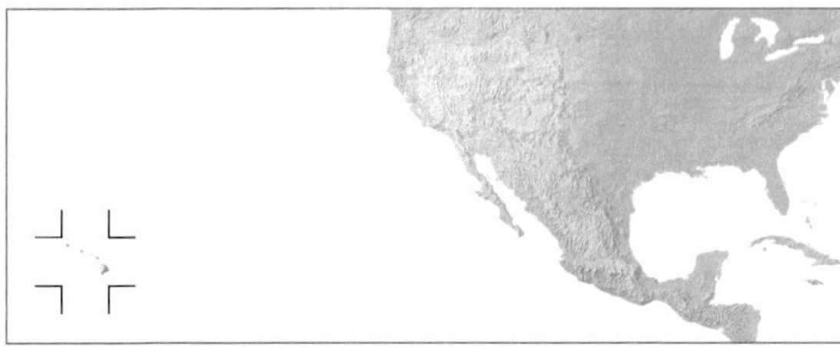

Elevation model: ETOPO-2 / **Resolution:** 4,000 m / **Height exaggeration:** 4.5 times / **Visualization:** shaded elevation model, pseudocolor / **Image processing:** German Remote Sensing Data Center / **Data source:** National Geophysical Data Center (NGDC)

Pages 174 / 175

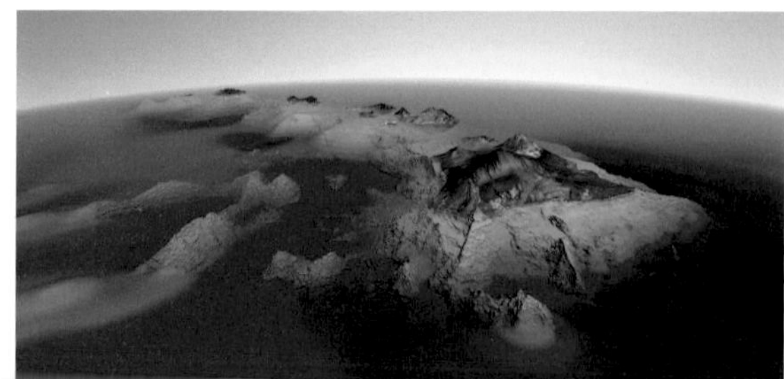

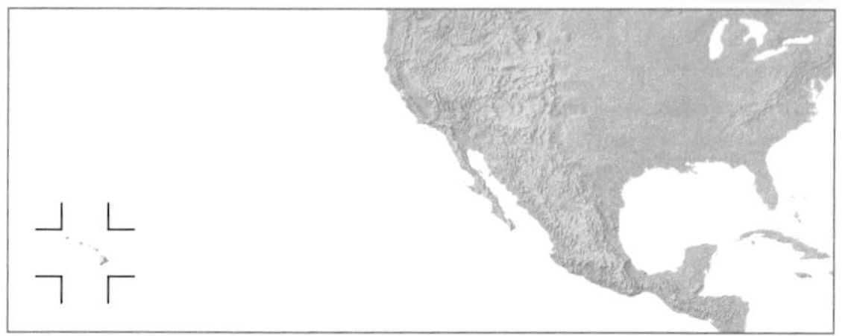

Satellite: Landsat-7 / **Sensor:** Enhanced Thematic Mapper (ETM+) – Mosaic / **Resolution:** 30 m / **Recorded:** July 3, 1999, January 2000, December 19, 2000 / **Elevation model:** NGDC Coastal Relief Model Vol. 10 / **Resolution:** 90 m / **Height exaggeration:** 4.5 times / **Visualization:** perspective view, gray ranges / **Spectral channels:** 0.63–0.69 µm / **Image processing:** German Remote Sensing Data Center / **Data source:** National Geophysical Data Center (NGDC); University of Maryland, Global Land Cover Facility (GLCF)–United States Geological Survey (USGS)

North America at a glance

This cloud-free overview of North America is in fact a mosaic of a number of different satellite pictures from the Moderate Imaging Spectroradiometer (MODIS). Each pixel represents 3,280 feet on the ground. The viewer is poised above Alaska, looking southeastward across the North American subcontinent. In the left half of the picture one can see the Canadian Shield with its landscape of lakes in dark green. These lakes are the result of the ice cover during the last ice age. Especially prominent on the extreme left edge are Hudson Bay and, in the background, the Great Lakes. Somewhat in from the Pacific Coast one can see the Rocky Mountains, some of their peaks covered with snow, extending diagonally from the lower left to the upper right. The Rockies are part of the North American Cordillera, a chain of mountains that extends from Alaska to Guatemala.

In the foreground, parallel to the Pacific Coast, lies the crest of Canada's Coast Range, which on the right becomes California's Sierra Nevada. Mountains are formed when two continental plates collide, and in that collision the layers of rock are folded and thrust upward over vast periods of time. The Rocky Mountains arose as the result of the subduction of the Pacific Plate beneath the North American Plate. At the right edge of the picture one can clearly see a straight line on the floor of the sea—the boundary between these plates. South of it are San Francisco Bay and the light green tones of the fertile San Joaquin Valley. The center of the upper part of the picture is occupied by the Great Plains. At the extreme right edge one can just see a part of the Gulf of Mexico.

Hawaii—hot spots and aging volcanoes

Here the earth's surface appears naked, without its covering of the waters of the Pacific, in shades of blue from dark to light. The volcanic Hawaiian Islands rise above the ocean surface in shades of green, yellow, and brown. Island follows island in a straight line, like a chain of beads. The line of volcanoes can be traced more than 2,000 miles to the west, before it suddenly changes direction and heads north, where it ends off the Russian mainland after a further 1,500 miles.

Volcanism is generally associated with fault zones or subduction zones, but Hawaii's volcanoes are far removed from any plate boundaries. Chains of volcanoes like this one are found in a number of places. In 1963 the geophysicist John Tuzo Wilson formulated his theory of hot spots to explain the origin of such chains. It suggests that the earth's crust moves across small spots where the mantle continuously thrusts up molten material. Successive volcanoes are formed as the hot spot's magma penetrates the crust and reaches the surface. As plates continue their movement, these volcanoes are moved farther and farther away from the hot spot; after thousands of years, cut off from their lava supply, they become extinct. Aging processes specific to volcanoes, the pressure of their own weight, and erosion reduce their size over the course of time until they are completely leveled or buried.

Hawaii, the highest mountain on earth

This computer-generated image shows the volcanic chain of the Hawaiian Islands in the middle of the Pacific Ocean. In the foreground lies the largest and southernmost of the islands, Hawaii. This island is dominated by the mighty crest of Mauna Loa, a volcano that is active to this day. In the overlay satellite image one can see a number of lava streams on its flanks that stand out as darker than the background. The younger Kilauea, also active, lies to the southwest near the coast. It is not very high, and can only be identified by its crater and its dark lava fields. In the northern part of the island Mauna Kea rises to a height of 13,796 feet, surpassing its younger brother Mauna Loa by 115 feet. It has not erupted for several thousand years, and erosion has left obvious traces. It is flanked by two other extinct volcanoes, Hualalai and Kohala.

Through the surface of the sea it is possible to make out the island's vast substructure, built up by the volcanoes over more than 800,000 years. The relatively flat slopes of the island surface give way to considerably steeper ones descending to the depths of the Pacific. On land the lava can flow out slowly, creating smooth relief forms, but when rapidly cooled in confrontation with water it creates more jagged rock formations. If one includes Hawaii's vast submarine foundation, Mauna Kea reaches a height of 31,824 feet, making it the world's tallest mountain.

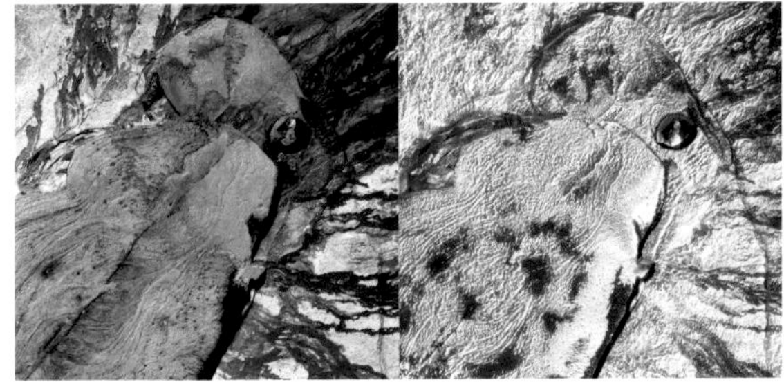

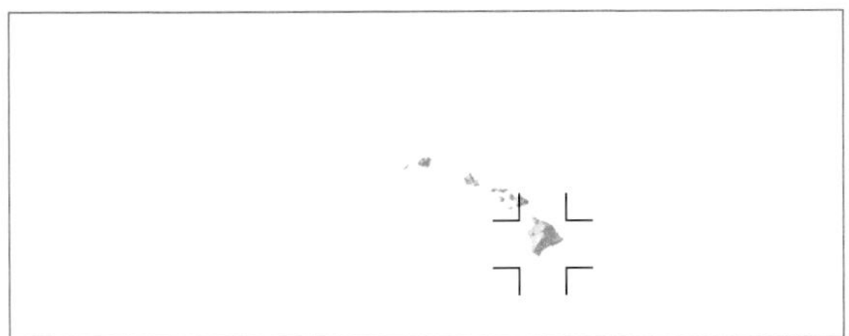

Satellite: Ikonos / **Resolution:** 1 m / **Recorded:** left, January 3, 2003, 21:07 UTC; right, January 3, 2002, 21:06 UTC / **Visualization:** true colors / **Spectral channels:** 0.63–0.69 µm, 0.52–0.60 µm, 0.45–0.52 µm / **Image processing:** German Remote Sensing Data Center / **Data source:** Space Imaging Inc.

The crater of Mauna Loa, Hawaii

Hawaii, or the Big Island as the natives call it, is the largest of the seven Hawaiian Islands. It is topped by Mauna Loa and Mauna Kea, the tallest mountains in the world measured from the sea floor, from which the shield volcano rises up 31,824 feet. These pictures show the crater of Mauna Loa on January 3, 2003 (left) and 2002 (right). The picture at the left clearly shows the structure of the lava flows and traces of volcanic activity. The large blue-gray area depicts the Mokuaweoweo caldera, a collapsed structure bordered in the north by the North Pit Crater (blue-gray) and the circular Lua Poholo. The round hole of the Lua Poholo pit crater was created by the collapse of the hardened lava surface after fluid lava beneath it flowed on. In the picture at the right we see the peak of Mauna Loa covered with snow. Even here, 19° north of the equator, snow regularly falls at 13,680 feet. In some areas the snow has already melted over larger areas; these may be spots of retained warmth within the caldera. According to one Polynesian legend, the volcanoes of the Big Island—especially Kilauea—are the home of the fire goddess, Pele.

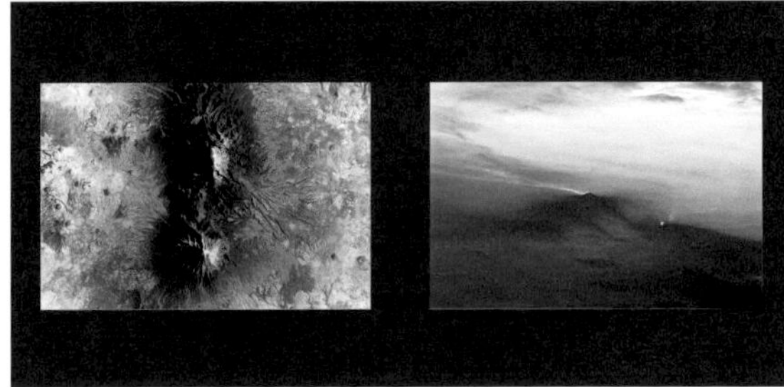

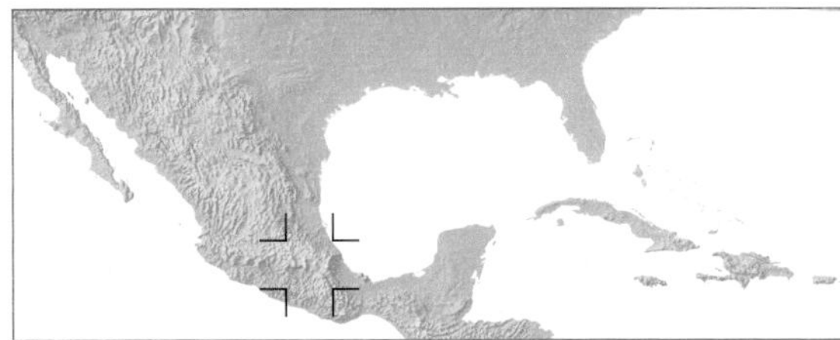

Satellite: International Space Station (ISS 04) / **Sensor:** photograph / **Recorded:** May 23, 2002, 13:19 UTC / **Visualization:** angled shot, true colors / **Image processing:** German Remote Sensing Data Center / **Data source:** Image Analysis laboratory, NASA Johnson Space Center, Roll E - Frame 12339

Satellite: International Space Station (ISS 01) / **Sensor:** photograph / **Recorded:** January 7, 2001, 13:33 UTC / **Visualization:** angled shot, true colors / **Image processing:** German Remote Sensing Data Center / **Data source:** Image Analysis Laboratory, NASA Johnson Space Center, Roll 335 - Frame 3

Smoking Mountain and Sleeping Woman

Both of these photographs were taken from the International Space Station. On the left is Mexico's Popocatépetl (17,887 feet), and on the right its 500-foot-shorter volcanic neighbor Iztaccíhuatl (17,342 feet). The two mountains' names, meaning "smoking mountain" and "sleeping woman," derive from an Aztec legend. In the left picture the dense coniferous forests that clothe the volcano's flanks can be seen in dark browns and greens. Beginning at an elevation of roughly 10,500 feet the forests give way to alpine meadows, which are now grazing land for cattle. The bare lower slopes of the crater appear in bright yellow above the meadows, and the snow-covered peak is white. Erosion gullies can be seen in the land surrounding the volcano, and in the extreme upper left corner the edge of Mexico City lies under a veil of smog.

In the picture at the right Popocatépetl appears in a wholly different light. In the twilight the picture is dominated by blues and reds owing to haze in the atmosphere. A banner of wind-drifted smoke is clearly visible at the volcano's peak. From this picture one gets a sense of the air pollution resulting from Mexico City's explosive growth since the 1970s. Aztec records tell of the first ascent of Popocatépetl, but they are contradictory, mentioning both the date 1289 and the period between 1502 and 1519. It is probable that a Spanish expedition led by Diego de Ordaz stood atop the peak in the year 1519.

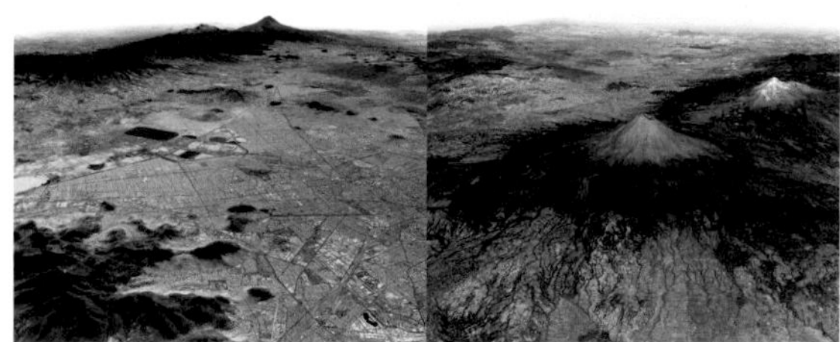

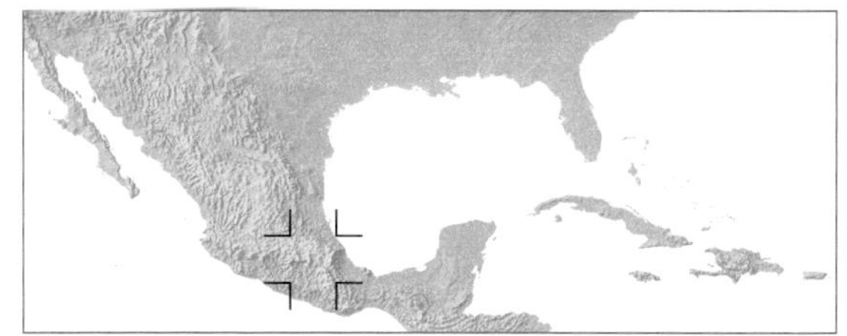

Satellite: Landsat-7 / **Sensor:** Enhanced Thematic Mapper (ETM+) / **Resolution:** 15 m / **Recorded:** March 21, 2000 / **Visualization:** perspective, true colors / **Spectral channels:** 0.63–0.69 µm, 0.53–0.61 µm, 0.45–0.52 µm / **Elevation model:** Shuttle Radar Topography Mission (SRTM), C-Band / **Resolution:** 90 m / **Height exaggeration:** 1.3 times / **Image processing:** German Remote Sensing Data Center / **Data source:** University of Maryland, Global Land Cover Facility (GLCF)-EarthSat, NASA

Mexico City without smog

These perspective views of the Mexico City region were produced by combining a high-resolution satellite picture with a digital elevation model. The picture at the left shows the densely populated region looking from northwest to southeast; the picture at the right shows the opposite view across the volcanoes from southeast to northwest.

In the foreground of the left picture we see Mexico City, a metropolis of 15 million (officially, but presumably more than 20 million) inhabitants, and thus the most populous city in the world. The major thoroughfares are clearly visible, as well as along the left, the city's reservoirs. In the background the chain of volcanoes dominated by Popocatépetl (right) and Iztaccíhuatl (left) rises majestically above the high plateau. At over 17,000 feet they tower nearly 10,000 feet above the plain. Up until the 1960s "Popo," as the Mexicans call it, could be seen lording over the city at all times. But since the unchecked growth of the metropolis beginning in the 1970s smog has increasingly obscured the volcano from view, though it is only around 40 miles away.

Many volcanologists and geologists consider Popocatépetl a nearly perfect stratovolcano. Since midnight on December 21, 1994, after more than fifty years of quiescence, the mountain has reawakened, regularly spewing large quantities of ash and gases into the atmosphere. It is monitored by Mexican and American volcanologists hoping to be able to predict further, possibly catastrophic, eruptions. Were the volcano to explode, the entire population of the region—including the Valley of Mexico with its 20 million people in the metropolis and the city of Puebla with another 5 million—could be endangered.

Pages 182 / 183

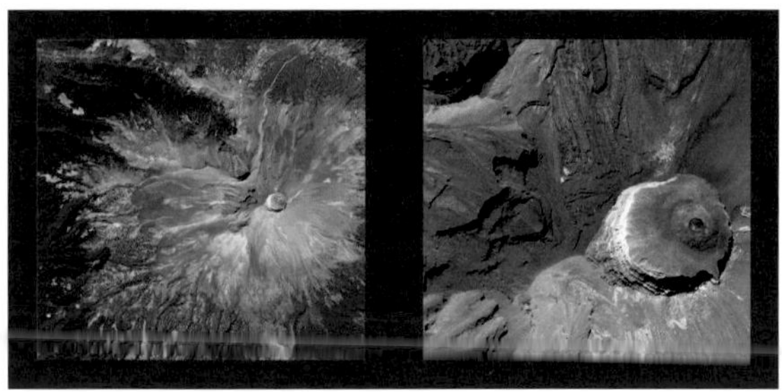

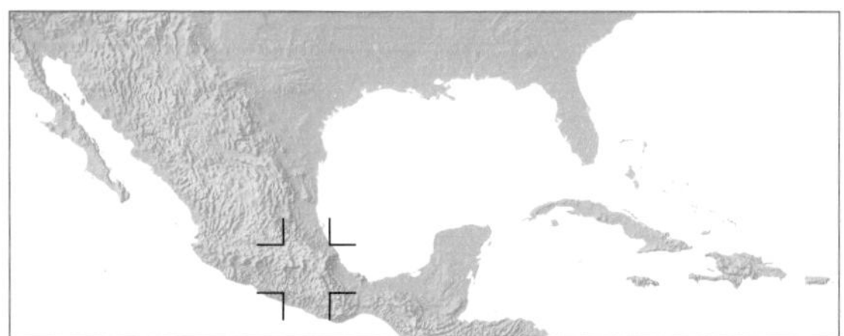

Satellite: Quickbird / Resolution: 60 cm / Recorded: March 7, 2003 / Visualization: true colors / Spectral channels: 0.63–0.69 µm, 0.52–0.60 µm, 0.45–0.52 µm / Image processing: German Remote Sensing Data Center / Data source: DigitalGlobe Inc.

Detailed view of Popocatépetl

The satellite picture on the left shows Popocatépetl's entire peak region at a resolution per pixel of roughly 60 centimeters on the ground. On the right is a detail of the crater itself. This crater is but one manifestation of the Ring of Fire, the string of volcanoes that circles the Pacific and also includes Mount St. Helens in the United States, Mount Fuji in Japan, Mount Pinatubo in the Philippines, and Cotopaxi in Ecuador. This ring of heightened volcanic activity runs along the edges of the great Pacific Plate. Some two-thirds of all the world's active volcanoes lie in this zone. The reason for such a high concentration of volcanoes is the subduction of one plate beneath another. In such areas of weakness in the earth's crust it is easier for magma to rise closer to the surface and create volcanoes. The results of this continuing activity over the past 900,000 years are evident in this picture: an inhospitable peak landscape with lava streams, ash fields, and a deep crater. Popocatépetl is considered one of the world's highly active volcanoes. Fifteen major eruptions have been recorded since the arrival of the Spanish in 1519.

Page 185

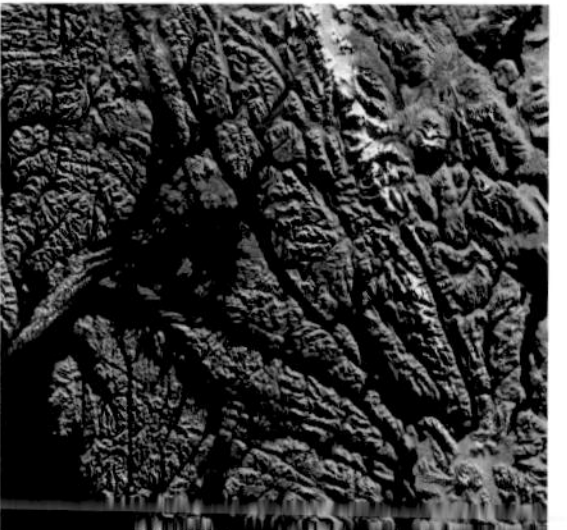

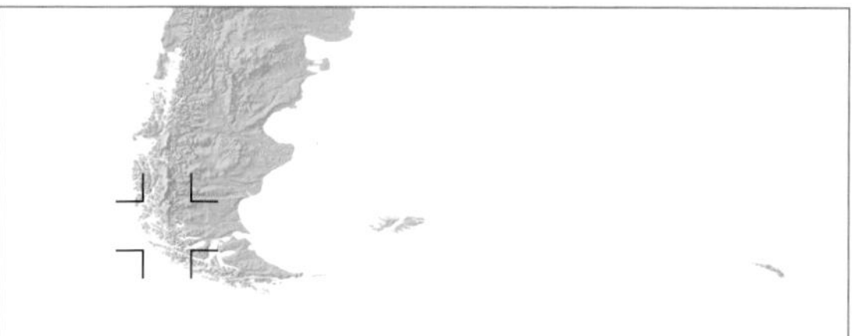

Satellite: Landsat-7 / Sensor: Enhanced Thematic Mapper (ETM+) / Resolution: 30 m / Recorded: May 7, 2001 / Visualization: pseudocolor / Spectral channels: 2.09–2.35 µm, 0.78–0.90 µm, 0.53–0.61 µm / Image processing: German Remote Sensing Data Center / Data source: University of Maryland, Global Land Cover Facility (GLCF)–EarthSat

The coastal landscape of Patagonia

This picture shows the Chilean side of Patagonia in the extreme south of South America. The south end of Patagonia's inland ice stands out from its surroundings as a band of cool shades of blue running north-south along the right side. This ice shield is the largest contiguous mass of ice outside the polar regions. A bit below the southern tip of the ice lies the 5,766-foot active volcano Mount Burney. The satellite image shows the southern edges of Bernardo O'Higgins National Park. With an area of about 13,500 square miles, it is the largest of Chile's more than thirty national parks. At the upper right edge a bit of the better-known Torres del Paine National Park is also visible. Slightly to the west of the ice mass in the upper right rises the peak of the Cerro Balmaceda, marking the south end of the Torres del Paine protected area. Tourism is now the chief source of income in the Chilean part of Patagonia. The Patagonian region is divided by the Andes into a western part, most of which belongs to Chile, and an eastern Argentine part. Because the Andes block clouds coming off the Pacific, the west side experiences heavy precipitation, making the Chilean Patagonia damp and cool. To the east of the mountain chain, by contrast, it is relatively dry.

Pages 186 / 187

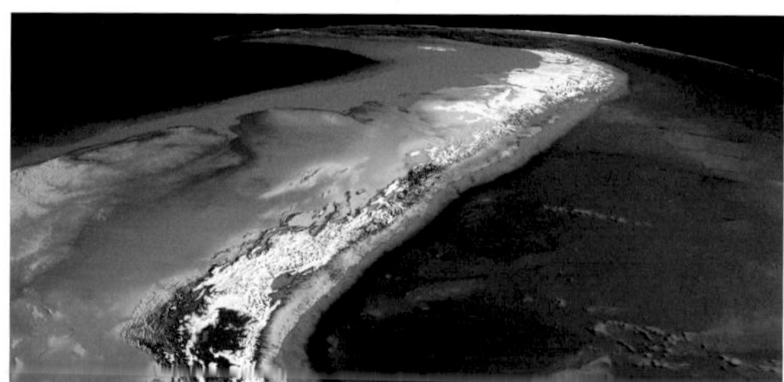

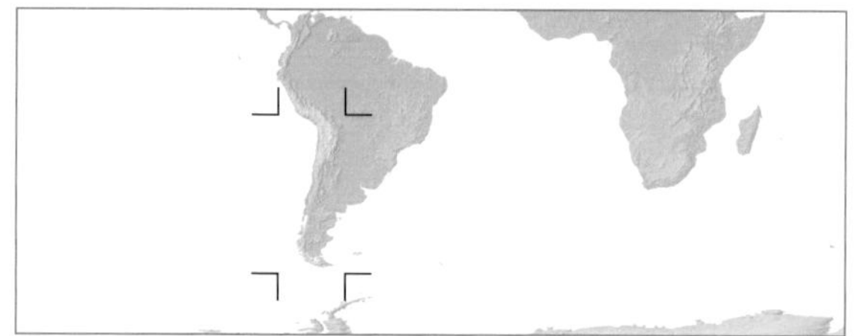

Elevation model: GTOPO-30, ETOPO-2 / Resolutions: 1,000 m, 2,000 m / Height exaggeration: 5 times / Visualization: perspective view, pseudocolor / Image processing: German Remote Sensing Data Center / Data source: NASA Goddard Space Flight Center; United States Geological Survey (USGS); National Geophysical Data Center (NGDC)

The Andes, the longest mountain range on earth

The relief image presents a view across much of the South American continent, from Peru in the northwest to Cape Horn, the southernmost spot on earth not covered in perpetual ice. Along the west coast, from Venezuela to Chile, stretches the world's longest mountain chain: the Andes.

The middle section of the Andes consists of two, in places three, parallel mountain chains—the Cordilleras. In a number of sections these lie far apart and surround a central plateau (altiplano). The east coast is bordered by extensive lower mountain systems, the Brazilian highlands and the Patagonian tableland in the south. Between these lies the Paraguay-Paraná Basin. To the southeast of the continent lie the British Falkland Islands (upper center).

The Andes were created in a subduction zone along the eastern Pacific. Here the oceanic Nazca Plate dips below the continental South American Plate. Rock from the ocean plate becomes molten at great depths and rises again as magma. Pressure from the collision and the related volcanic activity have thrust the Andes upward. At the present time the oceanic plate is sliding beneath the continental crust at a rate of roughly four inches a year. The subduction line is marked by a deep-sea trench along the continent's west coast—clearly visible in this image. As the oceanic plate makes its dive it carries with it great quantities of water into the depths. Because of their water content, the resulting magmas are less dense and rise to the surface. It is for this reason that especially explosive volcanoes are found near all the world's subduction zones—as here along the west coast of South America—which release water and carbon dioxide into the atmosphere.

Pages 188 / 189

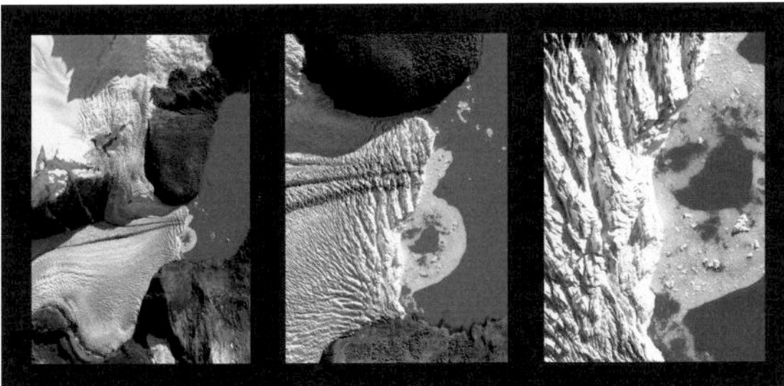

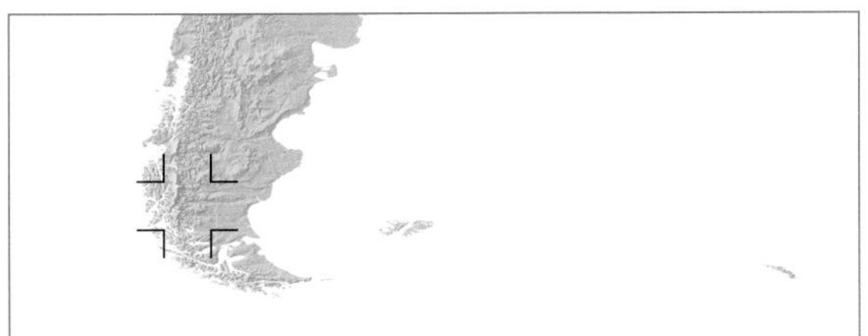

Satellite: Quickbird / **Resolution:** 60 cm / **Recorded:** May 21, 2003 / **Visualization:** true colors / **Spectral channels:** 0.63–0.69 µm, 0.52–0.60 µm, 0.45–0.52 µm / **Image processing:** German Remote Sensing Data Center / **Data source:** DigitalGlobe Inc.

Spegazzini Glacier next to Lake Argentino

This picture from the satellite Quickbird shows Spegazzini Glacier in Argentina in a level of detail previously unattained by civilian satellites. The glacier, named after the botanist Carlos Spegazzini, lies next to Lake Argentino. The name of the national park, Los Glaciares, makes it clear that this part of Patagonia is dominated by inland ice.

The ice river shown is fed by two glaciers at higher elevations: the Mayo Norte and the Peinta. In the center picture of this zoom sequence, but especially in the picture at right, we can see the wildly jagged surface of the glacier. In the left picture the obvious dark stripes on its surface are gravel moraines that the glacier has picked up on its long journey. Its ice edge at the shore of Lake Argentino presents one of the tallest vertical faces of any of the region's glaciers. The Spegazzini differs from the others in that it shows no signs of a retreat. All the others have become considerably smaller over the past few years as a result of global warming. The unusual blue-green, milky appearance of the water next to the ice face is directly related to the glacier. The cloudiness of this glacial milk comes from particles carried along by the ice that remain suspended in the water.

Pages 190 / 191

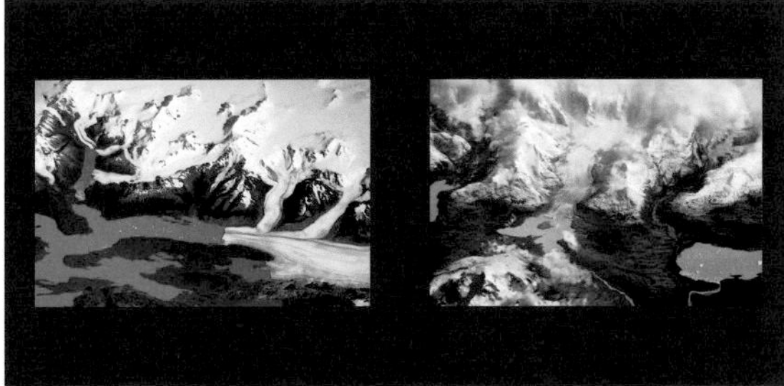

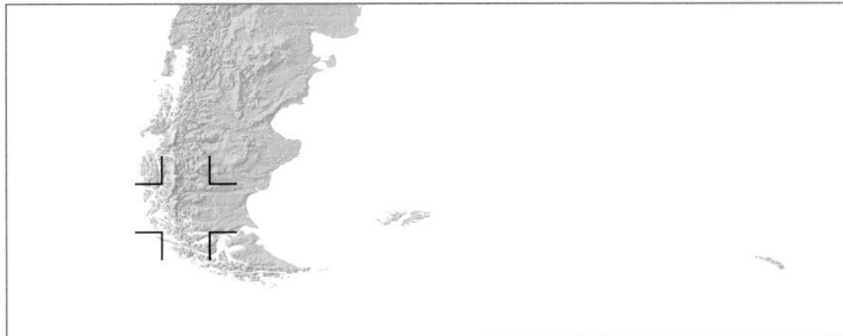

Satellite: International Space Station (ISS 06) / **Sensor:** photograph / **Recorded:** March 29, 2003, 15:47 UTC / **Visualization:** angled shot, true colors / **Image processing:** German Remote Sensing Data Center / **Data source:** Image Analysis Laboratory, NASA Johnson Space Center, Roll E - Frame 42086

Satellite: International Space Station (ISS 06) / **Sensor:** photograph / **Recorded:** March 19, 2003, 18:49 UTC / **Visualization:** angled shot, true colors / **Image processing:** German Remote Sensing Data Center / **Data source:** Image Analysis Laboratory, NASA Johnson Space Center, Roll E - Frame 39880

Left: Upsala Glacier next to Lake Argentino

The photograph at the left, from the International Space Station, looks to the southwest across a part of the national park Los Glaciares, with Lake Argentino, in Argentina. At the photo's right Upsala Glacier empties into the lake; at the upper left is the Onelli Glacier. At roughly 37 miles long and with an area of roughly 210 square miles, Upsala Glacier is the longest ice stream in South America and one of the largest in the world. It is fed by two smaller ones, which flow together at the top of the picture. The central moraines created by their confluence stand out against the ice surface as dark lines that join on Upsala Glacier. The rocks in front of the glacier (center) show traces of ice flow; they are polished smooth and present grooves in the direction of the glacier's path. Roughly sixty years ago Upsala Glacier reached across roughly half of the now exposed rock in the center of the picture. The glacier was named after the city of Uppsala in Sweden, which sponsored the first expeditions into Patagonia's continental inland ice.

Right: The Last Hope

The picture on the right was also taken from the International Space Station, and shows the area surrounding Ultima Esperanza Fjord. This region in the south of Chile is dominated by the mighty masses of Patagonia's inland ice. Thousands of islands make the region a labyrinth in which it is almost impossible for inexperienced navigators to orient themselves. Such was the case with those who desperately searched for the entrance to the Strait of Magellan in 1558 under the command of Juan Ladrilleros. To them the fjord was truly an *ultima esperanza*—their last hope.

Pages 192 / 193

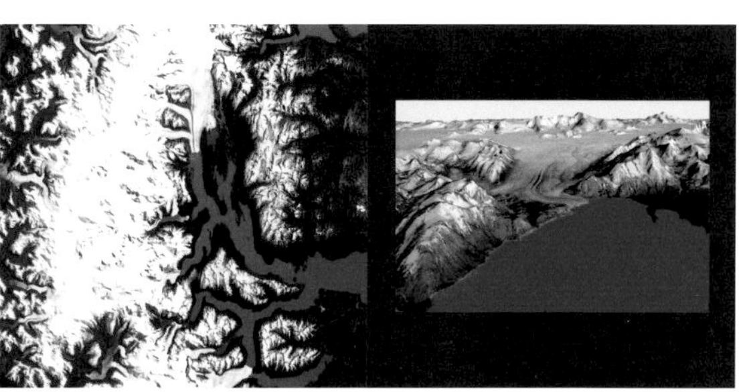

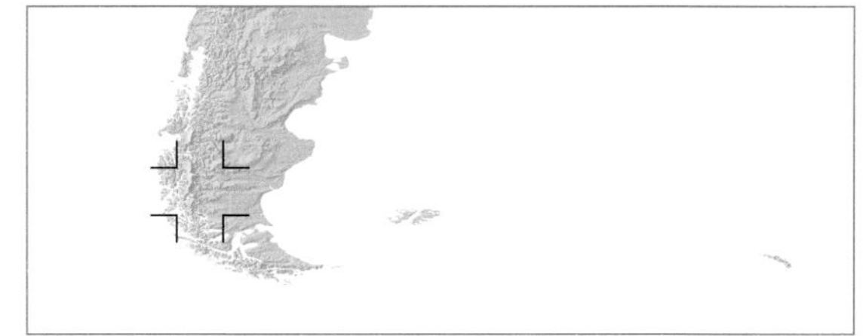

Satellite: Landsat-7 / **Sensor:** ETM+ / **Resolution:** 30 m / **Recorded:** October 14, 2001 / **Visualization:** true colors / **Spectral channels:** 0.63–0.69 µm, 0.53–0.61 µm, 0.45–0.52 µm / **Image processing:** German Remote Sensing Data Center / **Data source:** University of Maryland, GLCF-EarthSat

Satellite: Landsat-7 / **Sensor:** ETM+ / **Resolution:** 30 m / **Recorded:** October 14, 2001 / **Visualization:** perspective, true colors / **Spectral channels:** 0.63–0.69 µm, 0.53–0.61 µm, 0.45–0.52 µm / **Elevation model:** SRTM, C-Band / **Resolution:** 90 m / **Height exaggeration:** 1 time / **Image processing:** German Remote Sensing Data Center / **Data source:** University of Maryland, GLCF-EarthSat, NASA

Left: The glacial landscape of Patagonia

This photograph from the American Landsat satellite shows most impressively the dominance of the more than 180-mile-long inland ice on the border between Chile and Argentina. The last stragglers of the Andes extend to the south to the Strait of Magellan and Tierra del Fuego. In the left half of the picture lie the glaciers of Bernardo O'Higgins National Park in Chile. The right half shows mainly the region of Los Glaciares National Park in Argentina. Here we can see the greenish-blue western edges of Lake Argentino. In its milky waters there are white icebergs that have broken off from the face of the ice, which rises up 200 feet.

Right: View across Lake Viedma

High-resolution satellite data in combination with digital elevation models from the Shuttle Radar Topography Mission (SRTM) make it possible to produce virtual landscapes of even the most remote regions, as here in Patagonia. We are looking across Lake Viedma in Los Glaciares National Park toward the west onto Viedma Glacier. The glacier's gravel moraines stand out in shades of dark brown against the bluish-white ice. In the background stands the 11,129-foot Cerro Perito Moreno. Behind the mountains the Patagonian inland ice extends deep into Chilean territory. In the right foreground the Cerro Huemul rises to a height of 8,100 feet next to the lake.

Pages 196 / 197

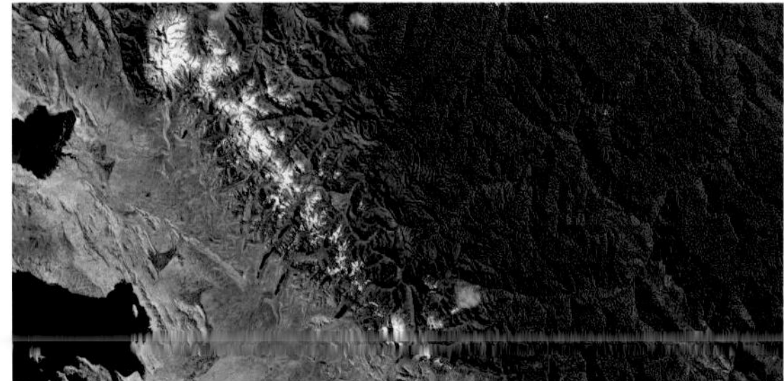

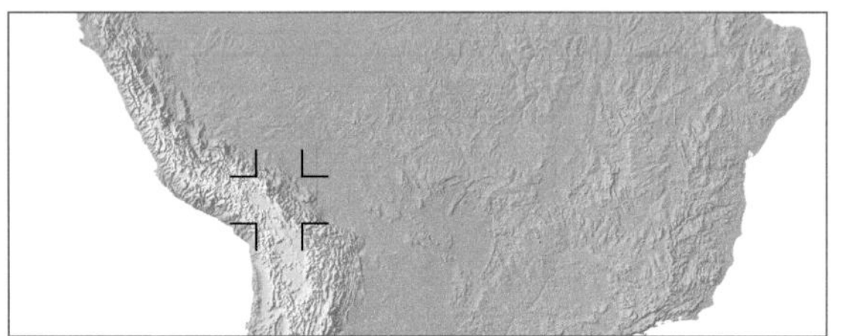

Satellite: Landsat-5 / **Sensor:** Thematic Mapper / **Resolution:** 30 m / **Recorded:** August 2, 1987 / **Visualization:** pseudocolor / **Spectral channels:** 0.76–0.90 µm, 0.63–0.69 µm, 0.52–0.60 µm / **Image processing:** German Remote Sensing Data Center / **Data source:** University of Maryland, Global Land Cover Facility (GLCF)–EarthSat

Pages 200 / 201

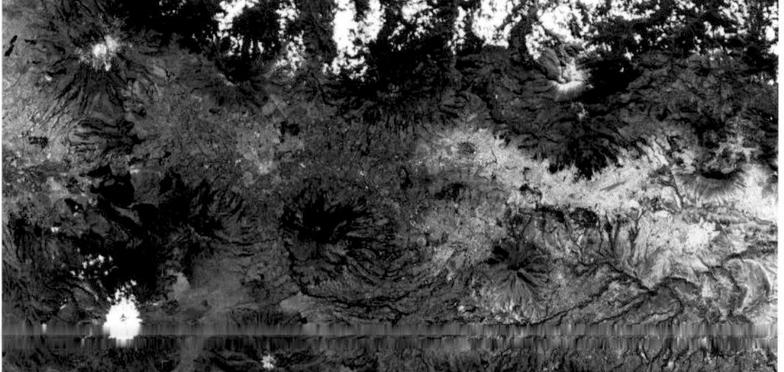

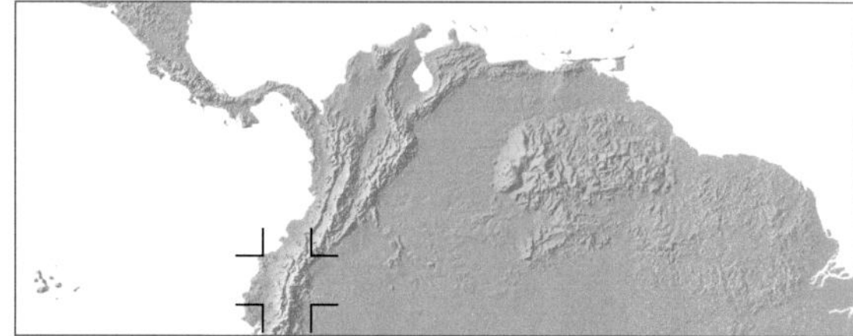

Satellite: Landsat-7 / **Sensor:** Enhanced Thematic Mapper (ETM+) / **Resolution:** 30 m / **Recorded:** November 14, 1999 / **Visualization:** true colors / **Spectral channels:** 0.63–0.69 µm, 0.52–0.60 µm, 0.45–0.52 µm / **Image processing:** German Remote Sensing Data Center / **Data source:** University of Maryland, Global Land Cover Facility (GLCF)–EarthSat

Pages 202 / 203

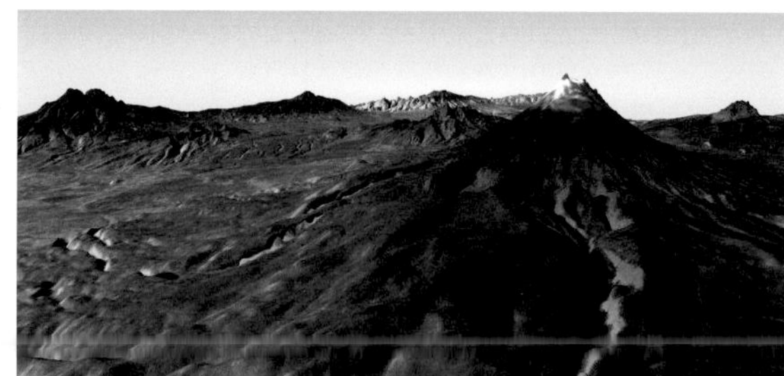

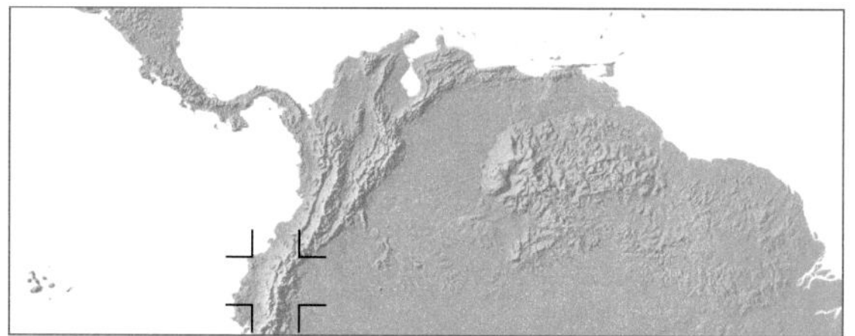

Elevation model: Shuttle Radar Topography Mission (SRTM), X-Band / **Resolution:** 30 m / **Height exaggeration:** 1.3 times / **Recorded:** February 2002 / **Visualization:** perspective, pseudocolor / **Image processing:** German Remote Sensing Data Center / **Data source:** German Aerospace Center

Bolivia's climate and vegetation zones

This image from Landsat-5 shows in white and brown the glaciated Cordillera Real of the Bolivian Andes running diagonally across the picture. This mountain chain is impressive for its high number of nearly 20,000-foot peaks, its glacial lakes, highly diverse rock formations, and waterfalls. One of its best-known mountains is Illampu (marker). At 20,873 feet it is, along with the somewhat taller neighboring Ancohuma (21,095 feet), a favorite goal for experienced mountain climbers. At the bottom edge of the picture stands another high peak, Huayna Potosí (19,996 feet), one of the "home mountains" to residents of La Paz. The eternal ice of the Cordillera Real runs through the picture like a dividing line. At the left edge one can see parts of Lake Titicaca, the highest navigable lake in the world and the largest lake in South America. Between Lake Titicaca and the Cordillera Real the highland basin of the altiplano extends in shades of brown.

At the eastern edge, the Cordillera Real gives way to the *yungas*: the mountain and cloud forests of Bolivia, with their deeply cut valleys and gorges. In this pseudocolor image vegetation appears red; it marks the dense growth and great biodiversity of these tropical valleys. Traveling from Bolivia's altiplano into the *yungas* one can experience almost all of South America's climate and vegetation zones; in a single day one passes from relatively dry highlands across snow and ice into tropical rain forest.

Cotopaxi: the once highest active volcano on earth

The highlands of the Andes occupy roughly a fourth of Ecuador's area. Here the Andes divide into two parallel mountain chains, the eastern and western Cordilleras. They are separated by a riftlike depression, through which the Pan American Highway threads past the capital of Quito. These northern highlands are a young and geologically active part of the Andes, the landscape having been shaped by volcanic activity and earthquakes. The highest elevation in the eastern Cordillera is 19,347-foot Cotopaxi (marker). This very symmetrical, cone-shaped stratovolcano is the second-tallest mountain in Ecuador. For many years it was considered the tallest active volcano on Earth, its last eruption in 1942. On its peak one can see an inner crater (roughly 650 feet in diameter) and an outer one (roughly 2,600 feet in diameter). Its far-reaching pyroclastic streams and numerous eruptions have left distinct marks on the volcano's surroundings. Its most violent eruptions were in 1744, 1768, and especially 1877, when streams of mud and ash (lahars) extended more than 60 miles to the Pacific Ocean and to the Amazon Basin. Its last significant eruption was in 1904. Directly in front of the mountain are three other volcanic peaks: Rumiñahui (15,492 feet), Sincholagua (16,053 feet), and Pasachoa (13,794 feet). In the upper part of the picture additional volcanoes describe the crest of the western Cordillera. At the foot of Pichincha (right center) lies Ecuador's capital, Quito, at 9,348 feet above sea level and home to 1.5 million people.

Avenida de los Volcanes—panorama of Cotopaxi

In the foreground of this perspective view rises snow-covered Cotopaxi. The cone-shaped stratovolcano, some 30 miles southeast of Quito, is at 19,347 feet, the second-tallest mountain in Ecuador. It towers nearly 10,000 feet above its surroundings. At its base it is roughly 14 miles wide. The German geologist Wilhelm Reiss reached the edge of its crater with his Columbian assistant Angel M. Escobar in 1872—presumably the first ascent. In the immediate vicinity one can see the peaks of the volcanoes Rumiñahui (15,492 feet), Pasachoa (13,794 feet), and Sincholagua (16,053 feet). In the background the volcanic peaks of the western Cordillera recede in a northerly direction. From left to right they are Iliniza Sur (17,267 feet), Iliniza Norte (16,818 feet), Corazon (15,718 feet), and Atacazo (14,642 feet). Though here partially obscured by the peak of Cotopaxi, one can also see the base of Pichincha (15,700 feet), dear to the hearts of Quito's residents.

On February 19, 2000, the space shuttle *Endeavor* flew over this extremely active volcanic zone of the Ecuadorean Andes. The digital elevation model derived from the data from this shuttle mission has a resolution of roughly 30 meters. With precise elevation models available, it is possible to depict this volcanic landscape in accurate detail. The crater of Cotopaxi and the gullies leading down from the peak are clearly visible. These gullies mark the courses of massive mudflows (lahars), some of which have caused damage as much as 180 miles away.

Pages 206 / 207

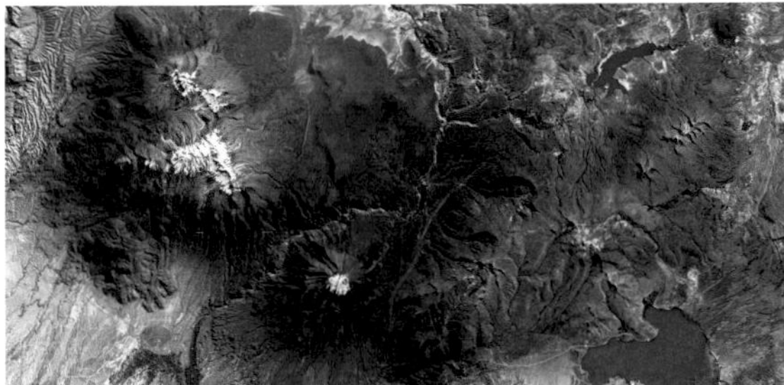

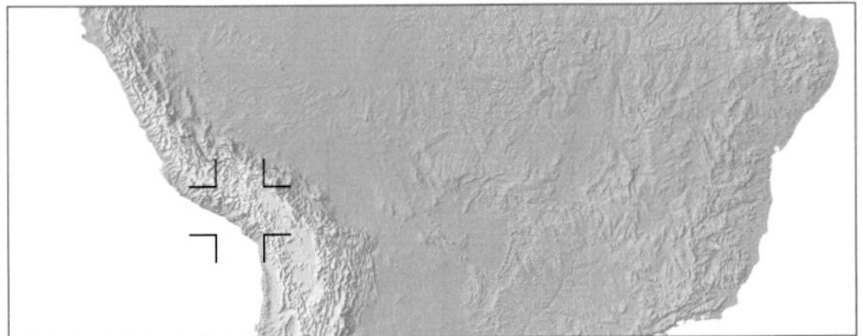

Satellite: Landsat-7 / **Sensor:** Enhanced Thematic Mapper (ETM+) / **Resolution:** 15 m / **Recorded:** May 10, 2001 / **Visualization:** true colors / **Spectral channels:** 0.63–0.69 µm, 0.52–0.60 µm, 0.45–0.52 µm / **Image processing:** German Remote Sensing Data Center / **Data source:** University of Maryland, Global Land Cover Facility (GLCF)–EarthSat

Pages 208 / 209

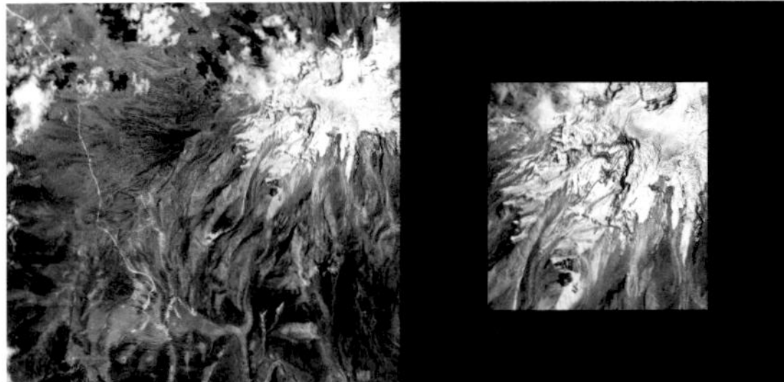

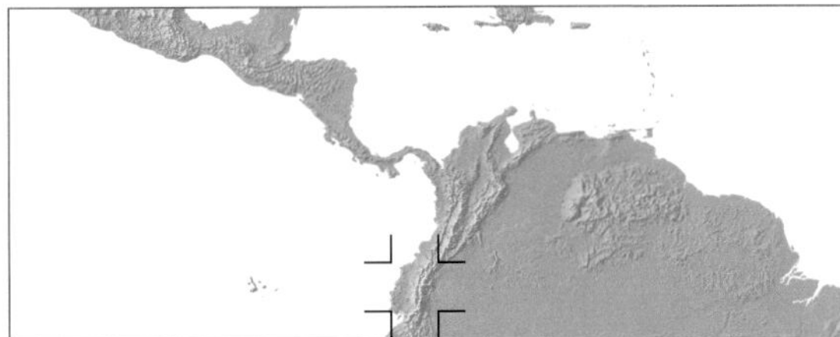

Satellite: Ikonos / **Resolution:** 1 m / **Recorded:** January 16, 2001, 15:51 UTC / **Visualization:** true colors / **Spectral channels:** 0.63–0.69 µm, 0.52–0.60 µm, 0.45–0.52 µm / **Image processing:** German Remote Sensing Data Center / **Data source:** Space Imaging Inc.

Pages 210 / 211

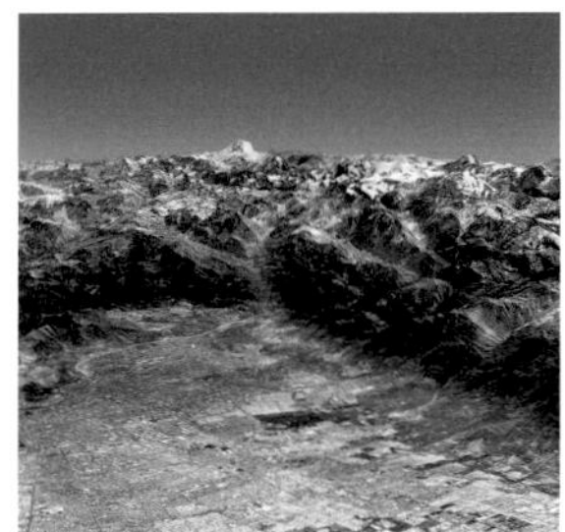

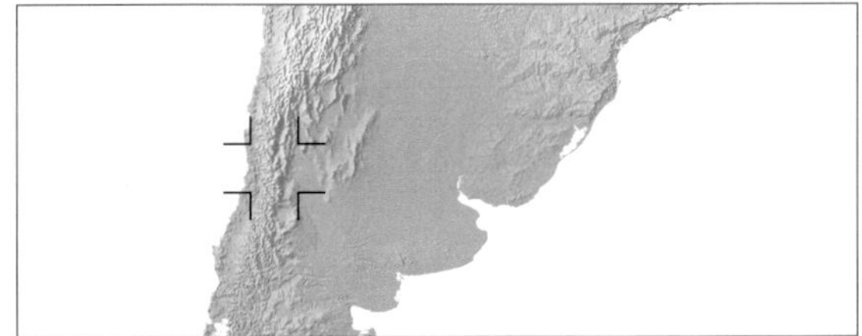

Satellite: Landsat-7 / **Sensor:** Enhanced Thematic Mapper (ETM+) / **Resolution:** 15 m / **Recorded:** December 26, 1999 / **Visualization:** perspective, true colors / **Spectral channels:** 0.63–0.69 µm, 0.52–0.60 µm, 0.45–0.52 µm / **Elevation model:** Shuttle Radar Topography Mission (SRTM), C-Band / **Resolution:** 90 m / **Height exaggeration:** 1.5 times / **Image processing:** German Remote Sensing Data Center / **Data source:** University of Maryland, Global Land Cover Facility (GLCF)–EarthSat

Volcanoes and Laguna Salinas

This image shows a portion of the western Cordillera of the Peruvian Andes. The marker in the left half of the picture shows the location of Peru's best-known active volcano, El Misti. The last documented eruption of this 19,101-foot peak occurred in 1948. Northwest of El Misti lies the likewise snow-covered and elongated peak of Chachani, 19,931 feet high. Both El Misti and Chachani are among the simpler, "non-technical" mountains of the Andes, which are climbed almost daily.

Between El Misti and Chachani runs the deeply cut valley of the Río Chile. To the right of the river stretches the puna landscape, a treeless plateau typical of Peru. At the lower left edge of the picture the edges of Arequipa can be identified by their green, irrigated areas. Because of its proximity to the active volcanoes, earthquakes are a daily fact of life in Peru's second-largest city. In June 2001 Arequipa, a UNESCO World Cultural Heritage site, was shaken by a strong earthquake. In the upper right half of the picture is the Fraile reservoir, which provides the city's drinking water. South of the reservoir, at an elevation of more than 13,000 feet, lies the salt lake Laguna Salinas (lower left in the right picture), home to a large number of rare flamingos. The entire Landsat image captures the major part of the protected area established in 1979 as the Reserva Nacional Salinas y Aguada Blanca.

Chimborazo—the highest mountain in the world?

Does the prominent ice cap seen in this picture crown the tallest mountain on earth? For a long time Ecuador's Chimborazo was considered the world's highest mountain, at 20,561 feet. It was only the discovery of Dhaulagiri in Nepal in 1808 that put it in second place. Since then it has slipped to ninety-ninth place on the list, but it has lost nothing of its former majestic appearance. As the satellite image on the right side shows in detail, the region's heavy precipitation leads to the formation of a shimmering crown of ice. The few green stretches at the right edge of the picture are home to vicuñas, very rare Andean camels. The true-color picture is dominated by the greenish-brown shades of the dry grasslands (*paramo*) typical of the tropical Andes above 10,000 feet. It was Alexander von Humboldt who first mapped the vegetation of Chimborazo. During his South American expedition in 1802 he even attempted to climb it, but was forced to turn back at a little over 19,000 feet. Even so, he set a long-standing altitude record, and in his report about the climb first described the symptoms of altitude sickness. The first successful ascent was accomplished in 1880 by Edward Whymper and the brothers Louis and Jean-Antoine Carrel. In terms of geology, Chimborazo is a volcano with two peaks. It lies in the western Cordillera of the Ecuadorean Andes. Although it last erupted more than 10,000 years ago, it has definitely exhibited volcanic activity since that time.

Chimborazo lies almost directly atop the equator, where the earth bulges out as a result of centrifugal force. The earth's radius is thus greater than at the poles. If one measures from the center of the earth, Chimborazo rises some 6,740 feet higher than Mount Everest, making it the unrecognized world's tallest mountain.

Aconcagua, the tallest mountain in the Andes

Looking from the southwest to the northeast, this perspective view shows the city of Santiago de Chile at the foot of the Andes. On the horizon, at a distance of roughly 60 miles, Aconcagua is clearly visible as a dome. The mountain itself lies across the Chilean border in Argentina. At 22,841 feet it is the tallest mountain in South America and the tallest outside Asia. On clear days one can even see the Pacific, about 100 miles away. The origin and meaning of the name Aconcagua are debated; one theory that is generally accepted has it that Aconcagua comes from the Indian and means "sentinel of stone." Aconcagua was first conquered on January 14, 1897, by the Swiss climber Matthias Zurbriggen. Favored above almost all the other Seven Summits—the highest mountains of the various continents—it is nowadays besieged by as many as 4,000 climbers a year. Because of its enormous height and unpredictable weather, also because the giant is often underestimated, only some 20 percent make it to the top.

Aconcagua dominates the landscape northeast of Santiago, the capital of Chile, at an altitude of some 2,000 feet. Greater Santiago is home to about 5.5 million people, roughly a third of the country's population. It was founded in 1541 on the banks of the Río Mapocho (center), which flows down out of the Andes and bisects the city from east to west. Also visible is the city's highly regular systematic street pattern.

About the German Aerospace Center

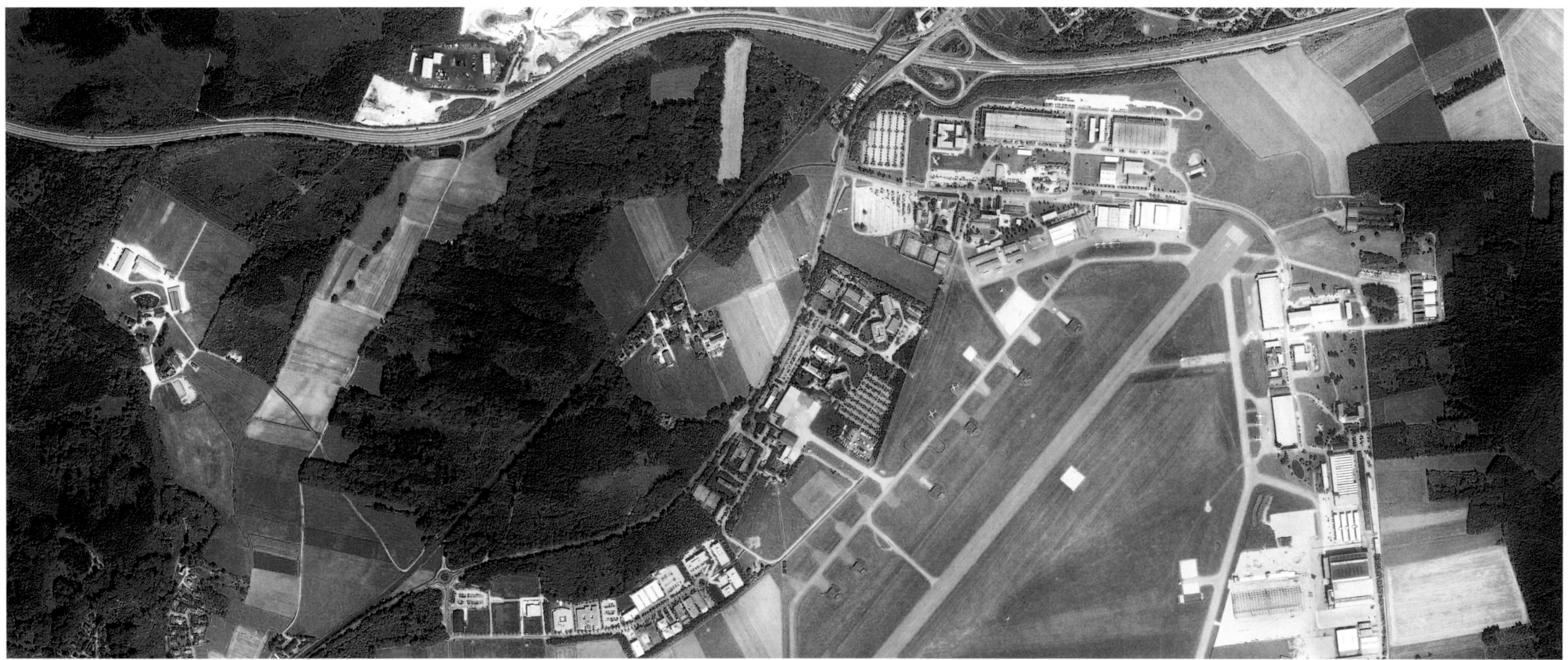

GERMAN AEROSPACE CENTER (DLR) www.dlr.de

The German Aerospace Center is the German national research facility for air and space travel, which also conducts research in energy technology and transportation. The German Aerospace Center is a member of the Herman von Helmholtz Community of German research centers. With headquarters in Cologne and eight locations total, it operates more than thirty institutes and facilities, employing some 5,000 people. The *Mountains from Space* project was directed by the German Remote Sensing Data Center.

GERMAN REMOTE SENSING DATA CENTER (DFD)

www.caf.dlr.de

The German Remote Sensing Data Center is an institute of the German Aerospace Center, with headquarters in Oberpfaffenhofen, near Munich, and a branch in Neustrelitz, in Mecklenburg-West Pomerania. The German Remote Sensing Data Center is committed to opening up the space-travel technology of "satellite remote sensing" to scientific, industrial, governmental, and public applications. To this end, it develops and produces informational products from earth-observation data for international programs and projects in collaboration with scientists and potential users. The data gathered is applied to research projects and practical uses for nature conservation, energy efficiency, planning, resource management, public safety and crisis mediation, and monitoring the climate and atmosphere. To acquire and process data, the German Remote Sensing Data Center operates an international network of ground stations; it registers information from a wide variety of observation satellites every day. The DFD data management and archival systems safeguard all collected information and make it available to users. DFD works closely with such international space organizations as the European Space Agency and NASA, as well as with industry and private enterprises, universities, and scientific facilities in executing its projects. One hundred fifty scientists and engineers are employed by the center. Together with the German Aerospace Center's Institute for Remote Sensing Methodology, it focuses on remote sensing applications.

The Ikonos satellite picture on this page shows the German Remote Sensing Data Center's Oberpfaffenhofen facility from a height of roughly 375 miles. In the immediate vicinity are buildings used for the air-travel industry and the Oberpfaffenhofen Airport. The work of the German Aerospace Center's institutes and other facilities is concentrated on the development and application of space-travel technologies, atmospheric research, earth observation, and the operation of the German space-travel control center.

Project Partners

DIGITALGLOBE INC. www.digitalglobe.com
Since 2001, DigitalGlobe, whose headquarters are in Longmont, Colorado, has operated Quickbird, the earth-observation satellite with the highest available resolution of 60 centimeters. The sharp detail of the images has opened up new opportunities for earth observation from space, for example in the fields of city and regional planning.

ENDOXON AG www.endoxon.ch
Endoxon is a leader in the development of products and services in the realm of geo-information in combination with the newest technology. It unites the tradition of Swiss cartography with the use of multimedia communications services (SMS, MMS, WAP, and WEB).

EUROPEAN SPACE AGENCY (ESA) www.esa.int
The ESA, with headquarters in Paris, is Europe's space-travel agency, representing fifteen countries. Its main focus is the design and realization of the European space-travel program. The ESA also operates scientific observation satellites and offers their data through partner organizations.

NATIONAL AERONAUTICS AND SPACE ADMINISTRATION (NASA) www.nasa.gov
NASA is the national space-travel organization in the United States, with research facilities located all around the country. The Johnson Space Center (JSC), the Goddard Space Flight Center (GSFC)—for this project its MODIS Rapid Response System—and the Jet Propulsion Laboratory (JPL), offer a variety of earth-observation data.

NATIONAL OCEANIC AND ATMOSPHERIC ADMINISTRATION (NOAA) www.noaa.gov
The NOAA, with its main headquarters in Washington, D.C., is a government agency with expertise in a number of different areas such as weather forecasting, setting fishing limits, oceanography, research, and air traffic. It operates a system of polar-orbit and geostationary satellites for environmental observation. The National Geophysical Data Center (NGDC) in Boulder, Colorado, is one of its three data centers.

SPACE IMAGING INC. www.spaceimaging.com
Space Imaging Inc., based in Thornton, Colorado, launched Ikonos on September 24, 1999, the first civilian earth-observation satellite with a resolution of 1 meter. Products derived from the data collected by Ikonos are available in the Carterra Archive of Space Imaging. European Space Imaging and Japan Space Imaging Corporation are among the regional organizations that distribute Ikonos data.

SPOTIMAGE / CENTRE NATIONAL D'ETUDES SPATIALES (CNES) www.spotimage.fr
Based in Toulouse, France, SpotImage has been the worldwide distributor of data and geo-information products from the French Spot satellites (with resolutions up to 2.5 meters) since 1986. The work of SpotImage is carried out on behalf of the French space-travel agency CNES. SpotImage also offers data from other earth-observation satellites.

SWISSPHOTO AG www.swissphoto.ch
Established in 1931 as Swissair Photo AG, Swissphoto AG, in Regensdorf-Watt, Switzerland, is today one of the largest providers of geomatic services and geo-data in Europe. Its offerings are varied, covering the entire range of airborne remote sensing from picture-taking flights to cartography, surveying, and engineering to the sale of geo-data and consulting.

UNIVERSITY OF MARYLAND, GLOBAL LAND COVER FACILITY (GLCF) www.glcf.umiacs.umd.edu
The GLCF is a service of the University of Maryland. It provides scientists and the interested public access to one of the largest archives of freely available satellite data from various sensors. The research work of the GLCF is focused on changes to the land surface.

UNITED STATES GEOLOGICAL SURVEY (USGS) – EROS DATA CENTER (EDC) www.earthexplorer.usgs.gov
The EROS Data Center, based in Sioux Falls, South Dakota, is a facility of the United States Geological Survey, and is the U.S. archive for remote sensing data relating to land surface. The archive contains aerial photographs, altitude data, satellite pictures, and a global coverage of Landsat data over a period of thirty years.

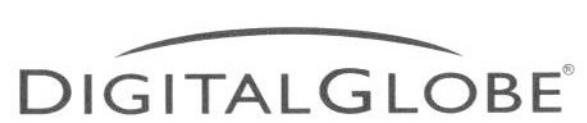

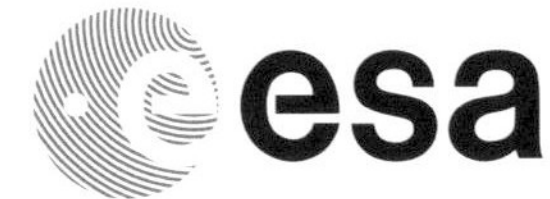

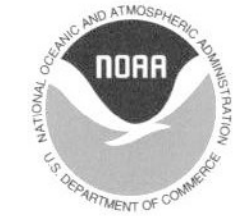

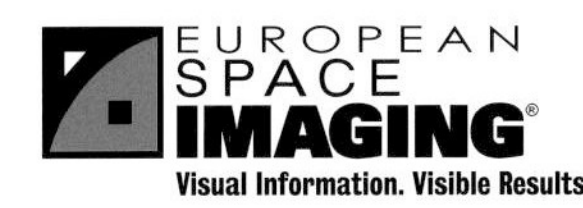

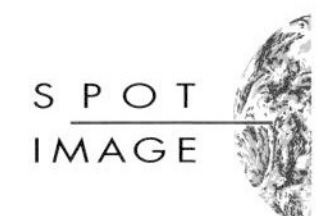

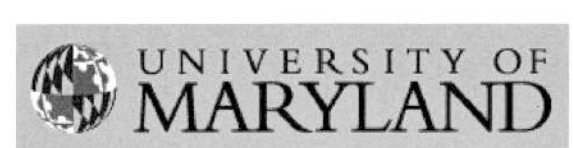

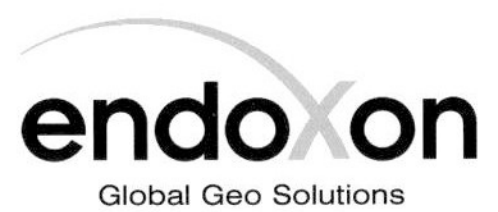

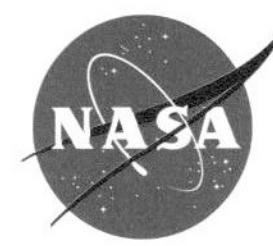

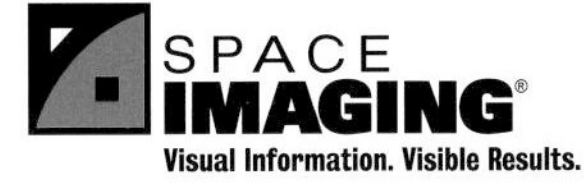

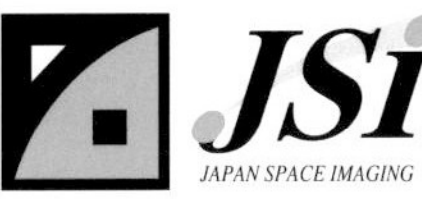

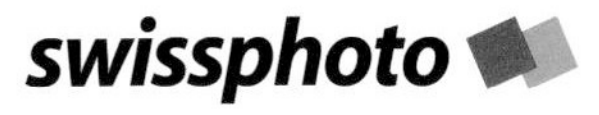

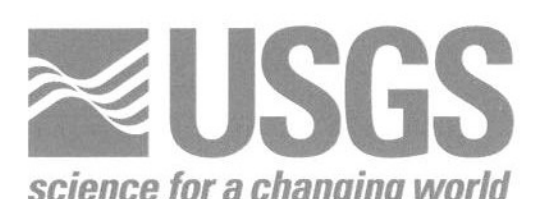

About the Authors

[STEFAN DECH]

Born in 1960, Dech studied geography, sociology, and political science at Würzburg University. He specialized early on in geo-scientific remote sensing with satellites, and went on to receive his PhD in the same field in 1990. Since 1987 he has worked at the German Center for Air and Space Travel, and beginning in 1998, he has been head of the German Remote Sensing Data Center. He has meanwhile pursued an active teaching career, first as a lecturer at universities in Eichstätt, Munich, and Heidelberg. Since 2001 he has been a professor at Würzburg University, holding a teaching chair in remote sensing at the Geographical Institute. His current research focuses primarily on environmentally-conscious subjects, especially the long-term development of terrestrial ecosystems using remote sensing and geographical information technology.

[RÜDIGER GLASER]

Born in 1959 in Ettlingen/Baden, Germany, Glaser received his PhD from Würzburg University in 1989. He was a professor of geography in Heidelberg from 2001 to 2004, and he has since served as director of the Institute for Physical Geography in Freiburg im Breisgau. In addition to remote exploration, his work concentrates on global change, environmental issues, and climate change. He has traveled extensively to study through North, Central, and South America, Africa, Arabia, Asia, and Europe. He is a member of the German Academy for German Culture, and the author of more than 100 publications, including the bestseller *1000 Jahre Wetter, Klima, Katastrophen; Klimageschichte Mitteleuropas* (*1,000 Years of Weather, Climate, Catastrophes; A History of the Central European Climate*).

[MAURICE HERZOG]

Maurice Herzog was born in 1919 in Lyon, France. As leader of the French Himalaya Expedition in 1950, he climbed (together with Louis Lachenal) the first eight-thousander, Annapurna in Nepal (26,545 feet). The conquest of the peak cost him his hands and feet, but his book about the climb became a bestseller, and President Charles de Gaulle later named him Minister of Sports (1958–1966) and the man who "once again [gave] French youth an ideal." Until 1978 he was a member of the National Assembly and mayor of Chamonix. Herzog now lives in Neuilly, near Paris, and in Chamonix.

[SIR EDMUND HILLARY]

Born in 1919 in Auckland, New Zealand, Sir Edmund Hillary is best known for his ascent of Mount Everest in 1953 with Tenzing Norgay. The son of a New Zealand beekeeper, he devoted himself to mountain climbing as a young man, and in 1951 and 1952 he took part in Eric Shipton's exploratory expeditions to Mount Everest and Cho-Oyu. Knighted by Queen Elizabeth II for his achievement, he also established the Himalayan Trust, which has constructed twenty-seven schools, two hospitals, drinking-water conduits, and airports for the Sherpas in their homeland, Solo Khumbu.

[ALEXANDER HUBER]

Alexander Huber, born in 1968 in Trostberg, Upper Bavaria, is a trained rescue worker, mountain guide, and graduate physicist. At the age of thirty he resolved to make a career of mountain climbing, and his solo free climbs (without ropes or a harness) in Yosemite Valley and in the Dolomites are legendary. In 1997 he and his team managed to conquer the 23,320-foot Latok II in the Karakorum by climbing the west wall in the style of American big wall climbing.

[RALF-PETER MÄRTIN]

Ralf-Peter Märtin was born in 1951 in Eisenach, Germany. He studied history and Germanistics in Berlin, where he earned his PhD with a dissertation on adventure novels. He has accompanied Reinhold Messner on numerous expeditions: into the kingdom of Mustang, through Tibet, into the Sahara, to the Mongolian Altai, and to Nanga Parbat. He currently lives in Frankfurt am Main where he works as a freelance journalist and non-fiction writer. His articles on historical and adventure subjects have appeared in *Die Zeit*, *Geo*, and *National Geographic*.

[REINHOLD MESSNER]

Born in South Tirol in 1944, Messner is the most famous high-mountain climber in the world. He was the first to climb all fourteen eight-thousanders, and the first to conquer Mount Everest without supplemental oxygen. In later years he turned to ice and desert trekking, and he has told of his experiences in numerous books and thousands of lectures. Today he is working on his "fifteenth eight-thousander"—the creation of a museum complex on the subject of mountains in his South Tirolean homeland.

[OSWALD OELZ]

Oswald Oelz was born in 1943 in Vorarlberg, Austria, and has become a well-recognized extreme mountain climber and physician. He climbed Mount Everest and Aconcagua with Reinhold Messner, and other tours have taken him to Manaslu, Makalu, and Shisha Pangma, to Mount Vinson, Mount McKinley, and Kilimanjaro. He demonstrated his skills as an expedition doctor in a spectacular rescue on Mount Kenya; as a high-altitude doctor he is the inventor of "Margherita cocktails" to prevent altitude sickness. He is the director of the medical clinic at the Triemli City Hospital in Zürich.

[CHRISTOPH RANSMAYR]

Christoph Ransmayr was born in 1954 in Wels, Upper Austria. He studied philosophy in Vienna and currently lives and works in West Cork, Ireland. His novels *The Terrors of Ice and Darkness*, *The Last World*, and *The Dog King* have been awarded numerous prizes, and to date have been translated into thirty languages. He is a friend of Reinhold Messner's, and together they have undertaken mountain treks and journeys through the Himalayas, Tibet, India, and Yemen. One of these he described in his story, "By the Shore of Lake Phoksundo", included here.

[STEPHEN VENABLES]

Born in 1954, Venables is one of the best-known British alpinists. He was the first to climb a number of peaks in the Himalayas and in South Georgia, but it was his new route across the east flank of Everest that made him famous. He has published eight books about his climbing experience, among them the award-winning photo documentary *To the Top: The Story of Mount Everest*. He currently writes radio and television features for the BBC on the subject of mountains, and is president of the British Alpine Club.

Translation from the German by Russell Stockman, except for Christoph Ransmayr's "Ballad of the Happy Return," and "By the Shore of Lake Phoksundo," translated from the German by John L. Woods

Editor, English-language edition: Samantha Topol
Design Coordinators, English-language edition: Brady McNamara and Neil Egan

Library of Congress Cataloging-in-Publication Data

[Berge aus dem All. English]
Mountains from space : peaks and ranges of the seven continents / [edited by] Stefan Dech ... [et al.].
p. cm.
Translation of: Berge aus dem All.
Includes bibliographical references and index.
ISBN 0-8109-5961-5 (alk. paper)
1. Aerial photography. 2. Photography of mountains. 3. Remote sensing. I. Dech, Stefan Werner.

TR810.B4713 2005
551.43'2'0222—dc22
2005015028

First published as *Berge aus dem All* in 2005 by Frederking & Thaler GmbH, München, www.frederking-thaler.de

Printed and bound in Germany
10 9 8 7 6 5 4 3 2 1

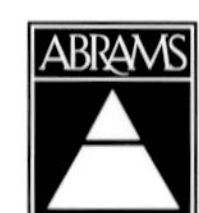

Harry N. Abrams, Inc.
100 Fifth Avenue
New York, NY 10011
www.abramsbooks.com

Abrams is a subsidiary of

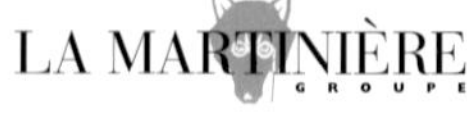

Concept: Professor Stefan Dech, Professor Rüdiger Glaser, Reinhold Messner, Dr. Robert Meisner

Project Direction: German Remote Sensing Data Center, DLR

Foreword: Professor Sigmar Wittig: "So Far, So Near"

Introductions: Professor Stefan Dech: "Remote Sensing with Satellites—Techniques, Uses, and Fascination"; Reinhold Messner: "The Big Picture—Mountains from Space"; Christoph Ransmayr: "The Ballad of the Happy Return"

Geoscientific Texts: Professor Rüdiger Glaser

Climbing and Literary Texts (see contents page): Maurice Herzog, Sir Edmund Hillary, Alexander Huber, Dr. Ralf-Peter Märtin, Reinhold Messner, Professor Oswald Oelz, Christoph Ransmayr, "By the Shore of Lake Phoksundo—Portrait of a Happy Man," in *Die Verbeugung des Riesen. Vom Erzählen* (S. Fischer Verlag GmbH, Frankfurt a. M., 2003), Stephen Venables

Picture Captions: Professor Stefan Dech, Dr. Robert Meisner, Dr. Thorsten Andresen, Nils Sparwasser

Scientific Data Preparation: Nils Sparwasser, Dr. Thorsten Andresen, Adelheid Craubner

Acknowledgments: The authors would like to thank the following people whose contributions have enriched this book: F. Baier, U. Beutelmüller, W. Dorigo, M. Eineder, T. Erbertseder, T. Esch. S. Glaser, U. Heek, U. Heiden, B. Hildenbrand, A. Hinterberger, J. Hoffmann, S. Holzwarth, M. Huber, T. Kemper, D. Kosmann, T. Kraus, C. Künzer, E. Paliouras, M. Pecher, P. Rastner, P. Reinartz, T. Riedlinger, G. Rücker, T. Ruppert, M. Schmidt, G. Strunz, H. Taubenböck, M. Vogel, D. Walter, K. Wisskirchen.

Photograph Credits: All images are reproduced courtesy the German Aerospace Center unless otherwise noted. (see Appendix p.211—p.239)
Satellite pictures for the scientific texts:
Page 23, 115: © 2005 German Aerospace Center
Page 29: © 2005 NASA, JSC
Page 49: © 2005 USGS, EROS Data Center
Pages 73, 169, 199, 205: © 2005 University of Maryland, GLCF - EarthSat
Page 139: © 2005 NASA, GSFC/ASTER Science Team; elevation model maps in the glossary section © 2005 German Aerospace Center, DLR: ETOPO-2, NASA/USGS

Authors' photos for the climbing and literary texts not otherwise credited by the authors:
Page 67: Oswald Oelz © 2005 Röbi Bösch
Page 91: Christoph Ransmayr and Reinhold Messner © 2005 FIRST LOOK - FLO 400669 - 13.10.1992 - Land der Berge "Julius Payer - Vom Ortler in die Arktis"
Page 143: Stephen Venables © 2005 Luke Hughes - North wall of the Eiger
Page 157: Alexander Huber © 2005 Heinz Zak

Bibliography

Albertz, J. *Einführung in die Fernerkundung—Grundlagen der Interpretation von Luft- und Satellitenbildern*. Darmstadt: Wissenschaftliche Buchgesellschaft, 2001.
Bätzing, W. *Die aktuellen Veränderungen von Umwelt, Wirtschaft, Gesellschaft und Bevölkerung in den Alpen*. Berlin: Umweltbundesamt, gefördert durch das Bundesministerium für Umwelt, Naturschutz und Reaktorsicherheit, 2002.
Birkenhauer, J. *Die Alpen—Gefährdeter Lebensraum im Gebirge, Problemräume Europas*. M. Strässer ed., Vol. 6, 2nd revised ed., Cologne: Aulis, 1996.
Bundesministerium für Umwelt, Naturschutz und Reaktorsicherheit (BMU). *Umweltziele im Alpenraum und Ansätze zu einem Monitoring durch Indikatoren—Abschlussbericht der Arbeitsgruppe "Bergspezifische Umweltqualitätsziele" der Alpenkonvention* (2. Mandatsphase), 2002.
Burga, C.A., F. Klötzli, and G. Grabherr, eds. *Gebirge der Erde—Landschaft, Klima, Pflanzenwelt*. Stuttgart: Ulmer, 2004.
Conservation International Center for Applied Biodiversity Science. *Designing Sustainable Landscapes*, 2000.
Hannah, L., and T.E. Lovejoy. *Climate Change and Biodiversity: Synergistic Impacts* (Advances in Applied Biodiversity Science 4), 2003.
Humboldt, Alexander von. *Kosmos—Entwurf einer Physischen Weltbeschreibung* [1845–62]. Frankfurt am Main: Eichborn, 2000.
Jeanneret, F., D. Wastl-Walter, U. Wiesmann, and M. Schwyn, eds. *Welt der Alpen—Gebirge der Welt. Ressourcen, Akteure, Perspektiven*. Bern: Haupt, 2003.
Jenson, J.R. *Remote Sensing of the Environment: An Earth Resource Perspective*. New Jersey: Prentice Hall, 2003.
Lillesand, T.M., and R.W. Kiefer. *Remote Sensing and Image Interpretation*. New York: Wiley & Son, 2004.
Rodrigues, A.S.L., S.J. Andelman, M.I. Bakarr, L. Boitani, T.M. Brooks, R.M. Cowling, L.D.C. Fishpool, G.A.B. da Fonseca, K.J. Gaston, M. Hoffmann, J.S. Long, P.A. Marquet, J.D. Pilgrim, R.L. Pressey, J. Schipper, W. Sechrest, S.N. Stuart, L.G. Underhill, R.W. Waller, M.E.J. Watts, and X. Yan. "Effectiveness of the Global Protected Area Network in Representing Species Diversity." *Nature*, vol. 248, 2004.
Schmincke, H.-U. *Vulkanismus*. Darmstadt: Wissenschaftliche Buchgesellschaft, 2000.
Veit, H. *Die Alpen—Geoökologie und Landschaftsentwicklung*. Stuttgart: Ulmer, 2002.
Zurick, D., and P.P. Karan. *Himalaya—Life on the Edge of the World*. Baltimore: Johns Hopkins University Press, 1999.